Ariano Irpino Families

–

The

D'Ausilio Family

(Francesco d'Ausilio
and
Angela Maria diStefano)

Ariano Irpino Families

-

The

D'Ausilio Family

(Francesco d'Ausilio
and
Angela Maria diStefano)

by

Frederick Fleischer

2055 Publishing

Published by

2055 Publishing

2055 Publishing
120 N South Rd.
Unit C, PMB 174
North Conway, NH 03860
www.2055publishing.com

Soft Cover ISBN-13: 979-8-9939063-0-0
Hard Cover ISBN-13: 979-8-9939063-1-7

Table of Contents

Dedication:

To my mother
Joan D'Ausilio Fleischer

Forward

This book is the results of many years of work on the genealogy of my mother's paternal family, the D'Ausilio family, from Ariano di Puglia (renamed to Ariano Irpino in 1930), Italy.

I began my research into this part of my family tree a few years before my mother passed away. I was looking forward to finding information to confirm some of my mother's stories about her family.

I have decided to publish now as I am getting older and have many other branches of the tree that I want to share before it gets too late. All my research would go to waste if I never actually get to share it with others. Maybe, it can be the foundation for others to continue.

The format of this book is designed to share the information for all descendants of the ancestors that are the farthest back that I could find. The majority of the information I have available is from the Family History Centers who have microfilms of most of the vital records from Ariano di Puglia/Irpino from 1809 to 1910. There are many descendants that have information available from other source especially if they emigrated to the United States.

There may be more information available from church records, however, that would require time and expenses to go to Ariano Irpino to do research. (As I finish this last edit, I have found that there are individuals that are posting digital images of Italian Church records online. I can hope that the records for Ariano will be done while I would be able to use them to do an expanded edition of this book.)

I am following the standard practice of not including information about living individuals in order to respect their privacy. I also decided to limit the coverage only up to the generation of my parents as later generations have many more individuals that are still living. I also will not include information for an individual if they have a living spouse.

I am also following the standard practice of assuming that someone isn't still living if they were born over 100 years ago, unless I have information to the contrary.

I have tried to make notations to indicate why there might be any missing information. However, the most likely cause is that I do not have access to the records due to government restrictions or an individual or family moved and I have not been able to locate where they went. I am working through the available records but without any indications where to look it is going to be like finding a needle in a haystack. I am encouraged by the current efforts to create indexes that can be searched so that it might be possible to make a more complete record in the future.

Acknowledgment

I would like to take a few words to thank Donna Troisi whose website https://arianoirpinogenealogy.weebly.com/ published indexes for the microfilmed vital records of Ariano Irpino. This has made researching the records easier, allowing me to make this book possible.

Notes

For convenience individuals are identified by a number and or letter. Direct descendants have a number with their spouses identified by the number and a lower case letter to identify order of spouse. Parents of the spouse use the spouse's number with an "F" for father or "M" for mother. Former spouses get an "X".

The ordering of the individuals is by date of birth per generation. I believe this is the best way to organize them. I have included an index at the end which puts everyone in alphabetic order.

Names can be spelled in different ways at different times as well as being subject to transcription errors. I will usually use the spelling I believe was used at the time.

Individuals will be listed by their birth names even if they eventually took their spouse's surname. In Italy wives do not take their husbands names so I felt it would be best to be consistent throughout the book. If someone took their spouse's name it will usually be reflected in the sources.

I will try to mention other names if it was usual to refer to someone by a name other than their birth name.

Ariano Irpino is the latest name for the town most of the family is from. The town was called just Ariano until 1858 when the name was changed to Ariano di Puglia. In 1930 the name was again changed to it's current one of Ariano Irpino. I have decided to just use the term Ariano, Italy regardless of the name in use at the time. It just made it easier for me and the reader should be able to determine the name that was in use by using the dates referenced above.

Most of the sources I used are available online. My primary sources are the previous mentioned index site, the LDS Church website (familysearch.org), and the website conceived and created by the Italian Directorate General for Archives, which contains the images of the original records from Italy (https://antenati.cultura.gov.it/?lang=en).

FIRST GENERATION

1) Francesco d'Ausilio

Francesco d'Ausilio(1) was born about 1733. Francesco d'Ausilio(1) died 13 June 1811 in Ariano, Italy. Francesco d'Ausilio(1) was a Coach-driver.

Francesco d'Ausilio(1) married Angela Maria diStefano(1a).

Angela Maria diStefano(1a) was born about 1735. Angela Maria diStefano(1a) died 16 July 1811 in Ariano, Italy. Angela Maria diStefano(1a) was a Homemaker.

Known Children of Francesco d'Ausilio(1) and Angela Maria diStefano(1a):

```
i)     Gennaro d'Ausilio(2) born about 1769
ii)    Nicoletta d'Ausilio(3) born about 1770
iii)   Vincenza d'Ausilio(4) born 1786
```

I have not found any records showing the parents for either Francesco d'Ausilio(1) or Angela Maria diStefano(1a).

Records that include Francesco d'Ausilio(1) and/or Angela Maria diStefano(1a):
* Ariano, Italy 1811 Death Act #216
* Ariano, Italy 1811 Death Act #265
* Ariano, Italy 1826 Death Act #168
* Ariano, Italy 1829 Death Act #90
* Ariano, Italy 1850 Death Act #43

2) Gennaro d'Ausilio

Gennaro d'Ausilio(2) was born in Ariano, Italy about 1769, the son of Francesco d'Ausilio(1) and Angela Maria diStefano(1a). Gennaro d'Ausilio(2) died on 4 March 1829 in Ariano, Italy. Gennaro d'Ausilio(2) was a coach-driver.

Gennaro d'Ausilio(2) married Angela Maria Peluso(2a) in Ariano, Italy.

Angela Maria Peluso(2a) was born about 1774 to Nicola Peluso(2aF) and Carmina Ienge(2aM). Angela Maria Peluso(2a) died 14 January 1834 in Ariano, Italy.

Known Children of Gennaro d'Ausilio(2) and Angela Maria Peluso(2a):

    i) Francesco Saverio d'Ausilio(5) born about 1797
    ii) Nicola Maria d'Ausilio(7) born about 1799

Records that include Gennaro d'Ausilio(2) and/or Angela Maria Peluso(2a):
- Ariano, Italy 1811 Death Act #216
- Ariano, Italy 1811 Death Act #265
- Ariano, Italy 1824 Marriage Act #22
- Ariano, Italy 1826 Marriage Act #32
- Ariano, Italy 1829 Death Act #90
- Ariano, Italy 1834 Death Act #21
- Ariano, Italy 1843 Death Act #73
- Ariano, Italy 1891 Death Act #249

3) Nicoletta d'Ausilio

Nicoletta d'Ausilio(3) was born about 1770 in Ariano, Italy to Francesco d'Ausilio(1) and Angela Maria diStefano(1a). Nicoletta d'Ausilio(3) died 8 February 1850 in Ariano, Italy.

Nicoletta d'Ausilio(3) married Francesco Saviero Marraffino(3a).

Francesco Saviero Marraffino(3a) - no records related to the birth, marriage, or death of Francesco Saviero Marraffino(3a) are currently available.

Known Children of Nicoletta d'Ausilio(3) and Francesco Saviero Marraffino(3a):

    i) Nicola Angelo Marraffino(6) born about 1798
    ii) Maria Angela Marraffino(8) born about 1801

Nicoletta d'Ausilio(3) also married Ferdinando Clericuzio(3b).

Ferdinando Clericuzio(3b) was born about 1784 to Francesco Clericuzio(3bF) and Carmina Maggese(3bM). Ferdinando Clericuzio(3b) died 29 October 1843 in Ariano, Italy. Ferdinando Clericuzio(3b) was a matchmaker.

Known Children of Nicoletta d'Ausilio(3) and Ferdinando Clericuzio(3b):

    i) Nicolantonio Clericuzio(9) born about 1808.
    ii) Francesco Saverio Clericuzio(10) born in 1810.
    iii) Colomba Clericuzio(11) born in 1812
    iv) Raffaele Clericuzio(12) born in 1815.

Records that include Nicoletta d'Ausilio(3), Francesco Saverio Marraffino(3a), and/or Ferdinando Clericuzio(3b):
- Ariano, Italy 1810 Birth Act #7
- Ariano, Italy 1811 Death Act #216
- Ariano, Italy 1811 Death Act #265
- Ariano, Italy 1812 Birth Act #446
- Ariano, Italy 1814 Death Act #335

- Ariano, Italy 1815 Birth Act #373
- Ariano, Italy 1824 Marriage Act #49
- Ariano, Italy 1824 Marriage Act #116
- Ariano, Italy 1837 Marriage Act #75
- Ariano, Italy 1838 Marriage Act #135
- Ariano, Italy 1842 Death Act #133
- Ariano, Italy 1843 Marriage Act #44
- Ariano, Italy 1843 Death Act #305
- Ariano, Italy 1846 Death Act #80
- Ariano, Italy 1850 Death Act #43
- Ariano, Italy 1857 Death Act #388
- Ariano, Italy 1858 Death Act #10
- Ariano, Italy 1875 Death Act #445

4) Vincenza d'Ausilio

Vincenza d'Ausilio(4) was born, around 1786, in Ariano, Italy, to Francesco d'Ausilio(1) and Angela Maria diStefano(1a). Vincenza d'Ausilio(4) died 19 July 1826 in Ariano, Italy. Vincenza d'Ausilio(4) was a seamstress, residing in the Parish of San Nicola.

Records that include Vincenza d'Ausilio(4):
- Ariano, Italy 1811 Death Act #216
- Ariano, Italy 1811 Death Act #265
- Ariano, Italy 1826 Death Act #168

THIRD GENERATION

5) Francesco Saverio d'Ausilio

Francesco Saverio d'Ausilio(5) was born about 1797, in Ariano, Italy, to Gennaro d'Ausilio(2) and Angela Maria Peluso(2a). Francesco Saverio d'Ausilio(5) died 5 March 1843 in Ariano, Italy. Francesco Saverio d'Ausilio(5) was a driver.

Francesco Saverio d'Ausilio(5) married Maria Rosa Salza(5a) on 8 March 1826 in Ariano, Italy.

Maria Rosa Salza(5a) who was born about 1805, in Ariano, Italy, to Giuseppe Salza(5aF) and Agata Maria LoCalzo(5aM). Maria Rosa Salza(5a) died 6 September 1840 in Ariano, Italy. Maria Rosa Salza(5a) was a spinner/seamstress.

Known children of Francesco Saverio d'Ausilio(5) and Maria Rosa Salza(5a):

    i) Mariangela d'Ausilio(15) born in 1827.
    ii) Maria Filomina d'Ausilio(21) born in 1830.

Records that include Francesco Saverio d'Ausilio(5) and/or Maria Rosa Salza(5a):
- Ariano, Italy 1826 Marriage Act #32
- Ariano, Italy 1827 Birth Act #36
- Ariano, Italy 1830 Birth Act #333
- Ariano, Italy 1840 Death Act #287
- Ariano, Italy 1843 Death Act #73
- Ariano, Italy 1844 Marriage Act #39
- Ariano, Italy 1851 Marriage Act #106
- Ariano, Italy 1867 Birth Act #228
- Ariano, Italy 1867 Death Act #597
- Ariano, Italy 1868 Birth Act #178
- Ariano, Italy 1889 Marriage Act #56

6) Nicola Angelo Marraffino

Nicola Angelo Marraffino(6) was born about 1798, in Ariano, Italy, to Francesco Saverio Marraffino(3a) and Nicoletta d'Ausilio(3). Nicola Angelo Marraffino(6) died 8 January 1858 in Ariano, Italy. Nicola Angelo Marraffino(6) was a shoemaker.

Nicola Angelo Marraffino(6) married Aurelina D'Agostino(6a) on 15 March 1824 in Ariano, Italy.

Aurelina D'Agostino(6a) was born about 1800, in Ariano, Italy, to Michele D'Agostino(6aF) and Rosa Orlando(6aM). Aurelina D'Agostino(6a) died between 1835 and 1848.

Known children of Nicola Angelo Marraffino(6) and Aurelina D'Agostino(6a):

    i) Maria Vincenza Marraffino(13) born in 1825.
    ii) Francesco Saverio Marraffino(17) born in 1827.
    iii) Maria Rosaria Marraffino(20) born in 1829.
    iv) Maria Rosaria Marraffino(22) born in 1831.
    v) Maria Michele Marraffino(25) born in 1833.
    vi) Antonio Marraffino(28) born in 1835.

Records that include Nicola Angelo Marraffino(6) and/or Aurelina D'Agostino(6a):
- Ariano, Italy 1824 Marriage Act #49
- Ariano, Italy 1825 Birth Act #102
- Ariano, Italy 1827 Birth Act #80
- Ariano, Italy 1829 Birth Act #431

- Ariano, Italy 1831 Death Act #6
- Ariano, Italy 1831 Birth Act #203
- Ariano, Italy 1833 Birth Act #223
- Ariano, Italy 1835 Birth Act #37
- Ariano, Italy 1848 Marriage Act #78
- Ariano, Italy 1858 Death Act #10
- Ariano, Italy 1867 Death Act #397
- Ariano, Italy 1871 Birth Act #653
- Ariano, Italy 1898 Death Act #33

7) Nicola Maria d'Ausilio

Nicola Maria d'Ausilio(7) was born around 1800, to Gennaro d'Ausilio(2) and Angela Maria Peluso(2a). Nicola Maria d'Ausilio(7) died 29 July 1891 in Ariano, Italy. Nicola Maria d'Ausilio(7) was a shoemaker.

Nicola Maria d'Ausilio(7) married Saveria Maria Petrosino(7a) on 16 February 1824 in Ariano, Italy.

Saveria Maria Petrosino(7a) was born about 1805, to Fillipo Petrosino(7aF) and Anna Maria Bruno(7aM). Saveria Maria Petrosino(7a) died 9 February 1875, in Ariano, Italy. Saveria Maria Petrosino(7a) was a seamstress.

Known children of Nicola Maria d'Ausilio(7) and Saveria Maria Petrosino(7a):

    i) Raimonda d'Ausilio(16) born in 1827.
    ii) Maria Guiseppa d'Ausilio(19) born in 1829.
    iii) Angelo Maria d'Ausilio(24) born in 1832.
    iv) Gennaro d'Ausilio(26) born in 1834.

Records that include Nicola Maria d'Ausilio(7) and Saveria Maria Petrosino(7a):
- Ariano, Italy 1824 Marriage Act #22
- Ariano, Italy 1827 Birth Act #66
- Ariano, Italy 1829 Birth Act #171
- Ariano, Italy 1832 Birth Act #187
- Ariano, Italy 1834 Birth Act #330
- Ariano, Italy 1849 Marriage Act #14
- Ariano, Italy 1850 Marriage Act #90
- Ariano, Italy 1852 Death Act #118
- Ariano, Italy 1854 Marriage Act #10
- Ariano, Italy 1855 Birth Act #116
- Ariano, Italy 1858 Marriage Act #97
- Ariano, Italy 1859 Birth Act #499
- Ariano, Italy 1867 Birth Act #574
- Ariano, Italy 1867 Birth Act #575
- Ariano, Italy 1870 Birth Act #114
- Ariano, Italy 1872 Birth Act #82
- Ariano, Italy 1872 Birth Act #83
- Ariano, Italy 1874 Birth Act #204
- Ariano, Italy 1875 Death Act #45
- Ariano, Italy 1891 Death Act #249

8) Maria Angela Marraffino

Maria Angela Marraffino(8) was born about 1806 in Ariano di Puglia. The daughter of Francesco Saverio Marraffino(3a) and Nicoletta d'Ausilio(3). Maria Angela Marraffino(8) died on 6 April 1846 in Ariano, Italy. Maria Angela Marraffino(8) was a spinner/seamstress.

Maria Angela Marraffino(8) married Domenico deDonato(8a) on 14 December 1824 in Ariano, Italy.

Domenico deDonato(8a)(also spelled diDonato) was born about 1796 in Ariano, Italy, to Filippo deDonato(8aF) and Anna Maria Grasso(8aM). Domenico deDonato(8a) also married Agata Scarpellino(8ab). Domenico deDonato(8a) died on 10 October 1868 in Ariano, Italy. Domenico deDonato(8a) was a shoemaker.

Known children of Maria Angela Marraffino(8) and Domenico deDonato(8a):

     i) Maria Raimonda deDonato (14) born in 1825
     ii) Maria Nicoletta deDonato(18) born in 1828
     iii) Michele deDonato(23) born in 1828
     iv) Luigi deDonato(27) born in 1835.
     v) Maria Concordia deDonato(29) born in 1839.
     vi) Marcello Francesco Saviero deDonato(31) born in 1840
     vii) Francesco Saverio deDonato(34) born in 1845

Records that include Maria Angela Marraffino(8) and/or Domenico deDonato(8a):
- Ariano, Italy 1824 Marriage Act #116
- Ariano, Italy 1825 Birth Act #489
- Ariano, Italy 1828 Birth Act #424
- Ariano, Italy 1831 Birth Act #340
- Ariano, Italy 1835 Birth Act #3
- Ariano, Italy 1837 Birth Act #541
- Ariano, Italy 1839 Death Act #594
- Ariano, Italy 1840 Birth Act #300
- Ariano, Italy 1845 Birth Act #156
- Ariano, Italy 1846 Death Act #80
- Ariano, Italy 1848 Marriage Act #86
- Ariano, Italy 1850 Marriage Act #101
- Ariano, Italy 1851 Marriage Act #56
- Ariano, Italy 1855 Marriage Act #141
- Ariano, Italy 1856 Birth Act #443
- Ariano, Italy 1857 Birth Act #511
- Ariano, Italy 1859 Birth Act #615
- Ariano, Italy 1861 Birth Act #76
- Ariano, Italy 1861 Death Act #2
- Ariano, Italy 1863 Birth Act #469
- Ariano, Italy 1866 Birth Act #422
- Ariano, Italy 1866 Birth Act #463
- Ariano, Italy 1866 Birth Act #603
- Ariano, Italy 1867 Death Act #216
- Ariano, Italy 1867 Death Act #988
- Ariano, Italy 1868 Birth Act #205
- Ariano, Italy 1868 Birth Act #262
- Ariano, Italy 1868 Death Act #383
- Ariano, Italy 1869 Birth Act #229
- Ariano, Italy 1869 Birth Act #632
- Ariano, Italy 1872 Birth Act #105
- Ariano, Italy 1892 Death Act #20
- Ariano, Italy 1898 Death Act #303

9) Nicolantonio Clericuzio

Nicolantonio Clericuzio(9) was born about 1809 to Ferdinando Clericuzio(3b) and Nicoletta D'Ausilio(3). Nicolantonio Clericuzio(9) died on 31 March 1842, in Ariano, Italy. Nicolantonio Clericuzio(9) was a matchmaker.

Nicolantonio Clericuzio(9), married Maria Rosaria Albanese(9a), on 21 October 1837 in Ariano, Italy.

Maria Rosaria Albanese(9a) was born on 6 February 1817, in Pietradefusi, Italy, to Giuseppe Albanese(9aF) and Orsola DiStefano(9aM). Maria Rosaria Albanese(9a) died on 5 January 1905, in Ariano, Italy.

Known children of Nicolantonio Clericuzio(9) and Maria Rosaria Albanese(9a):

     i) Angelo Antonio Clericuzio(30) in 1838
     ii) Nicoletta Clericuzio(33) in 1841

Maria Rosaria Albanese(9a) also married Antonio Cardinale(9ab) and had child(ren).

Records that include Nicolantonio Clericuzio(9) and/or Maria Rosaria Albanese(9a):
- Pietradefusi, Italy 1817 Birth Act #21
- Ariano, Italy 1837 Marriage Act #75
- Ariano, Italy 1838 Birth Act #117
- Ariano, Italy 1841 Birth Act #250
- Ariano, Italy 1841 Death Act #184
- Ariano, Italy 1842 Death Act #133
- Ariano, Italy 1843 Marriage Act #40
- Ariano, Italy 1863 Death Act #210
- Ariano, Italy 1905 Death Act #1-II

10) Francesco Saverio Clericuzio

Francesco Saverio Clericuzio(10) was born on 2 January 1810, in Ariano, Italy, to Ferdinando Clericuzio(3a) and Nicoletta D'Ausilio(3). Francesco Saverio Clericuzio(10) died on 14 August 1814, in Ariano, Italy.

Records that include Francesco Saverio Clericuzio(10):
- Ariano, Italy 1810 Birth Act #7
- Ariano, Italy 1814 Death Act #335

11) Colomba Clericuzio

Colomba Clericuzio(11) was born on 22 September 1812, in Ariano, Italy, to Ferdinando Clericuzio(3a) and Nicoletta D'Ausilio(3). Colomba Clericuzio(11) died on 13 December 1875, in Ariano, Italy. Colomba Clericuzio(11) was a seamstress.

Colomba Clericuzio(11) married Antonio Covotta(11a), on 31 December 1838 in Ariano, Italy.

Antonio Covotta(11a) was born on 29 November 1812, in Ariano, Italy, to Giuseppe Covotta(11aF) and Anna Maria diDonato(11aM). Antonio Covotta(11a) died on 1 March 1884, in Ariano, Italy. Antonio Covotta(11a) was a farmhand.

Known children of Antonio Covotta(11a)and Colomba Clericuzio(11):

    i) Raffaele Covotta(31) born in 1840
    ii) Anna Maria Covotta(34) born in 1842
    iii) Gaetano Covotta(37) born in 1845
    iv) Gaetano Covotta(39) born in 1848

Records that include Colomba Clericuzio(11) and/or Antonio Covotta(11a):
- Ariano, Italy 1812 Birth Act #446
- Ariano, Italy 1812 Birth Act #517
- Ariano, Italy 1838 Marriage Act #155
- Ariano, Italy 1840 Birth Act #169
- Ariano, Italy 1840 Death Act #196
- Ariano, Italy 1842 Birth Act #225
- Ariano, Italy 1845 Birth Act #173
- Ariano, Italy 1846 Death Act #111
- Ariano, Italy 1848 Birth Act #105
- Ariano, Italy 1867 Marriage Act #39
- Ariano, Italy 1868 Birth Act #111
- Ariano, Italy 1871 Birth Act #4
- Ariano, Italy 1874 Birth Act #119
- Ariano, Italy 1875 Marriage Act #26
- Ariano, Italy 1875 Death Act #407
- Ariano. Italy 1875 Death Act #445
- Ariano, Italy 1890 Marriage Act #89
- Ariano, Italy 1915 Death Act #303

12) Raffaele Clericuzio

Raffaele Clericuzio(12) was born on 27 August 1815, in Ariano, Italy, to Ferdinando Clericuzio(3a)and Nicoletta D'Ausilio(3). Raffaele Clericuzio(12) died on 31 December 1857 in Ariano, Italy. Raffaele Clericuzio(12) was a matchmaker.

Raffaele Clericuzio(12) married Maria Teresa Scaperotta/Perotta(12a) on 25 March 1843 in Ariano, Italy.

Maria Teresa Scaperotta/Perotta(12a) was born on 14 July 1815, in Ariano, Italy, to Antonio Perotta(12aF) and Saveria Scauzillo(12aM). Maria Teresa Scaperotta/Perotta(12a) died on 17 February 1903, in Ariano, Italy.

Maria Teresa Scaperotta/Perotta(12a) was previously married to Filippo Puorro(12aX).

Known children of Raffaele Clericuzio(12) and Maria Teresa Scaperotta/Perotta(12a):

> i) Maria Carmina Clericuzio(35) born in 1843.
> ii) Maria Consiglia Clericuzio(38) born in 1845.
> iii) Maria Amalia Clericuzio(40) born in 1849

Records that include Raffaele Clericuzio(12) and/or Maria Teresa Scaperotta/Perotta(12a):

- Ariano, Italy 1815 Birth Act #322
- Ariano, Italy 1815 Birth Act #373
- Ariano, Italy 1843 Birth Act #538
- Ariano, Italy 1843 Marriage Act #44
- Ariano, Italy 1845 Birth Act #175
- Ariano, Italy 1849 Birth Act #115
- Ariano, Italy 1857 Death Act #388
- Ariano, Italy 1867 Birth act #241
- Ariano, Italy 1870 Birth Act #637
- Ariano, Italy 1870 Birth Act #638
- Ariano, Italy 1871 Death Act #66
- Ariano, Italy 1877 Marriage Act #111
- Ariano, Italy 1903 Death Act #64

FOURTH GENERATION

13) Maria Vincenza Marraffino

Maria Vincenza Marraffino(13) was born on 28 February 1825, in Ariano, Italy, to Nicolangelo Marraffino(6) and Aurelina D'Agostino(6a). Maria Vincenza Marraffino(13) died on 24 January 1898 in Ariano, Italy. Maria Vincenza Marraffino(13) was a Housewife.

Maria Vincenza Marraffino(13) married Gaetano Fiorenza(13a), on 1 June 1848 in Ariano, Italy.

Gaetano Fiorenza(13a) was born on 21 May 1823, in Ariano, Italy, to Nicola Fiorenza(13aF) and Rosa Panzetta(13aM). Gaetano Fiorenza(13a) died on 8 February 1898 in Ariano, Italy. Gaetano Fiorenza(13a) was an embroiderer.

Known children of Maria Vincenza Marraffino(13) and Gaetano Fiorenza(13a):

> i) Maria Rosa Fiorenza(43) born in 1849.
> ii) Nicola Fiorenza(47) born in 1851.
> iii) Aurelia Fiorenza(55) born in 1854.
> iv) Maria Rosa Fiorenza(65) born in 1857.
> v) Rosa Fiorenza(69) born in 1859.
> vi) Giovanni Fiorenza(79) born in 1862.
> vii) Mariantonia Fiorenza(91) born in 1865.
> viii) Antonio Fiorenza(111) born in 1871.

Records that include Gaetano Fiorenza(13a) and/or Maria Vincenza Marraffino(13):

- Ariano, Italy 1823 Birth Act #247
- Ariano, Italy 1825 Birth Act #102
- Ariano, Italy 1848 Birth Act #78
- Ariano, Italy 1849 Birth Act #465
- Ariano, Italy 1850 Death Act #228
- Ariano, Italy 1851 Birth Act #460
- Ariano, Italy 1854 Birth Act #377
- Ariano, Italy 1857 Birth Act #426
- Ariano, Italy 1858 Death Act #152
- Ariano, Italy 1859 Birth Act #202
- Ariano, Italy 1862 Birth Act #299
- Ariano, Italy 1863 Death Act #6
- Ariano, Italy 1865 Birth Act #239
- Ariano, Italy 1867 Death Act #485
- Ariano, Italy 1871 Birth Act #653
- Ariano, Italy 1872 Death Act #77
- Ariano, Italy 1879 Marriage Act #1
- Ariano, Italy 1886 Marriage Act #86
- Ariano, Italy 1885 Marriage Act #36
- Ariano, Italy 1898 Death Act #33
- Ariano, Italy 1898 Death Act #68

14) Maria Raimonda deDonato

Maria Raimonda deDonato(14) was born on 11 November 1825, in Ariano, Italy, to Domenico deDonato(8a) and Mariangela Marraffino(8). Maria Raimonda deDonato(14) died on 14 April 1909, in Ariano, Italy.

Maria Raimonda deDonato(14) married Oto Maria Perrina(14a) on 3 October 1850 in Ariano, Italy.

Oto Maria Perrina(14a) was born on 5 June 1819, in Ariano, Italy, to Leonardantonio Perrina(14aF) and Anna diGruttola(14aM). Oto Maria Perrina(14a) died on 12 February 1881 in Ariano, Italy. Oto Maria Perrina(14a) was a farm-laborer.

Known children of Maria Raimonda deDonato(14) married Oto Maria Perrina(14a):

i) Mariangela Perrina(49) born in 1852.
ii) Filomena Perrina(53) born in 1853.
iii) Raffaele Perrina(58) born in 1855.
iv) Mariangela Perrina(67) born in 1858.
v) Anna Perrina(76) born in 1860.
vi) Filomena Perrina(82) born in 1862.
vii) Francesco Paolo Perrina(90) born in 1865.
viii) Maria Giovanna Perrina(105) born in 1869.

Records that include Maria Raimonda deDonato(14) and/or Oto Maria Perrina(14a):

- Ariano, Italy 1819 Birth Act #276
- Ariano, Italy 1825 Birth Act #489
- Ariano, Italy 1850 Marriage Act #101
- Ariano, Italy 1852 Birth Act #272
- Ariano, Italy 1853 Birth Act #526
- Ariano, Italy 1854 Death Act #428
- Ariano, Italy 1854 Death Act #440
- Ariano, Italy 1855 Birth Act #371
- Ariano, Italy 1858 Birth Act #50
- Ariano, Italy 1860 Birth Act #160
- Ariano, Italy 1862 Birth Act #384
- Ariano, Italy 1865 Birth Act #72
- Ariano, Italy 1869 Birth Act #229
- Ariano, Italy 1876 Marriage Act #132
- Ariano, Italy 1876 Marriage Act #133
- San Nicola Baronia, Italy 1879 Marriage Act #7
- Ariano, Italy 1881 Death Act #93
- Ariano, Italy 1883 Marriage Act #26
- San Nicola, Baronia, Italy 1884 Marriage Act #4
- Ariano, Italy 1892 Marriage Act #29
- Ariano, Italy 1909 Death Act #156

15) Mariangela d'Ausilio

Mariangela d'Ausilio(15) was born on 19 January 1827, in Ariano, Italy, to Francesco Saverio d'Ausilio(5) and Rosa Salza(5a). Mariangela d'Ausilio(15) died on 28 August 1906 in Ariano, Italy. Mariangela d'Ausilio(15) was a farmhand.

Mariangela d'Ausilio(15) was married to Domenico Fodarella(15a) and Liberatore Covotta(15b).

Mariangela d'Ausilio(15) married Domenico Fodarella(15a) on 2 May 1844 in Ariano, Italy.

Domenico Fodarella(15a) was born about 1802 to Giuseppe Fodarella(15aF) and Anna Maria Viscio(15aM). Domenico Fodarella(15a) died on 18 June 1886, in Ariano, Italy. Domenico Fodarella(15a) was a farmhand.

Known children of Mariangela d'Ausilio(15) and Domenico Fodarella(15a):

i) Raffaele Fodarella(41) born in 1845
ii) Maria Concordia Fodarella(42) born in 1848
iii) Lorenzo Fodarella(48) born in 1852
iv) Anna Maria Fodarella(57) born in 1855
v) Maria Francesca Fodarella(64) born in 1857
vi) Giuseppe Fodarella(73) born in 1859
vii) Mariantonia Fodarella(79) born in 1861
viii) Antonio Maria Fodarella(89) born in 1864
ix) Oto Maria Fodarella(102) born in 1868

Mariangela d'Ausilio(15) married Liberatore Covotta(15b) on 11 May 1889 in Ariano, Italy.

Liberatore Covotta(15b) was born on 7 November 1828, in Ariano, Italy, to Leonardo Covotta(15bF) and Giuseppa diPalma(15bM). Liberatore Covotta(15b) died on 13 December 1906, in Ariano, Italy. Liberatore Covotta(15b) was a farmhand.

Records that include Mariangela d'Ausilio(15), Domenico Fodarella(15a), and/or Liberatore Covotta(15b):

- Ariano, Italy 1827 Birth Act #36
- Ariano, Italy 1828 Birth Act #498
- Ariano, Italy 1844 Marriage Act #39
- Ariano, Italy 1845 Birth Act#424
- Ariano, Italy 1848 Birth Act #436
- Ariano, Italy 1852 Birth Act #5
- Ariano, Italy 1854 Death Act #113
- Ariano, Italy 1855 Birth Act #224
- Ariano, Italy 1857 Birth Act #241
- Ariano, Italy 1859 Birth Act #548
- Ariano, Italy 1860 Death Act #6
- Ariano, Italy 1861 Birth Act #357
- Ariano, Italy 1864 Birth Act #511
- Ariano, Italy 1868 Birth Act #178
- Ariano, Italy 1868 Marriage Record #140
- Ariano, Italy 1870 Birth Act #422
- Ariano, Italy 1872 Death Act #120
- Ariano, Italy 1874 Marriage act #80
- Ariano, Italy 1875 Marriage Act #83
- Ariano, Italy 1876 Marriage Act #111
- Ariano, Italy 1879 Marriage Act #241
- Ariano, Italy 1885 Marriage Act #4
- Ariano, Italy 1886 Death Act #228
- Ariano, Italy 1888 Death Act #290
- Ariano, Italy 1889 Marriage Act #56
- Ariano, Italy 1906 Death Act #216
- Ariano, Italy 1906 Death Act #25-II
- Ariano, Italy 1909 Death Act #142
- Ariano, Italy 1911 Death Act #49
- Ariano, Italy 1927 Death Act #139
- Ariano, Italy 1931 Death Act #103

16) Raimonda d'Ausilio

Raimonda d'Ausilio(16) was born on 5 February 1827, in Ariano, Italy, to Nicola Maria D'Ausilio(7) and Saveria Maria Petrosino(7a).

Raimonda D'Ausilio(16) married Raimondo diVitto(16a) on 12 September 1850 in Ariano, Italy.

Raimondo diVitto(16a) was born on 1 February 1821, in Ariano, Italy, to Michele diVitto(16aF) and Mariantonia Lombardi(16aM). Raimondo diVitto(16a) & his father, Michele diVitto(16aF), signed their names as "Vitto". Raimondo diVitto(16a) was a shoemaker.

Known children of Raimonda D'Ausilio(16) and Raimondo diVitto(16a):

    i) Gennaro diVitto(50) born in 1852
    ii) Michele diVitto(54) born in 1854
    iii) Maria Rosa diVitto(59) born in 1856
    iv) Antonio diVitto(82) born in 1863
    v) Pietro Paolo diVitto(90) born in 1865

Records that include Raimonda D'Ausilio(16)and/or Raimondo diVitto(16a):
- Ariano, Italy 1821 Birth Act #54
- Ariano, Italy 1827 Birth Act #66
- Ariano, Italy 1850 Marriage Act #90
- Ariano, Italy 1852 Birth Act #489

- Ariano, Italy 1854 Birth Act #328
- Ariano, Italy 1856 Birth Act #199
- Ariano. Italy 1863 Birth Act #139
- Ariano, Italy 1865 Birth Act #290
- Ariano, Italy 1867 Death Act #994
- Ariano, Italy 1871 Death Act #214

17) Francesco Saverio Marraffino

Francesco Saverio Marraffino(17) was born on 15 February 1827, in Ariano, Italy, to Nicolangelo Marraffino(6) and Aurelina D'Agostino(6a).

Records that include Francesco Saverio Marraffino(17):
- Ariano, Italy 1827 Birth Act #80

18) Maria Nicoletta deDonato

Maria Nicoletta deDonato(18) was born on 17 September 1828, in Ariano, Italy, to Domenico deDonato(8a) and Mariangela Marraffino(8). Maria Nicoletta deDonato(18) died on 7 September 1867, in Ariano, Italy.

Maria Nicoletta deDonato(18) married Liberatore Perrina(18a) on 15 June 1848 in Ariano, Italy.

Liberatore Perrina(18a) was born on 25 May 1828, in Ariano, Italy, to Leonardantonio Perrina(18aF) and Anna diGruttola(18aM). Liberatore Perrina(18a) died on 19 June 1898, in Ariano, Italy.

Liberatore Perrina(18a) married Maria Nicoletta deDonato(18), Carmela Ferraro(18ab) and Rosa Albanese(18ac).

Known children of Maria Nicoletta deDonato(18) and Liberatore Perrina(18a):

     i) Anna Maria Perrina(45) born in 1850
     ii) Mariangela Perrina(46) born in 1851
     iii) Angela Perrina(52) born in 1852
     iv) Ciriaco Perrina(62) born in 1857
     v) Francesco Perrina(67) born in 1858
     vi) Angelo Maria Perrina(74) born in 1859
     vii) Mariangela Perrina(77) born in 1861
     viii) Michele Perrina(88) born in 1864
     ix) Raimonda Perrina(95) born in 1866

Records that include Maria Nicoletta(18) deDonato and/or Liberatore Perrina(18a):
- Ariano, Italy 1828 Birth Act #275
- Ariano, Italy 1828 Birth Act #424
- Ariano, Italy 1848 Marriage Act #86
- Ariano, Italy 1850 Birth Act #94
- Ariano, Italy 1851 Birth Act #190
- Ariano, Italy 1851 Death Act #152
- Ariano, Italy 1852 Birth Act #559
- Ariano, Italy 1857 Birth Act #55
- Ariano, Italy 1857 Death Act #138
- Ariano, Italy 1858 Birth Act #290
- Ariano, Italy 1858 Death Act #435
- Ariano, Italy 1859 Birth Act #518
- Ariano, Italy 1864 Birth Act #182
- Ariano, Italy 1866 Birth Act #463
- Ariano, Italy 1867 Death Act #974
- Ariano, Italy 1867 Death Act #988
- Ariano, Italy 1874 Marriage Act #21
- Ariano, Italy 1876 Marriage Act #82
- Ariano, Italy 1886 Marriage Act #92
- Ariano, Italy 1888 Marriage Act #59
- Ariano, Italy 1891 Marriage Act #97

- Ariano, Italy 1898 Death Act #213
- Ariano, Italy 1913 Marriage Act #71
- Ariano, Italy 1933 Death Act #258
- Ariano, Italy 1935 Death Act #250

19) Maria Guiseppa D'Ausilio

Maria Guiseppa D'ausilio(19) was born on 18 March 1829, in Ariano, Italy, to Nicola Maria D'Ausilio(7) and Saveria Maria Petrosino(7a). Maria Guiseppa D'ausilio(19) died on 26 February 1890 in Grottaminarda, Italy. Maria Guiseppa D'ausilio(19) was an industrialist.

Maria Guiseppa D'ausilio(19) was married to Pasquale Orlando(19a), Raffaele Giovanni Altanese(19b) and Domenico Altanese(19c).

Maria Guiseppa D'ausilio(19) married Pasquale Orlando(19a) on 12 February 1849 in Ariano, Italy.

Pasquale Orlando(19a) was born 9 June 1823 in Orsara, Italy to Antonio Orlando(19aF) and Isabella Gianpaolo(19aM). Pasquale Orlando(19a) died on 20 October 1854 in Orsara, Italy. Pasquale Orlando(19a) was a shoemaker.

Known children of Maria Guiseppa D'ausilio(19)and Pasquale Orlando(19a):

> i) Giuseppe Orlando(44) born in 1850

Maria Guiseppa D'ausilio(19) married Raffaele Giovanni Altanese(19b) on 29 October 1858 in Ariano, Italy. Raffaele Giovanni Altanese(19b) was previously married to Maria Giuseppa de Marco(19bX).

Raffaele Giovanni Altanese(19b) was born between 1807 and 1817, in Secondigliano, Italy, to Giuseppe Altanese(19bcF) and Agnese Borganali(19bcM). Raffaele Giovanni Altanese(19b) died 8 September 1868 in Grottaminarda, Italy. Raffaele Giovanni Altanese(19b) was a merchant.

Known children of Maria Guiseppa D'ausilio(19) and Raffaele Giovanni Altanese(19b):

> i) Maria Agnese Altanese(70) born in 1859
> ii) Cosimo Altanese(87) born in 1864

Maria Guiseppa D'ausilio(19) married Domenico Augelo Giovanni Altanese(19c), on 16 February 1870 in Grottaminarda, Italy.

Domenico Augelo Giovanni Altanese(19c) was born about 1813 in Secondigliano, Italy, to Giuseppe Altanese(19bcF) and Agnese Borganali(19bcM). Domenico Augelo Giovanni Altanese(19c) died on 3 July 1880 in Grottaminarda, Italy. Domenico Augelo Giovanni Altanese(19c) was a foundry worker.

Known children of Maria Guiseppa D'ausilio(19) and Domenico Augelo Giovanni Altanese(19c):

> i)Raffaela Altanese(115) born in 1872

Records that include Maria Guiseppa D'ausilio(19), Pasquale Orlando(19a), Raffaele Giovanni Altanese(19b) and/or Domenico Augelo Giovanni Altanese(19c):
- Ariano, Italy 1829 Birth Act #171
- Orsara, Italy 1823 Birth Act #89
- Ariano, Italy 1849 Marriage Act #14
- Orsara, Italy 1850 Birth Act #14
- Orsara, Italy 1850 Death Act #140
- Orsara, Italy 1854 Death Act #199
- Ariano, Italy 1858 Marriage Act #97
- Grottaminarda, Italy 1859 Birth Act #155
- Grottaminarda, Italy 1864 Birth Act #36
- Grottaminarda, Italy 1867 Death Act #140
- Grottaminarda, Italy 1868 Death Act #71
- Grottaminarda, Italy 1870 Marriage Act #10

- Grottaminarda, Italy 1872 Birth Act #110
- Grottaminarda, Italy 1873 Death Act #3
- Ariano, Italy 1874 Birth Act #119
- Ariano, Italy 1874 Death Act #349
- Grottaminarda, Italy 1880 Death Act #83
- Grottaminarda, Italy 1890 Death Act #20
- Ariano, Italy 1891 Marriage Act# 97

20) Maria Rosaria Marraffino

Maria Rosaria Marraffino(20) was born on 3 October 1829, in Ariano, Italy, to Nicolangelo Maria Marraffino(6) and Aurelina D'Agostino(6a). Maria Rosaria Marraffino(20) died on 4 January 1831 in Ariano, Italy.

Records that include Maria Rosaria Marraffino(20):
- Ariano, Italy 1829 Birth Act #431
- Ariano, Italy 1831 Death Act #6

21) Maria Filomina d'Ausilio

Maria Filomina D'Ausilio(21) was born on 20 July 1830, in Ariano, Italy, to Francesco Saverio d'Ausilio(5) and Rosa Salza(5a). Maria Filomina D'Ausilio(21) died on 8 August 1867, in Ariano, Italy. Maria Filomina D'Ausilio(21) was a farmhand/laborer.

Maria Filomina d'Ausilio(21) married Antonio Giorgione(21a) on 21 August 1851 in Ariano, Italy.

Antonio Giorgione(21a) was born on 8 April 1828, in Ariano, Italy, to Oto Giorgione(21aF) and Eleonora Ciano(21aM). Antonio Giorgione(21a) died on 22 November 1878, in Ariano, Italy. Antonio Giorgione(21a) was a farmhand/laborer.

Antonio Giorgione(21a) also married Maria Raffaella Scarpellino(21ab).

Known children of Maria Filomina d'Ausilio(21) and Antonio Giorgione(21a):

  i) Rosa Giorgione(51) born in 1852
  ii) Maria Liberia Giorgione(60) born in 1856
  iii) Luigi Giorgione(71) born in 1859
  iv) Raffaele Giorgione(80) born in 1862
  v) Luigi (Louis) Giorgione/George(86) born in 1864
  vi) Francesco Paulo Giorgione(97) born in 1867

Records that include Maria Filomina D'ausilio(21) and/or Antonio Giorgione(21a):
- Ariano, Italy 1828 Birth Act #194
- Ariano, Italy 1830 Birth Act #333
- Ariano, Italy 1851 Marriage Act #106
- Ariano, Italy 1852 Birth Act #505
- Ariano, Italy 1856 Birth Act #401
- Ariano, Italy 1859 Birth Act #336
- Ariano, Italy 1861 Death Act #408
- Ariano, Italy 1862 Birth Act #35
- Ariano, Italy 1864 Birth Act #138
- Ariano, Italy 1865 Death Act #300
- Ariano, Italy 1867 Birth Act #228
- Ariano, Italy 1867 Death Act #757
- Ariano, Italy 1867 Death Act #597
- Ariano, Italy 1871 Marriage Act #83
- Ariano, Italy 1878 Death Act #319
- Ariano, Italy 1883 Marriage Act #95
- Ariano, Italy 1886 Marriage Act #102

- "New York, New York City Municipal Deaths, 1795-1949", database, FamilySearch (https://www.familysearch.org/ark:/61903/1:1:2W1T-8LW : 3 June 2020), Fannie Dansilio in entry for Louis George, 1921.
- Ariano, Italy 1938 Death Act #105
- Ariano, Italy 1940 Death Act #288

22) Maria Rosaria Marraffino

Maria Rosaria Marraffino(22) was born on 8 April 1831, in Ariano, Italy, to Nicolangelo Marraffino (6) and Aurelina D'Agostino(6a). Maria Rosaria Marraffino(22) died on 18 July 1867, in Ariano, Italy. Maria Rosaria Marraffino(22) was a spinner.

Records that include Maria Rosaria Marraffino(22):
- Ariano, Italy 1831 Birth Act #203
- Ariano, Italy 1867 Death Act #397

23) Michele deDonato

Michele deDonato(23) was born on 5 August 1831, in Ariano, Italy, to Domenico deDonato(8a) and Mariangela Marraffino(8). Michele deDonato(23) died on 16 January 1892 in Ariano, Italy. Michele deDonato(23) was a Dominican Friar.

Records that include Michele deDonato(23):
- Ariano, Italy 1831 Birth Act #340
- Ariano, Italy 1892 Death Act #20

24) Angelo Maria D'Ausilio

Angelo Maria D'Ausilio(24) was born on 2 April 1832, in Ariano, Italy, to Nicola Maria D'Ausilio(7) and Saveria Maria Petrosino(7a). Angelo Maria D'Ausilio(24) died on 6 December 1900 in Ariano, Italy. Angelo Maria D'Ausilio(24) was a Shoemaker.

Angelo Maria D'Ausilio(24) married Maria Concetta Grasso(24a) on 9 February 1854 in Ariano, Italy.

Maria Concetta Grasso(24a) was born on 1 May 1836, in Ariano, Italy, to Gabriele Grasso(24aF) and Maria Clemenzia Rendesi(24aM).

Known children of Angelo Maria D'Ausilio(24) and Maria Concetta Grasso(24a):

    i) Gabriele D'ausilio(56) born in 1855
    ii) Pasquale D'ausilio(63) born in 1857
    iii) Anna Maria D'Ausilio(72) born in 1859
    iv) Nicola Maria D'Ausilio(83) born in 1863
    v) Anna Saveria D'ausilio(92) born in 1865
    vi) Oto Maria D'ausilio(99) born in 1867
    vii) Mario Carmelo (Carmine) D'ausilio(100) born in 1867
    viii) Gabriele D'ausilio(107) born in 1870
    ix) Anna Saveria D'Ausilio(112) born in 1872
    x) Maria Silveria D'Ausilio(113) born in 1872
    xi) Maria Francesca D'Ausilio(117) born in 1874
    xii) Giovanni Battista (John B.) D'ausilio(120) born in 1877
    xiii) Salvatore Antonio D'ausilio(124) born in 1879
    xiv) Carminantonio D'ausilio(127) born in 1883

Records that include Angelo Maria D'Ausilio(24) and/or Maria Concetta Grasso(24a):
- Ariano, Italy 1832 Birth Act #187
- Ariano, Italy 1836 Birth Act #194
- Ariano, Italy 1854 Marriage Act #10
- Ariano, Italy 1855 Birth Act #116
- Ariano, Italy 1861 Death Act #211
- Ariano, Italy 1865 Birth Act #237
- Ariano, Italy 1867 Birth Act #574
- Ariano, Italy 1867 Birth Act #575

- Ariano, Italy 1869 Death Act #385
- Ariano, Italy 1870 Birth Act #114
- Ariano, Italy 1871 Death Act #91
- Ariano, Italy 1871 Death Act #232
- Ariano, Italy 1872 Birth Act #82
- Ariano, Italy 1872 Birth Act #83
- Ariano, Italy 1874 Birth Act #204
- Ariano, Italy 1877 Birth Act #162
- Ariano, Italy 1877 Death Act #17
- Ariano, Italy 1883 Birth Act #183
- Ariano, Italy 1883 Death Act #90
- Ariano, Italy 1898 Marriage Act #PII.16
- Ariano, Italy 1899 Marriage Act #34
- Ariano, Italy 1900 Death Act #386
- Ariano, Italy 1903 Marriage Act #51
- New Haven, CT 7 July 1904 Marriage Record

25) Maria Michele Marraffino

Maria Michele Marraffino(25) was born on 22 May 1833, in Ariano, Italy, to Nicolangelo Marraffino(6) and Aurelina D'Agostino(6a).

Records that include Maria Michele Marraffino(25):
- Ariano, Italy 1833 Birth Act #223

26) Gennaro D'Ausilio

Gennaro D'Ausilio(26) was born on 5 August 1834, in Ariano, Italy, to Nicola Maria D'Ausilio(7) and Saveria Maria Petrosino(7a). Gennaro D'Ausilio(26) died on 7 April 1852, in Ariano, Italy.

Records that include Gennaro D'Ausilio(26):
- Ariano, Italy 1834 Birth Act #330
- Ariano, Italy 1852 Death Act #118

27) Luigi deDonato

Luigi deDonato(27) was born on 4 January 1835, in Ariano, Italy, to Domenico deDonato(8a) and Mariangela Marraffino(8). Luigi deDonato(27) died on 29 January 1916 in Ariano, Italy. Luigi deDonato(27) was a shoemaker.

Luigi deDonato(27) married Angela Maria Miedico(27a) on 2 December 1855 in Ariano, Italy.

Angela Maria Miedico(27a) was born on 15 August 1826, in Ariano, Italy, to Giuseppe Miedico(27aF) and Maria Rosa Mainiero(27aM). Angela Maria Miedico(27a) died on 9 January 1894 in Ariano, Italy. Angela Maria Miedico(27a) was a farmhand.

Known children of Luigi deDonato(27) and Angela Maria Miedico(27a):

    i) Domenico deDonato(61) born in 1856
    ii) Concetta deDonato(66) born in 1857
    iii) Agata deDonato(75) born in 1859
    iv) Marcello deDonato(78) born in 1861
    v) Maria Carmela deDonato(85) born in 1863
    vi) Raimonda deDonato(96) born in 1866
    vii) Raimonda deDonato(104) born in 1868

Records that include Luigi deDonato(27) and/or Angela Maria Miedico(27a):
- Ariano, Italy 1826 Birth Act #344
- Ariano, Italy 1835 Birth Act #3
- Ariano, Italy 1855 Marriage Act #141
- Ariano, Italy 1856 Birth Act #443
- Ariano, Italy 1857 Birth Act #511
- Ariano, Italy 1859 Birth Act #615
- Ariano, Italy 1860 Death Act #86

- Ariano, Italy 1861 Birth Act #76
- Ariano, Italy 1863 Birth Act #469
- Ariano, Italy 1866 Birth Act #603
- Ariano, Italy 1867 Death Act #216
- Ariano, Italy 1868 Birth Act #262
- Ariano, Italy 1881 Marriage Act #79
- Ariano, Italy 1883 Marriage Act #20
- Ariano, Italy 1894 Death Act #11
- Ariano, Italy 1916 Death Act #29
- Ariano, Italy 1930 Death Act #274

28) Antonio Marraffino

Antonio Marraffino(28) was born on 18 January 1835, in Ariano, Italy, to Nicolangelo Marraffino(6) and Aurelina D'Agostino(6a).

Records that include Antonio Marraffino(28):
- Ariano, Italy 1835 Birth Act #37

29) Maria Concordia diDonato

Maria Concordia diDonato(29) was born on 30 December 1837, in Ariano, Italy, to Domenico diDonato(8a) and Mariangela Marraffino(8). Maria Concordia diDonato(29) died on 7 October 1839, in Ariano, Italy.

Records that include Maria Concordia diDonato(29):
- Ariano, Italy 1837 Birth Act #541
- Ariano, Italy 1839 Death Act #594

30) Angelo Antonio Clericuzio

Angelo Antonio Clericuzio(30) was born on 17 March 1838, in Ariano, Italy, to Nicolantonio Clericuzio(9) and Maria Rosaria Albanese(9a). He died on 13 June 1863, in Ariano, Italy. Angelo Antonio Clericuzio(30) was a farmhand.

Records that include Angelo Antonio Clericuzio(30):
- Ariano, Italy 1838 Birth Act #117
- Ariano, Italy 1863 Death Act #210

31) Raffaele Covotta

Raffaele Covotta(31) was born on 6 May 1840, in Ariano, Italy, to Antonio Covotta (11a) and Colomba Clericuzio(11). Raffaele Covotta(31) died on 29 May 1840, in Ariano, Italy.

Records that include Raffaele Covotta(31):
- Ariano, Italy 1840 Birth Act #169
- Ariano, Italy 1840 Death Act #196

32) Marcello Francesco Saviero deDonato

Marcello Francesco Saviero deDonato(32) was born on 27 September 1840, in Ariano, Italy, to Domenico deDonato(8a) and Mariangela Marraffino(8). Marcello Francesco Saviero deDonato(32) died on 2 January 1861 in Ariano, Italy. Marcello Francesco Saviero deDonato(32) was a landlord.

Records that include Marcello Francesco Saviero deDonato(32):
- Ariano, Italy 1840 Birth Act #300
- Ariano, Italy 1861 Death Act #2

33) Nicoletta Clericuzio

Nicoletta Clericuzio(33) was born on 17 May 1841, in Ariano, Italy, to Nicolantonio Clericuzio(9) and Maria Rosaria Albanese(9a). Nicoletta Clericuzio(33) died on 28 July 1841 in Ariano, Italy.

Records that include Nicoletta Clericuzio(33):
- Ariano, Italy 1841 Birth Act #250

• Ariano, Italy 1841 Death Act #184

34) Anna Maria Covotta

Anna Maria Covotta(34) was born on 21 July 1842, in Ariano, Italy, to Antonio Covotta(11a) and Colomba Clericuzio(11). Anna Maria Covotta(34) died on 7 November 1875 in Ariano, Italy. Anna Maria Covotta(34) was a housewife

Anna Maria Covotta(34) married Oto Stella(34a) on 27 May 1867 in Ariano, Italy.

Oto Stella(34a) was born on 22 February 1841, in Ariano, Italy, to Pellagrino Stella(34aF) and Faustina Spagnuolo(34aM). Oto Stella(34a) died on 30 May 1908, in Ariano, Italy. Oto Stella(34a) was a mediator.

Known children of Anna Maria Covotta(34) and Oto Stella(34a):

     i) Agostino Stella(101) born in 1868
     ii) Antonio Stella(110) born in 1871
     iii) Marianna Stella(116) born in 1874
     iv) Marianna Stella(118) born in 1875

Oto Stella(34a) later married Anna Maria Albanese(34ab) and had children.

Records that include Anna Maria Covotta(34) and/or Oto Stella(34a):
• Ariano, Italy 1841 Birth Act #76
• Ariano, Italy 1842 Birth Act #225
• Ariano, Italy 1867 Marriage Act #39
• Ariano, Italy 1868 Birth Act #111
• Ariano, Italy 1871 Birth Act #4
• Ariano, Italy 1874 Birth Act #119
• Ariano, Italy 1874 Death Act#349
• Ariano, Italy 1875 Birth Act # 496
• Ariano, Italy 1875 Death Act #407
• Ceppaloni, Italy 1896 Marriage Act #13
• Ariano, Italy 1897 Marriage Act #83
• Ariano, Italy 1908 Death Act #166

35) Maria Carmina Clericuzio

Maria Carmina Clericuzio(35) was born on 25 November 1843, in Ariano, Italy, to Raffaele Clericuzio(12) and Maria Teresa Perrotta(12a). Maria Carmina Clericuzio(35) died 12 September 1911 in Ariano, Italy. Maria Carmina Clericuzio(35) was a laundress.

Maria Carmina Clericuzio(35) married Antonio Grasso(35a) on 15 September 1877 in Ariano, Italy

Antonio Grasso(35a) was born on 8 February 1847, in Ariano, Italy, to Angelo Grasso(35aF) and Colomba di Paolo(35aM). Antonio Grasso(35a) died 17 November 1925 in Ariano, Italy. Antonio Grasso(35a) was a farm hand.

Records that include Maria Carmina Clericuzio(35) and/or Antonio Grasso(35a):
• Ariano, Italy 1843 Birth Act #538
• Ariano, Italy 1847 Birth Act #75
• Ariano, Italy 1877 Marriage Act #111
• Ariano, Italy 1911 Death Act #199
• Ariano, Italy 1925 Death Act #286

36) Francesco Saverio deDonato

Francesco Saverio deDonato(36) was born on 28 April 1845, in Ariano, Italy, to Domenico deDonato(8a) and Mariangela Marraffino(8). Francesco Saverio deDonato(36) died on 5 September 1898, in Ariano, Italy. Francesco Saverio deDonato(36) was a shoemaker.

Francesco Saverio deDonato(36) married Concetta Melito(36a).

Concetta Melito(36a) was born on 30 October 1846, in Ariano, Italy, to Nicolantonio Melito(36aF) and Maria Michele Graziano(36aM). Concetta Melito(36a) died on 1 February 1889, in Ariano, Italy. Concetta Melito(36a) was a spinner.

Known children of Francesco Saverio deDonato(36) and Concetta Melito(36a):

> i) Domenico deDonato(94) born in 1866
> ii) Domenico deDonato(103) born in 1868
> iii) Michele deDonato(106) born in 1869
> iv) Angela deDonato(114) born in 1872
> v) Eustachio deDonato(121) born in 1877
> vi) Rosaria deDonato(123) born in 1879
> vii) Luigi deDonato(126) born in 1882
> viii) Pietro deDonato(128) born in 1884
> ix) Angela deDonato(130) born in 1887

Records that include Francesco Saverio deDonato(36) and/or Concetta Melito(36a)

- Ariano, Italy 1845 Birth Act #156
- Ariano, Italy 1846 Birth Act #439
- Ariano, Italy 1866 Birth Act #422
- Ariano, Italy 1867 Death Act #569
- Ariano, Italy 1868 Birth Act #205
- Ariano, Italy 1869 Birth Act #632
- Ariano, Italy 1872 Birth Act #105
- Ariano, Italy 1875 Death Act #78
- Ariano, Italy 1877 Birth Act #380
- Ariano, Italy 1878 Death Act #90
- Ariano, Italy 1879 Birth Act #519
- Ariano, Italy 1882 Birth Act #174
- Ariano, Italy 1888 Birth Act #449
- Ariano, Italy 1889 Death Act #40
- Ariano, Italy 1889 Death Act #354
- Ariano, Italy 1894 Marriage Act #134
- Ariano, Italy 1898 Death Act #303
- Ariano, Italy 1908 Marriage Act #77
- Ariano, Italy 1909 Marriage Act #100

37) Gaetano Covotta

Gaetano Covotta(37) was born on 10 May 1845, in Ariano, Italy, to Antonio Covotta(11a) and Colomba Clericuzio(11). Gaetano Covotta(37) died on 22 May 1846, in Ariano, Italy.

Records that include Gaetano Covotta(37):
    Ariano, Italy 1845 Birth Act#173
    Ariano, Italy 1846 Death Act#111

38) Maria Consiglia Clericuzio

Maria Consiglia Clericuzio(38) was born on 12 May 1845, in Ariano, Italy, to Raffaele Clericuzio(12) and Maria Teresa Perrotta(12a). Maria Consiglia Clericuzio(38) died on 16 February 1871, in Ariano, Italy. Maria Consiglia Clericuzio(38) was a laundress.

Known children of Maria Consiglia Clericuzio(38):

> i) Giuseppe Vittorio Clericuzio(95) born in 1867
> ii) Adelina Clericuzio(108) born in 1870
> iii) Metilda Francesca Clericuzio(109) born in 1870

Records that include Maria Consiglia Clericuzio(38):
- Ariano, Italy 1845 Birth Act #175
- Ariano, Italy 1867 Birth Act #241
- Ariano, Italy 1867 Death Act #361
- Ariano, Italy 1870 Birth Act #636

- Ariano, Italy 1870 Birth Act #637
- Ariano, Italy 1871 Death Act #30
- Ariano, Italy 1871 Death Act #66

39) Gaetano Covotta

Gaetano Covotta(39) was born on 29 February 1848, in Ariano, Italy, to Antonio Covotta(11a) and Colomba Clericuzio(11). Gaetano Covotta(39) died on 24 December 1915, in Ariano, Italy. Gaetano Covotta(39) was a tailor.

Gaetano Covotta(39) married Giovanna di Franza(39a) and Raffaela Macchiaverna(39b).

Gaetano Covotta(39) married Giovanna Di Franza(39a) on 4 February 1875 in Ariano, Italy.

Giovanna Di Franza(39a) was born on 29 August 1850, in Ariano, Italy, to Michele di Franza(39aF) and Carosino Grasso(39aM). Giovanna Di Franza(39a) died on 27 August 1887 in Ariano, Italy. Giovanna Di Franza(39a) was a seamstress.

Known children of Gaetano Covotta(39) and Giovanna Di Franza(39a):

      i) Antonio Covotta(119) born in 1876
      ii) Michele Covotta(122) born in 1879
      iii) Raffaele Covotta(125) born about 1882
      iv) Maria Covotta(129) born in 1885

Gaetano Covotta(39) married Raffaela Macchiaverna(39b) on 23 August 1890 in Ariano, Italy.

Raffaela Macchiaverna(39b) was born on 25 May 1847, in Ariano, Italy, to Giovanni Macchiaverna(39bF) and Mariangela Zerella(39bM). Raffaela Macchiaverna(39b) died on 28 October 1910 in Ariano, Italy. Raffaela Macchiaverna(39b) was a seamstress.

Records that include Gaetano Covotta(39), Giovanna Di Franza(39a), and/or Raffaela Macchiaverna(39b):

- Ariano, Italy 1847 Birth Act #268
- Ariano, Italy 1848 Birth Act #105
- Ariano, Italy 1850 Birth Act #409
- Ariano, Italy 1875 Marriage Act #26
- Ariano, Italy 1876 Birth Act #16
- Ariano, Italy 1879 Birth Act #43
- Ariano, Italy 1885 Birth Act #673
- Ariano, Italy 1887 Death Act #289
- Ariano, Italy 1889 Death Act #385
- Ariano, Italy 1889 Death Act #389
- Ariano, Italy 1890 Marriage Act #89
- Ariano, Italy 1904 Marriage Act #93
- Ariano, Italy 1910 Death Act #374
- Ariano, Italy 1915 Death Act #303

40) Maria Amalia Clericuzio

Maria Amalia Clericuzio(40) was born on 19 February 1849, in Ariano, Italy, to Raffaele Clericuzio(12) and Maria Teresa Perrotta(12a).

Records that include Maria Amalia Clericuzio(40):
- Ariano, Italy 1849 Birth Act #115

FIFTH GENERATION

41) Raffaele Fodarella

Raffaele Fodarella(41) was born on 29 November 1845, in Ariano, Italy, to Domenico Fodarella(15a) and Mariangela d'Ausilio(15). Raffaele Fodarella(41) died on 13 March 1854, in Ariano, Italy.

Records that include Raffaele Fodarella(41):
- Ariano, Italy 1845 Birth Act #424
- Ariano, Italy 1854 Death Act #113

42) Maria Concordia Fodarella

Maria Concordia Fodarella(42) was born on 15 October 1848, in Ariano, Italy, to Domenico Fodarella(15a) and Mariangela d'Ausilio(15). Maria Concordia Fodarella(42) died 12 February 1911 in Ariano, Italy. Maria Concordia Fodarella(42) was a farm laborer.

Maria Concordia Fodarella(42) married Liberatore Tiso(42a) on 8 October 1868 in Ariano, Italy.

Liberatore Tiso(42a) was born on 6 June 1846, in Ariano, Italy, to Vincenzo Tiso(42aF) and Loreta Graziano(42aM). Liberatore Tiso(42a) died 11 November 1909. Liberatore Tiso(42a) was a farm laborer.

Known children of Maria Concordia Fodarella(42) and Liberatore Tiso(42a):

    i) Vincenzo Tiso(131) born in 1870
    ii) Mariangela Tiso(133) born about 1873
    iii) Filomena Tiso(136) born in 1876
    iv) Mariangela Tiso(153) born about 1880
    v) Oto (Ottone) Tiso(169) born in 1883

Records that include Maria Concordia Fodarella(42) and/or Liberatore Tiso(42a):
- Ariano, Italy 1846 Birth Act #252
- Ariano, Italy 1848 Birth Act #436
- Ariano, Italy 1868 Marriage Act #140
- Ariano, Italy 1870 Birth Act #422
- Ariano, Italy 1876 Birth Act #403
- Ariano, Italy 1880 Birth Act #340
- Ariano, Italy 1881 Death Act #320
- Ariano, Italy 1883 Birth Act #257
- Ariano, Italy 1894 Death Act #162
- Ariano, Italy 1909 Death Act #347
- Ariano, Italy 1911 Death Act #49

43) Maria Rosa Fiorenza

Maria Rosa Fiorenza(43) was born on 21 October 1849, in Ariano, Italy, to Gaetano Fiorenza(13a) and Maria Vincenza Marraffino(13). Maria Rosa Fiorenza(43) died on 23 August 1850 in Ariano, Italy.

Records that include Maria Rosa Fiorenza(43):
- Ariano, Italy 1849 Birth Act #465
- Ariano, Italy 1850 Death Act #228

44) Giuseppe Orlando

Giuseppe Orlando(44) was born on 25 January 1850, in Orsara, Italy, to Pasquale Orlando(19a) and Maria Guiseppa d'Ausilio(19). Giuseppe Orlando(44) died on 15 September 1850 in Orsara, Italy.

Records that include Giuseppe Orlando(44):
- Orsara, Italy 1850 Birth Act #14
- Orsara, Italy 1850 Death Act #140

45) Anna Maria Perrina

Anna Maria Perrina(45) was born on 18 February 1850, in Ariano, Italy, to Liberatore Perrina(18a) and Maria Nicoletta deDonato(18). Anna Maria Perrina(45) died 10 November 1933 in Ariano, Italy. Anna Maria Perrina(45) was a farm laborer.

Anna Maria Perrina(45) married Lorenzo Grasso(45a), on 5 February 1874 in Ariano, Italy.

Lorenzo Grasso(45a) was born on 16 November 1850, in Ariano, Italy, to Giovanbattista Grasso(45aF) and Raffaella Ciano(45aM). Lorenzo Grasso(45a) died on 21 March 1935, in Ariano, Italy. Lorenzo Grasso(45a) was a farm laborer.

Known children of Anna Maria Perrina(45) and Lorenzo Grasso(45a):

    i) Antonio Grasso(140) born in 1877
    ii) Lucia Grasso(149) born in 1879
    iii) Giovanni Battista Grasso(162) born in 1881
    iv) Raffaella Grasso(173) born in 1884
    v) Maria Raffaella Grasso(185) born in 1885
    vi) Michele Grasso(211) born about 1888
    vii) Carmela Grasso(223) born in 1890
    viii) Giovanbattista Grasso(240) born in 1892

Records that include Anna Maria Perrina(45) and Lorenzo Grasso(45a):
* Ariano, Italy 1850 Birth Act #94
* Ariano, Italy 1850 Birth Act #544
* Ariano, Italy 1874 Marriage Act #21
* Ariano, Italy 1877 Birth Act #333
* Ariano, Italy 1879 Birth Act #322
* Ariano, Italy 1880 Death Act #392
* Ariano, Italy 1880 Death Act #425
* Ariano, Italy 1881 Birth Act #608
* Ariano, Italy 1882 Death Act #61
* Ariano, Italy 1884 Birth Act #166
* Ariano, Italy 1884 Death Act #396
* Ariano, Italy 1885 Birth Act #646
* Ariano, Italy 1886 Death Act #282
* Ariano, Italy 1889 Birth Act #146
* Ariano, Italy 1889 Death Act #119
* Ariano, Italy 1892 Birth Act #570
* Ariano, Italy 1893 Death Act #243
* Ariano, Italy 1911 Marriage Act #82
* Ariano, Italy 1933 Death Act #258
* Ariano, Italy 1935 Death Act #96
* Ariano, Italy 1935 Death Act #202

46) Mariangela Perrina

Mariangela Perrina(46) was born on 24 April 1851, in Ariano, Italy, to Liberatore Perrina(18a) and Maria Nicoletta deDonato(18). Mariangela Perrina(46) died on 5 May 1851, in Ariano, Italy.

Records that include Mariangela Perrina(46):
* Ariano, Italy 1851 Birth Record #190
* Ariano, Italy 1851 Death Record #152

47) Nicola Fiorenza

Nicola Fiorenza(47) was born on 7 November 1851, in Ariano, Italy, to Gaetano Fiorenza(13a) and Maria Vincenza Marraffino(13). Nicola Fiorenza(47) died on 18 May 1935 in Ariano, Italy. Nicola Fiorenza(47) was a farm hand.

Nicola Fiorenza(47) married Concetta Ruggiero(47a) and Maria Carmela Iannone(47b).

Nicola Fiorenza(47) married Concetta Ruggiero(47a) 13 July 1882 in Ariano, Italy.

Concetta Ruggiero(47a) was born on 9 August 1853, in Ariano, Italy, to Domenico Ruggiero(47aF) and Maria Clericuzio(47aM). Concetta Ruggiero(47a) died on 25 March 1921 in Ariano, Italy. Concetta Ruggiero(47a) was a Housekeeper.

Nicola Fiorenza(47) married Maria Carmela Iannone(47b) on 5 August 1922 in Ariano, Italy.

Maria Carmela Iannone(47b) was born on 17 July 1853, in Montecalvo, Italy, to Giuseppe Iannone(47bF) and Maria Antonia Stiscia(47bM). Maria Carmela Iannone(47b) died on 22 January 1933 in Ariano, Italy. Maria Carmela Iannone(47b) was a farm laborer.

Maria Carmela Iannone(47b) was previously married to Lorenzo Ionno(47bX).

Records that include Nicola Fiorenza(47), Concetta Ruggiero(47a) and/or Maria Carmela Iannone(47b):
- Ariano, Italy 1851 Birth Act #460
- Ariano, Italy 1853 Birth Act #397
- Montecalvo, Italy 1853 Birth Act #106
- Montecalvo, Italy 1871 Marriage Act #27
- Ariano, Italy 1882 Marriage Act #65
- Ariano, Italy 1921 Death Act #104
- Ariano, Italy 1922 Marriage Act #115
- Ariano, Italy 1933 Death Act #20
- Ariano, Italy 1937 Death Act #II.B.8

48) Lorenzo Fodarella

Lorenzo Fodarella(48) was born on 4 January 1852, in Ariano, Italy, to Domenico Fodarella(15a) and Mariangela d'Ausilio(15). Lorenzo Fodarella(48) died 29 April 1927 in Ariano, Italy. Lorenzo Fodarella(48) was a farm laborer.

Lorenzo Fodarella(48) married Maria Fransesca Paola Dotolo(48a) on 4 November 1876 in Ariano, Italy.

Maria Fransesca Paola Dotolo(48a) was born on 30 May 1856, in Ariano, Italy, to Giuseppe Dotolo(48aF) and Raimonda Caputo(48aM).

Known children of Lorenzo Fodarella(48) and Maria Fransesca Paola Dotolo(48a):

    i) Domenico Fodarella(141) born in 1877
    ii) Mariangela Fodarella(146) born in 1879
    iii) Mariantonia Fodarella(152) born in 1880
    iv) Giuseppantonio Fodarella(161) born in 1881
    v) Domenico Fodarella(174) born in 1884
    vi) Luigi Fodarella(188) born in 1886
    vii) Maria Raimonda Fodarella(203) born in 1887
    viii) Otomaria Fodrella(214) born in 1889
    ix) Mariangela Fodarella(229) born in 1891
    x) Carmela Fodarella(244) born in 1893

Records that include Lorenzo Fodarella(48) and/or Maria Fransesca Paola Dotolo(48a):
- Ariano, Italy 1852 Birth Act #5
- Ariano, Italy 1856 Birth Act #321
- Ariano, Italy 1876 Marriage Act #111
- Ariano, Italy 1877 Birth Act #477
- Ariano, Italy 1878 Death Act #233
- Ariano, Italy 1879 Birth Act #57
- Ariano, Italy 1879 Death Act #140
- Ariano, Italy 1880 Birth Act #236

- Ariano, Italy 1881 Birth Act #571
- Ariano, Italy 1884 Birth Act #215
- Ariano, Italy 1886 Birth Act #11
- Ariano, Italy 1887 Birth Act #733
- Ariano, Italy 1889 Birth Act #635
- Ariano, Italy 1891 Birth Act #320
- Ariano, Italy 1893 Birth Act #110
- Ariano, Italy 1901 Marriage Act #27
- Ariano, Italy 1909 Marriage Act #93
- Ariano, Italy 1910 Marriage Act #93
- Ariano, Italy 1919 Marriage Act #86
- Ariano, Italy 1927 Death Act #139

49) Mariangela Perrina

Mariangela Perrina(49) was born on 28 April 1852, in Ariano, Italy, to Oto Maria Perrina (14a) and Maria Raimonda deDonato(14). Mariangela Perrina(49) died on 18 September 1854, in Ariano, Italy.

Records that include Mariangela Perrina(49):
- Ariano, Italy 1852 Birth Act #272
- Ariano, Italy 1854 Death Act #428

50) Gennaro diVitto

Gennaro diVitto(50) was born on 27 September 1852, in Ariano, Italy, to Raimondo di Vitto(16a) and Raimonda D'Ausilio(16).

Records that include Gennaro diVitto(50):
- Ariano, Italy 1852 Birth Act #489

51) Rosa Giorgione

Rosa Giorgione(51) was born on 8 October 1852, in Ariano, Italy, to Antonio Giorgione(21a) and Maria Filomina d'Ausilio(21). Rosa Giorgione(51) died on 28 April 1938 in Ariano, Italy. Rosa Giorgione(51) was a farm hand.

Rosa Giorgione(51) married Giuseppe Miressi(51a) on 4 September 1871 in Ariano, Italy.

Giuseppe Miressi(51a) was born on 30 December 1841, in Ariano, Italy, to Nicolangelo Miressi(51aF) and Serafina Lo Conte(51aM). Giuseppe Miressi(51a) died on 4 January 1925 in Ariano, Italy. Giuseppe Miressi(51a) was a farm hand.

Giuseppe Miressi(51a) previously married Concetta Pescatore(51aX).

Known children of Rosa Giorgione(51) and Giuseppe Miressi(51a):

    i) Nicolantonio Miressi(132) born in 1872
    ii) Filomena Miressi(134) born in 1874
    iii) Agata Miressi(142) born in 1877
    iv) Generoso Miressi(145) born in 1878
    v) Generoso Miressi(160) born in 1881
    vi) Biagio Miressi(172) born in 1884
    vii) Maria Miressi(192) born in 1886
    viii) Giovanni Miressi(226) born in 1891
    ix) Ciriaco Miressi(273) born in 1896
    x) Angela Miressi(291) born in 1898

Records that include Rosa Giorgione(51) and/or Giuseppe Miressi(51a):
- Ariano, Italy 1841 Birth Act #568
- Ariano, Italy 1852 Birth Act #505
- Ariano, Italy 1871 Marriage Act #83
- Ariano, Italy 1872 Birth Act #490
- Ariano, Italy 1874 Birth Act #575
- Ariano, Italy 1877 Birth Act #483

- Ariano, Italy 1877 Death Act #293
- Ariano, Italy 1878 Birth Act #426
- Ariano, Italy 1880 Death Act #560
- Ariano, Italy 1880 Death Act #574
- Ariano, Italy 1881 Birth Act #526
- Ariano, Italy 1884 Birth Act #68
- Ariano, Italy 1886 Birth Act #295
- Ariano, Italy 1891 Birth Act #248
- Ariano, Italy 1894 Marriage Act #84
- Ariano, Italy 1896 Birth Act #637
- Ariano, Italy 1898 Birth Act #518
- Ariano, Italy 1900 Marriage Act #89
- Ariano, Italy 1903 Marriage Act #86
- Ariano, Italy 1905 Marriage Act #29
- Ariano, Italy 1905 Marriage Act #105
- Ariano, Italy 1911 Marriage Act #47
- Ariano, Italy 1911 Marriage Act #103
- "New York, County Marriages, 1847-1848; 1908-1936", , FamilySearch (https://www.familysearch.org/ark:/61903/1:1:XVPV-9Z4 : Sat Mar 09 17:00:47 UTC 2024), Entry for John Mirissi and Ginseppe Miresse, 23 December 1917.
- Ariano, Italy 1920 Marriage Act #68
- Ariano, Italy 1925 Death Act #4
- Ariano, Italy 1938 Death Act #105
- Ariano, Italy 1950 Marriage Act #P.II.B.5

52) Angela Perrina

Angela Perrina(52) was born on 12 November 1852, in Ariano, Italy, to Liberatore Perrina(18a) and Maria Nicoletta deDonato(18). Angela Perrina(52) died 16 September 1935 in Ariano, Italy. Angela Perrina(52) was a farm laborer.

Angela Perrina(52) married Nicola Maria Di Lillo(52a), on 14 September 1876 in Ariano, Italy.

Nicola Maria Di Lillo(52a) was born on 18 September 1850, in Ariano, Italy, to Francesco di Lillo(52aF) and Lucia Perrina(52aM). Nicola Maria Di Lillo(52a) died on 20 September 1931 in Ariano, Italy. Nicola Maria Di Lillo(52a) was a farm laborer.

Known children of Angela Perrina(52) and Nicola Maria Di Lillo(52a):

    i) Maria Giuseppa Di Lillo(147) born in 1879
    ii) Mariantonia Di Lillo(155) born in 1880
    iii) Angelo Maria Di Lillo(170) born in 1883
    iv) Francesco di Lillo(184) born in 1885
    v) Pasquale Di Lillo(215) born in 1889
    vi) Pasquale Di Lillo(249) born in 1893

Records that include Angela Perrina(52) and/or Nicola Maria Di Lillo(52a):
- Ariano, Italy 1850 Birth Act #447
- Ariano, Italy 1852 Birth Act #559
- Ariano, Italy 1876 Marriage Act #82
- Ariano, Italy 1879 Birth Act #183
- Ariano, Italy 1879 Death Act #433
- Ariano, Italy 1880 Birth Act #489
- Ariano, Italy 1882 Death Act #294
- Ariano, Italy 1883 Birth Act #273
- Ariano, Italy 1884 Death Act #346
- Ariano, Italy 1885 Birth Act #682
- Ariano, Italy 1889 Birth Act #640
- Ariano, Italy 1891 Death Act #40
- Ariano, Italy 1893 Birth Act #364
- Ariano, Italy 1894 Death Act #345

- Ariano, Italy 1907 Marriage Act #110
- Ariano, Italy 1909 Death Act #328
- Ariano, Italy 1931 Death Act #195
- Ariano, Italy 1935 Death Act #250

53) Filomena Perrina

Filomena Perrina(53) was born on 11 November 1853, in Ariano, Italy, to Oto Maria Perrina(14a) and Maria Raimonda deDonato(14). Filomena Perrina(53) died on 23 September 1854, in Ariano, Italy.

Records that include Filomena Perrina(53):
Ariano, Italy 1853 Birth Act #526
Ariano, Italy 1854 Death Act #440

54) Michele diVitto

Michele diVitto(54) was born on 8 September 1854, in Ariano, Italy, to Raimondo diVitto(16a) and Raimonda D'Ausilio(16). Michele diVitto(54) died on 16 July 1871 in Ariano, Italy. Michele diVitto(54) was a scribe.

Records that include Michele diVitto(54):
- Ariano, Italy 1854 Birth Act #328
- Ariano, Italy 1871 death Act #214

55) Aurelia Fiorenza

Aurelia Fiorenza(55) was born on 18 October 1854, in Ariano, Italy, to Gaetano Fiorenza(13a) and Maria Vincenza Marraffino(13). Aurelia Fiorenza(55) died on 14 February 1925 in Ariano, Italy. Aurelia Fiorenza(55) was a farmhand.

Aurelia Fiorenza(55) married Lorenzo Scauzillo(55a) and Pasqualantonio Pietracola(55b).

Aurelia Fiorenza(55) married Lorenzo Scauzillo(55a) on 2 January 1879 in Ariano, Italy.

Lorenzo Scauzillo(55a) was born on 27 May 1851, in Ariano, Italy, to Otantonio Scauzillo(55aF) and Rosaria Lo Conte(55aM). Lorenzo Scauzillo(55a) died on 23 August 1883 in Ariano, Italy. Lorenzo Scauzillo(55a) was a farmhand.

Known children of Aurelia Fiorenza(55) and Lorenzo Scauzillo(55a):

   i) Maria Rosaria Scauzillo(150) born in 1879
   ii) Gaetano Scauzillo(164) born in 1882

Aurelia Fiorenza(55) married Pasqualantonio Pietracola(55b) on 16 April 1885 in Ariano, Italy.

Pasqualantonio Pietracola(55b) was born on 19 January 1862 in Ariano, Italy to Raffaele Pietracola(55bF) and Caterina Bernardo(55bM). Pasqualantonio Pietracola(55b) died 2 March 1934 in Ariano, Italy. Pasqualantonio Pietracola(55b) was a farmhand.

Known children of Aurelia Fiorenza(55) and Pasqualantonio Pietracola(55b):

   i) Mariangela Pietracola(189) born in 1886
   ii) Antonio Pietracola(212) born in 1889
   iii) Maria Carmelo Pietracola(237) born in 1892

Records that include Aurelia Fiorenza(55), Lorenzo Scauzillo(55a) and/or Pasqualantonio Pietracola(55b):
- Ariano, Italy 1851 Birth Act #239
- Ariano, Italy 1854 Birth Act #377
- Ariano, Italy 1862 Birth Act #28
- Ariano, Italy 1879 Marriage Act #1
- Ariano, Italy 1879 Birth Act #482
- Ariano, Italy 1882 Birth Act #170
- Ariano, Italy 1883 Death Act #243

- Ariano, Italy 1885 Marriage Act #36
- Ariano, Italy 1886 Birth Act #45
- Ariano, Italy 1888 Birth Act #164
- Ariano, Italy 1889 Birth Act #164
- Ariano, Italy 1892 Birth Act #320
- Ariano, Italy 1903 Marriage Act #18
- "New York, New York City Marriage Records, 1829-1938", , FamilySearch (https://www.familysearch.org/ark:/61903/1:1:244Q-4WZ : Sat Mar 09 04:31:53 UTC 2024), Entry for Gaetano Scanzillo and Giovannina Grassi, 7 Sep 1905.
- Ariano, Italy 1913 Marriage Act #31
- Ariano, Italy 1925 Death Act #41
- Ariano, Italy 1934 Death Act #65

56) Gabriele D'Ausilio

Gabriele D'ausilio(56) was born on 18 March 1855, in Ariano, Italy, to Angelo Maria D'Ausilio(24) and Maria Concetta Grasso(24a). Gabriele D'ausilio(56) died on 25 May 1861, in Ariano, Italy.

Records that include Gabriele D'ausilio(56):
- Ariano, Italy 1855 Birth Act #116
- Ariano, Italy 1861 Death Act #211

57) Anna Maria Fodarella

Anna Maria Fodarella(57) was born on 31 May 1855, in Ariano, Italy, to Domenico Fodarella(15a) and Mariangela d'Ausilio(15). Anna Maria Fodarella(57) died on 11 June 1888 in Ariano, Italy. Anna Maria Fodarella(57) was a farm laborer.

Anna Maria Fodarella(57) married Vincenzo Manganiello(57a) on 1 October 1874 in Ariano, Italy.

Vincenzo Manganiello(57a) was born on 25 October 1850, in Ariano, Italy, to Ciriaco Manganiello(57aF) and Maria Michele Scrima(57aM). Vincenzo Manganiello(57a) died on 10 May 1929, in Ariano, Italy. Vincenzo Manganiello(57a) was a farm laborer.

Vincenzo Manganiello(54a) also married Vincenza Rogazzo(57ab) and Anna Maria Tirano(57ac).

Known children of Anna Maria Fodarella(57) and Vincenzo Manganiello(57a):

i) Concetta Manganiello(135) born in 1875
ii) Michele Manganiello(138) born in 1877
iii) Maria Annuziata Manganiello(148) born in 1879
iv) Ciriaco Manganiello(159) born in 1881
v) Maria Carmela Manganiello(168) born in 1883
vi) Raimondo Manganiello(182) born in 1885

Records that include Anna Maria Fodarella(57) and/or Vincenzo Manganiello(57a):
- Ariano, Italy 1855 Birth Act #371
- Ariano, Italy 1850 Birth Act #504
- Ariano, Italy 1855 Birth Act #224
- Ariano, Italy 1874 Marriage Act #80
- Ariano, Italy 1875 Birth Act #539
- Ariano, Italy 1877 Birth Act #235
- Ariano, Italy 1879 Birth Act #186
- Ariano, Italy 1881 Birth Act #430
- Ariano, Italy 1883 Birth Act #134
- Ariano, Italy 1885 Birth Act #546
- Ariano, Italy 1888 Death Act #290
- Ariano, Italy 1899 Marriage Act #18
- Ariano, Italy 1905 Marriage Act #3
- Ariano, Italy 1909 Marriage Act #72

- Ariano, Italy 1920 Marriage Act #86
- Ariano, Italy 1927 Marriage Act #15
- Ariano, Italy 1929 Death Act #176
- Ariano, Italy 1932 Death Act #51
- Ariano, Italy 1937 Death Act #219
- Ariano, Italy 1956 Death Act #52

58) Raffaele Perrina

Raffaele Perrina(58) was born on 9 October 1855, in Ariano, Italy, to Oto Maria Perrina(14a) and Maria Raimonda deDonato(14). Raffaele Perrina(58) sailed to the United States on 24 April 1901 on board the ship Sempiane, arriving in New York, NY. On 3 June 1907 Raffaele Perrina(58) became an American Citizen, Raffaele Perrina(58) was listed as a Sexton. Raffaele Perrina(58) died on 24 February 1944 in Schenectady, NY.

Raffaele Perrina(58) married Maria Lucia Gesa(58a), on 8 October 1879 in San Nicola, Italy.

Maria Lucia Gesa(58a) was born on 13 December 1857, in San Sossio, Italy to Carmine Gesa(58aF) and Maria Saveria Pennacchio(58aM). Maria Lucia Gesa(58a) sailed to the United States arriving in New York on 21 November 1903 on the ship SS Perugia. Maria Lucia Gesa(58a) died on 25 May 1944 in Schenectady, NY.

Known children of Raffaele Perrina(58) and Maria Lucia Gesa(58a):

  i) Antonio Perrina(139) born in 1877
  ii) Maria Perrina(154) born in 1880
  iii) Concetta Perrina(157) born about 1881
  iv) Michelangelo Perrina(176) born in 1884
  v) Vittorio Perrino(187) born in 1885
  vi) Maria Perrina(202) born in 1887
  vii) Antonio Perrina(224) born in 1890
  viii) Concetta Felicia Perrina(238) born in 1892
  ix) Elisabetta Perrina(256) born in 1894
  x) Michelangelo Perrina(275) born in 1897
  xi) Elisabetta Giovanna Perrina(301) born in 1900

Records that include Raffaele Perrina(58) and Maria Lucia Gesa(58a):
- Ariano, Italy 1855 Birth Act #371
- San Sossio Baronia, Italy 1857 Birth Act #88
- San Nicola Baronia, Italy 1877 Birth Act #27
- San Nicola Baronia, Italy 1880 Birth Act #20
- San Nicola Baronia, Italy 1880 Death Act #19
- Castel Baronia, Italy 1884 Death #36
- San Nicola Baronia, Italy 1885 Birth Act #41
- San Nicola Baronia, Italy 1888 Death Act #40
- Castel Baronia, Italy 1889 Death Act #1
- Castel Baronia, Italy 1889 Death Act #2
- Castel Baronia, Italy 1892 Birth Act #26
- Castel Baronia, Italy 1894 Birth Act #33
- Castel Baronia, Italy 1897 Birth Act #23
- "New York Passenger Arrival Lists (Ellis Island), 1892-1924", , FamilySearch (https://www.familysearch.org/ark:/61903/1:1:JFYG-93G : Sun Mar 10 06:51:48 UTC 2024), Entry for M. Lucia Gesa and Raffaele Perrino, 1903.
- "New York, County Naturalization Records, 1791-1980", , FamilySearch (https://www.familysearch.org/ark:/61903/1:1:7WZM-S2PZ : Fri Mar 08 21:11:12 UTC 2024), Entry for Raffaele Perrino and Lucy Perrino, 1906.
- "United States Census, 1910," database with images, FamilySearch (https://familysearch.org/ark:/61903/1:1:M596-H5L : accessed 14 July 2023), Antonio Perrino in household of Raffaele Perrino, Schenectady Ward 7, Schenectady, New York, United States; citing enumeration district (ED) ED 196, sheet 10A, family 211, NARA microfilm publication T624 (Washington D.C.: National Archives and Records Administration, 1982), roll 1078; FHL microfilm 1,375,091.

- "New York, County Marriages, 1847-1848; 1908-1936", , FamilySearch (https://www.familysearch.org/ark:/61903/1:1:FFT7-4MK : Sun Mar 10 17:29:29 UTC 2024), Entry for Vittorio Perrino and Raffaele, 27 October 1910.
- "St. John the Baptist, Schenectady, New York, Marriages (May 1854 – Jun 2009)", American-Canadian Genealogical Society, Manchester, NH, page 576
- "New York State Census, 1915", database, FamilySearch (https://www.familysearch.org/ark:/61903/1:1:K9P8-7CH : 3 June 2022), Ralph Perrino, 1915.
- "New York State Census, 1925," database, FamilySearch (https://familysearch.org/ark:/61903/1:1:KSHH-T5G : 8 November 2014), Ralph Perrino, Schenectady Ward 14, A.D. 02, E.D. 01, Schenectady, New York, United States; records extracted by Ancestry and images digitized by FamilySearch; citing p. 14, line 17, New York State Archives, Albany.
- "United States Census, 1930," database with images, FamilySearch (https://www.familysearch.org/ark:/61903/1:1:X4T1-X6H : accessed 14 July 2023), Ralph Peraino, Schenectady, Schenectady, New York, United States; citing enumeration district (ED) ED 83, sheet 6B, line 54, family 118, NARA microfilm publication T626 (Washington D.C.: National Archives and Records Administration, 2002), roll 1646; FHL microfilm 2,341,380.
- "United States Census, 1940", , FamilySearch (https://www.familysearch.org/ark:/61903/1:1:KQ3C-F5Z : Sun Jul 14 04:45:47 UTC 2024), Entry for Michael Perrino and Rose Perrino, 1940.
- "St. Anthony, Schenectady, New York, Deaths (Oct 1916 –Jun 2007)", American-Canadian Genealogical Society, Manchester, NH, page 293

59) Maria Rosa diVitto

Maria Rosa diVitto(59) [birth record has last name as Vitto] was born on 2 April 1856, in Ariano, Italy, to Raimondo diVitto(16a) and Raimonda D'Ausilio(16).

Records that include Maria Rosa diVitto(59):
- Ariano, Italy 1856 Birth Act #199

60) Maria Libera Giorgione

Maria Liberia Giorgione(60) was born on 29 July 1856, in Ariano, Italy, to Antonio Giorgione(21a) and Maria Filomina d'Ausilio(21). Maria Liberia Giorgione(60) died on 13 October 1865, in Ariano, Italy.

Records that include Maria Libera Giorgione(60):
- Ariano, Italy 1856 Birth Act #401
- Ariano, Italy 1865 Death Act #300

61) Domenico deDonato

Domenico deDonato(61) was born on 31 August 1856, in Ariano, Italy, to Luigi deDonato(27) and Angela Maria Miedico(27a).

Domenico deDonato(61) married Anna Maria Coppola(61a) on 1 February 1883 in Ariano, Italy.

Anna Maria Coppola(61a) was born on 21 November 1859, in Ariano, Italy, to Leonardo Coppola(61aF) and Clementina Vernacchia(61aM). Anna Maria Coppola(61a) died 2 January 1935 in Ariano, Italy. Anna Maria Coppola(61a) was a domestic.

Known children of Domenico deDonato(61) and Anna Maria Coppola(61a):

    i) Luigi Anselmo deDonato(175) born in 1884
    ii) Generoso deDonato(197) born in 1887
    iii) Generoso deDonato(210) born in 1888
    iv) Pasquale Leonardo Pietro deDonato(222) born in 1890
    v) Clementina DeDonato(266) born in 1897

Records that include Domenico deDonato(61) and/or Anna Maria Coppola(61a):
* Ariano, Italy 1856 Birth Act #443
* Ariano, Italy 1859 Birth Act #534
* Ariano, Italy 1883 Marriage Act #20
* Ariano, Italy 1884 Birth Act #428
* Ariano, Italy 1885 Death Act #193
* Ariano, Italy 1887 Birth Act #345
* Ariano, Italy 1888 Birth Act #617
* Ariano, Italy 1888 Death Act #78
* Ariano, Italy 1888 Death Act #485
* Ariano, Italy 1890 Birth Act #84
* Ariano, Italy 1893 Death Act #35
* Ariano, Italy 1897 Birth Act #82
* Ariano, Italy 1898 Death Act #342
* Ariano, Italy 1935 Death Act #4

62) Ciriaco Perrina

Ciriaco Perrina(62) was born on 4 February 1857, in Ariano, Italy, to Liberatore Perrina(18a) and Maria Nicoletta deDonato(18). Ciriaco Perrina(62) died on 23 April 1857, in Ariano, Italy.

Records that include Ciriaco Perrina(62):
* Ariano, Italy 1857 Birth Act #55
* Ariano, Italy 1857 Death Act #138

63) Pasquale D'Ausilio

Pasquale D'ausilio(63) was born on 15 May 1857, in Ariano, Italy, to Angelo Maria D'Ausilio(24) and Maria Concetta Grasso(24a). Pasquale D'ausilio(63) died on 27 April 1940, in Ariano, Italy. Pasquale D'ausilio(63) was a property owner.

Pasquale D'ausilio(63) married Maria Loretta Scauzillo(63a) on 11 May 1882 in, Ariano Italy.

Maria Loretta Scauzillo(63a) was born on 12 February 1856, in Ariano, Italy, to Michele Scauzillo(63aF) and Mariantonia diFuria(63aM). Maria Loretta Scauzillo(63a) was a housewife.

Records that include Pasquale D'ausilio(63) and/or Maria Loretta Scauzillo(63a):
* Ariano, Italy 1856 Birth Act #79
* Ariano, Italy 1857 Birth Act #231
* Ariano, Italy 1882 Marriage Act #44
* Ariano, Italy 1940 Death Act #116

64) Maria Francesca Fodarella

Maria Francesca Fodarella(64) was born on 22 May 1857, in Ariano, Italy, to Domenico Fodarella(15a) and Mariangela d'Ausilio(15). Maria Francesca Fodarella(64) died 2 April 1909 in Ariano, Italy. Maria Francesca Fodarella(64) was a farmhand.

Maria Francesca Fodarella(64) married Giuseppe Manganiello(64a) on 7 August 1875 in Ariano, Italy.

Giuseppe Manganiello(64a) was born on 22 August 1847, in Ariano, Italy, to Ciriaco Manganiello(64aF) and Maria Michele Scrima(64aM). Giuseppe Manganiello(64a) died on 14 October 1913 in Ariano, Italy. Giuseppe Manganiello(64a) was a farm laborer.

Known children of Maria Francesca Fodarella(64) and Giuseppe Manganiello(64a):

i) Maria Michele Manganiello(137) born in 1876
ii) Mariangela Manganiello(151) born in 1879
iii) Mariantonia Manganiello(163) born in 1882

    iv) Mariantonia Manganiello(171) in 1883
    v) Ciriaco (Jerry) Manganiello(180) born in 1885
    vi) Carmela Manganiello(205) born in 1888
    vii) Concordia Manganiello(267) born in 1896

Records that include Maria Francesca Fodarella(64) and/or Giuseppe Manganiello(64a):

- Ariano, Italy 1847 Birth Act #391
- Ariano, Italy 1857 Birth Act #241
- Ariano, Italy 1875 Marriage Act #83
- Ariano, Italy 1876 Birth Act #610
- Ariano, Italy 1879 Birth Act #595
- Ariano, Italy 1882 Birth Act #130
- Ariano, Italy 1882 Death Act #96
- Ariano, Italy 1883 Birth Act #485
- Ariano, Italy 1885 Birth Act #369
- Ariano, Italy 1888 Birth Act #24
- Ariano, Italy 1896 Birth Act #24
- Ariano, Italy 1903 Death Act #10
- Ariano, Italy 1906 Marriage Act #97
- Ariano, Italy 1907 Marriage Act #39
- Ariano, Italy 1909 Death Act #142
- Ariano, Italy 1913 Death Act #226
- "Ohio Deaths, 1908-1953", , FamilySearch (https://www.familysearch.org/ark:/61903/1:1:X642-KVZ : Sun Mar 10 20:45:35 UTC 2024), Entry for Mary Grasso and Joseph Ameno, 1922.
- Ariano, Italy 1934 Death Act #133

65) Maria Rosa Fiorenza

Maria Rosa Fiorenza(65) was born on 24 October 1857, in Ariano, Italy, to Gaetano Fiorenza(13a) and Maria Vincenza Marraffino(13). She died on 16 April 1858, in Ariano, Italy.

Records that include Maria Rosa Fiorenza(65):

- Ariano, Italy 1857 Birth Act #426
- Ariano, Italy 1858 Death Act #152

66) Concetta DeDonato

Concetta deDonato(66) was born on 27 December 1857, in Ariano, Italy, to Luigi deDonato(27) and Angela Maria Miedico(27a).Concetta deDonato(66) died on 9 August 1930 in Ariano, Italy. Concetta deDonato(66) was a housekeeper.

Concetta deDonato(66) married Giuseppe Scaglione(66a) on 10 September 1881 in Ariano, Italy.

Giuseppe Scaglione(66a) was born on 9 March 1855, in Ariano, Italy, to Filippo Scaglione(66aF) and Carmina Gelormino(66aM). Giuseppe Scaglione(66a) died on 23 February 1932 in Ariano, Italy. Giuseppe Scaglione(66a) was a mason.

Known children of Concetta deDonato(66) and Giuseppe Scaglione(66a):

    i) Luigi Scaglione(181) born about 1885
    ii) Tommaso Scaglione(199) born about 1887

Records that include Concetta deDonato(66) and/or Giuseppe Scaglione(66a):

- Ariano, Italy 1855 Birth Act #105
- Ariano, Italy 1857 Birth Act #511
- Ariano, Italy 1881 Marriage Act #79
- Ariano, Italy 1885 Birth Act #426
- Ariano, Italy 1887 Birth Act #519
- Ariano, Italy 1888 Death Act #210
- Ariano, Italy 1888 Death Act #267
- Ariano, Italy 1930 Death Act #274
- Ariano, Italy 1932 Death Act #71

67) Mariangela Perrina

Mariangela Perrina(67) was born on 30 January 1858, in Ariano, Italy, to Oto Maria Perrina(14a) and Maria Raimonda deDonato(14). Mariangela Perrina(67) was a farm laborer.

Mariangela Perrina(67) married Gabriele Ninfadoro(67a), on 14 December 1876 in Ariano, Italy.

Gabriele Ninfadoro(67a) was a foundling, born on 31 January 1850, in Ariano, Italy. Gabriele Ninfadoro(67a) died on 14 January 1935 in Ariano, Italy. Gabriele Ninfadoro(67a) was a farm laborer.

Known children of Mariangela Perrina(67) and Gabriele Ninfadoro(67a):

      i) Anna Maria Ninfadoro(143) born in 1878
      ii) Maria Ninfadoro(156) born in 1880
      iii) Oto Ninfadoro(165) born in 1882
      iv) Antonio Ninfadoro(179) born in 1885
      v) Concetta Ninfadoro(191) born in 1888
      vi) Giovanni Ninfadoro(243) born in 1893

Records that include Mariangela Perrina(67) and/or Gabriele Ninfadoro(67a):
- Ariano, Italy 1850 Birth Act #45
- Ariano, Italy 1858 Birth Act #50
- Ariano, Italy 1876 Marriage Act #133
- Ariano, Italy 1878 Birth Act #8
- Ariano, Italy 1880 Birth Act #555
- Ariano, Italy 1880 Death Act #472
- Ariano, Italy 1882 Birth Act #162
- Ariano, Italy 1885 Birth Act #358
- Ariano, Italy 1885 Death Act #304
- Ariano, Italy 1888 Birth Act #344
- Ariano, Italy 1893 Birth Act #60
- Ariano, Italy 1896 Death Act #300
- Ariano, Italy 1907 Marriage Act #39
- Ariano, Italy 1907 Marriage Act #67
- Ariano, Italy 1915 Marriage Act #68
- Ariano, Italy 1934 Death Act #133
- Ariano, Italy 1935 Death Act #21

68) Francesco Paolo Perrina

Francesco Paolo Perrina(68) was born on 12 July 1858, in Ariano, Italy, to Liberatore Perrina(18a) and Maria Nicoletta deDonato(18). Francesco Paolo Perrina(68) died on 16 December 1858, in Ariano, Italy.

Records that include Francesco Paolo Perrina(68):
- Ariano, Italy 1858 Birth Act #290
- Ariano, Italy 1858 Death Act #435

69) Rosa Fiorenza

Rosa Fiorenza(69) was born on 5 April 1859, in Ariano, Italy, to Gaetano Fiorenza(13a) and Maria Vincenza Marraffino(13).

Rosa Fiorenza(69) married Domenico Ciccarelli(69a) on 9 November 1886 in Ariano, Italy.

Domenico Ciccarelli(69a) was born on 22 March 1854, in Ariano, Italy, to Raffaele Ciccarelli(69aF) and Concetta Iannarone(69aM). Domenico Ciccarelli(69a) died 21 February 1935 in Ariano, Italy. Domenico Ciccarelli(69a) was a farm laborer.

Domenico Ciccarelli(69a) was previously married to Maria Luigia Cirillo(69aX).

Known children of Rosa Fiorenza(69) and Domenico Ciccarelli(69a):

i) Nicola Ciccarelli(241) born in 1892
ii) Vincenzo Ciccarelli(288) born in 1898
iii) Carmine Ciccarelli(309) born in 1901

Records that include Rosa Fiorenza(69) and/or Domenico Ciccarelli(69a):
- Ariano, Italy 1854 Birth Act #138
- Ariano, Italy 1859 Birth Act #202
- Ariano, Italy 1886 Marriage Act #86
- Ariano, Italy 1893 Birth Act #3
- Ariano, Italy 1898 Birth Act #353
- Ariano, Italy 1901 Birth Act #388
- Ariano, Italy 1912 Marriage Act #9
- Ariano, Italy 1923 Death Act #II.C.15
- Ariano, Italy 1935 Death Act #65

70) Maria Agnese Altanese

Maria Aganese Altanese(70) was born on 29 October 1859 in Grottaminarda, Italy to Raffaele Giovanni Albanese(19b) and Maria Guiseppa D'Ausilio(19). Maria Aganese Altanese(70) died on 25 December 1867.

Records that include Maria Aganese Altanese(70):
- Grottaminarda, Italy 1859 Birth Act #155
- Grottaminarda, Italy 1867 Death Act #140

71) Luigi Giorgione

Luigi Giorgione(71) was born on 20 June 1859 to Antonio Giorgione(21a) and Maria Filomina d'Ausilio(21). Luigi Giorgione(71) died on 2 September 1861, in Ariano, Italy.

Records that include Luigi Giorgione(71):
- Ariano, Italy 1859 Birth Acts #336
- Ariano, Italy 1861 Death Acts #408

72) Anna Maria D'Ausilio

Anna Maria D'Ausilio(72) was born on 2 October 1859, in Ariano, Italy, to Angelo Maria D'Ausilio(24) and Maria Concetta Grasso(24a). Anna Maria D'Ausilio(72) arrived in New York, on board the ship SS Werra, on 7 October 1894 with three of her children to live in Bridgeport, CT with her husband Pasquale Antonio Anastasio(72a). Anna Maria D'Ausilio(72) died on 4 January 1926 in Racine, WI.

Anna Maria D'Ausilio(72) married Pasquale Antonio Anastasio(72a) on 11 February 1882 in Ariano, Italy.

Pasquale Antonio Anastasio(72a) was born on 16 December 1858, in Ariano, Italy, to Francesco Paulo d'Anastasio(72aF) and Maria Clementina Schiavo(72aM). Pasquale Antonio Anastasio(72a) became a citizen of the United States of America on 24 October 1898 in Waterbury, CT. Pasquale Antonio Anastasio(72a) died on 30 September 1917, in St. Louis, MO. Pasquale Antonio Anastasio(72a) was buried in Calvary Cemetery, St. Louis, MO. Pasquale Antonio Anastasio(72a) was a mason.

Known children of Anna Maria D'Ausilio(72) and Pasquale Antonio Anastasio(72a):

i) Francesco (Frank) Paul Anastasio(166) born in 1882
ii) Gabriele Anastasio(178) born in 1885
iii) Nicola Maria Anastasio(230) born in 1891
iv) Clementina Anastasio (259) born in 1894
v) Concetta Anastasio(271) born in 1896
vi) Helen Elvera Anastasio(308) born in 1901

Records that include Anna Maria D'Ausilio(72) and/or Pasquale Antonio Anastasio(72a):
- Ariano, Italy 1858 Birth Act #492

- Ariano, Italy 1859 Birth Act #499
- Ariano, Italy 1882 Marriage Act #17
- Ariano, Italy 1882 Birth Act #633
- Ariano, Italy 1885 Birth Act #167
- Ariano, Italy 1891 Birth Act #576
- Ariano, Italy 1894 Birth Act #521
- "New York Passenger Arrival Lists (Ellis Island), 1892-1924", , FamilySearch (https://www.familysearch.org/ark:/61903/1:1:JX36-9M5 : Fri Mar 08 16:06:42 UTC 2024), Entry for Anna Di Aurilio, 1895.
- "United States Census, 1900", , FamilySearch (https://www.familysearch.org/ark:/61903/1:1:M97Z-VHB : Thu Apr 11 18:23:28 UTC 2024), Entry for Anastasia Pasquale and Mary Pasquale, 1900.
- "New York Passenger Arrival Lists (Ellis Island), 1892-1924", , FamilySearch (https://www.familysearch.org/ark:/61903/1:1:JFLV-PYF : Fri Mar 08 04:58:58 UTC 2024), Entry for Giovannbattista d'Ansilio and Anastasi, 1902.
- "New York Passenger Arrival Lists (Ellis Island), 1892-1924", , FamilySearch (https://www.familysearch.org/ark:/61903/1:1:JFKP-ZYX : Sun Mar 10 13:06:46 UTC 2024), Entry for Nicola D' Ausilio and P Anastasia, 1902.
- "United States Census, 1910", , FamilySearch (https://www.familysearch.org/ark:/61903/1:1:MLMM-7YC : Fri Mar 08 21:46:08 UTC 2024), Entry for Pasquale Unastasio and Maria Unastasio, 1910.
- "Find a Grave Index," database, FamilySearch (https://www.familysearch.org/ark:/61903/1:1:QVK1-FHPW : 10 June 2021), Pasquale Anastasio, ; Burial, Saint Louis, St. Louis City, Missouri, United States of America, Calvary Cemetery and Mausoleum; citing record ID 52281260, Find a Grave, http://www.findagrave.com.
- Find a Grave Index," database, FamilySearch (https://www.familysearch.org/ark:/61903/1:1:Q231-LS7H : 10 July 2020), Anna Mary Anastasio, ; Burial, , ; citing record ID , Find a Grave, http://www.findagrave.com.

73) Giuseppe Fodarella

Giuseppe Fodarella(73) was born on 23 November 1859, in Ariano, Italy, to Domenico Fodarella(15a) and Mariangela d'Ausilio(15). Giuseppe Fodarella(73) died on 6 January 1860, in Ariano, Italy

Records that include Giuseppe Fodarella(73):
- Ariano, Italy 1859 Birth Act #548
- Ariano, Italy 1860 Death Act #6

74) Angelo Maria Perrina

Angelo Maria Perrina(74) was born on 14 December 1859, in Ariano, Italy, to Liberatore Perrina(18a) and Maria Nicoletta deDonato(18).

Angelo Maria Perrina(74) married Tommasina Paduano(74a) on 18 September 1886 in Ariano, Italy.

Tommasina Paduano(74a) was born on 15 March 1870, in Ariano, Italy, to Giuseppe Paduano(74aF) and Antonia Genita(74aM). Tommasina Paduano(74a) died 23 April 1935 in Ariano, Italy. Tommasina Paduano(74a) was a farm laborer.

Known children of Angelo Maria Perrina(74) and Tommasina Paduano(74a):

    i) Liberatore Perrina(200) born in 1887
    ii) Mariantonia Perrina(213) born in 1889
    iii) Rosaria Perrina(227) born in 1891
    iv) Pasquale Perrina(246) born in 1893
    v) Pasqualina Perrina(265) born in 1895
    vi) Pasquale (Patsy) Perrino(287) born in 1898
    vii) Salvatore Perrina(302) born in 1900
    viii) Maria Rosaria Perrina(334) born in 1906

ix) Maria Carssina Perrina(347) born in 1910

Records that include Angelo Maria Perrina(74) and/or Tommasina Paduano(74a):
- Ariano, Italy 1859 Birth Act #518
- Ariano, Italy 1870 Birth Act #166
- Ariano, Italy 1886 Marriage Act #92
- Ariano, Italy 1887 Birth Act #548
- Ariano, Italy 1889 Birth Act #34
- Ariano, Italy 1891 Birth Act #264
- Ariano, Italy 1893 Birth Act #127
- Ariano, Italy 1894 Death Act #250
- Ariano, Italy 1895 Birth Act #448
- Ariano, Italy 1898 Birth Act #348
- Ariano, Italy 1898 Death Act #158
- Ariano, Italy 1900 Birth Act #595
- Ariano, Italy 1921 Marriage Act #284
- Ariano, Italy 1922 Marriage Act #49
- Ariano, Italy 1906 Birth Act #536
- Ariano, Italy 1910 Birth Act #218
- Ariano, Italy 1910 Death Act #162
- "Massachusetts State Vital Records, 1841-1925", , FamilySearch (https://www.familysearch.org/ark:/61903/1:1:N4FF-42C : Thu May 23 01:09:26 UTC 2024), Entry for Liberatore Perrino and Carmenella Gammaroto, 26 Apr 1911.
- Ariano, Italy 1913 Marriage Act #36
- "New York, New York City Marriage Records, 1829-1938", , FamilySearch (https://www.familysearch.org/ark:/61903/1:1:Q2C6-W1ZZ : Sat Mar 09 05:34:35 UTC 2024), Entry for Pasquale Perrino and Fanny Masuces, 6 September 1925.
- Ariano, Italy 1935 Death Act #127
- Ariano, Italy 1990 Death Act #12

75) Agata DeDonato

Agata deDonato(75) was born on 31 December 1859, in Ariano, Italy, to Luigi deDonato(27) and Angela Maria Miedico(27a). Agata deDonato(75) died on 24 March 1860, as an infant, in Ariano, Italy

Records that include Agata deDonato(75):
- Ariano, Italy 1859 Birth Act #615
- Ariano, Italy 1860 Death Act #86

76) Anna Perrina

Anna Perrina(76) was born on 22 March 1860, in Ariano, Italy, to Oto Maria Perrina(14a) and Maria Raimonda deDonato(14).

Anna Perrina(76) married Crescenzo Grasso(76a) on 14 December 1876 in Ariano, Italy.

Crescenzo Grasso(76a) was born on 14 July 1852, in Ariano, Italy, to Floriano Grasso(76aF) and Rosa Vernacchia(76aM). Crescenzo Grasso(76a) died on 13 February 1933 in Ariano, Italy. Crescenzo Grasso(76a) was a farmhand.

Known children of Anna Perrina(76) and Crescenzo Grasso(76a):

    i) Rosa Grasso(144) born in 1878
    ii) Raimonda Grasso(158) born in 1881
    iii) Maria Giuseppa Grasso(167) born in 1882
    iv) Raimonda Grasso(177) born in 1885
    v) Giovanna Grasso(196) born in 1887
    vi) Floriano Grasso(258) born in 1894
    vii) Antonio Grasso(276) born in 1897
    vii) Maria Grasso(296) born in 1899

Records that include Anna Perrina(76) and/or Crescenzo Grasso(76a):
- Ariano, Italy 1852 Birth Act #377
- Ariano, Italy 1860 Birth Act #160

- Ariano, Italy 1876 Marriage Act #132
- Ariano, Italy 1878 Birth Act #342
- Ariano, Italy 1881 Birth Act #123
- Ariano, Italy 1881 Death Act #383
- Ariano, Italy 1882 Birth Act #647
- Ariano, Italy 1885 Birth Act #111
- Ariano, Italy 1886 Death Act #475
- Ariano, Italy 1887 Birth Act #257
- Ariano, Italy 1894 Birth Act #455
- Ariano, Italy 1897 Birth Act #353
- Ariano, Italy 1899 Birth Act #646
- "Italia, Avellino, Stato Civile (Archivio di Stato), 1809-1947", FamilySearch (https://www.familysearch.org/ark:/61903/1:1:6ZZF-J49R : Fri Apr 04 16:36:34 UTC 2025), Entry for Maria Grasso and Crescenzo Grasso, 12 Nov 1899.
- "Italia, Avellino, Stato Civile (Archivio di Stato), 1809-1947", FamilySearch (https://www.familysearch.org/ark:/61903/1:1:6ZKJ-WFQJ : Fri Apr 04 16:37:20 UTC 2025), Entry for Antonio Grasso and Crescenzo Grasso, 14 Jun 1897.
- Ariano, Italy 1933 Death Act #47
- "New York, New York City Marriage Records, 1829-1938", FamilySearch (https://www.familysearch.org/ark:/61903/1:1:244Q-4WZ : Sat Mar 09 04:31:53 UTC 2024), Entry for Gaetano Scanzillo and Giovannina Grassi, 7 Sep 1905.

77) Mariangela Perrina

Mariangela Perrina(77) was born about 1861, in Ariano, Italy, to Liberatore Perrina(18a) and Maria Nicoletta deDonato(18). Mariangela Perrina(77) died on 4 September 1867, in Ariano, Italy.

Records that include Mariangela Perrina(77):
- Ariano, Italy 1867 Death Act #974

78) Marcello deDonato

Marcello deDonato(78) was born on 23 February 1861, in Ariano, Italy, to Luigi deDonato(27) and Angela Maria Miedico(27a). In 1910 Marcello deDonato(78) was a baker in Ribeirão Pires, Brazil.

Marcello deDonato(78) married Maria Rosa Politano(78a) on 27 March 1886.

Maria Rosa Politano(78a) was born on 16 March 1863, in Paduli, Italy, to Giuseppe Politano(78aF) and Carmina Massimiano(78aM).

Known children of Marcello deDonato(78) and Maria Rosa Politano(78a):

  i) Angela deDonato(194) born in 1886
  ii) Luigi deDonato(201) born in 1887
  iii) Luigi deDonato(219) born in 1889
  iv) Giuseppe deDonato(234) born in 1892
  v) Maria Luigia deDonato(253) born in 1894
  vi) Angelina DeDonato(270) born in 1896
  vii) Carmella deDonato(281) born in 1897
  viii) Concetta DeDonato(292) born in 1899
  ix) Antonio DeDonato(303) born in 1901
  x) Conceição DeDonato(333) born in 1905

Records that include Marcello deDonato(78) and/or Maria Rosa Politano(78a):
- Ariano, Italy 1861 Birth Act #76
- Paduli, Italy 1863 Birth Act #356
- "Italia, Benevento, Stato Civile (Archivio di Stato), 1810-1942", , FamilySearch (https://www.familysearch.org/ark:/61903/1:1:QGK5-YJLH : Mon Jul 22 17:14:20 UTC 2024), Entry for Angela De Donato and Marcello De Donato, 24 Sep 1886.
- Paduli, Italy 1886 Birth Act #114
- Paduli, Italy 1887 Birth Act #171
- Paduli, Italy 1889 Birth Act #187

- "Italia, Benevento, Stato Civile (Archivio di Stato), 1810-1942", , FamilySearch (https://www.familysearch.org/ark:/61903/1:1:QL2J-MZ6D : Sun Mar 10 13:18:32 UTC 2024), Entry for Luigi di Donato and Marcello di Donato, 11 novembre 1889.
- Paduli, Italy 1892 Birth Act #39
- Paduli, Italy 1894 Birth Act #133
- "Brasil, São Paulo, Registro Civil, 1925-1995", , FamilySearch (https://www.familysearch.org/ark:/61903/1:1:6VWW-KZQ2 : Sat Mar 09 13:16:54 UTC 2024), Entry for Marcello Roque and Miguel Rinaldo, 0019.
- "Brasil, São Paulo, Registro Civil, 1925-1995", , FamilySearch (https://www.familysearch.org/ark:/61903/1:1:6V6P-X48Q : Fri Mar 08 09:15:53 UTC 2024), Entry for Marcello de Donato and José Forte, 22 de junho de 1934.
- "Brasil, São Paulo, Registro Civil, 1925-1995", , FamilySearch (https://www.familysearch.org/ark:/61903/1:1:6J1X-V8XT : Wed Mar 20 23:57:17 UTC 2024), Entry for Henrique Colombo and João Machadere, 19 de março de 1932.
- "Brasil, São Paulo, Registros da Igreja Católica, 1640-2012", , FamilySearch (https://www.familysearch.org/ark:/61903/1:1:6DGX-24PJ : Fri Mar 08 12:11:37 UTC 2024), Entry for Conceição and Marcello de Donato, 29 de junho de 1906.
- "Brasil, São Paulo, Registro Civil, 1925-1995", , FamilySearch (https://www.familysearch.org/ark:/61903/1:1:6VD1-FY7M : Fri May 17 09:51:21 UTC 2024), Entry for Maria Rinaldi and Carmen Rinaldo, 8 September 1932.
- "Brasil, São Paulo, Registro Civil, 1925-1995", , FamilySearch (https://www.familysearch.org/ark:/61903/1:1:6V4D-QFTY : Sun Mar 10 06:58:24 UTC 2024), Entry for Miguel Caba Ra and Elias Isbara, 1906.
- "Brasil, São Paulo, Registro Civil, 1925-1995", , FamilySearch (https://www.familysearch.org/ark:/61903/1:1:6V4K-YGFS : Sun Mar 10 16:39:38 UTC 2024), Entry for Angelina Donato and Marcello Donato, 1909.
- "Brasil, São Paulo, Registro Civil, 1925-1995", , FamilySearch (https://www.familysearch.org/ark:/61903/1:1:6VW4-2MFT : Fri Mar 08 19:16:39 UTC 2024), Entry for Rosa de Donato and Antonio de Donato, 0011.
- "Brasil, São Paulo, Registro Civil, 1925-1995", , FamilySearch (https://www.familysearch.org/ark:/61903/1:1:6V44-PQ4V : Sun Mar 10 17:12:48 UTC 2024), Entry for Luiz de Donato and Antonio Ferreira de Moraes, 18 de junho de 1901.
- "Brasil, São Paulo, Registro Civil, 1925-1995", , FamilySearch (https://www.familysearch.org/ark:/61903/1:1:6XZT-PGW5 : Wed Mar 06 08:39:51 UTC 2024), Entry for Carenela de Donato and Marcelo de Donato, 11 Jun 1967.
- "Brasil, São Paulo, Registro Civil, 1925-1995", , FamilySearch (https://www.familysearch.org/ark:/61903/1:1:6VWW-M7XC : Thu Mar 07 23:38:06 UTC 2024), Entry for Miguel Rinaldi and Marcelo de Donato, 0008.
- "Brasil, São Paulo, Registro Civil, 1925-1995", , FamilySearch (https://www.familysearch.org/ark:/61903/1:1:6V45-FP45 : Sat Mar 09 21:32:02 UTC 2024), Entry for Roza Napolitana and Pedro Isbara, 1902.
- "Brasil, São Paulo, Registros da Igreja Católica, 1640-2012", , FamilySearch (https://www.familysearch.org/ark:/61903/1:1:6DGX-6XGL : Fri Mar 08 10:45:42 UTC 2024), Entry for Concetta Guidonato and Marcello Guidonato, 15 de maio de 1899.
- "Brasil, São Paulo, Registro Civil, 1925-1995", , FamilySearch (https://www.familysearch.org/ark:/61903/1:1:65V2-SFY1 : Fri Mar 08 15:01:32 UTC 2024), Entry for Carmela de Donato and Marcelo de Donato, 11 de junho de 1967.
- "Brasil, São Paulo, Registro Civil, 1925-1995", , FamilySearch (https://www.familysearch.org/ark:/61903/1:1:6VSV-36GM : Fri May 17 07:53:52 UTC 2024), Entry for Paulo Zenorim and Honrrique Crombo, dezembro de 1930.
- https://www.dgabc.com.br/Noticia/278934/ribeirao-pires-a-terceira-forca-economica-em-1910-

- "Brasil, São Paulo, Registro Civil, 1925-1995", , FamilySearch (https://www.familysearch.org/ark:/61903/1:1:6XZ6-BKF5 : Fri Jul 05 19:47:46 UTC 2024), Entry for Angelina Donato and Marcelo Donato, 22 Jan 1934.
- "Brasil, São Paulo, Registro Civil, 1925-1995", , FamilySearch (https://www.familysearch.org/ark:/61903/1:1:65R8-ZNTT : Sat Mar 09 05:26:17 UTC 2024), Entry for Angelina de Lourdes Silva and Marcelo de Donato, 13 de abril de 1946.

79) Mariantonia Fodarella

Mariantonia Fodarella(79) was born on 9 October 1861, in Ariano, Italy, to Domenico Fodarella(15a) and Mariangela d'Ausilio(15). Mariantonia Fodarella(79) died on 9 May 1931, in Ariano, Italy. Mariantonia Fodarella(79) was a farmhand.

Mariantonia Fodarella(79) married Raimondo Manganiello(79a) on 10 January 1885 in Ariano, Italy.

Raimondo Manganiello(79a) was born on 13 February 1856, in Ariano, Italy, to Vincenzo Manganiello(79aF) and Luigia Rogazzo(79aM). Raimondo Manganiello(79a) died 9 December 1932 in Ariano, Italy. Raimondo Manganiello(79a) was a farmhand.

Known children of Mariantonia Fodarella(79) and Raimondo Manganiello(79a):

    i) Vincenzo Manganiello(193) born in 1886
    ii) Mariangela Manganiello(255) born in 1894
    iii) Oto Manganiello(286) born in 1898
    iv) Mariannina Manganiello(305) born in 1901

Records that include Mariantonia Fodarella(79) and/or Raimondo Manganiello(79a):
- Ariano, Italy 1856 Birth Act #84
- Ariano, Italy 1861 Birth Act #357
- Ariano, Italy 1885 Marriage Act #4
- Ariano, Italy 1886 Birth Act #340
- Ariano, Italy 1894 Birth Act #343
- Ariano, Italy 1898 Birth Act #165
- Ariano, Italy 1901 Birth Act #163
- Ariano, Italy 1910 Marriage Act #88
- Ariano, Italy 1913 Marriage Act #78
- Ariano, Italy 1913 Death Act #111
- "New York Passenger Arrival Lists (Ellis Island), 1892-1924", , FamilySearch (https://www.familysearch.org/ark:/61903/1:1:J667-92V : Fri Mar 08 03:37:39 UTC 2024), Entry for Oto Manganiello and Raimondo Manganiello, 1920.
- Ariano, Italy 1924 Marriage Act #131
- Ariano, Italy 1927 Marriage Act #60
- Ariano, Italy 1931 Death Act #103
- Ariano, Italy 1932 Death Act #297
- Ossining, New York 1932 Death Act #154

80) Raffaele Giorgione

Raffaele Giorgione(80) was born on 22 January 1862, in Ariano, Italy, to Antonio Giorgione(21a) and Maria Filomina d'Ausilio(21). Raffaele Giorgione(80) died on 21 December 1940, in Ariano, Italy. Raffaele Giorgione(80) was a farmhand.

Raffaele Giorgione(80) married Carmina Salvioli(80a), on 13 September 1883, in Ariano, Italy.

Carmina Salvioli(80a) was a foundling born on 4 July 1868, in Ariano, Italy.

Known children of Raffaele Giorgione(80) and Carmina Salvioli(80a):

    i) Antonia Giorgione(191) born in 1886

ii) Filomena Giorgione(216) born in 1889
iii) Giuseppe Giorgione(228) born in 1891
iv) Filomena Giorgione(248) born in 1893
v) Giuseppe (Joseph) Giorgione/George(263) born in 1895
vi) Antonio Giorgione(278) born in 1897
vii) Rosa Giorgione(300) born in 1900
viii) Maria Luigia Giorgione(316) born in 1902
ix) Francesco Paolo Giorgione(328) born in 1905
x) Nicola Giorgione(356) born in 1911

Records that include Raffaele Giorgione(80) and/or Carmina Salvioli(80a):
- Ariano, Italy 1862 Birth Act #35
- Ariano, Italy 1868 Birth Act #305
- Ariano, Italy 1883 Marriage Act #95
- Ariano, Italy 1886 Birth Act #181
- Ariano, Italy 1886 Death Act #166
- Ariano, Italy 1889 Birth Act #50
- Ariano, Italy 1889 Death Act #190
- Ariano, Italy 1891 Birth Act #309
- Ariano, Italy 1892 Death Act #429
- Ariano, Italy 1893 Birth Act #337
- Ariano, Italy 1895 Birth Act #393
- Ariano, Italy 1897 Birth Act #374
- Ariano, Italy 1900 Birth Act #234
- Ariano, Italy 1902 Birth Act #257
- Ariano, Italy 1905 Birth Act #214
- Ariano, Italy 1912 Death Act #15
- Ariano, Italy 1920 Marriage Act #105
- Ariano, Italy 1922 Marriage Act #159
- Ariano, Italy 1925 Marriage Act #23
- Ariano, Italy 1932 Marriage Act #P.II.A.111
- Ariano, Italy 1940 Death Act #288

81) Giovanni Fiorenza

Giovanni Fiorenza(81) was born on 23 June 1862, in Ariano, Italy, to Gaetano Fiorenza(13a) and Maria Vincenza Marraffino(13). Giovanni Fiorenza(81) died on 4 January 1863, in Ariano, Italy.

Records that include Giovanni Fiorenza(81):
- Ariano, Italy 1862 Birth Act #299
- Ariano, Italy 1863 Death Act #6

82) Filomena Perrina

Filomena Perrina(82) was born on 31 August 1862, in Ariano, Italy, to Oto Maria Perrina(14a) and Maria Raimonda deDonato(14).
Filomena Perrina(82) married Michele Ciasullo(82a) on 15 February 1883 in Ariano, Italy

Michele Ciasullo(82a) was born on 15 December 1856, in Ariano, Italy, to Fedele Ciasullo(82aF) and Raimonda Zecchino(82aM). Michele Ciasullo(82a) died 11 September 1904 in Ariano, Italy.

Known children of Filomena Perrina(82) and/or Michele Ciasullo(82a):

i) Raimonda Ciasullo(183) born in 1885
ii) Filippo Ciasullo(204) born in 1887
iii) Giovanna (Jenny) Ciasullo(221) born about 1889/90
iv) Antonia Ciasullo(231) born in 1892
v) Mariangela Ciasullo(232) born in 1892
vi) Fedele Ciasullo(254) born in 1894
vii) Pasquale Ciasullo(306) born in 1901
viii) Mariangela Ciasullo(325) born in 1904

Records that include Filomena Perrina(82) and/or Michele Ciasullo(82a):
- Ariano, Italy 1885 Birth Act#612

- Ariano, Italy 1887 Birth Act#745
- Ariano, Italy 1888 Death Act#378
- Ariano, Italy 1892 Birth Act#1
- Ariano, Italy 1892 Birth Act#2
- Ariano, Italy 1894 Birth Act#164
- Ariano, Italy 1901 Birth Act#220
- Ariano, Italy 1902 Death Act#22
- Ariano, Italy 1904 Death Act#333
- Ariano, Italy 1904 Birth Act#338
- Ariano, Italy 1907 Marriage Act#15
- Ariano, Italy 1908 Death Act#45
- Ariano, Italy 1908 Marriage Act#137
- Ariano, Italy 1920 Marriage Act#140

83) Nicola Maria D'Ausilio

Nicola Maria D'Ausilio(83) was born on 23 February 1863, in Ariano, Italy, to Angelo Maria D'Ausilio(24) and Maria Concetta Grasso(24a). Nicola Maria D'Ausilio(83) died on 2 June 1932, in Ariano, Italy. Nicola Maria D'Ausilio(83) was a property owner.

Nicola Maria D'Ausilio(83) married Giustina Mariano(83a) on 10 January 1885 in Ariano, Italy.

Giustina Mariano(83a) was born on 27 March 1850, in Ariano, Italy, to Gabriele Mariano(81aF) and Raimonda Savino(83aM). Giustina Mariano(83a) died on 21 February 1923 in Ariano, Italy. Giustina Mariano(83a) was a laborer.

Known children of Nicola Maria D'Ausilio(83) and Giustina Mariano(83a):

      i) Leopoldo D'ausilio(190) born in 1886
      ii) Concetta D'Ausilio(207) born in 1888
      iii) Maria Concetta D'Ausilio(220) born in 1889
      iv) Leopoldo D'Ausilio(242) born in 1893
      v) Raimonda D'Ausilio(272) born in 1896

Records that include Nicola Maria D'Ausilio(83) and/or Giustina Mariano(83a):
- Ariano, Italy 1850 Birth Act #163
- Ariano, Italy 1863 Birth Act #94
- Ariano, Italy 1885 Marriage Act #5
- Ariano, Italy 1886 Birth Act #73
- Ariano, Italy 1888 Birth Act #75
- Ariano, Italy 1889 Birth Act #701
- Ariano, Italy 1889 Death Act #358
- Ariano, Italy 1889 Death Act #409
- Ariano, Italy 1893 Birth Act #53
- Ariano, Italy 1896 Birth Act #599
- Ariano, Italy 1896 Death Act #81
- Ariano, Italy 1922 Marriage Act #13
- Ariano, Italy 1923 Death Act #55
- Ariano, Italy 1932 Death Act #144

84) Antonio diVitto

Antonio Di Vitto(84) was born on 25 March 1863, in Ariano, Italy, to Raimondo di Vitto(16a) and Raimonda D'Ausilio(16).

Note: I have only located Antonio Di Vitto(84)'s birth record. It has a partially legible notation on it saying that on 5 Feb 1885 Antonio Di Vitto(84) married someone named Maria. There is no marriage recorded in Ariano, Italy for him. I have not located a record in any other location.

Records that include Antonio Di Vitto(84):
- Ariano, Italy 1863 Birth Acts #139

85) Maria Carmela DeDonato

Maria Carmela deDonato(85) was born on 25 November 1863, in Ariano, Italy, to Luigi deDonato(27) and Angela Maria Miedico(27a). Maria Carmela deDonato(85) died on 2 October 1945 in Los Angeles, CA. Maria Carmela deDonato(85) was a housewife.

Maria Carmela deDonato(85) married Vincenzo (James) Lombardi(85a) in 1887.

Vincenzo (James) Lombardi(85a) was born on 8 July 1868, in Apice, Italy, to Feliciano Lombardi(85aF) and Filomena Zullo(85aM). Vincenzo (James) Lombardi(85a) died on 2 January 1948 in Los Angeles, California. Vincenzo (James) Lombardi(85a) was the owner of a macaroni factory.

Known children of Maria Carmela deDonato(85) and Vincenzo (James) Lombardi(85a):

    i) Feliciano Lombardi(198) born in 1887
    ii) Feliciano Lombardi(218) born in 1889
    iii) Feliciano (Phillip White) Lombardi(236) born in 1892
    iv) Saverio Lombardi(223) born in 1894
    v) Saverio Lombardi(261) born in 1895
    vi) Adamo Lombardi(282) born in 1897
    vii) Adamo (Adam Carl) Lombardi(312) born in 1902

Records that include Maria Carmela deDonato(85) and/or Vincenzo (James) Lombardi(85a):

- Ariano, Italy 1863 Birth Act #469
- Apice Italy 1868 Birth Act #63
- "Italia, Benevento, Stato Civile (Archivio di Stato), 1810-1942", , FamilySearch (https://www.familysearch.org/ark:/61903/1:1:QLK5-668S : Sun Mar 10 16:41:58 UTC 2024), Entry for Vincenzo Lombardi and Feliciano Lombardi, 8 luglio 1868.
- Apice Italy 1887 Birth Act #82
- "Italia, Benevento, Stato Civile (Archivio di Stato), 1810-1942", , FamilySearch (https://www.familysearch.org/ark:/61903/1:1:QLKP-P6QN : Sun Mar 10 04:16:09 UTC 2024), Entry for Feliciano Lombardi and Vincenzo Lombardi, 6 luglio 1887.
- Apice Italy 1889 Birth Act #81
- "Italia, Benevento, Stato Civile (Archivio di Stato), 1810-1942", , FamilySearch (https://www.familysearch.org/ark:/61903/1:1:QLK5-874L : Sat Mar 09 19:02:35 UTC 2024), Entry for Feliciano Lombardi and Vincenzo Lombardi, 2 giugno 1889.
- Apice Italy 1892 Birth Act #69
- "Italia, Benevento, Stato Civile (Archivio di Stato), 1810-1942", , FamilySearch (https://www.familysearch.org/ark:/61903/1:1:QGJ2-CZDK : Fri Mar 08 18:49:21 UTC 2024), Entry for Feliciano Lombardi and Vincenzo Lombardi, 18 maggio 1892.
- Apice Italy 1894 Birth Act #21
- "Italia, Benevento, Stato Civile (Archivio di Stato), 1810-1942", , FamilySearch (https://www.familysearch.org/ark:/61903/1:1:QGJ2-LW8G : Sun Mar 10 16:35:25 UTC 2024), Entry for Saverio Lombardi and Vincenzo Lombardi, 24 gennaio 1894.
- Apice Italy 1895 Birth Act #29
- "Italia, Benevento, Stato Civile (Archivio di Stato), 1810-1942", , FamilySearch (https://www.familysearch.org/ark:/61903/1:1:QLKP-RKY2 : Fri Mar 08 19:33:31 UTC 2024), Entry for Saverio Lombardi and Vincenzo Lombardi, 21 febbraio 1895.
- "Brasil, São Paulo, Registro Civil, 1925-1995", , FamilySearch (https://www.familysearch.org/ark:/61903/1:1:6YG4-Z5RL : Sat Jul 27 10:00:10 UTC 2024), Entry for Adamo Lombardi and Vincenzo Lombardi, 23 de outubro de 1898.
- "New York Passenger Arrival Lists (Ellis Island), 1892-1924", , FamilySearch (https://www.familysearch.org/ark:/61903/1:1:JX6K-7ZP : Thu Mar 07 01:49:04 UTC 2024), Entry for Feliciano Lombardi and Vincenzo, 1907.

- "United States Census, 1910", , FamilySearch
  (https://www.familysearch.org/ark:/61903/1:1:X39X-C53 : Fri Mar 08
  11:50:32 UTC 2024), Entry for James Lombardi and Carmelo Lombardi,
  1910.
- "New York State Census, 1915", , FamilySearch
  (https://www.familysearch.org/ark:/61903/1:1:K9FH-PVN : 4 June
  2022), Vincent Lombardi, 1915.
- "United States Census, 1920", , FamilySearch
  (https://www.familysearch.org/ark:/61903/1:1:MCFH-DK2 : Sun Mar 10
  06:14:48 UTC 2024), Entry for Vincent Lombardi and Casowasy
  Lombardi, 1920.
- Bridgeport, CT, Marriages July – September Pages 1 – 244 #51
- "United States Census, 1930", , FamilySearch
  (https://www.familysearch.org/ark:/61903/1:1:XMPM-77Y : Fri Mar 08
  01:23:40 UTC 2024), Entry for James Lombardi and Carmello Lombardi,
  1930.
- "New York, New York City Marriage Records, 1829-1938", ,
  FamilySearch (https://www.familysearch.org/ark:/61903/1:1:24D8-
  P23 : Tue Feb 20 17:49:15 UTC 2024), Entry for Philip H. Lombardi
  and Sylvia Noris Coari, 2 Dec 1931.
- "United States Census, 1940", , FamilySearch
  (https://www.familysearch.org/ark:/61903/1:1:K9CH-4ND : Mon Mar 11
  01:26:11 UTC 2024), Entry for Vincent Lombardi and Maria C
  Lombardi, 1940.
- "California, World War II Draft Registration Cards, 1940-1945", ,
  FamilySearch (https://www.familysearch.org/ark:/61903/1:1:QGXY-G3SC
  : Sat Mar 09 14:25:46 UTC 2024), Entry for Adam C Lombardi and
  Carmela Lombardi, 15 February 1942.
- "California, County Marriages, 1850-1953", , FamilySearch
  (https://www.familysearch.org/ark:/61903/1:1:K8XM-H19 : Sat Mar 09
  11:20:48 UTC 2024), Entry for Adam Carl Lombardi and Francisca Rico
  Nuno, 21 August 1944.
- "California, County Birth and Death Records, 1800-1994", ,
  FamilySearch (https://www.familysearch.org/ark:/61903/1:1:QGY2-DTMV
  : Sat Mar 09 17:26:47 UTC 2024), Entry for Vincent Lombardi, 2
  January 1948.
- "California Death Index, 1940-1997," database, FamilySearch
  (https://familysearch.org/ark:/61903/1:1:VGB3-VP8 : 26 November
  2014), Vincent Lombardi, 02 Jan 1948; Department of Public Health
  Services, Sacramento.
- "California, County Birth and Death Records, 1800-1994", ,
  FamilySearch (https://www.familysearch.org/ark:/61903/1:1:QGT5-4T43
  : Sun Mar 10 00:13:55 UTC 2024), Entry for Vincent Lombardi and
  Feliciano Lombardi, 2 January 1948.
- "California, County Birth and Death Records, 1800-1994", ,
  FamilySearch (https://www.familysearch.org/ark:/61903/1:1:QGPX-C9FT
  : Thu Mar 07 10:24:20 UTC 2024), Entry for Philip White Lombardi
  and Vincent Lombardi, 22 April 1961.
- "California, County Birth and Death Records, 1800-1994", ,
  FamilySearch (https://www.familysearch.org/ark:/61903/1:1:8LNW-JQZM
  : Sun Mar 10 02:02:39 UTC 2024), Entry for Saverio aka Sam Lombardi
  and Vincenzo Apice Lombardi, 10 Sep 1978.
- "California Deaths and Burials, 1776-2000", , FamilySearch
  (https://www.familysearch.org/ark:/61903/1:1:HGWN-6VPZ : Tue Mar 19
  19:08:17 UTC 2024), Entry for Saverio aka Sam Lombardi and Vincenzo
  Apice Lombardi, 13 September 1978.
- "California Deaths and Burials, 1776-2000", , FamilySearch
  (https://www.familysearch.org/ark:/61903/1:1:HG4Q-WKW2 : Tue Mar 19
  15:38:19 UTC 2024), Entry for Saverio Lombardi and Vincenzo Apice
  Lombardi, 13 September 1978.
- "California Death Index, 1940-1997," database, FamilySearch
  (https://familysearch.org/ark:/61903/1:1:VGP8-HWX : 26 November
  2014), Didonato in entry for Adam Carl Lombardi, 15 Mar 1988;
  Department of Public Health Services, Sacramento.
- "California Deaths and Burials, 1776-2000", , FamilySearch
  (https://www.familysearch.org/ark:/61903/1:1:HGWT-QGT2 : 8 April
  2022), Vincent Lombardi in entry for Adam Carl Lombardi, 1988.

- "Find a Grave Index," database, FamilySearch (https://www.familysearch.org/ark:/61903/1:1:QVKS-83YB : 12 December 2022), Carmela Donato Lombardi, ; Burial, Culver City, Los Angeles, California, United States of America, Holy Cross Cemetery; citing record ID 37622288, Find a Grave, http://www.findagrave.com.
- "Find a Grave Index," database, FamilySearch (https://www.familysearch.org/ark:/61903/1:1:QVKS-83BM : 22 November 2022), Vincent Lombardi, ; Burial, Culver City, Los Angeles, California, United States of America, Holy Cross Cemetery; citing record ID 37622276, Find a Grave, http://www.findagrave.com.
- "California Death Index, 1940-1997," , FamilySearch (https://familysearch.org/ark:/61903/1:1:VPKM-KQL : 26 November 2014), Carmela M Lombardi, 02 Oct 1945; Department of Public Health Services, Sacramento.
- "California, County Birth and Death Records, 1800-1994", FamilySearch (https://www.familysearch.org/ark:/61903/1:1:QP7Q-4M9J : Sun Mar 10 08:59:22 UTC 2024), Entry for Carmela M Lombardi and Louis D Donato, 2 October 1945.
- "California, County Birth and Death Records, 1800-1994", FamilySearch (https://www.familysearch.org/ark:/61903/1:1:QP4Y-T8Y2 : Sun Mar 10 14:05:34 UTC 2024), Entry for Carmela M Lombardi, 2 October 1945.

86) Luigi (Louis) Giorgione/George

Luigi (Louis) Giorgione/George(86) was born on 5 March 1864, in Ariano, Italy, to Antonio Giorgione(21a) and Maria Filomina d'Ausilio(21). Luigi (Louis) Giorgione/George(86) died on 12 August 1921 in Manhattan, NY. Luigi (Louis) Giorgione/George(86) was a flagman.

Luigi (Louis) Giorgione/George(86) married Maria Giovanna Perillo(86a) on 12 August 1886 in Ariano, Italy.

Maria Giovanna (Jennie) Perillo(86a) was born on 28 November 1862, in Ariano, Italy, to Giuseppe Perillo(86aF) and Maria Michele LaLuna(86aM). Maria Giovanna Perillo(86a) boarded the SS Algeria in Naples, Italy on 28 November 1905, arriving in New York on 18 December 1905. Maria Giovanna Perillo(86a) died 16 December 1945 in New York.

Known children of Luigi (Louis) Giorgione/George(86) and Maria Giovanna Perillo(86a):

i) Antonio (Anthony) Giorgione/George(206) born in 1889
ii) Raffaele Giorgione(233) born in 1892
iii) Michele Giorgione(264) born in 1895
iv) Carmine (Carmen Louis) Giorgione/George(290) born in 1898
v) Maria Silveria Francesca (Frances) Giorgione/George(311) born in 1901
vi) Rose Louise Giorgione(339) born in 1907

Records that include Luigi (Louis) Giorgione/George(86) and/or Maria Giovanna Perillo(86a):
- Ariano, Italy 1862 Birth Act #525
- Ariano, Italy 1864 Birth Act #138
- Ariano, Italy 1886 Marriage Act #102
- Ariano, Italy 1888 Birth Act #31
- Ariano, Italy 1892 Birth Act #14
- Ariano, Italy 1892 Death Act #47
- Ariano, Italy 1895 Birth Act #441
- Ariano, Italy 1898 Birth Act #421
- Ariano, Italy 1901 Birth Act #623
- "New York State Census, 1915", database, FamilySearch (https://www.familysearch.org/ark:/61903/1:1:K9GM-56F : 1 June 2022), Louie George, 1915.
- "New York, County Marriages, 1847-1848; 1908-1936", , FamilySearch (https://www.familysearch.org/ark:/61903/1:1:XVPZ-459 : Mon Mar 11 01:14:09 UTC 2024), Entry for Ralph Benjamin George and Louis George, 13 June 1920.

- "New York Marriages, 1686-1980", database, FamilySearch (https://familysearch.org/ark:/61903/1:1:HWJL-9GPZ : 21 January 2020), Louis George in entry for Ralph Benjamin George, 1920.
- "New York, County Marriages, 1847-1848; 1908-1936", , FamilySearch (https://www.familysearch.org/ark:/61903/1:1:Q2MT-CCJ9 : Fri Mar 08 04:24:10 UTC 2024), Entry for Theodore Taft Garber and Edward William Garber, December 1926.
- "United States Census, 1930", , FamilySearch (https://www.familysearch.org/ark:/61903/1:1:X4R1-NCJ : Sun Mar 10 15:50:00 UTC 2024), Entry for Anthony George and Jennie George, 1930.
- "New York, County Marriages, 1847-1848; 1908-1936", , FamilySearch (https://www.familysearch.org/ark:/61903/1:1:Q2MT-54YV : Sat Mar 09 21:42:13 UTC 2024), Entry for Michael William George and Louis George, February 1930.
- "United States, Social Security Numerical Identification Files (NUMIDENT), 1936-2007", database, FamilySearch (https://www.familysearch.org/ark:/61903/1:1:6K4V-V6WP : 11 February 2023), Anthony George, .
- "United States Census, 1940", FamilySearch (https://www.familysearch.org/ark:/61903/1:1:KQGP-XN8 : Sun Mar 10 21:26:22 UTC 2024), Entry for Anthony George and Joseph George, 1940.
- "New York, New York City Municipal Deaths, 1795-1949", database, FamilySearch (https://www.familysearch.org/ark:/61903/1:1:2WPV-GM6 : 13 May 2022), Louis in entry for Ralph George, 1944.
- "United States, Social Security Numerical Identification Files (NUMIDENT), 1936-2007", database, FamilySearch (https://www.familysearch.org/ark:/61903/1:1:6K97-KZWX : 10 February 2023), Louis George in entry for Rose Louise Garber, .
- "New York, County Marriages, 1847-1848; 1908-1936", , FamilySearch (https://www.familysearch.org/ark:/61903/1:1:KZ9S-P4Y : Sat Mar 09 03:18:45 UTC 2024), Entry for Anthony Amodio and Philip Amodio, 9 December 1923.
- "New York, New York City Municipal Deaths, 1795-1949", database, FamilySearch (https://www.familysearch.org/ark:/61903/1:1:2W1T-8LQ : 3 June 2020), Louis George, 1921.
- "Find a Grave Index," database, FamilySearch (https://familysearch.org/ark:/61903/1:1:QVV6-PJ9Y : 27 July 2019), Lewis George, 1921; Burial, Middletown, Orange, New York, United States of America, Hillside Cemetery; citing record ID 12946100, Find a Grave, http://www.findagrave.com.

87) Cosimo Altanese

Cosimo Altanese(87) was born on 22 March 1864 in Grottaminarda, Italy, to Raffaele Giovanni Altanese(19b) and Maria Guiseppa D'Ausilio(19). Cosimo Altanese(87) sailed on the SS Sempiona, from Naples, Italy, arriving in New York on 26 June 1899. Cosimo Altanese(87) is listed in the 1910 US and 1915 NJ Censuses as living in Newark, New Jersey. Cosimo Altanese(87) sailed on the SS Duilio leaving on 10 October 1927 from Naples, Italy arriving in New York on 17 October 1927. Cosimo Altanese(87) owned an Ice Cream Store.

Cosimo Altanese(87) married Margarita Galgothia Alfonsina Romano(87a) on 13 March 1886 in Grottaminarda, Italy.

Margarita Galgothia Alfonsina Romano(87a) was born 21 December 1863, in Grottaminarda, Italy, to Generoso Romano(87aF) and Filomena Iannarona(87aM). Margarita Galgothia Alfonsina Romano(87a) died June 1919 in Newark, NJ.

Known children of Cosimo Altanese(87) and Margarita Galgothia Alfonsina Romano(87a):

    i) Raffaela Maria Giuseppe Altanese(195) born in 1887
    ii) Raffaela Altanese(208) born about 1888
    iii) Filomena Maria Rosalia Altanese(235) born in 1892
    iv) Raffaele Altanese(257) born in 1894
    v) Filomena Altanese(283) born in 1897

Records that include Cosimo Altanese(87) and Margarita Galgothia Alfonsina Romano(87a):

- Grottaminarda, Italy 1863 Birth Act #177
- Grottaminarda, Italy 1864 Birth Act #36
- Grottaminarda, Italy 1886 Marriage Act #13
- Grottaminarda, Italy 1887 Birth Act #24
- Grottaminarda, Italy 1892 Birth Act #59
- Grottaminarda, Italy 1894 Birth Act #107
- Grottaminarda, Italy 1895 Death Act #91
- Grottaminarda, Italy 1895 Death Act #98
- Grottaminarda, Italy 1897 Birth Act #101
- Grottaminarda, Italy 1900 Death Act #3
- "New York Passenger Arrival Lists (Ellis Island), 1892-1924", database with images, FamilySearch (https://familysearch.org/ark:/61903/1:1:JXZ4-4J3 : 2 March 2021), Cosmo Altanese, 1899.
- "United States Census, 1910", database with images, FamilySearch (https://www.familysearch.org/ark:/61903/1:1:MKTT-DGB : Tue Jul 18 16:31:25 UTC 2023), Entry for Cosno Altanese and Margaret Altanese, 1910.
- "New Jersey State Census, 1915", database with images, FamilySearch (https://www.familysearch.org/ark:/61903/1:1:QV9Q-QR2P : Tue Apr 04 16:11:11 UTC 2023), Entry for Charles Altanese and Margaret Altanese, 1915.9
- "New York, New York Passenger and Crew Lists, 1909, 1925-1957," database with images, FamilySearch (https://familysearch.org/ark:/61903/1:1:KXGS-VQM : 2 March 2021), Cosimo Altanese, 1927; citing Immigration, New York, New York, United States, NARA microfilm publication T715 (Washington, D.C.: National Archives and Records Administration, n.d.).
- "New Jersey, Death Index, 1901-1903; 1916-1929", , FamilySearch (https://www.familysearch.org/ark:/61903/1:1:66NK-94K3 : Sat Mar 09 10:46:30 UTC 2024), Entry for Margherita Altanese, Jun 1919.

88) Michele Perrina

Michele Perrina(88) was born on 2 April 1864, in Ariano, Italy, to Liberatore Perrina(18) and Maria Nicoletta deDonato(18a).

Michele Perrina(88) married Maria Grazia Caraglia(88a) on 1 October 1891 in Ariano, Italy.

Maria Grazia Caraglia(88a) was born 22 May 1872, in Villanova del Battista, Italy, to Michele Caraglia(88aF) and Maria Michele Cusano(88aM). Maria Grazia Caraglia(88a) died 14 June 1954 in Ariano, Italy.

Known children of Michele Perrina(88) and Maria Grazia Caraglia(88a):

    i) Maria Felicita Perrina(239) born in 1892
    ii) Antonio Perrina(260) born in 1895
    iii) Luigi Perrina(277) born in 1897
    iv) Giuseppa Perrina(297) born in 1899
    v) Luigi Ermino Perrina(314) born in 1902
    vi) Angelo Perrina(326) born in 1904
    vii) Maria Amalia Perrina(336) born in 1907
    viii) Arminio Perrina(345) born about 1909
    ix) Maria Amalia Perrina(353) born in 1911
    x) Arminio Perrina(359) born in 1914
    xi) Arminio Perrina(V294) born in 1919

Records that include Michele Perrina(88) and/or Maria Grazia Caraglia(88a):
- Ariano, Italy 1864 Birth Act #182
- Villanova del Battista, Italy 1872 Birth Act #35
- Ariano, Italy 1891 Marriage Act #97
- Ariano, Italy 1892 Birth Act #380
- Ariano, Italy 1895 Birth Act #47
- Ariano, Italy 1896 Death Act #166

- Ariano, Italy 1897 Birth Act #363
- Ariano, Italy 1899 Birth Act #676
- Ariano, Italy 1900 death Act #159
- Ariano, Italy 1902 Birth Act #94
- Ariano, Italy 1904 Birth Act #497
- Ariano, Italy 1907 Birth Act #163
- Ariano, Italy 1907 Death Act #336
- Ariano, Italy 1910 Death Act #68
- Ariano, Italy 1911 Birth Act #339
- Ariano, Italy 1912 Marriage Act #30
- Ariano, Italy 1914 Birth Act #3
- Ariano, Italy 1914 Death Act #183
- Ariano, Italy 1919 Birth Act #345
- Ariano, Italy 1921 Marriage Act #151
- Ariano, Italy 1924 Marriage Act #24
- Ariano, Italy 1938 Marriage Act #P.IIA.67

89) Antonio Maria Fodarella

Antonio Maria Fodarella(89) was born on 18 November 1864, in Ariano, Italy, to Domenico Fodarella(15a) and Mariangela d'Ausilio(15). Antonio Maria Fodarella(89) died on 9 March 1872, in Ariano, Italy.

Records that include Antonio Maria Fodarella(89):
- Ariano, Italy 1864 Birth Act #511
- Ariano, Italy 1872 Death Act #120

90) Francesco Paolo Perrina

Francesco Paolo Perrina(90) was born on 13 February 1865, in Ariano, Italy, to Oto Maria Perrina(14a) and Maria Raimonda deDonato(14). Francesco Paolo Perrina(90) was a miller.

Francesco Paolo Perrina(90) married Maria Cristina Sofia Leone(90a) and Nicolina Merlucci(90b).

Francesco Paolo Perrina(90) married Maria Cristina Sofia Leone(90a) on 4 September 1884 in San Nicola Baronia, Italy.

Maria Cristina Sofia Leone(90a) was born on 22 May 1861 in San Nicola Baronia, Italy, to Giovanni Leone(90aF) and Camilla Iacoviello(90aM). Maria Cristina Sofia Leone(90a) died 4 October 1905 in Castel Baronia, Italy.

Known children of Francesco Paolo Perrina(90) and Maria Cristina Sofia Leone(90a);

      i) Oto Maria Perrina(186) born in 1885
      ii) Carmine Perrina(247) born in 1893
      iii) Emmiddio Giovanni Perrina(269) born in 1896
      iv) Giovannina Perrina(285) born in 1898
      v) Maria Raimonda Perrina(304) born in 1902

Francesco Paolo Perrina(90) married Nicolina Merlucci(90b) on 7 December 1905 in Flumeri, Italy.

Nicolina Merlucci(90b) was born on 4 May 1877 in Flumeri, Italy, to Pasquale Merlucci(90bF) and Maria Constadina Feola(90bM).

Records that include Francesco Paolo Perrina(90), Maria Cristina Sofia Leone(90a), and/or Nicolina Merlucci(90b):
- Castel Baronia, Italy 1861 Birth Act #17
- Ariano, Italy 1865 Birth Act #72
- Flumeri, Italy 1877 Birth Act #17
- San Nicola Baronia, Italy 1885 Marriage Act #4
- San Nicola Baronia, Italy 1885 Birth Act #41
- San Nicola Baronia 1888, death Act #40
- Castel Baronia, Italy 1893 Birth Act #18

- Castel Baronia, Italy 1896 Birth Act #17
- Castel Baronia, Italy 1896 Death Act #30
- Castel Baronia, Italy 1898 Birth Act #1
- Castel Baronia, Italy 1901 Birth Act #7
- Castel Baronia, Italy 1905 Death Act #31
- "New York Passenger Arrival Lists (Ellis Island), 1892-1924", , FamilySearch (https://www.familysearch.org/ark:/61903/1:1:JJYR-427 : Fri Feb 09 15:01:15 UTC 2024), Entry for Carmine Perrino and Francesco, 22 Mar 1912.
- Flumeri, Italy 1905 Marriage Act #15
- Flumeri, Italy 1919 Marriage Act #13
- Flumeri, Italy 1923 Marriage Act #4
- Flumeri, Italy 1929 Death Act #26

91) Mariantonia Fiorenza

Mariantonia Fiorenza(91) was born on 25 May 1865, in Ariano, Italy, to Gaetano Fiorenza(13a) and Maria Vincenza Marraffino(13). Mariantonia Fiorenza(91) died on 30 July 1867, in Ariano, Italy.

Records that include Mariantonia Fiorenza(91):
- Ariano, Italy 1865 Birth Act #239
- Ariano, Italy 1867 Death Act #485

92) Anna Saveria D'Ausilio

Anna Saveria D'ausilio(92) was born on 25 May 1865, in Ariano, Italy, to Angelo Maria D'Ausilio (24) and Maria Concetta Grasso(24a). Anna Saveria D'ausilio(92) died on 9 July 1871, in Ariano, Italy.

Records that include Anna Saveria D'ausilio(92):
- Ariano, Italy 1865 Birth Act #237
- Ariano, Italy 1871 Death Act #232

93) Pietro Paolo di Vitto

Pietro Paolo Di Vitto(93) was born on 4 July 1865, in Ariano, Italy, to Raimondo di Vitto(16a) and Raimonda D'Ausilio(16). Pietro Paolo Di Vitto(93) died on 9 September 1867, in Ariano, Italy.

Records that include Pietro Paolo Di Vitto(93):
- Ariano, Italy 1865 Birth Act #290
- Ariano, Italy 1867 Death Act #994

94) Domenico DeDonato

Domenico deDonato(94) was born on 21 July 1866, in Ariano, Italy, to Francesco Saverio deDonato(36) and Concetta Melito(36a). Domenico deDonato(94) died on 7 August 1867, in Ariano, Italy.

Records that include Domenico deDonato(94):
- Ariano, Italy 1866 Birth Act #422
- Ariano, Italy 1867 Death Act #569

95) Raimonda Perrina

Raimonda Perrina(95) was born on 11 August 1866, in Ariano, Italy, to Liberatore Perrina(18a) and Maria Nicoletta deDonato(18b).

Raimonda married Raffaele Di Lillo(95a) and Michele Scaperrotta(95b).

Raimonda Perrina(95) married Raffaele Di Lillo(95a) on 14 June 1888 in Ariano, Italy.

Raffaele Di Lillo(95a) was born on 6 February 1853, in Ariano, Italy, to Francesco di Lillo(95aF) and Lucia Perrina(95aM). Raffaele Di Lillo(95a) died on 9 Jun 1907 in Ariano, Italy.

Known children of Raimonda Perrina(95) and Raffaele Di Lillo(95a):

    i) Angelo Michele Di Lillo(217) born in 1889
    ii) Maria Antonia di Lillo(225) born in 1891
    iii) Giovanna Di Lillo(250) born in 1893
    iv) Maria Carmela di Lillo(251) born in 1893
    v) Angelo Michele di Lillo(237) born in 1896
    vi) Rosa di Lillo(279) born in 1897
    vii) Nicola di Lillo(272) born in 1902
    viii) Angelo Maria di Lillo(322) born in 1904

Raimonda Perrina(95) married Michele Scaperrotta(95b) on 5 June 1913 in Ariano, Italy.

Michele Scaperrotta(95b) was born on 16 July 1850, in Ariano, Italy, to Giovanni Scaperrotta(92aF) and Maria Magnino(92aM).

Records that include Raimonda Perrina(95), Raffaele Di Lillo(95a), and/or Michele Scaperrotta(95b):
   • Ariano, Italy 1850 Birth Act #345
   • Ariano, Italy 1853 Birth Act #68
   • Ariano, Italy 1866 Birth Act #463
   • Ariano, Italy 1888 Marriage Act #59
   • Ariano, Italy 1889 Birth Act #260
   • Ariano, Italy 1891 Birth Act #55
   • Ariano, Italy 1893 Birth Act #592
   • Ariano, Italy 1893 Birth Act #593
   • Ariano, Italy 1894 Death Act #303
   • Ariano, Italy 1896 Birth Act #211
   • Ariano, Italy 1896 Death Act #191
   • Ariano, Italy 1897 Birth Act #424
   • Ariano, Italy 1902 Birth Act #303
   • Ariano, Italy 1902 Death Act #204
   • Ariano, Italy 1904 Birth Act #184
   • Ariano, Italy 1907 Death Act #192
   • Ariano, Italy 1913 Marriage Act #71
   • Ariano, Italy 1925 Marriage Act #102
   • Ariano, Italy 1930 Marriage Act #II.A.94
   • Ariano, Italy 1983 Death Act #50

96) Raimonda deDonato

Raimonda deDonato(96) was born on 11 November 1866, in Ariano, Italy, to Luigi deDonato(27) and Angela Maria Miedico(27a). Raimonda deDonato(96) died on 14 June 1867, in Ariano, Italy.

Records that include Raimonda deDonato(96):
   • Ariano, Italy 1866 Birth Act #603
   • Ariano, Italy 1867 Death Act #216

97) Francesco Paulo Giorgione

Francesco Paulo Giorgione(97) was born on 27 April 1867, in Ariano, Italy, to Antonio Giorgione(21a) and Maria Filomina d'Ausilio(21). Francesco Paulo Giorgione(97) died on 19 August 1867, in Ariano, Italy.

Records that include Francesco Paulo Giorgione(97):
   • Ariano, Italy 1867 Birth Act #228
   • Ariano, Italy 1867 Death Act #757

98) Giuseppe Vittorio Emmanuel Clericuzio

Giuseppe Vittorio Emmanuele Clericuzio(98) was born on 29 April 1867, in Ariano, Italy, to Maria Consiglia Clericuzio(38). Giuseppe Vittorio Emmaneule Clericuzio(98) died on 14 July 1867, in Ariano, Italy.

Records that include Giuseppe Vittorio Emmaneule Clericuzio(98):
- Ariano, Italy 1867 Birth Act #241
- Ariano, Italy 1867 Death Act #361

99) Oto Maria D'Ausilio

Oto Maria D'ausilio(99) was born on 13 December 1867, in Ariano, Italy, to Angelo Maria D'Ausilio(24) and Maria Concetta Grasso(24a). Oto Maria D'ausilio(99) died before 1935.

Oto Maria D'ausilio(99) married Maria Gabriella Giannario(99a), on 5 December 1898 in Ariano, Italy.

Maria Gabriella Giannario(99a) was born on 17 September 1876, in Ariano, Italy, to Antonio Giannario(99aF) and Maria Giovanna Grasso(99aM). Maria Gabriella Giannario(99a) died 16 August 1929 in Rome, Italy.

Known children of Oto Maria D'ausilio(99) and Maria Gabriella Giannario(99a):

    i) Alfredo D'Ausilio(295) born in 1899
    ii) Alfredo D'Ausilio(307) born in 1901
    iii) Giulio D'Ausilio(341) born in 1908

Records that include Oto Maria D'ausilio(99) and/or Maria Gabriella Giannario(99a):
- Ariano, Italy 1867 Birth Act #574
- Ariano, Italy 1876 Birth Act #460
- Ariano, Italy 1898 Marriage Act #PII.16
- Ariano, Italy 1899 Birth Act #496
- Ariano, Italy 1900 Death Act #262
- Forlì (provincia di Forlì-Cesena), Italy 1901 Birth Act #371
- "Italia, Forlì-Cesena, Forlì, Stato Civile (Archivio di Stato), 1800-1815, 1866-1930", , FamilySearch (https://www.familysearch.org/ark:/61903/1:1:Q2Q3-2XTT : Fri Mar 08 17:21:26 UTC 2024), Entry for Alfredo d'Ausilio and Oto Maria d'Ausilio, 17 Apr 1901.
- Rome, Italy 1908 Birth Act #1013B.916
- "Italia, Roma, Stato Civile (Archivio di Stato), 1863-1930", , FamilySearch (https://www.familysearch.org/ark:/61903/1:1:4TMG-QDPZ : Fri Mar 08 19:11:12 UTC 2024), Entry for Maria Gabriella Gianuario and Antonio, 16 agosto 1929.

100) Mario Carmelo (Carmine) D'ausilio

Mario Carmelo (Carmine) D'ausilio(100), also recorded as Carmine D'Ausilio, was born on 13 December 1867, in Ariano, Italy, to Angelo Maria D'Ausilio(24) and Maria Concetta Grasso(24a). Mario Carmelo (Carmine) D'ausilio(100) died on 22 November 1869, in Ariano, Italy.

Records that include Mario Carmelo (Carmine) D'ausilio(100):
- Ariano, Italy 1867 Birth Act #575
- Ariano, Italy 1869 Death Act #385

101) Agostino Stella

Agostino Stella(101) was born on 26 February 1868, in Ariano, Italy, to Oto Stella(34a) and Anna Maria Covotta(34).

Agostino Stella(101) married Eugenia Donisi(101a) on 31 August 1896 in Ceppaloni, Italy.

Eugenia Donisi(101a) was born about 1875, in Ceppaloni, Italy, to Giuseppe Donisi(101aF) and Anna Maria Barone(101aM).

Known children of Agostino Stella(101) and Eugenia Donisi(101a):

    i) Oto Emilio Stella(284) born in 1897
    ii) Eugenio Stella(317) born in 1902

Records that include Agostino Stella(101) and/or Eugenia Donisi(101a):
- Ariano, Italy 1868 Birth Act #111
- Ceppaloni, Italy 1896 Marriage Act #13
- "Italia, Benevento, Stato Civile (Archivio di Stato), 1810-1942", , FamilySearch (https://www.familysearch.org/ark:/61903/1:1:QLK5-H8C6 : Sat Mar 09 06:26:04 UTC 2024), Entry for Oto Emilio Stella and Agostino Stella, 19 novembre 1897.
- "Italia, Benevento, Stato Civile (Archivio di Stato), 1810-1942", , FamilySearch (https://www.familysearch.org/ark:/61903/1:1:QLK5-Q2B7 : Sun Mar 10 00:56:01 UTC 2024), Entry for Eugenio Stella and Agostino Stella, 18 maggio 1902.

102) Oto Maria Fodarella

Oto Maria Fodarella(102) was born on 14 April 1868, in Ariano, Italy, to Domenico Fodarella(15a) and Mariangela d'Ausilio(15).

Records that include Oto Maria Fodarella(102):
- Ariano, Italy 1868 Birth Act #178

103) Domenico DeDonato

Domenico deDonato(103) was born on 3 May 1868, in Ariano, Italy, to Francesco Saverio deDonato(36) and Concetta Melito(36a).

Domenico deDonato(103) married Bridgida Carmosino(103a) on 16 October 1909 in Ariano, Italy.

Bridgida Carmosino(103a) was a foundling born on 8 October 1881, in Ariano, Italy.

Known children of Domenico deDonato(103) and Bridgida Carmosino(103a):

     i) Teresa Concetta deDonato(348) born in 1911
     ii) Elena deDonato(354) born in 1912
     iii) Guido Michele deDonato(361) born in 1914
     iv) Aldo deDonato(363) born in 1915
NOTE: There may be more children but the records are not available.

Records that include Domenico deDonato(103) and/or Bridgida Carmosino(103a):
- Ariano, Italy 1868 Birth Act #178
- Ariano, Italy 1881 Birth Act #P.II.51
- Ariano, Italy 1909 Marriage Act #100
- Ariano, Italy 1911 Birth Act #16
- Ariano, Italy 1912 Birth Act #211
- Ariano, Italy 1914 Birth Act #72
- Ariano, Italy 1915 Birth Act #573
- Ariano, Italy 1936 Marriage Act #P.II.77

104) Raimonda DeDonato

Raimonda deDonato(104) was born on 8 June 1868, in Ariano, Italy, to Luigi deDonato(27) and Angela Maria Miedico(27a).

Records that include Raimonda deDonato(104):
- Ariano, Italy 1868 Birth Act #262

105) Maria Giovanna Perrina

Maria Giovanna Perrina(105) was born on 10 April 1869, in Ariano, Italy, to Oto Maria Perrina(14a) and Maria Raimonda deDonato(14). Maria Giovanna Perrina(105) was a farmhand.

Maria Giovanna Perrina(105) married Filippo Ciasullo(105a) on 12 March 1892 in Ariano, Italy.

Filippo Ciasullo(105a) was born on 11 April 1868, in Ariano, Italy, to Fedele Ciasullo(105aF) and Raimonda Zecchino(105aM). Filippo Ciasullo(105a) was a farmhand.

Known children of Maria Giovanna Perrina(105) and Filippo Ciasullo(105a):

     i) Michele Ciasullo(245) born in 1893
     ii) Giuseppe Ciasullo(262) born in 1895
     iii) Anna Ciasullo(280) born in 1897
     iv) Assunta Ciasullo(293) born in 1899
     v) Michele Ciasullo(310) born in 1901
     vi) Michele Ciasullo(320) born in 1903
     vii) Raimonda Ciasullo(332) born in 1905
     viii) Pasqualina Ciasullo(340) born in 1908
     ix) Pasqualina Ciasullo(346) born in 1910
     x) Maria Archina Ciasullo(357) born in 1912

Records that include Maria Giovanna Perrina(105) and/or Filippo Ciasullo(105a):

- Ariano, Italy 1868 Birth Act #190
- Ariano, Italy 1869 Birth Act #229
- Ariano, Italy 1892 Marriage Act #29
- Ariano, Italy 1893 Birth Act #225
- Ariano, Italy 1894 Death Act #404
- Ariano, Italy 1895 Birth Act #220
- Ariano, Italy 1897 Birth Act #432
- Ariano, Italy 1899 Birth Act #486
- Ariano, Italy 1899 Death Act #58
- Ariano, Italy 1901 Birth Act #519
- Ariano, Italy 1902 death Act #175
- Ariano, Italy 1903 Birth Act #240
- Ariano, Italy 1904 Death Act #68
- Ariano, Italy 1905 Birth Act #638
- Ariano, Italy 1906 Death Act #223
- Ariano, Italy 1908 Birth Act #248
- Ariano, Italy 1908 Death Act #323
- Ariano, Italy 1910 Birth Act #217
- Ariano, Italy 1912 Birth Act #198
- Ariano, Italy 1917 Death Act #73
- Ariano, Italy 1922 Marriage Act #29
- Ariano, Italy 1931 Marriage Act #P.II.A.4

106) Michele DeDonato

Michele deDonato(106) was born on 24 December 1869, in Ariano, Italy, to Francesco Saverio deDonato(36) and Concetta Melito(36a). On 4 November 1916 Michele deDonato(106) immigrated to Ellis Island, New York. Michele deDonato(106) died in Connecticut in 1953. Michele deDonato(106) is buried in St. Michael's Cemetery, Stratford, CT.

Michele deDonato(106) married Loreta di Vitto(106a) on 15 December 1894 in Ariano, Italy.

Loreta di Vitto(106a) was born on 11 April 1871, in Ariano, Italy, to Tobia di Vitto(106aF) and Filomena Ferraro(106aM). On 8 October 1917 Loreta di Vitto(106a) immigrated to Boston, Massachusetts. Loreta di Vitto(106a) died in 1946 in Connecticut. Loreta di Vitto(106a) is buried in St. Michael's Cemetery, Stratford, CT.

Known children of Michele deDonato(106) and Loreta di Vitto(106a):

     i) Domenico deDonato(274) born in 1897
     ii) Francesca deDonato(294) born in 1899
     iii) Domenico deDonato(319) born in 1902
     iv) Filippo deDonato(327) born in 1905
     v) Antonio deDonato(337) born in 1907
     vi) Angelo deDonato(355) born in 1911

Records that include Michele deDonato(106) and/or Loreta di Vitto(106a):
- Ariano, Italy 1869 Birth Act #632
- Ariano, Italy 1871 Birth Act #235

- Ariano, Italy 1894 Marriage Act #134
- Ariano, Italy 1897 Birth Act #111
- Ariano, Italy 1897 Death Act #85
- Ariano, Italy 1899 Birth Act #488
- Ariano, Italy 1902 Birth Act #438
- Ariano, Italy 1905 Birth Act #143
- Ariano, Italy 1907 Birth Act #285
- Ariano, Italy 1911 Birth Act #479
- "Massachusetts, Boston Passenger Lists Index, 1899-1940", , FamilySearch (https://www.familysearch.org/ark:/61903/1:1:Q2W6-MR9G : Sun Mar 10 21:42:23 UTC 2024), Entry for Loreta Di Donato, 1914.
- "New York Passenger Arrival Lists (Ellis Island), 1892-1924", , FamilySearch (https://www.familysearch.org/ark:/61903/1:1:JJHQ-BPX : Sat Mar 09 10:49:38 UTC 2024), Entry for Michele De Donato and Loreta, 1916.
- "Massachusetts, Boston Passenger Lists Index, 1899-1940", , FamilySearch (https://www.familysearch.org/ark:/61903/1:1:QKQX-WYT6 : Sat Mar 09 21:59:45 UTC 2024), Entry for Loreta Di Vitto, 1916.
- "Connecticut, Military Census Questionnaires, 1917", , FamilySearch (https://www.familysearch.org/ark:/61903/1:1:ZGW1-Q1T2 : Sat Mar 09 16:18:58 UTC 2024), Entry for Michele De Donato, 1917.
- "Massachusetts, Boston Passenger Lists, 1891-1943", , FamilySearch (https://www.familysearch.org/ark:/61903/1:1:QV94-M7LR : Fri Mar 08 11:20:48 UTC 2024), Entry for Loreta Di Vitto, 1917.
- "United States Census, 1920", , FamilySearch (https://www.familysearch.org/ark:/61903/1:1:MCFH-8FW : Sun Mar 10 18:51:31 UTC 2024), Entry for Michael Donato and Edith Donato, 1920.
- Bridgeport, CT, Marriages July- Sept 1923 #280
- Bridgeport, CT, Marriages Oct - Dec 1924 #29
- "United States Census, 1930", , FamilySearch (https://www.familysearch.org/ark:/61903/1:1:XMPM-4G4 : Fri Mar 08 19:33:27 UTC 2024), Entry for Michael De Donato and Lorita De Donato, 1930.
- "United States Census, 1940", , FamilySearch (https://www.familysearch.org/ark:/61903/1:1:KWMJ-DTY : Sun Mar 10 05:43:58 UTC 2024), Entry for Michael Dedonado and Loretta Dedonado, 1940.
- "Find a Grave Index," database, FamilySearch (https://www.familysearch.org/ark:/61903/1:1:6RJQ-TNBL : 29 January 2024), Loretta DeDonato, ; Burial, Stratford, Fairfield, Connecticut, United States of America, Saint Michael's Cemetery; citing record ID 262002031, Find a Grave, http://www.findagrave.com.
- "Connecticut Death Index, 1949-2001," , FamilySearch (https://familysearch.org/ark:/61903/1:1:VZLP-8LB : 9 December 2014), Micha Dedonato, 06 Jun 1953; from "Connecticut Death Index, 1949-2001," database, Ancestry (http://www.ancestry.com : 2003); citing Stratford, Fairfield, Connecticut, Connecticut Department of Health, Hartford.
- "Find a Grave Index," database, FamilySearch (https://www.familysearch.org/ark:/61903/1:1:6RJQ-TNY5 : 29 January 2024), Michael DeDonato, ; Burial, Stratford, Fairfield, Connecticut, United States of America, Saint Michael's Cemetery; citing record ID 262002019, Find a Grave, http://www.findagrave.com.

107) Gabriele D'Ausilio

Gabriele D'ausilio(107) was born on 18 February 1870, in Ariano, Italy, to Angelo Maria D'Ausilio(24) and Maria Concetta Grasso(24a). Gabriele D'ausilio(107) died on 6 March 1871 in Ariano, Italy.

Records that include Gabriele D'ausilio(107):
- Ariano, Italy 1870 Birth Act #114
- Ariano, Italy 1871 Death Act #91

108) Adelina Clericuzio

Adelina Clericuzio(108) was born on 16 December 1870, in Ariano, Italy, to Maria Consiglia Clericuzio(38). Adelina Clericuzio(108) died on 17 January 1871 in Ariano, Italy.

Records that include Adelina Clericuzio(108):
- Ariano, Italy 1870 Birth Act #636
- Ariano, Italy 1871 Death Act #30

109) Metilde Francesca Clericuzio

Metilda Francesca Clericuzio(109) was born on 16 December 1870, in Ariano, Italy, to Maria Consiglia Clericuzio(38).

Records that include Metilda Francesca Clericuzio(109):
- Ariano, Italy 1870 Birth Act #637

110) Antonio Stella

Antonio Stella(110) was born on 3 January 1871, in Ariano, Italy, to Oto Stella(34a) and Anna Maria Covotta(34). On 11 April 1905 Antonio Stella(110) boarded the Ship Equita in Naples, Italy. Antonio Stella(110) arrived in New York on 30 April 1905.

Antonio Stella(110) married Eugenia LoConte(110a) on 28 August 1897 in Ariano, Italy.

Eugenia LoConte(110a) was born on 6 January 1877, in Ariano, Italy, to Michele LoConte(110aF) and Maria Liberia Pagano(110aM).

Known children of Antonio Stella(110) and Eugenia LoConte(110a):

    i) Oto (Otino) Stella(289) born in 1898
    ii) Michele Stella(299) born in 1900
    iii) Vincenza Stella(313) in 1902
    iv) Maria Stella(321) born in 1904

Records that include Antonio Stella(110) and/or Eugenia LoConte(110a):
- Ariano, Italy 1871 Birth Act #4
- Ariano, Italy 1877 Birth Act #20
- Ariano, Italy 1897 Marriage Act #83
- Ariano, Italy 1898 Birth act #385
- Ariano, Italy 1900 Birth Act #98
- Ariano, Italy 1902 Birth Act #40
- Ariano, Italy 1904 Birth Act #65
- Ariano, Italy 1904 Death Act #93
- Ariano, Italy 1910 Death Act #329
- "New York Passenger Arrival Lists (Ellis Island), 1892-1924", , FamilySearch (https://www.familysearch.org/ark:/61903/1:1:JFQ4-LZK : Sun Mar 10 09:38:14 UTC 2024), Entry for Antonio Stella and Marino Lo Conte, 1905.
- "United States Census, 1910", , FamilySearch (https://www.familysearch.org/ark:/61903/1:1:X39X-JM7 : Fri Mar 08 08:21:13 UTC 2024), Entry for Giuseppe Vasallo and Rosa Vasallo, 1910.
- "New York Passenger Arrival Lists (Ellis Island), 1892-1924", , FamilySearch (https://www.familysearch.org/ark:/61903/1:1:J6HJ-7PJ : Fri Mar 08 16:31:24 UTC 2024), Entry for Oto Stella and Eugenia Lo Conte, 1920.
- "United States Census, 1930", , FamilySearch (https://www.familysearch.org/ark:/61903/1:1:X7DZ-NK3 : Fri Mar 08 21:24:25 UTC 2024), Entry for Tony Stella and Jennie Stella, 1930.
- "United States Census, 1940", , FamilySearch (https://www.familysearch.org/ark:/61903/1:1:KQM8-RTY : Mon Mar 11 02:04:53 UTC 2024), Entry for Antonio Stella and Eugenia Stella, 1940.

111) Antonio Fiorenza

Antonio Fiorenza(111) was born on 18 December 1871, in Ariano, Italy, to Gaetano Fiorenza(13a) and Maria Vincenza Marraffino(13). Antonio Fiorenza(111) died on 17 February 1872 in Ariano, Italy.

Records that include Antonio Fiorenza(111):
- Ariano, Italy 1871 Birth Act #653
- Ariano, Italy 1872 Death Act #77

112) Anna Saveria D'Ausilio

Anna Saveria D'Ausilio(112) was born on 8 February 1872, in Ariano, Italy, to Angelo Maria D'Ausilio(24) and Maria Concetta Grasso(24a).

Anna Saveria D'Ausilio(112) married Giuseppe Angelica(112a) on 3 June 1903 in Ariano, Italy.

Giuseppe Angelica(112a) was born on 27 October 1861, in Campofiorito, Italy, to Stefano Angelica(112aF) and Lucia di Liberto(112aM). Giuseppe Angelica(112b) died 26 June 1929 in Rome, Italy.

Known children of Anna Saveria D'Ausilio(112) and Giuseppe Angelica(112a):

        i) Pasquale Angelica(323) born in 1904
        ii) Angelo Angelica(331) born in 1905
        iii) Angelo Angelica(338) born in 1907
        iv) Antonio Angelica(349) born in 1911
        v) Luigi Angelica(350) born in 1911
        vi) Biagio Angelica(365) born in 1916
        Note: records after 1916 are not currently available

Records that include Anna Saveria D'Ausilio(112), and/or Giuseppe Angelica(112a):
- Campofiorito, Italy 1861 Birth Act #41
- Ariano, Italy 1872 Birth Act #82
- Ariano, Italy 1903 Marriage Act #51
- Rome, Italy 1904 Birth Act #2343 a-804
- Rome, Italy 1905 Birth Act #2346-B844
- Rome, Italy 1906 Death Act #326pa616
- Rome, Italy 1907 Birth Act #2161-B896
- Rome, Italy 1911 Birth Act #1628-4a 1090
- Rome, Italy 1911 Birth Act #1629-4a 1090
- Rome, Italy 1911 Death Act #2919
- Rome, Italy 1916 Birth Act #2079-1-1366
- "Italia, Roma, Stato Civile (Archivio di Stato), 1863-1930", , FamilySearch (https://www.familysearch.org/ark:/61903/1:1:4KGK-33MM : Sat Mar 09 06:17:35 UTC 2024), Entry for Giuseppe Angelica and Stefano, 26 giugno 1929.

113) Maria Silveria D'Ausilio

Maria Silveria D'Ausilio(113) was born on 8 February 1872, in Ariano, Italy, to Angelo Maria D'Ausilio(24) and Maria Concetta Grasso(24a). Maria Silveria D'Ausilio(113) died on 15 January 1877 in Ariano, Italy.

Records that include Maria Silveria D'Ausilio(113):
- Ariano, Italy 1872 Birth Act #83
- Ariano, Italy 1877 Death Act #17

114) Angela DeDonato

Angela deDonato(114) was born on 17 February 1872, in Ariano, Italy, to Francesco Saverio deDonato(36) and Concetta Melito(36a). Angela deDonato(114) died on 4 March 1875 in Ariano, Italy.

Records that include Angela deDonato(114):
- Ariano, Italy 1872 Birth Act #105
- Ariano, Italy 1875 Death Act #78

115) Raffaela Altanese

Raffaela Altanese(115) was born on 24 July 1872, in Grottaminarda, Italy, to Dominico Augelo Giovanni Altanese(19c) and Maria Guiseppa D'Ausilio(19). Raffaela Altanese(115) died 8 January 1873 in Grottaminarda, Italy.

Records that include Raffaela Altanese(115):
- Grottaminarda, Italy 1872 Birth Act #110
- Grottaminarda, Italy 1873 Death Act #3

116) Marianna Stella

Marianna Stella(116) was born on 22 February 1874, in Ariano, Italy, to Oto Stella(34a) and Anna Maria Covotta(34). Marianna Stella(116) died on 2 September 1874 in Ariano, Italy.

Records that include Marianna Stella(116):
- Ariano, Italy 1874 Birth Act #119
- Ariano, Italy 1874 Death Act #349

117) Maria Francesca D'Ausilio

Maria Francesca D'Ausilio(117) was born on 14 April 1874, in Ariano, Italy, to Angelo Maria D'Ausilio(24) and Maria Concetta Grasso(24a). On 15 August 1901 Maria Francesca D'Ausilio(117) boarded the ship SS Treve in Naples, Italy, arriving in New York, NY on 26 August 1901. Maria Francesca D'Ausilio(117) was going to be living with her brother-in-law's, Pasquale Antonio Anastasio(72a), family in Waterbury, CT.

Records that include Maria Francesca D'Ausilio(117):
- Ariano, Italy 1874 Birth Act #204
- "New York, Passenger Arrival Lists (Ellis Island), 1892-1925", FamilySearch (https://www.familysearch.org/ark:/61903/1:1:JFJG-7ZL : Tue Apr 15 08:34:22 UTC 2025), Entry for M.O Francesca D'Aulcsio and Pasquale Anostazio, 26 Aug 1901.

NOTE: I have not found any other records for Maria Francesca D'Ausilio(117), however, there is a mention in the March 31, 1927 issue of the Waterbury Republican newspaper account of her brother, Giovanni Battista (John B.) D'ausilio(120) that states "… and a sister, Mrs. Francesca Briguglio of 61 Bishop Street, this city, when asked about her brother this morning, shouted "He's crazy, he's crazy," adding t[h]at he had disgraced the family."

Searches of the 1929 Price and Lee City Directory for Waterbury, Naugatuck, and Watertown show that there was a Frank Briguglio residing at 61 Bishop Street, however, the listing has his wife's name as Paolina.
The 1920 and 1930 Censuses also list him at the same address and his wife as Paulina.

118) Marianna Stella

Marianna Stella(118) was stillborn on 31 October 1875, in Ariano, Italy, to Oto Stella(34a) and Anna Maria Covotta(34a).

Records that include Marianna Stella(118):
- Ariano, Italy 1875 Birth Act # 496

119) Antonio Covotto

Antonio Covotta(119) was born on 5 January 1876, in Ariano, Italy, to Gaetano Covotta(39) and Giovanna di Franza(39a). Only record for Antonio Covotta(119) is birth record, with notation of marriage added.

Antonio Covotta(119) married Maria Giovanna D'Onofrio(119a) on 17 September 1905 in Castelfranco, Italy.

Maria Giovanna D'Onofrio(119a) No information other than date and place of marriage known.

Records that include Antonio Covotta(119) and/or Maria Giovanna D'Onofrio(119a):
Ariano, Italy 1876 Birth Act #16

120) Giovanni Battista (John B.) D'Ausilio

Giovanni Battista (John B.) D'ausilio(120) was born on 16 May 1877, in Ariano, Italy, to Angelo Maria D'Ausilio(24) and Maria Concetta Grasso(24a). On 17 May 1902 Giovanni Battista (John B.) D'ausilio(120) boarded the ship SS Marco Minghitti in Naples Italy, arriving in New York on 02 Jun 1902. In 31 August 1915 Giovanni Battista (John B.) D'ausilio(120) returned to Italy to serve in the Italian Army during WWI. Giovanni Battista (John B.) D'ausilio(120) achieved the rank of 1st Sargent machine-gunner. On 26 November 1916 Giovanni Battista (John B.) D'ausilio(120) was wounded and sent to the hospital of Bari to recover. Giovanni Battista (John B.) D'ausilio(120) was released from service on 5 December 1918. Giovanni Battista (John B.) D'ausilio(120) was awarded the memorial and Victory Medals. Giovanni Battista (John B.) D'ausilio(120) returned to the United States on the ship SS Argentina sailing from Naples, Italy on 18 December 1919, arriving in New York on 7 January 1920. On 30 March 1927 Giovanni Battista (John B.) D'ausilio(120) entered the Italian Consulate in New Haven, CT and shot the Vice-consul in the face with a sawed off shotgun. On 3 July 1927 Giovanni Battista (John B.) D'ausilio(120) was found to be insane and was sentenced to 15 years in the Connecticut State Hospital for the Insane. Giovanni Battista (John B.) D'ausilio(120) died on 2 August 1958 in Preston, Connecticut. Giovanni Battista (John B.) D'ausilio(120) was buried in St. Bernard Cemetery in New Haven, CT(Unmarked grave). Giovanni Battista (John B.) D'ausilio(120) was an Undertaker, Editor, Publisher, and Boot Finisher.

Giovanni Battista (John B.) D'ausilio(120) married Catherina Viola(120a) on 3 July 1904 at St. Michael's Church in New Haven, CT. They divorced in 1925.

Catherina Viola(120a) was born on 22 December 1885, in Cervinara, Italy, to Nunzio Viola(120aF) and Angelina Marie Valanta(120aM). In 1915 Catherina Viola(120a) returned to Italy with her family. Catherina Viola(120a) returned to the United Sates on the ship SS Belvedere that left Naples, Italy on 14 June 1920, arriving in New York on 8 July 1920. Catherina Viola(120a) died on 29 September 1965, in Bridgeport, Connecticut. Catherina Viola(120a) was buried on 2 October 1965 in Saint Michael's Cemetery, Stratford, CT (Name on grave marker is Catherina D'Ausilio).

Catherina Viola(120a) also married Francesco Laluna(335aF) and Sebastiano Aquilia(120ac).

Known children of Giovanni Battista (John B.) D'ausilio(120) and Catherina Viola(120a):

> i) Concetta D'Ausilio(329) born in 1905
> ii) Liberatore (Leon) D'Ausilio(335) born in 1907
> iii) Felice(Felix) D'Ausilio(346) born in 1908
> iv) Letizia (Leatrice) D'ausilio(351) born in 1911

Records that include Giovanni Battista (John B.) D'ausilio(120) and/or Catherina Viola(120a):
- Ariano, Italy 1877 Birth Act #162
- Cervinara, Italy 1885 Birth Act #345
- "New York, New York, Index to Passengers Lists of Vessels, 1897-1902", FamilySearch (https://www.familysearch.org/ark:/61903/1:1:ZKHD-HKPZ : Sat Apr 12 15:20:09 UTC 2025), Entry for Giovanni Cattesta d'Ausilio, 1902.
- New York, Passenger Arrival Lists (Ellis Island), 1892-1925", FamilySearch (https://www.familysearch.org/ark:/61903/1:1:JFLV-PYF : Tue Apr 15 17:46:03 UTC 2025), Entry for Giovannbattista D'Ansilio and Anastasi, 02 Jun 1902.
- New Haven, CT 7 July 1904 Marriage Record
- Bridgeport, CT 1905 Birth Record #42
- Bridgeport, CT 1907 Birth Record #500

- United States, Census, 1910", FamilySearch (https://www.familysearch.org/ark:/61903/1:1:MK2L-1FY : Sat Mar 09 10:39:59 UTC 2024), Entry for John B Durslio and Katherine Durslio, 1910.
- Milford, CT 30 December 1908 Birth Record
- https://collections.ctdigitalarchive.org/node/375603
- New York, Passenger Arrival Lists (Ellis Island), 1892-1925", FamilySearch (https://www.familysearch.org/ark:/61903/1:1:J6H2-7TL : Tue Apr 15 11:20:21 UTC 2025), Entry for Giov. Battista D'Ausilio and Caterina Viola, 07 Jan 1920.
- New York, Passenger Arrival Lists (Ellis Island), 1892-1925", FamilySearch (https://www.familysearch.org/ark:/61903/1:1:J6X1-3Q7 : Tue Apr 15 04:17:56 UTC 2025), Entry for Caterina Violo and Antonio, 08 Jul 1920.
- Bridgeport, CT October 1929 Marriage Record #127
- United States, Census, 1930", FamilySearch (https://www.familysearch.org/ark:/61903/1:1:XM53-7WR : Fri Jan 17 01:28:41 UTC 2025), Entry for Giovanni d'Ansilio, 1930.
- United States, Census, 1940", FamilySearch (https://www.familysearch.org/ark:/61903/1:1:K712-3DZ : Mon Jan 20 10:58:28 UTC 2025), Entry for Giovanni D'Ausilio, 1940.
- Pennsylvania, County Marriages, 1775-1991", FamilySearch (https://www.familysearch.org/ark:/61903/1:1:VFQQ-P8S : Sat Mar 09 04:13:07 UTC 2024), Entry for Felix d'Ausillio and Lucille Maria Rae, 1947.
- "Pennsylvania, County Marriages, 1775-1991", FamilySearch (https://www.familysearch.org/ark:/61903/1:1:VFQ8-86Y : Sat Jul 13 23:28:31 UTC 2024), Entry for Felix d'Austilio and John B., 6 Jan 1948.
- United States, Census, 1950", FamilySearch (https://www.familysearch.org/ark:/61903/1:1:6FMX-QT52 : Tue Mar 18 06:20:33 UTC 2025), Entry for Ethel Turkington and Catherine Crouch, 19 April 1950.
- Connecticut, Death Index, 1949-2001", FamilySearch (https://www.familysearch.org/ark:/61903/1:1:VZLR-5BD : Wed Feb 19 09:04:24 UTC 2025), Entry for Giova D'Ausilio, 02 Aug 1958.
- Preston, CT August 1958 Death Record #232
- Find a Grave Index", FamilySearch (https://www.familysearch.org/ark:/61903/1:1:ZRFD-CSW2 : Tue Apr 01 00:44:52 UTC 2025), Entry for Caterina D'Ausilio.
- Bridgeport, CT September 1999 Death Record #78
- Waterbury American, Waterbury, Connecticut, Thursday Evening March 31, 1927, page 1, "FORMER LOCAL MAN IS HELD FOR SHOOTING VICE-CONSUL WITH SAWEDOFF SHOTGUN".
- Waterbury American, Waterbury, Connecticut, Friday Evening April 1, 1927, page 1, "WOUNDED CONSUL FIGHTS FOR LIFE".
- Waterbury American, Waterbury, Connecticut, Thursday Evening April 7, 1927, page 1, "D'AUSILIO CASE GIVEN SETBACK".
- Waterbury American, Waterbury, Connecticut, Thursday Evening April 2`1, 1927, page 3, "DECICCO CONTINUES BATTLE FOR LIFE".
- Waterbury American, Waterbury, Connecticut, Tuesday Evening July 5, 1927, page 1, "INSANE GUNMAN IS SENT TO HOSPITAL".

NOTE: There are many newspaper articles from many different locations. These listed are the ones referenced. There are more articles available on the Library of Congress Website, www.loc.gov

121) Eustachio DeDonato

Eustachio deDonato(121) was born on 10 July 1877, in Ariano, Italy, to Francesco Saverio deDonato(36) and Concetta Melito(36a). Eustachio deDonato(121) died on 26 March 1878 in Ariano, Italy.

Records that include Eustachio deDonato(121):
- Ariano, Italy 1877 Birth Act #380
- Ariano, Italy 1878 Death Act #90

122) Michele Covotta

Michele Covotta(122) was born on 23 January 1879, in Ariano, Italy, to Gaetano Covotta(39) and Giovanna di Franza(39a).

Michele Covotta(122) married Antonetta Bilotta(122a) on 29 September 1904 in Ariano, Italy.

Antonetta Bilotta(122a) was born on 13 October 1881, in Ariano, Italy, to Serafino Bilotta(122aF) and Maria Carmina Ardito(122aM). Antonetta Bilotta(122a) died on 28 April 1928 in Ariano. Italy. Antonetta Bilotta(122a)

Known children of Michele Covotta(122) and Antonetta Bilotta(122a):

    i) Giovannina Covotta(330) born in 1905
    ii) Gaetano Giuseppe Luciano Covotta(358) born in 1912

Records that include Michele Covotta(122) and/or Antonetta Bilotta(122a):
* Ariano, Italy 1879 Birth Act #43
* Ariano, Italy 1881 Birth Act #499
* Ariano, Italy 1904 Marriage Act #93
* Ariano, Italy 1905 Birth Act #452
* Ariano, Italy 1912 Birth Act #355
* Ariano, Italy 1928 Death Act #99

123) Rosaria DeDonato

Rosaria deDonato(123) was born on 5 October 1879, in Ariano, Italy, to Francesco Saverio deDonato(36) and Concetta Melito(36a).

Records that include Rosaria deDonato(123):
* Ariano, Italy 1879 Birth Act #519

124) Salvatore Antonio D'Ausilio

Salvatore Antonio D'ausilio(124) was born on 20 November 1879, in Ariano, Italy, to Angelo Maria D'Ausilio(24) and Maria Concetta Grasso(24a). On 15 August 1901 Salvatore Antonio D'ausilio(124) boarded the ship SS Treve in Naples, Italy, arriving in New York, NY on 26 August 1901. Salvatore Antonio D'ausilio(124) was a Funeral Director in East Boston, Mass. In 1924, Salvatore Antonio D'ausilio(124) was naturalized in Maynard, MA. Salvatore Antonio D'ausilio(124) died in 1952 in Boston, MA.

Salvatore Antonio D'ausilio(124) married Giovanna Colucci(124a) on 24 March 1899 in Ariano, Italy.

Giovanna Colucci(124a) was born on 11 April 1880, in Ariano, Italy, to Romualdo Colucci(124aF) and Maria Libera Grillo(124aM). Giovanna Colucci(124a) boarded the ship SS Trojan Prince, in Naples, Italy, on 28 October 1902, arriving in New York, NY on 14 November 1902. Giovanna Colucci(124a) died before 1950.

Known children of Salvatore Antonio D'ausilio(124) and Giovanna Colucci(124a):

    i) Concetta D'Ausilio(298) born in 1900
    ii) Pasquale D'Ausilio(315) born in 1902
    iii) Angela Maria D'Ausilio(324) born in 1904

Records that include Salvatore Antonio D'ausilio(124) and/or Giovanna Colucci(124a):
* Ariano, Italy 1880 Birth Act #212
* Ariano, Italy 1899 Marriage Act #34
* Ariano, Italy 1900 Birth Act #68
* Ariano, Italy 1902 Birth Act #101
* Waterbury, CT 1904 Birth Records
* "New York Passenger Arrival Lists (Ellis Island), 1892-1924", , FamilySearch (https://www.familysearch.org/ark:/61903/1:1:JFJG-7ZG : Sat Mar 09 15:14:09 UTC 2024), Entry for Salvatore d'Anlisio and Pasquale Anostazio, 1901.

- "New York Passenger Arrival Lists (Ellis Island), 1892-1924", , FamilySearch (https://www.familysearch.org/ark:/61903/1:1:JFLS-XQ7 : Sat Mar 09 06:08:01 UTC 2024), Entry for Grovanna Calucei and Salvatore Dansilio, 1902.
- "New York Passenger Arrival Lists (Ellis Island), 1892-1924", , FamilySearch (https://www.familysearch.org/ark:/61903/1:1:JFZY-V3L : Sun Mar 10 05:36:50 UTC 2024), Entry for Gerardo Colucci and Salvatore d'Ansilio, 1906.
- "United States Census, 1910", , FamilySearch (https://www.familysearch.org/ark:/61903/1:1:MK2G-NS5 : Mon Mar 11 00:38:29 UTC 2024), Entry for Salvatore Dansilio and Jennie Dansilio, 1910.
- "United States World War I Draft Registration Cards, 1917-1918", database with images, FamilySearch (https://www.familysearch.org/ark:/61903/1:1:KZJP-X7C : 30 June 2024), Salvatore d'Ausilio, 1917-1918.
- "New York Passenger Arrival Lists (Ellis Island), 1892-1924", , FamilySearch (https://www.familysearch.org/ark:/61903/1:1:J6H2-7TL : Sun Mar 10 05:33:19 UTC 2024), Entry for Giov. Battista d'Ausilio and Caterina Viola, 1920.
- "Massachusetts, United States Naturalization Records, 1790-1991", FamilySearch (https://www.familysearch.org/ark:/61903/1:1:65MS-CBBY : Thu Apr 10 02:41:56 UTC 2025), Entry for Salvatore d'Ausilio and Giovannina, 18 Nov 1921.
- "Massachusetts, United States Naturalization Records, 1790-1991", , FamilySearch (https://www.familysearch.org/ark:/61903/1:1:QPCM-8CFM : Sat Mar 09 14:43:38 UTC 2024), Entry for Salvatore d'Ausilio, 1924.
- "Massachusetts Naturalization Index, 1906-1966," , FamilySearch (https://familysearch.org/ark:/61903/1:1:XL1K-1ZF : 4 December 2014), Salvatore D'Ausilio, 1924; from "Index to Petitions and Records of Naturalizations of the U.S. and District Courts for the District of Massachusetts, 1907-1966," database, Fold3.com (http://www.fold3.com : n.d.); citing NARA microfilm publication M1545 (Washington, D.C.: National Archives and Records Administration, n.d.), roll 7.
- "United States Census, 1930", , FamilySearch (https://www.familysearch.org/ark:/61903/1:1:XQ5G-9D4 : Thu Mar 07 16:52:48 UTC 2024), Entry for Salvatore Dauselio and Jennie Dauselio, 1930.
- "United States Census, 1950", , FamilySearch (https://www.familysearch.org/ark:/61903/1:1:6F38-C2LK : Fri Oct 06 17:29:06 UTC 2023), Entry for Nick M Dragoni and Angela M Dragoni, 10 April 1950.
- "United States, Social Security Numerical Identification Files (NUMIDENT), 1936-2007", database, FamilySearch (https://www.familysearch.org/ark:/61903/1:1:6KM3-MD16 : 10 February 2023), Salvatore Dusilio in entry for Concetta Bellofatto, .
- "United States, Social Security Numerical Identification Files (NUMIDENT), 1936-2007", database, FamilySearch (https://www.familysearch.org/ark:/61903/1:1:6KMW-Q39J : 10 February 2023), Salvatore Dausilio, .
- "United States, Social Security Numerical Identification Files (NUMIDENT), 1936-2007", database, FamilySearch (https://www.familysearch.org/ark:/61903/1:1:6KMW-Q39J : 10 February 2023), Salvatore Dausilio, .

125) Raffaele Covotta

Raffaele Covotta(125) was born about 1882 to Gaetano Covotta(39) and Giovanna di Franza(39a). Raffaele Covotta(125) died on 9 December 1889 in Ariano, Italy.

Records that include Raffaele Covotta(125):
- Ariano, Italy 1889 Death Act #389

126) Luigi DeDonato

Luigi deDonato(126) was born on 18 March 1882, in Ariano, Italy, to Francesco Saverio deDonato(36) and Concetta Melito(36a).

Luigi deDonato(126) married Caterina Montecalvo(126a) on 23 July 1908 in Ariano, Italy.

Caterina Montecalvo(126a) was born on 25 November 1886, in Ariano, Italy. Caterina Montecalvo(126a) was a foundling.

Known children of Luigi deDonato(126) and Caterina Montecalvo(126a):

> i) Lorenza Concetta deDonato(360) in 1913
> ii) Antonetta DeDonato(466) born about 1916

Records that include Luigi deDonato(126) and Caterina Montecalvo(126a):
* Ariano, Italy 1882 Birth Act #174
* Ariano, Italy 1886 Birth Act #35/II
* Ariano, Italy 1908 Marriage Act #77
* Ariano, Italy 1913 Birth Act #442
* Ariano, Italy 1919 Death Act #292
* "Italia, Benevento, Stato Civile (Archivio di Stato), 1810-1942", , FamilySearch (https://www.familysearch.org/ark:/61903/1:1:QLKP-5V64 : Fri Mar 08 03:49:07 UTC 2024), Entry for Aurelio Petruccelli and Raffaele Petruccelli, 24 ottobre 1936.

127) Carminantonio D'Ausilio

Carminantonio D'ausilio(127) was born on 14 March 1883, in Ariano, Italy, to Angelo Maria D'Ausilio(24) and Maria Concetta Grasso(24a). Carminantonio D'ausilio(127) died on 18 March 1883 in Ariano, Italy.

Records that include Carminantonio D'ausilio(127):
* Ariano, Italy 1883 Birth Act #183
* Ariano, Italy 1883 Death Act #90

128) Pietro DeDonato

Pietro deDonato(128) was born on 30 April 1884, in Ariano, Italy, to Francesco Saverio deDonato(36) and Concetta Melito(36a). Pietro deDonato(128) died on 30 May 1963 in Torino, Italy.

Pietro deDonato(128) married Rosa Bilancione(128a) on 2 May 1907 in Ariano, Italy.

Rosa Bilancione(128a) was born 1 July 1883, in Ariano, Italy. Rosa Bilancione(128a) was a foundling.

Known children of Pietro deDonato(128) and Rosa Bilancione(128a):

> i) Maria Libera deDonato(342) born in 1908
> ii) Michele deDonato(343) born in 1910
> iii) Pasquale deDonato(352) born in 1912
> iv) Francesco deDonato(362) born in 1914
> v) Giuseppe deDonato(364) born in 1916

Records that include Pietro deDonato(128) and/or Rosa Bilancione(128a):
* Ariano, Italy 1883 Birth Act #PII 21
* Ariano, Italy 1884 Birth Act #273
* Ariano, Italy 1907 Marriage Act #59
* Ariano, Italy 1908 Birth Act #524
* Ariano, Italy 1910 Birth Act #278
* Ariano, Italy 1912 Birth Act #29
* Ariano, Italy 1914 Birth Act #174
* Ariano, Italy 1918 Death Act #193

- Ariano, Italy 1918 Death Act #339
- Ariano, Italy 1929 Marriage Act #68
- Ariano, Italy 1934 Marriage Act #P.II.A.172
- Ariano, Italy 1939 Marriage Act #129

129) Maria Covotta

Maria Covotta(129) was born on 4 December 1885, in Ariano, Italy, to Gaetano Covotta(39) and Giovanna di Franza(39a). Maria Covotta(129) died on 3 December 1889 in Ariano, Italy.

Records that include Maria Covotta(129):
- Ariano, Italy 1885 Birth Act #673
- Ariano, Italy 1889 Death Act #385

130) Angela DeDonato

Angela deDonato(130) was born on 12 July 1887, in Ariano, Italy, to Francesco Saverio deDonato(36) and Concetta Melito(36a). Angela deDonato(127) died on 16 November 1889 in Ariano, Italy.

Records that include Angela deDonato(130):
- Ariano, Italy 1887 Birth Act #449
- Ariano, Italy 1889 Death Act #354

NOTE: Ariano, Italy 1889 Death Act #354 lists the age as 2 months, I believe this is an error as no death record for Angela deDonato(130) born in 1887 exist, nor is there any birth record in 1889 for another Angela deDonato.

SIXTH GENERATION

131) Vincenzo Tiso

Vincenzo Tiso(131) was born on 8 August 1870, in Ariano, Italy, to Liberatore Tiso(42a) and Maria Concordia Fodarella(42). Vincenzo Tiso(131) died on 25 May 1939 in Ariano, Italy. Vincenzo Tiso(131) was a farm laborer.

Vincenzo Tiso(131) married Giovanna Portogallo(131a) on 11 November 1899 in Ariano, Italy.

Giovanna Portogallo(131a) was born on 25 June 1881, in Ariano, Italy, to Bonaventura Portogallo(131aF) and Clorinda Grasso(131aM). Giovanna Portogallo(131a) died on 21 April 1963 in Ariano, Italy.

Known children of Vincenzo Tiso(131)and Giovanna Portogallo(131a):

      i) Liberato Tiso(373) born in 1901
      ii) Clorinda Mariantonia Tiso(380) born in 1904
      iii) Gabriella Tiso(396) born in 1907
      iv) Carmela Tiso(415) born in 1910
      v) Concordia Tiso(478) born in 1917

Records that include Vincenzo Tiso(131)and/or Giovanna Portogallo(131a):
- Ariano, Italy 1870 Birth Act #422
- Ariano, Italy 1881 Birth Act #304
- Ariano, Italy 1899 Marriage Act #94
- Ariano, Italy 1901 Birth Act #149
- Ariano, Italy 1904 Birth Act #30
- Ariano, Italy 1907 Birth Act #578
- Ariano, Italy 1910 Birth Act #231
- Ariano, Italy 1917 Birth Act #60
- Ariano, Italy 1924 Marriage Act #147
- Ariano, Italy 1928 Marriage Act #40
- Ariano, Italy 1931 Marriage Act #P.II.A.85
- Ariano, Italy 1936 Marriage Act #36
- Ariano, Italy 1939 Death Act #153
- Ariano, Italy 1984 Death Act #154

132) Nicolantonio Miressi

Nicolantonio Miressi(132) was born on 3 October 1872, in Ariano, Italy, to Giuseppe Miressi(51a) and Rosa Giorgione(51). Nicolantonio Miressi(132) died on 28 January 1953 in Ariano, Italy.

Nicolantonio Miressi(132) married Giovanna Giardino(132a), Maria Rosa Caso(132b), Maria Michele Monaco(132c) and Mariantonia Ciccarelli(132d).

Nicolantonio Miressi(132) married Giovanna Giardino(132a) on 13 September 1894 in Ariano, Italy.

Giovanna Giardino(132a) was born on 21 October 1871, in Ariano, Italy, to Francesco Paolo Giardino(132aF) and Rosaria Iannarone(132aM). Giovanna Giardino(132a) died 1 Jun 1900 in Ariano, Italy.

Known children of Nicolantonio Miressi(132) and Giovanna Giardino(132a):

      i) Francesco Paolo Miressi(367) born in 1895
      ii) Giuseppe Miressi(368) born in 1895
      iii) Giuseppe Miressi(369) born in 1897
      iv) Angelo Maria Miressi(370) born in 1898

Nicolantonio Miressi(132) married Maria Rosa Caso(132b) on 22 October 1900 in Ariano, Italy.

Maria Rosa Caso(132b) was born on 2 June 1876, in Ariano, Italy, to Lorenzo Caso(132bF) and Raffaela Monaco(132bM). Maria Rosa Caso(132b) died on 16 November 1902 in Ariano, Italy.

Known children of Nicolantonio Miressi(132) and Maria Rosa Caso(132b):

      i) Giovannina Miressi(374) in 1901

Nicolantonio Miressi(132) married Maria Michele Monaco(132c) on 19 October 1903 in Ariano, Italy.

Maria Michele Monaco(132c) was born on 12 January 1876, in Ariano, Italy, to Oto Maria Monaco(132cF) and Anna Maria Grasso(132cM). Maria Michele Monaco(132c) died on 29 February 1908 in Ariano, Italy.

Known children of Nicolantonio Miressi(132) and Maria Michele Monaco(132c):

      i) Giuseppe Miressi(383) born in 1904
     ii) Virgilia Miressi(399) born in 1908

Nicolantonio Miressi(132) married Mariantonia Ciccarelli(132d) on 6 April 1911 in Ariano, Italy.

Mariantonia Ciccarelli(132d) was born on 20 December 1874, in Ariano Italy, to Giuseppantonio Ciccarelli(132dF) and Caterina Grasso(132dM). Mariantonia Ciccarelli(132d) died on 21 January 1947 in Ariano Italy.

I have not found any records of children for Nicolantonio Miressi(132) and Mariantonia Ciccarelli(132d).

Mariantonia Ciccarelli(132d) had previously married Antonio Riccio(132dX).

Records that include Nicolantonio Miressi(132), Giovanna Giardino(132a), Maria Rosa Caso(132b), Maria Michele Monaco(132c) and/or Mariantonia Ciccarelli(132d):
- Ariano, Italy 1871 Birth Act #542
- Ariano, Italy 1872 Birth Act #490
- Ariano, Italy 1874 Birth Act #569
- Ariano, Italy 1876 Birth Act #24
- Ariano, Italy 1894 Marriage Act #84
- Ariano, Italy 1895 Birth Act #691
- Ariano, Italy 1895 Birth Act #690
- Ariano, Italy 1895 Death Act #425
- Ariano, Italy 1897 Birth Act #14
- Ariano, Italy 1897 Death Act #330
- Ariano, Italy 1898 Birth Act #161
- Ariano, Italy 1900 Marriage Act #89
- Ariano, Italy 1901 Birth Act #457
- Ariano, Italy 1902 Death Act #393
- Ariano, Italy 1903 Marriage Act #86
- Ariano, Italy 1904 Birth Act #358
- Ariano, Italy 1904 Death Act #339
- Ariano, Italy 1908 Birth Act #99
- Ariano, Italy 1908 Death Act #61
- Ariano, Italy 1908 Death Act #69
- Ariano, Italy 1911 Marriage Act #47
- Ariano, Italy 1947 Death Act #20
- Ariano, Italy 1953 Death Act #17

133) Mariangela Tiso

Mariangela Tiso(133) was born about 1873, in Ariano Italy, to Liberatore Tiso(42a) and Maria Concordia Fodarella(42).

Mariangela Tiso(133) married Gerardino Bianchi(133a) on 18 October 1902 in Ariano, Italy.

Gerardino Bianchi(133a) was born 21 July 1873, in Fontanarosa, Italy to unknown parents(foundling). Gerardino Bianchi(133a) died 6 February 1925, in Ariano, Italy. Gerardino Bianchi(133a) was a pasta maker.

Known children of Mariangela Tiso(133) and Gerardino Bianchi(133a):

    i) Francesco Vincenzo Liberato Bianchi(379) born in 1903
    ii) Oto Maria Carmine Bianchi(388) born in 1906
    iii) Liberato Amendeo Anselmo Bianchi(406) born in 1908
    iv) Oto Maria Carmelo (Otto M.) Bianchi(422) born in 1911

Records that include Mariangela Tiso(133) and Gerardino Bianchi(133a):
- Ariano, Italy 1873 Birth Act #358
- Ariano, Italy 1902 Marriage Act #84
- Ariano, Italy 1903 Birth Act #537
- Ariano, Italy 1906 Birth Act #215
- Ariano, Italy 1908 Birth Act #546
- Ariano, Italy 1910 Death Act #228
- Ariano, Italy 1925 Death Act #26
- Ariano, Italy 1930 Marriage Act #II.A.4

134) Filomena Miressi

Filomena Miressi(134) was born on 24 December 1874, in Ariano, Italy, to Giuseppe Miressi(51a) and Rosa Giorgione(51). Filomena Miressi(134) died 6 December 1880 in Ariano, Italy.

Records that include Filomena Miressi(134):
- Ariano, Italy 1874 Birth Act #575
- Ariano, Italy 1880 Death Act #574

135) Concetta Manganiello

Concetta Manganiello(135) was born on 8 December 1875, in Ariano, Italy, to Vincenzo Manganiello(57a) and Anna Maria Fodarella(57). Concetta Manganiello(135) died 5 November 1937 in Ariano, Italy.

Concetta Manganiello(135) married Nicola Maria d'Antuono(135a) on 18 February 1899 in Ariano, Italy.

Nicola Maria d'Antuono(135a) was born on 2 November 1874, in Ariano, Italy, to Gabriele d'Antuono(135aF) and Camina del Vecchio(135aM). Nicola Maria d'Antuono(135a) died 8 May 1918 in Ariano, Italy.

Known children of Concetta Manganiello(135) and Nicola Maria d'Antuono(135a):

    i) Gabriele D'Antuono(372) born in 1899
    ii) Gabriele D'Antuono(375) born in 1902
    iii) Elena D'Antuono(384) born in 1904
    iv) Angiolina d'Antuono(397) born in 1908
    v) Maria Archina D'Antuono(426) born in 1911

Records that include Concetta Manganiello(135) and/or Nicola Maria d'Antuono(135a):
- Ariano, Italy 1874 Birth Act #491
- Ariano, Italy 1875 Birth Act #539
- Ariano, Italy 1899 Marriage Act #18
- Ariano, Italy 1899 Birth Act #692
- Ariano, Italy 1901 Death Act #65
- Ariano, Italy 1902 Birth Act #17
- Ariano, Italy 1902 Death Act #65
- Ariano, Italy 1904 Birth Act #431
- Ariano, Italy 1905 Death Act #76
- Ariano, Italy 1908 Birth Act #24
- Ariano, Italy 1911 Birth Act #513
- Ariano, Italy 1918 Death Act #133
- Ariano, Italy 1937 Death Act #219
- Ariano, Italy 1940 Marriage Act #99

136) Filomena Tiso

Filomena Tiso(136) was born on 8 August 1876, in Ariano, Italy, to Liberatore Tiso(42a) and Maria Concordia Fodarella(42). Filomena Tiso(136) died on 25 April 1894, in Ariano, Italy. Filomena Tiso(136) was a farm laborer.

Records that include Filomena Tiso(136):
- Ariano, Italy 1876 Birth Act #403
- Ariano, Italy 1894 Death Act #162

137) Maria Michele Manganiello

Maria Michele Manganiello(137) was born on 21 December 1876, in Ariano, Italy, to Giuseppe Manganiello(64a) and Maria Francesca Fodarella(64). Maria Michele Manganiello(137) died on 13 January 1903 in Ariano, Italy.

Records that include Maria Michele Manganiello(137):
- Ariano, Italy 1876 Birth Act #610
- Ariano, Italy 1903 Death Act #10

138) Michele Manganiello

Michele Manganiello(138) was born on 19 April 1877, in Ariano, Italy, to Vincenzo Manganiello(57a) and Anna Maria Fodarella(57). Michele Manganiello(138) died on 22 February 1956 in Ariano, Italy.

Michele Manganiello(138) married Pasqualina Miniscalco(138a) on 12 January 1905 in Ariano, Italy.

Pasqualina Miniscalco(138a) was born on 12 February 1882, in Ariano, Italy, to Giuseppe Miniscalco(138aF) and Rosaria de Stefano(138aM).

Known children of Michele Manganiello(138) and Pasqualina Miniscalco(138a):

- i) Maria Manganiello(378) born in 1903
- ii) Virginia Manganiello(413) born in 1910
- iii) Raimondo Manganiello(528) born about 1923

Records that include Michele Manganiello(138) and/or Pasqualina Miniscalco(138a):
- Ariano, Italy 1877 Birth Act #235
- Ariano, Italy 1882 Birth Act #103
- Ariano, Italy 1905 Marriage Act #3
- Ariano, Italy 1903 Birth Act #443
- Ariano, Italy 1910 Birth Act #93
- Ariano, Italy 1910 Death Act #330
- Ariano, Italy 1924 Marriage Act #2
- Ariano, Italy 1924 Death Act #280
- Ariano, Italy 1956 Death Act #52
- Ariano, Italy 1996 Death Act #115

139) Antonio Perrina

Antonio Perrina(139) was born on 27 June 1877 in San Nicola Baronia, Italy, to Raffaele Perrina(58) and Maria Lucia Gesa(58a) Antonia Perrina died on 5 January 1889, in Castel Baronia, Italy.

Records that include Antonio Perrina(139):
- San Nicola Baronia, Italy 1877 Birth Act #27
- Castel Baronia, Italy 1889 Death Act #1

140) Antonio Grasso

Antonio Grasso(140) was born on 13 July 1877, in Ariano, Italy, to Lorenzo Grasso(45a) and Anna Maria Perrina(45). Antonio Grasso(140) died on 12 September 1880 in Ariano, Italy.

Records that include Antonio Grasso(140):
- Ariano, Italy 1877 Birth Act #333
- Ariano, Italy 1880 Death Act #425

141) Domenico Fodarella

Domenico Fodarella(141) was born on 24 September 1877, in Ariano, Italy, to Lorenzo Fodarella(48) and Maria Fransesca Paola Dotolo(48a). Domenico Fodarella(141) died on 30 August 1878 in Ariano, Italy.

Records that include Domenico Fodarella(141):
- Ariano, Italy 1877 Birth Act #477
- Ariano, Italy 1878 Death Act #233

142) Agata Miressi

Agata Miressi(142) was born on 28 September 1877, in Ariano, Italy, to Giuseppe Miressi(51a) and Rosa Giorgione(51). Agata Miressi(142) died on 5 October 1877 in Ariano, Italy.

Records that include Agata Miressi(142):
- Ariano, Italy 1877 Birth Act #483
- Ariano, Italy 1877 Death Act #293

143) Anna Maria Ninfadoro

Anna Maria Ninfadoro(143) was born on 5 January 1878, in Ariano, Italy, to Gabriele Ninfadoro(67a) and Mariangela Perrina(67). Anna Maria Ninfadoro(143) died on 8 October 1880 in Ariano, Italy.

Records that include Anna Maria Ninfadoro(143):
- Ariano, Italy 1878 Birth Act #8
- Ariano, Italy 1880 Death Act #472

144) Rosa Grasso

Rosa Grasso(144) was born on 16 July 1878, in Ariano, Italy, to Crescenzo Grasso(76a) and Anna Perrina(76). Rosa Grasso(144) boarded the ship SS Marco Minchetto on March 27 1901, in Naples, Italy, arriving in New York, NY on 13 April 1901.

Rosa Grasso(144) married Francesco Paolo Vernacchia(144a) on 8 January 1898, in Ariano, Italy.

Francesco Paolo Vernacchia(144a) was born on 1 December 1875, in Ariano, Italy, to Angelo Vernacchia(144aF) and Vincenza deDonato(144aM). On March 27 1901 boarded the ship SS Marco Minchetto arriving in New York, NY on 13 April 1901. Francesco Paolo Vernacchia(144a) became a citizen of the United States on 1 April 1913 in New York, NY.

Known children of Rosa Grasso(144) and Francesco Paolo Vernacchia(144a):

  i) Angelo Vernacchia(371) born in 1899
  ii) John Vernacchia(377) born in 1903
  iii) Vincenza Vernacchia(385) born in 1905
  iv) Immacolota (Concetta) Vernacchia(391) born in 1907
  v) Angelo (Charles) Vernacchia(405) born in 1908
  vi) Giovanni (John) Vernacchia(416) born in 1910
  vii) Aurora (Mary) Vernacchia(432) born in 1912

Records that include Rosa Grasso(144) and/or Francesco Paolo Vernacchia(144a):
- Ariano, Italy 1875 Birth Act #544
- Ariano, Italy 1878 Birth Act #342
- Ariano, Italy 1898 Marriage Act #1
- Ariano, Italy 1899 Birth Act #5
- "New York, New York City Births, 1846-1909", FamilySearch (https://www.familysearch.org/ark:/61903/1:1:2W87-D2H : Wed Mar 12 02:42:58 UTC 2025), Entry for Giuvannino Vemacchia and Francesco Femacchia, 16 Sep 1903.

- "New York, New York City Municipal Deaths, 1795-1949", FamilySearch (https://www.familysearch.org/ark:/61903/1:1:2WDJ-SFS : Wed Mar 26 17:25:53 UTC 2025), Entry for Creycerzio Vernacchia and Francesco Vernacchia, 21 Jan 1903.
- "New York, County Naturalization Records, 1791-1980", FamilySearch (https://www.familysearch.org/ark:/61903/1:1:QP8L-56R7 : Fri Apr 11 23:17:17 UTC 2025), Entry for Francesco Paolo Vernacchia and Rosa Grasso, 1912.
- "New York, New York City Municipal Deaths, 1795-1949", FamilySearch (https://www.familysearch.org/ark:/61903/1:1:2WDV-22S : Wed Mar 26 17:26:08 UTC 2025), Entry for John Vernacchio and Paulo Vernacchio, 21 Jan 1906.
- "New York, New York City Births, 1846-1909", FamilySearch (https://www.familysearch.org/ark:/61903/1:1:2WHN-48C : Wed Mar 12 01:37:48 UTC 2025), Entry for Concettina Vernacchio and Franceno Taolo Vernacchio, 08 Dec 1906.
- "New York, State Census, 1915", , FamilySearch (https://www.familysearch.org/ark:/61903/1:1:K9FC-ZB1 : 4 June 2022), Frank Vernachio, 1915.
- "United States, World War I Draft Registration Cards, 1917-1918", FamilySearch (https://www.familysearch.org/ark:/61903/1:1:7N84-CLMM : Tue Apr 29 06:13:13 UTC 2025), Entry for Francesco Paolo Vernacchio and Rosa Vernacchio, from 1917 to 1918.
- "United States, Census, 1920", FamilySearch (https://www.familysearch.org/ark:/61903/1:1:MJPD-KYN : Thu Jan 16 03:46:43 UTC 2025), Entry for Frank Vernacchia and Rose Vernacchia, 1920.
- "United States, Census, 1930", FamilySearch (https://www.familysearch.org/ark:/61903/1:1:X76D-NTR : Tue Jul 16 02:48:15 UTC 2024), Entry for Paul Vernacchia and Rose Vernacchia, 1930.
- "United States, Census, 1940", FamilySearch (https://www.familysearch.org/ark:/61903/1:1:KQL9-WYR : Thu Jul 11 06:07:18 UTC 2024), Entry for Frank Vernanhio and Rose Vernanhio, 1940.
- "United States, Census, 1950", FamilySearch (https://www.familysearch.org/ark:/61903/1:1:6XTR-JPDS : Tue Mar 19 02:08:33 UTC 2024), Entry for Frank Vernacchia and Rose Vernacchia, 1 April 1950.
- "New York, New York City Marriage Records, 1829-1938", FamilySearch (https://www.familysearch.org/ark:/61903/1:1:Q2CF-7VG3 : Fri Mar 08 20:27:02 UTC 2024), Entry for Frank Messina and Mary Vernacchia, 26 July 1933.
- "New York, New York City Marriage Records, 1829-1938", FamilySearch (https://www.familysearch.org/ark:/61903/1:1:Q2CF-3W93 : Sun Mar 10 12:06:47 UTC 2024), Entry for John Hernacchia and Antoinrtte Cappabianca, 24 June 1932.
- "New York, New York City Marriage Records, 1829-1938", FamilySearch (https://www.familysearch.org/ark:/61903/1:1:Q2CV-9MYW : Sun Mar 10 15:03:30 UTC 2024), Entry for Charles Vernacchia and Concetta Ferrande, 18 April 1926.
- "New York, New York City Marriage Records, 1829-1938", FamilySearch (https://www.familysearch.org/ark:/61903/1:1:Q2CJ-GN99 : Sun Mar 10 22:48:03 UTC 2024), Entry for Franck Solomene and Vincenza Vernacclio, 25 August 1929.
- "New York, New York City Marriage Records, 1829-1938", FamilySearch (https://www.familysearch.org/ark:/61903/1:1:Q2CJ-BDCB : Fri Mar 08 22:37:18 UTC 2024), Entry for Joseph Colette and Concetta Vernacchi, 29 September 1924.
- "United States, Social Security Numerical Identification Files (NUMIDENT), 1936-2007", FamilySearch (https://www.familysearch.org/ark:/61903/1:1:6K97-SJZB : Sat Apr 26 02:23:25 UTC 2025), Entry for Mary Messina and Frank P Vernacchio.
- "New York, U.S. District and Circuit Court Naturalization Records, 1824-1991", FamilySearch (https://www.familysearch.org/ark:/61903/1:1:6BZ2-LG2Y : Tue Apr 15 16:35:57 UTC 2025), Entry for Francesco Paolo Vernacchia, 6 Feb 1903.

- https://www.findagrave.com/memorial/136982424/john-vernacchia
- https://www.findagrave.com/memorial/136982368/angelo-vernacchia

145) Generoso Miressi

Generoso Miressi(145) was born on 9 September 1878, in Ariano, Italy, to Giuseppe Miressi(51a) and Rosa Giorgione(51). Generoso Miressi(145) died 2 December 1880 in Ariano, Italy.

Records that include Generoso Miressi(145):
- Ariano, Italy 1878 Birth Act #426
- Ariano, Italy 1880 Death Act #560

146) Mariangela Fodarella

Mariangela Fodarella(146) was born on 27 January 1879, in Ariano, Italy, to Lorenzo Fodarella(48) and Maria Fransesca Paola Dotolo(48a). Mariangela Fodarella(146) died on 9 May 1879 in Ariano, Italy.

Records that include Mariangela Fodarella(146):
- Ariano, Italy 1879 Birth Act #57
- Ariano, Italy 1879 Death Act #140

147) Maria Giuseppa Di Lillo

Maria Giuseppa Di Lillo(147) was born 18 March 1879, in Ariano, Italy, to Nicola Maria di Lillo(51a) and Angela Perrina(52). Maria Giuseppa Di Lillo(147) died on 1 November 1879 in Ariano, Italy.

Records that include Maria Giuseppa Di Lillo(147):
- Ariano, Italy 1879 Birth Act #183
- Ariano, Italy 1879 Death Act #433

148) Maria Annuziata Manganiello

Maria Annuziata Manganiello(148) was stillborn on 25 March 1879, in Ariano, Italy, to Vincenzo Manganiello(57a)and Anna Maria Fodarella(57).

Records that include Maria Annuziata Manganiello(148):
- Ariano, Italy 1879 Birth Act #186

149) Lucia Grasso

Lucia Grasso(149) was born on 20 June 1879, in Ariano, Italy, to Lorenzo Grasso(45a) and Anna Maria Perrina(45). Lucia Grasso(149) died on 24 August 1880 in Ariano, Italy.

Records that include Lucia Grasso(149):
- Ariano, Italy 1879 Birth Act #322
- Ariano, Italy 1880 Death Act #392

150) Maria Rosaria Scauzillo

Maria Rosaria Scauzillo(150) was born on 18 September 1879, in Ariano, Italy, to Lorenzo Scauzillo(55a) and Aurelia Fiorenza(55).

Maria Rosaria Scauzillo(150) married Agostino Mancino(150a) on 3 February 1903 in Ariano, Italy.

Agostino Mancino(150a) was born on 12 September 1879 in Ariano. Italy to Luigi Mancino(150aF) and Mariantonia DiGrottola(150aM).

Known children of Maria Rosaria Scauzillo(150) and Agostino Mancino(150a):

i) Luigi Mancino(381) born in 1903
ii) Antonio Mancino(393) born in 1907
iii) Amelia Mancino(420) born in 1910

Records that include Maria Rosaria Scauzillo(150) and/or Agostino Mancino(150a):

- Ariano, Italy 1879 Birth Act #482
- Ariano, Italy 1879 Birth Act #497
- Ariano, Italy 1903 Marriage Act #18
- Ariano, Italy 1903 Birth Act #606
- Ariano, Italy 1907 Birth Act #21
- Ariano, Italy 1910 Birth Act #613
- Ariano, Italy 1925 Marriage Act #11
- Ariano, Italy 1929 Marriage Act #IIA40
- Ariano, Italy 1936 Marriage Act #PIIA3
- Ariano, Italy 1983 Death Act #1

151) Mariangela Manganiello

Mariangela Manganiello(151) was born on 15 November 1879, in Ariano, Italy, to Giuseppe Manganiello(64a) and Maria Fransesca Fodarella(63). On 20 February 1915 Mariangela Manganiello(151) boarded the ship SS Duca Degli Abruzzi, in Naples, Italy. Mariangela Manganiello(151) arrived in New York City on 8 March 1918 with her daughter Rosa Grasso(403) to travel to Canton, OH to be with her husband Domenico Grasso(151a). Rosa Grasso(403) died on 26 February 1922 in Canton, OH. Mariangela Manganiello(151) was buried in Calvary Cemetery, Massillon, OH.

Mariangela Manganiello(151) married Domenico Grasso(151a) on 10 November 1906 in Ariano, Italy.

Domenico Grasso(151a) was born on 30 August 1879, in Ariano, Italy, to Michele Grasso(151aF) and Giustiniana Iodice(151aM). Domenico Grasso(151a) died on 14 February 1963 in Canton, Ohio. Domenico Grasso(151a)was buried in Calvary Cemetery, Massillon, OH.

Domenico Grasso(151a) also married Carmela Stark(151ab).

Known children of Mariangela Manganiello(151) and Domenico Grasso(151a):

i) Rosa Grasso(403) born in 1908

Records that include Mariangela Manganiello(151) and/or Domenico Grasso(151a):

- Ariano, Italy 1879 Birth Act #457
- Ariano, Italy 1879 Birth Act #595
- Ariano, Italy 1908 Birth Act #259
- "New York, Passenger Arrival Lists (Ellis Island), 1892-1925", FamilySearch (https://www.familysearch.org/ark:/61903/1:1:JJ4Q-6WY : Tue Apr 15 08:39:53 UTC 2025), Entry for Rosa Grasso and Michele Grasso, 08 Mar 1915.
- "United States World War I Draft Registration Cards, 1917-1918", database with images, FamilySearch (https://www.familysearch.org/ark:/61903/1:1:4MCY-DYN2 : 10 July 2024), Ciriaco Manganiello, 1917-1918.
- "Ohio, Deaths, 1908-1953", FamilySearch (https://www.familysearch.org/ark:/61903/1:1:X642-KVZ : Sat Jan 18 19:54:57 UTC 2025), Entry for Mary Grasso and Joseph Ameno, 26 Feb 1922.
- "United States, Census, 1930", FamilySearch (https://www.familysearch.org/ark:/61903/1:1:X4C2-P6D : Sun Jul 21 18:28:12 UTC 2024), Entry for Dominic Grasso and Carmel Grasso, 1930.
- "United States, Census, 1940", FamilySearch (https://www.familysearch.org/ark:/61903/1:1:KWP7-9XR : Tue Jul 09 06:36:35 UTC 2024), Entry for Domenic Grasso and Carmela Grasso, 1940.
- "United States, Census, 1950", FamilySearch (https://www.familysearch.org/ark:/61903/1:1:6XB6-7MSN : Tue Mar 18 04:18:46 UTC 2025), Entry for Dominic Grasso and Carmel Grasso, 7 April 1950.

- "Find a Grave Index", FamilySearch (https://www.familysearch.org/ark:/61903/1:1:QV2R-Z9MN : Thu Apr 03 13:20:14 UTC 2025), Entry for Mary Grasso.
- "United States, World War II Draft Registration Cards, 1942", FamilySearch (https://www.familysearch.org/ark:/61903/1:1:X5HK-7Z6 : Mon Apr 28 16:26:52 UTC 2025), Entry for Domenico Grasso, 1942.
- "United States, Social Security Numerical Identification Files (NUMIDENT), 1936-2007", database, FamilySearch (https://www.familysearch.org/ark:/61903/1:1:6K3K-X3TY : 10 February 2023), Domenico Grasso in entry for Rose Mancuso, .
- "United States, Social Security Death Index," , FamilySearch (https://familysearch.org/ark:/61903/1:1:J1HN-M2N : 9 January 2021), Domenico Grasso, Feb 1963; citing U.S. Social Security Administration, Death Master File, database (Alexandria, Virginia: National Technical Information Service, ongoing).
- "Ohio, Death Index, 1908-1932, 1938-1944, and 1958-2007", FamilySearch (https://www.familysearch.org/ark:/61903/1:1:VKB6-J4J : Tue Feb 25 09:15:06 UTC 2025), Entry for Dominic Grasso and , 14 Feb 1963.
- "Find a Grave Index", FamilySearch (https://www.familysearch.org/ark:/61903/1:1:QV2R-Z9MF : Tue Apr 01 14:59:30 UTC 2025), Entry for Dominick Grasso.

152) Mariantonia Fodarella

Mariantonia Fodarella(152) was born on 22 April 1880, in Ariano, Italy, to Lorenzo Fodarella(48) and Maria Fransesca Paola Dotolo(48a). Mariantonia Fodarella(152) died on 14 January 1957 in Ariano, Italy.

Mariantonia Fodarella(152) married Ciriaco Panza(152a) on 9 February 1901 in Ariano, Italy.

Ciriaco Panza(152a) was born on 20 April 1875, in Ariano, Italy, to Francesco Panza(152aF) and Rosa Pratola(152aM).

Known children of Mariantonia Fodarella(152) and Ciriaco Panza(152a):

   i) Raffaele Panza(376) born in 1902
   ii) Maria Rosa Panza(382) born in 1904
   iii) Lorenzo Panza(410) born about 1909
   iv) Giuseppe Panza(445) born in 1913

Records that include Mariantonia Fodarella(152) and/or Ciriaco Panza(152a):
- Ariano, Italy 1875 Birth Act #188
- Ariano, Italy 1880 Birth Act #236
- Ariano, Italy 1901 Marriage Act #27
- Ariano, Italy 1902 Birth Act #336
- Ariano, Italy 1904 Birth Act #199
- Ariano, Italy 1913 Birth Act #533
- Ariano, Italy 1925 Marriage Act #125
- Ariano, Italy 1926 Marriage Act #90
- Ariano, Italy 1939 Marriage Act #2
- Ariano, Italy 1939 Marriage Act #12

153) Mariangela Tiso

Mariangela Tiso(153) was born 3 July 1880, in Ariano, Italy, to Liberatore Tiso(42a) and Maria Concordia Fodarella(42). Mariangela Tiso(153) died on 10 August 1881 in Ariano, Italy.

Records that include Mariangela Tiso(153):
- Ariano, Italy 1880 Birth Act #340
- Ariano, Italy 1881 Death Act #320

154) Maria Perrina

Maria Perrina(154) was born on 15 June 1880, in San Nicola Baronia, Italy, to Raffaele Perrina(58) and Maria Lucia Gesa(58a). Maria Perrina(154) died 29 June 1880 in San Nicola Baronia, Italy.

Records that include Maria Perrina(154):
- San Nicola Baronia, Italy 1880 Birth Act #20
- San Nicola Baronia, Italy 1880 Death Act #19

155) Mariantonia Di Lillo

Mariantonia Di Lillo(155) was born on 24 October 1880, in Ariano, Italy, to Nicola Maria di Lillo(51a) and Angela Perrina(52). Mariantonia Di Lillo(155) died on 18 July 1882 in Ariano, Italy.

Records that include Mariantonia Di Lillo(155):
- Ariano, Italy 1880 Birth Act #489
- Ariano, Italy 1882 Death Act #294

156) Maria Ninfadoro

Maria Ninfadoro(156) was born on 15 December 1880, in Ariano, Italy, to Gabriele Ninfadoro(67a) and Mariangela Perrina(67). Maria Ninfadoro(156) died on 2 October 1885 in Ariano, Italy.

Records that include Maria Ninfadoro(156):
- Ariano, Italy 1880 Birth Act #555
- Ariano, Italy 1885 Death Act #304

157) Concetta Perrina

Concetta Perrina(157) was born about 1881, in Castel Baronia, Italy, to Raffaele Perrina(58) and Maria Lucia Gesa(58a). Concetta Perrina(157) died on 13 December 1889 in Castel Baronia, Italy.

Records including Concetta Perrina(157):
- Castel Baronia, Italy 1889 Death Act #2

NOTE: Castel Baronia, Italy Birth records for 1881 & 1882 are not available. Birth date calculated from death record.

158) Raimonda Grasso

Raimonda Grasso(158) was born on 5 March 1881, in Ariano, Italy, to Crescenzo Grasso(76a) and Anna Perrina(76). Raimonda Grasso(158) died on 19 September 1881 in Ariano, Italy.

Records that include Raimonda Grasso(158):
- Ariano, Italy 1881 Birth Act #123
- Ariano, Italy 1881 Death Act #383

159) Ciriaco Manganiello

Ciriaco Manganiello(159) was born on 14 September 1881, in Ariano, Italy, to Vincenzo Manganiello(57a) and Anna Maria Fodarella(57).

Ciriaco Manganiello(159) married Maria Concetta Mauro(159a) on 3 February 1927 in Ariano, Italy.

Maria Concetta Mauro(159a) was born on 28 February 1899, in Ariano, Italy, to Francesco Mauro(159aF) and Anna Maria Campagnola(159aM).

Records that include Ciriaco Manganiello(159) and/or Maria Concetta Mauro(159a):
- Ariano, Italy 1881 Birth Act #430
- Ariano, Italy 1899 Birth Act #156
- Ariano, Italy 1927 Marriage Act #15

160) Generoso Miressi

Generoso Miressi(160) was born on 31 October 1881, in Ariano, Italy, to Giuseppe Miressi(51a) and Rosa Giorgione(51). Generoso Miressi(160) sailed to Boston, MA on 7 May 1907. Generoso Miressi(160) died on 24 October 1954 in New Rochelle, NY.

Generoso Miressi(160) married Maria Luigia Iannarone(160a) on 31 August 1905 in Ariano, Italy.

Maria Luigia Iannarone(160a) was born on 1 February 1882, in Ariano, Italy, to Giocchino Iannarone(160aF) and Maria Teresa di Iesu(160aM).

Known children of Generoso Miressi(160) and Maria Luigia Iannarone(160a):

i) Maria Rosa Maria Domenica Maria Libera Miressi(390) born in 1906
ii) Teresa Miressi(412) born about 1910
iii) Joseph Miressi(434) born in 1912
iv) Giacchino / John (Jack) Miressi(449) born in 1914
v) Carmela Miressi(464) born about 1916
vi) Angelina Miressi(486) born about 1919

Records that include Generoso Miressi(160) and/or Maria Luigia Iannarone(160a):

- Ariano, Italy 1881 Birth Act #526
- Ariano, Italy 1882 Birth Act #86
- Ariano, Italy 1905 Marriage Act #105
- Ariano, Italy 1906 Birth Act #458
- "New York, Passenger Arrival Lists (Ellis Island), 1892-1925", FamilySearch (https://www.familysearch.org/ark:/61903/1:1:JF9H-HN5 : Tue Apr 15 05:25:14 UTC 2025), Entry for M. Luisa Ganna..One and Teresa, 06 Dec 1909.
- "New York, Passenger Arrival Lists (Ellis Island), 1892-1925", FamilySearch (https://www.familysearch.org/ark:/61903/1:1:JF9H-HNR : Tue Apr 15 05:20:24 UTC 2025), Entry for Rosa Mireasio and Teresa, 06 Dec 1909.
- "United States, Census, 1910", FamilySearch (https://www.familysearch.org/ark:/61903/1:1:M54W-J3S : Thu Jul 18 05:40:42 UTC 2024), Entry for Generoso Miresse and Maria L Miresse, 1910.
- "New York, State Census, 1915", database, FamilySearch (https://www.familysearch.org/ark:/61903/1:1:K95C-G7W : 1 June 2022), Generoso Miressi, 1915.
- "United States, World War I Draft Registration Cards, 1917-1918", FamilySearch (https://www.familysearch.org/ark:/61903/1:1:W72H-F1N2 : Tue Apr 29 04:02:46 UTC 2025), Entry for Generoso or Samuel J Miresse or Tinto and Marie Miresse, from 1917 to 1918.
- "United States, Census, 1930", FamilySearch (https://www.familysearch.org/ark:/61903/1:1:X4G6-NM9 : Tue Jul 09 21:44:43 UTC 2024), Entry for Generoso Miressi and Mary L Miressi, 1930.
- "United States, Census, 1940", FamilySearch (https://www.familysearch.org/ark:/61903/1:1:KQQ9-ZSV : Mon Jul 15 03:57:09 UTC 2024), Entry for Generoso Miresi and Marie Miresi, 1940.
- "United States, World War II Draft Registration Cards, 1942", FamilySearch (https://www.familysearch.org/ark:/61903/1:1:QKV7-6V8K : Mon Apr 28 21:24:00 UTC 2025), Entry for Generoso Maresi and Maria Maresi, 26 Apr 1942.
- "North Carolina, Deaths, 1931-1994", FamilySearch (https://www.familysearch.org/ark:/61903/1:1:FGFY-69D : Mon Oct 07 22:07:05 UTC 2024), Entry for Joseph John Miressi and Generosa Miressi, 1994.
- "North Carolina, Department of Archives and History, Index to Vital Records, 1800-2000", FamilySearch (https://www.familysearch.org/ark:/61903/1:1:QPTH-SPVM : Fri Feb 14 06:56:08 UTC 2025), Entry for Joseph John Miressi and Generosa Miressi, 5 Jul 1994.

- "United States, Social Security Numerical Identification Files (NUMIDENT), 1936-2007", FamilySearch (https://www.familysearch.org/ark:/61903/1:1:6KM5-XBBP : Sat Apr 26 00:04:24 UTC 2025), Entry for Angelina Miressi and Generoso Miressi.
- "United States, Social Security Numerical Identification Files (NUMIDENT), 1936-2007", FamilySearch (https://www.familysearch.org/ark:/61903/1:1:6K9S-BHPV : Sat Apr 26 02:13:50 UTC 2025), Entry for Jack J Miressi and Generoso Miressi.
- "United States, Social Security Numerical Identification Files (NUMIDENT), 1936-2007", FamilySearch (https://www.familysearch.org/ark:/61903/1:1:6K9C-RG4Q : Sat Apr 26 02:34:23 UTC 2025), Entry for Theresa Marie Miressi and Gerald Miressi.
- "United States, Social Security Numerical Identification Files (NUMIDENT), 1936-2007", FamilySearch (https://www.familysearch.org/ark:/61903/1:1:6K93-TDYF : Fri Apr 25 19:43:03 UTC 2025), Entry for Joseph J Miressi and Genarose Miressi.
- "North Carolina, Deaths and Burials, 1898-1994", database, FamilySearch (https://familysearch.org/ark:/61903/1:1:HH9K-55MM : 21 January 2020), Generosa Miressi in entry for Joseph John Miressi, .
- "United States, Social Security Numerical Identification Files (NUMIDENT), 1936-2007", FamilySearch (https://www.familysearch.org/ark:/61903/1:1:6KMT-2FMK : Sat Apr 26 15:46:52 UTC 2025), Entry for Generoso Miressi.

161) Giuseppantonio Fodarella

Giuseppantonio Fodarella(161) was born on 20 November 1881, in Ariano, Italy, to Lorenzo Fodarella(48) and Maria Fransesca Paola Dotolo(48a). On 6 March 1906, Giuseppantonio Fodarella(161) sailed from Naples, Italy on the SS Vincenzio Florio, arriving in New York, NY on 22 March 1906. Giuseppantonio Fodarella(161) died 5 February 1907 in New York, NY. Giuseppantonio Fodarella(161) was buried in St. Raymond's Cemetery.

Records that include Giuseppantonio Fodarella:
- Ariano, Italy 1881 Birth Act #571
- "New York Book Indexes to Passenger Lists, 1906-1942", , FamilySearch (https://www.familysearch.org/ark:/61903/1:1:Q23J-RV8K : Thu Mar 07 10:38:28 UTC 2024), Entry for G Antonio Fodarella, 1906.
- "New York Passenger Arrival Lists (Ellis Island), 1892-1924", , FamilySearch (https://www.familysearch.org/ark:/61903/1:1:JFFP-SM6 : Mon Mar 11 01:32:15 UTC 2024), Entry for G. Antonio Fodarella and Pasquale Parra, 1906.
- "New York, New York City Municipal Deaths, 1795-1949", database, FamilySearch (https://www.familysearch.org/ark:/61903/1:1:2WDK-LLK : 3 June 2020), Guiseppa Fatarella, 1907.
- Ariano, Italy 1907 Death Act ##P.II.33

162) Giovanni Battista Grasso

Giovanni Battista Grasso(162) was born on 17 December 1881, in Ariano, Italy, to Lorenzo Grasso(45a) and Anna Maria Perrina(45). Giovanni Battista Grasso(162) died on 9 February 1882 in Ariano, Italy.

Records that include Giovanni Battista Grasso(162):
- Ariano, Italy 1881 Birth Act #608
- Ariano, Italy 1882 Death Act #61

163) Mariantonia Manganiello

Mariantonia Manganiello(163) was born on 22 February 1882, in Ariano, Italy, to Giuseppe Manganiello(64a) and Maria Fransesca Fodarella(63). Mariantonia Manganiello(163) died on 28 February 1882 in Ariano, Italy.

Records that include Mariantonia Manganiello(163):
- Ariano, Italy 1882 Birth Act #130
- Ariano, Italy 1882 Death Act #96

164) Gaetano Scauzillo

Gaetano Scauzillo(164) was born on 16 March 1882, in Ariano, Italy, to Lorenzo Scauzillo(55a) and Aurelia Fiorenza(55). Gaetano Scauzillo(164) died in 1954 in Bronx, NY.

Gaetano Scauzillo(164) married Giovanna Grasso(196) (Gaetano Scauzillo(164)'s third cousin) on 7 September 1905 in Bronx, NY.

Giovanna Grasso(196) was born on 1 April 1887, in Ariano, Italy, to Crescenzo Grasso(76a) and Anna Perrina(76). Giovanna Grasso(196) died in 1962 in Bronx, NY.

Known children of Gaetano Scauzillo(164) and Giovanna Grasso(196):

- i) Lorenzo Scauzillo(389) born in 1906
- ii) Carmela Scanzillo(394) born in 1907
- iii) Aurelia Scanzillo(407) born in 1908
- iv) Virginia Scanzillo(431) born in 1912
- v) Lorenzo Scanzillo(476) born in 1916
- vi) Anthony Scanzillo(520) born in 1922

Records that include Gaetano Scauzillo(164) and/or Giovanna Grasso(196):
- Ariano, Italy 1882 Birth Act #170
- Ariano, Italy 1887 Birth Act #257
- "New York, New York City Marriage Records, 1829-1938", , FamilySearch (https://www.familysearch.org/ark:/61903/1:1:244Q-4WZ : Sat Mar 09 04:31:53 UTC 2024), Entry for Gaetano Scanzillo and Giovannina Grassi, 7 Sep 1905.
- "New York, New York City Births, 1846-1909," , FamilySearch (https://familysearch.org/ark:/61903/1:1:2W81-1FD : 11 February 2018), Gaetano Scanzillo in entry for Lorenzo Scanzillo, 14 Apr 1906; citing Manhattan, New York, New York, United States, reference cn 2031 New York Municipal Archives, New York; FHL microfilm 2,023,140.
- "New York, New York City Municipal Deaths, 1795-1949", database, FamilySearch (https://www.familysearch.org/ark:/61903/1:1:2719-474 : 13 May 2022), Gastano Scauzillo in entry for Lorenzo Scauzillo, 1906.
- "New York, New York City Births, 1846-1909," , FamilySearch (https://familysearch.org/ark:/61903/1:1:2W8H-5M2 : 11 February 2018), Gaetano Scanzilla in entry for Anleria Scanzilla, 28 Oct 1908; citing Manhattan, New York, New York, United States, reference 8022 New York Municipal Archives, New York; FHL microfilm 2,023,262.
- "New York, County Naturalization Records, 1791-1980", , FamilySearch (https://www.familysearch.org/ark:/61903/1:1:QPZB-C541 : Fri Mar 08 19:23:41 UTC 2024), Entry for Gaetano Scanzillo and Giovannino Grasso Scanzillo, 1913.
- "United States World War I Draft Registration Cards, 1917-1918", database with images, FamilySearch (https://www.familysearch.org/ark:/61903/1:1:W7VL-FR3Z : 10 July 2024), Gaetano Scanzillo, 1917-1918.
- "United States Census, 1920", , FamilySearch (https://www.familysearch.org/ark:/61903/1:1:MJG5-1XL : Sat Apr 13 04:57:08 UTC 2024), Entry for Gaetano Scanzilla and Jannie Scanzilla, 1920.
- "United States Census, 1930", , FamilySearch (https://www.familysearch.org/ark:/61903/1:1:X7D4-SB4 : Mon Jul 08 16:00:27 UTC 2024), Entry for Gaetano Scanzillo and Guanina Scanzillo, 1930.
- "United States Census, 1940", , FamilySearch (https://www.familysearch.org/ark:/61903/1:1:KQBN-826 : Sat Mar 09 01:41:31 UTC 2024), Entry for Gaetano Scanzillo and Jennie Scanzillo, 1940.

- "New York, New York City, World War II Draft Registration Cards, 1940-1947", , FamilySearch (https://www.familysearch.org/ark:/61903/1:1:WQYH-HVMM : Sun Mar 10 10:38:46 UTC 2024), Entry for Anthony Salvatore Scanzillo and Montgomery Ward, 30 Jun 1942.
- "United States Census, 1950", , FamilySearch (https://www.familysearch.org/ark:/61903/1:1:6XYM-9X8P : Tue Mar 19 16:01:57 UTC 2024), Entry for Virginia Scanzillo and Gaetano Scanzillo, 10 April 1950.
- "Find a Grave Index," database, FamilySearch (https://www.familysearch.org/ark:/61903/1:1:Q2DK-RCDG : 11 January 2023), Gaetano Scanzillo, ; Burial, Bronx, Bronx, New York, United States of America, Old Saint Raymond's Cemetery; citing record ID 172164315, Find a Grave, http://www.findagrave.com.
- "Find a Grave Index," database, FamilySearch (https://www.familysearch.org/ark:/61903/1:1:Q2DK-RC8P : 11 January 2023), Giovannina Scanzillo, ; Burial, Bronx, Bronx, New York, United States of America, Old Saint Raymond's Cemetery; citing record ID 172164402, Find a Grave, http://www.findagrave.com.
- "United States, Social Security Numerical Identification Files (NUMIDENT), 1936-2007", database, FamilySearch (https://www.familysearch.org/ark:/61903/1:1:6K9W-WS6K : 10 February 2023), Thomas Scanzilla in entry for Lorenzo Joseph Scanzillo, .
- "United States, Social Security Numerical Identification Files (NUMIDENT), 1936-2007", database, FamilySearch (https://www.familysearch.org/ark:/61903/1:1:6K9W-498X : 10 February 2023), Gaetano Scanzillo in entry for Anthony Scanzillo, .

165) Oto Ninfadoro

Oto Ninfadoro(165) was born on 24 November 1882, in Ariano, Italy, to Gabriele Ninfadoro(67a) and Mariangela Perrina(67). Oto Ninfadoro(165) Sailed from Naples, Italy on 27 March 1901. Oto Ninfadoro(165) arrived in New York on 13 April 1901. Oto Ninfadoro(165) was naturalized as a citizen of the United States on 28 February 1916. Oto Ninfadoro(165) died 27 October 1954 in Schenectady, NY.

Oto Ninfadoro(165) married Antonia Costanzo(165a) on 4 July 1907 in Ariano, Italy.

Antonia Costanzo(165a) was born on 17 January 1882, in Ariano, Italy, to Crescenzo Costanzo(165aF) and Maria Rosa Capozzi(165aM).

Known children of Oto Ninfadoro(165) and Antonia Costanzo(165a):

    i) Gabriel Ninfadoro(402) born in 1908
    ii) Anthony Ninfadoro(411) born in 1909
    iii) Eleonora Ninfadoro(439) born in 1913
    iv) Edward Ninfadoro(471) born in 1916

Records that include Oto Ninfadoro(165) and Antonia Costanzo(165a):
- Ariano, Italy 1882 Birth Act #40
- Ariano, Italy 1882 Birth Act #162
- Ariano, Italy 1904 Marriage Act #67
- "New York, County Naturalization Records, 1791-1980," database with images, FamilySearch (https://www.familysearch.org/ark:/61903/1:1:QRCN-GXPZ : 8 April 2021), Oto Ninfavoro or Ninfadoro, 1913; citing Naturalization, New York, United States, citing multiple County Clerk offices of New York; FHL microfilm 005411575.
- "New York, County Naturalization Records, 1791-1980," database with images, FamilySearch (https://www.familysearch.org/ark:/61903/1:1:QRCN-GXT2 : 8 April 2021), Oto Ninfadoro, 1915; citing Naturalization, New York, United States, citing multiple County Clerk offices of New York; FHL microfilm 005411575.

- "New York, County Naturalization Records, 1791-1980," database with images, FamilySearch (https://www.familysearch.org/ark:/61903/1:1:QRCN-GFW2 : 8 April 2021), Oto Ninfadoro, 1916; citing Naturalization, New York, United States, citing multiple County Clerk offices of New York; FHL microfilm 005411575.
- "United States World War I Draft Registration Cards, 1917-1918", database with images, FamilySearch (https://www.familysearch.org/ark:/61903/1:1:KXB8-CX2 : 26 December 2021), Otto Ninfadoro, 1917-1918.
- "United States Census, 1920", , FamilySearch (https://www.familysearch.org/ark:/61903/1:1:MVSC-2F2 : Sat Mar 09 12:04:52 UTC 2024), Entry for Otto Infator and Antonette Infator, 1920.
- "United States Census, 1930", , FamilySearch (https://www.familysearch.org/ark:/61903/1:1:X4TB-9PG : Wed Mar 06 06:37:33 UTC 2024), Entry for Otto Ninafodora and Antoinette Ninafodora, 1930.
- "United States Census, 1940", database with images, FamilySearch (ark:/61903/1:1:KQY5-TLS : Fri Jun 09 01:04:33 UTC 2023), Entry for Otto Ninfadoro and Antoinette Ninfadoro, 1940.
- "United States World War II Draft Registration Cards, 1942," database with images, FamilySearch (https://familysearch.org/ark:/61903/1:1:QKVQ-VJPN : 2 May 2023), Otto Ninfadoro, 25 Apr 1942; citing NARA microfilm publication M1936, M1937, M1939, M1951, M1962, M1964, M1986, M2090, and M2097 (Washington D.C.: National Archives and Records Administration, n.d.).
- "United States 1950 Census", database, FamilySearch (ark:/61903/1:1:6XYM-TS35 : Mon Jan 30 03:21:29 UTC 2023), Entry for Otto Ninfadore and Anthony Ninfadore, 15 April 1950.
- "New York, State Death Index, 1880-1956", database, FamilySearch (https://www.familysearch.org/ark:/61903/1:1:QGP3-28JV : 23 March 2023), Otto Ninfadora, 1954.
- "United States, Social Security Numerical Identification Files (NUMIDENT), 1936-2007", database, FamilySearch (https://www.familysearch.org/ark:/61903/1:1:6KMT-DGXS : 10 February 2023), Otto Ninfadoro, .

166) Francesco (Frank) Paul Anastasio

Francesco (Frank) Paul Anastasio(166) was born on 29 November 1882, in Ariano, Italy, to Pasquale Antonio Anastasio(72a) and Anna Maria D'Ausilio(72). Francesco (Frank) Paul Anastasio(166) boarded the SS Werra in Naples, Italy, arriving in New York City on 7 October 1895. Francesco (Frank) Paul Anastasio(166) died on 9 April 1958 in Racine, WI.

Francesco (Frank) Paul Anastasio(166) married Hilda (Gilda) Marcotti(166a) on 18 May 1908, in St. Louis, MO.

Hilda (Gilda) Marcotti(166a) was born about 1887, in Italy. Hilda (Gilda) Marcotti(166a) died on 2 March 1962 in Wisconsin.

NOTE: I have found an unverified reference to Hilda (Gilda) Marcotti(166a) being the daughter of Giovanni Battistia Marcati and Giuseppina Bendelli possibly from Santa Maria Capua Vetere, Italy.

Known children of Francesco (Frank) Paul Anastasio(166) and Hilda (Gilda) Marcotti(166a):

   i) Pasquale (Pat) Anastasio(409) born in 1909
   ii) Anna Mary Anastasio(414) born in 1910
   iii) John B Anastasio(429) born in 1911
   iv) Edward Paul Anastasio(451) born in 1914
   v) Rudolph William Anastasio(477) born in 1916
   vi) Clara Evelyn Anastasio(504) born in 1920
   vii) Living person and/or spouse.

Records that include Francesco (Frank) Paul Anastasio(166) and/or Hilda (Gilda) Marcotti(166a):

- Ariano, Italy 1882 Birth Act #633
- "New York, Passenger Arrival Lists (Ellis Island), 1892-1925", FamilySearch (https://www.familysearch.org/ark:/61903/1:1:JX36-9MR : Thu May 15 01:48:46 UTC 2025), Entry for Francesco Anastasio, 7 October 1895.
- "United States, Census, 1900", FamilySearch (https://www.familysearch.org/ark:/61903/1:1:M97Z-VHB : Tue Jan 14 04:44:47 UTC 2025), Entry for Anastasia Pasquale and Mary Pasquale, 1900.
- "Missouri, County Marriage, Naturalization, and Court Records, 1800-1991", FamilySearch (https://www.familysearch.org/ark:/61903/1:1:668N-M5DY : Sat Mar 09 04:02:54 UTC 2024), Entry for Frank P Anastasio and , 2 May 1908.
- "Missouri, County Marriage, Naturalization, and Court Records, 1800-1991", FamilySearch (https://www.familysearch.org/ark:/61903/1:1:6698-PT75 : Sat Mar 09 18:40:47 UTC 2024), Entry for Frank P Anastasis and Gilda Marcati, 18 May 1908.
- "United States, Census, 1910", FamilySearch (https://www.familysearch.org/ark:/61903/1:1:MK2G-BVS : Sun Mar 10 04:02:48 UTC 2024), Entry for Frank Anastasio and Gilda Anastasio, 1910.
- "United States, World War I Draft Registration Cards, 1917-1918", FamilySearch (https://www.familysearch.org/ark:/61903/1:1:7DD2-JW6Z : Tue Apr 29 08:52:37 UTC 2025), Entry for Frank Paul Anastasio and Hilda Anastasio, from 1917 to 1918.
- "United States, World War I Draft Registration Cards, 1917-1918", FamilySearch (https://www.familysearch.org/ark:/61903/1:1:K878-4NS : Mon Apr 28 23:29:18 UTC 2025), Entry for Frank Paul Anastasio, from 1917 to 1918.
- "United States, Census, 1920", FamilySearch (https://www.familysearch.org/ark:/61903/1:1:MFL9-JJ6 : Fri Jan 17 12:10:17 UTC 2025), Entry for Frank P Anastasio and Gilda Anastasio, 1920.
- "United States, Census, 1930", FamilySearch (https://www.familysearch.org/ark:/61903/1:1:X9SJ-2LK : Mon Jul 15 18:03:34 UTC 2024), Entry for Frank Anastasio and Hilda Anastasio, 1930.
- "United States, Census, 1940", FamilySearch (https://www.familysearch.org/ark:/61903/1:1:K7J6-HTQ : Sat Mar 09 04:26:52 UTC 2024), Entry for Frank P Anastascio and Jilda Anastascio, 1940.
- "United States, World War II Draft Registration Cards, 1942", FamilySearch (https://www.familysearch.org/ark:/61903/1:1:X59X-PXQ : Mon Apr 28 17:56:41 UTC 2025), Entry for Frank Paul Anastasio, 1942.
- "United States, Census, 1950", FamilySearch (https://www.familysearch.org/ark:/61903/1:1:6FMB-ZH8X : Mon Mar 17 21:01:41 UTC 2025), Entry for Frank P Anastasio and Jilda Anastasio, April 3, 1950.
- "United States, Social Security Numerical Identification Files (NUMIDENT), 1936-2007", FamilySearch (https://www.familysearch.org/ark:/61903/1:1:6KQF-RS1X : Sat Apr 26 05:12:43 UTC 2025), Entry for Anna M Kanetzke and Anna Mary Anastasio.
- "United States, Social Security Numerical Identification Files (NUMIDENT), 1936-2007", FamilySearch (https://www.familysearch.org/ark:/61903/1:1:6KQR-3NZB : Sat Apr 26 17:19:16 UTC 2025), Entry for Rudolf W Anastasio and Frank P Anastasio.
- "United States, Social Security Numerical Identification Files (NUMIDENT), 1936-2007", FamilySearch (https://www.familysearch.org/ark:/61903/1:1:6KQJ-LPF8 : Sat Apr 26 05:28:13 UTC 2025), Entry for Frank Paul Anastasio.
- https://journaltimes.newspapers.com/article/the-journal-times-obituary-for-frank-p/83018176/

167) Maria Giuseppa Grasso

Maria Giuseppa Grasso(167) was born on 30 Nov 1882, in Ariano, Italy, to Crescenzo Grasso(76a) and Anna Perrina(76). Maria Giuseppa Grasso(167) died in May 1975 in Mount Vernon, NY.

Maria Giuseppa Grasso(167) married Luigi Leggiadro(167a) on 7 October 1906 in Bronx, NY.

Luigi Leggiadro(167a) was a foundling born in Ariano, Italy on 8 March 1881. Luigi Leggiadro(167a) sailed on 27 Jan 1901 from Naples, Italy arriving in New York, NY on 20 February 1901 on the ship Perugia. Luigi Leggiadro(167a) became a Citizen of The United States on 28 July 1913 in New York. Luigi Leggiadro(167a) died in January 1968 in Mount Vernon, NY.

Known children of Maria Giuseppa Grasso(167) and Luigi Leggiadro(167a):

    i) Giovannina Leggiadro(396) born in 1907.

Records that include Maria Giuseppa Grasso(167) and/or Luigi Leggiadro(167a):
- Ariano, Italy 1881 Birth Act #PII.13
- Ariano, Italy 1882 Birth Act #647
- "New York, Passenger Arrival Lists (Ellis Island), 1892-1925", FamilySearch (https://www.familysearch.org/ark:/61903/1:1:JFPS-13D : Thu May 15 01:48:00 UTC 2025), Entry for Luigi Leggiadro and Pasquale Tauga, 16 February 1903.
- "New York, County Naturalization Records, 1791-1980", FamilySearch (https://www.familysearch.org/ark:/61903/1:1:QP1D-QYF5 : Sat Apr 12 00:28:31 UTC 2025), Entry for Luigi Leggiadro and Maria Grasso, 1913.
- "United States, World War I Draft Registration Cards, 1917-1918", FamilySearch (https://www.familysearch.org/ark:/61903/1:1:7NZ8-34MM : Tue Apr 29 06:09:37 UTC 2025), Entry for Luigi Leggiadri and Maria Leggiadri, from 1917 to 1918.
- "New York, New York City Marriage Records, 1829-1938", FamilySearch (https://www.familysearch.org/ark:/61903/1:1:Q2CJ-JZXW : Sun Mar 10 07:38:21 UTC 2024), Entry for Anthony Melito and Miss Jennie Leggiadro, 19 March 1927.
- "United States, World War II Draft Registration Cards, 1942", FamilySearch (https://www.familysearch.org/ark:/61903/1:1:F3J4-KPY : Tue Apr 29 05:05:04 UTC 2025), Entry for Luigi Leggiadro, 1942.
- "United States, Census, 1950", FamilySearch (https://www.familysearch.org/ark:/61903/1:1:6XYS-LG4M : Wed Mar 20 18:54:32 UTC 2024), Entry for Maria Leggiadro and Luigi Leggiadro, 1 April 1950.
- "United States, Social Security Death Index," database, FamilySearch (https://familysearch.org/ark:/61903/1:1:VSJS-VYC : 7 January 2021), Luigi Leggiadro, Jan 1968; citing U.S. Social Security Administration, Death Master File, database (Alexandria, Virginia: National Technical Information Service, ongoing).
- "United States, Social Security Death Index," database, FamilySearch (https://familysearch.org/ark:/61903/1:1:JB5F-LJZ : 7 January 2021), Maria Leggiadro, May 1975; citing U.S. Social Security Administration, Death Master File, database (Alexandria, Virginia: National Technical Information Service, ongoing).

168) Maria Carmela Manganiello

Maria Carmela Manganiello(168) was born on 18 February 1883, in Ariano, Italy, to
Vincenzo Manganiello(57a) and Anna Maria Fodarella(57).

Maria Carmela Manganiello(168) married Giovanni Ruggiero(168a) on 8 April 1920 in Ariano, Italy.

Giovanni Ruggiero(168a) was born on 22 January 1896, in Ariano, Italy, to Gabriele Ruggiero(168aF) and Carmina Maraio(168aM).

Records that include Maria Carmela Manganiello(168) and/or Giovanni Ruggiero(168a):
- Ariano, Italy 1883 Birth Act #134
- Ariano, Italy 1896 Birth Act #60
- Ariano, Italy 1920 Marriage Act #86

169) Oto (Ottone) Tiso

Oto (Ottone) Tiso(169), also known as Ottone Tiso, was born on 18 April 1883, in Ariano, Italy, to Liberatore Tiso(42a) and Maria Concordia Fodarella(42). Oto (Ottone) Tiso(169) sailed on, the SS Palatia, from Naples, Italy on 13 May 1902, arriving in New York City on 28 May 1902. Oto (Ottone) Tiso(169) died in 1934 in New Jersey.

Oto (Ottone) Tiso(169) married Mary Senese(169a).

Mary Senese(169a) was born about June 1893 in Italy. Mary Senese(169a) died in 1968 in New Jersey.

Mary Senese(169a) also married Willam Sidoli(161ab).

Known children of Oto (Ottone) Tiso(169) and Mary Senese(169a):

- i) Dora Tiso(423) born in 1911
- ii) Anna M. Tiso(443) born in 1913
- iii) Josephine Tiso(470) born in 1916
- iv) Angelina M. Tiso(482) born in 1917
- v) Alberto Tiso(495) born in 1919
- vi) Eleanor Marie Tiso(515) born in 1921
- vii) Robert Otto Tiso(554) born in 1926
- viii) Armand O. Tiso(566) born in 1929

Records that include Oto (Ottone) Tiso(169) and/or Mary Senese(169a):
- Ariano, Italy 1883 Birth Act #257
- "New York Passenger Arrival Lists (Ellis Island), 1892-1924", database with images, FamilySearch (https://familysearch.org/ark:/61903/1:1:JFKG-RTG : 2 March 2021), Ottone Tiso, 1902.
- "New Jersey State Census, 1915", database with images, FamilySearch (ark:/61903/1:1:QV9Q-SFNP : Wed Apr 05 19:55:00 UTC 2023), Entry for Ottone Tiso and Mary Tiso, 1915.
- "United States World War I Draft Registration Cards, 1917-1918", database with images, FamilySearch (https://www.familysearch.org/ark:/61903/1:1:KZJR-JQ6 : 31 December 2021), Ottone Tiso, 1917-1918.
- "United States Census, 1920", database with images, FamilySearch (https://www.familysearch.org/ark:/61903/1:1:M451-X6W : 2 February 2021), Ottone Tiso, 1920.
- "United States, Census, 1930", FamilySearch (https://www.familysearch.org/ark:/61903/1:1:X4DG-XPV : Fri Mar 08 18:34:06 UTC 2024), Entry for Ottone Liso and Mary H Liso, 1930.
- "United States, Census, 1940", FamilySearch (https://www.familysearch.org/ark:/61903/1:1:K4BX-LGY : Sun Mar 10 17:21:28 UTC 2024), Entry for William Sidoli and Mary Sidoli, 1940.
- "United States, Social Security Numerical Identification Files (NUMIDENT), 1936-2007", database, FamilySearch (https://www.familysearch.org/ark:/61903/1:1:6K9V-68JG : 10 February 2023), Otto Tiso in entry for Robert Tiso, .
- "United States, Social Security Numerical Identification Files (NUMIDENT), 1936-2007", database, FamilySearch (https://www.familysearch.org/ark:/61903/1:1:6K9Z-TQ1L : 10 February 2023), Otto Tiso in entry for Eleanor Marie Tiso, .
- "United States, Social Security Numerical Identification Files (NUMIDENT), 1936-2007", database, FamilySearch (https://www.familysearch.org/ark:/61903/1:1:6K96-C5GT : 10 February 2023), Ottone Tiso in entry for Armand Tiso, .

- "United States, Social Security Numerical Identification Files (NUMIDENT), 1936-2007", database, FamilySearch (https://www.familysearch.org/ark:/61903/1:1:6K9X-T398 : 10 February 2023), Ottone Tiso in entry for Josephine Albanese, .
- "Find a Grave Index", FamilySearch (https://www.familysearch.org/ark:/61903/1:1:QVLZ-3YXR : Fri Apr 04 06:44:26 UTC 2025), Entry for Otto Tiso.
- "United States, GenealogyBank Historical Newspaper Obituaries, 1815-2013", FamilySearch (https://www.familysearch.org/ark:/61903/1:1:Q5QR-GHC5 : Thu Mar 14 23:23:45 UTC 2024), Entry for Mr William E Sidoli and William F Sidoll, 17 Jul 1964.

170) Angelo Maria Di Lillo

Angelo Maria Di Lillo(170) was born on 30 April 1883, in Ariano, Italy, to Nicola Maria di Lillo(51a) and Angela Perrina(52). Angelo Maria Di Lillo(170) died 21 October 1884 in Ariano, Italy.

Records that include Angelo Maria Di Lillo(170):
- Ariano, Italy 1883 Birth Act #273
- Ariano, Italy 1884 Death Act #346

171) Mariantonia Manganiello

Mariantonia Manganiello(171) was stillborn on 3 September 1883, in Ariano, Italy, to Giuseppe Manganiello(64a) and Maria Fransesca Fodarella (63).

Records that include Mariantonia Manganiello(171):
- Ariano, Italy 1883 Birth Act #485

172) Biagio Miressi

Biagio Miressi(172) was born on 3 February 1884, in Ariano, Italy, to Giuseppe Miressi(51a) and Rosa Giorgione(51).

Biagio Miressi(172) married Lucia Grasso(172a) on 5 October 1911 in Ariano, Italy.

Lucia Grasso(172a) was born on 2 September 1892, in Ariano, Italy, to Savino Grasso(172aF) and Angela Maria Mincolelli(172aM).

Known children of Biagio Miressi(172) and Lucia Grasso(172a):

i) Giovanni Miressi(574) born in 1930

Records that include Biagio Miressi(172) and/or Lucia Grasso(172a):
- Ariano, Italy 1884 Birth Act #68
- Ariano, Italy 1892 Birth Act #475
- Ariano, Italy 1911 Marriage Act #103
- Ariano, Italy 1931 Death Act #102

173) Raffaella Grasso

Raffaella Grasso(173) was born on 16 March 1884, in Ariano, Italy, to Lorenzo Grasso(45a) and Anna Maria Perrina (44). Raffaella Grasso(173) died on 30 November 1884 in Ariano, Italy.

Records that include Raffaella Grasso(173):
- Ariano Italy 1884 Birth Act #166
- Ariano, Italy 1884 Death Act #396

174) Domenico Fodarella

Domenico Fodarella(174) was born on 4 April 1884, in Ariano, Italy, to Lorenzo Fodarella(48) and Maria Fransesca Paola Dotolo(48a).

Records that include Domenico Fodarella(174):
- Ariano Italy 1884 Birth Act #215

175) Luigi Anselmo deDonato

Luigi Anselmo deDonato(175) was born 30 July 1884, in Ariano, Italy, to Domenico deDonato(60a) and Anna Maria Coppola(60). Luigi Anselmo deDonato(175) died on 28 July 1885 in Ariano, Italy.

Records that include Luigi Anselmo deDonato(175):
- Ariano Italy 1884 Birth Act #428
- Ariano, Italy 1885 Death Act #193

176) Michelangelo Perrina

Michelangelo Perrina(176) was born on 15 December 1884 in Castel Baronia, Italy to Rafaele Perrina(57) and Maria Lucia Gesa(58a). Michelangelo Perrina(176) died on 24 December 1884 in Castel Baronia, Italy.

Records that include Michelangelo Perrina(176):
- Castel Baronia, Italy 1884 Death #36

NOTE: 1884 Birth records for Castel Baronia are not available. Birth date calculated from Death Record.

177) Raimonda Grasso

Raimonda Grasso(177) was born on 6 February 1885, in Ariano, Italy, to Crescenzo Grasso(76a) and Anna Perrina(76). Raimonda Grasso(177) died on 26 December 1886 in Ariano, Italy.

Records that include Raimonda Grasso(177):
- Ariano, Italy 1885 Birth Act #111
- Ariano, Italy 1886 Death Act #475

178) Gabriele Anastasio

Gabriele Anastasio(178) was born on 28 February 1885, in Ariano, Italy, to Pasquale Antonio Anastasio(72a) and Anna Maria D'Ausilio(72).

Records that include Gabriele Anastasio(178):
- Ariano Italy 1885 Birth Act #167

179) Antonio Ninfadoro

Antonio Ninfadoro(179) was born on 21 May 1885, in Ariano, Italy, to Gabriele Ninfadoro(67a) and Mariangela Perrina(67). Antonio Ninfadoro(179) died on 23 February 1952 in Ariano, Italy.

Antonio Ninfadoro(179) married Maria Carmela Dioguardi(179a) on 23 August 1915 in Ariano, Italy.

Maria Carmela Dioguardi(179a) was born 18 July 1889 to Luigi Dioguardi(179aF) and Marianna Mastantuono(179aM).

Known children of Antonio Ninfadoro(179) and Maria Carmela Dioguardi(179a):

- i) Gabriele Giovanni Ninfadoro(474) born about 1916
- ii) Enrico Ninfadoro(489) born about 1918

Records that include Antonio Ninfadoro(179) and/or Maria Carmela Dioguardi(179a):
- Ariano Italy 1885 Birth Act #358
- Ariano Italy 1889 Birth Act #495
- Ariano, Italy 1915 Marriage Act #68
- Zungoli, Italy 1916 Birth Act #35
- Ariano Italy 1918 Death Act #635
- Ariano, Italy 1937 Marriage Act #P.II.B.14

180) **Ciriaco (Jerry) Manganiello**

Ciriaco (Jerry) Manganiello(180) was born on 28 May 1885, in Ariano, Italy, to Giuseppe Manganiello(64a) and Maria Fransesca Fodarella(63). Ciriaco (Jerry) Manganiello(180) traveled to the United States at least three times. On 26 February 1907 Ciriaco (Jerry) Manganiello(180) boarded the ship SS Königin Luise in Naples, Italy, arriving in New York on 10 March 1904. On 31 May 1907, Ciriaco (Jerry) Manganiello(180) boarded the ship SS Königin Luise in Naples, Italy, arriving in New York on 14 June 1907. On 2 July 1927, Ciriaco (Jerry) Manganiello(180) boarded the ship SS Conte Rosso in Naples, Italy, arriving in New York on 12 July 1927. Ciriaco (Jerry) Manganiello(180) became a citizen of the United States on 2 April 1923 in Boston, MA.

Records that include Ciriaco (Jerry) Manganiello(180):
- Ariano Italy 1885 Birth Act #369
- "New York Passenger Arrival Lists (Ellis Island), 1892-1924", , FamilySearch (https://www.familysearch.org/ark:/61903/1:1:JFBT-S2J : Wed Jul 10 09:51:00 UTC 2024), Entry for Ciriaco Manganiello and Domenico Grassi, 10 Mar 1904.
- "New York Passenger Arrival Lists (Ellis Island), 1892-1924", , FamilySearch (https://www.familysearch.org/ark:/61903/1:1:JXJ5-3T5 : Sat Mar 09 06:04:24 UTC 2024), Entry for Ciriaco Manganiello and Michele Manganiello, 1907.
- "United States World War I Draft Registration Cards, 1917-1918", database with images, FamilySearch (https://www.familysearch.org/ark:/61903/1:1:4MCY-DYN2 : 10 July 2024), Ciriaco Manganiello, 1917-1918.
- "New York, New York Passenger and Crew Lists, 1909, 1925-1957", , FamilySearch (https://www.familysearch.org/ark:/61903/1:1:KXLG-PXB : Sat Mar 09 11:06:48 UTC 2024), Entry for Ciriaco Manganiello, 1927.
- "United States, Census, 1940", FamilySearch (https://www.familysearch.org/ark:/61903/1:1:K4VC-H9P : Wed Jan 15 01:29:25 UTC 2025), Entry for Raymond Gentile and Victoria Gentile, 1940.
- "United States World War II Draft Registration Cards, 1942", , FamilySearch (https://www.familysearch.org/ark:/61903/1:1:V12V-C3S : Sat Feb 24 04:23:58 UTC 2024), Entry for Jerry Manganiello, 1942.

181) **Luigi Scaglione**

Luigi Scaglione(181) was born 5 July 1885, in Ariano, Italy, to Giuseppe Scaglione(66a) and Concetta deDonato(66). Luigi Scaglione(181) died on 11 April 1888 in Ariano, Italy.

Records that include Luigi Scaglione(181):
- Ariano Italy 1885 Birth Act #426
- Ariano Italy 1888 Death Act #210

182) **Raimondo Manganiello**

Raimondo Manganiello(182) was born on 17 September 1885, in Ariano, Italy, to Vincenzo Manganiello(57a) and Anna Maria Fodarella(57). Raimondo Manganiello(182) died 7 February 1932 in Ariano, Italy. Raimondo Manganiello(182) was a farm laborer.

Raimondo Manganiello(182) married Maria Giovanna Paone(182a) on 5 August 1909 in Ariano, Italy.

Maria Giovanna Paone(182a) was born on 1 August 1886, in Ariano, Italy, to Raffaele Paone(182aF) and Raffaela Guardabascio(182aM).

Known children of Raimondo Manganiello(182) and Maria Giovanna Paone(182a):

  i) Genoveffa Carmna Maria Manganiello(419) born in 1910
  ii) Ida Manganiello(467) born in 1916

Records that include Raimondo Manganiello(182) and/or Maria Giovanna Paone(182a):

- Ariano Italy 1885 Birth Act #546

- Ariano Italy 1886 Birth Act #421
- Ariano Italy 1909 Marriage Act #72
- Ariano Italy 1910 Birth Act #629
- Ariano Italy 1916 Birth Act #3
- Ariano Italy 1932 Death Act #51
- Ariano Italy 1938 Marriage Act #P.IIA.125
- Ariano Italy 1956 Marriage Act #26

183) Raimonda Ciasullo

Raimonda Ciasullo(183) was born on 28 October 1885, in Ariano, Italy, to Michele Ciasullo(82a) and Filomena Perrina(82).

Raimonda Ciasullo(183) married Angelo Maria Riccio(183a) on 2 February 1907 in Ariano, Italy.

Angelo Maria Riccio(183a) was born on 14 March 1882, in Ariano, Italy, to Pietro Riccio(183aF)(221aF) and Anna Ardito(W183aM)(W221aM).

Known children of Raimonda Ciasullo(183) and Angelo Maria Riccio(183a):

    i) Marianna Riccio(400) born in 1908
    ii) Pietro Riccio(440) born in 1913
    iii) Maria Michela Riccio(460) born in 1915
    iv) Marianna Riccio(561) born in 1928

Records that include Raimonda Ciasullo(183) and/or Angelo Maria Riccio(183a):
- Ariano, Italy 1882 Birth Act #173
- Ariano, Italy 1885 Birth Act #612
- Ariano, Italy 1907 Marriage Act #15
- Ariano, Italy 1908 Birth Act #118
- Ariano, Italy 1909 Death Act #81
- Ariano, Italy 1913 Birth Act #14
- Ariano, Italy 1915 Birth Act #298
- Ariano, Italy 1916 Death Act #111
- Ariano, Italy 1928 Death Act #172
- Ariano, Italy 1936 Marriage Act #P.IIA.17

184) Francesco di Lillo

Francesco di Lillo(184) was born on 4 November 1885, in Ariano, Italy, to Nicola Maria di Lillo(51a) and Angela Perrina(52). Francesco di Lillo(184) died 30 October 1909 in Ariano, Italy.

Francesco di Lillo(184) married Concetta Perrina(184a) on 9 November 1907 in Ariano, Italy.

Concetta Perrina(184a) was born 4 December 1883, in Ariano, Italy, to Leonardo Perrina(184aF) and Maddalena di Maina(184aM).

Concetta Perrina(184a) also married Raffaele diPaola(184ab).

Known children of Francesco di Lillo(184) and Concetta Perrina(184a):

    i) Angela di Lillo(401) born in 1908

Records that include Francesco di Lillo(184) and/or Concetta Perrina(184a):
- Ariano, Italy 1883 Birth Act #646
- Ariano, Italy 1885 Birth Act #622
- Ariano, Italy 1907 Marriage Act #110
- Ariano, Italy 1908 Birth Act #139
- Ariano, Italy 1909 Death Act #328
- Ariano, Italy 1924 Marriage Act #24

185) Maria Raffaella Grasso

Maria Raffaella Grasso(185) was born on 16 November 1885, in Ariano, Italy, to Lorenzo Grasso(45a) and Anna Maria Perrina(45). Maria Raffaella Grasso(185) died on 22 August 1886 in Ariano, Italy.

Records that include Maria Raffaella Grasso(185):
- Ariano, Italy 1885 Birth Act #646
- Ariano, Italy 1886 Death Act #282

186) Oto Maria Perrina

Oto Maria Perrina(186) was born on 13 December 1885, in San Nicola Baronia, Italy, to Francesco Paolo Perrina(90) and Maria Sofia Leone(87a). Oto Maria Perrina(186) died 5 December 1888 in San Nicola Baronia, Italy.

Records that include Oto Maria Perrina(186):
- San Nicola Baronia, Italy 1885 Birth Act #41
- San Nicola Baronia, Italy 1888 Death Act #40

187) Vittorio Perrino

Vittorio Perrino(187), also known as Victor C. Perrino, was born on 28 December 1885, in San Nicola Baronia, Italy, to Raffaele Perrina(58) and Maria Lucia Gesa(58a). On 24 April 1901 Vittorio Perrino(187) sailed from Naples, Italy, on the SS Sympione, arriving in New York on 12 May 1901. Vittorio Perrino(187) became a United States Citizen on 27 January 1913, in Schenectady, NY. Vittorio Perrino(187) died 4 November 1936 in Schenectady, NY. Vittorio Perrino(187) was an Insurance Salesman.

On 24 October 1910 Vittorio Perrino(187) married Carmela Ricci(187a) on 27 October 1910 in Schenectady, NY.

Carmela Ricci(187a) was born about 1892 in Italy, to Vincenzo Ricci(187aF) and Raffaela Casozzo(187aM).

Known Children of Vittorio Perrino(187) and Carmela Ricci(187a):

   i) Victor Vincent Perrino(425) born in 1911
   ii) Edward Laurie Perrino(454) born in 1914
   iii) Eleanor Margaret Perrino(505) born in 1920
   iv) Dorothy Lillian Perrino(506) born in 1920

Records that include Vittorio Perrino(187) and/or Carmela Ricci(187a):
- San Nicola Baronia, Italy 1885 Birth Act #41
- "New York, New York, Index to Passengers Lists of Vessels, 1897-1902", , FamilySearch (https://www.familysearch.org/ark:/61903/1:1:Z76B-PP3Z : Sat Mar 09 18:12:39 UTC 2024), Entry for Vittorio Perrino, 1901.
- "New York, County Naturalization Records, 1791-1980", , FamilySearch (https://www.familysearch.org/ark:/61903/1:1:QPC6-JCZZ : Sun Mar 10 13:38:42 UTC 2024), Entry for Vittorio Perrino, 1910.
- "New York, County Marriages, 1847-1848; 1908-1936", , FamilySearch (https://www.familysearch.org/ark:/61903/1:1:FFT7-4MK : Sun Mar 10 17:29:29 UTC 2024), Entry for Vittorio Perrino and Raffaele, 27 October 1910.
- "St. John the Baptist, Schenectady, New York, Marriages (May 1854 – Jun 2009)", American-Canadian Genealogical Society, Manchester, NH, page 576
- "New York, County Naturalization Records, 1791-1980", , FamilySearch (https://www.familysearch.org/ark:/61903/1:1:QPC6-JCZ6 : Sat Mar 09 11:48:01 UTC 2024), Entry for Vittorio Perrino, 1913.
- "United States Census, 1920", , FamilySearch (https://www.familysearch.org/ark:/61903/1:1:MVSH-71T : Sat Jul 20 13:35:39 UTC 2024), Entry for Victor Perrino, Sr and Carrie Perrino, 1920.

- "United States Census, 1930", , FamilySearch (https://www.familysearch.org/ark:/61903/1:1:X4T1-VDJ : Mon Jul 08 19:59:28 UTC 2024), Entry for Victor C Perrino and Carrie Perrino, 1930.
- "New York, New York City, World War II Draft Registration Cards, 1940-1947", , FamilySearch (https://www.familysearch.org/ark:/61903/1:1:WZ9F-SW3Z : Sat Mar 09 03:15:01 UTC 2024), Entry for Victor Vincent Perrino and Unemployed, 16 Oct 1940.
- "Vermont Vital Records, 1760-2008," , FamilySearch (https://familysearch.org/ark:/61903/1:1:KFR6-9DB : 6 December 2014), Victor in entry for Victor Vincent Perrino and Louise Teresa Gararano, Marriage, 16 Aug 1942, Rutland, Vermont, United States; from "Vermont, Birth Records, 1909-2008," "Vermont, Death Records, 1909-2008," "Vermont, Marriage Records, 1909-2008," and "Vermont, Vital Records, 1720-1908." Ancestry (http://www.ancestry.com : 2010); citing Vital Records Office, Vermont Department of Health, Burlington and New England Historic Genealogical Society, Boston.

188) Luigi Fodarella

Luigi Fodarella(188) was born on 4 January 1886, in Ariano, Italy, to Lorenzo Fodarella(48) and Maria Fransesca Paola Dotolo(48a).

Luigi Fodarella(188) married Giuditta Marrone(188a) on 30 September 1909 in Ariano, Italy.

Giuditta Marrone(188a) was a foundling, born on 4 April 1886, in Ariano, Italy.

Known children of Luigi Fodarella(188) and Giuditta Marrone(188a):

i) Lorenzo Fodarella(421) born in 1911
ii) Raffaele Fodarella(441) born in 1913
iii) Francesca Paula Fodarella(459) born in 1915

Records that include Luigi Fodarella(188) and/or Giuditta Marrone(188a):
- Ariano, Italy 1886 Birth Act #11
- Ariano, Italy 1886 Birth Act #II-15
- Ariano, Italy 1909 Marriage Act #93
- Ariano, Italy 1911 Birth Act #38
- Ariano, Italy 1913 Birth Act #142
- Ariano, Italy 1915 Birth Act #257
- Ariano, Italy 1916 Death Act #201
- Ariano, Italy 1935 Marriage Act #P.IIA.21

189) Mariangela Pietracola

Mariangela Pietracola(189) was born 16 January 1886 in Ariano, Italy to Pasquale Pietracola(54b) and Aurelia Fiorenza(55).

Records that include Mariangela Pietracola(189):
- Ariano, Italy 1886 Birth Act #45

190) Leopoldo D'ausilio

Leopoldo D'ausilio(190) was born on 6 February 1886, in Ariano, Italy, to Nicola Maria D'Ausilio(83) and Giustina Mariano(83a). Leopoldo D'ausilio(190) died on 24 December 1889 in Ariano, Italy.

Records that include Leopoldo D'ausilio(190):
- Ariano, Italy 1886 Birth Act #73
- Ariano, Italy 1889 Death Act #409

191) Antonia Giorgione

Antonia Giorgione(191) was born on 19 March 1886, in Ariano, Italy, to Raffaele Giorgione(80) and Carmina Salvioli(80a). Antonia Giorgione(191) died on 2 April 1886 in Ariano, Italy.

Records that include Antonia Giorgione(191):
- Ariano, Italy 1886 Birth Act #181
- Ariano, Italy 1886 Death Act #166

192) Maria Miressi

Maria Miressi(192) was born on 13 May 1886, in Ariano, Italy, to Giuseppe Miressi 584 and Rosa Giorgione 583.

Maria Miressi(192) married Pasquale Gentile(192a) on 9 February 1905 in Ariano, Italy.

Pasquale Gentile(192a) was a foundling born on 21 March 1875, in Ariano, Italy.

Known children of Maria Miressi(192) and Pasquale Gentile(192a):

  i) Rosina Gentile(387) born in 1906
  ii) Maria Virginia Gentile(404) born in 1908
  iii) Angela Gentile(418) born in 1910

Records that include Maria Miressi(192) and/or Pasquale Gentile(192a):
- Ariano, Italy 1875 Birth Act #PII.20
- Ariano, Italy 1886 Birth Act #295
- Ariano, Italy 1925 Marriage Act #29
- Ariano, Italy 1906 Birth Act #7
- Ariano, Italy 1908 Birth Act #449
- Ariano, Italy 1910 Birth Act #575
- Ariano, Italy 1927 Marriage Act #38

193) Vincenzo Manganiello

Vincenzo Manganiello(193) was born on 9 June 1886, in Ariano, Italy, to Raimondo Manganiello(79a) and Mariantonia Fodarella(79). Vincenzo Manganiello(193) died 16 May 1913 in Ariano, Italy.

Vincenzo Manganiello(193) married Elena Morante(193a) on 20 October 1910 in Ariano, Italy.

Elena Morante(193a) was a foundling, born on 11 May 1884, in Ariano, Italy.

Elena Morante(193a) married Vincenzo Manganiello(193) and Pasquale Grasso(181ab).

Known children of Vincenzo Manganiello(193) and Elena Morante(193a):

  i) Raimondo Carmine Manganiello(427) born in 1911

Records that include Vincenzo Manganiello(193) and/or Elena Morante(193a):
- Ariano, Italy 1884 Birth Act #II-12
- Ariano, Italy 1886 Birth Act #340
- Ariano, Italy 1910 Marriage Act #88
- Ariano, Italy 1911 Birth Act #519
- Ariano, Italy 1913 Death Act #111
- Ariano, Italy 1935 Marriage Act #PIIA.41

194) Angela deDonato

Angela deDonato(194) was born on 24 September 1886, in Paduli, Italy, to Marcello deDonato(78) and Maria Rosa Politano(78a). Angela deDonato(194) died 13 April 1946 in Ribeirao Pires, Brazil.

Angela deDonato(194) married Luis Dos Santos(194a).

Luis Dos Santos(194a) [no information found except for mention in death record for Angela deDonato(194)].

Angela deDonato(194) and Luis Dos Santos(194a) had child(ren).

Records that include Angela deDonato(194) and/or Luis Dos Santos(194a):
- "Italia, Benevento, Stato Civile (Archivio di Stato), 1810-1942", , FamilySearch (https://www.familysearch.org/ark:/61903/1:1:QGK5-YJLH : Mon Jul 22 17:14:20 UTC 2024), Entry for Angela De Donato and Marcello De Donato, 24 Sep 1886.
- "Brasil, São Paulo, Registro Civil, 1925-1995", , FamilySearch (https://www.familysearch.org/ark:/61903/1:1:6XZ6-BKF5 : Fri Jul 05 19:47:46 UTC 2024), Entry for Angelina Donato and Marcelo Donato, 22 Jan 1934.
- "Brasil, São Paulo, Registro Civil, 1925-1995", , FamilySearch (https://www.familysearch.org/ark:/61903/1:1:65R8-ZNTT : Sat Mar 09 05:26:17 UTC 2024), Entry for Angelina de Lourdes Silva and Marcelo de Donato, 13 de abril de 1946.

195) Raffaela Maria Giuseppa Altanese

Raffaela Maria Giuseppa Altanese(195) was born 8 February 1887 in Grottaminarda, Italy to Cosimo Altanese(87) and Margarita Galgothia Alfonsina Romano(87a). Raffaela Maria Giuseppa Altanese(195) died 18 February 1887 in Grottaminarda, Italy.

Records that include Raffaela Maria Giuseppa Altanese:
- Grottaminarda, Italy 1887 Birth Act #24
- Grottaminarda, Italy 1887 Death Act #21

196) Giovanna Grasso

Giovanna Grasso(196) was born on 1 April 1887, in Ariano, Italy, to Crescenzo Grasso(76a) and Anna Perrina(76). Giovanna Grasso(196) died in 1962 in Bronx, NY.

Giovanna Grasso(196) married Gaetano Scauzillo(164) (Giovanna Grasso(196)'s third cousin) on 7 September 1905 in Bronx, NY.

Gaetano Scauzillo(164) was born on 16 March 1882, in Ariano, Italy, to Lorenzo Scauzillo(55a) and Aurelia Fiorenza(55). Gaetano Scauzillo(164) died in 1954 in Bronx, NY.

Known children of Giovanna Grasso(196) and Gaetano Scauzillo(164):

- i) Lorenzo Scauzillo(389) born in 1906
- ii) Carmela Scanzillo(394) born in 1907
- iii) Aurelia Scanzillo(407) born in 1908
- iv) Virginia Scanzillo(431) born in 1912
- v) Lorenzo Scanzillo(476) born in 1916
- vi) Anthony Scanzillo(520) born in 1922

Records that include Gaetano Scauzillo(164) and/or Giovanna Grasso(196):
- Ariano, Italy 1882 Birth Act #170
- Ariano, Italy 1887 Birth Act #257
- "New York, New York City Marriage Records, 1829-1938", , FamilySearch (https://www.familysearch.org/ark:/61903/1:1:244Q-4WZ : Sat Mar 09 04:31:53 UTC 2024), Entry for Gaetano Scanzillo and Giovannina Grassi, 7 Sep 1905.
- "New York, New York City Births, 1846-1909," , FamilySearch (https://familysearch.org/ark:/61903/1:1:2W81-1FD : 11 February 2018), Gaetano Scanzillo in entry for Lorenzo Scanzillo, 14 Apr 1906; citing Manhattan, New York, New York, United States, reference cn 2031 New York Municipal Archives, New York; FHL microfilm 2,023,140.
- "New York, New York City Municipal Deaths, 1795-1949", database, FamilySearch (https://www.familysearch.org/ark:/61903/1:1:2719-474 : 13 May 2022), Gastano Scauzillo in entry for Lorenzo Scauzillo, 1906.
- "New York, New York City Births, 1846-1909," , FamilySearch (https://familysearch.org/ark:/61903/1:1:2W8H-5M2 : 11 February 2018), Gaetano Scanzilla in entry for Anleria Scanzilla, 28 Oct 1908; citing Manhattan, New York, New York, United States, reference 8022 New York Municipal Archives, New York; FHL microfilm 2,023,262.

- "New York, County Naturalization Records, 1791-1980", , FamilySearch (https://www.familysearch.org/ark:/61903/1:1:QPZB-C541 : Fri Mar 08 19:23:41 UTC 2024), Entry for Gaetano Scanzillo and Giovannino Grasso Scanzillo, 1913.
- "United States World War I Draft Registration Cards, 1917-1918", database with images, FamilySearch (https://www.familysearch.org/ark:/61903/1:1:W7VL-FR3Z : 10 July 2024), Gaetano Scanzillo, 1917-1918.
- "United States Census, 1920", , FamilySearch (https://www.familysearch.org/ark:/61903/1:1:MJG5-1XL : Sat Apr 13 04:57:08 UTC 2024), Entry for Gaetano Scanzilla and Jannie Scanzilla, 1920.
- "United States Census, 1930", , FamilySearch (https://www.familysearch.org/ark:/61903/1:1:X7D4-SB4 : Mon Jul 08 16:00:27 UTC 2024), Entry for Gaetano Scanzillo and Guanina Scanzillo, 1930.
- "United States Census, 1940", , FamilySearch (https://www.familysearch.org/ark:/61903/1:1:KQBN-826 : Sat Mar 09 01:41:31 UTC 2024), Entry for Gaetano Scanzillo and Jennie Scanzillo, 1940.
- "New York, New York City, World War II Draft Registration Cards, 1940-1947", , FamilySearch (https://www.familysearch.org/ark:/61903/1:1:WQYH-HVMM : Sun Mar 10 10:38:46 UTC 2024), Entry for Anthony Salvatore Scanzillo and Montgomery Ward, 30 Jun 1942.
- "United States Census, 1950", , FamilySearch (https://www.familysearch.org/ark:/61903/1:1:6XYM-9X8P : Tue Mar 19 16:01:57 UTC 2024), Entry for Virginia Scanzillo and Gaetano Scanzillo, 10 April 1950.
- "Find a Grave Index," database, FamilySearch (https://www.familysearch.org/ark:/61903/1:1:Q2DK-RCDG : 11 January 2023), Gaetano Scanzillo, ; Burial, Bronx, Bronx, New York, United States of America, Old Saint Raymond's Cemetery; citing record ID 172164315, Find a Grave, http://www.findagrave.com.
- "Find a Grave Index," database, FamilySearch (https://www.familysearch.org/ark:/61903/1:1:Q2DK-RC8P : 11 January 2023), Giovannina Scanzillo, ; Burial, Bronx, Bronx, New York, United States of America, Old Saint Raymond's Cemetery; citing record ID 172164402, Find a Grave, http://www.findagrave.com.
- "United States, Social Security Numerical Identification Files (NUMIDENT), 1936-2007", database, FamilySearch (https://www.familysearch.org/ark:/61903/1:1:6K9W-WS6K : 10 February 2023), Thomas Scanzilla in entry for Lorenzo Joseph Scanzillo, .
- "United States, Social Security Numerical Identification Files (NUMIDENT), 1936-2007", database, FamilySearch (https://www.familysearch.org/ark:/61903/1:1:6K9W-498X : 10 February 2023), Gaetano Scanzillo in entry for Anthony Scanzillo, .

197) Generoso deDonato

Generoso deDonato(197) was born 1 May 1887, in Ariano, Italy, to Domenico deDonato(61) and Anna Maria Coppola(61a). Generoso deDonato(197) died on 18 February 1888 in Ariano, Italy.

Records that include Generoso deDonato(197):
- Ariano, Italy 1887 Birth Act #345
- Ariano, Italy 1888 Death Act #78

198) Feliciano Lombardi

Feliciano Lombardi(198) was born on 6 July 1887, in Apice, Italy, to Vincenzo (James) Lombardi(85a) and Maria Carmela deDonato(85). Feliciano Lombardi(198) died before 1889.

Records that include Feliciano Lombardi(198):
- Apice Italy 1887 Birth Act #82

- "Italia, Benevento, Stato Civile (Archivio di Stato), 1810-1942", , FamilySearch (https://www.familysearch.org/ark:/61903/1:1:QLKP-P6QN : Sun Mar 10 04:16:09 UTC 2024), Entry for Feliciano Lombardi and Vincenzo Lombardi, 6 luglio 1887.

199) Tommaso Scaglione

Tommaso Scaglione(199) was born 19 August 1887, in Ariano, Italy, to Giuseppe Scaglione(66a) and Concetta deDonato(66). Tommaso Scaglione(199) died on 16 May 1888 in Ariano, Italy.

Records that include Tommaso Scaglione(199):
- Ariano, Italy 1887 Birth Act #519
- Ariano, Italy 1888 Death Act #267

200) Liberatore Perrina

Liberatore Perrina(200) was born on 5 September 1887, in Ariano, Italy, to Angelo Maria Perrina(74) and Tommasina Paduano(74a). On 7 March 1906 Liberatore Perrina(200) boarded the ship SS Florida arriving on 23 March 1906 at Ellis Island, NY. Liberatore Perrina(200) died in 1942 in Boston, MA. Liberatore Perrina(200) was buried on 1 July 1942 in Calvary Cemetery, Concord, NH.

Liberatore Perrina(200) married Carmenella Gammaroto(200a) on 26 April 1911 in Boston, MA.

Carmenella Gammaroto(200a) was born on 17 September 1884, in Ariano, Italy, to Domenico A Gammaroto(200aF) and Francesca Meninno(200aM). Carmenella Gammaroto(200a) died February 1974 in New Hampshire.

Known Children of Liberatore Perrina(200) married Carmenella Gammaroto(200a):

    i) Teresa Alba Perrino(437) born in 1912
    ii) Angelo Mario Perrino(481) born in 1917
    iii) Mary Jenuvieve Perrino(514) born in 1921

Records that include Liberatore Perrina(200) married Carmenella Gammaroto(200a):
- Ariano, Italy 1884 Birth Act #501
- Ariano, Italy 1887 Birth Act #548
- "New York Passenger Arrival Lists (Ellis Island), 1892-1924", database with images, FamilySearch (https://familysearch.org/ark:/61903/1:1:JFFG-3JW : 2 March 2021), Liberatore Perrina, 1906.
- "Massachusetts State Vital Records, 1841-1925", database with images, FamilySearch (https://www.familysearch.org/ark:/61903/1:1:N4FF-42C : 4 November 2022), Liberatore Perrino and Carmenella Gammaroto, 1911.
- "Massachusetts State Vital Records, 1841-1925", database with images, FamilySearch (https://www.familysearch.org/ark:/61903/1:1:Q282-J39B : 24 November 2022), Liberatore Perrino and Carmenella Gammaroto, 1911.
- "United States World War I Draft Registration Cards, 1917-1918", database with images, FamilySearch (https://www.familysearch.org/ark:/61903/1:1:KZJ7-QTZ : 1 January 2022), Librotore Perrino, 1917-1918.
- "United States Census, 1920", database with images, FamilySearch (https://www.familysearch.org/ark:/61903/1:1:MH8R-RXT : 2 February 2021), Liberatore Perrino, 1920.
- "United States Census, 1930," database with images, FamilySearch (https://www.familysearch.org/ark:/61903/1:1:X7NK-BXM : accessed 11 July 2023), Liberatone Perrino, Concord, Merrimack, New Hampshire, United States; citing enumeration district (ED) ED 30, sheet 9A, line 39, family 196, NARA microfilm publication T626 (Washington D.C.: National Archives and Records Administration, 2002), roll 1304; FHL microfilm 2,341,039.

- "New Hampshire Death Records, 1654-1947," database with images, FamilySearch (https://familysearch.org/ark:/61903/1:1:FSKM-JXH : 22 February 2021), Liberatore Perrino, ; citing , Bureau Vital Records and Health Statistics, Concord; FHL microfilm 2,297,072.
- "Find A Grave Index," database, FamilySearch (https://www.familysearch.org/ark:/61903/1:1:DMGF-X1T2 : 12 May 2022), Liberatore Perrino, ; Burial, Concord, Merrimack, New Hampshire, United States of America, Calvary Cemetery; citing record ID 214492645, Find a Grave, http://www.findagrave.com.
- "New Hampshire Marriage Records, 1637-1947", , FamilySearch (https://www.familysearch.org/ark:/61903/1:1:FLX1-S4T : Sat Mar 09 05:45:30 UTC 2024), Entry for Albert Defelice and Teresa Alba Perrino, 1942.
- "Vermont, Town Clerk, Vital and Town Records, 1732-2005," database with images, FamilySearch (https://familysearch.org/ark:/61903/1:1:QPQX-9BS2 : 3 March 2021), Liberatore Perrino in entry for Albert De Felice and Teresa Alba Perrino, 5 Apr 1942; citing Marriage, Concord, Essex, Vermont, United States, various town clerks and records divisions, Vermont; FHL microfilm 005486629.
- "New Hampshire Marriage Records, 1637-1947", , FamilySearch (https://www.familysearch.org/ark:/61903/1:1:FLD1-VDL : Sat Mar 09 14:51:46 UTC 2024), Entry for Angelo M. Perrino and Lurline M. Dawson, 1944.
- "United States, Social Security Numerical Identification Files (NUMIDENT), 1936-2007", database, FamilySearch (https://www.familysearch.org/ark:/61903/1:1:6KM3-S7G1 : 10 February 2023), Mary Perrino, .
- "United States Social Security Death Index," database, FamilySearch (https://familysearch.org/ark:/61903/1:1:JPML-9QM : 7 January 2021), Carminella Perrino, Feb 1974; citing U.S. Social Security Administration, Death Master File, database (Alexandria, Virginia: National Technical Information Service, ongoing).
- "United States, Social Security Numerical Identification Files (NUMIDENT), 1936-2007", database, FamilySearch (https://www.familysearch.org/ark:/61903/1:1:6KMS-4Y67 : 10 February 2023), Teresa Alba Perrino, .
- "United States, Social Security Numerical Identification Files (NUMIDENT), 1936-2007", database, FamilySearch (https://www.familysearch.org/ark:/61903/1:1:6KM3-S7G1 : 10 February 2023), Mary Perrino, .

201) Luigi deDonato

Luigi deDonato(201) was born on 4 December 1887, in Paduli, Italy, to Marcello deDonato(78) and Maria Rosa Politano(78a). Luigi deDonato(201) died before 1889.
NOTE: Death records for Paduli at that time are not currently available.

Records that include Luigi deDonato(201):
- "Italia, Benevento, Stato Civile (Archivio di Stato), 1810-1942", , FamilySearch (https://www.familysearch.org/ark:/61903/1:1:QGJ2-HT9B : Fri Mar 08 09:19:04 UTC 2024), Entry for Luigi di Donato and Marcello di Donato, 4 dicembre 1887.

202) Maria Perrina

Maria Perrina(202) was born on 24 December 1887 in San Nicola, Italy to Raffaele Perrina(58) and Maria Lucia Gesa(58a).

Maria Perrina(202) married Angelo DeMeo(202a).

Angelo DeMeo(202a) was born on 15 November 1881, in Italy. Angelo DeMeo(202a) died on 29 November 1945 in Schenectady, NY.

Known Children of Maria Perrina(202) and Angelo DeMeo(202a):

    i) Lucy DeMeo(386) born in 1905
    ii) Teresina (Teresa) DeMeo(392) born about 1907

    iii) Rosina (Rose) DeMeo(408) born about 1909
    iv) Giovanni Raffaele (John) DeMeo(438) born about 1913
    v) Ralph Pasquale DeMeo(456) born about 1915
    vi) Michael Angelo DeMeo(475) born in 1916
    vii) Angelo DeMeo JR(503) born about 1921

Records that include Maria Perrina(202) and Angelo DeMeo(202a):
- "New York, New York City Births, 1846-1909," , FamilySearch
  (https://familysearch.org/ark:/61903/1:1:27YZ-1F7 : 11 February
  2018), Anglo De Meo in entry for Lucia De Meo, 27 Oct 1905; citing
  Manhattan, New York, New York, United States, reference v 8 cn 3589
  New York Municipal Archives, New York; FHL microfilm 2,022,302.
- "United States Census, 1910", , FamilySearch
  (https://www.familysearch.org/ark:/61903/1:1:M596-RYZ : Sun Mar 10
  01:00:22 UTC 2024), Entry for Angelo Demeo and Mary F Demeo, 1910.
- "New York State Census, 1915", , FamilySearch
  (https://www.familysearch.org/ark:/61903/1:1:K9P8-MYC : 3 June
  2022), Mary Demas in entry for Angelo Demas, 1915.
- "United States World War I Draft Registration Cards, 1917-1918",
  database with images, FamilySearch
  (https://www.familysearch.org/ark:/61903/1:1:WDY6-WXZM : 10 July
  2024), Angelo Demeo, 1917-1918.
- "United States Census, 1920", , FamilySearch
  (https://www.familysearch.org/ark:/61903/1:1:MVS4-RRY : Fri Mar 08
  05:51:12 UTC 2024), Entry for Angelo Demeo and Mary Demeo, 1920.
- "New York State Census, 1925", , FamilySearch
  (https://www.familysearch.org/ark:/61903/1:1:KSHH-T5Q : Thu Jul 18
  06:19:01 UTC 2024), Entry for Angelo De Meo, 1925.
- "United States Census, 1930", , FamilySearch
  (https://www.familysearch.org/ark:/61903/1:1:X4TT-YB5 : Mon Mar 11
  01:35:37 UTC 2024), Entry for Angelo De Meo and Mary De Meo, 1930.
- "United States World War II Draft Registration Cards, 1942", ,
  FamilySearch (https://www.familysearch.org/ark:/61903/1:1:QKV7-SWF5
  : Fri Feb 23 22:49:01 UTC 2024), Entry for Angelo De Meo and Mary
  De Meo, 26 Apr 1942.
- "Find a Grave Index," database, FamilySearch
  (https://www.familysearch.org/ark:/61903/1:1:CVDC-GRZM : 6 August
  2020), Angelo DeMeo, ; Burial, Schenectady, Schenectady, New York,
  United States of America, Saint John the Baptist Cemetery; citing
  record ID 205398476, Find a Grave, http://www.findagrave.com.
- "United States, Social Security Numerical Identification Files
  (NUMIDENT), 1936-2007", database, FamilySearch
  (https://www.familysearch.org/ark:/61903/1:1:6K9S-NPFD : 10
  February 2023), Angelo Demeo in entry for Michael Angelo Demeo, .
- "St. Anthony, Schenectady, New York, deaths (Oct 1916 -Jun 2007)",
  American-Canadian Genealogical Society, Manchester, NH, page 113

203) Maria Raimonda Fodarella

Maria Raimonda Fodarella(203) was born about December 1887, in Ariano, Italy,
to Lorenzo Fodarella(48) and Maria Fransesca Paola Dotolo(48a).

Maria Raimonda Fodarella(203) married Nicola Sicuranza(203a) on 20 October
1910 in Ariano, Italy.

Nicola Sicuranza(203a) was born on 9 May 1886, in Ariano, Italy, to Francesco
Sicuranza(203aF) and Concetta Sisbarra(203aM).

Known Children of Maria Raimonda Fodarella(203) and Nicola Sicuranza(203a):

    i) Concetta Angiolina Sicuranza(430) born in 1912
    ii) Francesco Sicuranza(449) born in 1914

Records that include Maria Raimonda Fodarella(203) and/or Nicola
Sicuranza(203a):
- Ariano, Italy 1886 Birth Act #287
- Ariano, Italy 1887 Birth Act #733
- Ariano, Italy 1910 Marriage Act #93

- Ariano, Italy 1912 Birth Act #33
- Ariano, Italy 1914 Birth Act #68

204) Filippo Ciasullo

Filippo Ciasullo(204) was born about December 1887, in Ariano, Italy, to Michele Ciasullo(82a) and Filomena Perrina(82). Filippo Ciasullo(204) died 26 August 1888 in Ariano, Italy.

Records that include Filippo Ciasullo:
- Ariano, Italy 1887 Birth Act #745
- Ariano, Italy 1888 Death Act #378

NOTE: The birth record is not available but was indexed.

NOTE: Many Ariano birth records for the years 1888 - 1890 no longer exist.

205) Carmela Manganiello

Carmela Manganiello(205) was born 8 January 1888, in Ariano, Italy, to Giuseppe Manganiello(64a) and Maria Fransesca Fodarella(63). Carmela Manganiello(205) died on 20 May 1934 in Ariano, Italy.

Carmela Manganiello(205) married Francesco Paolo Lo Conte(205a) on 2 March 1907 in Ariano, Italy.

Francesco Paolo Lo Conte(205a) was born on 18 June 1887, in Ariano, Italy, to Antonio Lo Conte(205aF) and Anna Maria Miedico(205aM). Francesco Paolo Lo Conte(205a) died 17 June 1934 in Ariano, Italy.

Known Children of Carmela Manganiello(205) and Francesco Paolo Lo Conte(205a):

   i) Maria Lo Conte(398) born in 1908
   ii) Giuseppe Lo Conte(435) born in 1912
   iii) Antonio Lo Conte(454) born in 1914
   iv) Angiolina Lo Conte(492) born about 1919

Records that include Carmela Manganiello(205) and/or Francesco Paolo Lo Conte(205a):
- Ariano, Italy 1887 Birth Act #414
- Ariano, Italy 1888 Birth Act #24
- Ariano, Italy 1907 Marriage Act #39
- Ariano, Italy 1908 Birth Act #95
- Ariano, Italy 1912 Birth Act #416
- Ariano, Italy 1914 Birth Act #576
- Ariano, Italy 1921 Death Act #261
- Ariano, Italy 1934 Death Act #133
- Ariano, Italy 1934 Death Act #151

206) Antonio (Anthony) Giorgione/George

Antonio (Anthony) Giorgione/George(206) was born on 5 or 9 January 1888 in Ariano, Italy, to Luigi (Louis) Giorgione/George(86) and Maria Giovanna Perillo(86a).

Records that include Antonio (Anthony) Giorgione/George(206):
- Ariano, Italy 1888 Birth Act #31
- "New York State Census, 1915", , FamilySearch (https://www.familysearch.org/ark:/61903/1:1:K9GM-56V : 1 June 2022), Tony George in entry for Louie George, 1915.
- "United States World War I Draft Registration Cards, 1917-1918", , FamilySearch (https://www.familysearch.org/ark:/61903/1:1:KXBQ-N1G : 30 June 2024), Antonio Giorgione, 1917-1918.
- "United States World War I Draft Registration Cards, 1917-1918", database with images, FamilySearch (https://www.familysearch.org/ark:/61903/1:1:WDH6-MTW2 : 10 July 2024), Antonio Giorgione, 1917-1918.

- "United States Census, 1930", , FamilySearch
  (https://www.familysearch.org/ark:/61903/1:1:X4R1-NCJ : Sun Mar 10
  15:50:00 UTC 2024), Entry for Anthony George and Jennie George,
  1930.
- "United States Census, 1940", , FamilySearch
  (https://www.familysearch.org/ark:/61903/1:1:KQGP-XN8 : Sun Mar 10
  21:26:22 UTC 2024), Entry for Anthony George and Joseph George,
  1940.
- "United States World War II Draft Registration Cards, 1942", ,
  FamilySearch (https://www.familysearch.org/ark:/61903/1:1:QKVQ-N35D
  : Sat Feb 24 00:53:58 UTC 2024), Entry for Anthony George and
  Joanna George, 25 Apr 1942.
- "United States, Social Security Numerical Identification Files
  (NUMIDENT), 1936-2007", database, FamilySearch
  (https://www.familysearch.org/ark:/61903/1:1:6K4V-V6WP : 11
  February 2023), Anthony George, .

NOTE: Most birth records for 1888 not available - information gained from
index for that year.

207) Concetta D'Ausilio

Concetta D'Ausilio(207) was born in January or February 1888, in Ariano,
Italy, to Nicola Maria D'Ausilio(83) and Giustina Mariano(83a). Concetta
D'Ausilio(207) died on 12 November 1889, in Ariano, Italy.

Records that include Concetta D'Ausilio(207):
- Ariano, Italy 1888 Birth Act #75
- Ariano, Italy 1889 Death Act #340

NOTE: Most birth records for 1888 not available - information gained from
index for that year.

208) Raffaela Altanese

Raffaela Altanese(208) was born about 1888 in Grottaminarda, Italy to Cosimo
Altanese(87) and Margarita Galgothia Alfonsina Romano(87a). Raffaela
Altanese(208) died on 12 December 1895 in Grottaminarda, Italy.

Records that include Raffaela Altanese(208):
- Grottaminarda, Italy 1895 Death Act #98

209) Concetta Ninfadoro

Concetta Ninfadoro(209) was born 16 June 1888, in Ariano, Italy, to Gabriele
Ninfadoro(67a) and Mariangela Perrina(66a). Concetta Ninfadoro(209) died on 13
July 1896 in Ariano, Italy.

Records that include Concetta Ninfadoro(209):
- Ariano, Italy 1888 Birth Act #344
- Ariano, Italy 1896 Death Act #306

210) Generoso deDonato

Generoso deDonato(210) was born 10 November 1888, in Ariano, Italy, to
Domenico deDonato(61) and Anna Maria Coppola(61a). Generoso deDonato(210) died
on 3 December 1888, in Ariano, Italy.

Records that include Generoso deDonato(210):
- Ariano, Italy 1888 Birth Act #617
- Ariano, Italy 1888 Death Act #485

NOTE: Birth record not available - information gained from index for that
year.

211) Michele Grasso

Michele Grasso(211) was born about July 1888, in Ariano, Italy, to Lorenzo
Grasso(45a) and Anna Maria Perrina(45). Michele Grasso(211) died on 2 April
1889, in Ariano, Italy.

Records that include Michele Grasso(211):
- Ariano, Italy 1889 Death Act #119

212) Antonio Pietracola

Antonio Pietracola(212) was born 8 March 1889 in Ariano, Italy to Pasqualantonio Pietracola(55b) and Aurelia Fiorenza(55).

Antonio Pietracola(212) married Marianna Ciano(212a) on 23 February 1913 in Ariano, Italy.

Marianna Ciano(212a) was born on 30 April 1886 in Ariano, Italy to Generoso Ciano(212aF) and Concordia d'Amico(212aM). Marianna Ciano(212a) died on 21 February 1920 in Teano, Italy.

Known Children of Antonio Pietracola(212) and Marianna Ciano(212a):

  i) Pasquale Pietracola(453) born in 1914

Records that include Antonio Pietracola(212) and Marianna Ciano(212a):
  • Ariano, Italy 1886 Birth Act #277
  • Ariano, Italy 1888 Birth Act #164
  • Ariano, Italy 1913 Marriage Act #31
  • Ariano, Italy 1914 Birth Act #328
  • Ariano, Italy 1921 Death Act #II.A1

213) Mariantonia Perrina

Mariantonia Perrina(213) was born 14 January 1889, in Ariano, Italy, to Angelo Maria Perrina(74) and Tommasina Paduano(74a).

Mariantonia Perrina(213) married Angelo Pannese(213a) on 6 March 1913 in Ariano, Italy.

Angelo Pannese(213a) was born on 14 April 1889, in Ariano, Italy, to Ciriaco Pannese(213aF) and Vincenza Lo Surdo(213aM).

Known Children of Mariantonia Perrina(213) and Angelo Pannese(213a):

  i) Maria Vincenza Pannese(448) born in 1914
  ii) Tommasina Pannese(510) born about 1920

Records that include Mariantonia Perrina(213) and/or Angelo Pannese(213a):
  • Ariano, Italy 1889 Birth Act #34
  • Ariano, Italy 1889 Birth Act #271
  • Ariano, Italy 1913 Marriage Act #36
  • Ariano, Italy 1914 Birth Act #58
  • Ariano, Italy 1925 Death Act #161
  • Ariano, Italy 1937 Marriage Act #PIIA160

214) Otomaria Fodarella

Otomaria Fodrella(214) was born 14 October 1889 in Ariano, Italy to Lorenzo Fodarella(48) and Maria Fransesca Paola Dotolo(48a).

Otomaria Fodrella(214) married Angela Maria Riccio(214a) on 25 September 1919 in Ariano, Italy.

Angela Maria Riccio(214a) was born on 30 January 1893 in Ariano, Italy to Giovanni Riccio(214aF) and Concetta Mingolelli(214aM).

Records that include Otomaria Fodrella(214) and/or Angela Maria Riccio(214a):
  • Ariano, Italy 1889 Birth Act #635
  • Ariano, Italy 1893 Birth Act #70
  • Ariano, Italy 1919 Marriage Act #86

215) Pasquale Di Lillo

Pasquale Di Lillo(215) was born 16 October 1889, in Ariano, Italy, to Nicola Maria di Lillo(51a) and Angela Perrina(52). Pasquale Di Lillo(215) died on 5 February 1891, in Ariano, Italy.

Records that include Pasquale Di Lillo:
- Ariano, Italy 1889 Birth Act #640
- Ariano, Italy 1891 Death Act #40

216) Filomena Giorgione

Filomena Giorgione(216) was born 18 January 1889, in Ariano, Italy, to Raffaele Giorgione(80) and Carmina Salvioli(80a). Filomena Giorgione(216) died on 11 July 1889, in Ariano, Italy.

Records that include Filomena Giorgione(216):
- Ariano, Italy 1889 Birth Act #50
- Ariano, Italy 1889 Death Act #190

217) Angelo Michele Di Lillo

Angelo Michele Di Lillo(217) was born 11 April 1889, in Ariano, Italy, to Raffaele Di Lillo(95a) and Raimonda Perrina(95). Angelo Michele Di Lillo(217) died on 14 February 1890, in Ariano, Italy.

Records that include Angelo Michele Di Lillo(217):
- Ariano, Italy 1889 Birth Act #260
- Ariano, Italy 1890 Death Act #91

218) Feliciano Lombardi

Feliciano Lombardi(218) was born on 2 June 1889, in Apice, Italy, to Vincenzo (James) Lombardi(85a) and Maria Carmela deDonato(85). Feliciano Lombardi(218) died before 1892 when the parents had another son they named Feliciano, however, the Apice, Italy death records are not available for that period.

Records that include Feliciano Lombardi(218):
- Apice, Italy 1889 Birth Act #81
- "Italia, Benevento, Stato Civile (Archivio di Stato), 1810-1942", , FamilySearch (https://www.familysearch.org/ark:/61903/1:1:QL2J-MZ6D : Sun Mar 10 13:18:32 UTC 2024), Entry for Luigi di Donato and Marcello di Donato, 11 novembre 1889.

219) Luigi deDonato

Luigi deDonato(219) was born on 11 November 1889 in Paduli, Italy to Marcello deDonato(78) and Maria Rosa Politano(78a).

Records that include Luigi deDonato(219):
- Paduli, Italy 1889 Birth Act #187

220) Maria Concetta D'Ausilio

Maria Concetta D'Ausilio(220) was born on 16 November 1889, in Ariano, Italy, to Nicola Maria D'Ausilio(83) and Giustina Mariano(83a).

Records that include Maria Concetta D'Ausilio(220):
- Ariano, Italy 1889 Birth Act #701

221) Giovanna(Jenny) Ciasullo

Giovanna (Jenny) Ciasullo(221) was born about 29 November 1889, in Ariano, Italy, to Michele Ciasullo(82a) and Filomena Perrina(82). Giovanna (Jenny) Ciasullo(221) died September 1972 in Schenectady, NY.

Giovanna (Jenny) Ciasullo(221) married Raffaele Riccio(221a) on 5 November 1908 in Ariano, Italy.

Raffaele Riccio(221a) was born on 28 May 1885, in Ariano, Italy, to Pietro Riccio(183aF)(221aF) and Anna Ardito(183aM)(221aM). Raffaele Riccio(221a) emigrated to the United States on board the ship SS America, arriving in New York on 27 March 1912 from Naples, Italy. Raffaele Riccio(221a) died July 1965 in Schenectady, NY.

Known children of Giovanna (Jenny) Ciasullo(221) and Raffaele Riccio(221a):

> i) Anna Riccio(424) born in 1911
> ii) Filomena Riccio(447) born in 1913
> iii) Michael Sam Riccio(463) born in 1915
> iv) Anthony Riccio(483) born in 1917
> v) Peter Attilio Riccio(491) born in 1918
> vi) Angelo H Riccio(518) born in 1921
> vii) Philomena (Filomena) B Riccio(522) born in 1922

Records that include Giovanna (Jenny) Ciasullo(221) and/or Raffaele Riccio(221a):

- Ariano, Italy 1885 Birth Act #368
- Ariano, Italy 1889 Birth Act #724
- Ariano, Italy 1908 Marriage Act #137
- Ariano, Italy 1911 Birth Act #402
- Ariano, Italy 1913 Birth Act #668
- "New York Passenger Arrival Lists (Ellis Island), 1892-1924", , FamilySearch (https://www.familysearch.org/ark:/61903/1:1:JJ51-H3L : Sat Mar 09 01:09:04 UTC 2024), Entry for Raffaele Riccio and Giovanna, 1912.
- "United States World War I Draft Registration Cards, 1917-1918", database with images, FamilySearch (https://www.familysearch.org/ark:/61903/1:1:WZNL-VSMM : 10 July 2024), Raffaele Riccio, 1917-1918.
- "New York, County Naturalization Records, 1791-1980", , FamilySearch (https://www.familysearch.org/ark:/61903/1:1:74NT-LGW2 : Sat Mar 09 17:22:53 UTC 2024), Entry for Raffael Riccio and Jennie, 1920.
- "New York, County Naturalization Records, 1791-1980", , FamilySearch (https://www.familysearch.org/ark:/61903/1:1:74MG-CRT2 : Thu Mar 07 10:13:15 UTC 2024), Entry for Raphael Riccio and Giovannina, 1928.
- "United States Census, 1930", , FamilySearch (https://www.familysearch.org/ark:/61903/1:1:X4TB-187 : Fri Mar 08 12:10:26 UTC 2024), Entry for Ralph Riccio and Jennie Riccio, 1930.
- "United States Census, 1940", , FamilySearch (https://www.familysearch.org/ark:/61903/1:1:K79V-TYQ : Sat Mar 09 17:46:14 UTC 2024), Entry for Ralph Riccio and Jennie Riccio, 1940.
- "United States World War II Draft Registration Cards, 1942", , FamilySearch (https://www.familysearch.org/ark:/61903/1:1:QKVQ-1KWJ : Sat Feb 24 00:26:06 UTC 2024), Entry for Ralph Riccio and Riccio, 26 Apr 1942.
- "United States Census, 1950", , FamilySearch (https://www.familysearch.org/ark:/61903/1:1:6XR7-3VHN : Wed Mar 20 20:19:14 UTC 2024), Entry for Ralph Riccio and Jennie Riccio, 27 April 1950.
- "United States Social Security Death Index," , FamilySearch (https://familysearch.org/ark:/61903/1:1:JBGD-Q2Z : 7 January 2021), Ralph Riccio, Jul 1965; citing U.S. Social Security Administration, Death Master File, database (Alexandria, Virginia: National Technical Information Service, ongoing).
- "United States Social Security Death Index," , FamilySearch (https://familysearch.org/ark:/61903/1:1:JR97-MZP : 7 January 2021), Jennie Riccio, Sep 1972; citing U.S. Social Security Administration, Death Master File, database (Alexandria, Virginia: National Technical Information Service, ongoing).
- "United States, Social Security Numerical Identification Files (NUMIDENT), 1936-2007", database, FamilySearch (https://www.familysearch.org/ark:/61903/1:1:6K9W-38HP : 10 February 2023), Ralph Riccio in entry for Michael Sam Riccio, .
- "United States, Social Security Numerical Identification Files (NUMIDENT), 1936-2007", database, FamilySearch (https://www.familysearch.org/ark:/61903/1:1:6KML-8K12 : 10 February 2023), Ralph Riccio in entry for Peter Attilio Riccio, .

222) Pasquale Leonardo Pietro deDonato

Pasquale Leonardo Pietro deDonato(222) was born 8 February 1890, in Ariano, Italy, to Domenico deDonato(61) and Anna Maria Coppola(61a). Pasquale Leonardo Pietro deDonato(222) died on 2 February 1893, in Ariano, Italy.

Records that include Pasquale Leonardo Pietro deDonato(222):
* Ariano, Italy 1890 Birth Act #84
* Ariano, Italy 1893 Death Act #35

223) Carmela Grasso

Carmela Grasso(223) was born 26 February 1890, in Ariano, Italy, to Lorenzo Grasso(45a) and Anna Maria Perrina(44a). Carmela Grasso(223) was a farmhand/laborer.

Carmela Grasso(223) married Antonio Zarrillo(223a) on 10 August 1911 in Ariano, Italy.

Antonio Zarrillo(223a) was born 22 June 1887, in Ariano, Italy, to Michelangelo Zarrillo(223aF) and Rosa loConte(223aM).

Known Children of Carmela Grasso(223) and Antonio Zarrillo(223a):

i) Domenico Zarrillo(586) born about 1932

Records that include Carmela Grasso(223) and/or Antonio Zarrillo(223a):
* Ariano, Italy 1887 Birth Act #82
* Ariano, Italy 1889 Birth Act #146
* Ariano, Italy 1911 Marriage Act #82
* Ariano, Italy 1933 Death Act #60

224) Antonio Perrina

Antonio Perrina(224) was born on 23 March 1890 in Castel Baronia, Italy to Raffaele Perrina(58) and Maria Lucia Gesa(58a). Antonio Perrina(224) lived in Schenectady, NY.

Records that include Antonio Perrina(224):
* "United States Census, 1910," database with images, FamilySearch (https://familysearch.org/ark:/61903/1:1:M596-H5L : accessed 14 July 2023), Antonio Perrino in household of Raffaele Perrino, Schenectady Ward 7, Schenectady, New York, United States; citing enumeration district (ED) ED 196, sheet 10A, family 211, NARA microfilm publication T624 (Washington D.C.: National Archives and Records Administration, 1982), roll 1078; FHL microfilm 1,375,091.
* "New York State Census, 1915", database, FamilySearch (https://www.familysearch.org/ark:/61903/1:1:K9P8-7C8 : 3 June 2022), Anthony Perrino in entry for Ralph Perrino, 1915.
* "United States World War I Draft Registration Cards, 1917-1918", database with images, FamilySearch (https://www.familysearch.org/ark:/61903/1:1:WZNT-SQZM : 10 July 2024), Anthony Perrino, 1917-1918.
* "United States World War I Draft Registration Cards, 1917-1918", database with images, FamilySearch (https://www.familysearch.org/ark:/61903/1:1:KXB8-CPJ : 26 December 2021), Anthony Perrino, 1917-1918.

225) Maria Antonia di Lillo

Maria Antonia di Lillo(225) was born on 20 January 1891, in Ariano, Italy, to Raffaele di Lillo 658 and Raimonda Perrina 657.

Maria Antonia di Lillo(225) married Angelo Maria Baviello(225a) on 12 June 1913 in Ariano, Italy.

Angelo Maria Baviello(225a) was born on 2 December 1894, in Ariano, Italy, to Oto Maria Baviello(225aF) and Carmina Faretra(225aM). Angelo Maria Baviello(225a) died 12 September 1976 in Ariano, Italy.

Known Children of Maria Antonia di Lillo(225) and Angelo Maria Baviello(225a):

> i) Oto Baviello(498) born in 1918
> ii) Edigio Baviello(575) born in 1930

Records that include Maria Antonia di Lillo(225) and/or Angelo Maria Baviello(225a):

- Ariano, Italy 1891 Birth Act #55
- Ariano, Italy 1894 Birth Act #646
- Ariano, Italy 1913 Marriage Act #71
- Ariano, Italy 1918 Birth Act #246
- Ariano, Italy 1931 Death Act #104
- Ariano, Italy 1939 Marriage Act #30

226) Giovanni Miressi

Giovanni Miressi(226) was born on 2 April 1891, in Ariano, Italy, to Giuseppe Miressi(51a) and Rosa Giorgione(51). Giovanni Miressi(226)Joined the United States Army on July 22, 1918 and was discharged 30 December 1918. Giovanni Miressi(226) was naturalized in May's Landing, NJ on 21 December 1918. Giovanni Miressi(226) died on 29 July 1977 in Middletown, NY.

Giovanni Miressi(226) married Florence Emily Wilson(226a) on 23 December 1917 in Middletown, NY.

Florence Emily Wilson(226a) was born 3 April 1894 in England to William Henry Wilson(226aF) and Mary Ann Orton(226aM). Florence Emily Wilson(226a) died in 1944 in Manhattan, New York. Florence Emily Wilson(226a) was buried 7 July 1944 in Phillipsburg, NY.

Known Children of Giovanni Miressi(226) and Florence Emily Wilson(226a):

> i) Frances Eva Miressi(487) born in 1918
> ii) Rosalind Miressi(497) born in 1919
> iii) John William Miressi(540) born in 1924
> * Giovanni Miressi(226) and Florence Emily Wilson(226a) also
>   have Living Children and/or children's spouse(s).

Records that include Giovanni Miressi(226) and/or Florence Emily Wilson(226a):

- Ariano, Italy 1891 Birth Act #248
- "United States World War I Draft Registration Cards, 1917-1918", database with images, FamilySearch (https://www.familysearch.org/ark:/61903/1:1:KZJ1-2Z1 : 31 December 2021), Giovanni Miressi, 1917-1918.
- "United States World War I Draft Registration Cards, 1917-1918", database with images, FamilySearch (https://www.familysearch.org/ark:/61903/1:1:7DF5-GZZM : 6 July 2024), Giovanni Miressi, 1917-1918.
- "United States, Veterans Administration Master Index, 1917-1940", , FamilySearch (https://www.familysearch.org/ark:/61903/1:1:W99W-N6T2 : Sat Mar 09 17:30:43 UTC 2024), Entry for Giovanni Miressi, 30 December 1918.
- "New Jersey, County Naturalization Records, 1749-1986", , FamilySearch (https://www.familysearch.org/ark:/61903/1:1:6CBT-B12L : Sun Mar 10 22:39:22 UTC 2024), Entry for Yiovanni Miressi and Lorence Emily, 21 Dec 1918.
- "New York, County Marriages, 1847-1848; 1908-1936," database with images, FamilySearch (https://familysearch.org/ark:/61903/1:1:XVPV-9Z4 : 9 March 2021), John Mirissi, 23 Dec 1917, New York, United States; citing ref. ID 9135, county clerk offices from various counties, New York; FHL microfilm 829,655.
- "United States Census, 1920", , FamilySearch (https://www.familysearch.org/ark:/61903/1:1:MV9F-9G9 : Sat Mar 09 10:15:10 UTC 2024), Entry for John Miressie and Florence Miressie, 1920.
- "United States Census, 1930", , FamilySearch (https://www.familysearch.org/ark:/61903/1:1:X4R1-4DV : Sun Mar 10 13:51:06 UTC 2024), Entry for John Miressi, 1930.

- "United States Census, 1940", , FamilySearch (https://www.familysearch.org/ark:/61903/1:1:KQGP-K5S : Sun Jul 14 13:44:31 UTC 2024), Entry for John Miressi and Florence Miressi, 1940.
- "United States World War II Draft Registration Cards, 1942", , FamilySearch (https://www.familysearch.org/ark:/61903/1:1:QKVQ-PYK5 : Sat Feb 24 00:40:05 UTC 2024), Entry for John Miressi and Florence Miressi, 27 Apr 1942.
- "New York, New York City Municipal Deaths, 1795-1949", database, FamilySearch (https://www.familysearch.org/ark:/61903/1:1:2WPV-668 : 13 May 2022), Florence Miressi, 1944.
- "Find A Grave Index," database, FamilySearch (https://www.familysearch.org/ark:/61903/1:1:QVVW-423J : 1 April 2023), Florence E. Wilson Miressi, ; Burial, Phillipsburg, Orange, New York, United States of America, Wallkill Cemetery; citing record ID 8871826, Find a Grave, http://www.findagrave.com.
- "United States Census, 1950", , FamilySearch (https://www.familysearch.org/ark:/61903/1:1:6XPZ-ZBX5 : Thu Oct 05 22:40:54 UTC 2023), Entry for John Miressi, April 8, 1950.
- "United States Social Security Death Index," , FamilySearch (https://familysearch.org/ark:/61903/1:1:JKNV-BZC : 7 January 2021), John Miressi, Jul 1977; citing U.S. Social Security Administration, Death Master File, database (Alexandria, Virginia: National Technical Information Service, ongoing).
- "Find a Grave Index," database, FamilySearch (https://www.familysearch.org/ark:/61903/1:1:QVVW-4KCK : 1 April 2023), John Miressi, ; Burial, Phillipsburg, Orange, New York, United States of America, Wallkill Cemetery; citing record ID 8871823, Find a Grave, http://www.findagrave.com.
- "United States, Social Security Numerical Identification Files (NUMIDENT), 1936-2007", database, FamilySearch (https://www.familysearch.org/ark:/61903/1:1:6KMR-JXNW : 10 February 2023), John Miressi in entry for John William Miressi, .

227) Rosaria Perrina

Rosaria Perrina(227) was born on 7 April 1891, in Ariano, Italy, to Angelo Maria Perrina(74) and Tommasina Paduano(74a). Rosaria Perrina(227) died on 17 April 1898 in Ariano, Italy.

Records that include Rosaria Perrina(227):
- Ariano, Italy 1891 Birth Act #264
- Ariano, Italy 1898 Death Act #158

228) Giuseppe Giorgione

Giuseppe Giorgione(228) was born on 23 April 1891, in Ariano, Italy, to Raffaele Giorgione(80) and Carmina Salvioli(80a). Giuseppe Giorgione(228) died on 17 November 1892 in Ariano, Italy.

Records that include Giuseppe Giorgione(228):
- Ariano, Italy 1891 Birth Act #309
- Ariano, Italy 1892 Death Act #429

229) Mariangela Fodarella

Mariangela Fodarella(229) was born on 30 April 1891, in Ariano, Italy, to Lorenzo Fodarella(48) and Maria Fransesca Paola Dotolo(48a). Mariangela Fodarella(229) died on 23 October 1962 in Ariano, Italy.

Records that include Mariangela Fodarella(229):
- Ariano, Italy 1891 Birth Act #320

230) Nicola Maria Anastasio

Nicola Maria Anastasio(230) was born on 25 September 1891, in Ariano, Italy, to Pasquale Antonio Anastasio(72a) and Anna Maria D'Ausilio(72). Nicola Maria Anastasio(230) lived in St. Louis, MO in 1910.

Records that include Nicola Maria Anastasio(230):
- Ariano, Italy 1891 Birth Record #576
- "United States Census, 1910," database with images, FamilySearch (https://familysearch.org/ark:/61903/1:1:MLMM-7Y8), Nicolo Unastasio in household of Pasquale Unastasio, St Louis Ward 26, St Louis (Independent City), Missouri, United States; citing enumeration district (ED) ED 416, sheet 5A, family 104, NARA microfilm publication T624 (Washington D.C.: National Archives and Records Administration, 1982), roll 822; FHL microfilm 1,374,835.

231) Antonia Ciasullo

Antonia Ciasullo(231) was born on 2 January 1892, in Ariano, Italy, to Michele Ciasullo(82a) and Filomena Perrina(82).

Records that include Antonia Ciasullo(231):
- Ariano, Italy 1892 Birth Act #1

232) Mariangela Ciasullo

Mariangela Ciasullo(232) was stillborn on 2 January 1892, in Ariano, Italy, to Michele Ciasullo(82a) and Filomena Perrina(82).

Records that include Mariangela Ciasullo(232):
- Ariano, Italy 1892 Birth Act #2

233) Raffaele Giorgione

Raffaele Giorgione(233) was born on 4 January 1892, in Ariano, Italy, to Luigi (Louis) Giorgione/George(86) and Maria Giovanna Perillo(86a). Raffaele Giorgione(233) died on 5 February 1892 in Ariano, Italy.

Records that include Raffaele Giorgione(233):
- Ariano, Italy 1892 Birth Act #14
- Ariano, Italy 1892 Death Act #47

234) Giuseppe deDonato

Giuseppe deDonato(234) was born on 13 April 1892, in Paduli, Italy, to Marcello deDonato(78) and Maria Rosa Politano(78a).

Records that include Giuseppe deDonato(234):
- Paduli, Italy 1892 Birth Act #39

235) Filomena Maria Rosaria Altanese

Filomena Maria Rosaria Altanese(235) was born 24 April 1892 in Grottaminarda, Italy to Cosimo Altanese(87) and Margharita Romano(87a). Filomena Maria Rosaria Altanese(235) died 2 November 1895 in Grottaminarda, Italy.

Records that include Filomena Maria Rosaria Altanese(235):
- Grottaminarda, Italy 1892 Birth Act #59
- Grottaminarda, Italy 1895 Death Act #91

236) Feliciano (Phillip White) Lombardi

Feliciano (Phillip White) Lombardi(236) was born on 18 May 1892, in Apice, Italy, to Vincenzo (James) Lombardi(85a) and Maria Carmela deDonato(85). On 21 April 1907 Feliciano (Phillip White) Lombardi(236) boarded the ship SS Creticin Naples, Italy. Feliciano (Phillip White) Lombardi(236) arrived in New York, NY on 6 May 1907. Feliciano (Phillip White) Lombardi(236) became a citizen of the United States on 12 November 1943 in Los Angeles, CA. Feliciano (Phillip White) Lombardi(236) was a Singing Teacher. Feliciano (Phillip White) Lombardi(236) died on 22 April 1961 in Los Angeles, CA.

Feliciano (Phillip White) Lombardi(236) married Mabel Grassie(236a) and Sylvia Noris Coari(236b).

Mabel Grassie(236a) was born about 1892, in New York, NY.

Known Children of Felici (Phillip White) Lombardi(236) and Mabel Grassie(236a):

    i) Eleanor Lombardi(436) born in 1912
    ii) George Vincent Lombardi(473) born in 1916

Feliciano (Phillip White) Lombardi(236) married Sylvia Noris Coari(236b) on 2 December 1931 in Mahattan, NY.

Sylvia Noris Coari(236b) was born on 30 July 1893, in New York, NY, to Luigi Noris Coari(236bF) and Rosa Neri(236bM). Sylvia Noris Coari(236b) died 9 October 1986 in Los Angeles, CA.

Known children of Feliciano (Phillip White) Lombardi(236) and Sylvia Noris Coari(236b):

    i)Raymond Coari Lombardi(516) born about 1922

Records that include Feliciano (Phillip White) Lombardi(236), Mabel Grassie (211a), and/or Sylvia Noris Coari(236b).
- Apice, Italy 1892 Birth Act #69
- "Italia, Benevento, Stato Civile (Archivio di Stato), 1810-1942", , FamilySearch (https://www.familysearch.org/ark:/61903/1:1:QGJ2-CZDK : Fri Mar 08 18:49:21 UTC 2024), Entry for Feliciano Lombardi and Vincenzo Lombardi, 18 maggio 1892.
- "New York Passenger Arrival Lists (Ellis Island), 1892-1924", , FamilySearch (https://www.familysearch.org/ark:/61903/1:1:JX6K-7ZP : Wed Jul 10 19:20:25 UTC 2024), Entry for Feliciano Lombardi and Vincenzo, 06 May 1907.
- "United States Census, 1910", , FamilySearch (https://www.familysearch.org/ark:/61903/1:1:X39X-C53 : Fri Mar 08 11:50:32 UTC 2024), Entry for James Lombardi and Carmelo Lombardi, 1910.
- "United States Census, 1900", , FamilySearch (https://www.familysearch.org/ark:/61903/1:1:MSJ2-STR : Thu Apr 11 20:47:56 UTC 2024), Entry for Louis Coari and Rosie Coari, 1900.
- "United States World War I Draft Registration Cards, 1917-1918", database with images, FamilySearch (https://www.familysearch.org/ark:/61903/1:1:W5Q2-QGW2 : 10 July 2024), Felice Lombardi, 1917-1918.
- "United States Census, 1920", database with images, FamilySearch (https://www.familysearch.org/ark:/61903/1:1:MJPX-9XJ : 2 February 2021), Mabel Lombardi in entry for Felice Lombardi, 1920.
- "United States Census, 1910", , FamilySearch (https://www.familysearch.org/ark:/61903/1:1:MKKV-GVL : Thu Mar 07 09:54:54 UTC 2024), Entry for Louis Coari and Rose Coari, 1910.
- "United States Census, 1920", , FamilySearch (https://www.familysearch.org/ark:/61903/1:1:MJPX-9XN : Thu Mar 07 22:40:59 UTC 2024), Entry for Felice Lombardi and Mabel Lombardi, 1920.
- "New York, New York City Marriage Records, 1829-1938", , FamilySearch (https://www.familysearch.org/ark:/61903/1:1:24D8-P23 : Tue Feb 20 17:49:15 UTC 2024), Entry for Philip H. Lombardi and Sylvia Noris Coari, 2 Dec 1931.
- "New York, New York City Marriage Records, 1829-1938", database, FamilySearch (https://www.familysearch.org/ark:/61903/1:1:Q2CF-FP8F : 17 August 2022), Mabelle Grassie in entry for Joseph Castroziavanni and Eleanor C Lombardi, 1936.
- "United States Census, 1940", , FamilySearch (https://www.familysearch.org/ark:/61903/1:1:K9CK-W43 : Sun Mar 10 11:32:40 UTC 2024), Entry for Phillip Lombardi and Sylvia Lombardi, 1940
- "United States World War II Draft Registration Cards, 1942", , FamilySearch (https://www.familysearch.org/ark:/61903/1:1:V4D4-DBS : Sat Feb 24 03:50:00 UTC 2024), Entry for Mr. Philip White Lombardi, 1942.

- "California, Southern District Court (Central) Naturalization Index, 1915-1976", , FamilySearch (https://www.familysearch.org/ark:/61903/1:1:KXQW-DRW : Tue Jul 09 15:52:39 UTC 2024), Entry for Philip White Or Feliciano Lombardi, 1943.
- "United States 1950 Census", database, FamilySearch (ark:/61903/1:1:6XT1-52SH : Tue Jul 11 05:12:00 UTC 2023), Entry for George V Lombardi and Joanne C Lombardi, 1 April 1950.
- "California Death Index, 1940-1997," , FamilySearch (https://familysearch.org/ark:/61903/1:1:VPCC-3MS : 26 November 2014), Philip W Lombardi, 22 Apr 1961; Department of Public Health Services, Sacramento.
- "California, County Birth and Death Records, 1800-1994", , FamilySearch (https://www.familysearch.org/ark:/61903/1:1:QGPX-C9FT : Thu Mar 07 10:24:20 UTC 2024), Entry for Philip White Lombardi and Vincent Lombardi, 22 April 1961.
- "United States, Social Security Numerical Identification Files (NUMIDENT), 1936-2007", database, FamilySearch (https://www.familysearch.org/ark:/61903/1:1:6KMR-MRM7 : 10 February 2023), George Vincent Lombardi, .
- "United States, Social Security Numerical Identification Files (NUMIDENT), 1936-2007", database, FamilySearch (https://www.familysearch.org/ark:/61903/1:1:6K44-7TYZ : 11 February 2023), Philip W Lombardi, .
- "Find A Grave Index," database, FamilySearch (https://www.familysearch.org/ark:/61903/1:1:Q2B1-VVHN : 7 August 2020), Mabelle Bassi, ; Burial, East Farmingdale, Suffolk, New York, United States of America, Saint Charles Cemetery; citing record ID 175792382, Find a Grave, http://www.findagrave.com.
- "United States Social Security Death Index," database, FamilySearch (https://familysearch.org/ark:/61903/1:1:JGH5-G6D : 11 January 2021), Sylvia Lombardi, Oct 1986; citing U.S. Social Security Administration, Death Master File, database (Alexandria, Virginia: National Technical Information Service, ongoing).
- "California Death Index, 1940-1997," , FamilySearch (https://familysearch.org/ark:/61903/1:1:VPF9-MY8 : 26 November 2014), Sylvia Coari Lombardi, 09 Oct 1986; Department of Public Health Services, Sacramento.

237) Maria Carmela Pietracola

Maria Carmelo Pietracola(237) was born on 23 June 1892, in Ariano, Italy to Pasqualantonio Pietracola(55b) and Aurelia Fiorenza(55).

Records that include Maria Carmelo Pietracola(237):
- Ariano, Italy 1892 Birth Act #320

238) Concetta Felicia Perrina

Concetta Felicia Perrina(238) was born on 8 July 1892, in Castel Baronia, Italy, to Raffaele Perrina(58) and Maria Lucia Gesa(58a). On 7 November 1903, Concetta Felicia Perrina(238) boarded the ship SS Perugia in Naples, Italy, arriving in New York, NY on 21 November 1903. Concetta Felicia Perrina(238) died on 12 May 1973 in Amsterdam, NY.

Concetta Felicia Perrina(238) married Ugo Miseno(238a) on 19 January 1911, in Schenectady, NY.

Ugo Miseno(238a) was born on 22 December 1885, in Solmona, Italy, to Lorenzo Miseno(238aF) and Francesca Susia(238aM). On 12 May 1902, Ugo Miseno(238a) sailed from Naples, Italy, on the ship Neckar, arriving in New York, NY on 26 May 1902. Ugo Miseno(238a) became a United States Citizen on 1 June 1920 in Amsterdam, NY. Ugo Miseno(238a) died on 8 July 1939, in Amsterdam, NY.

Known children of Concetta Felicia Perrina(238) and Ugo Miseno(238a):

i) Luciano Miseno(428) born in 1911
ii) Francesco Miseno(457) born in 1914
iii) Bruno Miseno(472) born in 1916

iv) Ugo Ralph Miseno(485) born in 1918

Records that include Concetta Felicia Perrina(238)and/or Ugo Miseno(238a):

- Castel Baronia, Italy 1892 Birth Act #26
- "Italia, Avellino, Stato Civile (Archivio di Stato), 1809-1947", , FamilySearch (https://www.familysearch.org/ark:/61903/1:1:7Z74-7Q2M : Sat Mar 09 17:27:21 UTC 2024), Entry for Concetta Felicia Perrino and Raffaele Perrino, 8 Jul 1892.
- "New York, New York, Index to Passengers Lists of Vessels, 1897-1902", , FamilySearch (https://www.familysearch.org/ark:/61903/1:1:6Z36-HF5D : Sat Mar 09 08:01:29 UTC 2024), Entry for Ugo Miseno, 1902.
- "New York Passenger Arrival Lists (Ellis Island), 1892-1924", , FamilySearch (https://www.familysearch.org/ark:/61903/1:1:JFYG-935 : Sun Mar 10 06:51:50 UTC 2024), Entry for Concetta Perrino and Raffaele Perrino, 1903.
- "United States Census, 1910", , FamilySearch (https://www.familysearch.org/ark:/61903/1:1:M596-H5V : Mon Jul 22 15:03:44 UTC 2024), Entry for Raffaele Perrino and Lucie Perrino, 1910.
- "New York, County Marriages, 1847-1848; 1908-1936", , FamilySearch (https://www.familysearch.org/ark:/61903/1:1:FFT7-26J : Fri Mar 08 17:33:51 UTC 2024), Entry for Ugo Miseno and Lorenzo, 19 January 1911.
- "St. John the Baptist, Schenectady, New York, Baptism (Oct 1854 – Jun 2009)", American-Canadian Genealogical Society, Manchester, NH, page 576
- "United States World War I Draft Registration Cards, 1917-1918", database with images, FamilySearch (https://www.familysearch.org/ark:/61903/1:1:WSWP-913Z : 10 July 2024), Ugo Miseno, 1917-1918.
- "New York, County Naturalization Records, 1791-1980", , FamilySearch (https://www.familysearch.org/ark:/61903/1:1:QPTW-8BMK : Mon Mar 11 01:57:06 UTC 2024), Entry for Ugo Miseno and Congetta, 1917.
- "New York, County Naturalization Records, 1791-1980", , FamilySearch (https://www.familysearch.org/ark:/61903/1:1:QP88-9BXG : Fri Mar 08 11:16:22 UTC 2024), Entry for Ugo Miseno and Congetta, 1917.
- "New York, County Naturalization Records, 1791-1980", , FamilySearch (https://www.familysearch.org/ark:/61903/1:1:KFXD-1XX : Fri Mar 08 01:50:26 UTC 2024), Entry for Ugo Miseno, 1920.
- "United States Census, 1920", , FamilySearch (https://www.familysearch.org/ark:/61903/1:1:MJGD-61J : Sun Mar 10 00:46:08 UTC 2024), Entry for Ugo Mireno and Concetta Mireno, 1920.
- "United States Census, 1930", , FamilySearch (https://www.familysearch.org/ark:/61903/1:1:X78V-MMP : Sun Mar 10 13:54:09 UTC 2024), Entry for Hugo Misseno and Conncetta Misseno, 1930.
- "New York, State Death Index, 1880-1956", , FamilySearch (https://www.familysearch.org/ark:/61903/1:1:QLB6-FVSJ : Thu Mar 07 21:23:57 UTC 2024), Entry for Ugo Miseno, 8 Jul 1939.
- "United States, Social Security Numerical Identification Files (NUMIDENT), 1936-2007", database, FamilySearch (https://www.familysearch.org/ark:/61903/1:1:6KMG-5FXC : 10 February 2023), Ugo Miseno, .
- "Find a Grave Index," database, FamilySearch (https://www.familysearch.org/ark:/61903/1:1:6FN2-ZG6G : 20 October 2022), Ugo Miseno Lombardi, ; Burial, Johnstown, Fulton, New York, United States of America, Mount Carmel Cemetery; citing record ID 237865735, Find a Grave, http://www.findagrave.com.
- "United States Census, 1940", , FamilySearch (https://www.familysearch.org/ark:/61903/1:1:KQ3M-2QT : Sun Jul 21 06:10:46 UTC 2024), Entry for Nickolas T Lombardi and Concetta Miseno, 1940.

- "United States Census, 1950", , FamilySearch (https://www.familysearch.org/ark:/61903/1:1:6X5W-XL1Q : Fri Oct 06 18:58:11 UTC 2023), Entry for Nicholas T Lombardi, Lombardi and Conccetta Miseno, 6 April 1950.
- "United States Social Security Death Index," database, FamilySearch (https://familysearch.org/ark:/61903/1:1:JKK3-46K : 7 January 2021), Concetta Miseno, May 1973; citing U.S. Social Security Administration, Death Master File, database (Alexandria, Virginia: National Technical Information Service, ongoing).
- "Find a Grave Index," database, FamilySearch (https://www.familysearch.org/ark:/61903/1:1:6FN2-DKX1 : 20 October 2022), Concetta Miseno, ; Burial, Johnstown, Fulton, New York, United States of America, Mount Carmel Cemetery; citing record ID 237986030, Find a Grave, http://www.findagrave.com.
- "United States, Social Security Numerical Identification Files (NUMIDENT), 1936-2007", database, FamilySearch (https://www.familysearch.org/ark:/61903/1:1:6KMG-QRCF : 10 February 2023), Ugo Miseno in entry for Lawrence Luciano Miseno, .

239) Maria Felicita Perrina

Maria Felicita Perrina(239) was born on 11 July 1892, in Ariano, Italy, to Michele Perrina(88) and Maria Grazia Caraglia(88a). Maria Felicita Perrina(239) died on 29 January 1969 in Villanova del Battista, Italy.

Maria Felicita Perrina(239) married Bennedetto Perrina(239a) on 7 March 1912 in Ariano, Italy.

Bennedetto Perrina(239a) was born on 16 February 1894, in Ariano, Italy, to Michele Perrina(239aF) and Maddalena Scarpellino(239aM).

Known Children of Maria Felicita Perrina(239) and Bennedetto Perrina(239a):

  i) Angelo Michele Perrina(444) born in 1913
  ii) Maria Maddalena Perrina(458) born about 1916
  iii) Raffaele Perrina(480) born in 1917

Records that include Maria Felicita Perrina(239) and/or Bennedetto Perrina(239a):
- Ariano, Italy 1892 Birth Act #380
- Ariano, Italy 1912 Marriage Act #30
- Villanova del Battista, Italy 1913 Birth Act #69
- Villanova del Battista, Italy 1914 Birth Act #107
- Villanova del Battista, Italy 1917 Death Act #19
- Villanova del Battista, Italy 1938 Marriage Act #7
- Villanova del Battista, Italy 2000 Death Act #5

240 Giovanbattista Grasso

Giovanbattista Grasso(240) was born on 28 October 1892, in Ariano, Italy, to Lorenzo Grasso(44) and Anna Maria Perrina(44a). Giovanbattista Grasso(240) died 13 August 1893 in Ariano, Italy.

Records that include Giovanbattista Grasso(240):
  Ariano, Italy 1892 Birth Act #570
  Ariano, Italy 1893 Death Act #243

241) Nicola Ciccarelli

Nicola Ciccarelli(241) was born on 31 December 1892, in Ariano, Italy, to Domenico Ciccarelli(69a) and Rosa Fiorenza(69).

Nicola Ciccarelli(241) married Lucia Mincolelli(241a) on 1 February 1912 in Ariano, Italy.

Lucia Mincolelli(241a) was born on 18 December 1893, in Ariano, Italy, to Antonio Mincolelli(241aF) and Maria Giuseppa Giorgione(241aM). Lucia Mincolelli(241a) died on 17 March 1958 in Ariano, Italy.

Known children of Nicola Ciccarelli(241) and Lucia Mincolelli(241a):

     i) Antonietta Ciccarelli(442) born in 1913
    ii) Dominica Ciccarelli(461) born in 1915

Records that include Nicola Ciccarelli(241) and/or Lucia Mincolelli(241a):
- Ariano, Italy 1893 Birth Act #3
- Ariano, Italy 1893 Birth Act #701
- Ariano, Italy 1912 Marriage Act #9
- Ariano, Italy 1913 Birth Act #69
- Ariano, Italy 1915 Birth Act #563
- Ariano, Italy 1917 Death Act #219
- Ariano, Italy 1931 Marriage Act #PIIA29

242) Leopoldo D'Ausilio

Leopoldo D'Ausilio(242) was born on 26 January 1893, in Ariano, Italy, to Nicola Maria D'Ausilio(83) and Giustina Mariano(83a). Leopoldo D'Ausilio(242) died on 9 May 1896 in Ariano, Italy.

Records that include Leopoldo D'Ausilio(242):
- Ariano, Italy 1893 Birth Act #53
- Ariano, Italy 1896 Death Act #81

243) Giovanni Ninfadoro

Giovanni Ninfadoro(243) was stillborn on 30 January 1893, in Ariano, Italy, to Gabriele Ninfadoro(67a) and Mariangela Perrina(67).

Records that include Giovanni Ninfadoro(243):
- Ariano, Italy 1893 Birth Act #60

244) Carmela Fodarella

Carmela Fodarella(244) was born on 15 February 1893, in Ariano, Italy, to Lorenzo Fodarella(48) and Maria Fransesca Paola Dotolo(48a).

Carmela Fodarella(244) married Pasquale Panza(244a) on 8 September 1927 in Ariano, Italy.

Pasquale Panza(244a) was born on 12 September 1881, in Ariano, Italy, to Francesco Panza(244aF) and Rosa Pratola(244aM).

Pasquale Panza(244a) previously married Maria Saveria Sicuranza(244aX).

Records that include Carmela Fodarella(244) and/or Pasquale Panza(244a):
- Ariano, Italy 1881 Birth Act #420
- Ariano, Italy 1893 Birth Act #110
- Ariano, Italy 1927 Marriage Act #139

245) Michele Ciasullo

Michele Ciasullo(245) was born on 8 April 1893, in Ariano, Italy, to Filippo Ciasullo(105a) and Maria Giovanna Perrina(105). Michele Ciasullo(245) died 23 November 1894 in Ariano, Italy.

Records that include Michele Ciasullo(245):
- Ariano, Italy 1893 Birth Act #225
- Ariano, Italy 1894 Death Act #404

246) Pasquale Perrina

Pasquale Perrina(246) was born on 24 February 1893, in Ariano, Italy, to Angelo Maria Perrina(74) and Tommasina Paduano(74a). Pasquale Perrina(246) died on 29 July 1894 in Ariano, Italy.

Records that include Pasquale Perrina(246):
- Ariano, Italy 1893 Birth Act #127

• Ariano, Italy 1894 Death Act #250

247) Carmine Perrina

Carmine Perrina(247) was born on 26 April 1893, in Castel Baronia, Italy, to Francesco Paolo Perrina(90) and Maria Cristina Sofia Leone(90a). Carmine Perrina(247) boarded the ship SS Taormina in Naples, Italy on 6 March 1912, arrived in New York on 12 March 1912. Carmine Perrina(247) served in the United States Military from 23 March 1918 to 5 June 1919. Carmine Perrina(247) was naturalized as a citizen of the United States on 21 June 1921 in Scranton, PA. Carmine Perrina(247) died in August of 1973 in Buffalo, NY.

Carmine Perrina(247) married Colomba di Pasquale(247a).

NOTE: There are some discrepancies in the records. Carmine Perrina(247)'s ship manifest, WWI draft card, declaration of Intention, and Petition for Naturalization, state that he is single. The 1920 Census shows him as married with children(the oldest being born in 1910, two years before he arrived in the United States).

Colomba di Pasquale(247a) was born 19 April 1890, in Teora, Italy, to Giovanni di Pasquale(247aF) and Maria Teresa Prudente(247aM). Colomba di Pasquale(247a) died 26 July 1957 in Buffalo, NY.

Known children on Carmine Perrina(247) and Colomba di Pasquale(247a):

    i) John Perrine(417) born in 1910
    ii) Paul (Frank) Perrine(433) born in 1912
    iii) Sofia (Susie) Perrine(446) born in 1913
    iv) Elena (Helen) Perrine(465) born about 1916
    v) Anthony Carmen Perrine(488) born in 1918
    vi) Ralph Carmen Perrine(531) born in 1923
    vii) Theresa Ann Perrine(551) born in 1926
    viii) Rena Perrine(569) born in 1929

Records that include Carmine Perrina(247) and/or Colomba di Pasquale(247a):
• Castel Baronia, Italy 1893 Birth Act #18
• "Italia, Avellino, Stato Civile (Archivio di Stato), 1809-1947", , FamilySearch (https://www.familysearch.org/ark:/61903/1:1:7FKQ-FY2M : Sun Mar 10 18:24:40 UTC 2024), Entry for Carmine Perrino and Francesco Paolo Perrino, 26 Apr 1893.
• https://www.phmc.state.pa.us/bah/dam/rg/di/r11_089_BirthIndexes/Birth_1910/1910%20-%20P.pdf page 133
• https://www.pa.gov/content/dam/copapwp-pagov/en/phmc/documents/archives/research-online/documents/1912%20-%20P.PDF page 137
• https://www.pa.gov/content/dam/copapwp-pagov/en/phmc/documents/archives/research-online/documents/1913-P.PDF page 130
• "United States World War I Draft Registration Cards, 1917-1918", database with images, FamilySearch (https://www.familysearch.org/ark:/61903/1:1:W8D6-3KPZ : 28 June 2024), Carmina or Carmino Perrine, 1917-1918.
• "New York Passenger Arrival Lists (Ellis Island), 1892-1924", database with images, FamilySearch (https://familysearch.org/ark:/61903/1:1:JJYR-427 : 2 March 2021), Carmine Perrino, 1912.
• "New York, County Naturalization Records, 1791-1980", , FamilySearch (https://www.familysearch.org/ark:/61903/1:1:78JR-TPMM : Thu Mar 07 14:06:24 UTC 2024), Entry for Carmino Perrino, 1915.
• "United States, Veterans Administration Master Index, 1917-1940", , FamilySearch (https://www.familysearch.org/ark:/61903/1:1:WSSL-HY6Z : Sun Mar 10 23:32:39 UTC 2024), Entry for Carmino Perrine, 5 June 1919.
• "United States, Enlisted and Officer Muster Rolls and Rosters, 1916-1939", , FamilySearch (https://www.familysearch.org/ark:/61903/1:1:6XHZ-RJN2 : Fri Mar 08 17:51:17 UTC 2024), Entry for Carmino Perrine, 23 May 1918.

- "United States, Enlisted and Officer Muster Rolls and Rosters, 1916-1939", , FamilySearch (https://www.familysearch.org/ark:/61903/1:1:8GCQ-MPT2 : Sat Mar 09 19:13:56 UTC 2024), Entry for Carmino Perrine, 31 July 1918.
- "United States, Enlisted and Officer Muster Rolls and Rosters, 1916-1939", , FamilySearch (https://www.familysearch.org/ark:/61903/1:1:8GC6-P3W2 : Wed Jul 24 03:06:08 UTC 2024), Entry for Carmino Perrine, 31 Aug 1918.
- "United States, Enlisted and Officer Muster Rolls and Rosters, 1916-1939", , FamilySearch (https://www.familysearch.org/ark:/61903/1:1:8GC4-9R3Z : Wed Jul 17 06:15:27 UTC 2024), Entry for Carmino Perrine, 8 Oct 1918.
- "United States, Enlisted and Officer Muster Rolls and Rosters, 1916-1939", , FamilySearch (https://www.familysearch.org/ark:/61903/1:1:8GCT-F7W2 : Sat Jul 06 12:45:28 UTC 2024), Entry for Carmine Perrine, 31 Oct 1918.
- "United States, Enlisted and Officer Muster Rolls and Rosters, 1916-1939", , FamilySearch (https://www.familysearch.org/ark:/61903/1:1:8GCQ-BKZM : Mon Jul 08 08:14:37 UTC 2024), Entry for Carmino Perrins, Nov 1918.
- "United States, Enlisted and Officer Muster Rolls and Rosters, 1916-1939", , FamilySearch (https://www.familysearch.org/ark:/61903/1:1:8GZP-3R6Z : Sat Mar 09 06:41:19 UTC 2024), Entry for Carmine Perrine, 30 November 1918.
- "United States, Enlisted and Officer Muster Rolls and Rosters, 1916-1939", , FamilySearch (https://www.familysearch.org/ark:/61903/1:1:8GC6-G8W2 : Thu Jul 18 00:03:07 UTC 2024), Entry for Carmino Perrine, 31 Jan 1919.
- "United States, Enlisted and Officer Muster Rolls and Rosters, 1916-1939", , FamilySearch (https://www.familysearch.org/ark:/61903/1:1:8GC1-P7W2 : Sat Mar 09 05:24:17 UTC 2024), Entry for Carmine Perrine, 30 April 1919.
- "United States, Enlisted and Officer Muster Rolls and Rosters, 1916-1939", , FamilySearch (https://www.familysearch.org/ark:/61903/1:1:8TZK-N4ZM : Sat Mar 09 21:58:23 UTC 2024), Entry for Carmine Perrine, 29 May 1919.
- "United States Census, 1920", , FamilySearch (https://www.familysearch.org/ark:/61903/1:1:MFY4-Q5M : Wed Mar 06 09:48:19 UTC 2024), Entry for O Dena Perine and Colombine Perine, 1920.
- "Pennsylvania, Middle District Court, Naturalization Records, 1901-1991", , FamilySearch (https://www.familysearch.org/ark:/61903/1:1:62SK-FLPN : Sun Mar 10 10:29:04 UTC 2024), Entry for Carmine Perrina, 21 Jun 1921.
- "Pennsylvania, Middle District Court, Naturalization Records, 1901-1991", database, FamilySearch (https://www.familysearch.org/ark:/61903/1:1:62SK-HX4K : 16 June 2023), Carmine Perrine, 1921.
- "Pennsylvania, Middle District Court, Naturalization Records, 1901-1991", , FamilySearch (https://www.familysearch.org/ark:/61903/1:1:62SK-C4MF : Fri Mar 08 10:27:10 UTC 2024), Entry for Carmine Perrine, 21 Jun 1921.
- "United States Census, 1930", , FamilySearch (https://www.familysearch.org/ark:/61903/1:1:X7CK-1B8 : Fri Jul 05 22:27:03 UTC 2024), Entry for Carmino Perrine and Columbia Perrine, 1930.
- "United States Census, 1940", , FamilySearch (https://www.familysearch.org/ark:/61903/1:1:KQ53-VDG : Tue Jul 23 10:44:20 UTC 2024), Entry for Carmen Perrone and Columba Perrone, 1940.
- "Pennsylvania, County Marriages, 1885-1950", , FamilySearch (https://www.familysearch.org/ark:/61903/1:1:Q2ZW-FS4V : Fri Mar 08 19:53:58 UTC 2024), Entry for Anthony Perrine and Anna Spinelli, March 1941.
- "United States World War II Draft Registration Cards, 1942", , FamilySearch (https://www.familysearch.org/ark:/61903/1:1:QKVQ-18RG : Fri Feb 23 22:55:30 UTC 2024), Entry for Carmino Perrine and Colomba Perrine, 26 Apr 1942.

- "Pennsylvania, World War II Draft Registration Cards, 1940-1945", , FamilySearch (https://www.familysearch.org/ark:/61903/1:1:Q2SJ-6YGP : Fri Feb 23 20:57:45 UTC 2024), Entry for Anthony Carmen Perrine and Carmen Perrine, 16 Oct 1940.
- "United States Census, 1950", , FamilySearch (https://www.familysearch.org/ark:/61903/1:1:6XTT-79WW : Thu Mar 21 00:15:09 UTC 2024), Entry for Carmine Perrino and Colombe Perrino, 10 April 1950.
- https://www.newspapers.com/article/the-buffalo-news-perrine-colomba-nee-d/148955383/
- "New York State Health Department, Genealogical Research Death Index, 1957-1963," , FamilySearch (https://familysearch.org/ark:/61903/1:1:2CHR-YF5 : 11 February 2018), Colomba Perrine, 26 Jul 1957; citing Death, Buffalo, Erie, New York, file #45239, New York State Department of Health—Vital Records Section, Albany.
- "United States, Social Security Numerical Identification Files (NUMIDENT), 1936-2007", database, FamilySearch (https://www.familysearch.org/ark:/61903/1:1:6KMJ-CRNK : 10 February 2023), Carmino Perrine in entry for Susie Constantino, .
- "United States Social Security Death Index," database, FamilySearch (https://familysearch.org/ark:/61903/1:1:JTBC-VWB : 7 January 2021), Carmino Perrine, Aug 1973; citing U.S. Social Security Administration, Death Master File, database (Alexandria, Virginia: National Technical Information Service, ongoing).
- https://www.amigone.com/obituaries/Rena-C-Cino?obId=12442027

248) Filomena Giorgione

Filomena Giorgione(248) was born on 29 May 1893, in Ariano, Italy, to Raffaele Giorgione(80) and Carmina Salvioli(80a).

Filomena Giorgione(248) married Michele Borelli(248a) on 13 May 1920 in Ariano, Italy.

Michele Borelli(248a) was a foundling born on 7 May 1896, in Ariano, Italy.

Records that include Filomena Giorgione(248) and/or Michele Borelli(221):
- Ariano, Italy 1893 Birth Act #337
- Ariano, Italy 1896 Birth Act #P.II.29
- Ariano, Italy 1920 Marriage Act #105

249) Pasquale Di Lillo

Pasquale Di Lillo(249) was born on 17 June 1893, in Ariano, Italy, to Nicola Maria di Lillo(51a) and Angela Perrina(52). Pasquale Di Lillo(249) died on 7 October 1894 in Ariano, Italy.

Records that include Pasquale Di Lillo(249):
- Ariano, Italy 1893 Birth Act #364
- Ariano, Italy 1894 Death Act #345

250) Giovanna Di Lillo

Giovanna Di Lillo(250) was born on 21 October 1893, in Ariano, Italy, to Raffaele Di Lillo(95a) and Raimonda Perrina(95). Giovanna Di Lillo(250) died on 17 September 1894 in Ariano, Italy.

Records that include Giovanna Di Lillo(250):
- Ariano, Italy 1893 Birth Act #592
- Ariano, Italy 1894 Death Act #303

251) Maria Carmela di Lillo

Maria Carmela di Lillo(251) was born on 21 October 1893, in Ariano, Italy, to Raffaele Di Lillo(95a) and Raimonda Perrina(95).

Maria Carmela di Lillo(251) married Giovanni Riccio(251a) on 10 June 1930 in Ariano, Italy.

Giovanni Riccio(251a) was born on 29 August 1906 in Ariano, Italy to Michele Riccio(251aF) and Raffaella Iannarone(251aM).

Records that include Maria Carmela di Lillo(251) and/or Giovanni Riccio(251a):
- Ariano, Italy 1893 Birth Act #593
- Ariano, Italy 1906 Birth Act #404
- Ariano, Italy 1930 Marriage Act #II.A.94

252) Saverio Lombardi

Saverio Lombardi(252) was born on 24 January 1894, in Apice, Italy, to Vincenzo (James) Lombardi(85a) and Maria Carmela deDonato(85). Saverio Lombardi(252) died before February 1895.

Records that include Saverio Lombardi(252):
- Apice, Italy 1894 Birth Act #21

253) Maria Luigia deDonato

Maria Luigia deDonato(253) was born on 20 February 1894, in Paduli, Italy, to Marcello deDonato(78) and Maria Rosa Politano(78a).

Records that include Maria Luigia deDonato(253):
- "Italia, Benevento, Stato Civile (Archivio di Stato), 1810-1942", , FamilySearch (https://www.familysearch.org/ark:/61903/1:1:QGJ2-ZF5D : Fri Mar 08 21:08:16 UTC 2024), Entry for Maria Luigia De Donato and Marcello De Donato, 20 febbraio 1894.

254) Fedele Ciasullo

Fedele Ciasullo(254) was born on 2 March 1894, in Ariano, Italy, to Michele Ciasullo(82a) and Filomena Perrina(82). Fedele Ciasullo(254) emigrated to the United States on 27 March 1911. Fedele Ciasullo(254) served in the United States Army between 21 September 1917 to 27 September 1919. Fedele Ciasullo(254) became a citizen of the United States on 25 June 1918, in Camp Devins, MA On 22 March 1920, Fedele Ciasullo(254) applied for a passport to "visit his mother" in Italy. Fedele Ciasullio(W227) returned to the United States with his wife on 22 December 1920. Fedele Ciasullo(254) died on 8 February 1948, in Schenectady, NY. Fedele Ciasullo was a tavern keeper.

Fedele Ciasullo(254) married Rosaria Mincolelli(254a) on 8 July 1920 in Ariano, Italy

Rosaria Mincolelli(254a) was born on 21 October 1897, in Ariano, Italy, to Leonardo Antonio Mincolelli(254aF) and Brigida Ciccorelli(254aM). Rosaria Mincolelli(254a) died May 1978 in Schenectady, NY.

Records that include Fedele Ciasullo(254) and/or Rosaria Mincolelli(254a):
- Ariano, Italy 1894 Birth Act #164
- Ariano, Italy 1897 Birth Act #573
- Ariano, Italy 1920 Marriage Act #140
- "United States World War I Draft Registration Cards, 1917-1918", database with images, FamilySearch (https://www.familysearch.org/ark:/61903/1:1:KXB8-7G1 : 26 December 2021), Fedele Ciasullo, 1917-1918.
- "United States World War II Draft Registration Cards, 1942", , FamilySearch (https://www.familysearch.org/ark:/61903/1:1:QKVQ-FCMV : Fri Feb 23 23:04:17 UTC 2024), Entry for Fedele Ciasullo and Rose Ciasullo, 27 Apr 1942.
- "United States Passport Applications, 1795-1925", , FamilySearch (https://www.familysearch.org/ark:/61903/1:1:QV5B-H7NN : Fri Mar 08 16:42:00 UTC 2024), Entry for Fedele Ciasullo, 1920.
- "United States Census, 1940", , FamilySearch (https://www.familysearch.org/ark:/61903/1:1:K79V-N1Y : Sat Mar 09 01:40:05 UTC 2024), Entry for Fedele Ciasullo and Rose Ciasullo, 1940.

- "United States, Veterans Administration Master Index, 1917-1940", , FamilySearch (https://www.familysearch.org/ark:/61903/1:1:QPZT-P999 : Sat Mar 09 11:45:17 UTC 2024), Entry for Fedele Ciasullo, 27 September 1919.
- "New York, State Death Index, 1880-1956", , FamilySearch (https://www.familysearch.org/ark:/61903/1:1:QGPN-5QKB : Sun Mar 10 12:20:33 UTC 2024), Entry for Fedele Ciasullo, 8 Feb 1948.
- "United States, Enlisted and Officer Muster Rolls and Rosters, 1916-1939", , FamilySearch (https://www.familysearch.org/ark:/61903/1:1:681T-STTG : Sat Mar 09 10:24:49 UTC 2024), Entry for Fedele Ciasullo, 31 January 1919.
- "United States, Enlisted and Officer Muster Rolls and Rosters, 1916-1939", , FamilySearch (https://www.familysearch.org/ark:/61903/1:1:681R-RL8D : Fri Mar 08 19:09:56 UTC 2024), Entry for Fedele Ciasullo, 31 August 1918.
- "United States, Enlisted and Officer Muster Rolls and Rosters, 1916-1939", , FamilySearch (https://www.familysearch.org/ark:/61903/1:1:CSJ8-2G6Z : Sat Mar 09 20:20:20 UTC 2024), Entry for Fedele Ciasullo, 21 September 1917.
- "United States, Enlisted and Officer Muster Rolls and Rosters, 1916-1939", , FamilySearch (https://www.familysearch.org/ark:/61903/1:1:CSJ8-YJT2 : Sat Mar 09 02:30:19 UTC 2024), Entry for Fedele Ciasullo, 21 September 1917.
- "United States, Enlisted and Officer Muster Rolls and Rosters, 1916-1939", , FamilySearch (https://www.familysearch.org/ark:/61903/1:1:CSJ8-GK2M : Sat Mar 09 03:44:23 UTC 2024), Entry for Fedele Ciasullo, 21 September 1917.
- "United States, Enlisted and Officer Muster Rolls and Rosters, 1916-1939", , FamilySearch (https://www.familysearch.org/ark:/61903/1:1:681R-L6PT : Sun Mar 10 11:36:42 UTC 2024), Entry for Fedele Ciasullo, 30 April 1919.
- "United States, Enlisted and Officer Muster Rolls and Rosters, 1916-1939", , FamilySearch (https://www.familysearch.org/ark:/61903/1:1:681B-DKJ5 : Wed Mar 06 00:05:30 UTC 2024), Entry for Fedele Ciasullo, 30 September 1919.
- "United States, Enlisted and Officer Muster Rolls and Rosters, 1916-1939", , FamilySearch (https://www.familysearch.org/ark:/61903/1:1:681R-RLC3 : Sun Mar 10 23:26:06 UTC 2024), Entry for Fedele Ciasullo, 31 December 1918.
- "United States, Enlisted and Officer Muster Rolls and Rosters, 1916-1939", , FamilySearch (https://www.familysearch.org/ark:/61903/1:1:CSJ8-P22M : Sat Mar 09 02:52:48 UTC 2024), Entry for Fedele Ciasullo, 21 September 1917.
- "United States, Enlisted and Officer Muster Rolls and Rosters, 1916-1939", , FamilySearch (https://www.familysearch.org/ark:/61903/1:1:6DMQ-2N1G : Sat Mar 09 08:52:25 UTC 2024), Entry for Fedele Ciasullo, 31 March 1919.
- "United States, Enlisted and Officer Muster Rolls and Rosters, 1916-1939", , FamilySearch (https://www.familysearch.org/ark:/61903/1:1:681T-7W4N : Sat Mar 09 15:51:51 UTC 2024), Entry for Fedele Ciasullo, 30 November 1918.
- "United States, Enlisted and Officer Muster Rolls and Rosters, 1916-1939", , FamilySearch (https://www.familysearch.org/ark:/61903/1:1:681R-G7CD : Fri Mar 08 13:23:46 UTC 2024), Entry for Fedele Ciasullo, 28 February 1919.
- United States, Enlisted and Officer Muster Rolls and Rosters, 1916-1939", , FamilySearch (https://www.familysearch.org/ark:/61903/1:1:6DMT-LV1C : Sun Mar 10 01:21:41 UTC 2024), Entry for Fedele Ciasullo, 31 July 1919.
- "United States, Enlisted and Officer Muster Rolls and Rosters, 1916-1939", , FamilySearch (https://www.familysearch.org/ark:/61903/1:1:681R-RDJM : Fri Mar 08 23:42:00 UTC 2024), Entry for Fedele Ciasullo, 31 August 1919.
- "United States, Enlisted and Officer Muster Rolls and Rosters, 1916-1939", , FamilySearch (https://www.familysearch.org/ark:/61903/1:1:681T-SRHH : Sun Mar 10 08:41:20 UTC 2024), Entry for Fedele Ciasullo, 30 June 1919.

- "United States, Enlisted and Officer Muster Rolls and Rosters, 1916-1939", , FamilySearch (https://www.familysearch.org/ark:/61903/1:1:CSJ8-12MM : Fri Mar 08 06:38:52 UTC 2024), Entry for Fedele Ciasullo, 21 September 1917.
- "United States, Enlisted and Officer Muster Rolls and Rosters, 1916-1939", , FamilySearch (https://www.familysearch.org/ark:/61903/1:1:681R-SWBL : Sun Mar 10 18:53:26 UTC 2024), Entry for Fedele Ciasullo, 31 May 1919.
- "United States, Enlisted and Officer Muster Rolls and Rosters, 1916-1939", , FamilySearch (https://www.familysearch.org/ark:/61903/1:1:CSJD-9H6Z : Sun Mar 10 07:39:47 UTC 2024), Entry for Fedele Ciasullo, 21 September 1917.
- "United States Social Security Death Index," database, FamilySearch (https://familysearch.org/ark:/61903/1:1:VML4-KXQ : 7 January 2021), Rose Ciasullo, May 1978; citing U.S. Social Security Administration, Death Master File, database (Alexandria, Virginia: National Technical Information Service, ongoing).
- "Find a Grave Index," database, FamilySearch (https://www.familysearch.org/ark:/61903/1:1:6PY3-QKKB : 8 March 2024), Fedele Ciasullo, ; Burial, Schenectady, Schenectady, New York, United States of America, Saint Joseph's Cemetery; citing record ID 260353438, Find a Grave, http://www.findagrave.com.
- "Find a Grave Index," database, FamilySearch (https://www.familysearch.org/ark:/61903/1:1:6PY3-M3PZ : 8 March 2024), Rose Mincolelli Ciasullo, ; Burial, Schenectady, Schenectady, New York, United States of America, Saint Joseph's Cemetery; citing record ID 260353439, Find a Grave, http://www.findagrave.com.

255) Mariangela Manganiello

Mariangela Manganiello(255) was born on 1 June 1894, in Ariano, Italy, to Raimondo Manganiello(79a) and Mariantonia Fodarella(79).

Mariangela Manganiello(255) married Antonio Moschella(255a) on 26 June 1913 in Ariano, Italy.

Antonio Moschella(255a) was born 30 October 1873 to Michele Moschella(255aF) and Maria Giovanna Melito(255aM).

Known children of Mariangela Manganiello(255) and Antonio Moschella(255a):

    i) Giovanna Moschella(452) born in 1914
    ii) Michele Moschella(462) born in 1915
    iii) Giuseppina Moschella(509) born about 1920
    iv) Antonietta Moschella(525) born about 1923

Records that include Mariangela Manganiello(255) and/or Antonio Moschella(255a):
- Ariano, Italy 1873 Birth Act #511
- Ariano, Italy 1894 Birth Act #343
- Ariano, Italy 1913 Marriage Act #78
- Ariano, Italy 1914 Birth Act #238
- Ariano, Italy 1914 Death Act #122
- Ariano, Italy 1915 Birth Act #595
- Ariano, Italy 1921 Death Act #200
- Ariano, Italy 1928 Death Act #137

256) Elisabetta Perrina

Elisabetta Perrina(256) was born on 8 July 1894, in Castel Baronia, Italy, to Raffaele Perrina(58) and Maria Lucia Gesa(58a). Elisabetta Perrina(256) died 16 August 1897 in Castel Baronia, Italy.

Records that include Elisabetta Perrina(256):
- Castel Baronia, Italy 1894 Birth Act #33
- Castel Baronia, Italy 1897 Death Act #25

257) Raffaele Altanese

Raffaele Altanese(257) was born on 20 July 1894 in Grottaminarda, Italy to Cosimo Altanese(87) and Margarita Galgothia Alfonsina Romano(87a). Raffaele Altanese(257) died 9 January 1900 in Grottaminarda, Italy.

Records that include Raffaele Altanese(257):
* Grottaminarda, Italy 1894 Birth Act #107
* Grottaminarda, Italy 1900 Death Act #3

258) Floriano Grasso

Floriano Grasso(258) was born on 15 August 1894, in Ariano, Italy, to Crescenzo Grasso(76a) and Anna Perrina(76). Floriano Grasso(258) died on 12 August 1895 in Ariano, Italy.

Records that include Floriano Grasso(258):
* Ariano, Italy 1894 Birth Act #455
* Ariano, Italy 1895 Death Act #228

259) Clementina Anastasio

Clementina Anastasio(259) was born on 19 September 1894, in Ariano, Italy, to Pasquale Antonio Anastasio(72a) and Anna Maria D'Ausilio(72). Clementina Anastasio(259) was brought aboard the ship SS Werra with her Mother and older brothers in Naples, Italy to arrive in New York City on 7 October 1895. Clementina Anastasio(259) died 17 March 1951 in St. Louis, MO.

Clementina Anastasio(259) married Domenick Zarlenga(259a) on 7 April 1913 in St. Louis, MO.

Domenick Zarlenga(259a) was born 26 December 1889, in Pietrabbondante, Italy, to Donatangelo Zarlenga(259aF) and Angela Zarlenga(259aM). Domenick Zarlenga(259a) died 27 June 1955 in St. Louis, MO.

Known children of Clementina Anastasio(259) and Domenick Zarlenga(259a):

    i) Dan A Zarlenga(469) born in 1916
    ii) Mary Angela Ann Zarlenga(479) born in 1917.
    iii) Lucian Angelo Zarlenga(501) born in 1920
    iv) Domenic Paul Zarlenga(571) born in 1929

Records that include Clementina Anastasio(259):
* Pietrabbondante, Italy 1889 Birth Act #115
* Ariano, Italy 1894 Birth Act #521
* "New York Passenger Arrival Lists (Ellis Island), 1892-1924", , FamilySearch (https://www.familysearch.org/ark:/61903/1:1:JX36-9WG : Fri Mar 08 16:06:42 UTC 2024), Entry for Clementina Anastasio, 1895.
* "United States Census, 1900", , FamilySearch (https://www.familysearch.org/ark:/61903/1:1:M97Z-VHB : Fri Aug 02 20:31:37 UTC 2024), Entry for Anastasia Pasquale and Mary Pasquale, 1900.
* "United States Census, 1910", , FamilySearch (https://www.familysearch.org/ark:/61903/1:1:MLMM-7YC : Fri Mar 08 21:46:08 UTC 2024), Entry for Pasquale Unastasio and Maria Unastasio, 1910.
* "Missouri, County Marriage, Naturalization, and Court Records, 1800-1991", , FamilySearch (https://www.familysearch.org/ark:/61903/1:1:6PKN-1RNF : Sat Mar 09 17:12:21 UTC 2024), Entry for Clementina Anastasio and , 7 Apr 1913.
* "Missouri, County Marriage, Naturalization, and Court Records, 1800-1991", , FamilySearch (https://www.familysearch.org/ark:/61903/1:1:6DTG-H59V : Thu Mar 07 13:20:47 UTC 2024), Entry for Domenick Zarlenga and , 7 Apr 1913.
* "Missouri, County Marriage, Naturalization, and Court Records, 1800-1991", , FamilySearch (https://www.familysearch.org/ark:/61903/1:1:6DY1-55BR : Sat Mar 09 16:23:01 UTC 2024), Entry for Domenick Qarlenga or Zarlenga and Clementina Anastasio, 27 Apr 1913.

- "United States World War I Draft Registration Cards, 1917-1918", database with images, FamilySearch (https://www.familysearch.org/ark:/61903/1:1:W8ZJ-2WW2 : 10 July 2024), Domenick Zarlenga, 1917-1918.
- "United States Census, 1930", , FamilySearch (https://www.familysearch.org/ark:/61903/1:1:XHJY-84K : Wed Jul 17 13:46:42 UTC 2024), Entry for Dominick Zarlingo and Clementine Zarlingo, 1930.
- "Missouri, Pre-WWII Adjutant General Enlistment Contracts, 1900-1941", , FamilySearch (https://www.familysearch.org/ark:/61903/1:1:6CB2-NCK8 : Sat Mar 09 03:04:54 UTC 2024), Entry for Lucian A Zarlenga and Dominic Zarlenga, 12 Aug 1937.
- "United States Census, 1940", , FamilySearch (https://www.familysearch.org/ark:/61903/1:1:K7HD-RP5 : Fri Mar 08 18:54:50 UTC 2024), Entry for Dominic Zarlenga and Clementine Zarlenga, 1940.
- "Missouri, Pre-WWII Adjutant General Enlistment Contracts, 1900-1941", , FamilySearch (https://www.familysearch.org/ark:/61903/1:1:6CBL-3DGY : Sat Mar 09 08:46:39 UTC 2024), Entry for Lucian Angelo Zarlenga and Dominic Zarlenga, 12 Aug 1940.
- "United States World War II Draft Registration Cards, 1942", , FamilySearch (https://www.familysearch.org/ark:/61903/1:1:QKVS-D87H : Fri Feb 23 18:13:53 UTC 2024), Entry for Dominick Zarlenga and Clementina Zarlenga, 25 Apr 1942.
- "United States Census, 1950", , FamilySearch (https://www.familysearch.org/ark:/61903/1:1:6FM2-4LJD : Tue Mar 19 23:33:08 UTC 2024), Entry for Dominick Zarlenga and Clementine Zarlenga, April 15, 1950
- "Find a Grave Index," database, FamilySearch (https://www.familysearch.org/ark:/61903/1:1:QVKL-VKPY : 30 May 2020), Clara Zarlenga, ; Burial, , ; citing record ID , Find a Grave, http://www.findagrave.com.
- "United States, Social Security Numerical Identification Files (NUMIDENT), 1936-2007", database, FamilySearch (https://www.familysearch.org/ark:/61903/1:1:6KWH-WZGG : 10 February 2023), Domineck Zarlenga, .
- "Find a Grave Index," database, FamilySearch (https://www.familysearch.org/ark:/61903/1:1:QVKL-VK5S : 9 June 2021), Domenick Zarlenga, ; Burial, Saint Louis, St. Louis City, Missouri, United States of America, Calvary Cemetery and Mausoleum; citing record ID 47035390, Find a Grave, http://www.findagrave.com.
- "United States, Social Security Numerical Identification Files (NUMIDENT), 1936-2007", database, FamilySearch (https://www.familysearch.org/ark:/61903/1:1:6KW3-JHRJ : 10 February 2023), Domenick Zarlenga in entry for Mary Angelaann Zarlenga, .
- "United States, Social Security Numerical Identification Files (NUMIDENT), 1936-2007", database, FamilySearch (https://www.familysearch.org/ark:/61903/1:1:6KW7-LXLD : 10 February 2023), Clara Anastasio in entry for Dominic Paul Zarlenga, .
- "United States, Social Security Numerical Identification Files (NUMIDENT), 1936-2007", database, FamilySearch (https://www.familysearch.org/ark:/61903/1:1:6KW7-LXLH : 10 February 2023), Dominic Zarlenga in entry for Dominic Paul Zarlenga, .

260) Antonio Perrina

Antonio Perrina(260) was born on 17 January 1895, in Ariano, Italy, to Michele Perrina(88) and Maria Grazia Caraglia(88a). Antonio Perrina(260) died on 4 April 1896 in Ariano, Italy.
Records that include Antonio Perrina(260):
- Ariano, Italy 1895 Birth Act #47
- Ariano, Italy 1896 Death Act #166

261) <u>Saverio Lombardi</u>

Saverio (Samuel) Lombardi(261) was born on 21 February 1895, in Apice, Italy, to Vincenzo (James) Lombardi(85a) and Maria Carmela deDonato(85). Saverio Lombardi(261) died on 10 September 1978 in Los Angeles, CA.

Saverio Lombardi(261) married Giovanna Prezioso(261a) on 9 July 1920 in Bridgeport, CT.

<u>Giovanna Prezioso</u>*(261a) was born on 27 August 1902, in Ariano, Italy, to Francesco Paolo Prezioso(261aF) and Caterina Ciasullo**(261aM). Giovanna Prezioso(261a) died in 1991.
* Name on Marriage Record is Jennie Josephine Prezioso.
** Name on Daughter's Marriage Record is Cath. Grasso.

Known children of Saverio Lombardi(261) and Giovanna Prezioso(261a):

    i) Carmen Lombardi(347) born in 1921
    ii) Felice Adam Lombardi(349) born in 1922
    iii) Delores Gloria Lombardi(353) born in 1923

Records that include Saverio Lombardi(261) and/or Giovanna Prezioso(261a):
* Ariano, Italy 1902 Birth Act #434
* Bridgeport, Connecticut Jul – Sep 1920 Marriage Records #51
* "Connecticut, Military Census Questionnaires, 1917", database, FamilySearch (https://www.familysearch.org/ark:/61903/1:1:ZVP9-J56Z : 8 July 2020), Samuel Lombardi, 1917.
* "United States Census, 1920", database with images, FamilySearch (ark:/61903/1:1:MCFH-DK2 : Thu Jul 13 18:37:31 UTC 2023), Entry for Vincent Lombardi and Casowasy Lombardi, 1920.
* "United States Census, 1930," database with images, FamilySearch (https://www.familysearch.org/ark:/61903/1:1:XMPM-771 : accessed 18 July 2023), Samuel Lombardi in household of James Lombardi, Bridgeport, Fairfield, Connecticut, United States; citing enumeration district (ED) ED 60, sheet , line , family , NARA microfilm publication T626 (Washington D.C.: National Archives and Records Administration, 2002), roll ; FHL microfilm .
* "United States Census, 1940", database with images, FamilySearch (ark:/61903/1:1:K97H-NYF : Fri Jul 14 13:01:19 UTC 2023), Entry for Sam Lombardis and Jennie Lombardis, 1940.
* "United States, Social Security Numerical Identification Files (NUMIDENT), 1936-2007", database, FamilySearch (https://www.familysearch.org/ark:/61903/1:1:6K4C-251L : 11 February 2023), Giovanna Lombardi, .

262) <u>Giuseppe Ciasullo</u>

Giuseppe Ciasullo(262) was born 21 March 1895, in Ariano, Italy, to Filippo Ciasullo(105a) and Maria Giovanna Perrina(105). On 20 February 1913 Giuseppe Ciasullo(262) boarded the ship SS America, arriving in New York City on 5 March 1913. Giuseppe Ciasullo(262) applied for United States Citizenship on 14 July 1920, in Schenectady, NY. Giuseppe Ciasullo(262) was granted United States Citizenship on 12 November 1926. Giuseppe Ciasullo(262) died July 1972, in Schenectady, NY.

Giuseppe Ciasullo(262) married Grace Castaldi(262a).

<u>Grace Castaldi</u>(262a) was born on 2 July 1903 in Salerno, Italy to Carmine Castaldi(262aF) and Consiglia Allegrette(262aM). Grace Castaldi(262a) died 18 May 1948 in Schenectady, NY.

Known Children of Giuseppe Ciasullo(262) and Grace Castaldi(262a):

    i) Jennie Ciasullo(T358) born in 1926
    ii) Living person and/or spouse
    iii) Deloris Ciasullo(592) born in 1933
    iv) Living person and/or spouse

Records that include Giuseppe Ciasullo(262) and/or Grace Castaldi(262a):
* Ariano, Italy 1895 Birth Act #220
* Salerno, Italy 1903 Birth Act #871

- "New York State Census, 1915", , FamilySearch (https://www.familysearch.org/ark:/61903/1:1:K9P8-7CN : 3 June 2022), Joseph Ciasullo in entry for Ralph Perrino, 1915.
- "New York, County Naturalization Records, 1791-1980", , FamilySearch (https://www.familysearch.org/ark:/61903/1:1:QPSP-D1WN : Sun Mar 10 18:28:51 UTC 2024), Entry for Joseph Ciasullo, 1920.
- "New York Passenger Arrival Lists (Ellis Island), 1892-1924", , FamilySearch (https://www.familysearch.org/ark:/61903/1:1:J6DM-M3F : Sun Mar 10 09:20:24 UTC 2024), Entry for Grazi...a Castaldi and Vincenzo Romano.
- "New York, County Naturalization Records, 1791-1980", , FamilySearch (https://www.familysearch.org/ark:/61903/1:1:QPXP-FDJ6 : Sun Mar 10 15:31:17 UTC 2024), Entry for Joseph or Giuseppe Ciasullo and Grace, 1926.
- "United States Census, 1930", , FamilySearch (https://www.familysearch.org/ark:/61903/1:1:X4TY-PGH : Sat Mar 09 21:13:12 UTC 2024), Entry for Joseph Ciasullo and Grace Ciasullo, 1930.
- "United States Census, 1940", , FamilySearch (https://www.familysearch.org/ark:/61903/1:1:KQY5-9BR : Fri Mar 08 20:57:12 UTC 2024), Entry for Joseph Ciasullo and Grace Ciasullo, 1940.
- "United States World War II Draft Registration Cards, 1942", , FamilySearch (https://www.familysearch.org/ark:/61903/1:1:QKVQ-FC4K : Sat Feb 24 00:52:17 UTC 2024), Entry for Joseph Ciasullo and Grace Ciasullo, 26 Apr 1942.
- "New York, State Death Index, 1880-1956", , FamilySearch (https://www.familysearch.org/ark:/61903/1:1:QGPN-PMM9 : Sun Mar 10 12:20:34 UTC 2024), Entry for Grace Ciasullo, 18 May 1948.
- "Find a Grave Index," database, FamilySearch (https://www.familysearch.org/ark:/61903/1:1:6PY3-M3PX : 8 March 2024), Grace Ciasullo, ; Burial, Schenectady, Schenectady, New York, United States of America, Saint Joseph's Cemetery; citing record ID 260353441, Find a Grave, http://www.findagrave.com.
- "United States Census, 1950", , FamilySearch (https://www.familysearch.org/ark:/61903/1:1:6XT1-KBSD : Tue Mar 19 15:06:03 UTC 2024), Entry for Connie M Cisaullo and Joseph Ciasullo, 10 April 1950.
- "United States Social Security Death Index," database, FamilySearch (https://familysearch.org/ark:/61903/1:1:JKGG-1Z7 : 7 January 2021), Giuseppe Ciasullo, Jul 1972; citing U.S. Social Security Administration, Death Master File, database (Alexandria, Virginia: National Technical Information Service, ongoing).
- "Find a Grave Index," database, FamilySearch (https://www.familysearch.org/ark:/61903/1:1:6PY3-M3PD : 8 March 2024), Joseph Ciasullo, ; Burial, Schenectady, Schenectady, New York, United States of America, Saint Joseph's Cemetery; citing record ID 260353440, Find a Grave, http://www.findagrave.com.
- "United States, GenealogyBank Obituaries, Births, and Marriages 1980-2014," database with images, FamilySearch (https://www.familysearch.org/ark:/61903/1:1:QVTQ-51Y2 : accessed 29 May 2024), Joseph Ciasullo in entry for Dolores N Perkins, Schenectady, New York, United States, 08 May 2013; from "Recent Newspaper Obituaries (1977 - Today)," database, GenealogyBank.com (http://www.genealogybank.com : 2014); citing Daily Gazette, The, born-digital text.

263) Giuseppe (Joseph) Giorgione/George

Giuseppe (Joseph) Giorgione/George(263) was born on 1 June 1895, in Ariano, Italy, to Raffaele Giorgione(80) and Carmina Salvioli(80a). Giuseppe (Joseph) Giorgione/George(263) boarded the ship SS America in June 1911 in Naples, Italy, arriving in New York City, Giuseppe (Joseph) Giorgione/George(263) was going to be living with his Uncle Luigi (Louis) Giorgione/George(86) in Middletown, NY.

Giuseppe (Joseph) Giorgione/George(263) died 5 May 1981 in Ogden, NY.

Giuseppe (Joseph) Giorgione/George(263) married Margherita Adele Maria Marasco(263a) on 23 May 1917 in Middletown, NY.

<u>Margherita Adele Maria Marasco</u>(263a) was born on 17 August 1898 in Taranto, Italy to Orzono Marasco(263aF) and Giuseppa DeRinaldi(263aM). Margherita Adele Maria Marasco(263a) died 8 January 1997 in Rochester, NY.

Known Children for Giuseppe (Joseph) Giorgione/George(263) and Margherita Adele Maria Marasco(263a):

     i) Raffaele (Ralph) Giorgione/George(490) born in 1919
     ii) Josephine Giorgione/George(502) born in 1920
     iii) Alfred Lorenzo Giorgione/George(512) born in 1921

Records that include Giuseppe (Joseph) Giorgione/George(263) and/or Margherita Adele Maria Marasco(263a):

- Ariano, Italy 1895 Birth Act #393
- Taranto, Italy 1898 Birth Act #1383
- "Italia, Taranto, Stato Civile (Archivio di Stato), 1809-1926", , FamilySearch (https://www.familysearch.org/ark:/61903/1:1:23P4-ZLT : Sun Mar 10 11:27:01 UTC 2024), Entry for Margherita Adele Maria Marasco and Oronzo Marasco, 17 Aug 1898.
- "New York, County Marriages, 1847-1848; 1908-1936", , FamilySearch (https://www.familysearch.org/ark:/61903/1:1:XVPJ-5M9 : Sun Mar 10 17:42:05 UTC 2024), Entry for Guiseppe Giorfione and Raffaele Giorgione, 23 May 1917.
- "United States World War I Draft Registration Cards, 1917-1918", database with images, FamilySearch (https://www.familysearch.org/ark:/61903/1:1:WDH6-MTZM : 10 July 2024), Giuseppe Giorgione, 1917-1918.
- "United States Census, 1920", , FamilySearch (https://www.familysearch.org/ark:/61903/1:1:MV9X-V8Z : Fri Mar 08 20:28:15 UTC 2024), Entry for Joseph George and Marguerite George, 1920.
- "United States Census, 1940", , FamilySearch (https://www.familysearch.org/ark:/61903/1:1:KQY5-9LC : Sat Mar 09 22:50:37 UTC 2024), Entry for Joseph George and Margret George, 1940.
- "United States World War II Draft Registration Cards, 1942", , FamilySearch (https://www.familysearch.org/ark:/61903/1:1:QKVQ-NM4N : Sat Feb 24 00:56:26 UTC 2024), Entry for Joseph George and Joseph George, 26 Apr 1942.
- "United States Census, 1950", , FamilySearch (https://www.familysearch.org/ark:/61903/1:1:6XTY-M8YG : Thu Oct 05 23:34:30 UTC 2023), Entry for Joseph George and Margaret George, 13 April 1950.
- "United States, Social Security Numerical Identification Files (NUMIDENT), 1936-2007", database, FamilySearch (https://www.familysearch.org/ark:/61903/1:1:6K42-G686 : 11 February 2023), Joseph George, .
- "Find a Grave Index," database, FamilySearch (https://www.familysearch.org/ark:/61903/1:1:QVK6-1M3X : 12 March 2024), Joseph George, ; Burial, Chili, Monroe, New York, United States of America, Grove Place Cemetery; citing record ID 39400266, Find a Grave, http://www.findagrave.com.
- "United States, Social Security Numerical Identification Files (NUMIDENT), 1936-2007", database, FamilySearch (https://www.familysearch.org/ark:/61903/1:1:6KMB-VGGV : 10 February 2023), Joseph George in entry for Alfred Lorenzo George, .
- "United States, Social Security Numerical Identification Files (NUMIDENT), 1936-2007", database, FamilySearch (https://www.familysearch.org/ark:/61903/1:1:6KMN-QN4M : 10 February 2023), Margaret George, .
- https://www.findagrave.com/memorial/263392711/margaret_george
- "United States Social Security Death Index," database, FamilySearch (https://familysearch.org/ark:/61903/1:1:JKVS-YQQ : 7 January 2021), Margaret George, 08 Jan 1997; citing U.S. Social Security Administration, Death Master File, database (Alexandria, Virginia: National Technical Information Service, ongoing).

- "United States, Social Security Numerical Identification Files (NUMIDENT), 1936-2007", database, FamilySearch (https://www.familysearch.org/ark:/61903/1:1:6KMB-K74J : 10 February 2023), Joseph George in entry for Ralph George, .

264) Michele (Michael William) Giorgione/George

Michele (Michael William) Giorgione/George(264) was born on 5 July 1895, in Ariano, Italy, to Luigi (Louis) Giorgione/George(86) and Maria Giovanna Perillo(86a). Michele Giorgione(264) boarded the SS Algeria in Naples, Italy on 28 November 1905, arriving in New York on 18 December 1905. Michele Giorgione(264) served in the United States Army from 23 July 1917 to 30 April 1919. Michele Giorgione(264) died April 1983 in Orange, NY.

Michele Giorgione(264) married Alma Sharp Terwilliger(264a) on 6 February 1930 in Orange, NY.

Alma Sharp Terwilliger(264a) was born on 10 October 1905 to John Terwilliger(264aF) and Alice Mary Andrews(264aM). Alma Sharp Terwilliger(264a) died in December 1987 in Goshen, NY.

Records that include Michele Giorgione(264) married Alma Sharp Terwilliger(264a):

- Ariano, Italy 1895 Birth Act #441
- "New York Passenger Arrival Lists (Ellis Island), 1892-1924", database with images, FamilySearch (https://familysearch.org/ark:/61903/1:1:JFHQ-4JW : 2 March 2021), Michele Giorgione, 1905.
- "New York Passenger Arrival Lists (Ellis Island), 1892-1924", , FamilySearch (https://www.familysearch.org/ark:/61903/1:1:JF3P-WZS : Sun Mar 10 00:44:58 UTC 2024), Entry for Michele Giorgione and Salvatore Grass, 1905.
- "United States Census, 1910", , FamilySearch (https://www.familysearch.org/ark:/61903/1:1:M598-W7R : Sun Mar 10 19:17:22 UTC 2024), Entry for John R Terwilliger and Alice Terwilliger, 1910.
- "United States World War I Draft Registration Cards, 1917-1918", database with images, FamilySearch (https://www.familysearch.org/ark:/61903/1:1:KXBQ-N15 : 26 December 2021), Michal Giorgione, 1917-1918.
- "United States, Veterans Administration Master Index, 1917-1940", , FamilySearch (https://www.familysearch.org/ark:/61903/1:1:783Q-78MM : Sat Mar 09 10:55:29 UTC 2024), Entry for Michael William George, 30 April 1919.
- "New York Records of the State National Guard, 1906-1954", , FamilySearch (https://www.familysearch.org/ark:/61903/1:1:QVJY-WCMV : Sat Mar 09 04:39:59 UTC 2024), Entry for Michael W George, 23 Jul 1917.
- "United States Census, 1920", , FamilySearch (https://www.familysearch.org/ark:/61903/1:1:MV9N-TZ2 : Fri Mar 08 14:29:49 UTC 2024), Entry for John Tewilliger and Alice Tewilliger, 1920.
- "United States Census, 1930", , FamilySearch (https://www.familysearch.org/ark:/61903/1:1:X4R1-NCJ : Sun Mar 10 15:50:00 UTC 2024), Entry for Anthony George and Jennie George, 1930.
- "United States Census, 1930", , FamilySearch (https://www.familysearch.org/ark:/61903/1:1:X4R1-K68 : Fri Mar 08 23:07:15 UTC 2024), Entry for Andrew N Carr and Violet M Carr, 1930.
- "New York, County Marriages, 1847-1848; 1908-1936", , FamilySearch (https://www.familysearch.org/ark:/61903/1:1:Q2MT-54YV : Sat Mar 09 21:42:13 UTC 2024), Entry for Michael William George and Louis George, February 1930.
- "United States Census, 1940", , FamilySearch (https://www.familysearch.org/ark:/61903/1:1:KQGP-L7S : Sun Mar 10 01:36:55 UTC 2024), Entry for Michael George and Alma George, 1940.

- "United States World War II Draft Registration Cards, 1942", ,
  FamilySearch (https://www.familysearch.org/ark:/61903/1:1:QKVQ-NQ55
  : Fri Feb 23 23:02:37 UTC 2024), Entry for Michael William George
  and Alma S George, 27 Apr 1942.
- "United States Census, 1950", , FamilySearch
  (https://www.familysearch.org/ark:/61903/1:1:6XY7-71C4 : Tue Oct 03
  21:30:15 UTC 2023), Entry for Michael W George and Elma S George,
  13 April 1950.
- "United States Social Security Death Index," database, FamilySearch
  (https://familysearch.org/ark:/61903/1:1:VMK2-H44 : 7 January
  2021), Michael George, Apr 1983; citing U.S. Social Security
  Administration, Death Master File, database (Alexandria, Virginia:
  National Technical Information Service, ongoing).
- "United States Social Security Death Index," database, FamilySearch
  (https://familysearch.org/ark:/61903/1:1:JPW6-T3G : 7 January
  2021), Alma George, Dec 1987; citing U.S. Social Security
  Administration, Death Master File, database (Alexandria, Virginia:
  National Technical Information Service, ongoing).

265) Pasqualina Perrina

Pasqualina Perrina(265) was born on 10 July 1895, in Ariano, Italy, to Angelo
Maria Perrina(74) and Tommasina Paduano(74a).

Pasqualina Perrina(265) married Giovanni Feriero(265a) on 31 March 1921 in
Ariano, Italy.

Giovanni Feriero(265a) was born 0n 24 May 1902, in Ariano, Italy, to Giuseppe
Feriero(265aF) and Maria Teresa Roviello(265aM). Giovanni Feriero(265a) died 5
May 1958 in Ariano, Italy.

Records that include Pasqualina Perrina(265) and/or Giovanni Feriero(265a):
- Ariano, Italy 1895 Birth Act #448
- Ariano, Italy 1902 Birth Act #284
- Ariano, Italy 1921 Marriage Act #53

266) Clementina DeDonato

Clementina DeDonato(266) was born 3 February 1897, in Ariano, Italy, to
Domenico deDonato(61) and Anna Maria Coppola(61a). Clementina DeDonato(266)
died on 15 October 1898, in Ariano Italy.

Records that include Clementina DeDonato(266):
- Ariano, Italy 1897 Birth Act #82
- Ariano, Italy 1896 Death Act #342

267) Concordia Manganiello

Concordia Manganiello(267) was stillborn on 11 January 1896, in Ariano, Italy,
to Giuseppe Manganiello(64a) and Maria Francesca Fodarella(64).

Records that include Concordia Manganiello(267):
- Ariano, Italy 1896 Birth Act #24

268) Angelo Michele DiLillo

Angelo Michele DiLillo(268) was born on 21 March 1896, in Ariano, Italy, to
Raffaele Di Lillo(95a) and Raimonda Perrina(95). Angelo Michele DiLillo(268)
died on 21 April 1896, in Ariano, Italy.

Records that include Angelo Michele DiLillo(268):
- Ariano, Italy 1896 Birth Act #211
- Ariano, Italy 1896 Death Act #191

269) Emmiddio Giovanni Perrina

Emmiddio Giovanni Perrina(269) was born on 21 April 1896, in Castel Baronia,
Italy, to Francesco Paolo Perrina(90) and Maria Cristina Sofia Leone(90a).
Emmiddio Giovanni Perrina(269) died 12 May 1896 in Castel Baronia, Italy.

Records that include Emmiddio Giovanni Perrina(269):
- Castel Baronia, Italy 1896 Birth Act #17
- Castel Baronia, Italy 1896 Death Act #30

270) Angelina DeDonato

Angelina DeDonato(270) born on 22 September 1896, in Sao Paulo, Brazil, to Marcello deDonato(78) and Maria Rosa Politano(78a).
NOTE: This is the only information I was able to locate. The registration in 1934 of Angelina DeDonato(270) birth in 1896.

Records that include Angelina DeDonato(270):
- "Brasil, São Paulo, Registro Civil, 1925-1995", , FamilySearch (https://www.familysearch.org/ark:/61903/1:1:6XZ6-BKF5 : Fri Jul 05 19:47:46 UTC 2024), Entry for Angelina Donato and Marcelo Donato, 22 Jan 1934.

271) Concetta Anastasio

Concetta Anastasio(271) was born in 23 August 1897, in Waterbury, CT, to Pasquale Antonio Anastasio(72a) and Anna Maria D'Ausilio(72). Concetta Anastasio(271) died 10 September 1985.

Concetta Anastasio(271) married Joseph Bonelli(271a) and Matthew Simon Gaina(271b).

Concetta Anastasio(271) married Joseph Bonelli(271a).

Joseph Bonelli(271a) was born 4 December 1887 in Licata, Italy, to Angelo Bonelli(271aF) and Angela Taselseth(271aM). On 2 April 1910, Joseph Bonelli(271a), boarded the ship "San Giovanni" in Palermo, Italy, arriving in New York City on 14 April 1910. Joseph Bonelli(271a) became a United States Citizen on 21 February 1918 in St. Louis, MO. Joseph Bonelli(271a) died(Homicide) 24 July 1929 in Detroit, MI.

Known Children of Concetta Anastasio(271) and Joseph Bonelli(271a):

    i) Angelina Bonelli(468) born in 1916
    ii) Mary Ann Bonelli(484) born in 1918
    iii) Angelo Bonelli(496) born in 1919
    iv) Josephine Bonelli(519) born in 1922
    v) Theresa Bonelli(542) born in 1925

Concetta Anastasio(271) married Matthew Simon Gaina(271b).

Matthew Simon Gaina(271b) was born on 4 November 1884, in Lithuania. Matthew Simon Gaina(271b) died in 1961, in Fountain, MI.

Records that include Concetta Anastasio(271), Joseph Bonelli(271a) and/or Matthew Simon Gaina(271b).
- "United States Census, 1900", , FamilySearch (https://www.familysearch.org/ark:/61903/1:1:M97Z-VHB : Fri Aug 02 20:31:37 UTC 2024), Entry for Anastasia Pasquale and Mary Pasquale, 1900.
- "United States Census, 1910", , FamilySearch (https://www.familysearch.org/ark:/61903/1:1:MLMM-7YC : Fri Mar 08 21:46:08 UTC 2024), Entry for Pasquale Unastasio and Maria Unastasio, 1910.
- "Missouri, County Naturalization Records, 1830-1985", , FamilySearch (https://www.familysearch.org/ark:/61903/1:1:6LTJ-29C8 : Thu Mar 07 02:43:21 UTC 2024), Entry for Joseph Bonelli, 21 Mar 1911.
- "United States, Missouri, Naturalization Records, 1843-1991", , FamilySearch (https://www.familysearch.org/ark:/61903/1:1:682D-LBVJ : Mon Mar 11 02:06:43 UTC 2024), Entry for Joseph Bonelli, 21 Mar 1911.

- "United States, Missouri, Naturalization Records, 1843-1991", , FamilySearch (https://www.familysearch.org/ark:/61903/1:1:6826-456Z : Sat Mar 09 10:54:22 UTC 2024), Entry for Joseph Bonelli and Concetta, 30 Apr 1917.
- "United States World War I Draft Registration Cards, 1917-1918", database with images, FamilySearch (https://www.familysearch.org/ark:/61903/1:1:WSC9-8GMM : 10 July 2024), Joseph Bonelli, 1917-1918.
- "United States, Missouri, Naturalization Records, 1843-1991", , FamilySearch (https://www.familysearch.org/ark:/61903/1:1:6826-456Z : Sat Mar 09 10:54:22 UTC 2024), Entry for Joseph Bonelli and Concetta, 30 Apr 1917.
- "Missouri, County Naturalization Records, 1830-1985", , FamilySearch (https://www.familysearch.org/ark:/61903/1:1:6GS7-JYK8 : Sat Mar 09 17:05:41 UTC 2024), Entry for Joseph Bonelli and Concetta, 21 Feb 1918.
- "United States, Missouri, Naturalization Records, 1843-1991", , FamilySearch (https://www.familysearch.org/ark:/61903/1:1:682J-HH6L : Fri Mar 08 09:45:52 UTC 2024), Entry for Joseph Bonelli and Concetta, 21 Feb 1918.
- "United States, Missouri, Naturalization Records, 1843-1991", , FamilySearch (https://www.familysearch.org/ark:/61903/1:1:68LS-JR92 : Fri Mar 08 22:45:20 UTC 2024), Entry for Joseph Bonelli, 22 Nov 1917.
- "United States Census, 1920", , FamilySearch (https://www.familysearch.org/ark:/61903/1:1:M887-HJN : Tue Jul 09 05:48:36 UTC 2024), Entry for Joseph Bonneli and Consetti Bonneli, 1920.
- "Michigan Death Certificates, 1921-1952", , FamilySearch (https://www.familysearch.org/ark:/61903/1:1:KF44-66X : Fri Mar 08 16:21:43 UTC 2024), Entry for Guiseppe Bonelli and Angelo Bonelli, 24 Jul 1929.
- "Find a Grave Index," database, FamilySearch (https://www.familysearch.org/ark:/61903/1:1:6BMQ-RG3H : 26 July 2024), Joseph/Joe, ; Burial, Detroit, Wayne, Michigan, United States of America, Mount Olivet Cemetery; citing record ID 271182539, Find a Grave, http://www.findagrave.com.
- "United States Census, 1930", , FamilySearch (https://www.familysearch.org/ark:/61903/1:1:X7SP-TPK : Sun Mar 10 23:23:02 UTC 2024), Entry for Causamo Stilo and Elvera Stilo, 1930.
- "Michigan Death Certificates, 1921-1952", , FamilySearch (https://www.familysearch.org/ark:/61903/1:1:KF4Z-QX5 : Fri Mar 08 15:54:39 UTC 2024), Entry for Angeline Bonelli and Joseph Bonelli, 14 Mar 1931.
- "Michigan Death Certificates, 1921-1952", , FamilySearch (https://www.familysearch.org/ark:/61903/1:1:KFWS-4LV : Fri Mar 08 16:06:18 UTC 2024), Entry for Angelo Bonelli and Joseph Bonelli, 02 Oct 1936.
- "United States Census, 1940", , FamilySearch (https://www.familysearch.org/ark:/61903/1:1:KH9W-QLW : Fri Jul 12 22:08:29 UTC 2024), Entry for Concetta H Athanas and Mary A Bonelli, 1940.
- "United States Census, 1940", , FamilySearch (https://www.familysearch.org/ark:/61903/1:1:K4G5-N83 : Wed Jul 17 06:22:29 UTC 2024), Entry for Matthew Gaina, 1940.
- "United States World War II Draft Registration Cards, 1942", , FamilySearch (https://www.familysearch.org/ark:/61903/1:1:J4ST-F6V : Sat Feb 24 03:28:12 UTC 2024), Entry for Matthew Simon Gaina, 1942.
- https://search.ancestry.com/cgi-bin/sse.dll?indiv=1&dbid=9093&h=4647908&tid=&pid=&usePUB=true&_phsrc=brq17604&_phstart=successSource
- https://search.ancestry.com/cgi-bin/sse.dll?viewrecord=1&r=an&db=Newspaperobits&indiv=try&h=584979959

- "Find a Grave Index," database, FamilySearch
  (https://www.familysearch.org/ark:/61903/1:1:QVLR-86WT : 23 July
  2024), Concetta Maria Anastasio Gaina, ; Burial, Louisville,
  Winston, Mississippi, United States of America, Memorial Park;
  citing record ID 104734136, Find a Grave,
  http://www.findagrave.com.
- "United States, Social Security Numerical Identification Files
  (NUMIDENT), 1936-2007", database, FamilySearch
  (https://www.familysearch.org/ark:/61903/1:1:6KQN-FGZ1 : 10
  February 2023), Conetta Anastasio in entry for Josephine Bonelli
  Jorgensen, .

272) Raimonda D'Ausilio

Raimonda D'Ausilio(272) was born on 12 November 1896, in Ariano, Italy, to
Nicola Maria D'Ausilio(83) and Giustina Mariano(83a).

Raimonda D'Ausilio(272) married Carmine Cappelluzzo(272a) on 25 January 1922
in Ariano, Italy.

Carmine Cappelluzzo(272a) was born on 16 May 1894, in Ariano, Italy, to Vito
Cappelluzzo(272aF) and Anna Maria Clericuzio(272aM).

Records that include Raimonda D'Ausilio(272) and/or Carmine Cappelluzzo(272a):
- Ariano, Italy 1894 Birth Act #313
- Ariano, Italy 1896 Birth Act #599
- Ariano, Italy 1922 Marriage Act #13

273) Ciriaco Miressi

Ciriaco Miressi(273) was stillborn on 16 December 1896, in Ariano, Italy, to
Giuseppe Miressi(51a) and Rosa Giorgione (50).

Records that include Ciriaco Miressi(273):
- Ariano, Italy 1896 Birth Act #637

274) Domenico deDonato

Domenico deDonato(274) was born on 19 February 1897, in Ariano, Italy, to
Michele deDonato(106) and Loreta di Vitto(106a). Domenico deDonato(274) died
on 10 March 1897, in Ariano, Italy.

Records that include Domenico deDonato(274):
- Ariano, Italy 1897 Birth Act #111
- Ariano, Italy 1897 Death Act #85

275) Michelangelo Perrina

Michelangelo Perrina(275) was born on 6 May 1897, in Castel Baronia, Italy, to
Raffaele Perrina(58) and Maria Lucia Gesa(58a). Michelangelo Perrina(275)
served as a private in the United States Army(Company D/107th Infantry) from
15 August 1918 to 12 April 1919. Michelangelo Perrina(275) died 6 March 1989
in Volusia, FL.

Michelangelo Perrina(275) married Rose Damiano(275a) on 4 October 1923 in
Schenectady, NY.

Rose Damiano(275a) was born on 04 May 1903, in New York, to Francesco
Damiano(275aF) and Maria Varasetta(275aM). Rose Damiano(275a) died on 18 Jul
1989 in Volusia, FL.

Known Children of Michelangelo Perrina(275) and/or Rose Damiano(275a):

    i) Ralph M. Perrino(537) born in 1924
    ii) Frances Michele Perrino(565) born in 1928

Records that include Michelangelo Perrina(275) and/or Rose Damiano(275a):
- Castel Baronia, Italy 1897 Birth Act #23

- "United States Census, 1910", , FamilySearch (https://www.familysearch.org/ark:/61903/1:1:M596-H5V : Mon Jul 22 15:03:44 UTC 2024), Entry for Raffaele Perrino and Lucie Perrino, 1910.
- "United States World War I Draft Registration Cards, 1917-1918", database with images, FamilySearch (https://www.familysearch.org/ark:/61903/1:1:W8FW-97W2 : 10 July 2024), Michael Perrino, 1917-1918.
- "United States, Veterans Administration Master Index, 1917-1940", , FamilySearch (https://www.familysearch.org/ark:/61903/1:1:WSSB-NPZM : Thu Mar 07 10:05:58 UTC 2024), Entry for Michael Perrino, 12 April 1919.
- "United States Census, 1920", , FamilySearch (https://www.familysearch.org/ark:/61903/1:1:MVS4-4ZB : Sat Mar 09 11:08:27 UTC 2024), Entry for Raffaele Perrino and Lucia Perrino, 1920.
- "United States Census, 1930", , FamilySearch (https://www.familysearch.org/ark:/61903/1:1:X4TT-MWS : Mon Jul 22 22:05:18 UTC 2024), Entry for Michael Purino and Rose Purino, 1930.
- "United States Census, 1940", , FamilySearch (https://www.familysearch.org/ark:/61903/1:1:KQ3C-F5Z : Sun Jul 14 04:45:47 UTC 2024), Entry for Michael Perrino and Rose Perrino, 1940.
- "United States Census, 1950", , FamilySearch (https://www.familysearch.org/ark:/61903/1:1:6XTY-YZ9F : Tue Mar 19 20:23:20 UTC 2024), Entry for Francis M Perrino and Rose C Salerno, 4 May 1950.
- "United States Social Security Death Index," database, FamilySearch (https://familysearch.org/ark:/61903/1:1:VSF6-GMH : 7 January 2021), Michael Perrino, 06 Mar 1989; citing U.S. Social Security Administration, Death Master File, database (Alexandria, Virginia: National Technical Information Service, ongoing).
- "United States, Social Security Numerical Identification Files (NUMIDENT), 1936-2007", database, FamilySearch (https://www.familysearch.org/ark:/61903/1:1:6KMG-SL1B : 10 February 2023), Michael Perrino, .
- "Florida Death Index, 1877-1998," database, FamilySearch (https://familysearch.org/ark:/61903/1:1:VV4W-MDR : 25 December 2014), Michael A Perrino, 06 Mar 1989; from "Florida Death Index, 1877-1998," index, Ancestry (www.ancestry.com : 2004); citing vol. , certificate number 35512, Florida Department of Health, Office of Vital Records, Jacksonville.
- "Find a Grave Index," database, FamilySearch (https://www.familysearch.org/ark:/61903/1:1:QVKZ-LCCR : 12 December 2022), Michael A. Perrino, ; Burial, Daytona Beach, Volusia, Florida, United States of America, Daytona Memorial Park; citing record ID 39847010, Find a Grave, http://www.findagrave.com.
- "Florida Death Index, 1877-1998," , FamilySearch (https://familysearch.org/ark:/61903/1:1:VV4W-MDT : 25 December 2014), Rose Perrino, 18 Jul 1989; from "Florida Death Index, 1877-1998," index, Ancestry (www.ancestry.com : 2004); citing vol. , certificate number 78241, Florida Department of Health, Office of Vital Records, Jacksonville.
- "United States, Social Security Numerical Identification Files (NUMIDENT), 1936-2007", database, FamilySearch (https://www.familysearch.org/ark:/61903/1:1:6K4C-MGRB : 11 February 2023), Rose Perrino, .
- "United States Social Security Death Index," database, FamilySearch (https://familysearch.org/ark:/61903/1:1:JG4P-QZ2 : 11 January 2021), Rose Perrino, 18 Jul 1989; citing U.S. Social Security Administration, Death Master File, database (Alexandria, Virginia: National Technical Information Service, ongoing).
- https://www.legacy.com/us/obituaries/dailygazette/name/ralph-perrino-obituary?id=17579971
- "St. Anthony, Schenectady, New York, Marriages (Oct 1916 -Jul 2006)", 2 Volumes, American-Canadian Genealogical Society, Manchester, NH, page 589

276) Antonio Grasso

Antonio Grasso(276) was born on 14 Jun 1897, in Ariano, Italy, to Crescenzo Grasso(76a) and Anna Perrina(76).

Antonio Grasso(276) married Mary Lombardi(276a) on 9 April 1923, 30 September 1923, and 24 September 1927* in Bronx, NY.
NOTE: 3 marriage records have been located, it is probable that only the last marriage date is correct probably due to circumstances not allowing the earlier marriage licenses from being used, More research is needed.

Mary Lombardi(276a) born on 23 March 1906, in Manhattan, NY, to Ferdinand Lombardi(276aF) and Josephine Mele(276aM).
NOTE: birth record list the family name as Lombardini.

Known Children of Antonio Grasso(276) and Mary Lombardi(276a):

   i) Gloria Grasso(579) born in 1931
   ii) Ferdinand (Fred Louis) Grasso(594) was born in 1934

Records that include Antonio Grasso(276) and/or Mary Lombardi(276a):
- "United States, Census, 1920", FamilySearch (https://www.familysearch.org/ark:/61903/1:1:MJG5-W5J : Fri Jan 10 19:13:55 UTC 2025), Entry for Frank Grasso and Mary Grasso, 1920.
- "New York, New York City Marriage Records, 1829-1938", FamilySearch (https://www.familysearch.org/ark:/61903/1:1:Q2C2-GPXB : Fri Mar 08 04:33:27 UTC 2024), Entry for Anthony Grasso and Mary Lombardi, 9 April 1923.
- "New York, New York City Marriage Records, 1829-1938", FamilySearch (https://www.familysearch.org/ark:/61903/1:1:Q2C2-GPZK : Sat Mar 09 09:05:40 UTC 2024), Entry for Anthony Grasso and Mary Lombardi, 30 September 1923.
- "New York, New York City Marriage Records, 1829-1938", FamilySearch (https://www.familysearch.org/ark:/61903/1:1:Q2CJ-J28G : Fri Mar 08 21:18:35 UTC 2024), Entry for Anthony Grasso and Mary Lombardi, 24 September 1927.
- "United States, Census, 1940", FamilySearch (https://www.familysearch.org/ark:/61903/1:1:KQMD-V2P : Fri Jul 19 06:08:08 UTC 2024), Entry for Anthony Grasso and Mary Grasso, 1940.
- "United States, Census, 1950", FamilySearch (https://www.familysearch.org/ark:/61903/1:1:6XT2-4X6Q : Tue Oct 03 16:45:26 UTC 2023), Entry for Fred Grasso and Anthony Grasso, 10 April 1950.
- https://dailyvoice.com/new-jersey/northernhighlands/obituaries/gloria-labollita-85-allendale-resident/698458/

277) Luigi Perrina

Luigi Perrina(277) was born on 21 June 1897, in Ariano, Italy, to Michele Perrina(88) and Maria Grazia Caraglia(88a). Luigi Perrina(277) died 16 April 1900 in Ariano, Italy.

Records that include Luigi Perrina(277):
- Ariano, Italy 1897 Birth Act #363
- Ariano, Italy 1900 Death Act #159

278) Antonio Giorgione

Antonio Giorgione(278) was born on 26 June 1897, in Ariano, Italy, to Raffaele Giorgione(80) and Carmina Salvioli(80a). Antonio Giorgione(278) died 2 February 1926 in the hospital of the incurables, San Lorenzo, Naples, Italy.

Antonio Giorgione(278) married Maria Liberata Vernacchia(278a) on 12 October 1922, in Ariano, Italy.

Maria Liberata Vernacchia(278a) was born on 14 May 1892, in Ariano, Italy, to Francesco Paolo Vernacchia(278aF) and Maria Serluca(278aM). Maria Liberata Vernacchia(278a) died 26 November 1976, in Ariano, Italy.

Maria Liberata Vernacchia(278a) was previously married to Nicola Fodarella(278aX).

Records that include Antonio Giorgione(278) and/or Maria Liberata Vernacchia(278a):
- Ariano, Italy 1892 Birth Act #87
- Ariano, Italy 1897 Birth Act #374
- Ariano, Italy 1922 Marriage Act #159
- Ariano, Italy 1926 Death Act #I.C.2
- Ariano, Italy 1976 Death Act #177

279) Rosa di Lillo

Rosa di Lillo(279) was born on 23 July 1897, in Ariano, Italy, to Raffaele Di Lillo(95a) and Raimonda Perrina(95).

Rosa di Lillo(279) married Gabriele de Lillo(279a) on 16 September 1920 in Ariano, Italy.

Gabriele de Lillo(279a) was born on 30 April 1895, in Ariano, Italy, to Michele de Lillo(279aF) and Maria Addolorata Santolino(279aM).

Records that include Rosa di Lillo(279) and/or Gabriele de Lillo(279a)
- Ariano, Italy 1895 Birth Act #316
- Ariano, Italy 1897 Birth Act #424
- Ariano, Italy 1920 Marriage Act #186

280) Anna Ciasullo

Anna Ciasullo(280) was born on 26 July 1897, in Ariano, Italy, to Filippo Ciasullo(105a) and Maria Giovanna Perrina(105). Anna Ciasullo(280) died on 11 February 1899 in Ariano, Italy.

Records that include Anna Ciasullo(280):
- Ariano, Italy 1897 Birth Act #432
- Ariano, Italy 1899 Death Act #58

281) Carmella DeDonato

Carmella deDonato(281) was born August 1897, in Paraíba, Brasil, to Marcello deDonato(78) and Maria Rosa Politano(78a). Carmella deDonato(281) was baptized 24 October 1897. Carmella deDonato(281) died 10 June 1967 in Santos, Santos, São Paulo, Brasil.

Carmella deDonato(281) married Luiz Cacetare(281a).

Luiz Cacetare(281a) no information found.

Records that include Carmella deDonato(281):
- "Brasil, São Paulo, Registro Civil, 1925-1995", , FamilySearch (https://www.familysearch.org/ark:/61903/1:1:65V2-SFY1 : Fri Mar 08 15:01:32 UTC 2024), Entry for Carmela de Donato and Marcelo de Donato, 11 de junho de 1967.

282) Adamo Lombardi

Adamo Lombardi(282) was born September 1897, in Brazil, to Vincenzo (James) Lombardi(85a) and Maria Carmela deDonato(85). Adamo Lombardi(282) died 23 October 1898 in Brás, Brazil.

Records that include Adamo Lombardi(282):
- "Brasil, São Paulo, Registro Civil, 1925-1995", , FamilySearch (https://www.familysearch.org/ark:/61903/1:1:6YG4-Z5RL : Sat Jul 27 10:00:10 UTC 2024), Entry for Adamo Lombardi and Vincenzo Lombardi, 23 de outubro de 1898.

283) Filomena Altanese

Filomena Altanese(283) was born on 17 September 1897, in Grottaminarda, Italy, to Cosimo Altanese(87) and Margarita Galgothia Alfonsina Romano(87a).

Records that include Filomena Altanese(283):
- Grottaminarda, Italy 1897 Birth Act #101
- "United States Census, 1910", , FamilySearch (https://www.familysearch.org/ark:/61903/1:1:MKTT-DGB : Fri Mar 08 06:34:11 UTC 2024), Entry for Cosno Altanese and Margaret Altanese, 1910.

284) Oto Emilio Stella

Oto Emilio Stella(284) was stillborn on 19 November 1897, in Ceppaloni, Italy, to Agostino Stella(101) and Eugenia Donisi(101a).

Records that include Oto Emilio Stella(284):
- Ceppaloni, Italy 1897 Birth Act #8 part II

285) Giovannina Perrina

Giovannina Perrina(285) was born on 2 January 1898, in Castel Baronia, Italy, to Francesco Paolo Perrina(90) and Maria Cristina Sofia Leone(90a). Giovannina Perrina(285) died 10 April 1979 in Flumeri, Italy.

Giovannina Perrina(285) married Michele Pennacchio(285a) on 21 September 1919 in Flumeri, Italy.

Michele Pennacchio(285a) was born on 8 March 1899, in San Sossio Baronia, Italy, to Giovanni Antonio Pennacchio(285aF) and Mariantonia Zizzo(285aM).

Records that include Giovannina Perrina(285) and/or Michele Pennacchio(285a):
- Castel Baronia, Italy 1898 Birth Act #1
- San Sossio Baronia, Italy 1899 Birth Act #15
- Flumeri, Italy 1919 Marriage Act #13

286) Oto Manganiello

Oto Manganiello(286) was born on 14 March 1898, in Ariano, Italy, to Raimondo Manganiello(79a) and Mariantonia Fodarella(79). Oto Manganiello(286) boarded the SS Patria, in Naples, Italy, on 17 July 1920, arrived in New York City, on 1 August 1920. Oto Manganiello(286) died 9 December 1932 in Ossining, NY.

Oto Manganiello(286) married Assunta Scrima(286a) on 9 May 1927 in Ariano, Italy.

Assunta Scrima(286a) was born on 10 October 1912, in Ariano, Italy, to Pasquale Scrima(286aF) and Clementina Albanese(286aM).

Assunta Scrima(286a) later married Giovanni Savino(286ab).

Records that include Oto Manganiello(286) and/or Assunta Serluca(249a):
- Ariano, Italy 1898 Birth Act #165
- Ariano, Italy 1912 Birth Act #506
- Ariano, Italy 1927 Marriage Act #60
- Ossining, NY 1932 Death Act #154

287) Pasquale (Patsy) Perrino

Pasquale (Patsy) Perrino(287) was born on 3 June 1898, in Ariano, Italy, to Angelo Maria Perrina(74) and Tommasina Paduano(74a). 19 June 1914 Pasquale (Patsy) Perrino(287) boarded the ship SS Verona in Naples, Italy arriving in New York City on 3 July 1914. Pasquale (Patsy) Perrino(287) became a United States Citizen on 19 September 1929 in Brooklyn, NY. Pasquale (Patsy) Perrino(287) died 22 October 1971 in Brooklyn, NY.

Pasquale (Patsy) Perrino(287) married Fioritta (Fanny) Masucci(287a) on 6 September 1925 in Brooklyn, NY.

Fioritta (Fanny) Masucci(287a) was born on 4 May 1903, in Villanova del Battista, Italy, to Carmine Masucci(287aF) and Pasqualina Barilla(287aM). On 29 May 1912 Fioritta (Fanny) Masucci(287a) boarded the ship SS San Gugliamo in Naples, Italy, arriving in New York City, on 11 June 1912.

Known children of Pasquale (Patsy) Perrino(287) and Fioritta (Fanny) Masucci(287a):

> i) Living Person or Spouse
> ii) Angelo Joseph Perrino(556) born in 1927
> iii) Living Person or Spouse

Records that include Pasquale (Patsy) Perrino(287) and/or Fioritta (Fanny) Masucci(287a):

- Ariano, Italy 1898 Birth Act #346
- Villanova del Battista, Italy 1903 Birth Act #25
- "New York Passenger Arrival Lists (Ellis Island), 1892-1924", , FamilySearch (https://www.familysearch.org/ark:/61903/1:1:JJRP-LYW : Sat Mar 09 08:06:23 UTC 2024), Entry for Fiorita Masucci and Concetta, 1912.
- "New York Passenger Arrival Lists (Ellis Island), 1892-1924", , FamilySearch (https://www.familysearch.org/ark:/61903/1:1:JJQ2-5PJ : Wed Sep 18 10:19:07 UTC 2024), Entry for Pasquale Perrina and Angelo, 1914.
- "New York, New York City Marriage Records, 1829-1938", , FamilySearch (https://www.familysearch.org/ark:/61903/1:1:Q2C6-W1ZZ : Sat Mar 09 05:34:35 UTC 2024), Entry for Pasquale Perrino and Fanny Masuces, 6 September 1925.
- "New York, U.S. District and Circuit Court Naturalization Records, 1824-1991", , FamilySearch (https://www.familysearch.org/ark:/61903/1:1:6L3Z-RZ6H : Thu Mar 07 22:36:53 UTC 2024), Entry for Pasquale Perrino and Fiorita, 18 Jan 1926.
- "New York, U.S. District and Circuit Court Naturalization Records, 1824-1991", , FamilySearch (https://www.familysearch.org/ark:/61903/1:1:6L37-JHZ7 : Wed Mar 06 05:16:00 UTC 2024), Entry for Pasquale Perrino and Fiorita, 18 Jan 1926.
- "New York, U.S. District and Circuit Court Naturalization Records, 1824-1991", , FamilySearch (https://www.familysearch.org/ark:/61903/1:1:6L3Z-K9N2 : Fri Mar 08 14:24:02 UTC 2024), Entry for Pasquale Perrino and Fioritta, 17 Jun 1929.
- "United States Census, 1930", , FamilySearch (https://www.familysearch.org/ark:/61903/1:1:X4LJ-KDX : Fri Mar 08 21:55:42 UTC 2024), Entry for Patsy Perrino and Fannie Perrino, 1930.
- "United States Census, 1940", , FamilySearch (https://www.familysearch.org/ark:/61903/1:1:KQLK-6DN : Sat Mar 09 18:14:25 UTC 2024), Entry for Pasquale Perrino and Fanny Perrino, 1940.
- "New York, New York City, World War II Draft Registration Cards, 1940-1947", , FamilySearch (https://www.familysearch.org/ark:/61903/1:1:WZ9J-7QT2 : Sat Mar 09 00:31:21 UTC 2024), Entry for Pasquale Perrino and New York City Transit System, 15 Feb 1942.
- "United States Census, 1950", , FamilySearch (https://www.familysearch.org/ark:/61903/1:1:6XRQ-T2GV : Wed Mar 20 21:41:17 UTC 2024), Entry for Patrick Perrino and Fannie Perrino, 8 April 1950.
- "United States Social Security Death Index," database, FamilySearch (https://familysearch.org/ark:/61903/1:1:JKK3-G2Q : 7 January 2021), Pasquale Perrino, Oct 1971; citing U.S. Social Security Administration, Death Master File, database (Alexandria, Virginia: National Technical Information Service, ongoing).
- "Find a Grave Index," database, FamilySearch (https://www.familysearch.org/ark:/61903/1:1:6NDP-3P4P : 24 August 2022), Patsy, ; Burial, , Suffolk, New York, United States of America, Saint Charles Cemetery; citing record ID 240244215, Find a Grave, http://www.findagrave.com.

- "United States, Social Security Numerical Identification Files (NUMIDENT), 1936-2007", database, FamilySearch (https://www.familysearch.org/ark:/61903/1:1:6K9X-KXY5 : 10 February 2023), Pasquale Perrino in entry for Angelo Joseph Perrino, .

288) Vincenzo Ciccarelli

Vincenzo Ciccarelli(288) was born on 4 June 1898, in Ariano, Italy, to Domenico Ciccarelli(69a) and Rosa Fiorenza(69). Vincenzo Ciccarelli(288) died 11 June 1898 in Ariano, Italy.

Records that include Vincenzo Ciccarelli(288):
- Ariano, Italy 1898 Birth Act #353
- Ariano, Italy 1898 Death Act #204

289) Oto (Otino) Stella

Oto (Otino) Stella(289) was born on 1 July 1898, in Ariano, Italy, to Antonio Stella(110) and Eugenia LoConte(110a). On 1920 Oto (Otino) Stella(289) boarded the ship SS Regino d'Italia, in Naples, Italy, arriving in New York on 30 April 1920. Oto (Otino) Stella(289) became a United States Citizen on 16 November 1927 in New York, NY. Oto (Otino) Stella(289) died on 3 December 1982 in Bronx, NY.*
* The date of death is from an unverified source.

Oto (Otino) Stella(289) married Maria Giovanna (Jennie) Merola(289a) on 23 July 1927 in New York, NY.

Maria Giovanna (Jennie) Merola(289a) was born on 5 March 1902, in Fisciano, Italy, to Giovanni Merola(289aF) and Carolina Scafuri(289aM). Maria Giovanna (Jennie) Merola(289a) arrived in New York, NY on 24 December 1919 on the ship SS Giuseppe Verde, from Naples, Italy. Maria Giovanna (Jennie) Merola(289a) died 2 February 1972 in Bronx, NY.

Known children of Oto (Otino) Stella(289) and Maria Giovanna (Jennie) Merola(289a):

- i) Anthony Joseph Stella(564) born in 1928
- ii) Eugenia Stella(572) born in 1929
- iii) Giovanni (John) Stella(577) born in 1931
- iv) Gloria Stella(602) born in 1939

Records that include Oto (Otino) Stella(289) and/or Maria Giovanna (Jennie) Merola(289a):
- Ariano, Italy 1898 Birth Act #385
- Fisciano, Italy 1902 Birth Act #43
- "New York Passenger Arrival Lists (Ellis Island), 1892-1924", , FamilySearch (https://www.familysearch.org/ark:/61903/1:1:J6HJ-7PJ : Fri Mar 08 16:31:24 UTC 2024), Entry for Oto Stella and Eugenia Lo Conte, 1920.
- "United States Census, 1940", , FamilySearch (https://www.familysearch.org/ark:/61903/1:1:KQL9-GV9 : Sun Jul 14 11:25:30 UTC 2024), Entry for Otino Stella and Jennie Stella, 1940.
- "New York, U.S. District and Circuit Court Naturalization Records, 1824-1991", , FamilySearch (https://www.familysearch.org/ark:/61903/1:1:W9GW-5MMM : Sat Mar 09 19:58:07 UTC 2024), Entry for Jennie or Giovanna Stella or Merola and Otino Stella.
- "New York, New York City, World War II Draft Registration Cards, 1940-1947", , FamilySearch (https://www.familysearch.org/ark:/61903/1:1:WWBY-FD3Z : Fri Mar 08 22:25:29 UTC 2024), Entry for Otino Stella and Unemployed.
- "New York, New York City, World War II Draft Registration Cards, 1940-1947", , FamilySearch (https://www.familysearch.org/ark:/61903/1:1:WWBL-G5N2 : Fri Mar 08 23:28:02 UTC 2024), Entry for Anthony Stella and Cc Ny, 20 Jun 1946.

- "United States Census, 1950", , FamilySearch
  (https://www.familysearch.org/ark:/61903/1:1:6X5Z-K51C : Mon Mar 18
  23:44:09 UTC 2024), Entry for Otino Stella and Jennie Stella, 18
  April 1950.
- https://www.nytimes.com/1972/02/21/archives/obituary-1-no-
  title.html
- "United States, Social Security Numerical Identification Files
  (NUMIDENT), 1936-2007", database, FamilySearch
  (https://www.familysearch.org/ark:/61903/1:1:6KMY-SK2V : 10
  February 2023), Otino Stella in entry for Anthony Joseph Stella, .

290) Carmine (Carmen Louis) Giorgione/George

Carmine (Carmen Louis) Giorgione/George(290) was born on 22 July 1898, in
Ariano, Italy, to Luigi Giorgione (84) and Maria Giovanna Perillo(86a).
Carmine (Carmen Louis) Giorgione/George(290) boarded the SS Algeria in Naples,
Italy on 28 November 1905, arriving in New York on 18 December 1905. Carmine
(Carmen Louis) Giorgione/George(290) died 4 March 1958 in New York.

Carmine (Carmen Louis) Giorgione/George(290) married Bertha Michalowski(290a).

Bertha Michalowski(290a) was born on 2 November 1904. Bertha Michalowski(290a)
died 20 February 1983 in New York.

Known children of Carmine (Carmen Louis) Giorgione/George(290) and Bertha
Michalowski(290a):

    i) Louis William George(494) born in 1919
    ii) Frances Roselyn George(546) born in 1925
    iii) Louise George(570) born in 1929

Records that include Carmine (Carmen Louis) Giorgione/George(290) and/or
Bertha Michalowski(290a):
- Ariano, Italy 1898 Birth Act #421
- "New York Passenger Arrival Lists (Ellis Island), 1892-1924", ,
  FamilySearch (https://www.familysearch.org/ark:/61903/1:1:JFHQ-
  4J4 : Fri Sep 20 03:13:14 UTC 2024), Entry for Carmine Giorgione
  and Luigi Giorgione, 1905.
- "New York State Census, 1915", database, FamilySearch
  (https://www.familysearch.org/ark:/61903/1:1:K9GM-56R : 1 June
  2022), Carman George in entry for Louie George, 1915.
- "United States World War I Draft Registration Cards, 1917-1918",
  database with images, FamilySearch
  (https://www.familysearch.org/ark:/61903/1:1:WDH5-NL2M : 10 July
  2024), Carman Louis George, 1917-1918.
- "United States Census, 1930", , FamilySearch
  (https://www.familysearch.org/ark:/61903/1:1:X4R1-RJV : Fri Sep 20
  03:41:55 UTC 2024), Entry for Carmin L George and Bertha C George,
  1930.
- "United States Census, 1940", , FamilySearch
  (https://www.familysearch.org/ark:/61903/1:1:KQG5-SHX : Tue Jul 16
  21:20:46 UTC 2024), Entry for Carmen George and Bertha M George,
  1940.
- "Ohio, County Marriages, 1789-2016", , FamilySearch
  (https://www.familysearch.org/ark:/61903/1:1:QPQ5-VBTJ : Sun Mar 10
  07:53:31 UTC 2024), Entry for Louis Wm George and Frances Rowley,
  26 October 1943.
- "United States Census, 1950", , FamilySearch
  (https://www.familysearch.org/ark:/61903/1:1:6XT5-S3N8 : Tue Mar 19
  04:47:32 UTC 2024), Entry for Carman L George and Bertha George, 5
  April 1950.
- "Find a Grave Index," database, FamilySearch
  (https://www.familysearch.org/ark:/61903/1:1:QVVW-4VVK : 1 April
  2023), Carman Louis George, ; Burial, Phillipsburg, Orange, New
  York, United States of America, Wallkill Cemetery; citing record ID
  9040500, Find a Grave, http://www.findagrave.com.

- "Find a Grave Index," , FamilySearch
  (https://www.familysearch.org/ark:/61903/1:1:QVVW-4K7D : 1 April
  2023), Bertha Michalowski, ; Burial, Phillipsburg, Orange, New
  York, United States of America, Wallkill Cemetery; citing record ID
  9040503, Find a Grave, http://www.findagrave.com.
- "United States, Social Security Numerical Identification Files
  (NUMIDENT), 1936-2007", database, FamilySearch
  (https://www.familysearch.org/ark:/61903/1:1:6K9Q-14S7 : 10
  February 2023), Carmen George in entry for Frances Roselyn
  George, .

291) Angela Miressi

Angela Miressi(291) was born on 20 September 1898, in Ariano, Italy, to
Giuseppe Miressi(51a) and Rosa Giorgione(51).

Angela Miressi(291) married Giovanni Zecchino(291a) and Nicola Luongo(291b).

Angela Miressi(291) married Giovanni Zecchino(291a) on 11 March 1920 in
Ariano, Italy.

Giovanni Zecchino(291a) was born on 10 September 1893, in Ariano, Italy, to
Michele Zecchino(291aF) and Maria Luigia Ceruolo(291aM). Giovanni
Zecchino(291a) died 30 March 1939 in Ariano, Italy.

Known children of Angela Miressi(291) and Giovanni Zecchino(291a):

    i) Attilio Zecchino(511) born in 1921
    ii) Gaetano Zecchino(521) born about 1922
    iii) Antonio Zecchino(534) born in 1924
    iv) Rosa Zecchino(588) born in 1933

Angela Miressi(291) married Nicola Luongo(291b) on 18 March 1950 in Melito,
Italy.

Nicola Luongo(291b) was born on 15 March 1895, in Melito Irpino, Italy, to
Cresenzo Luongo(291bF) and Elizabetta Muto(291bM).

Records that include Angela Miressi(291), Giovanni Zecchino(291a), and/or
Nicola Luongo(291b):
- Ariano, Italy 1893 Birth Act #518
- Melito Irpino, Italy 1895 Birth Act #25
- Ariano, Italy 1898 Birth Act #517
- Ariano, Italy 1920 Marriage Act #68
- Ariano, Italy 1921 Birth Act #35
- Ariano, Italy 1921 Death Act #17
- Ariano, Italy 1926 Death Act #293
- Ariano, Italy 1926 Death Act #351
- Ariano, Italy 1933 Death Act #138
- Ariano, Italy 1933 Death Act #109
- Ariano, Italy 1950 Marriage Act #P.II.B.5

292) Concetta deDonato

Concetta DeDonato(292) born on 29 April 1899, in São Paulo, Brasil, to
Marcello deDonato(78) and Maria Rosa Politano(78a). Concetta DeDonato(292)
died died 2 January 1901 in Aracá, Borba, Amazonas, Brasil.

Records that include Concetta DeDonato(292):
- "Brasil, São Paulo, Registros da Igreja Católica, 1640-2013", ,
  FamilySearch (https://www.familysearch.org/ark:/61903/1:1:6DGX-6XGL
  : Wed Jul 24 15:34:12 UTC 2024), Entry for Concetta Guidonato and
  Marcello Guidonato, 15 de maio de 1899.
- "Brasil, São Paulo, Registro Civil, 1925-2023", , FamilySearch
  (https://www.familysearch.org/ark:/61903/1:1:6YGM-8LNL : Sat Jul 27
  09:51:54 UTC 2024), Entry for Concetta Donato and Marcello Donato,
  2 de janeiro de 1901.

293) Assunta Ciasullo

Assunta Ciasullo(293) was born on 18 August 1899, in Ariano, Italy, to Filippo Ciasullo(105a) and Maria Giovanna Perrina(105). On 29 October 1932 Assunta Ciasullo(293) boarded the ship SS Conte Grande, in Naples, Italy. Assunta Ciasullo(293) arrived in New York, NY on 7 November 1932. Assunta Ciasullo(293) died 5 April 1959 in Schenectady, NY.

Assunta Ciasullo(293) married Antonio Vernacchia(293a) on 11 February 1922 in Ariano, Italy.

Antonio Vernacchia(293a) was born on 20 January 1896, in Ariano, Italy, to Francesco Vernacchia(293aF) and Maria Concetta Cetrone(293aM). Antonio Vernacchia(293a) served in the United States Army from 2 July 1918 until 28 June 1919. Antonio Vernacchia(293a) became a citizen of the United States on 27 June 1919 in Ohio. Antonio Vernacchia(293a) died 16 November 1992 in Schenectady, NY.

Antonio Vernacchia(293a) was previously married to Maria Vincenza Grasso(293aX) and had a child.

Known children of Assunta Ciasullo(293) and Antonio Vernacchia(293a):

    i) Concetta Mary Vernacchio(526) born in 1923
    ii) Phillip Vernacchio(536) born in 1924
    iii) Living person and/or spouse

Records that include Assunta Ciasullo(293) and/or Antonio Vernacchia(293a):
- Ariano, Italy 1896 Birth Act #49
- Ariano, Italy 1899 Birth Act #486
- "Ohio, World War I, Enrollment Cards, 1914-1918", , FamilySearch (https://www.familysearch.org/ark:/61903/1:1:7ZWX-13PZ : Sat Mar 09 08:24:28 UTC 2024), Entry for Antonio Vernacchio, 2 July 1918.
- "United States, Veterans Administration Master Index, 1917-1940", , FamilySearch (https://www.familysearch.org/ark:/61903/1:1:W7R8-QBMM : Fri Mar 08 00:56:59 UTC 2024), Entry for Antonio Vernacchio, 28 June 1919.
- "United States Passport Applications, 1795-1925", , FamilySearch (https://www.familysearch.org/ark:/61903/1:1:QV5B-F1QX : Sun Mar 10 17:56:49 UTC 2024), Entry for Antonio Vernacchio, 1919.
- "United States Passport Applications, 1795-1925", , FamilySearch (https://www.familysearch.org/ark:/61903/1:1:QV5Y-1GZJ : Sun Mar 10 12:21:19 UTC 2024), Entry for Antonio Vernacchio, 1921.
- Ariano, Italy 1922 Marriage Act #486
- "New York, New York Passenger and Crew Lists, 1909, 1925-1957", , FamilySearch (https://www.familysearch.org/ark:/61903/1:1:KXMK-3PP : Fri Mar 08 13:37:10 UTC 2024), Entry for Antonio Vernacchia, 1926.
- "United States Census, 1930", , FamilySearch (https://www.familysearch.org/ark:/61903/1:1:X4TY-PGH : Sat Mar 09 21:13:12 UTC 2024), Entry for Joseph Ciasullo and Grace Ciasullo, 1930.
- "New York, New York Passenger and Crew Lists, 1909, 1925-1957", , FamilySearch (https://www.familysearch.org/ark:/61903/1:1:24JT-VFV : Sat Mar 09 03:39:25 UTC 2024), Entry for Francesco Vernacchio, 1932.
- "United States Census, 1940", , FamilySearch (https://www.familysearch.org/ark:/61903/1:1:K79V-279 : Fri Mar 08 09:15:07 UTC 2024), Entry for Tony Vernacchio and Assunda Vernacchio, 1940.
- "United States World War II Draft Registration Cards, 1942", , FamilySearch (https://www.familysearch.org/ark:/61903/1:1:QKV7-FFG8 : Fri Feb 23 22:30:43 UTC 2024), Entry for Antonio Vernacchio and Assunta Vernacchio, 27 Apr 1942.
- "United States Census, 1950", , FamilySearch (https://www.familysearch.org/ark:/61903/1:1:6XP7-5F4V : Tue Oct 03 16:28:17 UTC 2023), Entry for Anthony Vernacchio and Susan Vernacchio, 19 April 1950.

- "New York State Health Department, Genealogical Research Death Index, 1957-1963," , FamilySearch (https://familysearch.org/ark:/61903/1:1:2CHV-9V8 : 11 February 2018), Philip Vernacchio, 14 Nov 1959; citing Death, Schenectady, Schenectady, New York, file #81042, New York State Department of Health—Vital Records Section, Albany.
- https://www.findagrave.com/memorial/141889792/philip_vernacchio
- "United States Social Security Death Index," database, FamilySearch (https://familysearch.org/ark:/61903/1:1:VMV3-BPG : 7 January 2021), Antonio Vernacchio, 16 Nov 1992; citing U.S. Social Security Administration, Death Master File, database (Alexandria, Virginia: National Technical Information Service, ongoing).
- "United States, Social Security Numerical Identification Files (NUMIDENT), 1936-2007", database, FamilySearch (https://www.familysearch.org/ark:/61903/1:1:6KMG-9491 : 10 February 2023), Antonio Vernacchio, .
- "Find a Grave Index," database, FamilySearch (https://www.familysearch.org/ark:/61903/1:1:QK1X-T65K : 7 March 2024), Antonio J. Vernacchio, ; Burial, Schenectady, Schenectady, New York, United States of America, Saint Joseph's Cemetery; citing record ID 141866909, Find a Grave, http://www.findagrave.com.
- https://www.findagrave.com/memorial/260004020/assunta_vernacchio
- https://www.findagrave.com/memorial/142035993/frank_vernacchio
- https://www.findagrave.com/memorial/259369980/concetta_mary_saccocio

294) Francesca deDonato

Francesca deDonato(294) was born on 21 August 1899, in Ariano, Italy, to Michele deDonato(106) and Loreta di Vitto(106a). On 8 October 1917 Francesca deDonato(294) immigrated to Boston, Massachusetts. Francesca deDonato(294) died 3 February 1938 in Bridgeport, CT.

Francesca deDonato(294) married Joseph Mingolello(294a) on 5 October 1918 in Bridgeport, CT.

Generoso (Joseph) Mincolelli/Mingolello(294a) was born on 04 October 1892, in Ariano, Italy, to Leonardantonio Mincolelli(294aF) and Giovanna Grasso(294aM). Joseph Mingolello(294a) emigrated to the United States in 1911.

Known children of Francesca deDonato(294) and Joseph Mingolello(294a):

    i) Giovanna (Jennie) Mingolello(499) born in 1919
    ii) Anthony (Tony) Mingolello(508) born in 1920
    iii) Ida Loretta Mingolello(530) born in 1923
    iv) Ralph George Mingolello(558) born in 1927
    v) Living person and/or spouse

Records that include Francesca deDonato(294) and/or Joseph Mingolello(294a):

- Ariano, Italy 1892 Birth Act #528
- Ariano, Italy 1899 Birth Act #488
- "Massachusetts, Boston Passenger Lists Index, 1899-1940", , FamilySearch (https://www.familysearch.org/ark:/61903/1:1:QKQX-WYTX : Sat Mar 09 21:59:44 UTC 2024), Entry for Francesca Di Vitto, 1916.
- Bridgeport, CT, Marriages October- November 1918, Marriage Act #18
- Bridgeport, CT, Births August 1919 #321
- Bridgeport, CT, Births October 1920 #467
- Bridgeport, CT, Births Dec 1927 #406
- "United States, Census, 1930", , FamilySearch (https://www.familysearch.org/ark:/61903/1:1:XMP8-M1P : Wed Mar 06 09:36:34 UTC 2024), Entry for Joe Mingolello and Francis Mingolello, 1930.
- Stratford, CT 1938 Deaths #24
- "United States, World War II Draft Registration Cards, 1942", , FamilySearch (https://www.familysearch.org/ark:/61903/1:1:X5LV-3Z7 : Sat Feb 24 04:41:35 UTC 2024), Entry for Joseph Mingolello, 1942.

- "Alabama County Marriages, 1711-1992", , FamilySearch (https://www.familysearch.org/ark:/61903/1:1:Q21X-17FX : Mon Mar 04 21:04:43 UTC 2024), Entry for Anthoney Mingolello and Joseph Mingolello, 10 Jun 1945.
- "United States, GenealogyBank Obituaries, Births, and Marriages, 1980-2015", , FamilySearch (https://www.familysearch.org/ark:/61903/1:1:QKLL-XJX7 : Sun Mar 10 01:19:56 UTC 2024), Entry for Anthony or Tony Anthony Mingolello and Joseph Mingolello, 16 Jan 2013.
- "Find a Grave Index," database, FamilySearch (https://www.familysearch.org/ark:/61903/1:1:66MH-H8SL : 31 May 2024), Tony, ; Burial, Derby, New Haven, Connecticut, United States of America, Mount Saint Peter Cemetery; citing record ID 234206147, Find a Grave, http://www.findagrave.com.
- "United States, Social Security Numerical Identification Files (NUMIDENT), 1936-2007", database, FamilySearch (https://www.familysearch.org/ark:/61903/1:1:6KMV-QW3L : 10 February 2023), Frances Dedonato in entry for Jennie Mingoletto, .
- Bridgeport, CT Deaths August 1988 #59
- "New York, New York City, Index to Passengers Arriving at New York City, compiled 1944-1948", , FamilySearch (https://www.familysearch.org/ark:/61903/1:1:7H32-TJMM : Sun Mar 10 12:57:34 UTC 2024), Entry for Geneasse Mincolelli, 1911.
- "United States, Census, 1950", , FamilySearch (https://www.familysearch.org/ark:/61903/1:1:6FM8-981D : Fri Oct 06 20:41:12 UTC 2023), Entry for Agnes Calogino and William Munphy, April 21, 1950.
- "United States, Index to Alien Case Files, 1940-2003," database, FamilySearch (https://www.familysearch.org/ark:/61903/1:1:6FY4-G2VD : 16 December 2022), Joseph Mingolello, 8 May 1911; citing Immigration, Alien Registration Number , "Index to Alien Case Files at the National Archives at Kansas City, ca. 1975 - 2012," NAID 5821836, Records of U.S. Citizenship and Immigration Services, 2003 - 2004, RG 566, National Archives at Kansas City.
- "New York, New York Passenger and Crew Lists, 1909, 1925-1958", , FamilySearch (https://www.familysearch.org/ark:/61903/1:1:2HHR-6MX : Sat Jul 20 23:12:28 UTC 2024), Entry for Generoso Mincolelli, 1955.
- "United States, Social Security Numerical Identification Files (NUMIDENT), 1936-2007", database, FamilySearch (https://www.familysearch.org/ark:/61903/1:1:6KMF-SK34 : 10 February 2023), Joseph Mingolello, .

295) Alfredo D'Ausilio

Alfredo D'Ausilio(295) was born on 27 August 1899, in Ariano, Italy, to Oto Maria D'ausilio(99) and Maria Gabriella Giannario(99a). Alfredo D'Ausilio(295) died on 21 August 1900 in Ariano, Italy.

Records that include Alfredo D'Ausilio(295):
- Ariano, Italy 1899 Birth Act #496
- Ariano, Italy 1900 Death Act #262

296) Maria Grasso

Maria Grasso(296) born on 12 Nov 1899 in Ariano, Italy, to Crescenzo Grasso(76a) and Anna Perrina(76). Maria Grasso(296) and Giovanni Cesarini(296a) boarded the ship Patria in Naples, Italy on 17 July 1920, arriving in New York, NY on 1 August 1920.

Maria Grasso(296) married Giovanni Cesarini(296a) on 30 October 1919 in Ariano, Italy.

Giovanni Cesarini(296a) was a foundling born in Ariano, Italy on 2 January 1895.
*On the ship manifest Giovanni Cesarini(296a) lists his nearest relative as his stepfather Vincenzo Giardino(296aSF).

Records that include Maria Grasso(296) and Giovanni Cesarini(296a):

- Ariano, Italy 1899 Birth Act #646
- Ariano, Italy 1919 Marriage Act #118
- Ariano, Italy 1895 Birth Act # P.II.1
- "New York, Passenger Arrival Lists (Ellis Island), 1892-1925", FamilySearch (https://www.familysearch.org/ark:/61903/1:1:J667-9ZQ : Tue Apr 15 04:26:35 UTC 2025), Entry for Giovanni Cesarini and Vincenzo Giardino, 30 Jul 1920.
- "New York, State Census, 1925", FamilySearch (https://www.familysearch.org/ark:/61903/1:1:KS9S-PPB : Sat Mar 09 18:17:36 UTC 2024), Entry for Mary Cesarini, 1925.

297) Giuseppa Perrina

Giuseppa Perrina(297) was born on 28 November 1899, in Ariano, Italy, to Michele Perrina(88) and Maria Grazia Caraglia(88a).

Giuseppa Perrina(297) married Pasquale Cusano(297a) on 13 October 1921 in Ariano, Italy.

Pasquale Cusano(297a) was born on 23 April 1888, in Ariano, Italy, to Nicola Cusano(297aF) and Carmina de Lillo(297aM).

Records that include Giuseppa Perrina(297) and/or Pasquale Cusano(297a):
- Ariano, Italy 1888 Birth Act #280
- Ariano, Italy 1899 Birth Act #676
- Ariano, Italy 1921 Marriage Act #151

298) Concetta D'Ausilio

Concetta D'Ausilio(298) was born on 20 January 1900, in Ariano, Italy, to Salvatore Antonio D'ausilio(124) and Giovanna Colucci(124a). Concetta D'Ausilio(298) died on 12 June 1997, in Wakefield, MA.

Concetta D'Ausilio(298) married Rocco Louis Bellofatto(298a) on 14 June 1930 in Boston, MA.

Rocco Louis Bellofatto(298a) was born on 10 April 1893, in Anzano, Italy, to Pasquale Bellofatto(298aF) and Angela Mastrangelo(298aM). Rocco Louis Bellofatto(298a) died on 29 September 1985 in East Boston, MA.

Rocco Louis Bellofatto(298a) was previously married to Gesuela Pettinato(298aX).

Known children of Concetta D'Ausilio(298) and Rocco Louis Bellofatto(298a):

    i) Salvatore Bellofatto(578) in 1931
    ii) Joseph Domenic Bellofatto(584) in 1932
    iii) Living person and/or spouse
    iv) Living person and/or spouse

Records that include Concetta D'Ausilio(298) and/or Rocco Louis Bellofatto(298a):
- "Italia, Foggia, Stato Civile (Archivio di Stato), 1809-1902", FamilySearch (https://www.familysearch.org/ark:/61903/1:1:6NTC-PFW9 : Tue Mar 11 19:32:30 UTC 2025), Entry for Rocco Luigi Bellofatto and Pasquale Bellofatto, 1 Apr 1893.
- Ariano, Italy 1900 Birth Act #68
- "United States, Census, 1910", , FamilySearch (https://www.familysearch.org/ark:/61903/1:1:MK2G-NS5 : Tue Jul 23 18:21:12 UTC 2024), Entry for Salvatore Dansilio and Jennie Dansilio, 1910.
- "Massachusetts, Suffolk, Boston Passenger Lists Index, 1899-1940", , FamilySearch (https://www.familysearch.org/ark:/61903/1:1:QKQ6-55QC : Fri Mar 08 10:07:51 UTC 2024), Entry for Rocco Bellofatto, 1911.
- "Massachusetts, Suffolk, Boston Passenger Lists Index, 1899-1940", , FamilySearch (https://www.familysearch.org/ark:/61903/1:1:Q2WD-PHFW : Sat Mar 09 23:35:16 UTC 2024), Entry for Rocco L Bellofatto, 1911.

- "Massachusetts, Suffolk, Boston Passenger Lists, 1891-1943", , FamilySearch (https://www.familysearch.org/ark:/61903/1:1:23XQ-Q52 : Sat Mar 09 12:28:07 UTC 2024), Entry for Rocco Luigi Bellafatto and M Angelo Bellafatto, 1911.

- "United States, World War I Draft Registration Cards, 1917-1918", , FamilySearch (https://www.familysearch.org/ark:/61903/1:1:4ZY2-RR3Z : Sat Nov 23 00:28:18 UTC 2024), Entry for Louis or Luis Ballafatto, from 1917 to 1918.

- "Massachusetts, Naturalization Index, 1906-1966," , FamilySearch (https://familysearch.org/ark:/61903/1:1:XG3V-BJ8 : 4 December 2014), Louis Bellofatto, 1918; from "Index to Petitions and Records of Naturalizations of the U.S. and District Courts for the District of Massachusetts, 1907-1966," database, Fold3.com (http://www.fold3.com : n.d.); citing NARA microfilm publication M1545 (Washington, D.C.: National Archives and Records Administration, n.d.), roll 2.

- "Massachusetts, Naturalization Index, 1906-1966," database, FamilySearch (https://familysearch.org/ark:/61903/1:1:XG3V-5MR : 4 December 2014), Louis Bellofatto, 1918; from "Index to Petitions and Records of Naturalizations of the U.S. and District Courts for the District of Massachusetts, 1907-1966," database, Fold3.com (http://www.fold3.com : n.d.); citing NARA microfilm publication M1545 (Washington, D.C.: National Archives and Records Administration, n.d.), roll 2.

- "Massachusetts, United States Naturalization Records, 1790-1991", , FamilySearch (https://www.familysearch.org/ark:/61903/1:1:QPH1-F2NQ : Mon Nov 25 16:45:41 UTC 2024), Entry for Louis Bellofatto, 1918.

- "United States, Veterans Administration Master Index, 1917-1940", , FamilySearch (https://www.familysearch.org/ark:/61903/1:1:QP8M-DX6B : Fri Mar 08 17:59:54 UTC 2024), Entry for Louis Bellofatto, 22 January 1919.

- "Massachusetts, State Vital Records, 1638-1927", , FamilySearch (https://www.familysearch.org/ark:/61903/1:1:QLGR-RD7K : Thu May 23 03:10:01 UTC 2024), Entry for Louis Bellofatto and Gesuela Pettinato, 12 Oct 1919.

- "Massachusetts, State Vital Records, 1638-1927", , FamilySearch (https://www.familysearch.org/ark:/61903/1:1:Q28J-PSVS : Thu May 23 02:59:45 UTC 2024), Entry for Louis Bellofatto and Gesuela Pettinato, 12 Oct 1919.

- "United States, Census, 1920", , FamilySearch (https://www.familysearch.org/ark:/61903/1:1:MFMC-Y9J : Sat Jul 06 12:33:15 UTC 2024), Entry for Salvatore Danselio and Jennie Danselio, 1920.

- "United States, Census, 1930", , FamilySearch (https://www.familysearch.org/ark:/61903/1:1:XQRK-F91 : Sat Jul 06 03:53:48 UTC 2024), Entry for Louis Bellofatto and Louis Bellofatto, 1930.

- "United States, Census, 1940", , FamilySearch (https://www.familysearch.org/ark:/61903/1:1:K4J6-N24 : Fri Mar 08 16:08:08 UTC 2024), Entry for Louis Bellorfatti and Concetta Bellorfatti, 1940.

- "United States, Census, 1940", , FamilySearch (https://www.familysearch.org/ark:/61903/1:1:K4J6-N24 : Fri Mar 08 16:08:08 UTC 2024), Entry for Louis Bellorfatti and Concetta Bellorfatti, 1940.

- "United States, World War II Draft Registration Cards, 1942", , FamilySearch (https://www.familysearch.org/ark:/61903/1:1:V12P-KKS : Sat Feb 24 04:57:34 UTC 2024), Entry for Louis Bellofatto, 1942.

- "United States, Census, 1950", , FamilySearch (https://www.familysearch.org/ark:/61903/1:1:6F3N-BJZN : Tue Feb 27 10:44:15 UTC 2024), Entry for Louis Bellofatto and Concetta Billofette, April 13, 1950.

- "United States, Social Security Death Index," database, FamilySearch (https://familysearch.org/ark:/61903/1:1:JP3F-DNT : 7 January 2021), Louis Bellofatto, Sep 1985; citing U.S. Social Security Administration, Death Master File, database (Alexandria, Virginia: National Technical Information Service, ongoing).

- "Massachusetts, Death Index, 1970-2003", database, FamilySearch (https://familysearch.org/ark:/61903/1:1:VZ5G-PL3 : 13 June 2019), Louis R Bellofatto, 1985.
- "Find a Grave Index", FamilySearch (https://www.familysearch.org/ark:/61903/1:1:X3LL-2K15 : Wed Jun 18 20:49:52 UTC 2025), Entry for Louis Bellofatto.
- "United States, Obituary Records, 2014-2023", , FamilySearch (https://www.familysearch.org/ark:/61903/1:1:XM41-V1J3 : Wed Nov 20 04:01:56 UTC 2024), Entry for Joseph Domenic Bellofatto and Rocco Luigi Bellofatto, 30 June 2021.
- "Massachusetts, Death Index, 1970-2003", , FamilySearch (https://familysearch.org/ark:/61903/1:1:VZRQ-T89 : 13 June 2019), Concetta Bellofatto, 1997
- "United States, Social Security Death Index," , FamilySearch (https://familysearch.org/ark:/61903/1:1:JK8G-VZK : 7 January 2021), Concetta Bellofatto, 12 Jun 1997; citing U.S. Social Security Administration, Death Master File, database (Alexandria, Virginia: National Technical Information Service, ongoing).
- "United States, Social Security Numerical Identification Files (NUMIDENT), 1936-2007", database, FamilySearch (https://www.familysearch.org/ark:/61903/1:1:6KM3-MD1Z : 10 February 2023), Concetta Bellofatto, .

299) Michele Stella

Michele Stella(299) was born on 6 February 1900, in Ariano, Italy, to Antonio Stella(110) and Eugenia LoConte(110a).

Records that include Michele Stella(299):
- Ariano, Italy 1900 Birth Act #98

300) Rosa Giorgione

Rosa Giorgione(300) was born on 21 April 1900, in Ariano, Italy, to Raffaele Giorgione(80) and Carmina Salvioli(80a).

Rosa Giorgione(300) married Pietro Savariello(300a) on 14 February 1925 in Ariano, Italy.

Pietro Savariello(300a) was born on 29 July 1900, in Ariano, Italy, to Ludovico Savariello(300aF) and Maria Luisa di Pippo(300aM).

Records that include Rosa Giorgione(300)and/or Pietro Savariello(300a):
- Ariano, Italy 1900 Birth Act #234
- Ariano, Italy 1900 Birth Act #404
- Ariano, Italy 1925 Marriage Act #23

301) Elisabetta Giovanna Perrina

Elisabetta Giovanna Perrina(301) was born on 21 November 1900, in Castel Baronia, Italy, to Raffaele Perrina(58) and Maria Lucia Gesa(58a). On 7 November 1903 Elisabetta Giovanna Perrina(301) boarded the ship SS Perugia arriving on 21 November 1903 in New York, NY. In 1910 Elisabetta Giovanna Perrina(301) was living in Schenectady, NY.

Records that include Elisabetta Giovanna Perrina(301):
- Castel Baronia, Italy 1900 Birth Act #23
- "New York Passenger Arrival Lists (Ellis Island), 1892-1924", , FamilySearch (https://www.familysearch.org/ark:/61903/1:1:JFYG-93G : Sun Mar 10 06:51:48 UTC 2024), Entry for M. Lucia Gesa and Raffaele Perrino, 1903.
- "New York, County Naturalization Records, 1791-1980", , FamilySearch (https://www.familysearch.org/ark:/61903/1:1:7WZM-S2PZ : Fri Mar 08 21:11:12 UTC 2024), Entry for Raffaele Perrino and Lucy Perrino, 1906.
- "United States Census, 1910", , FamilySearch (https://www.familysearch.org/ark:/61903/1:1:M596-H5V : Mon Jul 22 15:03:44 UTC 2024), Entry for Raffaele Perrino and Lucie Perrino, 1910.

302) Salvatore Perrina

Salvatore Perrina(302) was born on 6 December 1900, in Ariano, Italy, to Angelo Maria Perrina(74) and Tommasina Paduano(74a).

Salvatore Perrina(302) married Carmela di Lillo(302a) on 16 March 1922 in Ariano, Italy.

Carmela di Lillo(302a) was born on 14 April 1901, in Ariano, Italy, to Francesco Di Lillo(302aF) and Angela Scaperrotta(302aM).

Known children of Salvatore Perrina(302) and Carmela di Lillo(302a):

   i) Angelo Perrina(533) born about 1924

Records that include Salvatore Perrina(302) and/or Carmela di Lillo(302a):
   * Ariano, Italy 1900 Birth Act #598
   * Ariano, Italy 1901 Birth Act #230
   * Ariano, Italy 1922 Marriage Act #49
   * Ariano, Italy 1932 Death Act #13

303) Antonio DeDonato

Antonio DeDonato(303) was born on 18 Jun 1901, in Ribeirão Pires, São Paulo, Brazil, to Marcello deDonato(78) and Maria Rosa Politano(78a).

Antonio DeDonato(303) married Maria Rinaldi(303a).

Maria Rinaldi(303a) was born to Miguel Rinaldi(303aF) and Carmella Contivire(303aM).

Known Children of Antonio DeDonato(303) and Maria Rinaldi(303a):

   i) Carmina Rinaldi(500) born in 1920
   ii) Marcello Roque(523) born in 1922
   iii) Rosa De Donato(529) born in 1923
   iv) Luiz de Donato(539) born in 1924
   v) Pedro Miguel de Donato(548) born in 1926
   vi) Living person and/or spouse

Records that include Antonio DeDonato(303) and/or Maria Rinaldi(303a):
   * "Brasil, São Paulo, Registro Civil, 1925-2023", FamilySearch (https://www.familysearch.org/ark:/61903/1:1:6V44-PQ4V : Sat Aug 23 11:49:57 UTC 2025), Entry for Luiz de Donato and Antonio Ferreira de Moraes, 18 de junho de 1901.
   * "Brasil, São Paulo, Registro Civil, 1925-2023", FamilySearch (https://www.familysearch.org/ark:/61903/1:1:6VW7-R7DK : Sat Aug 23 11:09:59 UTC 2025), Entry for Maria Olinaldi and Carmel- A Rinaldi, 1923.
   * "Brasil, São Paulo, Registro Civil, 1925-2023", FamilySearch (https://www.familysearch.org/ark:/61903/1:1:6VW4-2MFT : Sat Aug 23 11:10:08 UTC 2025), Entry for Rosa de Donato and Antonio de Donato, 11 de outubro de 1924.
   * "Brasil, São Paulo, Registro Civil, 1925-2023", FamilySearch (https://www.familysearch.org/ark:/61903/1:1:65PV-BNRY : Sat Aug 23 12:18:24 UTC 2025), Entry for Luiz de Donato and Antonio de Donato, 1925.
   * "Brazil, Cemetery Records, 1799-2024", FamilySearch (https://www.familysearch.org/ark:/61903/1:1:X3NY-KLF5 : Tue Jun 10 22:44:27 UTC 2025), Entry for Pedro Miguel de Donato and Antonio de Donato, 18 Jun 1976.
   * "Brasil, São Paulo, Registro Civil, 1925-2023", FamilySearch (https://www.familysearch.org/ark:/61903/1:1:68JB-Q2NC : Wed Sep 03 16:54:30 UTC 2025), Entry for and , 6 October 1991.

304) Maria Raimonda Perrina

Maria Raimonda Perrina(304) was born on 22 February 1901, in Castel Baronia, Italy to Francesco Paolo Perrina(90) and Maria Cristina Sofia Leone(90a). Maria Raimonda Perrina(304) died on 20 May 1957 in Flumeri, Italy.

Maria Raimonda Perrina(304) married Guiseppe Del Sardo(304a) on 3 March 1923 in Flumeri, Italy.

Guiseppe Del Sardo(304a) was born on 22 May 1903, in Flumeri, Italy, to Francesco Antonio Del Sardo(304aF) and Angela Felicia Giacabbe(304aM). Guiseppe Del Sardo(304a) died 23 July 1987 in Flumeri, Italy.

Records that include Maria Raimonda Perrina(304) and/or Guiseppe Del Sardo(304a):
- Castel Baronia, Italy 1901 Birth Act #7
- Flumeri, Italy 1903 Birth Act #18
- Flumeri, Italy 1923 Marriage Act #4
- Flumeri, Italy 1957 Death Act #12
- Flumeri, Italy 1987 Death Act #17

305) Mariannina Manganiello

Mariannina Manganiello(305) was born on 11 March 1901, in Ariano , Italy, to Raimondo Manganiello(79a) and Mariantonia Fodarella(79).

Mariannina Manganiello(305) married Agostino LoCalzo(305a) on 26 October 1924 in Ariano, Italy.

Agostino LoCalzo(305a) was born on 17 February 1901, in Ariano, Italy, to Pasquale LoCalzo(305aF) and Maria Grazia Caso(305aM).

Records that include Mariannina Manganiello(305) and/or Agostino LoCalzo(305a):
- Ariano, Italy 1901 Birth Act #107
- Ariano, Italy 1901 Birth Act #163
- Ariano, Italy 1924 Marriage Act #131

306) Pasquale Ciasullo

Pasquale Ciasullo(306) was born on 9 April 1901, in Ariano, Italy, to Michele Ciasullo(82a) and Filomena Perrina(82). Pasquale Ciasullo(306) died 19 January 1903 in Ariano, Italy.

Records that include Pasquale Ciasullo(306):
- Ariano, Italy 1901 Birth Act #220
- Ariano, Italy 1902 Death Act #22

307) Alfredo D'Ausilio

Alfredo D'Ausilio(307) was born on 17 April 1901, in Forlì (provincia di Forlì-Cesena), Italy, to Oto Maria D'ausilio(99) and Maria Gabriella Giannario(99a).

Records that include Alfredo D'Ausilio(307):
- Forlì(provincia di Forlì-Cesena), Italy 1901 Birth Act #371

308) Helen Elvera Anastasio

Helen Elvera Anastasio(308) was born on 26 June 1901, in Waterbury, CT, to Pasquale Antonio Anastasio(72a) and Anna Maria D'Ausilio(72). Helen Elvera Anastasio(308) died on 22 February 1984, in Plainfield, IN. Helen Elvera Anastasio(308) was buried in Bachellor Cemetery, Fountain, MI.

Helen Elvera Anastasio(308) married Cosimo Stilo(308a) about 1917.

Cosimo Stilo(308a) was born on 22 August 1888, in Tripi, Italy, to Vito Stilo(308aF) and Antonia Belanda(308aM). On 11 April 1911 Cosimo Stilo(308a) boarded the ship SS Pomanic in the port of Messina, Italy. Cosimo Stilo(308a) arrived in Boston, MA on 25 April 1911. Cosimo Stilo(308a) served in the United States Army from 25 July 1918 to 2 December 1918. Cosimo Stilo(308a) was naturalized as a Citizen of the United States on 6 October 1928 in Racine, WI. Cosimo Stilo(308a) died on 11 March 1961. Cosimo Stilo(308a) was buried in Bachellor Cemetery, Fountain, MI.

Known children of Helen Elvera Anastasio(308) and Cosimo Stilo(308a):

      i) Victor Pasqual Stilo(493) in 1919
      ii) Annette M. Stilo(513) in 1921
      iii) Daniel Paul Stilo(541) born in 1925

Records that include Helen Elvera Anastasio(308) and/or Cosimo Stilo(308a):
- "Italia, Messina, Messina, Stato Civile (Tribunale), 1866-1939", FamilySearch (https://www.familysearch.org/ark:/61903/1:1:X323-KY1B : Wed Jun 18 01:11:37 UTC 2025), Entry for Cosimo Stilo and Vito Stilo, 22 Aug 1888.
- Waterbury, CT 1898-1902 Births Vol 5 pg289
- "New Hampshire, County Naturalization Records, 1771-2001", FamilySearch (https://www.familysearch.org/ark:/61903/1:1:CFVT-NXPZ : Fri Jan 17 09:31:42 UTC 2025), Entry for Cosimo Stilo, 31 Dec 1914.
- "United States, World War I Draft Registration Cards, 1917-1918", FamilySearch (https://www.familysearch.org/ark:/61903/1:1:WMXJ-C4T2 : Thu Jul 24 13:29:03 UTC 2025), Entry for Cosimo Stilo, Registration Card, 27 August 1918.
- "United States, Veterans Administration Master Index, 1917-1940", FamilySearch (https://www.familysearch.org/ark:/61903/1:1:WW2Y-TD2M : Fri Apr 25 23:56:47 UTC 2025), Entry for Cosimo Stilo, 2 Dec 1918.
- "United States, Census, 1920", FamilySearch (https://www.familysearch.org/ark:/61903/1:1:MCNL-VV4 : Thu Jan 16 10:28:30 UTC 2025), Entry for Cosemo Stilo and Elvera Stilo, 1920.
- "Wisconsin, County Naturalization Records, 1807-1992", FamilySearch (https://www.familysearch.org/ark:/61903/1:1:ZK72-XHT2 : Wed Jan 22 08:44:28 UTC 2025), Entry for Cosimo Stilo and Elvera Stilo, 26 Aug 1924.
- "Wisconsin, County Naturalization Records, 1807-1992", FamilySearch (https://www.familysearch.org/ark:/61903/1:1:ZNX1-82PZ : Sun Mar 10 21:13:31 UTC 2024), Entry for Cosimo Stilo and Elvera, 26 Aug 1924.
- "Illinois, Northern District Naturalization Index, 1840-1950", FamilySearch (https://www.familysearch.org/ark:/61903/1:1:XKGB-FD5 : Tue Apr 08 01:10:27 UTC 2025), Entry for Cosimo Stilo, 1928.
- "Wisconsin, County Naturalization Records, 1807-1992", FamilySearch (https://www.familysearch.org/ark:/61903/1:1:ZNFF-L6ZM : Sun Jan 12 13:56:03 UTC 2025), Entry for Cosimo Stilo and Elevera, 7 Jun 1928.
- "United States, Census, 1930", FamilySearch (https://www.familysearch.org/ark:/61903/1:1:X7SP-TPK : Sun Jan 19 00:36:31 UTC 2025), Entry for Causamo Stilo and Elvera Stilo, 1930.
- "United States, Census, 1940", FamilySearch (https://www.familysearch.org/ark:/61903/1:1:K7J8-X7Y : Wed Jan 22 06:44:17 UTC 2025), Entry for Cosimo Stilo and Helen E Stilo, 1940.
- "United States, Census, 1950", FamilySearch (https://www.familysearch.org/ark:/61903/1:1:6F9M-Q6TL : Wed Mar 20 07:07:01 UTC 2024), Entry for Cosimo Stilo and Helen E Stilo, April 1, 1950.
- "United States, Social Security Numerical Identification Files (NUMIDENT), 1936-2007", FamilySearch (https://www.familysearch.org/ark:/61903/1:1:6KQR-C1G7 : Sat Apr 26 17:20:50 UTC 2025), Entry for Cosimo Stilo.
- "Find a Grave Index", FamilySearch (https://www.familysearch.org/ark:/61903/1:1:QVVK-RS97 : Tue Apr 01 02:26:36 UTC 2025), Entry for Cosimo Stilo.

309) Carmine Ciccarelli

Carmine Ciccarelli(309) was born on 10 July 1901, in Ariano, Italy, to Domenico Ciccarelli(69a) and Rosa Fiorenza(69). Carmine Ciccarelli(309) died 21 September 1902 in Ariano, Italy.

Records that include Carmine Ciccarelli(309):
- Ariano, Italy 1901 Birth Act #388
- Ariano, Italy 1902 Death Act #307

310) Michele Ciasullo

Michele Ciasullo(310) was born on 12 October 1901, in Ariano, Italy, to Filippo Ciasullo(105a) and Maria Giovanna Perrina(105). Michele Ciasullo(310) died 26 May 1902 in Ariano, Italy.

Records that include Michele Ciasullo(310):
- Ariano, Italy 1901 Birth Act #519
- Ariano, Italy 1902 Death Act #175

311) Maria Silveria Francesca (Frances) Giorgione/George

Maria Silveria Francesca (Frances) Giorgione/George(311) was born on 9 December 1901, in Ariano, Italy, to Luigi (Louis) Giorgione/George(86) and Maria Giovanna Perillo(86a). Maria Silveria Francesca (Frances) Giorgione/George(311) died in 1942, in New York.

Maria Silveria Francesca (Frances) Giorgione/George(311) married Anthony Amodio(311a) on 9 December 1923 in Highland Mills, NY.

Anthony Amodio(311a) was born on 18 March 1892, in Naples, Bari, Italy, to Philip Amodio(311aF) and Angelina Marasciulo(311aM). Anthony Amodio(311a) served in the United States Army from 17 July 1918 to 6 December 1918. Anthony Amodio(311a) died 15 December 1965 in New York.

Known Children of Maria Silveria Francesca (Frances) Giorgione/George(311) and Anthony Amodio(311a):

  i) Angelina Antoinette Amodio(549) born in 1926
  ii) Felice Louis Amodio(567) born in 1929

Records that include Maria Silveria Francesca (Frances) Giorgione/George(311) and/or Anthony Amodio(311a):
- Ariano, Italy 1901 Birth Act #623
- "United States World War I Draft Registration Cards, 1917-1918", database with images, FamilySearch (https://www.familysearch.org/ark:/61903/1:1:WDJ2-L9W2 : 10 July 2024), Antonio Amodio, 1917-1918.
- "United States, Veterans Administration Master Index, 1917-1940", , FamilySearch (https://www.familysearch.org/ark:/61903/1:1:WW2Z-9QZM : Fri Mar 08 21:28:02 UTC 2024), Entry for Antonio William or Anthony Amodio, 6 December 1918.
- "United States, Veterans Administration Master Index, 1917-1940", , FamilySearch (https://www.familysearch.org/ark:/61903/1:1:QP8Z-5V18 : Sun Mar 10 20:20:31 UTC 2024), Entry for Antonio William or Anthony Amodio, 6 December 1918.
- "New York, County Marriages, 1847-1848; 1908-1936", , FamilySearch (https://www.familysearch.org/ark:/61903/1:1:KZ9S-P4Y : Sat Mar 09 03:18:45 UTC 2024), Entry for Anthony Amodio and Philip Amodio, 9 December 1923.
- "United States Census, 1930", , FamilySearch (https://www.familysearch.org/ark:/61903/1:1:X4R1-NC2 : Sun Jul 14 09:29:21 UTC 2024), Entry for Anthony Amodio and Frances Amodio, 1930.
- "United States Census, 1940", , FamilySearch (https://www.familysearch.org/ark:/61903/1:1:KQGP-8TT : Sat Mar 09 04:22:19 UTC 2024), Entry for Anthony Amodio and Frances Amodio, 1940.
- "United States World War II Draft Registration Cards, 1942", , FamilySearch (https://www.familysearch.org/ark:/61903/1:1:QKV7-JGZB : Sat Feb 24 00:24:37 UTC 2024), Entry for Anthony William Amodio and Francis Amodio, 27 Apr 1942.
- "Find a Grave Index," database, FamilySearch (https://www.familysearch.org/ark:/61903/1:1:QVVW-4VV2 : 1 April 2023), Frances George Amodio, ; Burial, Phillipsburg, Orange, New York, United States of America, Wallkill Cemetery; citing record ID 8871875, Find a Grave, http://www.findagrave.com.

- "United States Social Security Death Index," database, FamilySearch
  (https://familysearch.org/ark:/61903/1:1:JBG1-64W : 7 January
  2021), Anthony Amodio, Dec 1965; citing U.S. Social Security
  Administration, Death Master File, database (Alexandria, Virginia:
  National Technical Information Service, ongoing).
- "Find a Grave Index," database, FamilySearch
  (https://www.familysearch.org/ark:/61903/1:1:QVVW-4JYW : 6 June
  2024), Anthony Amodio, ; Burial, Phillipsburg, Orange, New York,
  United States of America, Wallkill Cemetery; citing record ID
  8871874, Find a Grave, http://www.findagrave.com.
- https://www.recordonline.com/story/news/2002/06/23/june-23-
  2002/51178787007/
- "United States, Social Security Numerical Identification Files
  (NUMIDENT), 1936-2007", database, FamilySearch
  (https://www.familysearch.org/ark:/61903/1:1:6K97-8NVS : 10
  February 2023), Frances George in entry for Angelina Antoinette
  Amodio, .
- "United States, Social Security Numerical Identification Files
  (NUMIDENT), 1936-2007", database, FamilySearch
  (https://www.familysearch.org/ark:/61903/1:1:6K9W-WF3X : 10
  February 2023), Frances George in entry for Felice Louis Amodio, .

312) Adamo (Adam Carl) Lombardi

Adamo (Adam Carl) Lombardi(312) was born on 14 January 1902, in Buenas Aires,
Argentina, to Vincenzo (James) Lombardi(85a) and Maria Carmela deDonato(85).
Adamo (Adam Carl) Lombardi(312) boarded the ship SS Florida, in Naples, Italy,
arriving in New York City on 27 September 1907. Adamo (Adam Carl)
Lombardi(312) became a citizen of the United States on 10 July 1946 in Los
Angeles, CA. Adamo (Adam Carl) Lombardi(312) died on 15 March 1988, in Los
Angeles, CA.

Adamo (Adam Carl) Lombardi(312) married Frances Rico Nuno(312a) on 21 August
1944 in Los Angeles, CA.

Frances Rico Nuno(312a) was born on 21 August 1912, in Leon, Mexico, to
Guillermo Nuno(312aF) and Ester Rico(312aM). Frances Rico Nuno(312a) became a
citizen of the United States on 28 March 1952 in Los Angeles, CA. Frances Rico
Nuno(312a) died on 16 June 2009 in California.

Known children of Adamo (Adam Carl) Lombardi(312) and Frances Rico Nuno(312a):

    i) Living person and/or spouse
    ii) Living person and/or spouse
    iii) Living person and/or spouse
    iv) Living person and/or spouse

Records that include Adamo (Adam Carl) Lombardi(312) and/or Frances Rico
Nuno(312a):

- "United States Census, 1910", , FamilySearch
  (https://www.familysearch.org/ark:/61903/1:1:X39X-C53 : Fri Mar 08
  11:50:32 UTC 2024), Entry for James Lombardi and Carmelo Lombardi,
  1910.
- "United States Census, 1920", , FamilySearch
  (https://www.familysearch.org/ark:/61903/1:1:MCFH-DK2 : Sun Mar 10
  06:14:48 UTC 2024), Entry for Vincent Lombardi and Casowasy
  Lombardi, 1920.
- "United States Census, 1930", , FamilySearch
  (https://www.familysearch.org/ark:/61903/1:1:XMPM-77Y : Fri Jul 05
  18:22:01 UTC 2024), Entry for James Lombardi and Carmello Lombardi,
  1930.
- "California, Naturalization Records, 1883-1991", FamilySearch
  (https://www.familysearch.org/ark:/61903/1:1:6TNJ-T2H8 : Tue Apr 29
  18:43:46 UTC 2025), Entry for Adam Carmine Lombardi, 22 May 1933.
- "California, Naturalization Records, 1883-1991", FamilySearch
  (https://www.familysearch.org/ark:/61903/1:1:6RB4-W7GP : Tue Apr 29
  19:05:09 UTC 2025), Entry for Adam Carmine Lombardi, 22 May 1933.

- "California, Naturalization Records, 1883-1991", FamilySearch (https://www.familysearch.org/ark:/61903/1:1:6RLF-L5W4 : Tue Apr 29 18:58:55 UTC 2025), Entry for Adam Carmine or Adamo Lombardi, 22 May 1933.
- "California, Southern District Court (Central) Naturalization Index, 1915-1976", , FamilySearch (https://www.familysearch.org/ark:/61903/1:1:KXQW-D52 : Fri Mar 08 11:19:35 UTC 2024), Entry for Adam Carl or Adamo Lombardi, 1936.
- "United States Census, 1940", , FamilySearch (https://www.familysearch.org/ark:/61903/1:1:K9CH-4ND : Mon Mar 11 01:26:11 UTC 2024), Entry for Vincent Lombardi and Maria C Lombardi, 1940.
- "California, World War II Draft Registration Cards, 1940-1945", , FamilySearch (https://www.familysearch.org/ark:/61903/1:1:QGXY-G3SC : Sat Mar 09 14:25:46 UTC 2024), Entry for Adam C Lombardi and Carmela Lombardi, 15 February 1942.
- "California, County Marriages, 1850-1953", , FamilySearch (https://www.familysearch.org/ark:/61903/1:1:K8XM-H19 : Sat Mar 09 11:20:48 UTC 2024), Entry for Adam Carl Lombardi and Francisca Rico Nuno, 21 August 1944.
- "United States Census, 1950", , FamilySearch (https://www.familysearch.org/ark:/61903/1:1:6XGL-6B7Z : Thu Mar 21 00:42:49 UTC 2024), Entry for Adam C Lombardi and Francis N Lombardi, 10 April 1950.
- "California, Southern District Court (Central) Naturalization Index, 1915-1976", , FamilySearch (https://www.familysearch.org/ark:/61903/1:1:KXQW-D5B : Fri Mar 08 06:00:15 UTC 2024), Entry for Frances Nuno Lombardi, 1952.
- "California Death Index, 1940-1997," database, FamilySearch (https://familysearch.org/ark:/61903/1:1:VGP8-HW6 : 26 November 2014), Adam Carl Lombardi, 15 Mar 1988; Department of Public Health Services, Sacramento.
- "California Deaths and Burials, 1776-2000", , FamilySearch (https://www.familysearch.org/ark:/61903/1:1:HGWT-QGPZ : 8 April 2022), Adam Carl Lombardi, 1988.
- "United States Social Security Death Index," , FamilySearch (https://familysearch.org/ark:/61903/1:1:V9T7-VM6 : 11 January 2021), Adam C Lombardi, 15 Mar 1988; citing U.S. Social Security Administration, Death Master File, database (Alexandria, Virginia: National Technical Information Service, ongoing).
- "United States, Social Security Numerical Identification Files (NUMIDENT), 1936-2007", database, FamilySearch (https://www.familysearch.org/ark:/61903/1:1:6K4W-RRG1 : 11 February 2023), Adam C Lombardi, .
- "United States Social Security Death Index," , FamilySearch (https://familysearch.org/ark:/61903/1:1:VQ9N-BZH : 12 January 2021), Frances Nuno Lombardi, 16 Jun 2009; citing U.S. Social Security Administration, Death Master File, database (Alexandria, Virginia: National Technical Information Service, ongoing).

313) Vincenza Stella

Vincenza Stella(313) was born on 14 January 1902, in Ariano, Italy, to Antonio Stella(110) and Eugenia LoConte(110a). Vincenza Stella(313) died 12 March 1904 in Ariano, Italy.

Records that include Vincenza Stella(313):
- Ariano, Italy 1902 Birth Act #40
- Ariano, Italy 1904 Death Act #93

314) Luigi Ermino Perrina

Luigi Ermino Perrina(314) was born on 20 February 1902, in Ariano, Italy, to Michele Perrina(88) and Maria Grazia Caraglia(88a). Luigi Ermino Perrina(314) died on 10 October 1976 in Ariano, Italy.

Luigi Ermino Perrina(314) married Angela De Lillo(401) on 7 February 1924 in Ariano, Italy.

Angela De Lillo(401)* was born on 2 March 1908, in Ariano, Italy, to Francesco diLillo(184) and Concetta Perrina(184a).
* Angela De Lillo(401) is also a D'Ausilio descendant.

Records that include Luigi Ermino Perrina(314) and/or Angela De Lillo(401):
* Ariano, Italy 1902 Birth Act #94
* Ariano, Italy 1908 Birth Act #139
* Ariano, Italy 1924 Marriage Act #24

315) Pasquale D'Ausilio

Pasquale D'Ausilio(315) was born on 26 February 1902, in Ariano, Italy, to Salvatore Antonio D'ausilio(124) and Giovanna Colucci(124a). Pasquale D'Ausilio(315) died on 28 March 1903, in Waterbury, CT. Pasquale D'Ausilio(315) was buried in Calvary Cemetery, Waterbury, CT.

Records that include Pasquale D'Ausilio(315):
* Ariano, Italy 1902 Birth Act #101
* Waterbury, CT 1903 Death Act #12

316) Maria Luigia Giorgione

Maria Luigia Giorgione(316) was born on 9 May 1902, in Ariano, Italy, to Raffaele Giorgione(80) and Carmina Salvioli(80a).

Maria Luigia Giorgione(316) married Luigi Graziano(316a) on 24 June 1920 in Ariano, Italy.

Luigi Graziano(316a) was born in 1889, in Ariano, Italy, to Michele Graziano(316aF) and Filomena Riccio(316aM).

Records that include Maria Luigia Giorgione(316) and Luigi Graziano(316a):
* Ariano, Italy 1889 Birth Act #441
* Ariano, Italy 1902 Birth Act #257
* Ariano, Italy 1920 Marriage Act #138

317) Eugenio Stella

Eugenio Stella(317) was born on 18 May 1902, in Ceppaloni, Italy, to Agostino Stella(101) and Eugenia Donisi(101a).

Eugenio Stella(317) married Josefina Emma Fasanelli De Polo(317a).

Josefina Emma Fasanelli De Polo(317a) was born in 1902, in Paraguay, to José Fasanelli Malinari(317aF) and Antonieta De Polo(317aM).
* Marriage information is from an unconfirmed source.

Records that include Eugenio Stella(317) and Josefina Emma Fasanelli De Polo(317a):
* Ceppaloni, Italy 1902 Birth Act #P.II.7
* "Italia, Benevento, Stato Civile (Archivio di Stato), 1810-1942", , FamilySearch (https://www.familysearch.org/ark:/61903/1:1:QLK5-Q2B7 : Sun Mar 10 00:56:01 UTC 2024), Entry for Eugenio Stella and Agostino Stella, 18 maggio 1902.
* "Paraguay, registros parroquiales, 1754-2015", , FamilySearch (https://www.familysearch.org/ark:/61903/1:1:ZCWQ-566Z : Sun Mar 10 05:36:37 UTC 2024), Entry for Josefina Emma Fasanelli de Polo and José Fasanelli, Mar 1902.
* "Paraguay, registros parroquiales, 1754-2015", , FamilySearch (https://www.familysearch.org/ark:/61903/1:1:Q2SH-T862 : Sun Mar 10 05:36:36 UTC 2024), Entry for Josefina Emma Fusanelli de Polo and José Fusanelli, 19 Mar 1902.

318) Nicola diLillo

Nicola diLillo(318) was born on 7 June 1902, in Ariano, Italy, to Raffaele Di Lillo(95a) and Raimonda Perrina(95).

Records that include Nicola diLillo(318):
* Ariano, Italy 1902 Birth Act #303

319) Domenico deDonato

Domenico deDonato(319) was born on 28 August 1902, in Ariano, Italy, to Michele deDonato(106) and Loreta di Vitto(106a). On 8 October 1917 Domenico deDonato(319) arrived in Boston, MA. Domenico deDonato(319) died on 15 July 1979 in Shelton, CT.

Domenico deDonato(319) married Anna Minotti(319a) on 1 September 1923 in Bridgeport, CT.

Anna Minotti(319a) was born on 7 March 1899, in Santa Croce Magliano, Italy, to Domenicantonio Minotti(319aF) and Lucia Rachele Maioribus(319aM). On 18 March 1921 Anna Minotti(319a) boarded the SS Duca d'Aosta, in Naples Italy, arriving in New York, NY on 31 March 1921. Anna Minotti(319a) died on 20 February 1998, in Milford, CT.

Known children of Domenico deDonato(319) and Anna Minotti(319a):

> i) Michael deDonato(538) born in 1924
> ii) Loretta DeDonato(563) born in 1928

Records that include Domenico deDonato(319) and/or Anna Minotti(319a):
- Santa Croce Magliano, Italy 1899 Birth Act #46
- Ariano, Italy 1902 Birth Act #438
- "New York Passenger Arrival Lists (Ellis Island), 1892-1924", , FamilySearch (https://www.familysearch.org/ark:/61903/1:1:J6VS-D68 : Fri Mar 08 20:30:11 UTC 2024), Entry for Anna Minotti and Domenicantonio, 1921.
- Bridgeport, CT, Marriage July - Sept 1923 #280
- Bridgeport, CT, July 1928 246 - 512 Birth Record #379
- "United States Census, 1940", , FamilySearch (https://www.familysearch.org/ark:/61903/1:1:KWMV-T5X : Fri Mar 08 07:43:14 UTC 2024), Entry for Domenick Dedonato and Anna Dedonato, 1940.
- "Connecticut, World War II Draft Registration Cards, 1940-1945", , FamilySearch (https://www.familysearch.org/ark:/61903/1:1:Q2CR-WF63 : Thu Mar 07 01:21:45 UTC 2024), Entry for Domenico De Donato and Anna De Donato, 16 Feb 1942.
- "United States Census, 1950", , FamilySearch (https://www.familysearch.org/ark:/61903/1:1:6FMX-76W1 : Thu Oct 05 02:16:58 UTC 2023), Entry for Anna Dendonato and Michael A Dendonato, 7 April 1950.
- "United States Social Security Death Index," database, FamilySearch (https://familysearch.org/ark:/61903/1:1:JKFV-1YM : 7 January 2021), Domenico Dedonato, Jul 1979; citing U.S. Social Security Administration, Death Master File, database (Alexandria, Virginia: National Technical Information Service, ongoing).
- "Connecticut Death Index, 1949-2001," database, FamilySearch (https://familysearch.org/ark:/61903/1:1:VZG6-GMY : 9 December 2014), Domin Dedonato, 15 Jul 1979; from "Connecticut Death Index, 1949-2001," database, Ancestry (http://www.ancestry.com : 2003); citing Shelton, , Connecticut, Connecticut Department of Health, Hartford.
- https://www.newspapers.com/article/the-bridgeport-telegram/33693041/
- "Connecticut Death Index, 1949-2001," , FamilySearch (https://familysearch.org/ark:/61903/1:1:VZGB-Y53 : 9 December 2014), Anna Dedonato, 20 Feb 1998; from "Connecticut Death Index, 1949-2001," database, Ancestry (http://www.ancestry.com : 2003); citing Milford, New Haven, Connecticut, Connecticut Department of Health, Hartford.
- "United States, Social Security Numerical Identification Files (NUMIDENT), 1936-2007", , FamilySearch (https://www.familysearch.org/ark:/61903/1:1:6KMV-Z2K3 : 10 February 2023), Anna Minotti Dedonato, .

320) Michele Ciasullo

Michele Ciasullo(320) was born on 8 May 1903, in Ariano, Italy, to Filippo Ciasullo(105a) and Maria Giovanna Perrina(105). Michele Ciasullo(320) died on 21 February 1904 in Ariano, Italy.

Records that include Michele Ciasullo(320):
- Ariano, Italy 1903 Birth Act #240
- Ariano, Italy 1904 Death Act #68

321) Maria Stella

Maria Stella(321) was born on 5 February 1904, in Ariano, Italy, to Antonio Stella(110) and Eugenia LoConte(110a). Maria Stella(321) died 19 September 1910 in Ariano, Italy.

Records that include Maria Stella(321):
- Ariano, Italy 1904 Birth Act #65
- Ariano, Italy 1910 Death Act #329

322) Angelo Maria di Lillo

Angelo Maria di Lillo(322) was born on 18 April 1904, in Ariano, Italy, to Raffaele di Lillo(95a) and Raimonda Perrina(95). Angelo Maria di Lillo(322) died on 16 March 1983 in Ariano, Italy.

Angelo Maria di Lillo(322) married Antonia lo Conte(322a) on 10 September 1925 in Ariano, Italy.

Antonia lo Conte(322a) was born on 3 February 1906, in Ariano, Italy, to Michele LoConte(322aF) and Maria Roseria Gelormini(322aM). Antonia LoConte(275) died 1 March 1981 in Ariano, Italy.

Records that include Angelo Maria di Lillo(322) and/or Antonia lo Conte(322a):
- Ariano, Italy 1904 Birth Act #184
- Ariano, Italy 1906 Birth Act #85
- Ariano, Italy 1925 Marriage Act #102
- Ariano, Italy 1981 Death Act #166
- Ariano, Italy 1983 Death Act #50

323) Pasquale Angelica

Pasquale Angelica(323) was born on 23 April 1904 in Rome, Italy to Giuseppe Angelica(112b) and Anna Saveria D'Ausilio(112). On 27 May 1920 Pasquale Angelica(323) boarded the ship SS Duca Degli Abruzzi, in Naples, Italy, arriving in New York on 9 Jun 1920. Pasquale Angelica(323) was going to Thompsonville, CT to be with his half-brother Carlo.

Records that include Pasquale Angelica(323):
- Rome, Italy 1904 Birth Act #2343-A-804
- "New York Passenger Arrival Lists (Ellis Island), 1892-1924", , FamilySearch (https://www.familysearch.org/ark:/61903/1:1:J6ZR-8TB : Sat Mar 09 10:41:56 UTC 2024), Entry for Pasquale Angelica and Giuseppe, 1920.

324) Angela Maria D'Ausilio

Angela Maria D'Ausilio(324) was born on 12 June 1904, in Waterbury, CT, to Salvatore Antonio D'ausilio(124) and Giovanna Colucci(124a). Angela Maria D'Ausilio(324) died on 6 September 1979, in Ipswich, MA.

Angela Maria D'Ausilio(324) married Nicola Giuseppe Amato Dragoni(324a) on 10 June 1922 in New York, NY.

Nicola Giuseppe Amato Dragoni(324a) was born on 5 March 1898, in Nusco, Italy, to Raffaele Dragoni(324aF) and Marianna Errico(324aM). On 19 October 1905 Nicola Giuseppe Amato Dragoni(324a) boarded the ship, SS Lombardia, in Naples, Italy. Nicola Giuseppe Amato Dragoni(324a) arrived in New York, NY on 3 November 1905. On 7 March 1944 Nicola Giuseppe Amato Dragoni(324a) became a citizen of the United States in Boston, MA. Nicola Giuseppe Amato Dragoni(324a) died on 11 October 1986 in Beverly, MA.

Known children of Angela Maria D'Ausilio(324) and Nicola Giuseppe Amato Dragoni(324a):

     i) Anna M. Dragoni(535) in 1924
     ii) John Dragoni(543) born in 1925
     iii) Rita Dragoni(576) born in 1930
     iv) Anthony E. Dragoni(580) born in 1931

Records that include Angela Maria D'Ausilio(324) and/or Nicola Giuseppe Amato Dragoni(324a):

- Nasco, Italy 1898 Birth Act #26
- "Italia, Avellino, Sant'Angelo dei Lombardi, Stato Civile (Tribunale), 1866-1910," images, FamilySearch (https://familysearch.org/ark:/61903/3:1:3QSQ-G97V-BWCJ? cc=2043434&wc=MPF4-929%3A348439701%2C348649301%2C348652201 : 22 May 2014), Avellino > Nusco > Nati 1885-1910 Pubblicazioni 1867-1910 > image 1148 of 2956; Tribunale di Sant'Angelo dei Lombardi (Sant'Angelo dei Lombardi Court and Criminal Court, Sant'Angelo dei Lombardi).
- "New York Passenger Arrival Lists (Ellis Island), 1892-1924", , FamilySearch (https://www.familysearch.org/ark:/61903/1:1:JF4X-P3P : Fri Jul 19 07:16:26 UTC 2024), Entry for Nicola Tragone and Raffle Tragone, 03 Nov 1905.
- "United States Census, 1910", , FamilySearch (https://www.familysearch.org/ark:/61903/1:1:MK2G-NS5 : Tue Jul 23 18:21:12 UTC 2024), Entry for Salvatore Dansilio and Jennie Dansilio, 1910.
- "United States Census, 1910", , FamilySearch (https://www.familysearch.org/ark:/61903/1:1:M5MV-JLL : Fri Mar 08 01:41:05 UTC 2024), Entry for Raphael Dragone and Annie Dragone, 1910.
- "New York, County Naturalization Records, 1791-1980", , FamilySearch (https://www.familysearch.org/ark:/61903/1:1:Q57R-HBBF : Thu Mar 07 00:28:10 UTC 2024), Entry for Nicholas Dragoni, 1917.
- "United States World War I Draft Registration Cards, 1917-1918", database with images, FamilySearch (https://www.familysearch.org/ark:/61903/1:1:WDY2-75PZ : 8 July 2024), Nicholas Michael Dragoni, 1917-1918.
- "United States Census, 1920", , FamilySearch (https://www.familysearch.org/ark:/61903/1:1:MFMC-Y9J : Sat Jul 06 12:33:15 UTC 2024), Entry for Salvatore Danselio and Jennie Danselio, 1920.
- "Massachusetts State Vital Records, 1841-1925", , FamilySearch (https://www.familysearch.org/ark:/61903/1:1:6PND-NJKK : Thu May 23 03:52:51 UTC 2024), Entry for John Dragoni and Nicola, 9 May 1925.
- "United States Census, 1930", , FamilySearch (https://www.familysearch.org/ark:/61903/1:1:XQ5G-9DC : Tue Jul 23 16:54:53 UTC 2024), Entry for Nicholas Dragoni and Angelina Dragoni, 1930.
- https://familysearch.org/ark:/61903/3:1:3Q9M-CSMV-FWGM-9? cat=1257420&i=844
- "United States Census, 1950", , FamilySearch (https://www.familysearch.org/ark:/61903/1:1:6F38-C2LK : Fri Oct 06 17:29:06 UTC 2023), Entry for Nick M Dragoni and Angela M Dragoni, 10 April 1950.
- "United States Social Security Death Index," database, FamilySearch (https://familysearch.org/ark:/61903/1:1:JKXL-B3D : 7 January 2021), Angela Dragoni, Sep 1979; citing U.S. Social Security Administration, Death Master File, database (Alexandria, Virginia: National Technical Information Service, ongoing).
- "Massachusetts Death Index, 1970-2003", , FamilySearch (https://familysearch.org/ark:/61903/1:1:VZYS-NYM : 13 June 2019), Angela M Dragoni, 1979.
- "United States Social Security Death Index," , FamilySearch (https://familysearch.org/ark:/61903/1:1:VMFD-BXM : 7 January 2021), Nicholas Dragoni, Oct 1986; citing U.S. Social Security Administration, Death Master File, database (Alexandria, Virginia: National Technical Information Service, ongoing).

- "Massachusetts Death Index, 1970-2003", , FamilySearch
  (https://familysearch.org/ark:/61903/1:1:VZ55-NV9 : 13 June 2019),
  Nicholas Dragoni, 1986.
- "United States, GenealogyBank Obituaries, Births, and Marriages
  1980-2014", , FamilySearch
  (https://www.familysearch.org/ark:/61903/1:1:QKPF-F5VN : Sat Mar 09
  06:46:02 UTC 2024), Entry for Mrs Anna M Dragoni Adams and Lawrence
  O Adams, 21 May 2011.
- "United States, Social Security Numerical Identification Files
  (NUMIDENT), 1936-2007", database, FamilySearch
  (https://www.familysearch.org/ark:/61903/1:1:6KM3-RG5P : 10
  February 2023), Nicholas Dragoni in entry for Rita Dragoni, .
- "Massachusetts State Vital Records, 1841-1925", , FamilySearch
  (https://www.familysearch.org/ark:/61903/1:1:6P6R-8HKH : Thu May 23
  03:54:08 UTC 2024), Entry for Anna Dragoni and Nicola Dragoni, 7
  Mar 1924.
- "United States, GenealogyBank Obituaries, Births, and Marriages
  1980-2014", , FamilySearch
  (https://www.familysearch.org/ark:/61903/1:1:QKRR-DNMY : Mon Jun 03
  18:55:45 UTC 2024), Entry for Mr Anthony E Dragoni and Nicholas
  Dragoni, 17 Aug 2006.

325) Mariangela Ciasullo

Mariangela Ciasullo(325) was born on 14 August 1904, in Ariano, Italy, to
Michele Ciasullo(82a) and Filomena Perrina(82). Mariangela Ciasullo(325) died
on 8 February 1908 in Ariano, Italy.

Records that include Mariangela Ciasullo(325):
- Ariano, Italy 1904 Birth Act #338
- Ariano, Italy 1908 Death Act #45

326) Angelo Perrina

Angelo Perrina(326) was born on 20 November 1904, in Ariano, Italy, to Michele
Perrina(88) and Maria Grazia Caraglia(88a).

Records that include Angelo Perrina(326):
- Ariano, Italy 1904 Birth Act #497

327) Filippo deDonato

Filippo deDonato(327) was born on 22 February 1905, in Ariano, Italy, to
Michele deDonato(106) and Loreta di Vitto(106a). On 8 October 1917, Filippo
deDonato(327) immigrated to Boston, MA. Filippo deDonato(327) became a United
States Citizen on 7 May 1940. Filippo deDonato(327) died on 10 May 1977 in
Bridgeport, CT.

Filippo deDonato(327) married Florence Cerino(327a) on 6 October 1924 in
Bridgeport, CT.

Florence Cerino(327a) was born on 7 November 1904, in Sepino, Italy, to
Giuseppe Cerino(327aF) and Lucy Verderamm(327aM). Florence Cerino(327a) died
on 28 February 1999 in Bridgeport, CT.

Known children of Filippo deDonato(327) and Florence Cerino(327a):

  i) Michael deDonato(557) born in 1927
  ii) Joseph DeDonato Sr.(568) born in 1929
  iii) Living Person and/or Spouse
  iv) Living Person and/or Spouse

Records that include Filippo deDonato(327) and/or Florence Cerino(327a):
Ariano, Italy 1905 Birth Act #143
- "United States Census, 1920", , FamilySearch
  (https://www.familysearch.org/ark:/61903/1:1:MCFH-8FW : Wed Jul 24
  19:29:25 UTC 2024), Entry for Michael Donato and Edith Donato,
  1920.
- Bridgeport, CT, Marriages Oct - Dec 1924 #29
- "Connecticut, Naturalization Records, 1795-1945", FamilySearch
  (https://www.familysearch.org/ark:/61903/1:1:6RQ1-CQQD : Wed May 28
  14:22:30 UTC 2025), Entry for Philip Dedonato and Fortunata, 31 Jan
  1925.

- "United States Census, 1930", , FamilySearch (https://www.familysearch.org/ark:/61903/1:1:XMPM-C9Q : Sat Mar 09 16:00:40 UTC 2024), Entry for Phillip Dedonato and Florence Dedonato, 1930.
- "Connecticut, Naturalization Records, 1795-1945", FamilySearch (https://www.familysearch.org/ark:/61903/1:1:6R79-J1RC : Wed May 28 14:22:27 UTC 2025), Entry for Philip or Filippo De Donato or Di Donato and Florence, 28 Aug 1936.
- "Connecticut, Naturalization Records, 1795-1945", FamilySearch (https://www.familysearch.org/ark:/61903/1:1:6R6M-NYSN : Wed May 28 14:54:07 UTC 2025), Entry for Philip or Filippo De Donato or Di Donato and Florence, 28 Aug 1936.
- "United States Census, 1940", , FamilySearch (https://www.familysearch.org/ark:/61903/1:1:KWMK-MGQ : Sun Mar 10 01:58:12 UTC 2024), Entry for Philip Dedonato and Florence Dedonato, 1940.
- "Connecticut, Naturalization Records, 1795-1945", FamilySearch (https://www.familysearch.org/ark:/61903/1:1:6R8G-3GPG : Wed May 28 14:52:06 UTC 2025), Entry for Philip De Donato and Florence, 7 May 1940.
- "Connecticut, World War II Draft Registration Cards, 1940-1945", , FamilySearch (https://www.familysearch.org/ark:/61903/1:1:Q2CR-WN4J : Sun Mar 10 12:20:42 UTC 2024), Entry for Philip De Donato and Philip De Donato, 16 Oct 1940.
- United States Census, 1950", , FamilySearch (https://www.familysearch.org/ark:/61903/1:1:6FMX-1KMM : Fri Oct 06 06:38:41 UTC 2023), Entry for Phillip De Donato and Florence De Donato, 1950.
- Bridgeport, CT Deaths May 1977 #58
- "United States Social Security Death Index," database, FamilySearch (https://familysearch.org/ark:/61903/1:1:JBLV-6M5 : 7 January 2021), Philip Dedonato, May 1977; citing U.S. Social Security Administration, Death Master File, database (Alexandria, Virginia: National Technical Information Service, ongoing).
- https://www.newspapers.com/newspage/60253816/
- Bridgeport, CT Deaths February 1999 #223
- "Find a Grave Index," database, FamilySearch (https://www.familysearch.org/ark:/61903/1:1:68JM-TK6C : 14 June 2023), Phillip DeDonato, ; Burial, Stratford, Fairfield, Connecticut, United States of America, Saint Michael's Cemetery; citing record ID 228225963, Find a Grave, http://www.findagrave.com.
- "Connecticut Death Index, 1949-2001," , FamilySearch (https://familysearch.org/ark:/61903/1:1:V647-4LZ : 9 December 2014), PHILI in entry for Florence De Donato, 28 Feb 1999; from "Connecticut Death Index, 1949-2001," database, Ancestry (http://www.ancestry.com : 2003); citing Bridgeport, Fairfield, Connecticut, Connecticut Department of Health, Hartford.

328) Francesco Paolo Giorgione

Francesco Paolo Giorgione(328) was born on 2 April 1905, in Ariano, Italy, to Raffaele Giorgione(80) and Carmina Salvioli(80a).

Francesco Paolo Giorgione(328) married Francesca DeVito(328a) on 8 October 1932 in Ariano, Italy.

Francesca DeVito(328a) was born on 2 January 1906, in Ariano, Italy, to Pasquale DeVito(328aF) and Anna Maria Vernacchia(328aM).

Records that include Francesco Paolo Giorgione(328) and/or Francesca DeVito(328a):
- Ariano, Italy 1905 Birth Act #214
- Ariano, Italy 1906 Birth Act #6
- Ariano, Italy 1932 Marriage Act #P.II.A.111

329) Concetta D'Ausilio

Concetta D'Ausilio(329) was born on 8 August 1905, in Bridgeport, CT, to Giovanni Battista (John B.) D'ausilio(120) and Catherina Viola(120a). Concetta D'Ausilio(329) died on 16 March 1910 in Waterbury, CT. Concetta D'Ausilio(329) was buried in Calvary Cemetery, Waterbury, CT.

Records that include Concetta D'Ausilio(329):
* Bridgeport, CT 1905 Birth Act #42
* Waterbury, CT 1910 Death Act #190

330) Giovannina Covotta

Giovannina Covotta(330) was born on 22 August 1905, in Ariano, Italy, to Michele Covotta(122) and Antonetta Bilotta(122a).

Giovannina Covotta(330) married Federico Capenone(330a) on 13 June 1953 in Rome, Italy.

Federico Capenone(330a). The marriage is referenced on the birth record of Giovannina Covotta(330), no further information has been located.

Records that include Giovannina Covotta(330) and/or Federico Capenone(330a):
* Ariano, Italy 1905 Birth Act #452

331) Angelo Angelica

Angelo Angelica(331) was born on 10 November 1905 in Rome, Italy to Giuseppe Angelica(112b) and Anna Saveria D'Ausilio(112). Angelo Angelica(331) died 22 Aug 1906 in Rome, Italy.

Records that include Angelo Angelica(331):
* Ariano, Italy 1905 Birth Act #2346.B844
* Ariano, Italy 1906 Death Act #326pa.616

332) Raimonda Ciasullo

Raimonda Ciasullo(332) was born on 19 November 1905, in Ariano, Italy, to Filippo Ciasullo(105a) and Maria Giovanna Perrina(105). Raimonda Ciasullo(332) died on 1 September 1906 in Ariano, Italy.

Records that include Raimonda Ciasullo(332):
* Ariano, Italy 1905 Birth Act #638
* Ariano, Italy 1906 Death Act #223

333) Conceição DeDonato

Conceição DeDonato(333) was born on 8 December 1905, in Bras, Sao Paulo, Brazil, to Marcello deDonato(78) and Maria Rosa Politano(78a). Conceição DeDonato(333) was baptized on 29 June 1906 in Brás, São Paulo, Brasil.

Conceição DeDonato(333) married Camillo Costa(333a).

Camillo Costa(333a) was born in Brazil to Jose Luiz Costa(333aF) and Maria Baptista(333aM).

Known Children of Conceição DeDonato(333) and Camillo Costa(333a):

    i) Maria Costa(532) born in 1924

Records that include Conceição DeDonato(333) and/or Camillo Costa(333a):
* "Brasil, São Paulo, Registros da Igreja Católica, 1640-2013", FamilySearch (https://www.familysearch.org/ark:/61903/1:1:6DGX-24PJ : Mon Jul 14 18:00:27 UTC 2025), Entry for Conceição and Marcello de Donato, 29 de junho de 1906.
* "Brasil, São Paulo, Registro Civil, 1925-2023", FamilySearch (https://www.familysearch.org/ark:/61903/1:1:6VW4-MYVD : Sat Aug 23 11:10:16 UTC 2025), Entry for Antenor Ferreira de Morais and Ca Millo Costa, 20 de setembro de 1924.

334) Maria Rosaria Perrina

Maria Rosaria Perrina(334) was born on 13 November 1906, in Ariano, Italy, to Angelo Maria Perrina(74) and Tommasina Paduano(74a). Maria Rosaria Perrina(334) died 18 January 1990 in Ariano, Italy.

Maria Rosaria Perrina(334) married Raffaele Cardinale(334a) on 14 September 1933 in Ariano, Italy.

Raffaele Cardinale(334a) was born on 23 November 1906, in Ariano, Italy to Domenico Cardinale(334aF) and Maria Summa(334aM).

Records that include Maria Rosaria Perrina(334) and Raffaele Cardinale(334a):
- Ariano, Italy 1906 Birth Act #536
- Ariano, Italy 1906 Birth Act #548
- Ariano, Italy 1933 Marriage Act #P.II.A.106
- Ariano, Italy 1990 Death Act #12

335) Liberatore (Leon) D'Ausilio

Liberatore (Leon) D'Ausilio(335) was born on 7 March 1907, in Bridgeport, CT, to Giovanni Battista (John B.) D'ausilio(120) and Catherina Viola(120a). Liberatore (Leon) D'Ausilio(335) was baptized at Holy Rosary Church, Bridgeport, CT. Liberatore (Leon) D'Ausilio(335) died on 15 September 1999 in Bridgeport, CT. Liberatore (Leon) D'Ausilio(335) was buried on 20 September 1999 in Saint Michael's Cemetery, Stratford, CT. Liberatore (Leon) D'Ausilio(335) was a plumber.

Liberatore (Leon) D'Ausilio(335) married Helen Eleanor LaLuna(335a) and Rose Vallillo(335b).

Liberatore (Leon) D'Ausilio(335) married Helen Eleanor LaLuna(335a) on 28 October 1929 in Bridgeport, CT. Liberatore (Leon) D'Ausilio(335) divorced Helen Eleanor LaLuna(335a) in 1938.

Helen Eleanor LaLuna(335a) was born on 12 August 1913, in Croton-on-Hudson, NY, to Francesco Laluna(335aF) and Antonia Maria Di Stephano(335aM). Helen Eleanor LaLuna(335a) died on 13 August 1992 in Bridgeport, CT.

Helen Eleanor LaLuna(335a) also married John Terris Kurtzenacker III(335ab).

Known children of Liberatore (Leon) D'Ausilio(335) and Helen Eleanor LaLuna(335a):

    i) John Louis D'Ausilio(573) born in 1929
    ii) Lillian Joyce D'Ausilio(582) born in 1931
    iii) Living person and/or spouse
    iv) Eleanor Jane D'ausilio(597) born in 1935
    v) Living person and/or spouse
    vi) Living person and/or spouse

Liberatore (Leon) D'Ausilio(335) married Rose Vallillo(335b) on 27 October 1945 in Bridgeport, CT.

Rose Vallillo(335b) was born on 6 February 1909, in Bridgeport, CT, to John Vallillo(335bF) and Antoinette Benedetto(335dM). Rose Vallillo(335b) died on 27 May 1974 in Bridgeport, CT. Rose Vallillo(335b) was buried in Saint Michael's Cemetery, Stratford, CT.

Records that include Liberatore (Leon) D'Ausilio(335), Helen Eleanor LaLuna(335a) and/or Rose Vallillo(335b):
- Bridgeport, CT 1907 Birth Act #500
- "United States Census, 1910", , FamilySearch (https://www.familysearch.org/ark:/61903/1:1:MK2L-1FY : Sat Mar 09 10:39:59 UTC 2024), Entry for John B Durslio and Katherine Durslio, 1910.
- Croton-on-Hudson, NY 1913 Birth Act #518
- "United States Census, 1920", , FamilySearch (https://www.familysearch.org/ark:/61903/1:1:MCFC-N6W : Thu Jul 11 17:35:15 UTC 2024), Entry for Frank La Luna and Maria La Luna, 1920.

- "United States Census, 1920", , FamilySearch (https://www.familysearch.org/ark:/61903/1:1:MCFH-475 : Thu Mar 07 15:23:17 UTC 2024), Entry for John Vallie and Antoinette Vallie, 1920.
- "New York Passenger Arrival Lists (Ellis Island), 1892-1924", , FamilySearch (https://www.familysearch.org/ark:/61903/1:1:JN27-PMF : Tue Jul 23 23:28:04 UTC 2024), Entry for Liberatore D'Ansilio, 26 Sep 1924.
- Bridgeport, CT 1929 Marriage Act #127
- "United States Census, 1930", , FamilySearch (https://www.familysearch.org/ark:/61903/1:1:XMGY-ZDN : Fri Jul 12 20:12:30 UTC 2024), Entry for Libero Pavsilio and Helen Dansilio, 1930.
- "United States Census, 1930", , FamilySearch (https://www.familysearch.org/ark:/61903/1:1:XMGB-4PJ : Fri Jul 19 19:33:10 UTC 2024), Entry for John Vallillo and Antoinette Vallillo, 1930.
- "United States Census, 1940", , FamilySearch (https://www.familysearch.org/ark:/61903/1:1:KWMF-GZ6 : Fri Mar 08 14:30:32 UTC 2024), Entry for Libero D Ansilio and Helen D Ansilio, 1940.
- "United States Census, 1940", , FamilySearch (https://www.familysearch.org/ark:/61903/1:1:KWMN-GP8 : Sat Mar 09 01:23:39 UTC 2024), Entry for John Vallillo and Antionette Vallillo, 1940.
- "Connecticut, World War II Draft Registration Cards, 1940-1945", , FamilySearch (https://www.familysearch.org/ark:/61903/1:1:Q2CR-WQP9 : Fri Mar 08 23:10:56 UTC 2024), Entry for Libero d'Ausilio and Helen d'Ausilio, 16 Oct 1940.
- Bridgeport, CT 1945 Marriage Act #129
- "United States Census, 1950", , FamilySearch (https://www.familysearch.org/ark:/61903/1:1:6FM8-9K1V : Fri Oct 06 03:02:30 UTC 2023), Entry for Leon Dausilio and Rose Dausilio, 3 April 1950.
- "United States Census, 1950", , FamilySearch (https://www.familysearch.org/ark:/61903/1:1:6FM6-7RRD : Thu Oct 05 11:11:44 UTC 2023), Entry for John T Kurtzenacker and Helen E Kurtzenacker, 1 April 1950.
- "Connecticut Death Index, 1949-2001," database, FamilySearch (https://familysearch.org/ark:/61903/1:1:V648-98F : 9 December 2014), LEON in entry for Rose Dausilio, 27 May 1974; from "Connecticut Death Index, 1949-2001," database, Ancestry (http://www.ancestry.com : 2003); citing Bridgeport, , Connecticut, Connecticut Department of Health, Hartfort.
- "United States Social Security Death Index," database, FamilySearch (https://familysearch.org/ark:/61903/1:1:JTRW-5M4 : 7 January 2021), Rose Dausilio, May 1974; citing U.S. Social Security Administration, Death Master File, database (Alexandria, Virginia: National Technical Information Service, ongoing).
- "Find a Grave Index," database, FamilySearch (https://www.familysearch.org/ark:/61903/1:1:QPRZ-WC6X : 13 June 2023), Rose DAusilio, ; Burial, Stratford, Fairfield, Connecticut, United States of America, Saint Michael's Cemetery; citing record ID 192645952, Find a Grave, http://www.findagrave.com.
- Bridgeport, CT 1992 Death Act #72
- "Find a Grave Index," database, FamilySearch (https://www.familysearch.org/ark:/61903/1:1:QPHV-FB2D : 12 May 2022), Helen Kurtzenacker, ; Burial, Bridgeport, Fairfield, Connecticut, United States of America, Park Cemetery; citing record ID 189953368, Find a Grave, http://www.findagrave.com.
- "United States, Social Security Numerical Identification Files (NUMIDENT), 1936-2007", database, FamilySearch (https://www.familysearch.org/ark:/61903/1:1:6KMV-V8TB : 10 February 2023), Helen Eleanor Dausilio, .

- "Connecticut Death Index, 1949-2001," , FamilySearch (https://familysearch.org/ark:/61903/1:1:VZGL-4FC : 9 December 2014), Helen E Kurtzenacker, 13 Aug 1992; from "Connecticut Death Index, 1949-2001," database, Ancestry (http://www.ancestry.com : 2003); citing Bridgeport, Fairfield, Connecticut, Connecticut Department of Health, Hartford.
- "United States Social Security Death Index," database, FamilySearch (https://familysearch.org/ark:/61903/1:1:VMNR-QPR : 7 January 2021), Helen E Kurtzenacker, Aug 1992; citing U.S. Social Security Administration, Death Master File, database (Alexandria, Virginia: National Technical Information Service, ongoing).
- "Connecticut Death Index, 1949-2001," database, FamilySearch (https://familysearch.org/ark:/61903/1:1:VZPJ-NRG : 9 December 2014), null in entry for Lillian D Landau, 21 Jan 1996; from "Connecticut Death Index, 1949-2001," database, Ancestry (http://www.ancestry.com : 2003); citing Shelton, Fairfield, Connecticut, Connecticut Department of Health, Hartford.
- "United States, Social Security Numerical Identification Files (NUMIDENT), 1936-2007", database, FamilySearch (https://www.familysearch.org/ark:/61903/1:1:6KMF-JZ7V : 10 February 2023), Leon Dausilio in entry for Lillian Joyce Dausilio, .
- Bridgeport, CT 1999 Death Act #78
- "Connecticut Death Index, 1949-2001," database, FamilySearch (https://familysearch.org/ark:/61903/1:1:VZP1-8PK : 9 December 2014), Liberatore L Dausilio, 1999; from "Connecticut Death Index, 1949-2001," database, Ancestry (http://www.ancestry.com : 2003); citing Bridgeport, Fairfield, Connecticut, Connecticut Department of Health, Hartford.
- "United States Social Security Death Index," database, FamilySearch (https://familysearch.org/ark:/61903/1:1:VS8Y-V27 : 7 January 2021), Leon Dausilio, 15 Sep 1999; citing U.S. Social Security Administration, Death Master File, database (Alexandria, Virginia: National Technical Information Service, ongoing).
- "Find a Grave Index," database, FamilySearch (https://www.familysearch.org/ark:/61903/1:1:QPRZ-J4ZR : 13 June 2023), Leon DAusilio, ; Burial, Stratford, Fairfield, Connecticut, United States of America, Saint Michael's Cemetery; citing record ID 192645828, Find a Grave, http://www.findagrave.com.
- "United States, Social Security Numerical Identification Files (NUMIDENT), 1936-2007", database, FamilySearch (https://www.familysearch.org/ark:/61903/1:1:6KMN-8JX2 : 10 February 2023), Leon Dausilio, .
- "United States, Social Security Numerical Identification Files (NUMIDENT), 1936-2007", database, FamilySearch (https://www.familysearch.org/ark:/61903/1:1:6KMV-ZK31 : 10 February 2023), Eleanor Jane Dausilio, .
- "United States, GenealogyBank Obituaries, Births, and Marriages 1980-2014", , FamilySearch (https://www.familysearch.org/ark:/61903/1:1:QVPP-YMND : Sun Jul 14 18:42:22 UTC 2024), Entry for Joan L Fleischer and Libero Or Leon D'Ausilio, 10 Apr 2012.

336) Maria Amalia Perrina

Maria Amalia Perrina(336) was born on 21 March 1907, in Ariano, Italy, to Michele Perrina(88) and Maria Grazia Caraglia(88a). Maria Amalia Perrina(336) died 8 December 1907 in Ariano, Italy.

Records that include Maria Amalia Perrina(336):
- Ariano, Italy 1907 Birth Act #163
- Ariano, Italy 1907 Death Act #336

337) Antonio deDonato

Antonio deDonato(337) was born on 5 June 1907, in Ariano, Italy, to Michele deDonato(106) and Loreta di Vitto(106a). On 8 October 1917, Antonio deDonato(337) immigrated to Boston, MA. Antonio deDonato(337) became a citizen of the United States of America on 6 February 1936 in Bridgeport, CT. Antonio deDonato(337) died on 6 May 1979 in Shelton, CT.

Antonio deDonato(337) married Mary Rosaria Cretella(337a) on 7 June 1927 in Stratford, CT.

Mary Rosaria Cretella(337a) was born on 16 April 1910, in Bridgeport, CT, to Antonio Cretella(337aF) and Antonetta Cargano(337aM). Mary Rosaria Cretella(337a) died on 6 October 1969 in Stratford, CT.

Known children of Antonio deDonato(337) and Mary Rosaria Cretella(337a):

    i) Michael DeDonato(589) in 1933
    ii) Antoinette DeDonato(599) born in 1935

Records that include Antonio deDonato(337) and/or Mary Rosaria Cretella(337a):

- Ariano, Italy 1907 Birth Act #285
- Bridgeport, CT, Births April 1910 #842
- "United States Census, 1920", , FamilySearch (https://www.familysearch.org/ark:/61903/1:1:MCFH-8FW : Wed Jul 24 19:29:25 UTC 2024), Entry for Michael Donato and Edith Donato, 1920.
- "United States Census, 1930", , FamilySearch (https://www.familysearch.org/ark:/61903/1:1:XMRS-5VY : Sat Mar 09 00:02:52 UTC 2024), Entry for Anthony De Donato, 1930.
- "United States Census, 1930", , FamilySearch (https://www.familysearch.org/ark:/61903/1:1:XMRS-5VB : Sat Mar 09 00:02:51 UTC 2024), Entry for Mary De Donato, 1930.
- Bridgeport, CT, Births May 1933 #105
- "United States Census, 1940", , FamilySearch (https://www.familysearch.org/ark:/61903/1:1:K71S-C8W : Fri Mar 08 05:05:36 UTC 2024), Entry for Mary Dedonato and Micheal Dedonato, 1940.
- "United States Census, 1950", , FamilySearch (https://www.familysearch.org/ark:/61903/1:1:6FMX-JJ72 : Tue Mar 19 16:49:54 UTC 2024), Entry for Anthony Dedonato and Mary Dedonato, 22 April 1950.
- "Connecticut Death Index, 1949-2001," , FamilySearch (https://familysearch.org/ark:/61903/1:1:VZ5H-NJH : 9 December 2014), Mary R Dedonato, 06 Oct 1969; from "Connecticut Death Index, 1949-2001," database, Ancestry (http://www.ancestry.com : 2003); citing Stratford, Fairfield, Connecticut, Connecticut Department of Health, Hartfort.
- https://www.newspapers.com/article/the-bridgeport-post-mary-dedonato-obit/34449919/
- "Find a Grave Index," database, FamilySearch (https://www.familysearch.org/ark:/61903/1:1:W6JP-T6W2 : 13 June 2023), Mary R Cretella DeDonato, ; Burial, Stratford, Fairfield, Connecticut, United States of America, Saint Michael's Cemetery; citing record ID 199916257, Find a Grave, http://www.findagrave.com.
- "Connecticut Death Index, 1949-2001," database, FamilySearch (https://familysearch.org/ark:/61903/1:1:VZ59-8CW : 9 December 2014), Antho Dedonato, 06 May 1979; from "Connecticut Death Index, 1949-2001," database, Ancestry (http://www.ancestry.com : 2003); citing Shelton, , Connecticut, Connecticut Department of Health, Hartfort.
- "United States Social Security Death Index," database, FamilySearch (https://familysearch.org/ark:/61903/1:1:JKF2-Q32 : 7 January 2021), Anthony Dedonato, May 1979; citing U.S. Social Security Administration, Death Master File, database (Alexandria, Virginia: National Technical Information Service, ongoing).
- "United States, Social Security Numerical Identification Files (NUMIDENT), 1936-2007", database, FamilySearch (https://www.familysearch.org/ark:/61903/1:1:6KMF-VNTS : 10 February 2023), Anthony Dedonato in entry for Nettie Marie Dedonato, .
- https://www.pisteyfuneralhome.com/obituaries/Michael-J-DeDonato?obId=577238

338) <u>Angelo Angelica</u>

Angelo Angelica(338) was born on 1 August 1907 in Rome, Italy to Giuseppe Angelica(112b) and Anna Saveria D'Ausilio(112).

Records that include Angelo Angelica(338):
- Rome, Italy 1907 Birth Act #2161.B.96

339) <u>Rose Louise Giorgione</u>

Rose Louise Giorgione(339) was born on 23 December 1907, in Middletown, NY, to Luigi (Louis) Giorgione/George(86) and Maria Giovanna Perillo(86a). Rose Louise Giorgione(339) died 19 March 1997 in Garland, TX.

Rose Louise Giorgione(339) married Theodore Taft Garber(339a) on 16 December 1926 in New York.

<u>Theodore Taft Garber</u>(339a) was born on 13 May 1908, in Augusta, VA, to William Garber(339aF) and Carrie Sandridge(339aM). Theodore Taft Garber(339a) died 23 June 1967.

Known children of Rose Louise Giorgione(339) and Theodore Taft Garber(339a):

- i) Jean Louise Garber(559) born in 1928
- ii) Theodore Anthony Garber(606) born in 1941

Records that include Rose Louise Giorgione(339) and/or Theodore Taft Garber(339a):
- "New York, Birth Indexes outside of New York City, 1881-1942", , FamilySearch (https://www.familysearch.org/ark:/61903/1:1:6FYD-R9J1 : Sun Mar 10 11:07:39 UTC 2024), Entry for Rose George, 24 Dec 1907.
- "Virginia, Birth Certificates, 1912-1913", , FamilySearch (https://www.familysearch.org/ark:/61903/1:1:QVBN-LNVS : Tue Jul 23 11:06:02 UTC 2024), Entry for Theodore T Garver and Edward W Garver, 13 May 1908.
- "United States Census, 1910", , FamilySearch (https://www.familysearch.org/ark:/61903/1:1:MPGN-QJZ : Sat Mar 09 18:30:00 UTC 2024), Entry for Edward W Garber and Sarah E Garber, 1910.
- "United States Census, 1920", , FamilySearch (https://www.familysearch.org/ark:/61903/1:1:MJJ2-QVZ : Sat Jul 13 05:22:31 UTC 2024), Entry for E W Garver and Carrie S Garver, 1920.
- "New York, County Marriages, 1847-1848; 1908-1936", , FamilySearch (https://www.familysearch.org/ark:/61903/1:1:Q2MT-CCJ9 : Sun Jul 07 14:36:33 UTC 2024), Entry for Theodore Taft Garber and Edward William Garber, 16 Dec 1926.
- "United States Census, 1930", , FamilySearch (https://www.familysearch.org/ark:/61903/1:1:X4R1-NC5 : Mon Mar 11 01:37:59 UTC 2024), Entry for Theodore Garber and Rose Garber, 1930.
- "United States Census, 1940", , FamilySearch (https://www.familysearch.org/ark:/61903/1:1:KQGP-XN8 : Sun Mar 10 21:26:22 UTC 2024), Entry for Anthony George and Joseph George, 1940.
- "United States Census, 1950", , FamilySearch (https://www.familysearch.org/ark:/61903/1:1:6XY7-1SV2 : Thu Oct 05 08:22:58 UTC 2023), Entry for Theodore T Garber and Rose L Garber, 5 April 1950.
- "United States, Social Security Numerical Identification Files (NUMIDENT), 1936-2007", , FamilySearch (https://www.familysearch.org/ark:/61903/1:1:6KMT-XB7Q : 10 February 2023), Rose George in entry for Jean Garber, .
- "United States Social Security Death Index," database, FamilySearch (https://familysearch.org/ark:/61903/1:1:JK22-RZQ : 7 January 2021), Theodore Garber, Jun 1967; citing U.S. Social Security Administration, Death Master File, database (Alexandria, Virginia: National Technical Information Service, ongoing).

- "United States, Social Security Numerical Identification Files (NUMIDENT), 1936-2007", database, FamilySearch (https://www.familysearch.org/ark:/61903/1:1:6KM5-9H2K : 10 February 2023), Theodore T Garber, .
- "Texas Death Index, 1964-1998," , FamilySearch (https://familysearch.org/ark:/61903/1:1:JV5S-624 : 5 December 2014), Rose Louise Garber, Dallas, Texas, United States; citing Department of State Health Services, Austin.
- "United States Social Security Death Index," database, FamilySearch (https://familysearch.org/ark:/61903/1:1:JKR9-8JW : 7 January 2021), Rose L Garber, 19 Mar 1997; citing U.S. Social Security Administration, Death Master File, database (Alexandria, Virginia: National Technical Information Service, ongoing).
- "United States, Social Security Numerical Identification Files (NUMIDENT), 1936-2007", database, FamilySearch (https://www.familysearch.org/ark:/61903/1:1:6K97-KZWX : 10 February 2023), Louis George in entry for Rose Louise Garber, .
- "Find a Grave Index," database, FamilySearch (https://www.familysearch.org/ark:/61903/1:1:QVVW-4VVP : 1 April 2023), Rose L. George, ; Burial, Phillipsburg, Orange, New York, United States of America, Wallkill Cemetery; citing record ID 9118365, Find a Grave, http://www.findagrave.com.

340) Pasqualina Ciasullo

Pasqualina Ciasullo(340) was born on 21 April 1908, in Ariano, Italy, to Filippo Ciasullo(105a) and Maria Giovanna Perrina(105). Pasqualina Ciasullo(340) died on 2 November 1908 in Ariano, Italy.

Records that include Pasqualina Ciasullo(340):
- Ariano, Italy 1908 Birth Act #248
- Ariano, Italy 1908 Death Act #323

341) Giulio D'Ausilio

Giulio D'Ausilio(341) was born 20 May 1908, in Rome, Italy, to Oto Maria D'ausilio(99) and Maria Gabriella Giannario(99a).

Giulio D'Ausilio(341) married Raffella Lanzi(341a) on 20 February 1935 in Vicenza, Italy.

Raffella Lanzi(341a) was born about 1911, in Cagli, Italy, to Augusto Lanzi(341aF) and Burisida Benneditti(341aM).

Records that include Giulio D'Ausilio(341) and/or Raffella Lanzi(341a):
- Rome, Italy 1908 Birth Act #1013B.916

342) Maria Libera deDonato

Maria Libera deDonato(342) was born on 27 September 1908, in Ariano, Italy, to Pietro deDonato(118) and Rosa Bilancione(118a).

Maria Libera deDonato(342) married Giuseppe Ciriaco Michele Covotta(342a) on 27 June 1929 in Ariano, Italy.

Giuseppe Ciriaco Michele Covotta(342a) was born on 1 February 1907, in Ariano, Italy, to Filippo Covotta(342aF) and Maria Giuseppa Spagnoletto(342aM).

Known children of Maria Libera deDonato(342) and Giuseppe Ciriaco Michele Covotta(342a):

i) Liberato Covotta(603) born in 1940

Records that include Maria Libera deDonato(342) and/or Giuseppe Ciriaco Michele Covotta(342a):
- Ariano, Italy 1907 Birth Act #66
- Ariano, Italy 1908 Birth Act #524
- Ariano, Italy 1929 Marriage Act #68
- Ariano, Italy 1940 Death Act #214

343) Michele deDonato

Michele deDonato(343) was born on 20 April 1910, in Ariano, Italy, to Pietro deDonato(128) and Rosa Bilancione(128a). Michele deDonato(343) died 5 October 1918 in Ariano, Italy.

Records that include Michele deDonato(343):
- Ariano, Italy 1910 Birth Act #278
- Ariano, Italy 1918 Death Act #339

344) Felice (Felix) D'Ausilio

Felice (Felix) D'Ausilio(344) was born on 21 December 1908, in Milford, CT, to Giovanni Battista (John B.) D'ausilio(120) and Catherina Viola(120a). Felice (Felix) D'Ausilio(344) died on 31 July 1954 in South Fayette, PA.

Known children of Felice (Felix) D'Ausilio(344):

i) Living Person and/or Spouse

Felice (Felix) D'Ausilio(344) married Laura Blaze(344a) on 6 January 1948 in Canton Township, PA. Felice (Felix) D'Ausilio(344) and Laura Blaze(344a) divorced.

Laura Blaze(344a) was born on 14 June 1922, in Cleveland, OH, to Frank Blaze(344aF) and Catherine Knopa(344aM). Laura Blaze(344a) died on 3 October 2004 in Washington, PA. Laura Blaze(344a) was buried on 6 October 2004 in Washington Cemetery, Washington, PA.

Laura Blaze(344a) also married Paul J. Woznick(344ab).

Records that include Felice (Felix) D'Ausilio(344):
- Milford, CT 1908 Birth Act 30 December 1908
- "United States Census, 1910", , FamilySearch (https://www.familysearch.org/ark:/61903/1:1:MK2L-1FY : Sat Mar 09 10:39:59 UTC 2024), Entry for John B Durslio and Katherine Durslio, 1910.
- "New York Passenger Arrival Lists (Ellis Island), 1892-1924", , FamilySearch (https://www.familysearch.org/ark:/61903/1:1:JN27-PMN : Thu Mar 07 14:08:31 UTC 2024), Entry for Felice d'Ansilio, 1924.
- "United States Census, 1930", , FamilySearch (https://www.familysearch.org/ark:/61903/1:1:XCZS-8H1 : Sat Mar 09 00:12:33 UTC 2024), Entry for Frank Blaze and Katherine Blaze, 1930.
- "United States Census, 1940", , FamilySearch (https://www.familysearch.org/ark:/61903/1:1:KQ7K-9X4 : Sat Jul 13 08:31:57 UTC 2024), Entry for Mary Hammond and Roy E Curtis, 1940.
- "United States Census, 1940", , FamilySearch (https://www.familysearch.org/ark:/61903/1:1:KQ7V-LQ3 : Fri Mar 08 08:15:41 UTC 2024), Entry for Mary Hammond and Roy E Curtis, 1940.
- "United States Census, 1940", , FamilySearch (https://www.familysearch.org/ark:/61903/1:1:KQCR-3WV : Sun Mar 10 00:50:34 UTC 2024), Entry for Frank Blaze and Catherine Blaze, 1940.
- "Pennsylvania, World War II Draft Registration Cards, 1940-1945", , FamilySearch (https://www.familysearch.org/ark:/61903/1:1:Q2SX-PSBP : Fri Feb 23 19:57:23 UTC 2024), Entry for Felix Dausilio and Litres Marseglia, 16 Oct 1940.
- "Pennsylvania, County Marriages, 1885-1950", , FamilySearch (https://www.familysearch.org/ark:/61903/1:1:VFQ9-Y3J : Tue Jul 23 18:44:49 UTC 2024), Entry for Felix Dausilio and John.
- "Pennsylvania, County Marriages, 1885-1950", , FamilySearch (https://www.familysearch.org/ark:/61903/1:1:VFQQ-P8S : Sat Mar 09 04:13:07 UTC 2024), Entry for Felix d'Ausillio and Lucille Maria Rae, 1947.

- "Pennsylvania, County Marriages, 1885-1950", , FamilySearch (https://www.familysearch.org/ark:/61903/1:1:VFQ8-86Y : Sat Jul 13 23:28:31 UTC 2024), Entry for Felix d'Austilio and John B., 6 Jan 1948.
- "United States Census, 1950", , FamilySearch (https://www.familysearch.org/ark:/61903/1:1:6XBV-FWMZ : Tue Mar 19 06:29:42 UTC 2024), Entry for Felix d'Ausilio and Fred L C Collinet, April 10, 1950.
- https://www.phmc.state.pa.us/bah/dam/rg/di/r11_090_DeathIndexes/Death_1954/D-54%20C-D.pdf
- "United States Social Security Death Index," database, FamilySearch (https://familysearch.org/ark:/61903/1:1:JG84-2JH : 11 January 2021), Laura Woznick, 03 Oct 2004; citing U.S. Social Security Administration, Death Master File, database (Alexandria, Virginia: National Technical Information Service, ongoing).
- "United States, Social Security Numerical Identification Files (NUMIDENT), 1936-2007", database, FamilySearch (https://www.familysearch.org/ark:/61903/1:1:6K9G-LVYP : 10 February 2023), Laura Blaze, .

345) Arminio Perrina

Arminio Perrina(345) was born about 1909, in Ariano, Italy, to Michele Perrina(88) and Maria Grazia Caraglia(88a). Arminio Perrina(345) died on 6 February 1910 in Ariano, Italy.

Records that include Arminio Perrina(345):
- Ariano, Italy 1910 Death Act #68

346) Pasqualina Ciasullo

Pasqualina Ciasullo(346) was born on 23 March 1910, in Ariano, Italy, to Filippo Ciasullo(105a) and Maria Giovanna Perrina(105).

Pasqualina Ciasullo(346) married Vincenzo Sanzio(346a) on 12 January 1931 in Ariano, Italy.

Vincenzo Sanzio(346a) was born on 19 July 1912, in Ariano, Italy, to Giuseppe Sanzio(346aF) and Loreta Pepe(346aM).

Records that include Pasqualina Ciasullo(346) and/or Vincenzo Sanzio(346a):
- Ariano, Italy 1910 Birth Act #217
- Ariano, Italy 1912 Birth Act #362
- Ariano, Italy 1931 Marriage Act #P.II.A.4

347) Maria Carssina Perrina

Maria Carssina Perrina(347) was born on 23 March 1910, in Ariano, Italy, to Angelo Maria Perrina(74) and Tommasina Paduano(74a). Maria Carssina Perrina(347) died 12 April 1910 in Ariano, Italy.

Records that include Maria Carssina Perrina(347):
- Ariano, Italy 1910 Birth Act #218
- Ariano, Italy 1910 Death Act #162

348) Teresa Concetta deDonato

Teresa Concetta deDonato(348) was born on 3 January 1911, in Ariano, Italy, to Domenico deDonato(103) and Bridgida Carmosino(103a). Teresa Concetta deDonato(348) died on 12 December 1995 in Grottaminarda, Italy.

Teresa Concetta deDonato(348) married Salvatore Belardi(348a) on 14 June 1936 in Naples, Italy.

Salvatore Belardi(348a) was born about 1904 in Naples, Italy to Luigi Belardi(348aF) and Lucia Ferrara(348aM).

Records that include Teresa Concetta deDonato(348) and/or Salvatore Belardi(348a):
- Naples, Italy 1907 Birth Act #383

- Ariano, Italy 1911 Birth Act #16
- Ariano, Italy 1936 Marriage Acts #PIIA.77

349) Antonio Angelica

Antonio Angelica(349) was born on 14 June 1911 in Rome, Italy to Giuseppe Angelica(112b) and Anna Saveria D'Ausilio(112). Antonio Angelica(349) died on 18 July 1911 in Rome, Italy.

Records that include Antonio Angelica(349):
- Rome, Italy 1911 Birth Act #1628 - 4a 1090
- Rome, Italy 1911 Death Act #2919

350) Luigi Angelica

Luigi Angelica(350) was born on 14 June 1911 in Rome, Italy to Giuseppe Angelica(112b) and Anna Saveria D'Ausilio(112).

Records that include Luigi Angelica(350):
- Rome, Italy 1911 Birth Act #1629 - 4a 1090

351) Letizia D'ausilio

Letizia (Leatrice) D'ausilio(351) was born on 25 June 1911, in Waterbury, CT, to Giovanni Battista (John B.) D'ausilio(120) and Catherina Viola(120a). Letizia (Leatrice) D'ausilio(351) died on 18 May 2007 in Bridgeport, CT.

Letizia (Leatrice) D'ausilio(351) married Luigi Marseglia(351a) on 28 July 1930 in Bridgeport, CT.

Luigi Marseglia(351a) was born on 22 August 1898, in Bovino, Italy, to Francesco Paolo Marseglia(351aF) and Maria Giuseppa d'Alessandro(351aM). Luigi Marseglia(351a) died on 26 August 1963 in Bridgeport, CT.

Known children of Letizia (Leatrice) D'ausilio(351) and Luigi Marseglia(351a):

   i) Living Person and/or Spouse
   ii) Living Person and/or Spouse

Records that include Letizia (Leatrice) D'ausilio(351) and/or Luigi Marseglia(351a):
- "Italia, Foggia, Stato Civile (Archivio di Stato), 1809-1902", FamilySearch (https://www.familysearch.org/ark:/61903/1:1:6B8Q-HL8F : Tue Mar 11 18:48:14 UTC 2025), Entry for Luigi Marseglia and Francesco Paolo Marseglia, 22 Aug 1898.
- Waterbury, CT 1911 Birth Record pg239
- "New York, New York Passenger and Crew Lists, 1909, 1925-1958", FamilySearch (https://www.familysearch.org/ark:/61903/1:1:24XJ-4PZ : Sat Apr 12 16:56:03 UTC 2025), Entry for Letizia Dausilio, 1929.
- "United States, Census, 1940", FamilySearch (https://www.familysearch.org/ark:/61903/1:1:KWMV-XVC : Thu Jan 23 23:58:20 UTC 2025), Entry for Louis Marseglia and Leatrice Marseglia, 1940.
- "Pennsylvania, World War II Draft Registration Cards, 1940-1945", FamilySearch (https://www.familysearch.org/ark:/61903/1:1:Q2SX-PSBP : Fri Feb 23 19:57:23 UTC 2024), Entry for Felix Dausilio and Litres Marseglia, 16 Oct 1940.
- "United States, Census, 1950", FamilySearch (https://www.familysearch.org/ark:/61903/1:1:6FMX-1ZLJ : Thu Mar 21 01:47:53 UTC 2024), Entry for Louis Marseglia and Leatrice Marseglia, 14 April 1950.
- "Alabama County Marriages, 1711-1992", FamilySearch (https://www.familysearch.org/ark:/61903/1:1:Q216-NB54 : Mon Mar 04 20:51:16 UTC 2024), Entry for Paul Marseglia and Louis Marseglia, 06 Jan 1953.
- "Connecticut, Death Index, 1949-2001", FamilySearch (https://www.familysearch.org/ark:/61903/1:1:VZPT-4YS : Wed Feb 19 11:03:06 UTC 2025), Entry for Louis Marseglia and LEAT, 26 Aug 1963.

- "Find a Grave Index", FamilySearch
  (https://www.familysearch.org/ark:/61903/1:1:QVVJ-LSDM : Mon Mar 31
  18:26:49 UTC 2025), Entry for Leatrice Dausilio Marseglia.
- "United States, Social Security Death Index," database,
  FamilySearch (https://familysearch.org/ark:/61903/1:1:VM4L-86T : 12
  January 2021), Leatrice Marseglia, 18 May 2007; citing U.S. Social
  Security Administration, Death Master File, database (Alexandria,
  Virginia: National Technical Information Service, ongoing).
- "United States, GenealogyBank Obituaries, Births, and Marriages,
  1980-2015", FamilySearch
  (https://www.familysearch.org/ark:/61903/1:1:QKG9-5HGM : Tue Jan 21
  12:35:23 UTC 2025), Entry for Mrs Leatrice Marseglia and Louis
  Marseglia, 27 May 2007.
- "United States, Social Security Numerical Identification Files
  (NUMIDENT), 1936-2007", FamilySearch
  (https://www.familysearch.org/ark:/61903/1:1:6KMJ-WQ4D : Fri Apr 25
  22:06:07 UTC 2025), Entry for Leatrice Dausilio and Giovanni
  Dausilio.

352) Pasquale deDonato

Pasquale deDonato(352) was born on 28 January 1912, in Ariano, Italy, to
Pietro deDonato(128) and Rosa Bilancione(128a).

Pasquale deDonato(352) married Rosina Manna(352a) on 12 October 1939 in
Ariano, Italy.

Rosina Manna(352a) was born about 1920, in Ariano, Italy, to Luigi
Manna(352aF) and Rosaria Farisco(352aM).

Records that include Pasquale deDonato(352) and/or Rosina Manna(352a):
- Ariano, Italy 1912 Birth Act #29
- Ariano, Italy 1939 Marriage Act #129

353) Maria Amalia Perrina

Maria Amalia Perrina(353) was born on 22 July 1914, in Ariano, Italy, to
Michele Perrina(88) and Maria Grazia Caraglia(88a).

Maria Amalia Perrina(353) married Angelo Iannarone(353a) on 3 November 1934 in
Ariano, Italy.

Angelo Iannarone(353a) was born on 3 November 1913 in Villanova de Battista,
Italy, to Sabato Iannarone(353aF) and Rosario Moscaritolo(353aM).

Records that include Maria Amalia Perrina(353) and/or Angelo Iannarone(353a):
- Villanova del Battista, Italy 1913 Birth Act #88
- Ariano, Italy 1913 Birth Act #339
- Ariano, Italy 1934 Marriage Act #P.II.A.157

354) Elena deDonato

Elena deDonato(354) was born on 16 April 1912 in Ariano, Italy to Domenico
deDonato(103) and Brigida Carmosino(103a).

Records that include Elena deDonato(354):
- Ariano, Italy 1912 Birth Act #211

355) Angelo deDonato

Angelo deDonato(355) was born on 11 October 1911, in Ariano, Italy, to
Michele deDonato(106) and Loreta di Vitto(106a). On 15 September Angelo
deDonato(355) boarded the ship SS Canopic, with his family, in Naples, Italy,
arriving in Boston, MA on 8 October 1917. Angelo deDonato(355) died on 29
August 1984 in Bridgeport, CT.

Angelo deDonato(355) married Mary Cirella(355a) on 13 October 1931 in
Bridgeport, CT.

<u>Mary Cirella</u>(355a) was born on 11 April 1912, in Westchester County, NY, to Andrew Cirella(355aF) and Tomasina Gointa(355aM). Mary Cirella(355a) died on 28 June 1999 in Trumbull, CT.

Known children of Angelo deDonato(355) and Mary Cirella(355a):

  i) Phyllis deDonato(368) born in 1931

Records that include Angelo deDonato(355) and/or Mary Cirella(355a):
- Ariano, Italy 1911 Birth Act #479
- "Massachusetts, Boston Passenger Lists Index, 1899-1940", , FamilySearch (https://www.familysearch.org/ark:/61903/1:1:QKQX-WYTV : Sat Mar 09 21:59:45 UTC 2024), Entry for Angelo Di Vitto, 1916.
- "United States Census, 1920", , FamilySearch (https://www.familysearch.org/ark:/61903/1:1:MCFH-8FW : Wed Jul 24 19:29:25 UTC 2024), Entry for Michael Donato and Edith Donato, 1920.
- "United States Census, 1930", , FamilySearch (https://www.familysearch.org/ark:/61903/1:1:XMPM-4G4 : Fri Mar 08 19:33:27 UTC 2024), Entry for Michael De Donato and Lorita De Donato, 1930.
- "United States Census, 1930", , FamilySearch (https://www.familysearch.org/ark:/61903/1:1:XMG1-VZF : Sun Jul 21 01:27:23 UTC 2024), Entry for Joseph Del Maggis and Tomasina Del Maggis, 1930.
- Bridgeport, CT 1931 Marriage Record
- City Of Bridgeport, Births, September 1931 #146
- "United States Census, 1940", , FamilySearch (https://www.familysearch.org/ark:/61903/1:1:KWMJ-K2F : Sun Mar 10 18:49:40 UTC 2024), Entry for Angelo Dedonato and Mary Dedonato, 1940.
- "Connecticut, World War II Draft Registration Cards, 1940-1945", , FamilySearch (https://www.familysearch.org/ark:/61903/1:1:Q2CR-WFQ7 : Mon Jul 08 23:11:22 UTC 2024), Entry for Angelo Dedonato and Mary Catherine Dedonato, 16 Oct 1940.
- "United States Social Security Death Index," database, FamilySearch (https://familysearch.org/ark:/61903/1:1:VS6Q-NPN : 7 January 2021), Angelo Dedonato, Aug 1984; citing U.S. Social Security Administration, Death Master File, database (Alexandria, Virginia: National Technical Information Service, ongoing).
- "Connecticut Death Index, 1949-2001," , FamilySearch (https://familysearch.org/ark:/61903/1:1:VZG4-H96 : 9 December 2014), Angelo Dedonato, 29 Aug 1984; from "Connecticut Death Index, 1949-2001," database, Ancestry (http://www.ancestry.com : 2003); citing Bridgeport, , Connecticut, Connecticut Department of Health, Hartfort.
- "Connecticut Death Index, 1949-2001," , FamilySearch (https://familysearch.org/ark:/61903/1:1:VZP8-LWY : 9 December 2014), Mary Dedonato, 28 Jun 1999; from "Connecticut Death Index, 1949-2001," database, Ancestry (http://www.ancestry.com : 2003); citing Trumbull, Fairfield, Connecticut, Connecticut Department of Health, Hartfort.
- "United States, Social Security Numerical Identification Files (NUMIDENT), 1936-2007", , FamilySearch (https://www.familysearch.org/ark:/61903/1:1:6KMN-KZHD : 10 February 2023), Mary Dedonato, .
- "United States Social Security Death Index," database, FamilySearch (https://familysearch.org/ark:/61903/1:1:JPQV-T6L : 7 January 2021), Mary Dedonato, 28 Jun 1999; citing U.S. Social Security Administration, Death Master File, database (Alexandria, Virginia: National Technical Information Service, ongoing).
- "Find a Grave Index," database, FamilySearch (https://www.familysearch.org/ark:/61903/1:1:QV22-JVFS : 13 June 2023), Mary Cirella DeDonato, ; Burial, Stratford, Fairfield, Connecticut, United States of America, Saint Michael's Cemetery; citing record ID 77283783, Find a Grave, http://www.findagrave.com.
- https://www.legacy.com/us/obituaries/ctpost/name/phyllis-mase-obituary?id=17732515

356) Nicola Giorgione

Nicola Giorgione(356) was born about 14 December 1911, in Ariano, Italy to Raffaele Giorgione(80) and Carmina Salvioli(80a). Nicola Giorgione(356) died 16 January 1912 in Ariano, Italy.

Records that include Nicola Giorgione(356):
* Ariano, Italy 1912 Death Act #15

357) Maria Archina Ciasullo

Maria Archina Ciasullo(357) was born on 10 April 1912, in Ariano, Italy, to Filippo Ciasullo(105a) and Maria Giovanna Perrina(105). Maria Archina Ciasullo(357) died on 15 March 1917 in Ariano, Italy.

Records that include Maria Archina Ciasullo(357):
* Ariano, Italy 1912 Birth Act #198
* Ariano, Italy 1917 Death Act #73

358) Gaetano Giuseppe Luciano Covotta

Gaetano Giuseppe Luciano Covotta(358) was born on 17 June 1912, in Ariano, Italy, to Michele Covotta(122) and Antonietta Bilotta(122a).

Gaetano Giuseppe Luciano Covotta(358) married Settemia Perini(358a) on 10 October 1948 in Rome, Italy.

Settemia Perini(358a) is mentioned in note on birth record of Gaetano Giuseppe Luciano Covotta(358), no other information has been found.

Records that include Gaetano Giuseppe Luciano Covotta(358) and/or Settemia Perini(358a):
* Ariano, Italy 1912 Birth Act #355

359) Arminio Perrina

Arminio Perrina(359) was born on 1 January 1914, in Ariano, Italy, to Michele Perrina(88) and Maria Grazia Caraglia(88a). Arminio Perrina(359) died on 14 September 1914 in Ariano, Italy.

Records that include Arminio Perrina(359):
* Ariano, Italy 1914 Birth Act #3
* Ariano, Italy 1914 Death Act #183

360) Lorenza Concetta deDonato

Lorenza Concetta deDonato(360) was born on 10 August 1913, in Ariano, Italy, to Luigi deDonato(126) and Caterina Montecalvo(126a).

Lorenza Concetta deDonato(360) married Aurelio Fedele Petruccelli(360a) on 24 October 1936 in Castelfranco in Miscano, Italy.

Aurelio Fedele Petruccelli(360a) was born on 29 September 1913, in Castelfranco in Miscano, Italy, to Raffaele Petruccelli(360aF) and Maria Inglese(360aM).

Records that include Lorenza Concetta deDonato(360) and/or Aurelio Fedele Petruccelli(360a):
* Ariano, Italy 1913 Birth Act #442
* "Italia, Benevento, Stato Civile (Archivio di Stato), 1810-1942", , FamilySearch (https://www.familysearch.org/ark:/61903/1:1:QGJ2-ZVPF : Sun Mar 10 22:20:03 UTC 2024), Entry for Aurelio Fedele Petruccelli and Raffaele Petruccelli, 17 settembre 1913.
* "Italia, Benevento, Stato Civile (Archivio di Stato), 1810-1942", , FamilySearch (https://www.familysearch.org/ark:/61903/1:1:QLKP-5V64 : Fri Mar 08 03:49:07 UTC 2024), Entry for Aurelio Petruccelli and Raffaele Petruccelli, 24 ottobre 1936.

361) Guido Michele deDonato

Guido Michele deDonato(361) was born on 27 January 1914 in Ariano, Italy to Domenic deDonato(103) and Bridgida Carmosino(103a).

Records that include Guido Michele deDonato(361):
* Ariano, Italy 1914 Birth Act #72

362) Francesco deDonato

Francesco deDonato(362) was born 11 March 1914 in Ariano, Italy, to Pietro deDonato(128) and Rosa Bilancione(128a).

Francesco deDonato(362) married Saveria Gelormino(362a) on 29 November 1934 in Ariano, Italy

Saveria Gelormino(362a) was born 5 November 1915, in Ariano, Italy, to Luigi Gelormino(362aF) and Adelina Savino(362aM).

Records that include Francesco deDonato(362) and/or Saveria Gelormino(362a):
* Ariano, Italy 1914 Birth Act #174
* Ariano, Italy 1915 Birth Act #577
* Ariano, Italy 1934 Marriage Act #P.II.A.172

363) Aldo deDonato

Aldo deDonato(363) was stillborn on 2 November 1915 in Ariano, Italy to Domenic deDonato(103) and Bridgida Carmosino(103a).

Record that include Aldo deDonato(363):
* Ariano, Italy 1915 Birth Record #573

364) Giuseppe deDonato

Giuseppe deDonato(364) was born about 25 March 1916, in Ariano, Italy, to Pietro deDonato(128) and Rosa Bilancione(128a). Giuseppe deDonato(364) died 20 July 1918 in Ariano, Italy.

Record that include Giuseppe deDonato(364):
* Ariano, Italy 1918 Death Act #193

365) Biagio Angelica

Biagio Angelica(365) was born on 27 April 1916 in Rome, Italy to Giuseppe Angelica(112b) and Anna Saveria D'Ausilio(112).

Record that include Biagio Angelica(365):
* Rome, Italy 1916 Birth Act #2075,vol7,p1,s1

366) Armino Perrina

Armino Perrina(366) was born 23 September 1917, in Ariano, Italy, to Michele Perrina(88) and Maria Grazia Caraglia(88a).

Armino Perrina(366) married Maria Luigia Perrina(366a) on 25 June 1938 in Ariano, Italy.

Maria Luigia Perrina(366a) was born on 2 April 1919, in Ariano, Italy, to Giovanna Perrina(366aF) and Rosina Meninno(366aM).

Records including Armino Perrina(366) and/or Maria Luigia Perrina(366a):
* Ariano, Italy 1917 Birth Act #345
* Ariano, Italy 1919 Birth Act #138
* Ariano, Italy 1938 Marriage Act #P.IIA.67

367) Francesco Paolo Miressi

Francesco Paolo Miressi(367) was stillborn on 2 December 1895, in Ariano, Italy, to Nicolantonio Miressi(132) and Giovanna Giardino(132a).

Records that include Francesco Paolo Miressi(367):
* Ariano Italy 1895 Birth Act #691

368) Giuseppe Miressi

Giuseppe Miressi(368) was born on 2 December 1895, in Ariano, Italy, to Nicolantonio Miressi(132) and Giovanna Giardino(132a). Giuseppe Miressi(368) died on 4 December 1895, in Ariano, Italy.

Records that include Giuseppe Miressi(368):
* Ariano, Italy 1895 Birth Act #690
* Ariano, Italy 1895 Death Act #425

369) Giuseppe Miressi

Giuseppe Miressi(369) was born on 5 January 1897, in Ariano, Italy, to Nicolantonio Miressi(132) and Giovanna Giardino(132a). Giuseppe Miressi(369) died on 21 September 1897, in Ariano, Italy.

Records that include Giuseppe Miressi(369):
* Ariano, Italy 1897 Birth Act #14
* Ariano, Italy 1897 Death Act #330

370) Angelo Maria Miressi

Angelo Maria Miressi(370) was born on 11 March 1898, in Ariano, Italy, to Nicolantonio Miressi(132) and Giovanna Giardino(132a).

Records that include Angelo Maria Miressi(370):
* Ariano, Italy 1898 Birth Act #161

371) Angelo Vernacchia

Angelo Vernacchia(371) was born on 1 January 1899, in Ariano, Italy, to Francesco Paolo Vernacchia(144a) and Rosa Grasso(144). Angelo Vernacchia(371) died in 1906. Angelo Vernacchia(371) was buried in Old Saint Raymond's Cemetery, Bronx, NY.

Records that include Angelo Vernacchia(371):
* Ariano, Italy 1899 Birth Act #5
* https://www.findagrave.com/memorial/136982368/angelo-vernacchia

372) Gabriele D'Antuono

Gabriele D'Antuono(372) was born on 5 December 1899, in Ariano, Italy, to Nicola Maria d'Antuono(135a) and Concetta Manganiello(135). Gabriele D'Antuono(372) died on 15 February 1901 in Ariano, Italy.

Records that include Gabriele D'Antuono(372):
* Ariano, Italy 1899 Birth Act #692
* Ariano, Italy 1901 Death Act #65

373) Liberato Tiso

Liberato Tiso(373) was born on 4 March 1901, in Ariano, Italy, to Vincenzo Tiso(131) and Giovanna Portogallo(131a).

Liberato Tiso(373) married Marietta Clericuzio(373a) on 15 November 1924 in Ariano, Italy.

Marietta Clericuzio(373a) was born on 10 December 1904, in Ariano, Italy, to Giuseppe Clericuzio(373aF) and Maria Rosaria Iannarone(373aM).

Liberato Tiso(373) and Marietta Clericuzio(373a) had child(ren).

Records that include Liberato Tiso(373) and/or Marietta Clericuzio(373a):
- Ariano, Italy 1901 Birth Act #149
- Ariano, Italy 1904 Birth Act #547
- Ariano, Italy 1924 Marriage Act #147

374) Giovannina Miressi

Giovannina Miressi(374) was born on 2 September 1901, in Ariano, Italy, to Nicolantonio Miressi(132) and Maria Rosa Caso(132b).

NOTE: Birth record mentions marriage 17 April 1922 to Maria Matteo[??] … writing is unclear as to spouse's name and where the marriage took place, and no record appears in Ariano.

Records that include Giovannina Miressi(374):
- Ariano, Italy 1901 Birth Act #457

375) Gabriele D'Antuono

Gabriele D'Antuono(375) was born on 1 January 1902, in Ariano, Italy, to Nicola Maria d'Antuono(135a) and Concetta Manganiello(135). Gabriele D'Antuono(375) died 6 March 1902 in Ariano, Italy.

Records that include Gabriele D'Antuono(375):
- Ariano, Italy 1902 Birth Act #17
- Ariano, Italy 1902 death Act #65

376) Raffaele Panza

Raffaele Panza(376) was born on 25 June 1902, in Ariano, Italy, to Ciriaco Panza(152a) and Mariantonia Fodarella(152).

Raffaele Panza(376) married Antonietta Fortunato(376a) on 15 October 1925 in Ariano, Italy.

Antonietta Fortunato(376a) was born on 6 May 1905, in Ariano, Italy, to Vincenzo Fortunato(376aF) and Lucrezia Lo Conte(376aM).

Records that include Raffaele Panza(376) and/or Antonietta Fortunato(376a):
- Ariano, Italy 1902 Birth Act #336
- Ariano, Italy 1905 Birth Act #275
- Ariano, Italy 1925 Marriage Act #125

377) John Vernacchia

John Vernacchia(377) was born on 3 Sep 1903, in New York, NY, to Francesco Paolo Vernacchia(144a) and Rosa Grasso(144). John Vernacchia(377) died in 1906. John Vernacchia(377) is buried in Old Saint Raymond's Cemetery, Bronx, NY.

Records that include John Vernacchia(377):
- "New York, New York City Municipal Deaths, 1795-1949", FamilySearch (https://www.familysearch.org/ark:/61903/1:1:2WDV-22S : Wed Mar 26 17:26:08 UTC 2025), Entry for John Vernacchio and Paulo Vernacchio, 21 Jan 1906.
- https://www.findagrave.com/memorial/136982424/john-vernacchia

378) Maria Manganiello

Maria Manganiello(378) was born on 19 September 1903, in Ariano, Italy, to Michele Manganiello(138) 361 and Pasqualina Miniscalco(138a). Maria Manganiello(378) died 16 July 1996 in Ariano. Italy.

Maria Manganiello(378) married Giuseppe Paone(378a) on 5 January 1924 in Ariano, Italy.

Giuseppe Paone(378a) was born on 3 October 1903, in Ariano, Italy, to Giuseppe Paone(378aF) and Raffaella Guardabascio(378aM).

Records that include Maria Manganiello(378) and/or Giuseppe Paone(378a):
- Ariano, Italy 1903 Birth Act #443
- Ariano, Italy 1903 Birth Act #469
- Ariano, Italy 1924 Marriage Act #2
- Ariano, Italy 1996 Death Act #115

379) Francesco Vincenzo Liberato Bianchi

Francesco Vincenzo Liberato Bianchi(379) was born on 12 November 1903, in Ariano, Italy, to Gerardino Bianchi(133a) and Mariangela Tiso(133). Francesco Vincenzo Liberato Bianchi(379) boarded the SS Providence on 2 April 1921 in Naples, Italy, arriving on 15 April 1921 in New York. Francesco Vincenzo Liberato Bianchi(379) became a United States Citizen on 30 September 1927 in Newark, NJ. Francesco Vincenzo Liberato Bianchi(379) died on 15 January 1970 in Florida.

Francesco Vincenzo Liberato Bianchi(379) married Jennie Guarraci(379a).

Jennie Guarraci(379a) was born about 1910 in Italy. Jennie Guarraci(379a) died 4 June 1965 in New Jersey.

Francesco Vincenzo Liberato Bianchi(379) and Jennie Guarraci(379a) had child(ren).

Records that include Francesco Vincenzo Liberato Bianchi(379) and/or Jennie Guarraci(379a):
- Ariano, Italy 1903 Birth Act #537
- "New Jersey Naturalization Records, 1796-1991", , FamilySearch (https://www.familysearch.org/ark:/61903/1:1:6PJJ-8PP3 : Sat Mar 09 05:15:06 UTC 2024), Entry for Frank Bianchi, 27 Apr 1927.
- "New Jersey Naturalization Records, 1796-1991", , FamilySearch (https://www.familysearch.org/ark:/61903/1:1:WB7X-B2ZM : Sat Mar 09 13:42:24 UTC 2024), Entry for Frank Bianchi, 1927.
- "New Jersey Naturalization Records, 1796-1991", , FamilySearch (https://www.familysearch.org/ark:/61903/1:1:6PJJ-8PPS : Sat Mar 09 10:37:46 UTC 2024), Entry for Frank or Francesco Bianchi, 10 Sep 1926.
- "New Jersey Naturalization Records, 1796-1991", , FamilySearch (https://www.familysearch.org/ark:/61903/1:1:6PJJ-V6TG : Sun Mar 10 16:55:00 UTC 2024), Entry for Frank Bianchi, 30 Sep 1927.
- "United States Census, 1930", , FamilySearch (https://www.familysearch.org/ark:/61903/1:1:X4DV-MX8 : Mon Mar 11 00:33:37 UTC 2024), Entry for Frank Bianchi and Jennie Bianchi, 1930.
- "United States Census, 1940", , FamilySearch (https://www.familysearch.org/ark:/61903/1:1:K4P1-LGV : Thu Mar 07 09:50:08 UTC 2024), Entry for Frank Bianchi and Jennie Bianchi, 1940.
- "United States 1950 Census", , FamilySearch (https://www.familysearch.org/ark:/61903/1:1:6F91-HPMG : Wed Mar 20 14:57:16 UTC 2024), Entry for Frank Bianski and Jennie Bianski, 1 April 1950.
- "Florida Death Index, 1877-1998," , FamilySearch (https://familysearch.org/ark:/61903/1:1:VVQC-T2P : 25 December 2014), Frank Bianchi, 11 Jan 1970; from "Florida Death Index, 1877-1998," index, Ancestry (www.ancestry.com : 2004); citing vol. , certificate number 1774, Florida Department of Health, Office of Vital Records, Jacksonville.
- "United States Social Security Death Index," database, FamilySearch (https://familysearch.org/ark:/61903/1:1:JK1B-34Q : 8 January 2021), Frank Bianchi, Jan 1970; citing U.S. Social Security Administration, Death Master File, database (Alexandria, Virginia: National Technical Information Service, ongoing).

- "Find a Grave Index," database, FamilySearch (https://www.familysearch.org/ark:/61903/1:1:4KJT-8W6Z : 25 May 2022), Jennie Bianchi, ; Burial, North Arlington, Bergen, New Jersey, United States of America, Holy Cross Cemetery and Mausoleum; citing record ID 204755233, Find a Grave, http://www.findagrave.com.
- "Find a Grave Index," database, FamilySearch (https://www.familysearch.org/ark:/61903/1:1:4KJT-876Z : 25 May 2022), Frank Bianchi, ; Burial, North Arlington, Bergen, New Jersey, United States of America, Holy Cross Cemetery and Mausoleum; citing record ID 204755224, Find a Grave, http://www.findagrave.com.

380) Clorinda Mariantonia Tiso

Clorinda Mariantonia Tiso(380) was born on 17 January 1904, in Ariano, Italy, to Vincenzo Tiso(123) and Giovanna Portogallo(123a).

Records that include Clorinda Mariantonia Tiso(380):
- Ariano, Italy 1904 Birth Act #30

381) Luigi Mancino

Luigi Mancino(381) was born on 23 December 1903, in Ariano, Italy, to Agostino Mancino(150a) and Maria Rosaria Scauzillo(150). Luigi Mancino(381) died 1 January 1983 in Ariano, Italy.

Luigi Mancino(381) married Rosaria Vitillo(381a) on 26 January 1925 in Ariano, Italy.

Rosaria Vitillo(381a) was born on 24 February 1906, in Ariano, Italy, to Ciriaco Vitillo(381aF) and Concetta Riccio(381aM).

Records that include Luigi Mancino(381) and/or Rosaria Vitillo(381a):
- Ariano, Italy 1903 Birth Act #606
- Ariano, Italy 1906 Birth Act #104
- Ariano, Italy, 1925 Marriages Act #11
- Ariano, Italy 1983 Death Act #1

382) Maria Rosa Panza

Maria Rosa Panza(382) was born on 24 April 1904, in Ariano, Italy, to Ciriaco Panza(152a) and Mariantonia Fodarella(152).

Maria Rosa Panza(382) married Domenico Luigi Casiodoro(382a) on 26 August 1926 in Ariano, Italy.

Domenico Luigi Casiodoro(382a) was born on 17 September 1903, in Ariano, Italy, to Giovanni Casiodoro(382aF) and Caterina Grasso(382aM).

Records that include Maria Rosa Panza(382) and/or Domenico Luigi Casiodoro(382a):
- Ariano, Italy 1903 Birth Act #440
- Ariano, Italy 1904 Birth Act #199
- Ariano, Italy 1926 Marriage Act #90

383) Giuseppe Miressi

Giuseppe Miressi(383) was born on 2 September 1904, in Ariano, Italy, to Nicolantonio Miressi(132) and Maria Michele Monaco(132c). Giuseppe Miressi(383) died 18 September 1904 in Ariano, Italy.

Records that include Giuseppe Miressi(383):
- Ariano, Italy 1904 Birth Act #358
- Ariano, Italy 1904 death Act #339

384) Elena D'Antuono

Elena D'Antuono(384) was born on 12 October 1904, in Ariano, Italy, to Nicola Maria d'Antuono(135a) and Concetta Manganiello(135). Elena D'Antuono(384) died on 28 February 1905 in Ariano, Italy.

Records that include Elena D'Antuono(384):
- Ariano, Italy 1904 Birth Act #431
- Ariano, Italy 1905 Death Act #76

385) Vincenza Vernacchia

Vincenza Vernacchia(385) was born on 14 April 1905, in New York, NY, to Francesco Paolo Vernacchia(144a) and Rosa Grasso(144). Vincenza Vernacchia(385) died 28 March 2003 in Yonkers, NY.

Vincenza Vernacchia(385) married Frank Solimene(385a) on 25 August 1929 in New York, NY.

Frank Solimene(385a) was born about 1904, in Italy, to Joseph Solimene(385aF) and Florence Yeredella(385aM).

Vincenza Vernacchia(385) and Frank Solimene(385a) had Child(ren).

Records that include Vincenza Vernacchia(385) and/or Frank Solimene(385a):
- "New York, State Census, 1915", , FamilySearch (https://www.familysearch.org/ark:/61903/1:1:K9FC-ZB1 : 4 June 2022), Frank Vernachio, 1915.
- "United States, Census, 1920", FamilySearch (https://www.familysearch.org/ark:/61903/1:1:MJPD-KYN : Thu Jan 16 03:46:43 UTC 2025), Entry for Frank Vernacchia and Rose Vernacchia, 1920.
- "New York, New York City Marriage Records, 1829-1938", FamilySearch (https://www.familysearch.org/ark:/61903/1:1:Q2CJ-GN99 : Sun Mar 10 22:48:03 UTC 2024), Entry for Franck Solomene and Vincenza Vernacclio, 25 August 1929.
- "United States, Census, 1930", FamilySearch (https://www.familysearch.org/ark:/61903/1:1:X766-2ZF : Fri Mar 08 12:33:49 UTC 2024), Entry for Frank Solomira and Vincenza Solomira, 1930.
- "United States, Census, 1940", FamilySearch (https://www.familysearch.org/ark:/61903/1:1:KQM8-27K : Sun Mar 10 17:39:22 UTC 2024), Entry for Frank Solimene and Vincenza Solimene, 1940.
- "United States, Census, 1950", FamilySearch (https://www.familysearch.org/ark:/61903/1:1:6XTR-CYKQ : Wed Mar 20 02:54:04 UTC 2024), Entry for J Rocco and Frank Solimene, 10 April 1950.
- "United States, Social Security Numerical Identification Files (NUMIDENT), 1936-2007", FamilySearch (https://www.familysearch.org/ark:/61903/1:1:6K93-SLX3 : Mon Oct 06 23:22:39 UTC 2025), Entry for Vincenza Solimene.

386) Lucy DeMeo

Lucy DeMeo(386) was born in 1906, in Schenectady, NY, to Angelo DeMeo(202a) and Maria Perrina(202).

Records that include Lucy DeMeo(386):
- "United States Census, 1910", , FamilySearch (https://www.familysearch.org/ark:/61903/1:1:M596-RYZ : Sun Mar 10 01:00:22 UTC 2024), Entry for Angelo Demeo and Mary F Demeo, 1910.
- "United States Census, 1920", , FamilySearch (https://www.familysearch.org/ark:/61903/1:1:MVS4-RRY : Fri Mar 08 05:51:12 UTC 2024), Entry for Angelo Demeo and Mary Demeo, 1920.
- "New York State Census, 1925", , FamilySearch (https://www.familysearch.org/ark:/61903/1:1:KSHH-T5H : Sat Mar 09 14:50:32 UTC 2024), Entry for Lucy De Meo, 1925.
- "United States Census, 1930", , FamilySearch (https://www.familysearch.org/ark:/61903/1:1:X4TT-YB5 : Mon Mar 11 01:35:37 UTC 2024), Entry for Angelo De Meo and Mary De Meo, 1930.

387) Rosina Gentile

Rosina Gentile(387) was stillborn on 5 January 1906, in Ariano, Italy, to Pasquale Gentile(192a) and Maria Miressi(192).

Records that include Rosina Gentile(387):
- Ariano, Italy 1906 Birth Act #7

388) Oto Maria Carmine Bianchi

Oto Maria Carmine Bianchi(388) was born on 18 April 1906, in Ariano, Italy, to Gerardino Bianchi(133a) and Mariangela Tiso(133). Oto Maria Carmine Bianchi(388) died on 14 June 1910 in Ariano, Italy.

Records that include Oto Maria Carmine Bianchi(388):
- Ariano, Italy 1906 Birth Act #215
- Ariano, Italy 1910 Death Act #228

389) Lorenzo Scauzillo

Lorenzo Scauzillo(389) was born on 14 April 1906, in New York, NY, to Gaetano Scauzillo(164) and Giovanna Grasso(196). Lorenzo Scauzillo(389) died 13 May 1906 in New York, NY.

Records that include Lorenzo Scauzillo(389):
- "New York, New York City Municipal Deaths, 1795-1949", database, FamilySearch (https://www.familysearch.org/ark:/61903/1:1:2719-474 : 13 May 2022), Gastano Scauzillo in entry for Lorenzo Scauzillo, 1906.

390) Maria Rosa Maria Domenica Maria Libera Miressi

Maria Rosa Maria Domenica Maria Libera Miressi(390) was born on 4 October 1906, in Ariano, Italy, to Generoso Miressi(160) and Maria Luigia Iannarone(160a). Maria Rosa Maria Domenica Maria Libera Miressi(390) boarded the ship SS Duca Di Genova, in Naples, Italy, with her mother on 24 November 1909, they arrived in New York, on 5 December 1909, to live with her father in New Rochelle, NY.

Records that include Maria Rosa Maria Domenica Maria Libera Miressi(390):
- Ariano, Italy 1906 Birth Act #458
- "New York Passenger Arrival Lists (Ellis Island), 1892-1924", , FamilySearch (https://www.familysearch.org/ark:/61903/1:1:JF9H-HNR : Sun Mar 10 18:31:06 UTC 2024), Entry for Rosa Mireasio and Teresa, 1909.
- "United States Census, 1910", , FamilySearch (https://www.familysearch.org/ark:/61903/1:1:M54W-J3S : Fri Mar 08 01:14:07 UTC 2024), Entry for Generoso Miresse and Maria L Miresse, 1910.
- "New York State Census, 1915", , FamilySearch (https://www.familysearch.org/ark:/61903/1:1:K95C-G7Z : 1 June 2022), Rosa Miressi in entry for Generoso Miressi, 1915.

391) Immacolota (Concetta) Vernacchia

Immacolota (Concetta) Vernacchia(391) was born on 8 December 1906, in Manhattan, NY, to Francesco Paolo Vernacchia(144a) and Rosa Grasso(144).

Records that include Immacolota (Concetta) Vernacchia(391):
- "New York, New York City Births, 1846-1909", FamilySearch (https://www.familysearch.org/ark:/61903/1:1:2WHN-48C : Wed Mar 12 01:37:48 UTC 2025), Entry for Concettina Vernacchio and Franceno Taolo Vernacchio, 08 Dec 1906.
- "United States, Census, 1920", FamilySearch (https://www.familysearch.org/ark:/61903/1:1:MJPD-KYN : Thu Jan 16 03:46:43 UTC 2025), Entry for Frank Vernacchia and Rose Vernacchia, 1920.

392) Teresina (Teresa) DeMeo

Teresina (Teresa) DeMeo(392) was born on 3 April 1907, in Schenectady, NY to Angelo DeMeo(202a) and Maria Perrina(202). Teresina (Teresa) DeMeo(392) died 27 April 1956 in Glenville, NY.

Teresina (Teresa) DeMeo(392) married Stanley Mortka(392a) on 28 November 1948 in Flushings, NY.

NOTE: Baptism and Death record indicates Teresina (Teresa) DeMeo(392) was married to Stanley Mortka(392a), however, I have been unable to find any further information.

Records that include Teresina (Teresa) DeMeo(392):
- "New York, Birth Indexes outside of New York City, 1881-1942", , FamilySearch (https://www.familysearch.org/ark:/61903/1:1:6FBH-ZB46 : Sat Mar 09 16:35:58 UTC 2024), Entry for Teresina Demeo, 3 Apr 1907.
- "St. Anthony, Schenectady, New York, Baptism (Sep 1912 - May 2007)", 2 Volumes American-Canadian Genealogical Society, Manchester, NH, page 263
- "United States Census, 1910", , FamilySearch (https://www.familysearch.org/ark:/61903/1:1:M596-RYZ : Sun Mar 10 01:00:22 UTC 2024), Entry for Angelo Demeo and Mary F Demeo, 1910.
- "United States Census, 1920", , FamilySearch (https://www.familysearch.org/ark:/61903/1:1:MVS4-RRY : Fri Mar 08 05:51:12 UTC 2024), Entry for Angelo Demeo and Mary Demeo, 1920.
- "United States Census, 1930", , FamilySearch (https://www.familysearch.org/ark:/61903/1:1:X4TT-YB5 : Mon Mar 11 01:35:37 UTC 2024), Entry for Angelo De Meo and Mary De Meo, 1930.
- "United States Census, 1950", , FamilySearch (https://www.familysearch.org/ark:/61903/1:1:6XTT-P885 : Tue Mar 19 18:53:16 UTC 2024), Entry for Stanley Mortker, 15 April 1950.
- "New York, State Death Index, 1880-1956", , FamilySearch (https://www.familysearch.org/ark:/61903/1:1:QGR2-WWLB : Sun Mar 10 07:16:24 UTC 2024), Entry for Theresa Mortka, 27 Apr 1956.
- "Find a Grave Index," database, FamilySearch (https://www.familysearch.org/ark:/61903/1:1:6ZWM-NXS8 : 8 March 2021), Theresa DeMeo Nortka, ; Burial, Schenectady, Schenectady, New York, United States of America, Saint John the Baptist Cemetery; citing record ID 220874172, Find a Grave, http://www.findagrave.com.

393) Antonio Mancino

Antonio Mancino(393) was born on 10 January 1907, in Ariano, Italy, to Agostino Mancino(150a) and Maria Rosaria Scauzillo(150).

Antonio Mancino(393) married Maria Saveria Puzo(393a) on 22 October 1929 in Ariano, Italy.

Maria Saveria Puzo(393a) was born on 5 October 1905, in Ariano, Italy, to Michele Puzo(393aF) and Rosa Comanzo(393aM).

Records that include Antonio Mancino(393) and/or Maria Saveria Puzo(393a):
- Ariano, Italy 1905 Birth Act #537
- Ariano, Italy 1907 Birth Act #21
- Ariano, Italy Marriage Act #IIA40

394) Carmela Scanzillo

Carmela Scanzillo(394) was born on 24 July 1907, in New York, NY, to Gaetano Scauzillo(164) and Giovanna Grasso(196). Carmela Scanzillo(394) died on 29 August 1985, in Bridgeport, CT.

Carmela Scanzillo(394) married Natalio Speranzo(394a) on 5 February 1928 in Bronx, NY.

Natalio Speranzo(394a) was born on 25 December 1901, in Ariano, Italy, to Emilio Speranzo(394aF) and Carmela D'Auria(394aM). On 2 June 1904 Natalio Speranzo(394a) arrived in New York, NY on the ship SS Calabria having boarded in Naples, Italy. Natalio Speranzo(394a) became a United States citizen in 1938. Natalio Speranzo(394a) died on 10 December 1954 in Bridgeport, CT.

Carmela Scanzillo(394) and Natalio Speranzo(394a) had child(ren).

Records that include Carmela Scanzillo(394) and/or Natalio Speranzo(394a):

- Ariano, Italy 1901 Birth Act#650
- "Connecticut, Military Census Questionnaires, 1917", , FamilySearch (https://www.familysearch.org/ark:/61903/1:1:Z21X-3DMM : Sat Mar 09 20:25:20 UTC 2024), Entry for Natalino Speranzo, 1917.
- "United States Census, 1920", , FamilySearch (https://www.familysearch.org/ark:/61903/1:1:MJG5-1XL : Sat Apr 13 04:57:08 UTC 2024), Entry for Gaetano Scanzilla and Jannie Scanzilla, 1920.
- "New York, New York City Marriage Records, 1829-1938", , FamilySearch (https://www.familysearch.org/ark:/61903/1:1:Q2CJ-K68M : Sat Mar 09 18:40:07 UTC 2024), Entry for Natalino Speranzo and Carmela Scanzilla, 5 February 1928.
- "United States Census, 1930", , FamilySearch (https://www.familysearch.org/ark:/61903/1:1:XMPM-PX2 : Sun Mar 10 22:33:32 UTC 2024), Entry for Natalino Speranzo and Carmilla Speranzo, 1930.
- "United States, New England Petitions for Naturalization Index, 1791-1906", , FamilySearch (https://www.familysearch.org/ark:/61903/1:1:VX5R-TZ5 : Fri Mar 08 17:42:00 UTC 2024), Entry for Natalino Speranzo, 1938.
- https://www.familysearch.org/ark:/61903/3:1:3Q9M-CSM4-43VV-3?i=1361&cat=1147528
- https://www.familysearch.org/ark:/61903/3:1:3Q9M-CSM4-43G5-P?i=1362&cat=1147528
- https://www.familysearch.org/ark:/61903/3:1:3Q9M-CSM4-4322-6?i=1363&cat=1147528
- United States Census, 1940", , FamilySearch (https://www.familysearch.org/ark:/61903/1:1:KWMV-SWH : Sun Mar 10 00:03:33 UTC 2024), Entry for Natalino Speranzo and Carmella Speranzo, 1940.
- "Connecticut, World War II Draft Registration Cards, 1940-1945", , FamilySearch (https://www.familysearch.org/ark:/61903/1:1:Q2CR-1D1G : Fri Mar 08 05:34:24 UTC 2024), Entry for Natalino Speranzo and Carmela Speranzo, 16 Feb 1942.
- "United States 1950 Census", , FamilySearch (https://www.familysearch.org/ark:/61903/1:1:6FM6-HN4H : Wed Mar 20 00:49:32 UTC 2024), Entry for Natalino Speranzo and Carmela Speranzo, 17 April 1950.
- "Connecticut Death Index, 1949-2001," database, FamilySearch (https://familysearch.org/ark:/61903/1:1:V67Y-DRZ : 9 December 2014), CARM in entry for Natal Speranzo, 10 Nov 1954; from "Connecticut Death Index, 1949-2001," database, Ancestry (http://www.ancestry.com : 2003); citing Bridgeport, Fairfield, Connecticut, Connecticut Department of Health, Hartford.
- "Connecticut Death Index, 1949-2001," , FamilySearch (https://familysearch.org/ark:/61903/1:1:VZP4-ZNY : 9 December 2014), Carmela A Speranzo, 29 Aug 1985; from "Connecticut Death Index, 1949-2001," database, Ancestry (http://www.ancestry.com : 2003); citing Bridgeport, , Connecticut, Connecticut Department of Health, Hartford.
- "United States, Social Security Numerical Identification Files (NUMIDENT), 1936-2007", database, FamilySearch (https://www.familysearch.org/ark:/61903/1:1:6KMF-3WMR : 10 February 2023), Natalino Speranzo, .
- "United States Social Security Death Index," database, FamilySearch (https://familysearch.org/ark:/61903/1:1:JKFV-HQM : 7 January 2021), Natalino Speranzo, Nov 1954; citing U.S. Social Security Administration, Death Master File, database (Alexandria, Virginia: National Technical Information Service, ongoing).
- "United States Social Security Death Index," , FamilySearch (https://familysearch.org/ark:/61903/1:1:JKF5-Q5Q : 7 January 2021), Carmela Speranzo, Aug 1985; citing U.S. Social Security Administration, Death Master File, database (Alexandria, Virginia: National Technical Information Service, ongoing).

- "Find a Grave Index," database, FamilySearch
  (https://www.familysearch.org/ark:/61903/1:1:QVVR-7BR3 : 7 March
  2024), Natalino Speranzo, ; Burial, Stratford, Fairfield,
  Connecticut, United States of America, Saint Michael's Cemetery;
  citing record ID 27376027, Find a Grave, http://www.findagrave.com.
- "Find a Grave Index," database, FamilySearch
  (https://www.familysearch.org/ark:/61903/1:1:QVVR-7BR9 : 7 March
  2024), Carmela A Scanzillo Speranzo, ; Burial, Stratford,
  Fairfield, Connecticut, United States of America, Saint Michael's
  Cemetery; citing record ID 27376039, Find a Grave,
  http://www.findagrave.com.

395) Giovannina (Jennie) Leggiadro

Giovannina (Jennie) Leggiadro(395) was born on 2 August 1907, in New York, NY,
to Luigi Leggiadro(167a) and Maria Giuseppa Grasso(167). Giovannina (Jennie)
Leggiadro(395) died October 1974 in New York.

Giovannina (Jennie) Leggiadro(395) married Otantonio (Anthony) Melito(395a) on
19 March 1927 in Bronx, NY.

Otantonio (Anthony) Melito(395a) was born 2 November 1903, in Ariano, Italy,
to Joseph Melito(395aF) and Angelina Popolo(395aM). Otantonio (Anthony)
Melito(395a) died 25 July 1988 in New York.

Giovannina (Jennie) Leggiadro(395) and Otantonio (Anthony) Melito(395a) had
child(ren).

Records that include Giovannina (Jennie) Leggiadro(395) and Otantonio
(Anthony) Melito(395a):
- Ariano, Italy 1903 Birth Act #525
- "United States, Census, 1920", FamilySearch
  (https://www.familysearch.org/ark:/61903/1:1:MJY4-HN1 : Wed Jan 22
  11:11:04 UTC 2025), Entry for Joseph Miletta and Angela Miletta,
  1920.
- "New York, New York City Marriage Records, 1829-1938", FamilySearch
  (https://www.familysearch.org/ark:/61903/1:1:Q2CJ-JZXW : Sun Mar 10
  07:38:21 UTC 2024), Entry for Anthony Melito and Miss Jennie
  Leggiadro, 19 March 1927.
- "United States, Census, 1940", FamilySearch
  (https://www.familysearch.org/ark:/61903/1:1:KQMZ-X2Z : Mon Jan 20
  06:46:44 UTC 2025), Entry for Anthony Melito and Jennie Melito,
  1940.
- "New York, New York City, World War II Draft Registration Cards,
  1940-1947", FamilySearch
  (https://www.familysearch.org/ark:/61903/1:1:W8WL-MV2M : Sat Apr 12
  20:17:25 UTC 2025), Entry for Anthony Melito and James King, 15 Feb
  1942.
- "United States, Census, 1950", FamilySearch
  (https://www.familysearch.org/ark:/61903/1:1:6XYM-P298 : Wed Mar 20
  18:54:32 UTC 2024), Entry for Anthony Melito and Jennie Melito, 1
  April 1950.
- "United States, Social Security Death Index," database,
  FamilySearch (https://familysearch.org/ark:/61903/1:1:JR9Z-H4S : 7
  January 2021), Jennie Melito, Oct 1974; citing U.S. Social
  Security Administration, Death Master File, database (Alexandria,
  Virginia: National Technical Information Service, ongoing).
- "United States, Social Security Death Index," database,
  FamilySearch (https://familysearch.org/ark:/61903/1:1:JKRV-GY7 : 7
  January 2021), Anthony Melito, 25 Jul 1988; citing U.S. Social
  Security Administration, Death Master File, database (Alexandria,
  Virginia: National Technical Information Service, ongoing).
- https://www.legacy.com/us/obituaries/poughkeepsiejournal/name/dolor
  es-colombo-obituary?id=17370102

396) Gabriella Tiso

Gabriella Tiso(396) was born on 7 December 1907, in Ariano, Italy, to Vincenzo
Tiso(131) and Giovanna Portogallo(131a).

Gabriella Tiso(396) married Raffaele Pastore(396a) on 12 April 1928 in Ariano, Italy.

Raffaele Pastore(396a) was born on 8 November 1906, in Ariano, Italy, to Nicoletta Pastore(396aM)[father unnamed]. Raffaele Pastore(396a) died 26 November 1984 in Ariano, Italy.

Records that include Gabriella Tiso(396) and/or Raffaele Pastore(396a):
- Ariano, Italy 1906 Birth Act #532
- Ariano, Italy 1907 Birth Act #578
- Ariano, Italy 1928 Marriage Act #40
- Ariano, Italy 1984 Death Act #154

397) Angiolina d'Antuono

Angiolina d'Antuono(397) was born on 10 January 1908, in Ariano, Italy, to Nicola Maria d'Antuono(135a) and Concetta Manganiello(135).

Angiolina d'Antuono(397) married Felico Colangelo(397a) on 24 August 1940 in Ariano, Italy.

Felico Colangelo(397a) was born on 30 August 1905, in Ariano, Italy, to Michele Colangelo(397aF) and Maria Gabriella Melito(397aM).

Records that include Angiolina d'Antuono(397) and/or Felico Colangelo(397a):
- Ariano, Italy 1905 Birth Act #469
- Ariano, Italy 1908 Birth Act #24
- Ariano, Italy 1940 Marriage Act #99

398) Maria LoConte

Maria LoConte(398) was born on 17 February 1908, in Ariano, Italy, to Francesco Paolo Lo Conte(205a) and Carmela Manganiello(205).

Maria LoConte(398) married Michele Borriello(398a) on 1 March 1928 in Ariano, Italy.

Michele Borriello(398a) was born on 21 August 1907, in Ariano, Italy, to Luigi Borriello(398aF) and Raffaella Schiavonne(398aM).

Records that include Maria LoConte(398) and/or Michele Borriello(398a):
- Ariano, Italy 1907 Birth Act #394
- Ariano, Italy 1908 Birth Act #95
- Ariano, Italy 1928 Marriage Act #18

399) Virgilia Miressi

Virgilia Miressi(399) was born on 20 February 1908, in Ariano, Italy, to Nicolantonio Miressi(132) and Maria Michele Monaco(132c). Virgilia Miressi(399) died on 25 February 1908 in Ariano, Italy.

Records that include Virgilia Miressi(399):
- Ariano, Italy 1908 Birth Act #99
- Ariano, Italy 1908 Death Act #61

400) Marianna Riccio

Marianna Riccio(400) was born on 27 February 1908, in Ariano, Italy, to Angelo Maria Riccio(183a) and Raimonda Ciasullo(183). Marianna Riccio(400) died 21 February 1909 in Ariano, Italy.

Records that include Marianna Riccio(400):
- Ariano, Italy 1908 Birth Act #118
- Ariano, Italy 1909 Death Act #81

401) Angela diLillo

Angela De Lillo(401) was born on 2 March 1908, in Ariano, Italy, to Francesco diLillo(184) and Concetta Perrina(184a).

Angela De Lillo(401) married Luigi Ermino Perrina(314) on 7 February 1924 in Ariano, Italy.

Luigi Ermino Perrina(314)* was born on 20 February 1902, in Ariano, Italy, to Michele Perrina(88) and Maria Grazia Caraglia(88a). Luigi Ermino Perrina(314) died on 10 October 1976 in Ariano, Italy.
* Luigi Ermino Perrina(314) is also D'Ausilio descendant.

Records that include Angela De Lillo(401) and/or Luigi Ermino Perrina(314):
- Ariano, Italy 1902 Birth Act #94
- Ariano, Italy 1908 Birth Act #139
- Ariano, Italy 1924 Marriage Act #24

402) Gabriel Ninfadoro

Gabriel Ninfadoro(402) was born on 24 March 1908, in Schenectady, NY, to Oto Ninfadoro(165) and Antonia Costanzo(165a). Gabriel Ninfadoro(402) died on April 1979, in Schenectady, NY. Gabriel Ninfadoro(402) was a stock clerk.

Gabriel Ninfadoro(402) married Carmella Romanella(402a).

Carmella Romanella(402a) was born on 16 October 1910, in Schenectady, NY, to Vincent Romanella(402aF) and Carmelia Carmello(402aM). Carmella Romanella(402a) died on 1 January 1986 in Schenectady, NY.

Records that include Gabriel Ninfadoro(402) and/or Carmella Romanella(402a):
- "United States Census, 1920", , FamilySearch (https://www.familysearch.org/ark:/61903/1:1:MVSC-KQM : Sat Mar 09 03:55:07 UTC 2024), Entry for Vincent Romanello and Carmelia Romanello, 1920.
- "United States Census, 1930", , FamilySearch (https://www.familysearch.org/ark:/61903/1:1:X4TB-9PG : Wed Mar 06 06:37:33 UTC 2024), Entry for Otto Ninafodora and Antoinette Ninafodora, 1930.
- "United States Census, 1930", , FamilySearch (https://www.familysearch.org/ark:/61903/1:1:X4T1-VMV : Thu Mar 07 23:45:49 UTC 2024), Entry for Carmela Romanella and Carmela Romanella, 1930.
- "United States Census, 1940", , FamilySearch (https://www.familysearch.org/ark:/61903/1:1:KQY5-TLS : Sun Mar 10 15:51:37 UTC 2024), Entry for Otto Ninfadoro and Antoinette Ninfadoro, 1940.
- "United States Census, 1940", , FamilySearch (https://www.familysearch.org/ark:/61903/1:1:KQY5-X8P : Thu Mar 07 12:37:40 UTC 2024), Entry for Carmela Romanella and Carmela Romanella, 1940.
- "United States 1950 Census", , FamilySearch (https://www.familysearch.org/ark:/61903/1:1:6XT1-N5GK : Tue Mar 19 19:50:22 UTC 2024), Entry for Gabriel Ninfadore and Carmela Ninfadore, 15 April 1950.
- "United States Social Security Death Index," database, FamilySearch (https://familysearch.org/ark:/61903/1:1:VMKS-72P : 7 January 2021), Gabriel Ninfadore, Apr 1979; citing U.S. Social Security Administration, Death Master File, database (Alexandria, Virginia: National Technical Information Service, ongoing).
- "United States Social Security Death Index," database, FamilySearch (https://familysearch.org/ark:/61903/1:1:JBP7-PZ5 : 7 January 2021), Carmela Ninfadore, Jan 1986; citing U.S. Social Security Administration, Death Master File, database (Alexandria, Virginia: National Technical Information Service, ongoing).
- "Sacred Heart, Schenectady, New York, Deaths (Mar 1904 -Jul 2001)", American-Canadian Genealogical Society, Manchester, NH, page 106

403) Rosa Grasso

Rosa Grasso(403) was born on 30 April 1908 in Ariano, Italy to Domenico Grasso(151a) and Mariangela Manganiello(151). Rosa Grasso(403) boarded the ship SS Duca Degli Abruzzi, with her mother, in Naples, Italy, on 24 February 1905, arriving in New York, on 9 March 1915. Rosa Grasso(403) died 10 February 2005 in Canton,OH.

Rosa Grasso(403) married Angelantonio (Angelo) Guarente/Guarendi(403a) and Joseph Mancuso(403b).

Angelantonio (Angelo) Guarente/Guarendi(403a) was born on 3 December 1896 in San Nicola Manfredi, Italy, to Nicola Guarente(403aF) and Catarina Maletesta(403aM). Angelantonio (Angelo) Guarente/Guarendi(403a) died on 20 September 1975 in Canton, OH.

Joseph Mancuso(403b) was born on 5 January 1897 in Italy. Joseph Mancuso(403b) died 13 December 1983 in Canton, OH. Joseph Mancuso(403b) was previously married to Carmela Raso(403bX)

Rosa Grasso(403) and Angelantonio (Angelo) Guarente/Guarendi(403a) had child(ren).

- Records that include Rosa Grasso(403), Angelantonio (Angelo) Guarente/Guarendi(403a), and/or Joseph Mancuso(403b):
- "Italia, Benevento, Stato Civile (Archivio di Stato), 1810-1942", , FamilySearch (https://www.familysearch.org/ark:/61903/1:1:QLKP-YMFD : Sat Mar 09 21:38:58 UTC 2024), Entry for Angelantonio Guarente and Nicola Guarente, 3 dicembre 1896.
- Ariano, Italy 1908 Birth Act#259
- "New York Passenger Arrival Lists (Ellis Island), 1892-1924", , FamilySearch (https://www.familysearch.org/ark:/61903/1:1:JJ4Q-6WY : Sun Mar 10 23:50:55 UTC 2024), Entry for Rosa Grasso and Michele Grasso, 1915.
- "United States World War I Draft Registration Cards, 1917-1918", database with images, FamilySearch (https://www.familysearch.org/ark:/61903/1:1:K6F9-HZ2 : 24 December 2021), Angelo Guarnt, 1917-1918.
- "United States Census, 1930", , FamilySearch (https://www.familysearch.org/ark:/61903/1:1:X4CP-24N : Sun Mar 10 07:55:58 UTC 2024), Entry for Tony Chiofolo and Rosa Chiofolo, 1930.
- "United States Census, 1930", , FamilySearch (https://www.familysearch.org/ark:/61903/1:1:X4C2-84G : Sun Mar 10 20:24:21 UTC 2024), Entry for Angelo Gorranto and Rose Gorranto, 1930.
- "United States Census, 1940", , FamilySearch (https://www.familysearch.org/ark:/61903/1:1:KWP7-T52 : Sat Mar 09 06:03:04 UTC 2024), Entry for Joseph Mancuso and Carmella Mancuso, 1940.
- "United States Census, 1940", , FamilySearch (https://www.familysearch.org/ark:/61903/1:1:KWP7-96J : Sat Mar 09 05:09:54 UTC 2024), Entry for Angelo Guarante and Rose Guarante, 1940.
- "United States 1950 Census", , FamilySearch (https://www.familysearch.org/ark:/61903/1:1:6XB9-2K42 : Tue Mar 19 02:16:24 UTC 2024), Entry for Carmela Mancuso and Mary Mancuso, 10 April 1950.
- "United States 1950 Census", , FamilySearch (https://www.familysearch.org/ark:/61903/1:1:6XBD-LF3Z : Thu Mar 21 00:28:46 UTC 2024), Entry for Rose N Guarendi and Nick R Guarendi, 7 April 1950.
- "Ohio Death Index, 1908-1932, 1938-1944, and 1958-2007", , FamilySearch (https://www.familysearch.org/ark:/61903/1:1:VKVG-V36 : 29 June 2021), Angelo Guarendi, 1975.
- "Ohio Death Index, 1908-1932, 1938-1944, and 1958-2007", database, FamilySearch (https://www.familysearch.org/ark:/61903/1:1:VKK7-FBQ : 30 June 2021), Joseph Mancuso, 1983.
- "United States Social Security Death Index," , FamilySearch (https://familysearch.org/ark:/61903/1:1:J2N5-JWB : 8 January 2021), Angelo Guarendi, Sep 1975; citing U.S. Social Security Administration, Death Master File, database (Alexandria, Virginia: National Technical Information Service, ongoing).

- "United States, Social Security Numerical Identification Files
  (NUMIDENT), 1936-2007", database, FamilySearch
  (https://www.familysearch.org/ark:/61903/1:1:6K3K-X3TT : 10
  February 2023), Rose Mancuso, .
- "Find a Grave Index," database, FamilySearch
  (https://www.familysearch.org/ark:/61903/1:1:QVGW-44BF : 1 April
  2023), Angelo Guarendi, ; Burial, Massillon, Stark, Ohio, United
  States of America, Calvary Cemetery; citing record ID 114662999,
  Find a Grave, http://www.findagrave.com.
- "Find a Grave Index," database, FamilySearch
  (https://www.familysearch.org/ark:/61903/1:1:QVGX-DQSS : 1 April
  2023), Joseph Mancuso, ; Burial, Massillon, Stark, Ohio, United
  States of America, Calvary Cemetery; citing record ID 115621312,
  Find a Grave, http://www.findagrave.com.
- "Find a Grave Index," database, FamilySearch
  (https://www.familysearch.org/ark:/61903/1:1:QVGW-44BR : 1 April
  2023), Rose Grasso Guarendi, ; Burial, Massillon, Stark, Ohio,
  United States of America, Calvary Cemetery; citing record ID
  114663000, Find a Grave, http://www.findagrave.com.

404) Maria Virginia Gentile

Maria Virginia Gentile(404) was born on 20 August 1908, in Ariano, Italy, to
Pasquale Gentile(192a) and Maria Miressi(192).

Records that include Maria Virginia Gentile(404):
- Ariano, Italy 1908 Birth Act #449

405) Angelo (Charles) Vernacchia

Angelo (Charles) Vernacchia(405) born on 10 September 1908, in New York,
to Francesco Paolo Vernacchia(144a) and Rosa Grasso(144). Angelo (Charles)
Vernacchia(405) died on 18 March 1976 in Miami, FL. Angelo (Charles)
Vernacchia(405) owned a bakery.

Angelo (Charles) Vernacchia(405) married Concetta Ferrante(405a) on 16 April
1926 in New York, NY.

Concetta Ferrante(405a) was born 29 October 1907, in Campobasso, Italy, to
Pasquale Ferrante(405aF) and Mary Del Grappo(405aM). Concetta Ferrante(405a)
sailed from Naples, Italy on the SS Prinzess Irene arriving in New York, NY on
21 November 1912. became a citizen of the United States 13 December 1944 in
the Southern District of New York. Concetta Ferrante(405a) died 28 February
1981 in Miami, FL.

Angelo (Charles) Vernacchia(405) and Concetta Ferrante(405a) had child(ren).

Records that include Angelo (Charles) Vernacchia(405) and/or Concetta
Ferrante(405a):
- "New York, State Census, 1915", , FamilySearch
  (https://www.familysearch.org/ark:/61903/1:1:K9FC-ZB1 : 4 June
  2022), Frank Vernachio, 1915.
- "United States, Census, 1920", FamilySearch
  (https://www.familysearch.org/ark:/61903/1:1:MJPD-KYN : Thu Jan 16
  03:46:43 UTC 2025), Entry for Frank Vernacchia and Rose Vernacchia,
  1920.
- "New York, New York City Marriage Records, 1829-1938", FamilySearch
  (https://www.familysearch.org/ark:/61903/1:1:Q2CV-9MYW : Sun Mar 10
  15:03:30 UTC 2024), Entry for Charles Vernacchia and Concetta
  Ferrande, 18 April 1926.
- "United States, Census, 1930", FamilySearch
  (https://www.familysearch.org/ark:/61903/1:1:X76D-W3Y : Fri Mar 08
  10:37:35 UTC 2024), Entry for Charles Vernacchio and Concetta
  Vernacchio, 1930.
- "New York, U.S. District and Circuit Court Naturalization Records,
  1824-1991", FamilySearch
  (https://www.familysearch.org/ark:/61903/1:1:716V-GLN2 : Sat Sep 06
  16:40:23 UTC 2025), Entry for Concetta Ferrante or Vernacchia and
  Charles, 1912.

- "United States, Census, 1940", FamilySearch
  (https://www.familysearch.org/ark:/61903/1:1:KQM8-5YH : Fri Mar 08
  09:56:42 UTC 2024), Entry for Charles Vernacchia and Concetta
  Vernacchia, 1940.
- "New York, New York City, World War II Draft Registration Cards,
  1940-1947", FamilySearch
  (https://www.familysearch.org/ark:/61903/1:1:WWLF-XWW2 : Sat Apr 12
  09:34:09 UTC 2025), Entry for Charles Angelo Vernacchia and Patsy
  Ferrante, 16 Oct 1940.
- https://www.nytimes.com/1945/03/10/archives/police-raid-curfew-
  speakeasy-wreck-bar-in-bronx-with-axes-squad.html
- "United States, Census, 1950", FamilySearch
  (https://www.familysearch.org/ark:/61903/1:1:6XP7-YNV3 : Thu Oct 05
  09:22:21 UTC 2023), Entry for Charles Vernacchia and Concetta
  Vernacchia, 10 April 1950.
- https://www.ancientfaces.com/person/charles-vernacchia-birth-1908-
  death-1976/12661371
- "Florida, Death Index, 1877-1998", FamilySearch
  (https://www.familysearch.org/ark:/61903/1:1:VV7K-KQL : Wed Feb 19
  02:45:59 UTC 2025), Entry for Charles A Vernacchia, 18 Mar 1976.
- "United States, Social Security Death Index," database,
  FamilySearch (https://familysearch.org/ark:/61903/1:1:JTBD-WP5 : 7
  January 2021), Charles Vernacchia, Mar 1976; citing U.S. Social
  Security Administration, Death Master File, database (Alexandria,
  Virginia: National Technical Information Service, ongoing).
- "United States, Social Security Death Index," database,
  FamilySearch (https://familysearch.org/ark:/61903/1:1:JTTZ-PY6 : 7
  January 2021), Concetta Vernacchia, Feb 1981; citing U.S. Social
  Security Administration, Death Master File, database (Alexandria,
  Virginia: National Technical Information Service, ongoing).
- "Florida, Death Index, 1877-1998", FamilySearch
  (https://www.familysearch.org/ark:/61903/1:1:VV87-ND3 : Wed Feb 19
  13:46:40 UTC 2025), Entry for Concetta Vernacchia, 28 Feb 1981.

406) Liberato Amendeo Anselmo Bianchi

Liberato Amendeo Anselmo Bianchi(406) was born on 3 October 1908, in Ariano, Italy, to Gerardino Bianchi(133a) and Mariangela Tiso(133).

Liberato Amendeo Anselmo Bianchi(406) married Filomena Guardabascio(406a) on 8 January 1930 in Ariano, Italy.

Filomena Guardabascio(406a) was born on 28 July 1905, in Ariano, Italy, to Francesco Paolo Guardabascio(406aF) and Marianna d'Agostino(406aM).

Records that include Liberato Amendeo Anselmo Bianchi(406) and/or Filomena Guardabascio(406a):
- Ariano, Italy 1905 Birth Act #400
- Ariano, Italy 1908 Birth Act #546
- Ariano, Italy 1930 Marriage Act #II.A.4

407) Aurelia Scanzillo

Aurelia Scanzillo(407) was born on 25 October 1908, in Ariano, Italy, to Gaetano Scauzillo(164) and Giovanna Grasso(196). Aurelia Scanzillo(407) died July 1987 in Dobbs Ferry, NY.

Aurelia Scanzillo(407) married Vito Rocco Mondo(407a).

Vito Rocco Mondo(407a) was born on 21 March 1907, in Bari, Italy to Rocco Mondo(407aF) and Teresa Mincieli(407aM). On 27 September 1907, in Naples, Italy, Vito Rocco Mondo(407a) emigrated to the United States, with his mother, on board the ship SS König Albert, arriving in New York on 10 October 1907. Vito Rocco Mondo(407a) was a mailman.

Aurelia Scanzillo(407) and Vito Rocco Mondo(407a) had Child(ren).

Records that include Aurelia Scanzillo(407) and/or Vito Rocco Mondo(407a):

- "New York, New York City Births, 1846-1909," database, FamilySearch
  (https://familysearch.org/ark:/61903/1:1:2W8H-5MG : 11 February
  2018), Anleria Scanzilla, 28 Oct 1908; citing Manhattan, New York,
  New York, United States, reference 8022 New York Municipal
  Archives, New York; FHL microfilm 2,023,262.
  "New York Passenger Arrival Lists (Ellis Island), 1892-1924", ,
  FamilySearch (https://www.familysearch.org/ark:/61903/1:1:JX2D-
  VMG : Sat Mar 09 13:35:33 UTC 2024), Entry for Vito Rocco Monno and
  Caterina, 1907.
- "United States Census, 1920", , FamilySearch
  (https://www.familysearch.org/ark:/61903/1:1:MJG5-1XL : Wed Mar 06
  20:43:44 UTC 2024), Entry for Gaetano Scanzilla and Jannie
  Scanzilla, 1920.
- "United States Census, 1920", , FamilySearch
  (https://www.familysearch.org/ark:/61903/1:1:MJ1F-KZ8 : Sun Mar 10
  21:56:37 UTC 2024), Entry for Rocco Mondo and Theresa Mondo, 1920.
- "United States Census, 1930", , FamilySearch
  (https://www.familysearch.org/ark:/61903/1:1:X7D7-14C : Sun Mar 10
  17:52:18 UTC 2024), Entry for Rocco Mando and Teresa Mando, 1930.
- "United States Census, 1940", , FamilySearch
  (https://www.familysearch.org/ark:/61903/1:1:KQBN-DM6 : Sun Mar 10
  08:56:28 UTC 2024), Entry for Victor Mondo and Aurelia Mondo, 1940.
- "New York, New York City, World War II Draft Registration Cards,
  1940-1947", , FamilySearch
  (https://www.familysearch.org/ark:/61903/1:1:W4W2-5JW2 : Sat Mar 09
  08:57:30 UTC 2024), Entry for Victor Mondo and U S Post Office.
- "United States 1950 Census", , FamilySearch
  (https://www.familysearch.org/ark:/61903/1:1:6XR4-6MT1 : Sat Oct 07
  00:41:13 UTC 2023), Entry for Victor Mondo and Aurelia Mondo, 13
  April 1950.
- "United States Social Security Death Index," , FamilySearch
  (https://familysearch.org/ark:/61903/1:1:JB5Z-2ZP : 7 January
  2021), Aurelia Mondo, Jul 1987; citing U.S. Social Security
  Administration, Death Master File, database (Alexandria, Virginia:
  National Technical Information Service, ongoing).

408) Rosina (Rose) DeMeo

Rosina (Rose) DeMeo(408) was born on 11 February 1909, in Schenectady, NY, to
Angelo DeMeo(202a) and Maria Perrina(202).

Rosina (Rose) DeMeo(408) married Joseph Calabrese(408a) on 12 April 1931, in
Schenectady, NY.

Joseph Calabrese(408a) was born on 27 December 1906, in Corona, NY, to
Bennedetto Calabrese(408aF) and Concetta DeMeo(408aM). Joseph Calabrese(408a)
was a carpenter.

Records that include Rosina (Rose) DeMeo(408) and/or Joseph Calabrese(408a):

- "United States Census, 1910", , FamilySearch
  (https://www.familysearch.org/ark:/61903/1:1:M596-RYZ : Sun Mar 10
  01:00:22 UTC 2024), Entry for Angelo Demeo and Mary F Demeo, 1910.
- "United States Census, 1910", , FamilySearch
  (https://www.familysearch.org/ark:/61903/1:1:M5HP-XRQ : Sat Mar 09
  12:32:13 UTC 2024), Entry for Beneddeto Calabrese and Concetta
  Calabrese, 1910.
- "United States Census, 1920", , FamilySearch
  (https://www.familysearch.org/ark:/61903/1:1:MVM3-97S : Fri Mar 08
  03:29:54 UTC 2024), Entry for Couchem Calabrese and Joseph
  Calabrese, 1920.
- "United States Census, 1920", , FamilySearch
  (https://www.familysearch.org/ark:/61903/1:1:MVS4-RRY : Fri Mar 08
  05:51:12 UTC 2024), Entry for Angelo Demeo and Mary Demeo, 1920.
- "United States Census, 1930", , FamilySearch
  (https://www.familysearch.org/ark:/61903/1:1:X4TT-YB5 : Mon Mar 11
  01:35:37 UTC 2024), Entry for Angelo De Meo and Mary De Meo, 1930.

- "United States Census, 1930", , FamilySearch
  (https://www.familysearch.org/ark:/61903/1:1:X4PK-2N6 : Thu Mar 07
  03:06:26 UTC 2024), Entry for Joseph Trezza and Concetta Trezza,
  1930.
- https://www.mes-racines.ca/fichiers/R%C3%A9pertoire%20BMS/Etats-
  Unis/New%20York/Schenectady/St-Anthony/Mariages%20-%201903-
  2006/Volume%201%20-%20A-I/St%20Anthony%20-%20M%20-%201903-2006%20-
  %20Aba-Iov.pdf
- "United States Census, 1940", , FamilySearch
  (https://www.familysearch.org/ark:/61903/1:1:KQYF-JDN : Sun Mar 10
  02:54:25 UTC 2024), Entry for Joseph Calabrese and Rose Calabrese,
  1940.
- "New York, New York City, World War II Draft Registration Cards,
  1940-1947", , FamilySearch
  (https://www.familysearch.org/ark:/61903/1:1:WW5F-C26Z : Sat Mar 09
  04:24:03 UTC 2024), Entry for Joseph Calabrese and Self, 16 Oct
  1940.
- "United States 1950 Census", , FamilySearch
  (https://www.familysearch.org/ark:/61903/1:1:6XRQ-22SD : Tue Mar 19
  20:26:01 UTC 2024), Entry for Joseph Calabrese and Rose Calabrese,
  10 April 1950.
- "United States, Social Security Numerical Identification Files
  (NUMIDENT), 1936-2007", database, FamilySearch
  (https://www.familysearch.org/ark:/61903/1:1:6K9Q-LTPK : 10
  February 2023), Rose M Demeo in entry for Dorothy Rose Calabrese, .
- "St. Anthony, Schenectady, New York, Marriages (Oct 1916 -Jul
  2006)", 2 Volumes, American-Canadian Genealogical Society,
  Manchester, NH, page 220

409) Pasquale (Pat) Anastasio

Pasquale (Pat) Anastasio(409) was born on 30 April 1909, in Ohio, to Francesco
(Frank) Paul Anastasio(166) and Hilda (Gilda) Marcotti(166a). Pasquale (Pat)
Anastasio(409) died on 15 September 1974, in Boca Raton, FL.

Pasquale (Pat) Anastasio(409) married Helen Janokowicz(409a).

Helen Janokowicz(409a) was born on 21 March 1916, in Wisconsin, to Egnitz
Janokowicz(409aF) and Mary Miszkowski(409aM). Helen Janokowicz(409a) died on 4
July 1985, in Boca Raton, FL.

Pasquale (Pat) Anastasio(409) and Helen Janokowicz(409a) had Child(ren).

Records that include Pasquale (Pat) Anastasio(409) and/or Helen
Janokowicz(409a):

- https://journaltimes.newspapers.com/article/the-journal-times-
  obituary-for-frank-p/83018176/
- "United States Census, 1910", , FamilySearch
  (https://www.familysearch.org/ark:/61903/1:1:MK2G-BVS : Sun Mar 10
  04:02:48 UTC 2024), Entry for Frank Anastasio and Gilda Anastasio,
  1910.
- "United States Census, 1920", , FamilySearch
  (https://www.familysearch.org/ark:/61903/1:1:MFLS-36K : Sat Mar 09
  01:06:44 UTC 2024), Entry for Egnitz Juankovitz and Mary
  Juankovitz, 1920.
- "United States Census, 1920", , FamilySearch
  (https://www.familysearch.org/ark:/61903/1:1:MFL9-JJ6 : Sun Mar 10
  05:10:16 UTC 2024), Entry for Frank P Anastasio and Gilda
  Anastasio, 1920.
- "United States Census, 1930", , FamilySearch
  (https://www.familysearch.org/ark:/61903/1:1:X9SJ-2LK : Sat Mar 09
  02:41:12 UTC 2024), Entry for Frank Anastasio and Hilda Anastasio,
  1930.
- "United States Census, 1930", , FamilySearch
  (https://www.familysearch.org/ark:/61903/1:1:X9SV-66P : Sat Mar 09
  23:45:14 UTC 2024), Entry for Tony A Wosyk and Mary Wosyk, 1930.

- "United States Census, 1940", , FamilySearch
  (https://www.familysearch.org/ark:/61903/1:1:K7J6-8M8 : Sun Mar 10
  17:31:45 UTC 2024), Entry for Pasquale Anastasio and Helen
  Anastasio, 1940.
- "United States 1950 Census", , FamilySearch
  (https://www.familysearch.org/ark:/61903/1:1:6FMB-VVD1 : Thu Oct 05
  18:18:05 UTC 2023), Entry for Pasquale Anastasio and Helen P
  Anastasio, April 4, 1950.
- "RecordAGrave Index", , FamilySearch
  (https://www.familysearch.org/ark:/61903/1:1:662J-W1QR : 11 July
  2023), Pat Anastasio, .
- "RecordAGrave Index", , FamilySearch
  (https://www.familysearch.org/ark:/61903/1:1:662N-H6VT : 11 July
  2023), Helen P Anastasio, .
- "Find a Grave Index," database, FamilySearch
  (https://www.familysearch.org/ark:/61903/1:1:QPHL-W5W9 : 25
  February 2022), Tony, ; Burial, Mount Pleasant, Racine, Wisconsin,
  United States of America, West Lawn Memorial Park; citing record ID
  190099301, Find a Grave, http://www.findagrave.com.
- "Find a Grave Index," database, FamilySearch
  (https://www.familysearch.org/ark:/61903/1:1:QPHL-Z5HY : 25
  February 2022), Mary, ; Burial, Mount Pleasant, Racine, Wisconsin,
  United States of America, West Lawn Memorial Park; citing record ID
  190099309, Find a Grave, http://www.findagrave.com.
- "Find a Grave Index," database, FamilySearch
  (https://www.familysearch.org/ark:/61903/1:1:QPHV-BHNX : 1 August
  2020), Pat Anastasio, ; Burial, Boca Raton, Palm Beach, Florida,
  United States of America, Boca Raton Municipal Cemetery and
  Mausoleum; citing record ID 187955341, Find a Grave,
  http://www.findagrave.com.
- "Find a Grave Index," database, FamilySearch
  (https://www.familysearch.org/ark:/61903/1:1:QPHV-JN4J : 25
  February 2022), Helen P Anastasio, ; Burial, Boca Raton, Palm
  Beach, Florida, United States of America, Boca Raton Municipal
  Cemetery and Mausoleum; citing record ID 187955345, Find a Grave,
  http://www.findagrave.com.
- "United States Social Security Death Index," database, FamilySearch
  (https://familysearch.org/ark:/61903/1:1:JYVF-F6P : 9 January
  2021), Pasquale Anastasio, Sep 1974; citing U.S. Social Security
  Administration, Death Master File, database (Alexandria, Virginia:
  National Technical Information Service, ongoing).
- "Florida Death Index, 1877-1998," database, FamilySearch
  (https://familysearch.org/ark:/61903/1:1:VVNX-W97 : 25 December
  2014), Pasquale Anastasio, 15 Sep 1974; from "Florida Death Index,
  1877-1998," index, Ancestry (www.ancestry.com : 2004); citing
  vol. , certificate number 64079, Florida Department of Health,
  Office of Vital Records, Jacksonville.
- "Florida Death Index, 1877-1998," database, FamilySearch
  (https://familysearch.org/ark:/61903/1:1:VVNG-DKY : 25 December
  2014), Helen P Anastasio, 04 Jul 1985; from "Florida Death Index,
  1877-1998," index, Ancestry (www.ancestry.com : 2004); citing
  vol. , certificate number 70513, Florida Department of Health,
  Office of Vital Records, Jacksonville.

410) Lorenzo Panza

Lorenzo Panza(410) was born on 23 June 1909, in Ariano, Italy, to Ciriaco
Panza(152a) and Maria Antonia Fodarella(152).

Lorenzo Panza(410) married Antonetta LoConte(410a) on 30 December 1938 in
Ariano, Italy.

Antonetta LoConte(410a) was born on 9 October 1913, in Ariano, Italy, to
Generoso LoConte(410aF) and Maria Giuseppa Bongo(410aM).

Records that include Lorenzo Panza(410) and Antonetta LoConte(410a):
- Ariano, Italy 1909 Birth Act #378
- Ariano, Italy 1913 Birth Act #538
- Ariano, Italy 1939 Marriage Act #2

411) Anthony Ninfadoro

Anthony Ninfadoro(411) was born on 10 August 1909, in Schenectady, NY, to Oto Ninfadoro(153) and Antonia Costanzo(153a). Anthony Ninfadoro(411) died in 16 April 1987, in Schenectady, NY. Anthony Ninfadoro(411) was a toolmaker.

Records that include Anthony Ninfadoro(411):
- "United States Census, 1930", , FamilySearch (https://www.familysearch.org/ark:/61903/1:1:X4TB-9PG : Wed Mar 06 06:37:33 UTC 2024), Entry for Otto Ninafodora and Antoinette Ninafodora, 1930.
- "United States Census, 1940", , FamilySearch (https://www.familysearch.org/ark:/61903/1:1:KQY5-TLS : Sun Mar 10 15:51:37 UTC 2024), Entry for Otto Ninfadoro and Antoinette Ninfadoro, 1940.
- "United States 1950 Census", , FamilySearch (https://www.familysearch.org/ark:/61903/1:1:6XYM-TS35 : Fri Oct 06 04:13:49 UTC 2023), Entry for Otto Ninfadore and Anthony Ninfadore, 15 April 1950.
- "United States Social Security Death Index," database, FamilySearch (https://familysearch.org/ark:/61903/1:1:JKLV-FZH : 7 January 2021), Anthony Ninfadoro, Apr 1987; citing U.S. Social Security Administration, Death Master File, database (Alexandria, Virginia: National Technical Information Service, ongoing).
- "Find a Grave Index," database, FamilySearch (https://www.familysearch.org/ark:/61903/1:1:6Z7T-CTP6 : 8 March 2021), Anthony Ninfadoro, ; Burial, Schenectady, Schenectady, New York, United States of America, Saint John the Baptist Cemetery; citing record ID 220094013, Find a Grave, http://www.findagrave.com.
- "Sacred Heart, Schenectady, New York, Deaths (Mar 1904 -Jul 2001)", American-Canadian Genealogical Society, Manchester, NH, page 106

412) Teresa Miressi

Teresa Miressi(412) was born on 23 September 1910, in New Rochelle, NY, to Generoso Miressi(160) and Maria Luigia Iannarone(160a). Teresa Miressi(412) died 30 April 1990 in New Rochelle, NY.

Teresa Miressi(412) married Vincenzo Serpillo(412a) on 2 October 1954 in Greenwich, CT.

Vincenzo Serpillo(412a) was born on 6 September 1893 in Atri, Italy, to Donato Serpillo(412aF) and Grazia Paracchia(412aM). Vincenzo Serpillo(412a) emigrated to the United States on 25 July 1913. Vincenzo Serpillo(412a) died in November 1969 in New Rochelle, NY.

Records that include Teresa Miressi(412) and/or Vincenzo Serpillo(412a):
- "New York Passenger Arrival Lists (Ellis Island), 1892-1924", , FamilySearch (https://www.familysearch.org/ark:/61903/1:1:JJ94-9Y8 : Thu Mar 07 20:56:07 UTC 2024), Entry for Vincenzo Serpillo and Giuseppe, 1913.
- "United States Census, 1930", , FamilySearch (https://www.familysearch.org/ark:/61903/1:1:X4G6-NM9 : Sat Mar 09 03:25:50 UTC 2024), Entry for Generoso Miressi and Mary L Miressi, 1930.
- "United States Census, 1940", , FamilySearch (https://www.familysearch.org/ark:/61903/1:1:KQQ9-ZSV : Sat Mar 09 07:00:44 UTC 2024), Entry for Generoso Miresi and Marie Miresi, 1940.
- "United States World War I Draft Registration Cards, 1917-1918", database with images, FamilySearch (https://www.familysearch.org/ark:/61903/1:1:KXYM-CVN : 26 December 2021), Vincenzo Serpillo, 1917-1918.
- "United States, Social Security Numerical Identification Files (NUMIDENT), 1936-2007", database, FamilySearch (https://www.familysearch.org/ark:/61903/1:1:6K9C-RG4Q : 10 February 2023), Theresa M Miressi, .

- "United States Social Security Death Index," database, FamilySearch (https://familysearch.org/ark:/61903/1:1:JR9W-K3T : 7 January 2021), Vincenzo Serpillo, Nov 1969; citing U.S. Social Security Administration, Death Master File, database (Alexandria, Virginia: National Technical Information Service, ongoing).
- "United States Social Security Death Index," database, FamilySearch (https://familysearch.org/ark:/61903/1:1:JRW9-WPK : 7 January 2021), Theresa Serpillo, 20 Apr 1990; citing U.S. Social Security Administration, Death Master File, database (Alexandria, Virginia: National Technical Information Service, ongoing).

413) Virginia Manganiello

Virginia Manganiello(413) was born on 3 February 1910, in Ariano, Italy, to Michele Manganiello(138) and Pasqualina Miniscalco(138a). Virginia Manganiello(413) died 20 September 1910 in Ariano, Italy.

Records that include Virginia Manganiello(413):
- Ariano, Italy 1910 Birth Act #93
- Ariano, Italy 1910 Death Act #330

414) Anna Mary Anastasio

Anna Mary Anastasio(414) was born on 31 March 1910, in Connecticut, to Francesco (Frank) Paul Anastasio(166) and Hilda (Gilda) Marcotti(166a). Anna Mary Anastasio(414) died on 30 October 1988, in Racine, WI.

Anna Mary Anastasio(414) married Henry Kanetzke(414a) on 23 November 1957 in Racine, WI.

Henry Kanetzke(414a) was born on 25 Nay 1903 in Racine, WI to Julius Kanetzke(414aF) and Hulda Kiebel(414aM). Henry Kanetzke(414a) died in April of 1984 in Racine, WI.

Henry Kanetzke(414a) was previously married to Margaret Sweetman(414aX).

Records that include Anna Mary Anastasio(414) and/or Henry Kanetzke(414a):
- "Wisconsin Birth Index, 1820-1907," , FamilySearch (https://familysearch.org/ark:/61903/1:1:VHH2-BHK : 4 December 2014), Henri Ranitzki, 25 May 1903; from "Wisconsin Births, 1820-1907," database, Ancestry (http://www.ancestry.com : 2000); citing Racine, Wisconsin, reel 0250, Wisconsin Department of Health and Family Services, Vital Records Division, Madison.
- "Wisconsin State Census, 1905", database with images, FamilySearch (https://www.familysearch.org/ark:/61903/1:1:MMQS-38T : 5 March 2022), Henry Kanetzke in entry for Julius Kanetzke, 1905.
- "United States Census, 1910", , FamilySearch (https://www.familysearch.org/ark:/61903/1:1:MK2G-BVS : Sun Mar 10 04:02:48 UTC 2024), Entry for Frank Anastasio and Gilda Anastasio, 1910.
- "United States Census, 1920", , FamilySearch (https://www.familysearch.org/ark:/61903/1:1:MFL9-JJ6 : Sun Mar 10 05:10:16 UTC 2024), Entry for Frank P Anastasio and Gilda Anastasio, 1920.
- "United States Census, 1920", , FamilySearch (https://www.familysearch.org/ark:/61903/1:1:MF2R-5ST : Sat Mar 09 02:28:49 UTC 2024), Entry for Kyloa Kanetzke and Fred Kanetzke, 1920.
- "United States Census, 1930", , FamilySearch (https://www.familysearch.org/ark:/61903/1:1:X9SV-7VN : Sun Mar 10 07:03:39 UTC 2024), Entry for Henry Kanetzke and Margaret Kanetzke, 1930.
- "United States Census, 1930", , FamilySearch (https://www.familysearch.org/ark:/61903/1:1:X9SJ-2LK : Sat Mar 09 02:41:12 UTC 2024), Entry for Frank Anastasio and Hilda Anastasio, 1930.

- "United States Census, 1940", , FamilySearch
  (https://www.familysearch.org/ark:/61903/1:1:K7J6-HTQ : Sat Mar 09
  04:26:52 UTC 2024), Entry for Frank P Anastascio and Jilda
  Anastascio, 1940.
- "United States Census, 1940", , FamilySearch
  (https://www.familysearch.org/ark:/61903/1:1:K7JQ-QYR : Sun Mar 10
  08:14:35 UTC 2024), Entry for Henry Kanetzke and Margaret Kanetzke,
  1940.
- "United States 1950 Census", , FamilySearch
  (https://www.familysearch.org/ark:/61903/1:1:6FMB-ZH8X : Tue Oct 03
  08:34:28 UTC 2023), Entry for Frank P Anastasio and Jilda
  Anastasio, April 3, 1950.
- "United States 1950 Census", , FamilySearch
  (https://www.familysearch.org/ark:/61903/1:1:6FMT-GPWX : Tue Oct 03
  09:28:27 UTC 2023), Entry for Augusta C Kanetzke and Henry W
  Kanetzke.
- http://digital.library.wisc.edu/1711.dl/wiarchives.uw-whs-ph03957
- https://journaltimes.newspapers.com/article/the-journal-times-
  obituary-for-frank-p/83018176/
- "Wisconsin Death Index, 1959-1997", , FamilySearch
  (https://www.familysearch.org/ark:/61903/1:1:V8SB-RJ5 : 8 January
  2022), Henry William Kanetzke, 1984.
- "Wisconsin Death Index, 1959-1997", , FamilySearch
  (https://www.familysearch.org/ark:/61903/1:1:V8SB-RJ6 : 8 January
  2022), Anna Mary Kanetzke, 1988.
- "United States Social Security Death Index," database, FamilySearch
  (https://familysearch.org/ark:/61903/1:1:JL3Q-P66 : 9 January
  2021), Henry Kanetzke, Apr 1984; citing U.S. Social Security
  Administration, Death Master File, database (Alexandria, Virginia:
  National Technical Information Service, ongoing).
- "United States Social Security Death Index," database, FamilySearch
  (https://familysearch.org/ark:/61903/1:1:J1XT-CMX : 9 January
  2021), A Mary Kanetzke, Oct 1988; citing U.S. Social Security
  Administration, Death Master File, database (Alexandria, Virginia:
  National Technical Information Service, ongoing).
- "United States, Social Security Numerical Identification Files
  (NUMIDENT), 1936-2007", database, FamilySearch
  (https://www.familysearch.org/ark:/61903/1:1:6KQF-RS1X : 10
  February 2023), A Mary Kanetzke, .

415) Carmela Tiso

Carmela Tiso(415) was born on 22 April 1910, in Ariano, Italy to Vincenzo Tiso(131) and Giovanna Portogallo(131a).

Carmela Tiso(415) married Paolo Ferriero(415a) on 8 June 1931 in Ariano, Italy.

Paolo Ferriero(415a) was born on 1 August 1906, in Ariano, Italy, to Carmine Ferriero(415aF) and Maria Liberata LoConte(415aM).

Records that include Carmela Tiso(415) and/or Paolo Ferriero(415a):
- Ariano, Italy 1906 Birth Act #373
- Ariano, Italy 1910 Birth Act #281
- Ariano, Italy 1931 Marriage Act #P.II.A.85

416) Giovanni (John) Vernacchia

Giovanni (John) Vernacchia(416) was born on 17 may 1910, to Francesco Paolo Vernacchia(144a) and Rosa Grasso(144). Giovanni (John) Vernacchia(416) died 12 January 1998.

Giovanni (John) Vernacchia(416) married Antoinette (Alice) Cappabianca(416a) on 24 June 1932 in New York, NY.

Antoinette (Alice) Cappabianca(416a) born 18 January 1912, in New York, to Frank Cappabianca(416aF) and Julia Guerra(416aM). Antoinette (Alice) Cappabianca(416a) died 29 November 1999, in Bronx, NY.

Giovanni (John) Vernacchia(416) and Antoinette (Alice) Cappabianca(416a) had child(red).

Records that include Giovanni (John) Vernacchia(416) and/or Antoinette (Alice) Cappabianca(416a):

- "New York, State Census, 1915", , FamilySearch (https://www.familysearch.org/ark:/61903/1:1:K9FC-ZB1 : 4 June 2022), Frank Vernachio, 1915.
- "New York, State Census, 1915", , FamilySearch (https://www.familysearch.org/ark:/61903/1:1:K9FC-TVC : 4 June 2022), Andonetta Capobianco in entry for Francesco Capobianco, 1915.
- "United States, Census, 1920", FamilySearch (https://www.familysearch.org/ark:/61903/1:1:MJPD-KYN : Thu Jan 16 03:46:43 UTC 2025), Entry for Frank Vernacchia and Rose Vernacchia, 1920.
- "United States, Census, 1920", FamilySearch (https://www.familysearch.org/ark:/61903/1:1:MJP6-7WY : Sat Jan 11 05:00:56 UTC 2025), Entry for Frank Cappabianca and Angelina Cappabianca, 1920.
- "United States, Census, 1930", FamilySearch (https://www.familysearch.org/ark:/61903/1:1:X76D-NTR : Tue Jul 16 02:48:15 UTC 2024), Entry for Paul Vernacchia and Rose Vernacchia, 1930.
- "New York, New York City Marriage Records, 1829-1938", FamilySearch (https://www.familysearch.org/ark:/61903/1:1:Q2CF-3W93 : Sun Mar 10 12:06:47 UTC 2024), Entry for John Hernacchia and Antoinrtte Cappabiance, 24 June 1932.
- "United States, Census, 1940", FamilySearch (https://www.familysearch.org/ark:/61903/1:1:KQL9-SQR : Sun Mar 10 05:49:38 UTC 2024), Entry for John Vernacchia and Alice Vernacchia, 1940.
- "New York, New York City, World War II Draft Registration Cards, 1940-1947", FamilySearch (https://www.familysearch.org/ark:/61903/1:1:WWLF-XWN2 : Sat Apr 12 14:24:06 UTC 2025), Entry for John Vernacchia and Herman Dressel, 16 Oct 1940.
- "United States, Census, 1950", FamilySearch (https://www.familysearch.org/ark:/61903/1:1:6XTR-8W3S : Tue Mar 19 10:25:08 UTC 2024), Entry for John Vernacchia and Alice Vernacchia, 2 April 1950.
- "United States, Social Security Death Index," database, FamilySearch (https://familysearch.org/ark:/61903/1:1:JTB4-L3K : 7 January 2021), John Vernacchia, 12 Jan 1998; citing U.S. Social Security Administration, Death Master File, database (Alexandria, Virginia: National Technical Information Service, ongoing).
- "United States, Social Security Numerical Identification Files (NUMIDENT), 1936-2007", FamilySearch (https://www.familysearch.org/ark:/61903/1:1:6KMR-7M5Y : Sat Apr 26 00:17:45 UTC 2025), Entry for John Vernacchia.
- "United States, Social Security Numerical Identification Files (NUMIDENT), 1936-2007", FamilySearch (https://www.familysearch.org/ark:/61903/1:1:6KMP-7Y5V : Fri Apr 25 22:22:52 UTC 2025), Entry for Alice Vernacchia.
- "United States, Social Security Death Index," database, FamilySearch (https://familysearch.org/ark:/61903/1:1:JBG6-GZ9 : 7 January 2021), Alice Vernacchia, 29 Nov 1999; citing U.S. Social Security Administration, Death Master File, database (Alexandria, Virginia: National Technical Information Service, ongoing).
- "United States, Obituary Records, 2014-2023", FamilySearch (https://www.familysearch.org/ark:/61903/1:1:XMF1-8S96 : Mon Nov 25 22:37:32 UTC 2024), Entry for Frank P Vernacchia and John Vernacchia, 2 February 2022.

417) John Perrine

John Perrine(417) born 29 July 1910 in Lackawanna County, PA, to Carmine Perrina(247) and Colomba di Pasquale(247a). John Perrine(417) died March 1985 in Erie County, NY.

John Perrine(417) married and divorced June Smith(417a).

June Smith(417a) was born 1 February 1921, in Ohio, to Alfred Smith(417aF) and Clara Loder(417aM). June Smith(417a) died 30 August 2008 in Depew, NY.

John Perrine(417) and June Smith(417a) had child(ren).

Records that include John Perrine(417) and June Smith(417a):
- https://www.phmc.state.pa.us/bah/dam/rg/di/r11_089_BirthIndexes/Birth_1910/1910%20-%20P.pdf page 133
- "United States Census, 1920", , FamilySearch (https://www.familysearch.org/ark:/61903/1:1:MFY4-Q5M : Wed Mar 06 09:48:19 UTC 2024), Entry for O Dena Perine and Colombine Perine, 1920.
- "United States Census, 1930", , FamilySearch (https://www.familysearch.org/ark:/61903/1:1:X7CK-1B8 : Fri Jul 05 22:27:03 UTC 2024), Entry for Carmino Perrine and Columbia Perrine, 1930.
- "United States Census, 1930", , FamilySearch (https://www.familysearch.org/ark:/61903/1:1:X7C6-HYR : Sun Mar 10 18:01:22 UTC 2024), Entry for Alfred J Smith and Clara Smith, 1930.
- "United States Census, 1940", , FamilySearch (https://www.familysearch.org/ark:/61903/1:1:KQ53-VDG : Tue Jul 23 10:44:20 UTC 2024), Entry for Carmen Perrone and Columba Perrone, 1940.
- "United States Census, 1950", , FamilySearch (https://www.familysearch.org/ark:/61903/1:1:6XRQ-FV9M : Tue Oct 03 09:54:23 UTC 2023), Entry for John Perrine and June Perrine, April 3, 1950.
- https://www.newspapers.com/article/the-buffalo-news-perrine-colomba-nee-d/148955383/
- "Virginia, Marriage Certificates, 1936-1988", , FamilySearch (https://www.familysearch.org/ark:/61903/1:1:QK9F-JPMW : Tue Jul 23 21:47:39 UTC 2024), Entry for Jessee Hipkiss and Earl Hipkiss, 13 Nov 1953.
- "United States Social Security Death Index," database, FamilySearch (https://familysearch.org/ark:/61903/1:1:VM2N-KQ3 : 7 January 2021), John Perrine, Mar 1985; citing U.S. Social Security Administration, Death Master File, database (Alexandria, Virginia: National Technical Information Service, ongoing).
- "United States, Residence Database, 1970-2024", database, FamilySearch (https://www.familysearch.org/ark:/61903/1:1:6Y4W-LQ8B : 19 June 2024), John Perrine, 1985.
- https://www.newspapers.com/newspage/875694146/
- "United States Social Security Death Index," database, FamilySearch (https://familysearch.org/ark:/61903/1:1:VS7X-NZD : 12 January 2021), June Hipkiss, 30 Aug 2008; citing U.S. Social Security Administration, Death Master File, database (Alexandria, Virginia: National Technical Information Service, ongoing).
- "Find a Grave Index," database, FamilySearch (https://www.familysearch.org/ark:/61903/1:1:QV2N-CXVZ : 15 July 2020), June Smith Hipkiss, 2008; Burial, , ; citing record ID , Find a Grave, http://www.findagrave.com.

418) Angela Gentile

Angela Gentile(418) was born on 8 October 1910, in Ariano, Italy, to Pasquale Gentile(192a) and Maria Miressi(192). Angela Gentile(418) arrived in Providence, RI, on board the ship SS Providence, on 8 July 1927. Angela Gentile(418) became a citizen of the United States on 28 April 1944, in Newark, NJ. Angela Gentile(418) died 4 December 1989 in East Orange, NJ.

Angela Gentile(418) married Raffaele (Ralph) Carbone(418a) on 31 March 1927 in Ariano, Italy.

<u>Raffaele (Ralph) Carbone</u>(418a) was born on 29 January 1898, in Ariano, Italy, to Antonio Carbone(418aF) and Concordia Romagna(418aM). Raffaele (Ralph) Carbone(418a) emigrated to the United States on 5 May 1914. Raffaele (Ralph) Carbone(418a) served in the United States Army Field Artillery from 30 September 1920 to 31 August 1921. Raffaele (Ralph) Carbone(418a) became a citizen of the United states on 8 May 1922 in Newark, NJ. Raffaele (Ralph) Carbone(418a) died May 1973 in New Jersey. Raffaele (Ralph) Carbone(418a) was a coal dealer.

Angela Gentile(418) and Raffaele (Ralph) Carbone(418a) had child(ren).

Records that include Angela Gentile(418) and/or Raffaele (Ralph) Carbone(418a):

- Ariano, Italy 1898 Birth Act #70
- Ariano, Italy 1910 Birth Act #575
- "United States, Enlisted and Officer Muster Rolls and Rosters, 1916-1939", , FamilySearch (https://www.familysearch.org/ark:/61903/1:1:68FR-P3NF : Sun Mar 10 05:38:50 UTC 2024), Entry for Ralph Carbone, 31 August 1921.
- "United States World War I Draft Registration Cards, 1917-1918", database with images, FamilySearch (https://www.familysearch.org/ark:/61903/1:1:7628-9M3Z : 6 July 2024), Ralph Carbone, 1917-1918.
- "New Jersey Naturalization Records, 1796-1991", , FamilySearch (https://www.familysearch.org/ark:/61903/1:1:6PKG-7JM9 : Fri Mar 08 17:05:53 UTC 2024), Entry for Ralph Carbone, 8 May 1922.
- "New Jersey Naturalization Records, 1796-1991", , FamilySearch (https://www.familysearch.org/ark:/61903/1:1:QPRY-8C7C : Sun Mar 10 16:09:13 UTC 2024), Entry for Ralph Carbone, 1922.
- Ariano, Italy 1927 Marriage Act #38
- "United States Census, 1930", , FamilySearch (https://www.familysearch.org/ark:/61903/1:1:X4DH-19S : Sun Mar 10 18:44:17 UTC 2024), Entry for Ralph Caibone and Angelina Carbone, 1930.
- "United States Census, 1940", , FamilySearch (https://www.familysearch.org/ark:/61903/1:1:K45L-VR1 : Fri Mar 08 17:13:31 UTC 2024), Entry for Ralph Carbone and Angela Carbone, 1940.
- "New Jersey Naturalization Records, 1796-1991", , FamilySearch (https://www.familysearch.org/ark:/61903/1:1:6PXJ-H5KJ : Sun Mar 10 04:41:28 UTC 2024), Entry for Angelina Carbone or Gentile and Ralph, 26 Jun 1943.
- "New Jersey Naturalization Records, 1796-1991", , FamilySearch (https://www.familysearch.org/ark:/61903/1:1:WYRQ-NQ2M : Sun Mar 10 14:47:43 UTC 2024), Entry for Angelina Carbone, 1944.
- "United States Census, 1950", , FamilySearch (https://www.familysearch.org/ark:/61903/1:1:6F9P-6W6H : Fri Oct 06 08:52:02 UTC 2023), Entry for Ralph Carbone and Angeline Carbone, 5 April 1950.
- "United States Social Security Death Index," database, FamilySearch (https://familysearch.org/ark:/61903/1:1:JKBL-MZX : 8 January 2021), Ralph Carbone, May 1973; citing U.S. Social Security Administration, Death Master File, database (Alexandria, Virginia: National Technical Information Service, ongoing).
- "United States Social Security Death Index," database, FamilySearch (https://familysearch.org/ark:/61903/1:1:JBTL-C6B : 8 January 2021), Angelina Carbone, 04 Dec 1989; citing U.S. Social Security Administration, Death Master File, database (Alexandria, Virginia: National Technical Information Service, ongoing).
- "United States, Social Security Numerical Identification Files (NUMIDENT), 1936-2007", database, FamilySearch (https://www.familysearch.org/ark:/61903/1:1:6K98-5FV6 : 10 February 2023), Angelina Carbone, .

- "Find a Grave Index," database, FamilySearch
  (https://www.familysearch.org/ark:/61903/1:1:QVLZ-78SP : 14 April
  2023), Angelina Carbone, ; Burial, East Hanover, Morris, New
  Jersey, United States of America, Gate of Heaven Cemetery and
  Mausoleum; citing record ID 92311671, Find a Grave,
  http://www.findagrave.com.

419) Genoveffa Carmna Maria Manganiello

Genoveffa Carmna Maria Manganiello(419) was born on 9 November 1910, in
Ariano, Italy, to Raimondo Manganiello(182) and Maria Giovanna Paone(182a).

Genoveffa Carmna Maria Manganiello(419) married Rocco Faratro(419a) on 5 April
1956 in Ariano, Italy.

Rocco Faratro(419a) Only record currently available is a margin note in the
birth record of Genoveffa Carmna Maria Manganiello(419).

Records that include Genoveffa Carmna Maria Manganiello(419) and/or Rocco
Faratro(419a):
- Ariano, Italy 1910 Birth Act #629
- Ariano, Italy 1956 Marriage Act #26

420) Amelia Mancino

Amelia Mancino(420) was born on 19 November 1910 in Ariano, Italy, to Agostino
Mancino(150a) and Maria Rosaria Scauzillo(150).

Amelia Mancino(420) married Antonio Pannese(420a)on 16 January 1936 in Ariano,
Italy.

Antonio Pannese(420a) was born on 7 May 1912, in Ariano, Italy, to Giovanni
Pannese(420aF) and Mariah Leonarda Mainiero(420aM).

Records that include Amelia Mancino(420) and/or Antonio Pannese(420a):
- Ariano, Italy 1910 Birth Act #613
- Ariano, Italy 1912 Birth Act #247
- Ariano, Italy 1936 Marriage Act #PIIA3

421) Lorenzo Fodarella

Lorenzo Fodarella(421) was born on 12 January 1911, in Ariano, Italy to Luigi
Fodarella(188) and Giuditta Marrone(188a).

Records that include Lorenzo Fodarella(421):
- Ariano, Italy 1911 Birth Act #18

422) Oto Maria Carmelo (Otto M.) Bianchi

Oto Maria Carmelo (Otto M.) Bianchi(422) was born on 12 January 1911, in
Ariano, Italy, to Gerardino Bianchi(133a) and Mariangela Tiso(133). Oto Maria
Carmelo (Otto M.) Bianchi(422) arrived in the United States (New York, NY) on
4 January 1956 on the ship SS Saturnia. Oto Maria Carmelo (Otto M.)
Bianchi(422) became a citizen of the United States on 1 May 1961 in New
Jersey. Oto Maria Carmelo (Otto M.) Bianchi(422) died on 2 December 1997 in
Essex, NJ. Oto Maria Carmelo (Otto M.) Bianchi(422) was buried in Holy Cross
Cemetery and Mausoleum, North Arlington, NJ. Oto Maria Carmelo (Otto M.)
Bianchi(422) was a barber.

Oto Maria Carmelo (Otto M.) Bianchi(422) married Olga Maria Balzano(422a) on
14 September 1947, in Trieste, Italy.

Olga Maria Balzano(422a) was born on 10 October 1924, in Reana del Rojale,
Italy. Olga Maria Balzano(422a) arrived in the United States (New York, NY) on
4 January 1956 on the ship SS Saturnia. Olga Maria Balzano(422a) became a
Citizen of the United States on 1 May 1961 in New Jersey. Olga Maria
Balzano(422a) died 3 July 2001 in New Jersey. Olga Maria Balzano(422a) was
buried in Holy Cross Cemetery and Mausoleum, North Arlington, NJ.

Oto Maria Carmelo (Otto M.) Bianchi(422) and Olga Maria Balzano(422a) had child(ren).

Records that include Oto Maria Carmelo (Otto M.) Bianchi(422) and/or Olga Maria Balzano(422a):

- Ariano, Italy 1911 Birth Act #37
- "New Jersey, Naturalization Records, 1796-1991", FamilySearch (https://www.familysearch.org/ark:/61903/1:1:QLGY-RCBC : Sat Apr 12 04:13:08 UTC 2025), Entry for Oto Maria Bianchi and Olga Balzano, 1956.
- "New Jersey, Naturalization Records, 1796-1991", FamilySearch (https://www.familysearch.org/ark:/61903/1:1:WBZC-FRW2 : Fri Apr 11 18:56:12 UTC 2025), Entry for Oto Maria Bianchi, 1961.
- "United States, Social Security Death Index," database, FamilySearch (https://familysearch.org/ark:/61903/1:1:JKYM-229 : 8 January 2021), Otto M Bianchi, 02 Dec 1997; citing U.S. Social Security Administration, Death Master File, database (Alexandria, Virginia: National Technical Information Service, ongoing).
- "United States, GenealogyBank Obituaries, Births, and Marriages, 1980-2015", FamilySearch (https://www.familysearch.org/ark:/61903/1:1:QKWG-2N8N : Tue Jul 23 12:54:48 UTC 2024), Entry for Mr Otto M Bianchi and Olga Bianchi, 03 Dec 1997.
- "United States, Social Security Numerical Identification Files (NUMIDENT), 1936-2007", FamilySearch (https://www.familysearch.org/ark:/61903/1:1:6K9N-6MJ2 : Sat Apr 26 16:22:37 UTC 2025), Entry for Otto M Bianchi.
- "Find a Grave Index", FamilySearch (https://www.familysearch.org/ark:/61903/1:1:4KJT-Y66Z : Tue Apr 01 07:24:21 UTC 2025), Entry for Otto M Bianchi.

423) Dora Tiso

Dora Tiso(423) was born about July 1911 in New Jersey, to Oto (Ottone) Tiso(169) and Mary Senese(169a).

Records that include Dora Tiso(423):

- "New Jersey State Census, 1915", , FamilySearch (https://www.familysearch.org/ark:/61903/1:1:QV9Q-SFNP : Mon Mar 11 01:12:03 UTC 2024), Entry for Ottone Tiso and Mary Tiso, 1915.

424) Anna Riccio

Anna Riccio(424) was born on 2 September 1911, in Ariano, Italy, to Raffaele Riccio(221a) and Giovanna (Jenny) Ciasullo(221). Anna Riccio(424) died 1 March 1992 in Schenectady, NY. Anna Riccio(424) was buried in St. John's Cemetery, Schenectady, NY.

Records that include Anna Riccio(424):

- Ariano, Italy 1911 Birth Act #402
- "United States Census, 1930", , FamilySearch (https://www.familysearch.org/ark:/61903/1:1:X4TB-187 : Fri Mar 08 12:10:26 UTC 2024), Entry for Ralph Riccio and Jennie Riccio, 1930.
- "United States Census, 1940", , FamilySearch (https://www.familysearch.org/ark:/61903/1:1:K79V-TYQ : Sat Mar 09 17:46:14 UTC 2024), Entry for Ralph Riccio and Jennie Riccio, 1940.
- "United States Census, 1950", , FamilySearch (https://www.familysearch.org/ark:/61903/1:1:6XR7-3VHN : Wed Mar 20 20:19:14 UTC 2024), Entry for Ralph Riccio and Jennie Riccio, 27 April 1950.
- "St. Luke, Schenectady, New York, Baptism and Burials(Jan 1916 – Sep 2003)", American-Canadian Genealogical Society, Manchester, NH, page 222

425) Victor Vincent Perrino

Victor Vincent Perrino(425) born on 17 October 1911, in Schenectady, NY, to Vittorio Perrino(187) and Carmela Ricci(187a). Victor Vincent Perrino(425) died 26 October 1981 in Albany, NY.

Victor Vincent Perrino(425) married Louise Teresa Garafano(425a) on 16 August 1942 in Rutland, VT.

Louise Teresa Garafano(425a) was born on 13 February 1915, in Rutland, VT, to Joseph T. Garafano(425aF) and Mary S. Schettini(425aM). Louise Teresa Garafano(425a) died 19 September 2004, in Schenectady, NY.

Records that include Victor Vincent Perrino(425) and/or Louise Teresa Garafano(425a):

- "St. John the Baptist, Schenectady, New York, Baptism (oct 1854 – Jun 2009)", American-Canadian Genealogical Society, Manchester, NH
- "United States Census, 1920", , FamilySearch (https://www.familysearch.org/ark:/61903/1:1:MVSH-71T : Sat Jul 20 13:35:39 UTC 2024), Entry for Victor Perrino, Sr and Carrie Perrino, 1920.
- "United States Census, 1930", , FamilySearch (https://www.familysearch.org/ark:/61903/1:1:X4T1-VDJ : Mon Jul 08 19:59:28 UTC 2024), Entry for Victor C Perrino and Carrie Perrino, 1930.
- "United States Census, 1930", , FamilySearch (https://www.familysearch.org/ark:/61903/1:1:XMZZ-WWP : Fri Mar 08 02:00:48 UTC 2024), Entry for Joseph Garafano and Mary S Garafano, 1930.
- "United States Census, 1940", , FamilySearch (https://www.familysearch.org/ark:/61903/1:1:VYHN-4GQ : Fri Mar 08 23:28:37 UTC 2024), Entry for Joseph Garafano and Mary Garafano, 1940.
- "New York, New York City, World War II Draft Registration Cards, 1940-1947", , FamilySearch (https://www.familysearch.org/ark:/61903/1:1:WZ9F-SW3Z : Sat Mar 09 03:15:01 UTC 2024), Entry for Victor Vincent Perrino and Unemployed, 16 Oct 1940.
- "Vermont Vital Records, 1760-2008," , FamilySearch (https://familysearch.org/ark:/61903/1:1:KFR1-3RB : 6 December 2014), Victor Vincent Perrino and Louise Teresa Garafano, Marriage, 16 Aug 1942, Rutland, Rutland, Vermont, United States; from "Vermont, Birth Records, 1909-2008," "Vermont, Death Records, 1909-2008," "Vermont, Marriage Records, 1909-2008," and "Vermont, Vital Records, 1720-1908." Ancestry (http://www.ancestry.com : 2010); citing Vital Records Office, Vermont Department of Health, Burlington and New England Historic Genealogical Society, Boston.
- "Vermont Vital Records, 1760-1954", , FamilySearch (https://www.familysearch.org/ark:/61903/1:1:VNRR-CYN : Sat Mar 09 05:17:19 UTC 2024), Entry for Victor Vincent Perrino and Victor Perrino, 16 Aug 1942.
- "Vermont Vital Records, 1760-2008," , FamilySearch (https://familysearch.org/ark:/61903/1:1:KFR6-9DY : 6 December 2014), Victor Vincent Perrino and Louise Teresa Gararano, Marriage, 16 Aug 1942, Rutland, Vermont, United States; from "Vermont, Birth Records, 1909-2008," "Vermont, Death Records, 1909-2008," "Vermont, Marriage Records, 1909-2008," and "Vermont, Vital Records, 1720-1908." Ancestry (http://www.ancestry.com : 2010); citing Vital Records Office, Vermont Department of Health, Burlington and New England Historic Genealogical Society, Boston.
- "Vermont Vital Records, 1760-1954", , FamilySearch (https://www.familysearch.org/ark:/61903/1:1:VN51-LR7 : Sat Mar 09 09:11:43 UTC 2024), Entry for Victor Vincent Perrino and Louise Teresa Garafano, 16 Aug 1942.
- "United States Census, 1950", , FamilySearch (https://www.familysearch.org/ark:/61903/1:1:6X5D-ZM8G : Tue Mar 19 17:12:06 UTC 2024), Entry for Victor V Perrino and Louise T Perrino, 10 April 1950.
- "United States Social Security Death Index," database, FamilySearch (https://familysearch.org/ark:/61903/1:1:VML3-CZP : 7 January 2021), Victor Perrino, Oct 1981; citing U.S. Social Security Administration, Death Master File, database (Alexandria, Virginia: National Technical Information Service, ongoing).

- "United States, Social Security Numerical Identification Files (NUMIDENT), 1936-2007", database, FamilySearch (https://www.familysearch.org/ark:/61903/1:1:6KMS-RH8Y : 10 February 2023), Louise Garafano Perrino, .
- "Sacred Heart, Schenectady, New York, Deaths (Mar 1904 -Jul 2001)", American-Canadian Genealogical Society, Manchester, NH, page 106
- "St. John the Baptist, Schenectady, New York, Beaths (Jan 1886 - Jun 2009)", 2 Volumes, American-Canadian Genealogical Society, Manchester, NH page 624

426) Maria Archina D'Antuono

Maria Archina D'Antuono(426) was born on 31 October 1911, in Ariano, Italy, to Nicola Maria d'Antuono(135a) and Concetta Manganiello(135).

Maria Archina D'Antuono(426) married Michele Puorro(426a) on 23 November 1931 in Ariano, Italy.

Michele Puorro(426a) was born about 1909, in Ariano, Italy, to Giuseppe Puorro(426aF) and Rosaria Costanzo(426aM).

Records that include Maria Archina D'Antuono(426) and/or Michele Puorro(426a):
- Ariano, Italy 1911 Birth Act #513
- Ariano, Italy 1931 Marriage Act #P.II.A.175

427) Raimondo Carmine Manganiello

Raimondo Carmine Manganiello(427) was born on 3 November 1911 in Ariano, Italy, to Vincenzo Manganiello(193) and Elena Morante(193a).

Raimondo Carmine Manganiello(427) married Maria Michele Comanzo(427a) on 4 April 1935 in Ariano, Italy.

Maria Michele Comanzo(427a) was born on 2 May 1910 in Ariano, Italy, to Pietro Comanzo(427aF) and Lucrezia Corsano(427aM). Maria Michele Comanzo(427a)died in Ariano, Italy, on 17 Dec 1981.

Records that include Raimondo Carmine Manganiello(427) and/or Maria Michele Comanzo(427a):
- Ariano, Italy 1910 Birth Act #302
- Ariano, Italy 1911 Birth Act #519
- Ariano, Italy 1935 Marriage Act #P.IIA.41

428) Luciano Miseno

Luciano Miseno(428) was born on 13 December 1911, in Amsterdam, NY, to Ugo Miseno(238a) and Ugo Concetta Felicia Perrina(238). Luciano Miseno(428) died 30 June 1988 in Amsterdam, NY

Luciano Miseno(428) married Clara C. [Zaklukiewicz] Zack(428a) on 2 May 1936 in New York.

Clara C. [Zaklukiewicz] Zack(428a) was born on 13 October 1917, to James Zaklukiewicz(428aF) and Mary M Brzezinska(428aM). Clara C. [Zaklukiewicz] Zack(428a) died 7 September 2011 in Amsterdam, NY.

Luciano Miseno(428) and Clara C. [Zaklukiewicz] Zack(428a) had child(ren).

Records that include Luciano Miseno(428) and/or Clara C. [Zaklukiewicz] Zack(428a):
- "New York, Birth Indexes outside of New York City, 1881-1942", , FamilySearch (https://www.familysearch.org/ark:/61903/1:1:6FH2-MZCB : Thu Mar 07 20:13:08 UTC 2024), Entry for Lucyanno Miseno, 13 Dec 1911.
- "New York, Birth Indexes outside of New York City, 1881-1942", , FamilySearch (https://www.familysearch.org/ark:/61903/1:1:6FFK-YB4Q : Fri Mar 08 03:33:03 UTC 2024), Entry for Clara C Zaklukiewics, 13 Oct 1917.

- "United States Census, 1920", , FamilySearch
  (https://www.familysearch.org/ark:/61903/1:1:MJGD-61J : Sun Mar 10
  00:46:08 UTC 2024), Entry for Ugo Mireno and Concetta Mireno, 1920.
- "United States Census, 1920", , FamilySearch
  (https://www.familysearch.org/ark:/61903/1:1:MJG6-88X : Sun Mar 10
  16:37:53 UTC 2024), Entry for James Zakluberwicz and Mary
  Zakluberwicz, 1920.
- "United States Census, 1930", , FamilySearch
  (https://www.familysearch.org/ark:/61903/1:1:X78V-MMP : Sun Mar 10
  13:54:09 UTC 2024), Entry for Hugo Misseno and Conncetta Misseno,
  1930.
- "United States Census, 1930", , FamilySearch
  (https://www.familysearch.org/ark:/61903/1:1:X78N-B5S : Wed Jul 17
  16:02:20 UTC 2024), Entry for James Zaklukiewicz and Mary
  Zaklukiewicz, 1930.
- "United States Census, 1950", , FamilySearch
  (https://www.familysearch.org/ark:/61903/1:1:6XY9-MXQG : Wed Mar 20
  21:59:45 UTC 2024), Entry for Lawrence Miseno and Clara C Miseno,
  10 April 1950.
- "United States Social Security Death Index," database, FamilySearch
  (https://familysearch.org/ark:/61903/1:1:JBPX-623 : 7 January
  2021), Lawrence L Miseno, 30 Jun 1988; citing U.S. Social Security
  Administration, Death Master File, database (Alexandria, Virginia:
  National Technical Information Service, ongoing).
- "United States, Social Security Numerical Identification Files
  (NUMIDENT), 1936-2007", database, FamilySearch
  (https://www.familysearch.org/ark:/61903/1:1:6KMG-QRCF : 10
  February 2023), Ugo Miseno in entry for Lawrence Luciano Miseno, .
- "Find a Grave Index," database, FamilySearch
  (https://www.familysearch.org/ark:/61903/1:1:6ND5-HXXV : 11 August
  2022), Lawrence L Miseno, ; Burial, Amsterdam, Montgomery, New
  York, United States of America, Saint Stanislaus Cemetery; citing
  record ID 240896813, Find a Grave, http://www.findagrave.com.
- "United States Social Security Death Index," database, FamilySearch
  (https://familysearch.org/ark:/61903/1:1:VHCC-F51 : 12 January
  2021), Clara C Miseno, 07 Sep 2011; citing U.S. Social Security
  Administration, Death Master File, database (Alexandria, Virginia:
  National Technical Information Service, ongoing).

429) John B Anastasio

John B Anastasio(429) was born on 20 December 1911, in Connecticut, to
Francesco (Frank) Paul Anastasio(166) and Hilda (Gilda) Marcotti(166a). John B
Anastasio(429) died on 24 November 1984, in Wisconsin.

John B Anastasio(429) married Helen Steinman(429a).

Helen Steinman(429a) was born in Wisconsin about 1913. Helen Steinman(429a)
was previously married to Frank Schaffer(429aX).

John B Anastasio(429) and Helen Steinman(429a) had child(ren).

Records that include John B Anastasio(429) and/or Helen Steinman(429a):
- "United States Census, 1920", , FamilySearch
  (https://www.familysearch.org/ark:/61903/1:1:MFL9-JJ6 : Sun Mar 10
  05:10:16 UTC 2024), Entry for Frank P Anastasio and Gilda
  Anastasio, 1920.
- "United States Census, 1930", , FamilySearch
  (https://www.familysearch.org/ark:/61903/1:1:X9SJ-2LK : Sat Mar 09
  02:41:12 UTC 2024), Entry for Frank Anastasio and Hilda Anastasio,
  1930.
- "United States Census, 1940", , FamilySearch
  (https://www.familysearch.org/ark:/61903/1:1:K7J6-HTQ : Sat Mar 09
  04:26:52 UTC 2024), Entry for Frank P Anastascio and Jilda
  Anastascio, 1940.
- "United States 1950 Census", , FamilySearch
  (https://www.familysearch.org/ark:/61903/1:1:6F93-CGRX : Fri Oct 06
  08:47:30 UTC 2023), Entry for Susan C Schaffer and John B
  Anastasio, Apr 1, 1950.

- https://journaltimes.newspapers.com/article/the-journal-times-
  obituary-for-frank-p/83018176/
- "Wisconsin Death Index, 1959-1997", , FamilySearch
  (https://www.familysearch.org/ark:/61903/1:1:V8SV-PMP : 8 January
  2022), John B Anastasio, 1984.

430) <u>Concetta Angiolina Sicuranza</u>

Concetta Angiolina Sicuranza(430) was born on 16 January 1912, in Ariano,
Italy, to Nicola Sicuranza(203a) and Maria Raimonda Foderella(203).

Records that include Concetta Angiolina Sicuranza(430):
- Ariano, Italy 1912 Birth Act #33

431) <u>Virgilia Scanzillo</u>

Virginia Scanzillo(431) was born on 12 April 1912, in New York, NY, to Gaetano
Scauzillo(164) and Giovanna Grasso(196).

Records that include Virginia Scanzillo(431):
- "United States Census, 1920", , FamilySearch
  (https://www.familysearch.org/ark:/61903/1:1:MJG5-1XL : Wed Mar 06
  20:43:44 UTC 2024), Entry for Gaetano Scanzilla and Jannie
  Scanzilla, 1920.
- "United States Census, 1930", , FamilySearch
  (https://www.familysearch.org/ark:/61903/1:1:X7D4-SB4 : Sun Mar 10
  21:34:02 UTC 2024), Entry for Gaetano Scanzillo and Guanina
  Scanzillo, 1930.
- "United States Census, 1940", , FamilySearch
  (https://www.familysearch.org/ark:/61903/1:1:KQBN-826 : Sat Mar 09
  01:41:31 UTC 2024), Entry for Gaetano Scanzillo and Jennie
  Scanzillo, 1940.
- "United States 1950 Census", , FamilySearch
  (https://www.familysearch.org/ark:/61903/1:1:6XYM-9X8P : Tue Mar 19
  16:01:57 UTC 2024), Entry for Virginia Scanzillo and Gaetano
  Scanzillo, 10 April 1950.

432) <u>Aurora (Mary) Vernacchia</u>

Aurora (Mary) Vernacchia(432) was born on 6 May 1912, in , to Francesco Paolo
Vernacchia(144a) and Rosa Grasso(144). Aurora (Mary) Vernacchia(432) died 20
August 1992, in Bronx, NY.

Aurora (Mary) Vernacchia(432) married Frank Messina(432a) on 26 July 1933, in
New York, NY.

<u>Frank Messina</u>(432a) was born on 11 March 1908, in Jersey City, NJ, to Mariano
Messina(432aF) and Fanny Messelotta(432aM). Frank Messina(432a) died 27
October 1998, in Bronx, NY.

Aurora (Mary) Vernacchia(432) and Frank Messina(432a) had child(ren).

Records that include Aurora (Mary) Vernacchia(432) and/or Frank Messina(432a):
- "New York, State Census, 1915", , FamilySearch
  (https://www.familysearch.org/ark:/61903/1:1:K9FC-ZB1 : 4 June
  2022), Frank Vernachio, 1915.
- "United States, Census, 1920", FamilySearch
  (https://www.familysearch.org/ark:/61903/1:1:MJPD-KYN : Thu Jan 16
  03:46:43 UTC 2025), Entry for Frank Vernacchia and Rose Vernacchia,
  1920.
- "United States, Census, 1920", FamilySearch
  (https://www.familysearch.org/ark:/61903/1:1:MJPD-1QY : Wed Jan 15
  21:13:21 UTC 2025), Entry for Fannie Messeni and Mensi Messeni,
  1920.
- "United States, Census, 1930", FamilySearch
  (https://www.familysearch.org/ark:/61903/1:1:X76D-NTR : Tue Jul 16
  02:48:15 UTC 2024), Entry for Paul Vernacchia and Rose Vernacchia,
  1930.

- "United States, Census, 1930", FamilySearch
  (https://www.familysearch.org/ark:/61903/1:1:X766-3J9 : Sat Mar 09
  19:33:05 UTC 2024), Entry for Fannie Messina and Vincent Messina,
  1930.
- "New York, New York City Marriage Records, 1829-1938", FamilySearch
  (https://www.familysearch.org/ark:/61903/1:1:Q2CF-7VG3 : Fri Mar 08
  20:27:02 UTC 2024), Entry for Frank Messina and Mary Vernacchia, 26
  July 1933.
- "New York, New York City, World War II Draft Registration Cards,
  1940-1947", FamilySearch
  (https://www.familysearch.org/ark:/61903/1:1:W485-5KPZ : Sat Apr 12
  14:45:33 UTC 2025), Entry for Frank Messina and None, 16 Oct 1940.
- "United States, Census, 1950", FamilySearch
  (https://www.familysearch.org/ark:/61903/1:1:6XTR-2QGL : Fri Oct 06
  13:33:40 UTC 2023), Entry for Frank Messina and Mary Messina, 3
  April 1950.
- "United States, Social Security Numerical Identification Files
  (NUMIDENT), 1936-2007", FamilySearch
  (https://www.familysearch.org/ark:/61903/1:1:6K97-SJZB : Sat Apr 26
  02:23:25 UTC 2025), Entry for Mary Messina and Frank P Vernacchio.
- "United States, Social Security Death Index," database,
  FamilySearch (https://familysearch.org/ark:/61903/1:1:JPHZ-SMP : 7
  January 2021), Frank Messina, 27 Oct 1998; citing U.S. Social
  Security Administration, Death Master File, database (Alexandria,
  Virginia: National Technical Information Service, ongoing).
- "United States, Social Security Numerical Identification Files
  (NUMIDENT), 1936-2007", FamilySearch
  (https://www.familysearch.org/ark:/61903/1:1:6KM5-KGB6 : Fri Apr 25
  22:54:50 UTC 2025), Entry for Maryann Aversa and Frank Messina.
- "United States, Social Security Numerical Identification Files
  (NUMIDENT), 1936-2007", FamilySearch
  (https://www.familysearch.org/ark:/61903/1:1:6KM1-37VH : Sat Apr 26
  15:50:43 UTC 2025), Entry for Frank P Messina and Frank Messina.

433) Paul (Frank) Perrine

Paul (Frank) Perrine(433) was born 31 May 1912, in Winton, PA, to Carmine
Perrina(247) and Colomba di Pasquale(247a). Paul (Frank) Perrine(433) died 22
Aug 1987 in Los Angeles, CA.

Paul (Frank) Perrine(433) married and divorced Dorothy Dale Davis(433a).

Dorothy Dale Davis(433a) was born 16 February 1920, in Pittsburg, TX, to Henry
Pierce Davis(433aF) and Virginia Mae Johnston(433aM). Dorothy Dale Davis(433a)
died November 1981 in Los Angeles, CA.

Dorothy Dale Davis(433a) later married James Widley Basford(433ab) and
(unknown) Gattis(433ac).

Paul (Frank) Perrine(433) and Dorothy Dale Davis(433a) had Child(ren).

Records that include Paul (Frank) Perrine(433) and/or Dorothy Dale
Davis(433a):
- https://www.pa.gov/content/dam/copapwp-
  pagov/en/phmc/documents/archives/research-online/documents/1912%20-
  %20P.PDF page 137
- "United States Census, 1920", , FamilySearch
  (https://www.familysearch.org/ark:/61903/1:1:MFY4-Q5M : Wed Mar 06
  09:48:19 UTC 2024), Entry for O Dena Perine and Colombine Perine,
  1920.
- "United States Census, 1930", , FamilySearch
  (https://www.familysearch.org/ark:/61903/1:1:X7CK-1B8 : Fri Jul 05
  22:27:03 UTC 2024), Entry for Carmino Perrine and Columbia Perrine,
  1930.
- "United States Census, 1940", , FamilySearch
  (https://www.familysearch.org/ark:/61903/1:1:KQ53-VDG : Tue Jul 23
  10:44:20 UTC 2024), Entry for Carmen Perrone and Columba Perrone,
  1940.
- "United States Census, 1950", , FamilySearch
  (https://www.familysearch.org/ark:/61903/1:1:6XGH-Q8P4 : Thu Oct 05
  16:06:19 UTC 2023), Entry for Frank P Perrine, 7 April 1950.

- "California Death Index, 1940-1997," database, FamilySearch (https://familysearch.org/ark:/61903/1:1:VPMX-XT5 : 26 November 2014), Frank Paul Perrine, 22 Aug 1987; Department of Public Health Services, Sacramento.
- "United States, Social Security Numerical Identification Files (NUMIDENT), 1936-2007", database, FamilySearch (https://www.familysearch.org/ark:/61903/1:1:6K93-VP9Z : 10 February 2023), Frank P Perrine, .
- "United States Social Security Death Index," database, FamilySearch (https://familysearch.org/ark:/61903/1:1:JPH3-B3J : 7 January 2021), Frank P Perrine, 22 Aug 1987; citing U.S. Social Security Administration, Death Master File, database (Alexandria, Virginia: National Technical Information Service, ongoing).
- https://www.newspapers.com/newspage/875694146/
- "Texas Birth Certificates, 1903-1935", , FamilySearch (https://www.familysearch.org/ark:/61903/1:1:X2TW-6ZN : Fri Mar 08 10:00:56 UTC 2024), Entry for Dorthia Dail Davis and H P Davis, 16 Feb 1920.
- "United States Census, 1930", , FamilySearch (https://www.familysearch.org/ark:/61903/1:1:SP4W-Q9R : Mon Jul 08 00:41:58 UTC 2024), Entry for Henry P Davis and May Davis, 1930.
- "California Birth Index, 1905-1995," database, FamilySearch (https://familysearch.org/ark:/61903/1:1:V277-P18 : 27 November 2014), Davis in entry for Sissa Diane Perrine, 10 Jan 1943; citing Los Angeles, California, United States, Department of Health Services, Vital Statistics Department, Sacramento.
- "California, County Marriages, 1850-1953", , FamilySearch (https://www.familysearch.org/ark:/61903/1:1:K82Z-HPK : Sat Mar 09 17:54:39 UTC 2024), Entry for James Widley Basford and Dorothy Dale Perrine, 24 September 1950.
- "United States Census, 1950", , FamilySearch (https://www.familysearch.org/ark:/61903/1:1:6XGS-3WSQ : Fri Oct 06 10:51:30 UTC 2023), Entry for Dorothy C Davis and Diane S Perrine, 3 April 1950.
- "California, County Marriages, 1850-1953", , FamilySearch (https://www.familysearch.org/ark:/61903/1:1:K82Z-HPK : Sat Mar 09 17:54:39 UTC 2024), Entry for James Widley Basford and Dorothy Dale Perrine, 24 September 1950.
- "California Death Index, 1940-1997," database, FamilySearch (https://familysearch.org/ark:/61903/1:1:VP6Q-MMB : 26 November 2014), Dorothy Dale Gattis, 23 Nov 1981; Department of Public Health Services, Sacramento.
- "United States Social Security Death Index," database, FamilySearch (https://familysearch.org/ark:/61903/1:1:VMMH-26X : 11 January 2021), Dorothy Gattis, Nov 1981; citing U.S. Social Security Administration, Death Master File, database (Alexandria, Virginia: National Technical Information Service, ongoing).

434) Joseph Miressi

Joseph Miressi(434) was born on 27 July 1912, in Westchester County, NY, to Generoso Miressi(160) and Maria Luigia Iannarone(160a). Joseph Miressi(434) died 5 July 1994 in Wilmington, NC.

Joseph Miressi(434) married Josephine (Julia) DeMicco(434a).

Josephine (Julia) DeMicco(434a) was born on 21 August 1906, in Italy, to Louis DeMicco(434aF) and Gelsomina (Josephine) Incerto(434aM). Josephine (Julia) DeMicco(434a) died 1 May 1974 in Pelham, NY.

Joseph Miressi(434) and/or Josephine (Julia) DeMicco(434a) had child(ren).

Records that include Joseph Miressi(434) and/or Josephine (Julia) DeMicco(434a):
- "United States Census, 1910", , FamilySearch (https://www.familysearch.org/ark:/61903/1:1:M5C9-FPW : Sun Mar 10 12:44:29 UTC 2024), Entry for Louis De Micco and Gelmina De Micco, 1910.

- "United States Census, 1920", , FamilySearch (https://www.familysearch.org/ark:/61903/1:1:MV34-K9S : Sat Mar 09 09:14:40 UTC 2024), Entry for Louis Demicco and Josephine Demicco, 1920.
- "United States Census, 1930", , FamilySearch (https://www.familysearch.org/ark:/61903/1:1:X4G6-NM9 : Sat Mar 09 03:25:50 UTC 2024), Entry for Generoso Miressi and Mary L Miressi, 1930.
- "United States Census, 1930", , FamilySearch (https://www.familysearch.org/ark:/61903/1:1:X4GZ-Y3T : Sun Mar 10 02:30:15 UTC 2024), Entry for Louis Demicco and Josephine Demicco, 1930.
- "United States Census, 1940", , FamilySearch (https://www.familysearch.org/ark:/61903/1:1:KQ3Y-YJL : Sun Mar 10 01:38:39 UTC 2024), Entry for Joseph Miressi and Josephine J Miressi, 1940.
- "United States 1950 Census", , FamilySearch (https://www.familysearch.org/ark:/61903/1:1:6XTY-L9J8 : Wed Mar 20 13:35:56 UTC 2024), Entry for Joseph Miressi and Josephine Miressi, 18 April 1950.
- "North Carolina Deaths and Burials, 1898-1994", database, FamilySearch (https://familysearch.org/ark:/61903/1:1:HH9K-5PT2 : 21 January 2020), Joseph John Miressi, .
- "United States Social Security Death Index," database, FamilySearch (https://familysearch.org/ark:/61903/1:1:JTBV-VZ3 : 7 January 2021), Josephine Miressi, May 1974; citing U.S. Social Security Administration, Death Master File, database (Alexandria, Virginia: National Technical Information Service, ongoing).
- "United States, Social Security Numerical Identification Files (NUMIDENT), 1936-2007", database, FamilySearch (https://www.familysearch.org/ark:/61903/1:1:6K93-TDYF : 10 February 2023), Joseph John Miressi, .
- "Find a Grave Index," database, FamilySearch (https://www.familysearch.org/ark:/61903/1:1:6PY3-2C1P : 8 November 2023), Josephine Julia DeMicco Miressi, ; Burial, New Rochelle, Westchester, New York, United States of America, Holy Sepulchre Cemetery; citing record ID 260523180, Find a Grave, http://www.findagrave.com.
- "Find a Grave Index," database, FamilySearch (https://www.familysearch.org/ark:/61903/1:1:6PY3-KHSY : 8 November 2023), John Joseph Miressi, ; Burial, New Rochelle, Westchester, New York, United States of America, Holy Sepulchre Cemetery; citing record ID 260522632, Find a Grave, http://www.findagrave.com.

435) Giuseppe LoConte

Giuseppe LoConte(435) was born on 30 August 1912 in Ariano, Italy, to Francesco Paolo LoConte(205a) and Carmela Manganiello(205).

Giuseppe LoConte(435) married Filomena Miedico(435a) on 22 February 1937 in Bivino, Italy.

Giuseppe LoConte(435) married Nicoletta Borgo(435b) on 2 may 1950.

NOTE:Marriages are noted on the birth record.

Records that include Giuseppe LoConte(435):
- Ariano, Italy 1912 Birth Act#416

436) Eleanor Lombardi

Eleanor Lombardi(436) was born 17 October 1912, in New York, NY, to Feliciano (Phillip White) Lombardi(236) and Mabel Grassie(236a). Eleanor Lombardi(436) died on 8 January 1999.

Eleanor Lombardi(436) married Giuseppe Castrogiovanni(436a) on 26 April 1936, in Kings, NY.

Giuseppe Castrogiovanni(436a) was born on 12 February 1913, in "Via Monte", Italy, to Francesco Castrogiovanni(436aF) and Mary Capillo(436aM). Giuseppe Castrogiovanni(436a) arrived in New York, NY, on 14 April 1918, on board the ship SS Sant'Anna. On 9 February 1937, Giuseppe Castrogiovanni(436a) applied for United States Citizenship. Giuseppe Castrogiovanni(436a) died on 19 December 1996, in New York. Giuseppe Castrogiovanni(436a) was a plumber.

Records that include Eleanor Lombardi(436) and/or Giuseppe Castrogiovanni(436a):

- "United States Census, 1920", , FamilySearch (https://www.familysearch.org/ark:/61903/1:1:MJPX-9XN : Thu Mar 07 22:40:59 UTC 2024), Entry for Felice Lombardi and Mabel Lombardi, 1920.
- "United States Census, 1930", , FamilySearch (https://www.familysearch.org/ark:/61903/1:1:X4N2-Q8Y : Fri Mar 08 12:04:44 UTC 2024), Entry for Frank Castro and Mary Castro, 1930.
- "New York, U.S. District and Circuit Court Naturalization Records, 1824-1991", , FamilySearch (https://www.familysearch.org/ark:/61903/1:1:621B-51YC : Thu Mar 07 09:26:28 UTC 2024), Entry for Giuseppe or Joseph Castregievanni and Eleanore, 9 Nov 1936.
- "New York, New York City Marriage Records, 1829-1938", , FamilySearch (https://www.familysearch.org/ark:/61903/1:1:Q2CF-FPC2 : Sat Mar 09 17:19:11 UTC 2024), Entry for Joseph Castroziavanni and Eleanor C Lombardi, 26 April 1936.
- "New York, New York City, World War II Draft Registration Cards, 1940-1947", , FamilySearch (https://www.familysearch.org/ark:/61903/1:1:WZHY-BMW2 : Sun Mar 10 11:19:29 UTC 2024), Entry for Joseph Frank Castrogiovanni or Castro and George E Curtis, 16 Oct 1940.
- "United States Census, 1940", , FamilySearch (https://www.familysearch.org/ark:/61903/1:1:KQR7-GMV : Sat Mar 09 07:35:47 UTC 2024), Entry for Joseph Castro and Eleanor Castro, 1940.
- "United States 1950 Census", , FamilySearch (https://www.familysearch.org/ark:/61903/1:1:6XR7-1DTL : Sat Oct 07 00:51:14 UTC 2023), Entry for Joseph Castro and Elenore Castro, 6 April 1950.
- "United States, Social Security Numerical Identification Files (NUMIDENT), 1936-2007", database, FamilySearch (https://www.familysearch.org/ark:/61903/1:1:6KML-8M8J : 10 February 2023), Joseph Frank Castrogiovanni, .
- "United States Social Security Death Index," database, FamilySearch (https://familysearch.org/ark:/61903/1:1:J5BB-C6Y : 7 January 2021), Joseph Castrogiovan, 19 Dec 1996; citing U.S. Social Security Administration, Death Master File, database (Alexandria, Virginia: National Technical Information Service, ongoing).
- "United States, Social Security Numerical Identification Files (NUMIDENT), 1936-2007", database, FamilySearch (https://www.familysearch.org/ark:/61903/1:1:6KMN-L3H4 : 10 February 2023), Eleanor Castrogiovanni, .
- "United States Social Security Death Index," database, FamilySearch (https://familysearch.org/ark:/61903/1:1:J51Z-D2H : 7 January 2021), Eleanor Castrogiova, 08 Jan 1999; citing U.S. Social Security Administration, Death Master File, database (Alexandria, Virginia: National Technical Information Service, ongoing).

437) Teresa Alba Perrino

Teresa Alba Perrino(437) was born on 7 November 1912, in Concord, NH, to Liberatore Perrina(200) and Carmenella Gammaroto(200a). Teresa Alba Perrino(437) died 8 September 2001 in Concord, NH.

Teresa Alba Perrino(437) married Albert DeFelice(437a) on 5 April, 1942 in Concord, NH.

Albert DeFelice(437a) was born on 17 Aug 1914 in Keene, NH, to Alexander DeFelice(437aF) and Avelina Buci(437aM). Albert DeFelice(437a) died on 16 January 1969 in Concord, NH.

Records that include Teresa Alba Perrino(437) and/or Albert DeFelice(437a):

- "United States Census, 1920", , FamilySearch
  (https://www.familysearch.org/ark:/61903/1:1:MH8R-RXT : Sat Mar 09
  02:30:10 UTC 2024), Entry for Liberatore Perrino and Carmela
  Perrino, 1920.

- "United States Census, 1930", , FamilySearch
  (https://www.familysearch.org/ark:/61903/1:1:X7NK-BXM : Sat Mar 09
  13:58:16 UTC 2024), Entry for Liberatone Perrino and Carmirella
  Perrino, 1930.

- "United States Census, 1940", , FamilySearch
  (https://www.familysearch.org/ark:/61903/1:1:VT94-72P : Sat Mar 09
  20:05:01 UTC 2024), Entry for Liberstore Perrins and Carmella
  Perrins, 1940.

- "United States Census, 1940", , FamilySearch
  (https://www.familysearch.org/ark:/61903/1:1:VYH2-WK8 : Sat Mar 09
  04:10:18 UTC 2024), Entry for Carlo Regione and Stephan Defelice,
  1940.

- "Vermont, Town Clerk, Vital and Town Records, 1732-2005", ,
  FamilySearch (https://www.familysearch.org/ark:/61903/1:1:QPQX-9B92
  : Sat Mar 09 04:23:04 UTC 2024), Entry for Albert De Felice and
  Teresa Alba Perrino, 5 April 1942.

- "United States World War II Army Enlistment Records, 1938-1946," ,
  FamilySearch (https://familysearch.org/ark:/61903/1:1:K85P-T16 : 5
  December 2014), Albert De Felice, enlisted 14 Apr 1941, Rutland,
  Vermont, United States; citing "Electronic Army Serial Number
  Merged File, ca. 1938-1946," database, The National Archives:
  Access to Archival Databases (AAD) (http://aad.archives.gov :
  National Archives and Records Administration, 2002); NARA NAID
  1263923, National Archives at College Park, Maryland.

- "New Hampshire Marriage Records, 1637-1947", , FamilySearch
  (https://www.familysearch.org/ark:/61903/1:1:FLX1-S4T : Sat Mar 09
  05:45:30 UTC 2024), Entry for Albert Defelice and Teresa Alba
  Perrino, 1942.

- "Vermont, Town Clerk, Vital and Town Records, 1732-2005", ,
  FamilySearch (https://www.familysearch.org/ark:/61903/1:1:QPQX-9B92
  : Sat Mar 09 04:23:04 UTC 2024), Entry for Albert De Felice and
  Teresa Alba Perrino, 5 April 1942.

- "United States, Social Security Numerical Identification Files
  (NUMIDENT), 1936-2007", database, FamilySearch
  (https://www.familysearch.org/ark:/61903/1:1:6KMS-4Y67 : 10
  February 2023), Teresa Alba Perrino, .

- "United States Social Security Death Index," database, FamilySearch
  (https://familysearch.org/ark:/61903/1:1:JK8F-WZ6 : 7 January
  2021), Albert Defelice, Jan 1969; citing U.S. Social Security
  Administration, Death Master File, database (Alexandria, Virginia:
  National Technical Information Service, ongoing).

- "Find a Grave Index," database, FamilySearch
  (https://www.familysearch.org/ark:/61903/1:1:6ZR3-K9W2 : 2 June
  2022), Teresa A Perrino DeFelice, ; Burial, Concord, Merrimack, New
  Hampshire, United States of America, Calvary Cemetery; citing
  record ID 226598504, Find a Grave, http://www.findagrave.com.

- "Find a Grave Index," database, FamilySearch
  (https://www.familysearch.org/ark:/61903/1:1:6ZR3-6Z48 : 2 June
  2022), Albert DeFelice, ; Burial, Concord, Merrimack, New
  Hampshire, United States of America, Calvary Cemetery; citing
  record ID 226598441, Find a Grave, http://www.findagrave.com.

438) Giovanni Raffaele (John) DeMeo

Giovanni Raffaele (John) DeMeo(438) was born on 28 November 1912, in
Schenectady, NY, to Angelo DeMeo(202a) and Maria Perrina(202). Giovanni
Raffaele (John) DeMeo(438) died on 7 November 2012 in Schenectady, NY.

Giovanni Raffaele (John) DeMeo(438) married Lucy Mary Dipasquale(438a) on 26
October 1957 in Schenectady, NY.

Lucy Mary Dipasquale(438a) was born on 7 March 1912 in Ballston Spa, NY, to
Anthony Dipasquale(438aF) and Mary N. Guide(438aM). Lucy Mary Dipasquale(438a)
died on 11 April 2001, in Schenectady, NY.

Giovanni Raffaele (John) DeMeo(438) and Lucy Mary Dipasquale(438a) had Child(ren).

Records that include Giovanni Raffaele (John) DeMeo(438) and/or Lucy Mary Dipasquale(438a):

- "St. Anthony, Schenectady, New York, Baptism (Sep 1912 - May 2007)", 2 Volumes American-Canadian Genealogical Society, Manchester, NH, page 262
- "United States Census, 1920", , FamilySearch (https://www.familysearch.org/ark:/61903/1:1:MVS4-RRY : Fri Mar 08 05:51:12 UTC 2024), Entry for Angelo Demeo and Mary Demeo, 1920.
- "United States Census, 1930", , FamilySearch (https://www.familysearch.org/ark:/61903/1:1:X4TT-YB5 : Mon Mar 11 01:35:37 UTC 2024), Entry for Angelo De Meo and Mary De Meo, 1930.
- "United States 1950 Census", , FamilySearch (https://www.familysearch.org/ark:/61903/1:1:6XYQ-7YHK : Thu Oct 05 17:34:17 UTC 2023), Entry for John R Demeo and Lucy M Demeo, May 6, 1950.
- "United States, Social Security Numerical Identification Files (NUMIDENT), 1936-2007", database, FamilySearch (https://www.familysearch.org/ark:/61903/1:1:6KM5-PW2N : 10 February 2023), Lucy Mary De Meo, .
- "United States Social Security Death Index," database, FamilySearch (https://familysearch.org/ark:/61903/1:1:VM2M-2PV : 7 January 2021), Lucy M Demeo, 11 Apr 2001; citing U.S. Social Security Administration, Death Master File, database (Alexandria, Virginia: National Technical Information Service, ongoing).
- "United States, Social Security Numerical Identification Files (NUMIDENT), 1936-2007", database, FamilySearch (https://www.familysearch.org/ark:/61903/1:1:6KM5-PW2N : 10 February 2023), Lucy Mary De Meo, .
- "United States Social Security Death Index," database, FamilySearch (https://familysearch.org/ark:/61903/1:1:K8BV-JY3 : 12 January 2021), John R Demeo, 07 Nov 2012; citing U.S. Social Security Administration, Death Master File, database (Alexandria, Virginia: National Technical Information Service, ongoing).
- "Find a Grave Index," database, FamilySearch (https://www.familysearch.org/ark:/61903/1:1:QVG6-WFPF : 3 July 2020), Lucy M De Meo, ; Burial, , ; citing record ID , Find a Grave, http://www.findagrave.com.
- "Find a Grave Index," database, FamilySearch (https://www.familysearch.org/ark:/61903/1:1:QVG6-WFP6 : 11 January 2023), John Ralph De Meo, ; Burial, Ballston Spa, Saratoga, New York, United States of America, Saint Marys Cemetery; citing record ID 117643252, Find a Grave, http://www.findagrave.com.

439) Eleonora Ninfadoro

Eleonora Ninfadoro(439) was born on 1 January 1913, in Schenectady, NY, to Oto Ninfadoro(165) and Antonia Costanzo(165a).

Records that include Eleonora Ninfadoro(439):

- "New York, Birth Indexes outside of New York City, 1881-1942", , FamilySearch (https://www.familysearch.org/ark:/61903/1:1:6FFG-ZHK2 : Sat Mar 09 05:58:35 UTC 2024), Entry for Alionore A Ninfadore, Jan 1913.
- "United States Census, 1930", , FamilySearch (https://www.familysearch.org/ark:/61903/1:1:X4TB-9PG : Mon Apr 15 09:09:11 UTC 2024), Entry for Otto Ninafodora and Antoinette Ninafodora, 1930.
- "United States Census, 1940", , FamilySearch (https://www.familysearch.org/ark:/61903/1:1:KQY5-TLS : Sun Mar 10 15:51:37 UTC 2024), Entry for Otto Ninfadoro and Antoinette Ninfadoro, 1940.

440) Pietro Riccio

Pietro Riccio(440) was born on 3 January 1913, in Ariano, Italy, to Angelo Maria Riccio(183a) and Raimonda Ciasullo(183). Pietro Riccio(440) died 31 May 1916 in Ariano, Italy.

Records that include Pietro Riccio(440):
- Ariano, Italy 1913 Birth Act #14
- Ariano, Italy 1916 Death Act #111

441) Raffaele Fodarella

Raffaele Fodarella(441) was born on 28 February 1913, in Ariano, Italy, to Luigi Fodarella(188) and Giuditta Marrone(188a). Raffaele Fodarella(441) died in Ariano, Italy on 11 October 1916.

Records that include Raffaele Fodarella(441):
- Ariano, Italy 1913 Birth Act #142
- Ariano, Italy, 1916 Death Act #201

442) Antonietta Ciccarelli

Antonietta Ciccarelli(442) was born on 1 August 1913, in Villanova del Battista, Italy, to Nicola Ciccarelli(241) and Lucia Mincolelli(241a). Antonietta Ciccarelli(442) died on 31 August 1958, in Ariano, Italy.

Antonietta Ciccarelli(442) married Giovanni Battista Zunino(442a), on 14 February 1931, in Martina Olba, Italy.

Giovanni Battista Zunino(442a) was born on 29 Aug 1886, in Martina Olba, Italy, to Giovanni Battista Zunino(442aF) and Luigia Zunino(442aM).

Records that include Antonietta Ciccarelli(442) and/or Giovanni Battista Zunino(442a):
- Villanova del Battista, Italy 1913 Birth Act #69
- Martina Olba, Italy 1886 Birth Act #42
- Ariano, Italy 1931 Marriage Act #PIIA29

443) Anna M. Tiso

Anna M. Tiso(443) was born on 23 August 1913, in Newark, NJ, to Oto (Ottone) Tiso(169) and Mary Senese(169a). Anna M. Tiso(443) died on July 1993 in New Jersey.

Anna M. Tiso(443) married Gerard (Jerry) P. Parcaro(443a).

Gerard (Jerry) P. Parcaro(443a) was born on 2 February 1911, in New Jersey, to Ralph Parcaro(443aF) and Margaret Falvino(443aM). Gerard (Jerry) P. Parcaro(443a) died on 12 July 1994 in Essex, NJ.

Records that include Anna M. Tiso(443) and/or Gerard (Jerry) P. Parcaro(443a):
- "New Jersey, Reclaim the Records, Geographic Birth Index, 1901-1929", , FamilySearch (https://www.familysearch.org/ark:/61903/1:1:6NQZ-4RV5 : Sat Mar 09 17:59:42 UTC 2024), Entry for Anna M. Tiso, 28 Aug 1913.
- "United States Census, 1920", , FamilySearch (https://www.familysearch.org/ark:/61903/1:1:M451-X6W : Sat Mar 09 14:37:36 UTC 2024), Entry for Ottone Tiso and Mary Tiso, 1920.
- "United States Census, 1920", , FamilySearch (https://www.familysearch.org/ark:/61903/1:1:M45L-F4J : Mon Mar 11 00:19:50 UTC 2024), Entry for Ralph Porcaro and Maggie Porcaro, 1920.
- "United States Census, 1930", , FamilySearch (https://www.familysearch.org/ark:/61903/1:1:X4DG-XPV : Fri Mar 08 18:34:06 UTC 2024), Entry for Ottone Liso and Mary H Liso, 1930.
- "United States Census, 1930", , FamilySearch (https://www.familysearch.org/ark:/61903/1:1:X4DB-N4R : Sun Mar 10 09:29:01 UTC 2024), Entry for Ralph Porcaro and Margaret Porcaro, 1930.
- "United States Census, 1940", , FamilySearch (https://www.familysearch.org/ark:/61903/1:1:K4B2-699 : Sun Mar 10 02:46:56 UTC 2024), Entry for Ralph Parcaro and Margaret Parcaro, 1940.

- "United States 1950 Census", , FamilySearch (https://www.familysearch.org/ark:/61903/1:1:6F9G-6914 : Fri Oct 06 03:51:35 UTC 2023), Entry for Jerry P Parcaro and Anna M Parcaro, 21 April 1950.
- "United States Social Security Death Index," database, FamilySearch (https://familysearch.org/ark:/61903/1:1:JR76-TX3 : 7 January 2021), Anna M Parcaro, Jul 1993; citing U.S. Social Security Administration, Death Master File, database (Alexandria, Virginia: National Technical Information Service, ongoing).
- "United States Social Security Death Index," database, FamilySearch (https://familysearch.org/ark:/61903/1:1:JBT7-624 : 7 January 2021), Jerry Parcaro, 12 Jul 1994; citing U.S. Social Security Administration, Death Master File, database (Alexandria, Virginia: National Technical Information Service, ongoing).
- "United States, Social Security Numerical Identification Files (NUMIDENT), 1936-2007", , FamilySearch (https://www.familysearch.org/ark:/61903/1:1:6K9D-7GWM : 10 February 2023), Anna M Parcaro, .
- "United States, Social Security Numerical Identification Files (NUMIDENT), 1936-2007", database, FamilySearch (https://www.familysearch.org/ark:/61903/1:1:6K96-NDQJ : 10 February 2023), Jerry Parcaro, .
- "Find a Grave Index," database, FamilySearch (https://www.familysearch.org/ark:/61903/1:1:QVLZ-3JTV : 12 March 2024), Anna Marie Parcaro, ; Burial, Bloomfield, Essex, New Jersey, United States of America, Glendale Cemetery; citing record ID 90554541, Find a Grave, http://www.findagrave.com.
- "Find a Grave Index," database, FamilySearch (https://www.familysearch.org/ark:/61903/1:1:QVLZ-3JYJ : 12 March 2024), Jerry, ; Burial, Bloomfield, Essex, New Jersey, United States of America, Glendale Cemetery; citing record ID 90554542, Find a Grave, http://www.findagrave.com.

444) Angelo Michele Perrina

Angelo Michele Perrina(444) was born on 29 September 1913, in Villanova del Battista, Italy, to Bennedetto Perrina(239a) and Maria Felicita Perrina(239). Angelo Michele Perrina(444) died 8 March 2000 in Villanova del Battista, Italy.

Records that include Angelo Michele Perrina(444):
- Villanova del Battista, Italy 1913 Birth Act #69
- Villanova del Battista, Italy 2000 Death Act #5 (Death date and Act# mentioned on birth record)

445) Giuseppe Panza

Giuseppe Panza(445) was born on 2 October 1913, in Ariano, Italy, to Ciriaco Panza(152a) and Mariantonia Fodarella(152).

Giuseppe Panza(445) married Vincenza loConte(445a) on 9 February 1939 in Ariano, Italy.

Vincenza loConte(445a) was born on 28 September 1911, in Ariano, Italy, to Generoso loConte(445aF) and Giuseppa Bongo(445aM). Vincenza loConte(445a) died on 26 December 1996 in Ariano, Italy.

Records that include Giuseppe Panza(445) and/or Vincenza loConte(445a):
- Ariano, Italy 1911 Birth Act #457
- Ariano, Italy 1913 Birth Act #533
- Ariano, Italy 1939 Marriage Act #12

446) Sofia (Susie) Perrine

Sofia (Susie) Perrine(446) born in 30 November 1913, in Winton, PA, to Carmine Perrina(247) and Colomba di Pasquale(247a). Sofia (Susie) Perrine(446) died 11 March 1999 in Buffalo, NY

Sofia (Susie) Perrine(446) married George Constantino(446a).

George Constantino(446a) was born on 22 November 1902, in Italy, to Orazio Constantino(446aF) and Jennie Ruffino(446aM). George Constantino(446a) died 26 January 1974 in Buffalo, NY.

Sofia (Susie) Perrine(446) and George Constantino(446a) had child(ren).

Records that include Sofia (Susie) Perrine(446) and/or George Constantino(446a):

- https://www.pa.gov/content/dam/copapwp-pagov/en/phmc/documents/archives/research-online/documents/1913-P.PDF page 130
- "United States Census, 1920", , FamilySearch (https://www.familysearch.org/ark:/61903/1:1:MFY4-Q5M : Wed Mar 06 09:48:19 UTC 2024), Entry for O Dena Perine and Colombine Perine, 1920.
- "United States Census, 1930", , FamilySearch (https://www.familysearch.org/ark:/61903/1:1:X7CK-1B8 : Fri Jul 05 22:27:03 UTC 2024), Entry for Carmino Perrine and Columbia Perrine, 1930.
- "United States Census, 1940", , FamilySearch (https://www.familysearch.org/ark:/61903/1:1:KQ53-VDG : Tue Jul 23 10:44:20 UTC 2024), Entry for Carmen Perrone and Columba Perrone, 1940."United States, Social Security Numerical Identification Files (NUMIDENT), 1936-2007", database, FamilySearch (https://www.familysearch.org/ark:/61903/1:1:6KMJ-CRNK : 10 February 2023), Carmino Perrine in entry for Susie Constantino, .
- "United States Census, 1940", , FamilySearch (https://www.familysearch.org/ark:/61903/1:1:KQBH-GT7 : Sat Mar 09 09:43:29 UTC 2024), Entry for George Constaantio and Susie Constaantio, 1940.
- "United States Census, 1950", , FamilySearch (https://www.familysearch.org/ark:/61903/1:1:6XTY-63JB : Tue Mar 19 05:34:00 UTC 2024), Entry for George Constantino and Susie Constantino, 2 April 1950.
- "United States Social Security Death Index," database, FamilySearch (https://familysearch.org/ark:/61903/1:1:JTT8-722 : 7 January 2021), Susie Constantino, 11 Mar 1999; citing U.S. Social Security Administration, Death Master File, database (Alexandria, Virginia: National Technical Information Service, ongoing).
- "United States, Social Security Numerical Identification Files (NUMIDENT), 1936-2007", database, FamilySearch (https://www.familysearch.org/ark:/61903/1:1:6KMJ-CRNN : 10 February 2023), Susie Constantino, .
- "Find a Grave Index," database, FamilySearch (https://www.familysearch.org/ark:/61903/1:1:6ZWM-CHMF : 15 June 2022), Susie Perrine Constantino, ; Burial, Cheektowaga, Erie, New York, United States of America, Holy Sepulchre Cemetery; citing record ID 220711366, Find a Grave, http://www.findagrave.com.
- "United States Social Security Death Index," database, FamilySearch (https://familysearch.org/ark:/61903/1:1:VSJ4-12X : 7 January 2021), George Constantino, Jan 1974; citing U.S. Social Security Administration, Death Master File, database (Alexandria, Virginia: National Technical Information Service, ongoing).
- "Find a Grave Index," database, FamilySearch (https://www.familysearch.org/ark:/61903/1:1:6ZWM-C4BG : 15 June 2022), George Constantino, ; Burial, Cheektowaga, Erie, New York, United States of America, Holy Sepulchre Cemetery; citing record ID 220711334, Find a Grave, http://www.findagrave.com.
- https://www.newspapers.com/newspage/875694146/
- "United States, Social Security Numerical Identification Files (NUMIDENT), 1936-2007", database, FamilySearch (https://www.familysearch.org/ark:/61903/1:1:6K9Q-RSVX : 10 February 2023), George Constantino in entry for Jenny Constantino, .

447) Filomena Riccio

Filomena Riccio(447) was stillborn on 15 December 1913, in Ariano, Italy, to Raffaele Riccio(221a) and Giovanna (Jenny) Ciasullo(221).

Records that include Filomena Riccio(447):
* Ariano, Italy 1913 Birth Act #668

448) Maria Vincenza Pannese

Maria Vincenza Pannese(448) was born on 23 January 1914, in Ariano, Italy, to Angelo Pannese(213a) and Mariantonia Perrina(213). Maria Vincenza Pannese(448) died on 19 June 1925 in Ariano, Italy.

Records that include Maria Vincenza Pannese(448):
* Ariano, Italy 1914 Birth Act #38
* Ariano, Italy 1925 Death Act #161

449) Francesco Sicuranza

Francesco Sicuranza(449) was born 25 January 1914 in Ariano, Italy, to Nicola Sicuranza(203a) and Maria Raimonda Fodarella(203).

Francesco Sicuranza(449) married Paolina Altavia(449a) on 5 April 1946 in Ariano, Italy.
NOTE: Marriage is noted in the margin of Birth Record.

Records that include Francesco Sicuranza(449) and/or Paolina Altavia(449a):
* Ariano, Italy 1914 Birth Act #68

450) Giacchino /John (Jack) Miressi

Giacchino /John (Jack) Miressi(450) was born 28 March 1914, in New York, to Generoso Miressi(160) and Maria Luigia Iannarone(160a). Giacchino /John (Jack) Miressi(450) died on 17 November 1996.

Giacchino /John (Jack) Miressi(450) married Rose Ferrara(450a).

Rose Ferrara(450a) was born on 2 December 1918, in New York, NY, to Joseph Ferrara(450aF) and Dora Uva(450aM). Rose Ferrara(450a) died on 2 July 1988.

Records that include Giacchino /John (Jack) Miressi(450) and Rose Ferrara(450a):
* "United States Census, 1930", , FamilySearch (https://www.familysearch.org/ark:/61903/1:1:X4G6-NM9 : Sat Mar 09 03:25:50 UTC 2024), Entry for Generoso Miressi and Mary L Miressi, 1930.
* "United States Census, 1940", , FamilySearch (https://www.familysearch.org/ark:/61903/1:1:K3TG-DDM : Fri Mar 08 21:52:57 UTC 2024), Entry for Jack Miressi and Rose Miressi, 1940.
* "New York, New York City, World War II Draft Registration Cards, 1940-1947", , FamilySearch (https://www.familysearch.org/ark:/61903/1:1:WCXF-5K6Z : Sun Mar 10 21:45:37 UTC 2024), Entry for Jack John Miressi and King Kullen Market, 16 Oct 1940.
* "United States 1950 Census", , FamilySearch (https://www.familysearch.org/ark:/61903/1:1:6XRW-9ZX8 : Wed Mar 20 22:52:08 UTC 2024), Entry for Doris Miresse and Linda Miresse, 7 April 1950.
* "United States, Social Security Numerical Identification Files (NUMIDENT), 1936-2007", , FamilySearch (https://www.familysearch.org/ark:/61903/1:1:6K9S-BHPV : 10 February 2023), Jack John Miressi, .
* "United States, Social Security Numerical Identification Files (NUMIDENT), 1936-2007", database, FamilySearch (https://www.familysearch.org/ark:/61903/1:1:6KM1-DQSH : 10 February 2023), Rose Marie Miressi, .
* "United States Social Security Death Index," , FamilySearch (https://familysearch.org/ark:/61903/1:1:JKPS-N25 : 7 January 2021), Rose Miressi, 02 Jul 1988; citing U.S. Social Security Administration, Death Master File, database (Alexandria, Virginia: National Technical Information Service, ongoing).

- "United States, Social Security Numerical Identification Files
  (NUMIDENT), 1936-2007", database, FamilySearch
  (https://www.familysearch.org/ark:/61903/1:1:6K98-N8YN : 10
  February 2023), Giacchino Miressi in entry for Marie Louise
  Miressi, .

451) <u>Edward Paul Anastasio</u>, Colonel, USAF

Edward Paul Anastasio(451), Colonel, USAF was born on 2 April 1914, in
Missouri, to Francesco (Frank) Paul Anastasio(166) and Hilda (Gilda)
Marcotti(166a). Edward Paul Anastasio(451) died on 09 April 1982, in Spokane,
WA. Edward Paul Anastasio(451) was a retired Colonel in the United States Air
Force.

Edward Paul Anastasio(451) married Katherine Patricia Reynolds(451a) on 30
November 1940 in Williamson, TX.

<u>Katherine Patricia Reynolds(451a)</u> was born on 12 October 1920, in Memphis, TX,
to Bryan W. Reynolds(451aF) and Bela L. Ford(451aM). Katherine Patricia
Reynolds(451a) died on 5 December 2005, in Spokane, WA.

Edward Paul Anastasio(451) and Katherine Patricia Reynolds(451a) had
child(ren).

Katherine Patricia Reynolds(451a) also married Felix Harlan(451ab) on 24
December 1987.

Records that include Edward Paul Anastasio(451) and/or Katherine Patricia
Reynolds(451a):

- "Texas Birth Certificates, 1903-1935", , FamilySearch
  (https://www.familysearch.org/ark:/61903/1:1:X2R5-6XJ : Sun Mar 10
  14:05:52 UTC 2024), Entry for Katherine Reynolds and Bryan W
  Reynolds, 12 Oct 1920.
- "United States Census, 1920", , FamilySearch
  (https://www.familysearch.org/ark:/61903/1:1:MFL9-JJ6 : Sun Mar 10
  05:10:16 UTC 2024), Entry for Frank P Anastasio and Gilda
  Anastasio, 1920.
- "United States Census, 1930", , FamilySearch
  (https://www.familysearch.org/ark:/61903/1:1:X9SJ-2LK : Sat Mar 09
  02:41:12 UTC 2024), Entry for Frank Anastasio and Hilda Anastasio,
  1930.
- "United States Census, 1930", , FamilySearch
  (https://www.familysearch.org/ark:/61903/1:1:HYKN-BZM : Sat Mar 09
  18:11:01 UTC 2024), Entry for Bryan W Reynolds and Lee B Reynolds,
  1930.
- "United States Census, 1940", , FamilySearch
  (https://www.familysearch.org/ark:/61903/1:1:K4QR-M9S : Sun Mar 10
  13:42:45 UTC 2024), Entry for Edw P Anastasis, 1940.
- "United States 1950 Census", , FamilySearch
  (https://www.familysearch.org/ark:/61903/1:1:6F64-Z2J5 : Wed Oct 04
  08:23:02 UTC 2023), Entry for Edward P Anastaria and Katherine P
  Anastaria, 10 April 1950.
- "Texas, County Marriage Records, 1837-1965", , FamilySearch
  (https://www.familysearch.org/ark:/61903/1:1:QV1H-53KQ : Sun Mar 10
  07:33:27 UTC 2024), Entry for Edward P Anastasio and Kathryn
  Patricia Reynolds, 30 Nov 1940.
- https://journaltimes.newspapers.com/article/the-journal-times-
  obituary-for-frank-p/83018176/
- "United States Social Security Death Index," database, FamilySearch
  (https://familysearch.org/ark:/61903/1:1:V3W3-MYM : 9 January
  2021), Edward Anastasio, Apr 1982; citing U.S. Social Security
  Administration, Death Master File, database (Alexandria, Virginia:
  National Technical Information Service, ongoing).
- "Washington Death Index, 1965-2014," database, FamilySearch
  (https://familysearch.org/ark:/61903/1:1:QLWS-9T25 : 13 July 2017),
  Edward P Anastasio, 09 Apr 1982, Spokane, Spokane, Washington,
  United States; from the Department of Health, Death Index, 1907-
  1960; 1965-2014, Washington State Archives, Digital Archives
  (https://www.digitalarchives.wa.gov/Collections/TitleInfo/472 :
  n.d.); Citing Washington State Department of Health.

- "United States, Social Security Numerical Identification Files (NUMIDENT), 1936-2007", database, FamilySearch (https://www.familysearch.org/ark:/61903/1:1:6K7K-RW69 : 10 February 2023), Kathryn Reynolds Deason, .

452) Giovanna Moschella

Giovanna Moschella(452) was born on 14 April 1914, in Ariano, Italy, to Antonio Moschella(255a) and Mariangela Manganiello(255). Giovanna Moschella(452) died on 10 Jun 1914 in Ariano, Italy.

Records that include Giovanna Moschella(452):
- Ariano, Italy 1914 Birth Act #238
- Ariano, Italy 1914 Death Act #122

453) Pasquale Pietracola

Pasquale Pietracola(453) was born on 4 June 1914, in Ariano, Italy, to Antonio Pietracola(212) and Marianna Ciano(212a).

Records that include Pasquale Pietracola(453):
- Ariano, Italy 1914 Birth Act #328

454) Edward Laurie Perrino

Edward Laurie Perrino(454) born on 1 September 1914, in Schenectady, NY, to Vittorio Perrino(187) and Carmela Ricci(187a). Edward Laurie Perrino(454) died March 1964 in Clearwater, FL.

Edward Laurie Perrino(454) married Mary A. Gignac(454a) on 6 April 1949 in Schenectady, NY.

Mary A. Gignac(454a) was born on 9 July 1913, in Schenectady, NY, to Eugene J. Gignac(454aF) and Agnes M. Martin(454aM). Mary A. Gignac(454a) died 21 December 1982 in Clearwater, FL.

Edward Laurie Perrino(454) and Mary A. Gignac(454a) had child(ren).

Records that include Edward Laurie Perrino(454) and/or Mary A. Gignac(454a):
- "New York, Birth Indexes outside of New York City, 1881-1942", , FamilySearch (https://www.familysearch.org/ark:/61903/1:1:6FDW-K392 : Fri Mar 08 14:09:05 UTC 2024), Entry for Mary A Gignac, 9 Jul 1913.
- "St. John the Baptist, Schenectady, New York, Baptism (oct 1854 – Jun 2009)", American-Canadian Genealogical Society, Manchester, NH
- "United States Census, 1920", , FamilySearch (https://www.familysearch.org/ark:/61903/1:1:MVSH-71T : Sat Jul 20 13:35:39 UTC 2024), Entry for Victor Perrino, Sr and Carrie Perrino, 1920.
- "United States Census, 1920", , FamilySearch (https://www.familysearch.org/ark:/61903/1:1:MVS4-81R : Sun Mar 10 21:28:23 UTC 2024), Entry for James Martin and Elizabeth Martin, 1920.
- "United States Census, 1930", , FamilySearch (https://www.familysearch.org/ark:/61903/1:1:X4T1-VDJ : Mon Jul 08 19:59:28 UTC 2024), Entry for Victor C Perrino and Carrie Perrino, 1930.
- "United States Census, 1930", , FamilySearch (https://www.familysearch.org/ark:/61903/1:1:X4TT-X6R : Tue Jul 16 00:38:44 UTC 2024), Entry for Louis Campochiaro and Agnes Campochiaro, 1930.
- "United States Census, 1940", , FamilySearch (https://www.familysearch.org/ark:/61903/1:1:KQ3C-K9V : Sat Mar 09 18:44:11 UTC 2024), Entry for Louis Campochiaro and Agnes M Campochiaro, 1940.
- "United States Census, 1950", , FamilySearch (https://www.familysearch.org/ark:/61903/1:1:6XPL-Y4QL : Wed Oct 04 20:46:01 UTC 2023), Entry for Edward L Perrino and Mary A Perrino, 3 April 1950.

- "United States, Social Security Numerical Identification Files (NUMIDENT), 1936-2007", , FamilySearch (https://www.familysearch.org/ark:/61903/1:1:6KMP-6YHJ : 10 February 2023), Edward L Perrino, .
- "Florida Death Index, 1877-1998," , FamilySearch (https://familysearch.org/ark:/61903/1:1:VVN2-XHF : 25 December 2014), Edward Laurie Perrino, Mar 1964; from "Florida Death Index, 1877-1998," index, Ancestry (www.ancestry.com : 2004); citing vol. 2567, certificate number 15274, Florida Department of Health, Office of Vital Records, Jacksonville.
- "United States Social Security Death Index," database, FamilySearch (https://familysearch.org/ark:/61903/1:1:JBGZ-H2C : 7 January 2021), Edward Perrino, Mar 1964; citing U.S. Social Security Administration, Death Master File, database (Alexandria, Virginia: National Technical Information Service, ongoing).
- "Find a Grave Index," database, FamilySearch (https://www.familysearch.org/ark:/61903/1:1:QVGV-GXKK : 6 July 2020), Edward Perrino, ; Burial, , ; citing record ID , Find a Grave, http://www.findagrave.com.
- "Florida Death Index, 1877-1998," database, FamilySearch (https://familysearch.org/ark:/61903/1:1:VV4W-MD5 : 25 December 2014), Mary A Perrino, 21 Dec 1982; from "Florida Death Index, 1877-1998," index, Ancestry (www.ancestry.com : 2004); citing vol. , certificate number 108045, Florida Department of Health, Office of Vital Records, Jacksonville.
- "United States Social Security Death Index," database, FamilySearch (https://familysearch.org/ark:/61903/1:1:JBRD-5Q7 : 7 January 2021), Mary Perrino, Dec 1982; citing U.S. Social Security Administration, Death Master File, database (Alexandria, Virginia: National Technical Information Service, ongoing).
- "Find a Grave Index," database, FamilySearch (https://www.familysearch.org/ark:/61903/1:1:QVGV-GXKL : 6 July 2020), Mary Perrino, ; Burial, , ; citing record ID , Find a Grave, http://www.findagrave.com.
- "St. Anthony, Schenectady, New York, Marriages (Oct 1916 -Jul 2006)", 2 Volumes, American-Canadian Genealogical Society, Manchester, NH, page 589

455) Antonio LoConte

Antonio LoConte(455) was born on 13 November 1914, in Ariano, Italy, to Francesco Paolo LoConte(205a) and Carmela Manganiello(205).

Records that include Antonio LoConte(455):
- Ariano, Italy 1914 Birth Act #576

456) Ralph Pasquale DeMeo

Ralph Pasquale DeMeo(456) was born on 27 October 1914 in Schenectady, New York, to Angelo DeMeo(202a) and Maria Perrina(202). Ralph Pasquale DeMeo(456) died March 1984 in Flushings, NY.

Ralph Pasquale DeMeo(456) married Eugenia(456).

Eugenia(456) was born on 15 December 1913 in New York. Eugenia(456) died April 1983 in Flushings, NY.

Ralph Pasquale DeMeo(456) and Eugenia(456) had child(ren).

Records that include Ralph Pasquale DeMeo(456) and/or Eugenia(456):
- "United States Census, 1920", , FamilySearch (https://www.familysearch.org/ark:/61903/1:1:MVS4-RRY : Fri Mar 08 05:51:12 UTC 2024), Entry for Angelo Demeo and Mary Demeo, 1920.
- "United States Census, 1930", , FamilySearch (https://www.familysearch.org/ark:/61903/1:1:X4TT-YB5 : Mon Mar 11 01:35:37 UTC 2024), Entry for Angelo De Meo and Mary De Meo, 1930.
- "United States Census, 1940", , FamilySearch (https://www.familysearch.org/ark:/61903/1:1:KQYF-JDN : Sun Mar 10 02:54:25 UTC 2024), Entry for Joseph Calabrese and Rose Calabrese, 1940.

- New York, New York City, World War II Draft Registration Cards,
  1940-1947", , FamilySearch
  (https://www.familysearch.org/ark:/61903/1:1:WZJY-VG2M : Sun Mar 10
  05:27:29 UTC 2024), Entry for Ralph Pasquale Demeo and Brooklyn
  Navy Yard, 16 Oct 1940.
- "Hawaii, Honolulu Passenger Lists, 1900-1953", , FamilySearch
  (https://www.familysearch.org/ark:/61903/1:1:QVR9-5866 : Sun Mar 10
  17:27:12 UTC 2024), Entry for Ralph P De Meo, 1940.
- "United States, California, List of United States Citizens Arriving
  at San Francisco, 1930-1949", , FamilySearch
  (https://www.familysearch.org/ark:/61903/1:1:WB7C-B73Z : Sun Mar 10
  16:14:24 UTC 2024), Entry for Ralph De Meo, 1940.
- "United States 1950 Census", , FamilySearch
  (https://www.familysearch.org/ark:/61903/1:1:6XRW-1PQV : Thu Oct 05
  18:42:36 UTC 2023), Entry for Ralph Demeo and Eugena Demeo, 10
  April 1950.
- "United States Social Security Death Index," database, FamilySearch
  (https://familysearch.org/ark:/61903/1:1:JYM4-2ZJ : 7 January
  2021), Eugenia Demeo, Apr 1983; citing U.S. Social Security
  Administration, Death Master File, database (Alexandria, Virginia:
  National Technical Information Service, ongoing).
- "Find a Grave Index," database, FamilySearch
  (https://www.familysearch.org/ark:/61903/1:1:Q2SS-CVBG : 7 August
  2020), Eugenia De Meo, ; Burial, Flushing, Queens, New York, United
  States of America, Mount Saint Mary Cemetery; citing record ID
  154136216, Find a Grave, http://www.findagrave.com.
- "United States Social Security Death Index," database, FamilySearch
  (https://familysearch.org/ark:/61903/1:1:JPZQ-KJC : 7 January
  2021), Ralph Demeo, Mar 1984; citing U.S. Social Security
  Administration, Death Master File, database (Alexandria, Virginia:
  National Technical Information Service, ongoing).
- "Find a Grave Index," database, FamilySearch
  (https://www.familysearch.org/ark:/61903/1:1:Q2SS-CNX5 : 7 August
  2020), Ralph De Meo, ; Burial, Flushing, Queens, New York, United
  States of America, Mount Saint Mary Cemetery; citing record ID
  154136962, Find a Grave, http://www.findagrave.com.

457) Francesco Miseno

Francesco Miseno(457) was born on 23 November 1914, in Amsterdam, NY, to Ugo
Miseno(238a) and Concetta Felicia Perrina(238). Francesco Miseno(457) died 25
Sept 1970 in Jacksonville, FL. Francesco Miseno(457) was buried in Mount
Carmel Cemetery, Johnstown, NY.

Records that include Francesco Miseno(457):
- "United States Census, 1920", , FamilySearch
  (https://www.familysearch.org/ark:/61903/1:1:MJGD-61J : Sun Mar 10
  00:46:08 UTC 2024), Entry for Ugo Mireno and Concetta Mireno, 1920.
- "United States Census, 1930", , FamilySearch
  (https://www.familysearch.org/ark:/61903/1:1:X78V-MMP : Sun Mar 10
  13:54:09 UTC 2024), Entry for Hugo Misseno and Conncetta Misseno,
  1930.
- "United States Census, 1940", , FamilySearch
  (https://www.familysearch.org/ark:/61903/1:1:KQ3M-2QT : Sun Jul 21
  06:10:46 UTC 2024), Entry for Nickolas T Lombardi and Concetta
  Miseno, 1940.
- "United States Census, 1950", , FamilySearch
  (https://www.familysearch.org/ark:/61903/1:1:6X5W-XL1Q : Fri Oct 06
  18:58:11 UTC 2023), Entry for Nicholas T Lombardi, Lombardi and
  Conccetta Miseno, 6 April 1950.
- "Florida Death Index, 1877-1998," , FamilySearch
  (https://familysearch.org/ark:/61903/1:1:VVFJ-F5L : 25 December
  2014), Francis J Miseno, 25 Feb 1970; from "Florida Death Index,
  1877-1998," index, Ancestry (www.ancestry.com : 2004); citing
  vol. , certificate number 10338, Florida Department of Health,
  Office of Vital Records, Jacksonville.

- "Find a Grave Index," database, FamilySearch (https://www.familysearch.org/ark:/61903/1:1:6FN2-DKF9 : 20 October 2022), Francis Miseno, ; Burial, Johnstown, Fulton, New York, United States of America, Mount Carmel Cemetery; citing record ID 237986031, Find a Grave, http://www.findagrave.com.

458) Maria Maddalena Perrina

Maria Maddalena Perrina(458) was born 2 December 1914 in Villanova de Battista, Italy, to Bennedetto Perrina(239a) and Maria Felicita Perrina(239).

Maria Maddalena Perrina(458) married Alfonso Ianniciello(458a) on 7 April 1938 in Villanova de Battista, Italy.

Alfonso Ianniciello(458a) was born on 9 January 1912 in Flumeri, Italy, to Bartolomes Ianniciello(458aF) and Bernice Rosaria Del Sardo(458aM). Alfonso Ianniciello(458a) was a farmer.

Maria Maddalena Perrina(458) and Alfonso Ianniciello(458a) had child(ren).

Records that include Maria Maddalena Perrina(458) and/or Alfonso Ianniciello(458a):
- Flumeri, Italy 1912 Birth Act #4
- Villanova del Battista, Italy 1914 Birth Act #107
- Villanova del Battista, Italy 1938 Marriage Act #7

459) Francesca Paula Fodarella

Francesca Paula Fodarella(459) was born 22 April 1915 in Ariano, Italy, to Luigi Fodarella(188) and Giuditta Marrone(188a).

Francesca Paula Fodarella(459) married Giuseppe Pierro(459a) on 11 February 1935 in Ariano, Italy.

Giuseppe Pierro(459a) was born on 24 February 1915 in Ariano, Italy, to Raffaele Pierro(459aF) and Maria Assunta Gagliardo(459aM)

Records that include Francesca Paula Fodarella(459) and/or Giuseppe Pierro(459a):
- Ariano, Italy 1915 Birth Act #173
- Ariano, Italy 1915 Birth Act #257
- Ariano, Italy 1935 Marriage Act #P-II-A21

460) Maria Michela Riccio

Maria Michela Riccio(460) was born on 19 May 1915, in Ariano, Italy, to Angelo Maria Riccio(183a) and Raimonda Ciasullo(183).

Maria Michela Riccio(460) married Oto Maria diMaina(460a) on 6 February 1936, in Ariano, Italy,

Oto Maria diMaina(460a) was born on 23 January 1914, in Ariano, Italy, to Ciriaco diMaina(460aF) and Saveria diVitto(460aM).

Records that include Maria Michela Riccio(460) and/or Oto Maria diMaina(460a):
- Ariano, Italy 1914 Birth Act #67
- Ariano, Italy 1915 Birth Act #298
- Ariano, Italy 1936 Marriage Act #P.IIA.17

461) Domenica Ciccarelli

Domenica Ciccarelli(461) was born on 30 October 1915, in Ariano, Italy, to Nicola Ciccarelli(241) and Lucia Mincolelli(241a). Domenica Ciccarelli(461) died on 2 September 1917 in Ariano, Italy.

Records that include Domenica Ciccarelli(461):
- Ariano, Italy 1915 Birth Act #563
- Ariano, Italy 1917 Death Act #219

462) Michele Moschella

Michele Moschella(462) was born on 12 November 1915, in Ariano, Italy, to Antonio Moschella(255a) and Mariangela Manganiello(255).

Records that include Michele Moschella(462):
- Ariano, Italy 1915 Birth Act #595

463) Michael Sam Riccio

Michael Sam Riccio(463) was born born on 4 December 1915, in Schenectady, NY, to Raffaele Riccio(221a) and Giovanna (Jenny) Ciasullo(221). Michael Sam Riccio(463) served in the United States Army during WWII. Michael Sam Riccio(463) died 14 March 2005 in Ardsley, NY. Michael Sam Riccio(463) was a grocery store owner.

Michael Sam Riccio(463) married Filomena (Fannie) Perillo(463a) April 28, 1940 at Our Lady of Perpetual Help Church in Ardsley, NY.

Filomena (Fannie) Perillo(463a) was born on 27 March 1916, in Ardsley, NY, to Giuseppe Perillo(463aF) and Maria Melito(463aM). Filomena (Fannie) Perillo(463a) died on date 2003 in Ardsley, NY.

Michael Sam Riccio(463) and Filomena (Fannie) Perillo(463a) had child(ren).

Records that include Michael Sam Riccio(463) and/or Filomena (Fannie) Perillo(463a):
- "United States Census, 1930", , FamilySearch (https://www.familysearch.org/ark:/61903/1:1:X4TB-187 : Fri Mar 08 12:10:26 UTC 2024), Entry for Ralph Riccio and Jennie Riccio, 1930.
- "United States Census, 1930", , FamilySearch (https://www.familysearch.org/ark:/61903/1:1:X4G7-H8F : Fri Mar 08 16:24:39 UTC 2024), Entry for Joseph Perillo and Marie Perillo, 1930.
- "United States Census, 1940", , FamilySearch (https://www.familysearch.org/ark:/61903/1:1:KQ5D-524 : Fri Mar 08 23:01:50 UTC 2024), Entry for Joseph Perillo and Mary Perillo, 1940.
- "United States World War II Army Enlistment Records, 1938-1946," database, FamilySearch (https://familysearch.org/ark:/61903/1:1:K85X-8Z5 : 5 December 2014), Michael S Riccio, enlisted 20 Mar 1945, New York City, New York, United States; citing "Electronic Army Serial Number Merged File, ca. 1938-1946," database, The National Archives: Access to Archival Databases (AAD) (http://aad.archives.gov : National Archives and Records Administration, 2002); NARA NAID 1263923, National Archives at College Park, Maryland.
- "United States Census, 1950", , FamilySearch (https://www.familysearch.org/ark:/61903/1:1:6XPP-15QV : Wed Mar 20 12:21:22 UTC 2024), Entry for Joseph Perillo and Maria Perillo, 5 May 1950.
- https://www.legacy.com/us/obituaries/lohud/name/filomena-riccio-obituary?id=48199530
- "United States, Social Security Numerical Identification Files (NUMIDENT), 1936-2007", database, FamilySearch (https://www.familysearch.org/ark:/61903/1:1:6K9W-38HP : 10 February 2023), Ralph Riccio in entry for Michael Sam Riccio, .
- "United States, Social Security Numerical Identification Files (NUMIDENT), 1936-2007", database, FamilySearch (https://www.familysearch.org/ark:/61903/1:1:6K9W-38HP : 10 February 2023), Ralph Riccio in entry for Michael Sam Riccio, .
- "United States Social Security Death Index," , FamilySearch (https://familysearch.org/ark:/61903/1:1:J5T2-CWL : 11 January 2021), Michael S Riccio, 14 Mar 2005; citing U.S. Social Security Administration, Death Master File, database (Alexandria, Virginia: National Technical Information Service, ongoing).
- https://www.edwardsdowdle.com/obituaries/Michael-Riccio?obId=25500594

464) Carmela Miressi

Carmela Miressi (464) was born 9 December 1915, in New Rochelle, NY, to Generoso Miressi(160) and Maria Luigia Iannarone(160a).

Records that include Carmela Miressi(334):
- "New York, Birth Indexes outside of New York City, 1881-1942", , FamilySearch (https://www.familysearch.org/ark:/61903/1:1:6FYJ-5845 : Fri Mar 08 13:11:22 UTC 2024), Entry for Carmela Miressi, 9 Dec 1915.
- "United States Census, 1920", , FamilySearch (https://www.familysearch.org/ark:/61903/1:1:MV3Z-67Q : Sat Mar 09 23:43:34 UTC 2024), Entry for Jenarosa Merrisi and Maria Merrisi, 1920.
- "United States Census, 1930", , FamilySearch (https://www.familysearch.org/ark:/61903/1:1:X4G6-NM9 : Sat Mar 09 03:25:50 UTC 2024), Entry for Generoso Miressi and Mary L Miressi, 1930.

465) Elena (Helen) Perrine

Elena (Helen) Perrine(465) was born about 1916, in Jessup, PA, to Carmine Perrina(247) and Colomba di Pasquale(247a). Elena (Helen) Perrine(465) died before 1957.
NOTE: I have not been able to locate any more information about this individual.

Records that include Elena (Helen) Perrine(465):
- "United States Census, 1920", , FamilySearch (https://www.familysearch.org/ark:/61903/1:1:MFY4-Q5M : Wed Mar 06 09:48:19 UTC 2024), Entry for O Dena Perine and Colombine Perine, 1920.
- "United States Census, 1930", , FamilySearch (https://www.familysearch.org/ark:/61903/1:1:X7CK-1B8 : Fri Jul 05 22:27:03 UTC 2024), Entry for Carmino Perrine and Columbia Perrine, 1930.
- https://www.newspapers.com/article/the-buffalo-news-perrine-colomba-nee-d/148955383/

466) Antonetta DeDonato

Antonetta DeDonato(466) was born about 1916, in Ariano, Italy, to Luigi deDonato(126) and Caterina Montecalvo(126a). Antonetta DeDonato(466) died on 20 June 1919 in Ariano, Italy.

Records that include Antonetta DeDonato(466):
- Ariano, Italy 1919 Death Act #292

467) Ida Manganiello

Ida Manganiello(467) was born on 1 January 1916, in Ariano, Italy, to Raimondo Manganiello(182) and Maria Giovanna Paone(182a).

Ida Manganiello(467) married Vincenzo Paone(467a) on 8 October 1938 in Ariano, Italy.

Vincenzo Paone(467a) was born on 22 December 1912, in Ariano, Italy to Pasquale Paone(467aF) and Filomena Adamini(467aM).

Records that include Ida Manganiello(467a) and Vincenzo Paone(467a):
- Ariano, Italy 1912 Birth Act #640
- Ariano, Italy 1916 Birth Act #3
- Ariano, Italy 1938 Marriage Act #PIIA.125

468) Angelina Bonelli

Angelina Bonelli(468) was born on 15 January 1916, in St. Louis, MO, to Joseph Bonelli(271a) and Concetta Anastasio(271). Angelina Bonelli(468) died on 14 March 1931 in Detroit, MI.

Records that include Angelina Bonelli(468):
- "United States Census, 1920", , FamilySearch
  (https://www.familysearch.org/ark:/61903/1:1:M887-HJN : Sat Mar 09
  17:39:56 UTC 2024), Entry for Joseph Bonneli and Consetti Bonneli,
  1920.
- "United States Census, 1930", , FamilySearch
  (https://www.familysearch.org/ark:/61903/1:1:X7SP-TPK : Sun Mar 10
  23:23:02 UTC 2024), Entry for Causamo Stilo and Elvera Stilo, 1930.
- "Michigan Death Certificates, 1921-1952", , FamilySearch
  (https://www.familysearch.org/ark:/61903/1:1:KF4Z-QX5 : Fri Mar 08
  15:54:39 UTC 2024), Entry for Angeline Bonelli and Joseph Bonelli,
  14 Mar 1931.
- "Find a Grave Index," database, FamilySearch
  (https://www.familysearch.org/ark:/61903/1:1:6NND-NMCX : 10 May
  2023), Angeline Bonelli, ; Burial, Detroit, Wayne, Michigan, United
  States of America, Mount Olivet Cemetery; citing record ID
  241565673, Find a Grave, http://www.findagrave.com.

469) Dan A Zarlenga

Dan A Zarlenga(469) was born on 19 January 1916, in St. Louis, MO, to Domenick
Zarlenga(259a) and Clementina Anastasio(259). Dan A Zarlenga(469) died on 17
October 1924 in St. Louis, MO.

Records that include Dan A Zarlenga(469):
- "United States Census, 1920", , FamilySearch
  (https://www.familysearch.org/ark:/61903/1:1:M8ZB-8SY : Sat Mar 09
  21:28:03 UTC 2024), Entry for Dominick Zasleoga and Clara Zasleoga,
  1920.
- "Find a Grave Index," database, FamilySearch
  (https://www.familysearch.org/ark:/61903/1:1:QVKL-VK5M : 9 June
  2021), Danny Zarlenga, ; Burial, Saint Louis, St. Louis City,
  Missouri, United States of America, Calvary Cemetery and Mausoleum;
  citing record ID 47035393, Find a Grave, http://www.findagrave.com.

470) Josephine Tiso

Josephine Tiso(470) was born on 6 March 1916, in Newark, NJ, to Oto (Ottone)
Tiso(169) and Mary Senese(169a). Josephine Tiso(470) died on 8 March 2001 in
Nutley, NJ.

Josephine Tiso(470) married Frank A. Albanese(470a).

Frank A. Albanese(470a) was born on 8 September 1908, in Newark, NJ to
Stephano Albanese(470aF) and Matida Arbucci(470aM). Frank A. Albanese(470a)
died 30 March 1992 in Nutley, NJ.

Records that include Josephine Tiso(470) and/or Frank A. Albanese(470a):
- "New Jersey, Reclaim the Records, Geographic Birth Index, 1901-
  1929", , FamilySearch
  (https://www.familysearch.org/ark:/61903/1:1:6N9V-L815 : Fri Mar 29
  03:00:46 UTC 2024), Entry for Frank Albanese, 8 September 1908.
- "United States Census, 1920", , FamilySearch
  (https://www.familysearch.org/ark:/61903/1:1:M451-X6W : Sat Mar 09
  14:37:36 UTC 2024), Entry for Ottone Tiso and Mary Tiso, 1920.
- "United States Census, 1930", , FamilySearch
  (https://www.familysearch.org/ark:/61903/1:1:X4DG-XPV : Fri Mar 08
  18:34:06 UTC 2024), Entry for Ottone Liso and Mary H Liso, 1930.
- "Find a Grave Index," database, FamilySearch
  (https://www.familysearch.org/ark:/61903/1:1:QVLZ-SWJP : 1 April
  2023), Josephine M. Albanese, ; Burial, Bloomfield, Essex, New
  Jersey, United States of America, Glendale Cemetery; citing record
  ID 90352083, Find a Grave, http://www.findagrave.com.
- "Find a Grave Index," database, FamilySearch
  (https://www.familysearch.org/ark:/61903/1:1:QVLZ-SWJZ : 1 April
  2023), Frank A Albanese, ; Burial, Bloomfield, Essex, New Jersey,
  United States of America, Glendale Cemetery; citing record ID
  90352080, Find a Grave, http://www.findagrave.com.

- "United States Social Security Death Index," database, FamilySearch (https://familysearch.org/ark:/61903/1:1:JKYK-DNG : 7 January 2021), Frank A Albanese, 30 Mar 1992; citing U.S. Social Security Administration, Death Master File, database (Alexandria, Virginia: National Technical Information Service, ongoing).
- "United States, Social Security Numerical Identification Files (NUMIDENT), 1936-2007", database, FamilySearch (https://www.familysearch.org/ark:/61903/1:1:6K9F-D6K6 : 10 February 2023), Frank A Albanese.
- United States, Social Security Numerical Identification Files (NUMIDENT), 1936-2007", database, FamilySearch (https://www.familysearch.org/ark:/61903/1:1:6K9X-T39C : 10 February 2023), Josephine Albanese, .

471) Edward Ninfadoro

Edward Ninfadoro(471) was born on 17 March 1916, in Schenectady, NY, to Oto Ninfadoro(165) and Antonia Costanzo(165a). Edward Ninfadoro(471) died on 20 March 1985 in Schenectady, NY.

Edward Ninfadoro(471) married Roslina Romanelli(471a) on 20 October 1946 in Schenectady, NY.

Roslina Theresa Romanelli(471a) was born on 29 October 1919 in Schenectady, NY, to Vincenzo (James) Romanelli(471aF) and Carmella Delorenzo(471aM). Roslina Romanelli(471a) died on 6 May 1996 in Schenectady, NY.

Records that include Edward Ninfadoro(471) and/or Roslina Romanelli(471a):
- "New York, Birth Indexes outside of New York City, 1881-1942", , FamilySearch (https://www.familysearch.org/ark:/61903/1:1:6F4L-3ZQT : Sun Mar 10 19:54:37 UTC 2024), Entry for Edward P Ninfadoro, 17 Mar 1916.
- "United States Census, 1920", , FamilySearch (https://www.familysearch.org/ark:/61903/1:1:MVSC-2F2 : Sat Mar 09 12:04:52 UTC 2024), Entry for Otto Infator and Antonette Infator, 1920.
- "United States Census, 1920", , FamilySearch (https://www.familysearch.org/ark:/61903/1:1:MVSC-KQM : Sat Mar 09 03:55:07 UTC 2024), Entry for Vincent Romanello and Carmelia Romanello, 1920.
- "United States Census, 1930", , FamilySearch (https://www.familysearch.org/ark:/61903/1:1:X4TB-9PG : Wed Mar 06 06:37:33 UTC 2024), Entry for Otto Ninafodora and Antoinette Ninafodora, 1930.
- "United States Census, 1930", , FamilySearch (https://www.familysearch.org/ark:/61903/1:1:X4T1-VMV : Thu Mar 07 23:45:49 UTC 2024), Entry for Carmela Romanella and Carmela Romanella, 1930.
- "United States Census, 1940", , FamilySearch (https://www.familysearch.org/ark:/61903/1:1:KQY5-TLS : Sun Mar 10 15:51:37 UTC 2024), Entry for Otto Ninfadoro and Antoinette Ninfadoro, 1940.
- "United States Census, 1940", , FamilySearch (https://www.familysearch.org/ark:/61903/1:1:KQY5-X8P : Thu Mar 07 12:37:40 UTC 2024), Entry for Carmela Romanella and Carmela Romanella, 1940.
- "United States World War II Army Enlistment Records, 1938-1946," , FamilySearch (https://familysearch.org/ark:/61903/1:1:K8R8-DBN : 5 December 2014), Edward P Ninfadoro, enlisted 16 Apr 1942, Albany, New York, United States; citing "Electronic Army Serial Number Merged File, ca. 1938-1946," database, The National Archives: Access to Archival Databases (AAD) (http://aad.archives.gov : National Archives and Records Administration, 2002); NARA NAID 1263923, National Archives at College Park, Maryland.
- "United States 1950 Census", , FamilySearch (https://www.familysearch.org/ark:/61903/1:1:6XYM-TS3T : Tue Mar 19 19:50:22 UTC 2024), Entry for Rosena T Ninfadore, 15 April 1950.
- "United States, Social Security Numerical Identification Files (NUMIDENT), 1936-2007", , FamilySearch (https://www.familysearch.org/ark:/61903/1:1:6KMV-P98T : 10 February 2023), Rosena Theresa Romanella, .

- "United States Social Security Death Index," database, FamilySearch (https://familysearch.org/ark:/61903/1:1:JP41-XJS : 7 January 2021), Edward Ninfadoro, Mar 1985; citing U.S. Social Security Administration, Death Master File, database (Alexandria, Virginia: National Technical Information Service, ongoing).
- "United States Social Security Death Index," database, FamilySearch (https://familysearch.org/ark:/61903/1:1:VMJB-G2N : 7 January 2021), Rosena Ninfadore, May 1996; citing U.S. Social Security Administration, Death Master File, database (Alexandria, Virginia: National Technical Information Service, ongoing).
- "Sacred Heart, Schenectady, New York, Deaths (Mar 1904 -Jul 2001)", American-Canadian Genealogical Society, Manchester, NH, page 106

472) Bruno Miseno

Bruno Miseno(472) was born on 22 May 1916, in Amsterdam, NY, to Ugo Miseno(238a) and Concetta Felicia Perrina(238). Bruno Miseno(472) died 13 July 1985 in Amsterdam, NY.

Bruno Miseno(472) married Emilie Monteleone(472a) on 3 July 1938.

Emilie Monteleone(472a) was born on 10 May 1917, in Utica, NY, to William Monteleone(472aF) and Angelina Mature(472aM). Emilie Monteleone(472a) died 5 August 2015, in Amsterdam, NY.

Bruno Miseno(472) and Emilie Monteleone(472a) had child(ren).

Records that include Bruno Miseno(472) and/or Emilie Monteleone(472a):
- "United States Census, 1920", , FamilySearch (https://www.familysearch.org/ark:/61903/1:1:MJGD-61J : Sun Mar 10 00:46:08 UTC 2024), Entry for Ugo Mireno and Concetta Mireno, 1920.
- "United States Census, 1920", , FamilySearch (https://www.familysearch.org/ark:/61903/1:1:MVMT-LC5 : Sat Jul 06 15:35:41 UTC 2024), Entry for William Monteleone and Angeline Monteleone, 1920.
- "United States Census, 1930", , FamilySearch (https://www.familysearch.org/ark:/61903/1:1:X78V-MMP : Sun Mar 10 13:54:09 UTC 2024), Entry for Hugo Misseno and Conncetta Misseno, 1930.
- "United States Census, 1930", , FamilySearch (https://www.familysearch.org/ark:/61903/1:1:X78N-FBB : Sat Jul 06 20:57:29 UTC 2024), Entry for Joseph Karam and Laura Karam, 1930.
- "United States Census, 1940", , FamilySearch (https://www.familysearch.org/ark:/61903/1:1:KQ39-96V : Tue Jul 09 20:51:49 UTC 2024), Entry for Bruno Mineso and Amelia Mineso, 1940.
- "United States Census, 1950", , FamilySearch (https://www.familysearch.org/ark:/61903/1:1:6XT1-GJ5Z : Wed Mar 20 21:59:45 UTC 2024), Entry for Bruno Miseno and Emilia Miseno, 10 April 1950.
- "United States Social Security Death Index," database, FamilySearch (https://familysearch.org/ark:/61903/1:1:JTTL-KMD : 7 January 2021), Bruno Miseno, Jul 1985; citing U.S. Social Security Administration, Death Master File, database (Alexandria, Virginia: National Technical Information Service, ongoing).
- "Find a Grave Index," database, FamilySearch (https://www.familysearch.org/ark:/61903/1:1:6NLZ-DPK7 : 12 September 2022), Bruno A Miseno, ; Burial, Amsterdam, Montgomery, New York, United States of America, Saint Michael Cemetery; citing record ID 242540608, Find a Grave, http://www.findagrave.com.

473) George Vincent Lombardi

George Vincent Lombardi(473) was born on 22 September 1916, in Bronx, NY, to Feliciano (Phillip White) Lombardi(236) and Mabel Grassie(236a). George Vincent Lombardi(473) died on 15 January 1993 in Nassau, NY. George Vincent Lombardi(473) was a musician.

George Vincent Lombardi(473) married Joanne Catherine Bonusiewicz(473a).

Joanne Catherine Bonusiewicz(473a) was born 4 November 1917 in Conshohocken, PA, to Stanley Bonusiewicz(473aF) and Laura Walachowski(473aM). Joanne Catherine Bonusiewicz(473a) died 27 March 2005 in Nassau, NY.

George Vincent Lombardi(473) and Joanne Catherine Bonusiewicz(473a) had Child(ren).

Records that include George Vincent Lombardi(473) and/or Joanne Catherine Bonusiewicz(473a):
- "United States Census, 1920", , FamilySearch (https://www.familysearch.org/ark:/61903/1:1:MJPX-9XN : Thu Mar 07 22:40:59 UTC 2024), Entry for Felice Lombardi and Mabel Lombardi, 1920.
- "New York, New York City, World War II Draft Registration Cards, 1940-1947", , FamilySearch (https://www.familysearch.org/ark:/61903/1:1:WH5M-R5W2 : Sat Mar 09 18:22:51 UTC 2024), Entry for George Vincent Lombardi and Self Employed, 16 Oct 1940.
- "United States 1950 Census", , FamilySearch (https://www.familysearch.org/ark:/61903/1:1:6XT1-52SH : Thu Oct 05 22:30:23 UTC 2023), Entry for George V Lombardi and Joanne C Lombardi, 1 April 1950.
- "New York, New York City Marriage Licenses Index, 1950-1995," , FamilySearch (https://www.familysearch.org/ark:/61903/1:1:QLST-D1NY : 16 February 2024), George Lombardi and Joan Power, 1961, Brooklyn, New York City, New York, United States;Marriage, Brooklyn, New York City, New York, United States, from Reclaim the Records, The NYC Marriage Index (http://www.nycmarriageindex.com : 2016); citing New York City Clerk's Office.
- "United States, Social Security Numerical Identification Files (NUMIDENT), 1936-2007", database, FamilySearch (https://www.familysearch.org/ark:/61903/1:1:6KMR-MRM7 : 10 February 2023), George Vincent Lombardi, .
- "United States Social Security Death Index," database, FamilySearch (https://familysearch.org/ark:/61903/1:1:JKVK-D6Y : 7 January 2021), George V Lombardi, 15 Jan 1993; citing U.S. Social Security Administration, Death Master File, database (Alexandria, Virginia: National Technical Information Service, ongoing).
- "Find a Grave Index," database, FamilySearch (https://www.familysearch.org/ark:/61903/1:1:QL7R-VTV5 : 7 August 2020), George V Lombardi, ; Burial, East Farmingdale, Suffolk, New York, United States of America, Saint Charles Cemetery; citing record ID 177753406, Find a Grave, http://www.findagrave.com.
- "United States, Social Security Numerical Identification Files (NUMIDENT), 1936-2007", database, FamilySearch (https://www.familysearch.org/ark:/61903/1:1:6KMP-SSKJ : 10 February 2023), Joanne Catherine Bonusiewicz, .
- "United States Social Security Death Index," database, FamilySearch (https://familysearch.org/ark:/61903/1:1:JTXS-P3L : 11 January 2021), Joanne Lombardi, 27 Mar 2005; citing U.S. Social Security Administration, Death Master File, database (Alexandria, Virginia: National Technical Information Service, ongoing).
- "Find a Grave Index," database, FamilySearch (https://www.familysearch.org/ark:/61903/1:1:QL7T-96YN : 7 August 2020), Joanne C Lombardi, ; Burial, East Farmingdale, Suffolk, New York, United States of America, Saint Charles Cemetery; citing record ID 177753628, Find a Grave, http://www.findagrave.com.

474) Gabriele Giovanni Ninfadoro

Gabriele Giovanni Ninfadoro(474) was born 23 June 1916, in Zungoli, Italy, to Antonio Ninfadoro(179) and Maria Carmela Dioguardi(179a).

Gabriele Giovanni Ninfadoro(474) married Emma Palladino(474a), on 11 December 1937 in Ariano, Italy.

Emma Rose Maria Matilde Palladino(474a) was born 1 April 1916, in Ottati, Italy, to Nicola Palladino(474aF) and Elisa Sabini(474aM).

Records that include Gabriele Giovanni Ninfadoro(474) and/or Emma Palladino(474a):

- Ottati, Italy 1916 Birth Act #10
- Zungoli, Italy 1916 Birth Act #35
- Ariano 1937 Marriage Act #P.II.B.14

475) Michael Angelo DeMeo

Michael Angelo DeMeo(475) was born on 22 August 1916 in Schenectady, NY, to Angelo DeMeo(202a) and Maria Perrina(202). Michael Angelo DeMeo(475) died 15 November 2007 in LaVita, CO.

Michael Angelo DeMeo(475) married Marie Helen Occhiuto(475a).

Marie Helen Occhiuto(475a) was born on 30 April 1916, in Fort Lee, NJ, to Louis Vincent Occhiuto(475aF) and Sabina Pallini(475aM). Marie Helen Occhiuto(475a) died on 30 December 1997 in LaVita, CO.

Michael Angelo DeMeo(475) and Marie Helen Occhiuto(475a) had child(ren).

Records that include Michael Angelo DeMeo(475) and/or Marie Helen Occhiuto(475a):

- "St. Anthony, Schenectady, New York, Baptism (Sep 1912 - May 2007)", 2 Volumes American-Canadian Genealogical Society, Manchester, NH, page 263
- "New Jersey, Reclaim the Records, Geographic Birth Index, 1901-1929", , FamilySearch (https://www.familysearch.org/ark:/61903/1:1:6N35-3TZW : Sat Mar 09 22:57:11 UTC 2024), Entry for Maria Occhinto, 30 Apr 1916.
- "United States Census, 1920", , FamilySearch (https://www.familysearch.org/ark:/61903/1:1:MVS4-RRY : Fri Mar 08 05:51:12 UTC 2024), Entry for Angelo Demeo and Mary Demeo, 1920.
- "United States Census, 1930", , FamilySearch (https://www.familysearch.org/ark:/61903/1:1:X4TT-YB5 : Mon Mar 11 01:35:37 UTC 2024), Entry for Angelo De Meo and Mary De Meo, 1930.
- "United States Census, 1930", , FamilySearch (https://www.familysearch.org/ark:/61903/1:1:X4PY-DPF : Fri Mar 08 16:12:42 UTC 2024), Entry for Vincent Orchinto and Sandy Orchinto, 1930.
- "United States Census, 1940", , FamilySearch (https://www.familysearch.org/ark:/61903/1:1:KQYF-JQN : Mon Mar 11 00:43:44 UTC 2024), Entry for Michael Demeo and Marie Demeo, 1940.
- "New York, New York City, World War II Draft Registration Cards, 1940-1947", , FamilySearch (https://www.familysearch.org/ark:/61903/1:1:WZJ1-RNPZ : Fri Mar 08 19:56:30 UTC 2024), Entry for Michael Angelo Demeo and Eastern Welded Products.
- "United States World War II Draft Registration Cards, 1942", , FamilySearch (https://www.familysearch.org/ark:/61903/1:1:F3FL-ZYH : Sat Feb 24 01:33:00 UTC 2024), Entry for Louis Vincent Occhiuto, 1942.
- "United States, Social Security Numerical Identification Files (NUMIDENT), 1936-2007", database, FamilySearch (https://www.familysearch.org/ark:/61903/1:1:6K9S-NPF8 : 10 February 2023), Michael Angelo Demeo, .
- "United States, Social Security Numerical Identification Files (NUMIDENT), 1936-2007", database, FamilySearch (https://www.familysearch.org/ark:/61903/1:1:6KMJ-L4GV : 10 February 2023), Marie Helen Occhiuto, .
- "United States Social Security Death Index," database, FamilySearch (https://familysearch.org/ark:/61903/1:1:JBGB-52C : 7 January 2021), Marie Demeo, 30 Dec 1997; citing U.S. Social Security Administration, Death Master File, database (Alexandria, Virginia: National Technical Information Service, ongoing).
- "United States, Social Security Numerical Identification Files (NUMIDENT), 1936-2007", database, FamilySearch (https://www.familysearch.org/ark:/61903/1:1:6K4Q-MGVD : 11 February 2023), James Robert Demeo, .

- "Find a Grave Index," database, FamilySearch
  (https://www.familysearch.org/ark:/61903/1:1:QV2Q-64JX : 10
  September 2021), Marie De Meo, ; Burial, La Veta, Huerfano,
  Colorado, United States of America, La Veta Cemetery; citing record
  ID 59309637, Find a Grave, http://www.findagrave.com.
- "Find a Grave Index," database, FamilySearch
  (https://www.familysearch.org/ark:/61903/1:1:QV2Q-64J6 : 10
  September 2021), Michael A De Meo, ; Burial, La Veta, Huerfano,
  Colorado, United States of America, La Veta Cemetery; citing record
  ID 59309594, Find a Grave, http://www.findagrave.com.

476) <u>Lorenzo Scanzillo</u>

Lorenzo Scanzillo(476) was born 13 September 1916, in New York, to Gaetano
Scauzillo(164) and Giovanna Grasso(196). Lorenzo Scanzillo(476) died 27 May
1996, in Bronx, NY. Lorenzo Scanzillo(476) was a mail handler.

Lorenzo Scanzillo(476) married Helen Marie Glovicko(476a).

<u>Helen Marie Glovicko</u>(476a)was born 3 April 1920, in Gary Lake, Indiana, to
Steve Glovicko(476aF) and Mary Sefcik(476aM). Helen Marie Glovicko(476a) died
13 Feb 2005 in Bronx, NY.

Records that include Lorenzo Scanzillo(476) and/or Helen Marie Glovicko(476a):
- "United States Census, 1920", , FamilySearch
  (https://www.familysearch.org/ark:/61903/1:1:MJG5-1XL : Wed Mar 06
  20:43:44 UTC 2024), Entry for Gaetano Scanzilla and Jannie
  Scanzilla, 1920.
- "United States Census, 1930", , FamilySearch
  (https://www.familysearch.org/ark:/61903/1:1:X7D4-SB4 : Sun Mar 10
  21:34:02 UTC 2024), Entry for Gaetano Scanzillo and Guanina
  Scanzillo, 1930.
- "United States Census, 1940", , FamilySearch
  (https://www.familysearch.org/ark:/61903/1:1:KQBN-826 : Sat Mar 09
  01:41:31 UTC 2024), Entry for Gaetano Scanzillo and Jennie
  Scanzillo, 1940.
- "United States Census, 1940", , FamilySearch
  (https://www.familysearch.org/ark:/61903/1:1:V1TL-BL4 : Fri Mar 08
  13:58:45 UTC 2024), Entry for Steve Glovicko and Helen Glovicko,
  1940.
- "New York, New York City, World War II Draft Registration Cards,
  1940-1947", , FamilySearch
  (https://www.familysearch.org/ark:/61903/1:1:WQTV-WR2M : Sun Mar 10
  05:38:59 UTC 2024), Entry for Larry Joseph Scanzilla and
  Unemployed, 16 Oct 1940.
- "United States 1950 Census", , FamilySearch
  (https://www.familysearch.org/ark:/61903/1:1:6XR4-PS2V : Fri Oct 06
  00:30:03 UTC 2023), Entry for Ralph Polombo and Lorenzo Scanzillo,
  17 April 1950.
- "United States Social Security Death Index," database, FamilySearch
  (https://familysearch.org/ark:/61903/1:1:VM21-861 : 7 January
  2021), Lorenzo Scanzillo, 27 May 1996; citing U.S. Social Security
  Administration, Death Master File, database (Alexandria, Virginia:
  National Technical Information Service, ongoing).
- "United States, Social Security Numerical Identification Files
  (NUMIDENT), 1936-2007", database, FamilySearch
  (https://www.familysearch.org/ark:/61903/1:1:6K9W-WS6V : 10
  February 2023), Lorenzo Joseph Scanzillo, .
- "Find a Grave Index," database, FamilySearch
  (https://www.familysearch.org/ark:/61903/1:1:Q2DK-RCXS : 11 January
  2023), Lorenzo Scanzillo, ; Burial, Bronx, Bronx, New York, United
  States of America, Old Saint Raymond's Cemetery; citing record ID
  172164353, Find a Grave, http://www.findagrave.com.
- "United States Social Security Death Index," database, FamilySearch
  (https://familysearch.org/ark:/61903/1:1:JKH5-NMW : 11 January
  2021), Helen Scanzillo, 13 Feb 2005; citing U.S. Social Security
  Administration, Death Master File, database (Alexandria, Virginia:
  National Technical Information Service, ongoing).

- "United States, Social Security Numerical Identification Files
  (NUMIDENT), 1936-2007", database, FamilySearch
  (https://www.familysearch.org/ark:/61903/1:1:6K32-GC2Y : 10
  February 2023), Helen Marie Glovicks, .

477) Rudolph William Anastasio

Rudolph William Anastasio(477) was born on 10 December 1916, in Racine, WI to
Francesco (Frank) Paul Anastasio(166) and Hilda (Gilda) Marcotti(166a).
Rudolph William Anastasio(477) died on 23 October 1994, in Racine, WI.

Rudolph William Anastasio(477) married June Elisabeth Evenson(477a), on 28
June 1941.

June Elisabeth Evenson(477a) was born on 17 November 1919, in Racine, WI, to
Einer Evenson(477aF) and Juliana Grass(477aM). June Elisabeth Evenson(477a)
died on 5 January 2001, in Racine, WI.

Rudolph William Anastasio(477) and June Elisabeth Evenson(477a) had
child(ren).

Records that include Rudolph William Anastasio(477) and/or June Elisabeth
Evenson(477a):
- "United States Census, 1920", , FamilySearch
  (https://www.familysearch.org/ark:/61903/1:1:MFL9-JJ6 : Sun Mar 10
  05:10:16 UTC 2024), Entry for Frank P Anastasio and Gilda
  Anastasio, 1920.
- "United States Census, 1920", , FamilySearch
  (https://www.familysearch.org/ark:/61903/1:1:MFLS-QLB : Sat Mar 09
  00:03:21 UTC 2024), Entry for Einar Evenson and Julia Evenson,
  1920.
- "United States Census, 1930", , FamilySearch
  (https://www.familysearch.org/ark:/61903/1:1:X9SJ-2LK : Sat Mar 09
  02:41:12 UTC 2024), Entry for Frank Anastasio and Hilda Anastasio,
  1930.
- "United States Census, 1930", , FamilySearch
  (https://www.familysearch.org/ark:/61903/1:1:X9SJ-1XR : Sat Mar 09
  20:34:17 UTC 2024), Entry for Einer Evenson and Julia M Evenson,
  1930.
- "United States Census, 1940", , FamilySearch
  (https://www.familysearch.org/ark:/61903/1:1:K7J6-HTQ : Sat Mar 09
  04:26:52 UTC 2024), Entry for Frank P Anastascio and Jilda
  Anastascio, 1940.
- "United States 1950 Census", , FamilySearch
  (https://www.familysearch.org/ark:/61903/1:1:6F93-YS91 : Sun Mar 24
  12:40:39 UTC 2024), Entry for Rudolph W Anastasio and June G
  Anastasio, 5 April 1950.
- "United States, Social Security Numerical Identification Files
  (NUMIDENT), 1936-2007", database, FamilySearch
  (https://www.familysearch.org/ark:/61903/1:1:6KQR-3NZB : 10
  February 2023), Rudolf William Anastasio, .
- "Wisconsin Death Index, 1959-1997", , FamilySearch
  (https://www.familysearch.org/ark:/61903/1:1:V8SV-PM5 : 8 January
  2022), Rudolf William Anastasio, 1994.
- https://journaltimes.newspapers.com/article/the-journal-times-
  obituary-for-frank-p/83018176/
- "United States, Social Security Numerical Identification Files
  (NUMIDENT), 1936-2007", database, FamilySearch
  (https://www.familysearch.org/ark:/61903/1:1:6KQL-MF5W : 10
  February 2023), June Elisabeth Evenson, .
- "United States Social Security Death Index," database, FamilySearch
  (https://familysearch.org/ark:/61903/1:1:JLS4-P3X : 9 January
  2021), June E Anastasio, 05 Jan 2001; citing U.S. Social Security
  Administration, Death Master File, database (Alexandria, Virginia:
  National Technical Information Service, ongoing).
- "Find a Grave Index," database, FamilySearch
  (https://www.familysearch.org/ark:/61903/1:1:Q231-LSWP : 10 July
  2020), Rudolf W. Anastasio, ; Burial, , ; citing record ID , Find a
  Grave, http://www.findagrave.com.

- "Find a Grave Index," database, FamilySearch (https://www.familysearch.org/ark:/61903/1:1:Q231-LSWS : 10 July 2020), June E. Anastasio, ; Burial, , ; citing record ID , Find a Grave, http://www.findagrave.com.

478) Concordia Tiso

Concordia Tiso(478) was born on 4 February 1917, in Ariano, Italy to Vincenzo Tiso(131) and Giovanna Portogallo(131a).

Concordia Tiso(478) married Giovanni Cuoco(478a) on 28 March 1939 in Ariano, Italy.

Giovanni Cuoco(478a) was born on 18 July 1918, in Ariano, Italy, to Gaetano Cuoco(478aF) and Carminella Impara(478aM).

Records that include Concordia Tiso(478) and/or Giovanni Cuoco(478a):
- Ariano, Italy 1917 Birth Act #60
- Ariano, Italy 1918 Birth Act #285
- Ariano, Italy 1939 Marriage Act #36

479) Mary Angela Ann Zarlenga

Mary Angela Ann Zarlenga(479) was born on 14 March 1917, in St. Louis, MO, to Domenick Zarlenga(259a) and Clementina Anastasio(259). Mary Angela Ann Zarlenga(479) died 7 December 2003, in St. Louis, MO. Mary Angela Ann Zarlenga(479) was buried at Calvary Cemetery and Mausoleum, St. Louis, MO.

Mary Angela Ann Zarlenga(479) married Francesco (Frank) Charles Castellano(479a) and August Francis Martorana(479b).

Mary Angela Ann Zarlenga(479) married Francesco (Frank) Charles Castellano(479a) between 1934 and 1940.

Francesco (Frank) Charles Castellano(479a) was born on 13 September 1906, in Casteltermini, Italy, to Carmelo Castellano(479aF) and Josephine D'Angelo(479aM). Princess Irene from Palermo, Italy. Francesco (Frank) Charles Castellano(479a) became a citizen of the United States 3 February 1939 in St. Louis, MO. Francesco (Frank) Charles Castellano(479a) died 25 September 1953, in St. Louis, MO. Francesco (Frank) Charles Castellano(479a) was buried at Calvary Cemetery and Mausoleum, St. Louis, MO.

Mary Angela Ann Zarlenga(479) and Francesco (Frank) Charles Castellano(479a) had child(ren).

Mary Angela Ann Zarlenga(479) married August Francis Martorana(479b) after 1982.

August Francis Martorana(479b) was born on 27 February 1916, in St. Louis, MO, to Antonino Martorana(479bF) and Alfonsa Cacciatore(479bM). August Francis Martorana(479b) died 1 September 1996 in St. Louis, MO. August Francis Martorana(479b) was buried at Resurrection Cemetery, Affton, MO.

August Francis Martorana(479b) was previously married to Geraldine L. Tedeschi(w479bX).

Records that include Mary Angela Ann Zarlenga(479), Francesco (Frank) Charles Castellano(479a) and/or August Francis Martorana(479b):
- "United States, Missouri, Naturalization Records, 1843-1991", FamilySearch (https://www.familysearch.org/ark:/61903/1:1:68LM-53CY : Thu Apr 24 06:03:23 UTC 2025), Entry for Frank Castellano, 7 Jul 1909.
- "Missouri, County Naturalization Records, 1830-1985", FamilySearch (https://www.familysearch.org/ark:/61903/1:1:6LN8-PF9J : Sun Mar 10 04:53:13 UTC 2024), Entry for Frank Castellano, 17 Sep 1924.
- "United States, Census, 1930", FamilySearch (https://www.familysearch.org/ark:/61903/1:1:XHJY-84K : Wed Jul 17 13:46:42 UTC 2024), Entry for Dominick Zarlingo and Clementine Zarlingo, 1930.
- "United States, Missouri, Naturalization Records, 1843-1991", FamilySearch (https://www.familysearch.org/ark:/61903/1:1:682Y-L5XZ : Thu Apr 24 06:42:32 UTC 2025), Entry for Frank Castellano, 9 Aug 1934.

- "United States, Missouri, Naturalization Records, 1843-1991", FamilySearch (https://www.familysearch.org/ark:/61903/1:1:68LK-LFL1 : Wed Apr 23 19:12:39 UTC 2025), Entry for Frank or Francesco Castellano, 9 Aug 1934.
- "United States, Missouri, Naturalization Records, 1843-1991", FamilySearch (https://www.familysearch.org/ark:/61903/1:1:68LV-QZ8N : Thu Apr 24 08:37:59 UTC 2025), Entry for Francesco aka Frank Castellano, 26 Oct 1938.
- "United States, Census, 1940", FamilySearch (https://www.familysearch.org/ark:/61903/1:1:K7HD-PDN : Sat Jan 18 20:56:21 UTC 2025), Entry for Frank C Castellano and Mary A Castellano, 1940.
- "United States, Census, 1940", FamilySearch (https://www.familysearch.org/ark:/61903/1:1:K7H8-XJW : Fri Jan 24 01:56:02 UTC 2025), Entry for Tony Martorana and Florence Martorana, 1940.
- "Missouri, World War II Draft Registration Cards, 1940-1945", FamilySearch (https://www.familysearch.org/ark:/61903/1:1:QLFM-F3WQ : Fri Apr 11 15:53:11 UTC 2025), Entry for Gus Frank Martorana and Florence Martorana, 16 Oct 1940.
- "Missouri, World War II Draft Registration Cards, 1940-1945", FamilySearch (https://www.familysearch.org/ark:/61903/1:1:QLX1-F9F8 : Fri Apr 11 15:15:16 UTC 2025), Entry for Frank Charles Castellano and Mary Castellano, 16 Oct 1940.
- "United States, Missouri, Naturalization Records, 1843-1991", FamilySearch (https://www.familysearch.org/ark:/61903/1:1:68LV-QZ8F : Wed Apr 23 18:18:59 UTC 2025), Entry for Frank aka Francesco Castellano, 9 Aug 1941.
- "Missouri, County Marriage, Naturalization, and Court Records, 1800-1991", FamilySearch (https://www.familysearch.org/ark:/61903/1:1:66ZB-3K5F : Fri Mar 08 03:06:59 UTC 2024), Entry for August F Martorana and Geraldine L Techeschi, 10 Sep 1944.
- "United States, Social Security Numerical Identification Files (NUMIDENT), 1936-2007", FamilySearch (https://www.familysearch.org/ark:/61903/1:1:6KW3-JHR8 : Sat Apr 26 07:32:43 UTC 2025), Entry for Mary Ann Castellano and Mary A Zarlenga.
- "United States, Social Security Death Index," database, FamilySearch (https://familysearch.org/ark:/61903/1:1:JLP4-ZM7 : 10 January 2021), Mary A Martorana, 07 Dec 2003; citing U.S. Social Security Administration, Death Master File, database (Alexandria, Virginia: National Technical Information Service, ongoing).
- https://www.findagrave.com/memorial/50740126/frank_charles-castellano
- "United States, Social Security Numerical Identification Files (NUMIDENT), 1936-2007", FamilySearch (https://www.familysearch.org/ark:/61903/1:1:6KWC-GNHX : Sat Apr 26 14:41:10 UTC 2025), Entry for August F Martorana and Antonino Martorana.
- "United States, Social Security Death Index," database, FamilySearch (https://familysearch.org/ark:/61903/1:1:JL5D-8YM : 10 January 2021), August F Martorana, 01 Sep 1996; citing U.S. Social Security Administration, Death Master File, database (Alexandria, Virginia: National Technical Information Service, ongoing).
- https://www.findagrave.com/memorial/211130342/august_francis-martorana
- "Find a Grave Index", FamilySearch (https://www.familysearch.org/ark:/61903/1:1:QVKL-F3M4 : Wed Apr 02 23:28:44 UTC 2025), Entry for Mary Angela Ann Zarlenga Martorana.

480) Raffaele Perrina

Raffaele Perrine(480) was born about 30 March 1917, in Villanova del Battista, Italy, to Bennedetto Perrina(239a) and Maria Felicita Perrina(239). Raffaele Perrine(480) died on 25 April 1917 in Villanova del Battista, Italy.

Records that include Raffaele Perrine(480):
- Villanova del Battista, Italy 1917 Death Act #19

481) Angelo Mario Perrino

Angelo Mario Perrino(481) was born on 30 April 1917, in Concord, NH, to Liberatore Perrina(200) and Carmenalla Gammaroto(200a). Angelo Mario Perrino(481) died 5 July 1985 in Hillsborough, NH.

Angelo Mario Perrino(481) married Lurline St Amand(481a) on 22 November 1944.

Lurline St Amand(481a) was born on 29 March 1914, in Concord, NH, to John H St Amand(481aF) and Catherine Peabody(481aM). Lurline St Amand(481a) died 17 September 1994 in Hillsborough, NH.

Lurline St Amand(481a) was previous marriage James R. Dawson(481aX).

Records that include Angelo Mario Perrino(481) and/or Lurline St Amand(481a):
- "United States Census, 1920", , FamilySearch (https://www.familysearch.org/ark:/61903/1:1:MH8R-RXT : Sat Mar 09 02:30:10 UTC 2024), Entry for Liberatore Perrino and Carmela Perrino, 1920.
- "United States Census, 1920", , FamilySearch (https://www.familysearch.org/ark:/61903/1:1:MH8R-NHD : Sun Mar 10 04:04:12 UTC 2024), Entry for John H St Amand and Katherine E St Amand, 1920.
- "United States Census, 1930", , FamilySearch (https://www.familysearch.org/ark:/61903/1:1:X7NK-BXM : Sat Mar 09 13:58:16 UTC 2024), Entry for Liberatone Perrino and Carmirella Perrino, 1930.
- "United States Census, 1930", , FamilySearch (https://www.familysearch.org/ark:/61903/1:1:X7NK-32F : Sun Mar 10 17:56:46 UTC 2024), Entry for John A St Stamand and Katherine St Stamand, 1930.
- "New Hampshire Marriage Records, 1637-1947", , FamilySearch (https://www.familysearch.org/ark:/61903/1:1:FLC5-B3S : Fri Mar 08 13:14:13 UTC 2024), Entry for James R. Dawson and Lurline St.amand, 1934.
- "United States Census, 1940", , FamilySearch (https://www.familysearch.org/ark:/61903/1:1:VT94-72P : Sat Mar 09 20:05:01 UTC 2024), Entry for Liberstore Perrins and Carmella Perrins, 1940.
- "United States Census, 1940", , FamilySearch (https://www.familysearch.org/ark:/61903/1:1:VT9W-QWW : Sat Mar 09 15:56:13 UTC 2024), Entry for James R Dawson and Lurline M Dawson, 1940.
- "New Hampshire Marriage Records, 1637-1947", , FamilySearch (https://www.familysearch.org/ark:/61903/1:1:FLD1-VDL : Sat Mar 09 14:51:46 UTC 2024), Entry for Angelo M. Perrino and Lurline M. Dawson, 1944.
- "New Hampshire, World War II Draft Registration Cards, 1940-1947," database, FamilySearch (https://familysearch.org/ark:/61903/1:1:QP8J-XHPD : 10 February 2024), Angelo Mario Perrino, 16 Oct 1940; records extracted by FamilySearch, images digitized by Ancestry.com; citing Draft Registration, Concord, Merrimack, New Hampshire, United States, Records extracted by FamilySearch. Images digitized by Ancestry.com. National Archives and Records Administration, Washington D.C.; FHL microfilm 00571.
- "United States 1950 Census", , FamilySearch (https://www.familysearch.org/ark:/61903/1:1:6X5D-GR24 : Tue Mar 19 23:59:32 UTC 2024), Entry for Angelo M Perrino and Lurline M Perrino, April 4, 1950.
- "United States Social Security Death Index," database, FamilySearch (https://familysearch.org/ark:/61903/1:1:JBK4-868 : 7 January 2021), Angelo Perrino, Jul 1985; citing U.S. Social Security Administration, Death Master File, database (Alexandria, Virginia: National Technical Information Service, ongoing).

- "Find a Grave Index," database, FamilySearch (https://www.familysearch.org/ark:/61903/1:1:6NDP-LQDX : 11 August 2022), Angelo M. Perrino, ; Burial, Manchester, Hillsborough, New Hampshire, United States of America, Mount Calvary Cemetery; citing record ID 240566454, Find a Grave, http://www.findagrave.com.
- "United States, Social Security Numerical Identification Files (NUMIDENT), 1936-2007", database, FamilySearch (https://www.familysearch.org/ark:/61903/1:1:6KMS-CXMG : 10 February 2023), Lurline St Amand Dawson, .
- "United States Social Security Death Index," , FamilySearch (https://familysearch.org/ark:/61903/1:1:JPSQ-4PJ : 7 January 2021), Lurline Perrino, 17 Sep 1994; citing U.S. Social Security Administration, Death Master File, database (Alexandria, Virginia: National Technical Information Service, ongoing).

482) Angelina M. Tiso

Angelina M. Tiso(482) was born on 31 October 1917, in Newark, NJ, to Oto (Ottone) Tiso(169) and Mary Senese(169a). Angelina M. Tiso(482) died 15 February 2012 in Newark, NJ.

Angelina M. Tiso(482) married Vincent James Pallitto(482a) in 1937.

Vincent James Pallitto(482a) was born on 8 August 1912, in Newark, NJ, to Anthony Pallitto(482aF) and Elizabeth Yacullo(482aM). Vincent James Pallitto(482a) died 8 April 2008 in Newark, NJ.

Angelina M. Tiso(482) and Vincent James Pallitto(482a) had child(ren).

Records that include Angelina M. Tiso(482) and/or Vincent James Pallitto(482a):
- "New Jersey, Reclaim the Records, Geographic Birth Index, 1901-1929", , FamilySearch (https://www.familysearch.org/ark:/61903/1:1:6NSF-1SFN : Thu Mar 07 10:17:14 UTC 2024), Entry for James Pallitto, 8 Aug 1912.
- "United States Census, 1920", , FamilySearch (https://www.familysearch.org/ark:/61903/1:1:M451-X6W : Sat Mar 09 14:37:36 UTC 2024), Entry for Ottone Tiso and Mary Tiso, 1920.
- "United States Census, 1930", , FamilySearch (https://www.familysearch.org/ark:/61903/1:1:X4DP-3XT : Sun Mar 10 23:46:12 UTC 2024), Entry for Anthony Pallitto and Elizabeth Pallitto, 1930.
- "United States Census, 1930", , FamilySearch (https://www.familysearch.org/ark:/61903/1:1:X4DG-XPV : Fri Mar 08 18:34:06 UTC 2024), Entry for Ottone Liso and Mary H Liso, 1930.
- "New Jersey, Bride Index, 1930-1938", , FamilySearch (https://www.familysearch.org/ark:/61903/1:1:QP4C-FBSV : Sun Mar 10 02:09:01 UTC 2024), Entry for Angelina Tiso and Vincent Pallitto, 1937.
- "United States Census, 1940", , FamilySearch (https://www.familysearch.org/ark:/61903/1:1:K4BX-LF1 : Sat Mar 09 02:36:08 UTC 2024), Entry for Vincent Pallitto and Angelina Pallitto, 1940.
- "United States 1950 Census", , FamilySearch (https://www.familysearch.org/ark:/61903/1:1:6F9G-QJ4L : Wed Mar 20 07:46:28 UTC 2024), Entry for Vincent Pallitto and Angelina Pallitto, 1 April 1950.
- "United States Social Security Death Index," database, FamilySearch (https://familysearch.org/ark:/61903/1:1:V31M-NPP : 12 January 2021), Vincent J Pallitto, 08 Apr 2008; citing U.S. Social Security Administration, Death Master File, database (Alexandria, Virginia: National Technical Information Service, ongoing).
- "Find a Grave Index," database, FamilySearch (https://www.familysearch.org/ark:/61903/1:1:QVLZ-3N2F : 10 September 2021), Angelina Tiso Pallitto, ; Burial, Bloomfield, Essex, New Jersey, United States of America, Glendale Cemetery; citing record ID 90263967, Find a Grave, http://www.findagrave.com.

- "Find a Grave Index," database, FamilySearch
  (https://www.familysearch.org/ark:/61903/1:1:QVLZ-3NL7 : 1 April
  2023), Vincent J. Pallitto, ; Burial, Bloomfield, Essex, New
  Jersey, United States of America, Glendale Cemetery; citing record
  ID 90554328, Find a Grave, http://www.findagrave.com.

483) Anthony Riccio

Anthony Riccio(483) was born in 1917, in New York, to Raffaele Riccio(221a)
and Giovanna (Jenny) Ciasullo(221).

Records that include Anthony Riccio(483):
- "United States Census, 1930", , FamilySearch
  (https://www.familysearch.org/ark:/61903/1:1:X4GN-27X : Sun Mar 10
  13:46:50 UTC 2024), Entry for Leonard Riccio and Jennie Riccio,
  1930.
- "United States Census, 1940", , FamilySearch
  (https://www.familysearch.org/ark:/61903/1:1:K79V-TYQ : Sat Mar 09
  17:46:14 UTC 2024), Entry for Ralph Riccio and Jennie Riccio, 1940.
- "United States Census, 1950", , FamilySearch
  (https://www.familysearch.org/ark:/61903/1:1:6XRQ-N1D2 : Wed Mar 20
  20:19:13 UTC 2024), Entry for Anthony Riccio and Evelyn Riccio, 27
  April 1950.

NOTE: This is the only information I could confirm for Anthony Riccio(483),
however, I found more information that I can not definitively connect to
Anthony Riccio(483) if it is correct the record for him should be:

*483) Anthony Riccio

Anthony Riccio(*483) was born on 30 March 1917, in Schenectady, NY, to
Raffaele Riccio(221a) and Giovanna (Jenny) Ciasullo(221). Anthony Riccio(*483)
died on 24 October 1972 in Schenectady, NY.

Anthony Riccio(*483) married Evelyn D'Agostino(*483a).

Evelyn D'Agostino(*483a) was born on 29 June 1924, in Schenectady, NY, to
Andrew James D'Agostino(*483aF) and Mary Antoinette Comunale(*483aM). Evelyn
D'Agostino(*483a) died on 9 August 2011 in Schenectady, NY.

Anthony Riccio(*483) and Evelyn D'Agostino(*483a) had child(ren).

Records that include Anthony Riccio(*483) and/or Evelyn D'Agostino(*483a):
- "New York, Birth Indexes outside of New York City, 1881-1942", ,
  FamilySearch (https://www.familysearch.org/ark:/61903/1:1:6FXL-W97Q
  : Sun Mar 10 16:18:16 UTC 2024), Entry for Antonio Ricci, 30 Mar
  1917.
- "United States Census, 1930", , FamilySearch
  (https://www.familysearch.org/ark:/61903/1:1:X4GN-27X : Sun Mar 10
  13:46:50 UTC 2024), Entry for Leonard Riccio and Jennie Riccio,
  1930.
- "United States Census, 1930", , FamilySearch
  (https://www.familysearch.org/ark:/61903/1:1:X4TY-RM4 : Thu Mar 07
  08:44:23 UTC 2024), Entry for Andrew Dagostino and Marry Dagostino,
  1930.
- "United States Census, 1940", , FamilySearch
  (https://www.familysearch.org/ark:/61903/1:1:K79V-TYQ : Sat Mar 09
  17:46:14 UTC 2024), Entry for Ralph Riccio and Jennie Riccio, 1940.
- "United States Census, 1940", , FamilySearch
  (https://www.familysearch.org/ark:/61903/1:1:KQY5-7WY : Fri Mar 08
  04:32:08 UTC 2024), Entry for Andrew d'Agostino and Mary
  d'Agostino, 1940.
- "United States World War II Army Enlistment Records, 1938-1946," ,
  FamilySearch (https://familysearch.org/ark:/61903/1:1:K8RC-LJ2 : 5
  December 2014), Anthony R Riccio, enlisted 13 Feb 1942, Cp Upton,
  Yaphank, New York, United States; citing "Electronic Army Serial
  Number Merged File, ca. 1938-1946," database, The National
  Archives: Access to Archival Databases (AAD)
  (http://aad.archives.gov : National Archives and Records
  Administration, 2002); NARA NAID 1263923, National Archives at
  College Park, Maryland.

- "United States Census, 1950", , FamilySearch
  (https://www.familysearch.org/ark:/61903/1:1:6XRQ-N1D2 : Wed Mar 20
  20:19:13 UTC 2024), Entry for Anthony Riccio and Evelyn Riccio, 27
  April 1950.
- "United States, Social Security Numerical Identification Files
  (NUMIDENT), 1936-2007", database, FamilySearch
  (https://www.familysearch.org/ark:/61903/1:1:6K99-DJNQ : 10
  February 2023), Anthony R Riccio, .
- "United States, Social Security Numerical Identification Files
  (NUMIDENT), 1936-2007", database, FamilySearch
  (https://www.familysearch.org/ark:/61903/1:1:6K99-DJNQ : 10
  February 2023), Anthony R Riccio, .
- "United States Social Security Death Index," database, FamilySearch
  (https://familysearch.org/ark:/61903/1:1:VQN2-1VH : 12 January
  2021), Evelyn Riccio, 09 Aug 2011; citing U.S. Social Security
  Administration, Death Master File, database (Alexandria, Virginia:
  National Technical Information Service, ongoing).

484) Mary Ann Bonelli

Mary Ann Bonelli(484) was born on 17 July 1917, in St. Louis, MO, to Joseph
Bonelli(271a) and Concetta Anastasio(271). Mary Ann Bonelli(484) died 4 July
2003 in Mesa, AZ.

Mary Ann Bonelli(484) married Thomas Elmo Gibson(484a) in 1941.

Thomas Elmo Gibson(484a) was born on 31 December 1913, in Kevil, KY, to
Charlie Thomas Gibson(484aF) and Osie Soloman(484aM). Thomas Elmo Gibson(484a)
died 27 Jun 2001 in Lansing, MI.

Mary Ann Bonelli(484) and Thomas Elmo Gibson(484a) had child(ren).

Records that include Mary Ann Bonelli(484) and/or Thomas Elmo Gibson(484a):
- "Kentucky, Vital Record Indexes, 1911-1999," , FamilySearch
  (https://www.familysearch.org/ark:/61903/1:1:QKHG-QC9G : 5 December
  2023), Thomas Gibson, 31 Dec 1913; citing Birth, Kentucky, United
  States, Kentucky Department for Libraries and Archives, Frankfort.
- "United States Census, 1920", , FamilySearch
  (https://www.familysearch.org/ark:/61903/1:1:M887-HJN : Sat Mar 09
  17:39:56 UTC 2024), Entry for Joseph Bonneli and Consetti Bonneli,
  1920.
- "United States Census, 1920", , FamilySearch
  (https://www.familysearch.org/ark:/61903/1:1:MHGP-CPP : Wed Jul 10
  17:21:14 UTC 2024), Entry for Charlie Gibson and Olie Gibson, 1920.
- United States Census, 1930", , FamilySearch
  (https://www.familysearch.org/ark:/61903/1:1:X7SP-TPK : Sun Mar 10
  23:23:02 UTC 2024), Entry for Causamo Stilo and Elvera Stilo, 1930.
- "United States Census, 1940", , FamilySearch
  (https://www.familysearch.org/ark:/61903/1:1:KH9W-QLW : Sat Mar 09
  23:26:34 UTC 2024), Entry for Concetta H Athanas and Mary A
  Bonelli, 1940.
- "United States Census, 1940", , FamilySearch
  (https://www.familysearch.org/ark:/61903/1:1:K755-WTC : Sun Jul 07
  01:18:19 UTC 2024), Entry for Charlie Gibson and Osie Gibson, 1940.
- "Michigan, World War II Draft Registration Cards, 1940-1947", ,
  FamilySearch (https://www.familysearch.org/ark:/61903/1:1:QPRC-9HTH
  : Sun Jul 14 05:25:49 UTC 2024), Entry for Thomas Elmo Gibson and
  A.C. Johnson Co., 16 Oct 1940.
- "United States Census, 1950", , FamilySearch
  (https://www.familysearch.org/ark:/61903/1:1:6F7W-ZKF8 : Wed Mar 20
  18:14:59 UTC 2024), Entry for Elwood Morgan and Idell Morgan, 10
  April 1950.
- "United States Social Security Death Index," database, FamilySearch
  (https://familysearch.org/ark:/61903/1:1:JRGK-VYZ : 9 January
  2021), Thomas E Gibson, 27 Jun 2001; citing U.S. Social Security
  Administration, Death Master File, database (Alexandria, Virginia:
  National Technical Information Service, ongoing).

- "United States, Social Security Numerical Identification Files (NUMIDENT), 1936-2007", database, FamilySearch (https://www.familysearch.org/ark:/61903/1:1:6KQC-VZGF : 10 February 2023), Thomas E Gibson, .
- "Find a Grave Index," database, FamilySearch (https://www.familysearch.org/ark:/61903/1:1:W6P4-7V2M : 23 July 2024), Thomas Elmo Gibson, ; Burial, La Center, Ballard, Kentucky, United States of America, Mount Pleasant Church Cemetery; citing record ID 201139449, Find a Grave, http://www.findagrave.com.
- "United States, Social Security Numerical Identification Files (NUMIDENT), 1936-2007", database, FamilySearch (https://www.familysearch.org/ark:/61903/1:1:6KQF-XSLX : 10 February 2023), Mary A Gibson, .
- "United States Social Security Death Index," database, FamilySearch (https://familysearch.org/ark:/61903/1:1:JRGY-CNL : 9 January 2021), Mary A Gibson, 04 Jul 2003; citing U.S. Social Security Administration, Death Master File, database (Alexandria, Virginia: National Technical Information Service, ongoing).
- "Find a Grave Index," database, FamilySearch (https://www.familysearch.org/ark:/61903/1:1:W6P4-7V6Z : 23 July 2024), Mary Ann Bonelli Gibson, ; Burial, La Center, Ballard, Kentucky, United States of America, Mount Pleasant Church Cemetery; citing record ID 201139447, Find a Grave, http://www.findagrave.com.

485) Ugo Ralph Miseno

Ugo Ralph Miseno(485) was born on 18 March 1918, in Amsterdam, NY, to Ugo Miseno(238a) and Concetta Felicia Perrina(238). Ugo Ralph Miseno(485) graduated from Sienna College, Loudonville, NY in 1943. Ugo Ralph Miseno(485) died 29 April 2007 in Piscataway, NJ.

Ugo Ralph Miseno(485) married Violet Perine(485a) after 1950.

Violet Perine(485a) was born on 7 February 1910, in Staten Island, NY. Violet Perine(485a) died 26 January 2015 in Flemington, NJ.

Ugo Ralph Miseno(485) and/or Violet Perine(485a) had child(ren).

Records that include Ugo Ralph Miseno(485) and/or Violet Perine(485a):
- "New York, Birth Indexes outside of New York City, 1881-1942", , FamilySearch (https://www.familysearch.org/ark:/61903/1:1:6XT7-RXNW : Sun Mar 10 18:24:18 UTC 2024), Entry for Hugo R Miseno, 18 Mar 1918.
- "United States Census, 1920", , FamilySearch (https://www.familysearch.org/ark:/61903/1:1:MJGD-61J : Sun Mar 10 00:46:08 UTC 2024), Entry for Ugo Mireno and Concetta Mireno, 1920.
- "United States Census, 1930", , FamilySearch (https://www.familysearch.org/ark:/61903/1:1:X78V-MMP : Sun Mar 10 13:54:09 UTC 2024), Entry for Hugo Misseno and Conncetta Misseno, 1930.
- https://siena.contentdm.oclc.org/digital/collection/SienaNP01/id/2051
- "United States World War II Army Enlistment Records, 1938-1946," , FamilySearch (https://familysearch.org/ark:/61903/1:1:K85D-SVZ : 5 December 2014), Ugo R Miseno, enlisted 15 Jan 1944, Albany, New York, United States; citing "Electronic Army Serial Number Merged File, ca. 1938-1946," database, The National Archives: Access to Archival Databases (AAD) (http://aad.archives.gov : National Archives and Records Administration, 2002); NARA NAID 1263923, National Archives at College Park, Maryland.
- "United States Census, 1950", , FamilySearch (https://www.familysearch.org/ark:/61903/1:1:6XT1-B8TJ : Tue Mar 19 15:33:24 UTC 2024), Entry for Magda R Stadler and Ethel Lambert, 10 April 1950.

- "United States Social Security Death Index," database, FamilySearch (https://familysearch.org/ark:/61903/1:1:JGJH-83K : 12 January 2021), Ugo R Miseno, 29 Apr 2007; citing U.S. Social Security Administration, Death Master File, database (Alexandria, Virginia: National Technical Information Service, ongoing).
- https://obits.nj.com/us/obituaries/hunterdoncountydemocrat/name/violet-miseno-obituary?id=18423733

486) Angelina Miressi

Angelina Miressi(486) was born on 4 July 1918, in New Rochelle, NY, to Generoso Miressi(160) and Maria Luigia Iannarone(160a). Angelina Miressi(486) died on 9 June 2002 in Lake Luzerne, NY.

Angelina Miressi(486) married Domenick Condello(486a) on 16 October 1940.

Domenick Condello(486a) was born on 1 July 1916, in Cittanova, Italy, to Joseph Condello(486aF) and Angelina Tropeano(486aM). Domenick Condello(486a) died 31 December 1994 in Lake Luzerne, NY.

Angelina Miressi(486) and Domenick Condello(486a) had child(ren).

Records that include Angelina Miressi(486) and/or Domenick Condello(486a):
- "New York, Birth Indexes outside of New York City, 1881-1942", , FamilySearch (https://www.familysearch.org/ark:/61903/1:1:6XT7-RXFD : Sun Mar 10 18:24:19 UTC 2024), Entry for Angela Miressi, 4 Jul 1918.
- "New York, New York Passenger and Crew Lists, 1909, 1925-1957", , FamilySearch (https://www.familysearch.org/ark:/61903/1:1:24NM-3KC : Thu Mar 07 13:45:41 UTC 2024), Entry for Domenico Condello, 1930.
- "United States, New York, Index to Passengers Arriving at New York City, compiled 1944-1948", , FamilySearch (https://www.familysearch.org/ark:/61903/1:1:7HL6-Y3ZM : Sat Mar 09 10:02:34 UTC 2024), Entry for Domenico Condello, 1930.
- "United States Census, 1940", , FamilySearch (https://www.familysearch.org/ark:/61903/1:1:KQMC-WL8 : Sun Mar 10 09:29:24 UTC 2024), Entry for Joseph Condello and Angelina Condello, 1940.
- "New York, New York City, World War II Draft Registration Cards, 1940-1947", , FamilySearch (https://www.familysearch.org/ark:/61903/1:1:WHL1-W36Z : Sun Mar 10 06:53:15 UTC 2024), Entry for Domenick Condello and William Shemin, 16 Oct 1940.
- "United States 1950 Census", , FamilySearch (https://www.familysearch.org/ark:/61903/1:1:6XT5-X19B : Tue Mar 19 02:20:26 UTC 2024), Entry for Domenick Condello and Angelina Condello, 10 April 1950.
- "United States 1950 Census", , FamilySearch (https://www.familysearch.org/ark:/61903/1:1:6XT5-X19B : Tue Mar 19 02:20:26 UTC 2024), Entry for Domenick Condello and Angelina Condello, 10 April 1950.
- "United States Social Security Death Index," database, FamilySearch (https://familysearch.org/ark:/61903/1:1:JTYJ-7JD : 7 January 2021), Domiinick Condello, 31 Dec 1994; citing U.S. Social Security Administration, Death Master File, database (Alexandria, Virginia: National Technical Information Service, ongoing).
- "United States, Social Security Numerical Identification Files (NUMIDENT), 1936-2007", database, FamilySearch (https://www.familysearch.org/ark:/61903/1:1:6KMB-F83W : 10 February 2023), Domenick Condello, .
- "United States, Social Security Numerical Identification Files (NUMIDENT), 1936-2007", database, FamilySearch (https://www.familysearch.org/ark:/61903/1:1:6KM5-XBBP : 10 February 2023), Angelina Condello, .

- "United States Social Security Death Index," database, FamilySearch (https://familysearch.org/ark:/61903/1:1:JBP6-8MZ : 7 January 2021), Angelina Condello, 09 Jun 2002; citing U.S. Social Security Administration, Death Master File, database (Alexandria, Virginia: National Technical Information Service, ongoing).
- "United States, Social Security Numerical Identification Files (NUMIDENT), 1936-2007", , FamilySearch (https://www.familysearch.org/ark:/61903/1:1:6KMT-LF2C : 10 February 2023), Angelina Miresia in entry for Donna Angela Condello, .
- "Find a Grave Index," database, FamilySearch (https://www.familysearch.org/ark:/61903/1:1:QVG6-NCKB : 10 September 2021), Angelina Condello, ; Burial, Lake Luzerne, Warren, New York, United States of America, Church of the Holy Infancy Cemetery; citing record ID 117111319, Find a Grave, http://www.findagrave.com.

487) Frances Eva Miressi

Frances Eva Miressi(487) was born on 21 July 1918, in Middletown, NY, to Giovanni Miressi(226) and Florence Emily Wilson(226a). Frances Eva Miressi(487) died 26 March 2008 in Middletown, NY.

Frances Eva Miressi(487) married Robert Eustacchio LoFrese(487a).

Robert Eustacchio LoFrese(487a) was born on 30 October 1914, in Cassano della Murge, Italy, to Joseph LoFrese(487aF) and Terese Colacicco(487aM). Robert Eustacchio LoFrese(487a)died March 1992 in Middletown, NY.

Records that include Frances Eva Miressi(487) married Robert Eustacchio LoFrese(487a):

- "New York, Birth Indexes outside of New York City, 1881-1942", , FamilySearch (https://www.familysearch.org/ark:/61903/1:1:6XT7-RXF6 : Sun Mar 10 18:24:17 UTC 2024), Entry for Frances E Miressi, 21 Jul 1918.
- "United States Census, 1920", , FamilySearch (https://www.familysearch.org/ark:/61903/1:1:MV9F-9G9 : Sat Mar 09 10:15:10 UTC 2024), Entry for John Miressie and Florence Miressie, 1920.
- "New York, New York Passenger and Crew Lists, 1909, 1925-1957", , FamilySearch (https://www.familysearch.org/ark:/61903/1:1:24XP-RPX : Thu Mar 07 17:23:11 UTC 2024), Entry for Eustacchio Lofrese, 1929.
- "United States Census, 1930", , FamilySearch (https://www.familysearch.org/ark:/61903/1:1:X4R1-4DK : Sun Mar 10 13:51:06 UTC 2024), Entry for Florence Miressi and Frances E Miressi, 1930.
- "United States Census, 1930", , FamilySearch (https://www.familysearch.org/ark:/61903/1:1:X7DT-9X9 : Fri Mar 08 10:20:09 UTC 2024), Entry for Joseph Lafresa and Therresa Lafresa, 1930.
- "United States Census, 1950", , FamilySearch (https://www.familysearch.org/ark:/61903/1:1:6XTR-3S63 : Sat Oct 07 01:02:50 UTC 2023), Entry for Eustachio Lofrese and Frances E Lofrese, 10 April 1950.
- "United States Social Security Death Index," database, FamilySearch (https://familysearch.org/ark:/61903/1:1:JPWF-S2R : 7 January 2021), Eustachio Lofrese, Mar 1992; citing U.S. Social Security Administration, Death Master File, database (Alexandria, Virginia: National Technical Information Service, ongoing).
- "United States, Social Security Numerical Identification Files (NUMIDENT), 1936-2007", database, FamilySearch (https://www.familysearch.org/ark:/61903/1:1:6KMB-VM2G : 10 February 2023), Robert Lofrese, .
- "United States Social Security Death Index," database, FamilySearch (https://familysearch.org/ark:/61903/1:1:V3BT-T68 : 12 January 2021), Frances E Lofrese, 26 Mar 2008; citing U.S. Social Security Administration, Death Master File, database (Alexandria, Virginia: National Technical Information Service, ongoing).

- https://www.legacy.com/us/obituaries/recordonline/name/frances-obituary?id=29195462

488) Anthony Carmen Perrine

Anthony Carmen Perrine(488) was born on 21 July or 21 August 1918, in Jessup, PA, to Carmine Perrina(247) and Colomba di Pasquale(247a). Anthony Carmen Perrine(488) died July 1984.

NOTE: Anthony Carmen Perrine(488)'s birth date is listed as 21 July 1918 on his death records, however, it is listed as 21 August 1918 on his WWII draft card and marriage license.

Anthony Carmen Perrine(488) married Anna Spinelli(488a) on 27 April 1941 in Philadelphia, PA.

Anna Spinelli(488a) was born on 20 June 1919, in Philadelphia, PA, to Joseph Spinelli(488aF) and Anna Galdi(488aM). Anna Spinelli(488a) died July 2015.

Anthony Carmen Perrine(488)and Anna Spinelli(488a) had child(ren).

Records that include Anthony Carmen Perrine(488) and/or Anna Spinelli(488a):

- "United States Census, 1920", , FamilySearch (https://www.familysearch.org/ark:/61903/1:1:MFY4-Q5M : Wed Mar 06 09:48:19 UTC 2024), Entry for O Dena Perine and Colombine Perine, 1920.
- "United States Census, 1930", , FamilySearch (https://www.familysearch.org/ark:/61903/1:1:X7CK-1B8 : Fri Jul 05 22:27:03 UTC 2024), Entry for Carmino Perrine and Columbia Perrine, 1930.
- "United States Census, 1920", , FamilySearch (https://www.familysearch.org/ark:/61903/1:1:MNMP-LML : Fri Mar 08 21:55:50 UTC 2024), Entry for Joseph Spinelli and Anna Spinelli, 1920.
- "United States Census, 1930", , FamilySearch (https://www.familysearch.org/ark:/61903/1:1:XH4Q-7M6 : Sat Mar 09 19:44:06 UTC 2024), Entry for Joseph Spinelli and Anna Spinelli, 1930.
- "United States Census, 1940", , FamilySearch (https://www.familysearch.org/ark:/61903/1:1:KQX9-R7Y : Wed Mar 06 16:42:53 UTC 2024), Entry for Daniel Spinelli and Anna Spinelli, 1940.
- "Pennsylvania, World War II Draft Registration Cards, 1940-1945", , FamilySearch (https://www.familysearch.org/ark:/61903/1:1:Q2SJ-6YGP : Fri Feb 23 20:57:45 UTC 2024), Entry for Anthony Carmen Perrine and Carmen Perrine, 16 Oct 1940.
- "Pennsylvania, Philadelphia Marriage Indexes, 1885-1951", , FamilySearch (https://www.familysearch.org/ark:/61903/1:1:JVQX-LHW : Sat Feb 24 04:20:57 UTC 2024), Entry for Anna Spinelli and Perrine, 1941.
- "Pennsylvania, Philadelphia Marriage Indexes, 1885-1951", , FamilySearch (https://www.familysearch.org/ark:/61903/1:1:ZW78-G6MM : Sat Feb 24 05:23:29 UTC 2024), Entry for Anthony Perrine and Spinelli, 1941.
- "Pennsylvania, County Marriages, 1885-1950", , FamilySearch (https://www.familysearch.org/ark:/61903/1:1:Q2ZW-FS4V : Mon Sep 02 04:17:41 UTC 2024), Entry for Anthony Perrine and Anna Spinelli, March 1941.
- "Pennsylvania, County Marriages, 1885-1950", , FamilySearch (https://www.familysearch.org/ark:/61903/1:1:Q2ZW-F9BL : Wed Jul 10 08:26:41 UTC 2024), Entry for Anthony Perrene and Anna Spinelli, 27 Apr 1941.
- https://www.newspapers.com/article/the-philadelphia-inquirer-marriage-of-go-111824388/
- "United States Census, 1950", , FamilySearch (https://www.familysearch.org/ark:/61903/1:1:6X13-B7WD : Wed Mar 20 19:48:49 UTC 2024), Entry for Anita M Perrine and Anthony J Perrine, 12 April 1950.

- https://www.newspapers.com/article/the-buffalo-news-perrine-colomba-nee-d/148955383/
- "United States Social Security Death Index," , FamilySearch (https://familysearch.org/ark:/61903/1:1:JY79-HZR : 8 January 2021), Anthony Perrine, Jul 1984; citing U.S. Social Security Administration, Death Master File, database (Alexandria, Virginia: National Technical Information Service, ongoing).
- "Find a Grave Index," database, FamilySearch (https://www.familysearch.org/ark:/61903/1:1:4KVB-1WW2 : 12 January 2023), Anthony Perrine, ; Burial, Torresdale, Philadelphia, Pennsylvania, United States of America, Saint Dominic Church Cemetery; citing record ID 205016617, Find a Grave, http://www.findagrave.com.

489) Enrico Ninfadoro

Enrico Ninfadoro(489) was born about September 1918, in Zungoli, Italy, to Antonio Ninfadoro(179) and Maria Carmela Dioguardi(179a). Enrico Ninfadoro(489) died on 2 December 1918, in Ariano, Italy.

Records that include Enrico Ninfadoro(489):
- Ariano, Italy 1918 Death Act #635

490) Raffaele (Ralph) Giorgione/George

Raffaele (Ralph) Giorgione/ George(490) was born on 10 October 1918, in Middletown, NY, to Giuseppe (Joseph) Giorgione/George(263) and Margherita Adele Maria Marasco(263a). Raffaele (Ralph) Giorgione/ George(490) died on 6 September 1996 in Lexington, SC.

Raffaele (Ralph) Giorgione/ George(490) married Lillian Evetta Shealy(490a).

Lillian Evetta Shealy(490a) was born on 23 February 1917, in Lexington, SC, to Pierce Rufus Shealy(490aF) and Lillian Agnes Jumper(490aM). Lillian Evetta Shealy(490a) died on 22 August 2014 in Lexington, SC.

Raffaele (Ralph) Giorgione/ George(490) and Lillian Evetta Shealy(490a) had child(ren).

Records that include Raffaele (Ralph) Giorgione/ George(490) and/or Lillian Evetta Shealy(490a):
- "New York, Birth Indexes outside of New York City, 1881-1942", , FamilySearch (https://www.familysearch.org/ark:/61903/1:1:6XKY-3MFJ : Fri Mar 08 23:55:37 UTC 2024), Entry for Ralph George, 10 Oct 1918.
- "United States Census, 1920", , FamilySearch (https://www.familysearch.org/ark:/61903/1:1:MV9X-V8Z : Fri Mar 08 20:28:15 UTC 2024), Entry for Joseph George and Marguerite George, 1920.
- "United States Census, 1920", , FamilySearch (https://www.familysearch.org/ark:/61903/1:1:M6ZL-286 : Thu Mar 07 04:57:33 UTC 2024), Entry for Pierce Shealy and Lillian Shealy, 1920.
- "United States Census, 1930", , FamilySearch (https://www.familysearch.org/ark:/61903/1:1:X78W-X9G : Sun Mar 10 20:48:01 UTC 2024), Entry for Joseph Giorgione and Margaret Giorgione, 1930.
- "United States Census, 1930", , FamilySearch (https://www.familysearch.org/ark:/61903/1:1:SPCY-34Q : Sun Mar 10 06:34:11 UTC 2024), Entry for Pierce B Shealey and Lillian A Shealey, 1930.
- "United States Census, 1940", , FamilySearch (https://www.familysearch.org/ark:/61903/1:1:KQY5-9LC : Sat Mar 09 22:50:37 UTC 2024), Entry for Joseph George and Margret George, 1940.
- "United States Census, 1940", , FamilySearch (https://www.familysearch.org/ark:/61903/1:1:K4DR-FXQ : Sun Mar 10 22:37:49 UTC 2024), Entry for Peirce R Shealy and Lillian Shealy, 1940.

- "United States Census, 1950", , FamilySearch
  (https://www.familysearch.org/ark:/61903/1:1:6XY4-9B98 : Wed Mar 20
  14:13:44 UTC 2024), Entry for Ralph George and Lillian S George, 14
  April 1950.
- "United States World War II Army Enlistment Records, 1938-1946," ,
  FamilySearch (https://familysearch.org/ark:/61903/1:1:KMJQ-HPC : 5
  December 2014), Ralph George, enlisted 31 Mar 1942, Ft Niagara,
  Youngstown, New York, United States; citing "Electronic Army Serial
  Number Merged File, ca. 1938-1946," database, The National
  Archives: Access to Archival Databases (AAD)
  (http://aad.archives.gov : National Archives and Records
  Administration, 2002); NARA NAID 1263923, National Archives at
  College Park, Maryland.
- "Find a Grave Index," database, FamilySearch
  (https://www.familysearch.org/ark:/61903/1:1:QVPM-P5FY : 12 March
  2024), Ralph George, ; Burial, Batesburg, Lexington, South
  Carolina, United States of America, Ridge Crest Memorial Park;
  citing record ID 134744351, Find a Grave,
  http://www.findagrave.com.
- "Find a Grave Index," database, FamilySearch
  (https://www.familysearch.org/ark:/61903/1:1:QVPM-P5FT : 17 July
  2020), Lillian Evetta Shealy George, 2014; Burial, , ; citing
  record ID , Find a Grave, http://www.findagrave.com.

491) Peter Attilio Riccio

Peter Attilio Riccio(491) was born on 26 December 1918, in Schenectady, NY, to
Raffaele Riccio(221a) and Giovanna (Jenny) Ciasullo(221). Peter Attilio
Riccio(491) served in the United States Army from July 1944 to May 1945. Peter
Attilio Riccio(491) died 15 July 2004 in Schenectady, NY.

Peter Attilio Riccio(491) married Marie diTorio(491a).

Marie diTorio(491a) was born on 29 May 1917, in Pietracupa, Italy, to Giuseppe
(Joseph) diTorio(491aF) and Theresa Sardella(491aM). Marie diTorio(491a) died
on 24 August 1993 in Schenectady, NY.

Peter Attilio Riccio(491) and Marie diTorio(491a) had child(ren).

Records that include Peter Attilio Riccio(491) and/or Marie diTorio(491a):
- "New York, County Naturalization Records, 1791-1980", ,
  FamilySearch (https://www.familysearch.org/ark:/61903/1:1:7WKN-NXN2
  : Fri Mar 08 08:42:48 UTC 2024), Entry for Joseph Giuseppe Di Torio
  and Theresa, 1927.
- "United States Census, 1930", , FamilySearch
  (https://www.familysearch.org/ark:/61903/1:1:X4TB-187 : Fri Mar 08
  12:10:26 UTC 2024), Entry for Ralph Riccio and Jennie Riccio, 1930.
- "United States Census, 1930", , FamilySearch
  (https://www.familysearch.org/ark:/61903/1:1:X4T1-Z2X : Thu Jul 18
  07:13:58 UTC 2024), Entry for Joseph Diiorio and Teresa Diiorio,
  1930.
- "United States Census, 1940", , FamilySearch
  (https://www.familysearch.org/ark:/61903/1:1:K79V-TYQ : Sat Mar 09
  17:46:14 UTC 2024), Entry for Ralph Riccio and Jennie Riccio, 1940.
- "United States Census, 1940", , FamilySearch
  (https://www.familysearch.org/ark:/61903/1:1:K79V-BHH : Sun Mar 10
  05:19:40 UTC 2024), Entry for Joseph Diorio and Theresa Diorio,
  1940.
- "United States World War II Army Enlistment Records, 1938-1946," ,
  FamilySearch (https://familysearch.org/ark:/61903/1:1:K8RC-BVQ : 5
  December 2014), Peter A Riccio, enlisted 12 Mar 1942, Cp Upton,
  Yaphank, New York, United States; citing "Electronic Army Serial
  Number Merged File, ca. 1938-1946," database, The National
  Archives: Access to Archival Databases (AAD)
  (http://aad.archives.gov : National Archives and Records
  Administration, 2002); NARA NAID 1263923, National Archives at
  College Park, Maryland.

- "United States World War II Army Enlistment Records, 1938-1946," , FamilySearch (https://familysearch.org/ark:/61903/1:1:KMJZ-L5K : 5 December 2014), Peter A Ricci, enlisted 23 Oct 1942, Rochester, New York, United States; citing "Electronic Army Serial Number Merged File, ca. 1938-1946," database, The National Archives: Access to Archival Databases (AAD) (http://aad.archives.gov : National Archives and Records Administration, 2002); NARA NAID 1263923, National Archives at College Park, Maryland.
- "United States, Social Security Numerical Identification Files (NUMIDENT), 1936-2007", database, FamilySearch (https://www.familysearch.org/ark:/61903/1:1:6KML-8K1K : 10 February 2023), Peter Attilio Riccio, .
- "United States Social Security Death Index," , FamilySearch (https://familysearch.org/ark:/61903/1:1:J5FJ-PPY : 11 January 2021), Peter A Riccio, 15 Jul 2004; citing U.S. Social Security Administration, Death Master File, database (Alexandria, Virginia: National Technical Information Service, ongoing).
- "Find a Grave Index," database, FamilySearch (https://www.familysearch.org/ark:/61903/1:1:QPRZ-9XN9 : 16 December 2020), Peter A. Riccio, ; Burial, Niskayuna, Schenectady, New York, United States of America, Most Holy Redeemer Cemetery; citing record ID 192414137, Find a Grave, http://www.findagrave.com.
- "United States, Social Security Numerical Identification Files (NUMIDENT), 1936-2007", database, FamilySearch (https://www.familysearch.org/ark:/61903/1:1:6K9Q-Y9Q6 : 10 February 2023), Marie Diorio, .
- "St. Luke, Schenectady, New York, Baptism and Burials(Jan 1916 – Sep 2003)", American-Canadian Genealogical Society, Manchester, NH, page 222
- "Find a Grave Index," database, FamilySearch (https://www.familysearch.org/ark:/61903/1:1:QPRZ-X2H3 : 16 December 2020), Marie Riccio, ; Burial, Niskayuna, Schenectady, New York, United States of America, Most Holy Redeemer Cemetery; citing record ID 192414175, Find a Grave, http://www.findagrave.com.

492) Angiolina LoConte

Angiolina LoConte(492) was born about 1919, in Ariano, Italy, to Francesco Paolo LoConte(205a) and Carmela Manganiello(205). Angiolina LoConte(492) died on 23 November 1923, in Ariano, Italy.

Records that include Angiolina LoConte(492):
- Ariano, Italy 1922 Death Act#261

493) Victor Pasqual Stilo

Victor Pasqual Stilo(493) was born on 21 April 1919, in Milford Hill, NH, to Cosimo Stilo(363a) and Helen Elvera Anastasio(363). Victor Pasqual Stilo(493) died on 17 January 1992 in Racine, WI. Victor Pasqual Stilo(493) was buried in West Lawn Memorial Park, Mount Pleasant, WI.

Victor Pasqual Stilo(493) married Josephine L. Coyne(493a) and Ramona Violet Josephine Rundquist(493b).

Josephine L. Coyne(493a) was born about 10 August 1925 in Wisconsin, to Joseph Coyne(493aF) and Agnita Brotherson(493aM). Josephine L. Coyne(493a) died on 29 January 2008 in Racine, WI.

Victor Pasqual Stilo(493) married Ramona Violet Josephine Rundquist(493b) on 19 November 1966 in Racine, Wisconsin.

Ramona Violet Josephine Rundquist(493b) was born on 14 August 1930, in Chisago, MN, to Walter Rundquist(493bF) and Hulda Josephena Sophina Rydoon(493bM). Ramona Violet Josephine Rundquist(493b) died on 26 July 2013, in Berlin, WI. Ramona Violet Josephine Rundquist(493b) was buried in West Lawn Memorial Park, Mount Pleasant, WI.

Records that include Victor Pasqual Stilo(493), Josephine L. Coyne(493a), and/or Ramona Violet Josephine Rundquist(493b):
- "United States Census, 1920", , FamilySearch (https://www.familysearch.org/ark:/61903/1:1:MCNL-VV4 : Sun Mar 10 15:00:17 UTC 2024), Entry for Cosemo Stilo and Elvera Stilo, 1920.

- "United States Census, 1930", , FamilySearch
  (https://www.familysearch.org/ark:/61903/1:1:X7SP-TPK : Sun Mar 10
  23:23:02 UTC 2024), Entry for Causamo Stilo and Elvera Stilo, 1930.
- "United States Census, 1930", , FamilySearch
  (https://www.familysearch.org/ark:/61903/1:1:X9SN-49W : Sun Mar 10
  00:22:45 UTC 2024), Entry for Joseph Coyne and Agnita Coyne, 1930.
- "United States Census, 1940", , FamilySearch
  (https://www.familysearch.org/ark:/61903/1:1:K7J8-X7Y : Sat Mar 09
  13:14:36 UTC 2024), Entry for Cosimo Stilo and Helen E Stilo, 1940.
- "United States Census, 1940", , FamilySearch
  (https://www.familysearch.org/ark:/61903/1:1:K7JD-B3J : Thu Mar 07
  20:15:31 UTC 2024), Entry for Joseph Coyne and Agneta Coyne, 1940.
- "United States Census, 1940", , FamilySearch
  (https://www.familysearch.org/ark:/61903/1:1:K7N2-C2D : Sat Mar 09
  08:14:37 UTC 2024), Entry for Erwin W Raudquist and Minnie
  Raudquist, 1940.
- "United States World War II Army Enlistment Records, 1938-1946,"
  database, FamilySearch
  (https://familysearch.org/ark:/61903/1:1:K8Y2-LYY : 5 December
  2014), Victor P Stilo, enlisted 30 Jun 1942, Milwaukee, Wisconsin,
  United States; citing "Electronic Army Serial Number Merged File,
  ca. 1938-1946," database, The National Archives: Access to Archival
  Databases (AAD) (http://aad.archives.gov : National Archives and
  Records Administration, 2002); NARA NAID 1263923, National Archives
  at College Park, Maryland.
- "United States 1950 Census", , FamilySearch
  (https://www.familysearch.org/ark:/61903/1:1:6FMY-L911 : Wed Mar 20
  04:01:44 UTC 2024), Entry for Joseph E Coyne and Agneta S Coyne, 10
  April 1950.
- "United States, Social Security Numerical Identification Files
  (NUMIDENT), 1936-2007", database, FamilySearch
  (https://www.familysearch.org/ark:/61903/1:1:6KQK-M1WS : 10
  February 2023), Victor Pat Stilo, .
- "United States Social Security Death Index," database, FamilySearch
  (https://familysearch.org/ark:/61903/1:1:V3BZ-VJZ : 12 January
  2021), Josephine L Stilo, 29 Jan 2008; citing U.S. Social Security
  Administration, Death Master File, database (Alexandria, Virginia:
  National Technical Information Service, ongoing).
- "United States Social Security Death Index," database, FamilySearch
  (https://familysearch.org/ark:/61903/1:1:K5M8-T2J : 12 January
  2021), Ramona V Stilo, 26 Jul 2013; citing U.S. Social Security
  Administration, Death Master File, database (Alexandria, Virginia:
  National Technical Information Service, ongoing).
- "Find a Grave Index," database, FamilySearch
  (https://www.familysearch.org/ark:/61903/1:1:QVG5-X12J : 15 June
  2022), Victor Pasqual Stilo, ; Burial, Mount Pleasant, Racine,
  Wisconsin, United States of America, West Lawn Memorial Park;
  citing record ID 127082061, Find a Grave,
  http://www.findagrave.com.
- "Find a Grave Index," database, FamilySearch
  (https://www.familysearch.org/ark:/61903/1:1:QVG5-X12N : 2 July
  2020), Ramona Violet Josephine Stilo, 2013; Burial, , ; citing
  record ID , Find a Grave, http://www.findagrave.com.

494) Louis William George

Louis William George(494) was born on 15 February 1919, in Middletown, NY, to
Carmine (Carmen Louis) Giorgione/George(290) and Bertha Michalowski(290a).
Louis William George(494) died December 1982.

Louis William George(494) married Frances (Margaret) Rowley(494a) on 26
October 1943 in Mahoning County, OH.

Frances (Margaret) Rowley(494a) was born on 12 April 1922, in Youngstown, OH,
to Frank Blaine Rowley(494aF) and Edith Heater(494aM).

Louis William George(494) and Frances (Margaret) Rowley(494a) had child(ren).

Records that include Louis William George(494) and/or Frances (Margaret) Rowley(494a):

- "New York, Birth Indexes outside of New York City, 1881-1942", , FamilySearch (https://www.familysearch.org/ark:/61903/1:1:6F4T-CS1J : Sun Mar 10 00:03:42 UTC 2024), Entry for Lewis W George, 15 Feb 1919.
- "United States Census, 1930", , FamilySearch (https://www.familysearch.org/ark:/61903/1:1:X4R1-RJV : Fri Sep 20 03:41:55 UTC 2024), Entry for Carmin L George and Bertha C George, 1930.
- "United States Census, 1930", , FamilySearch (https://www.familysearch.org/ark:/61903/1:1:X4ZX-W4D : Fri Mar 08 01:00:32 UTC 2024), Entry for Frank B Rowley and Edith Rowley, 1930.
- "United States Census, 1940", , FamilySearch (https://www.familysearch.org/ark:/61903/1:1:K429-H2Y : Sat Mar 09 02:11:36 UTC 2024), Entry for Louis W George, 1940.
- "United States Census, 1940", , FamilySearch (https://www.familysearch.org/ark:/61903/1:1:KWG4-QBZ : Sun Mar 10 16:07:26 UTC 2024), Entry for Frank B Rowley and Edith Rowley, 1940.
- "United States Census, 1950", , FamilySearch (https://www.familysearch.org/ark:/61903/1:1:6XTR-KYRZ : Wed Mar 20 12:24:31 UTC 2024), Entry for Louis W George and Margaret George, 3 April 1950.
- "United States Social Security Death Index," database, FamilySearch (https://familysearch.org/ark:/61903/1:1:VMK8-PWP : 7 January 2021), Louis George, Dec 1982; citing U.S. Social Security Administration, Death Master File, database (Alexandria, Virginia: National Technical Information Service, ongoing).

495) Alberto Tiso

Alberto Tiso(495) was born on 25 October 1919, in Newark, NJ, to Oto (Ottone) Tiso(169) and Mary Senese(169a). Alberto Tiso(495) died on June 1924 in Newark, NJ.

Records that include Alberto Tiso(495):

- "New Jersey, Reclaim the Records, Geographic Birth Index, 1901-1929", , FamilySearch (https://www.familysearch.org/ark:/61903/1:1:6NQ9-ZNHN : Sun Mar 10 07:53:57 UTC 2024), Entry for Alberto Tiso, 25 Oct 1919.
- "United States Census, 1920", , FamilySearch (https://www.familysearch.org/ark:/61903/1:1:M451-X6W : Sat Mar 09 14:37:36 UTC 2024), Entry for Ottone Tiso and Mary Tiso, 1920.
- "New Jersey, Death Index, 1901-1903; 1916-1929", , FamilySearch (https://www.familysearch.org/ark:/61903/1:1:8DJZ-RX6Z : Sat Mar 09 07:55:44 UTC 2024), Entry for Albert Tiso, Jun 1924.

496) Angelo Bonelli

Angelo Bonelli(496) was born on 28 November 1919, in St. Louis, MO, to Joseph Bonelli(271a) and Concetta Anastasio(271). Angelo Bonelli(496) died on 2 October 1936, in Detroit, MI.

Records that include Angelo Bonelli(496):

- "United States Census, 1920", , FamilySearch (https://www.familysearch.org/ark:/61903/1:1:M887-HJN : Sat Mar 09 17:39:56 UTC 2024), Entry for Joseph Bonneli and Consetti Bonneli, 1920.
- "United States Census, 1930", , FamilySearch (https://www.familysearch.org/ark:/61903/1:1:X7SP-TPK : Sun Mar 10 23:23:02 UTC 2024), Entry for Causamo Stilo and Elvera Stilo, 1930.
- "Michigan Death Certificates, 1921-1952", , FamilySearch (https://www.familysearch.org/ark:/61903/1:1:KFWS-4LV : Fri Mar 08 16:06:18 UTC 2024), Entry for Angelo Bonelli and Joseph Bonelli, 02 Oct 1936.

- "Find a Grave Index," database, FamilySearch (https://www.familysearch.org/ark:/61903/1:1:QPR3-Y35V : 10 May 2023), Angelo Bonelli, ; Burial, Detroit, Wayne, Michigan, United States of America, Mount Olivet Cemetery; citing record ID 158822780, Find a Grave, http://www.findagrave.com.

497) Rosalind Miressi

Rosalind Miressi(497) was born on 11 December 1919, in Middletown, NY, to Giovanni (John) Miressi(266) and Florence Emily Wilson(226a). Rosalind Miressi(497) died 28 November, 2010 in Louisville, KY.

Rosalind Miressi(497) married John Mosher(497a).

John Mosher(497a) was born 11 April 1917, in New York, to John Mosher(497aF) and Katherine Van Dohlen(497aM). John Mosher(497a) died 15 May 1994 in Middletown, NY.

Records that include Rosalind Miressi(497) and/or John Mosher(497a):
- "New York, Birth Indexes outside of New York City, 1881-1942", , FamilySearch (https://www.familysearch.org/ark:/61903/1:1:6FJ9-TR1G : Sat Mar 09 00:54:05 UTC 2024), Entry for John C Mosher, 11 Apr 1917.
- "New York, Birth Indexes outside of New York City, 1881-1942", , FamilySearch (https://www.familysearch.org/ark:/61903/1:1:6FJ9-TR1G : Sat Mar 09 00:54:05 UTC 2024), Entry for John C Mosher, 11 Apr 1917.
- "United States Census, 1920", , FamilySearch (https://www.familysearch.org/ark:/61903/1:1:MV9F-9G9 : Sat Mar 09 10:15:10 UTC 2024), Entry for John Miressie and Florence Miressie, 1920.
- "New York, Birth Indexes outside of New York City, 1881-1942", , FamilySearch (https://www.familysearch.org/ark:/61903/1:1:6FJ9-TR1G : Sat Mar 09 00:54:05 UTC 2024), Entry for John C Mosher, 11 Apr 1917.
- "United States Census, 1930", , FamilySearch (https://www.familysearch.org/ark:/61903/1:1:X4R1-4DK : Sun Mar 10 13:51:06 UTC 2024), Entry for Florence Miressi and Frances E Miressi, 1930.
- "United States Census, 1930", , FamilySearch (https://www.familysearch.org/ark:/61903/1:1:X4TM-9FB : Fri Mar 08 08:55:26 UTC 2024), Entry for John Mosher and Catherine M Mosher, 1930.
- "United States Census, 1940", , FamilySearch (https://www.familysearch.org/ark:/61903/1:1:KQGP-K5S : Sun Mar 10 00:13:39 UTC 2024), Entry for John Miressi and Florence Miressi, 1940.
- "United States World War II Army Enlistment Records, 1938-1946," , FamilySearch (https://familysearch.org/ark:/61903/1:1:KMX4-C2T : 5 December 2014), John C Mosher, enlisted 13 Feb 1942, New York City, New York, United States; citing "Electronic Army Serial Number Merged File, ca. 1938-1946," database, The National Archives: Access to Archival Databases (AAD) (http://aad.archives.gov : National Archives and Records Administration, 2002); NARA NAID 1263923, National Archives at College Park, Maryland.
- "United States Social Security Death Index," database, FamilySearch (https://familysearch.org/ark:/61903/1:1:VSHK-1P5 : 12 January 2021), Rosalind Mosher, 28 Nov 2010; citing U.S. Social Security Administration, Death Master File, database (Alexandria, Virginia: National Technical Information Service, ongoing).
- "United States, Social Security Numerical Identification Files (NUMIDENT), 1936-2007", database, FamilySearch (https://www.familysearch.org/ark:/61903/1:1:6KMB-JJ1Q : 10 February 2023), John Christopher Mosher, .
- "United States Social Security Death Index," database, FamilySearch (https://familysearch.org/ark:/61903/1:1:VMVJ-44D : 7 January 2021), John C Mosher, 15 May 1994; citing U.S. Social Security Administration, Death Master File, database (Alexandria, Virginia: National Technical Information Service, ongoing).

- "Find a Grave Index," database, FamilySearch (https://www.familysearch.org/ark:/61903/1:1:QK1X-R7DB : 3 April 2023), John C. Mosher, ; Burial, Phillipsburg, Orange, New York, United States of America, Wallkill Cemetery; citing record ID 139530098, Find a Grave, http://www.findagrave.com.
- "Find a Grave Index," database, FamilySearch (https://www.familysearch.org/ark:/61903/1:1:QV2H-4L66 : 1 April 2023), Rosalind M. Miressi Mosher, ; Burial, Phillipsburg, Orange, New York, United States of America, Wallkill Cemetery; citing record ID 62875660, Find a Grave, http://www.findagrave.com.

498) Oto Baviello

Oto Baviello(498) was born 1 June 1918 in Ariano, Italy to Antonio Maria Baviello(225a) and Maria Antonia di Lillo(225).

Oto Baviello(498) married Elena De Lillo(498a) on 20 March 1939 in Ariano, Italy.

Elena De Lillo(498a) was born on 26 January 1924 in Ariano, Italy to Tommaso De Lillo(498aF) and Maria Liberia Cusano(498aM).

Records that include Oto Baviello(498) and/or Elena De Lillo(498a):
- Ariano, Italy 1918 Birth Act #246
- Ariano, Italy 1924 Birth Act #85
- Ariano, Italy 1939 Marriage Act #30

499) Jennie Mingolello

Giovanna (Jennie) Mingolello(499) was born on 27 August 1919, in Bridgeport, CT, to Joseph Mingolello(294a) and Francesca deDonato(294). Giovanna (Jennie) Mingolello(499) died 7 August 1988 in Bridgeport, CT. Giovanna (Jennie) Mingolello(499) was buried in St. Micheal's Cemetery in Stratford, CT.

Giovanna (Jennie) Mingolello(499) married Leonardo Anthony Altieri(499a) on 27 February 1943 in Stratford, CT.

Leonardo Anthony Altieri(499a) was born on 30 Jun 1918, in Bridgeport, CT, to Antonio Altieri(499aF) and Elise Guerra(499aM). Leonardo Anthony Altieri(499a) died on 16 July 2002 in Trumbull, CT.

Giovanna (Jennie) Mingolello(499) and Leonardo Anthony Altieri(499a)had children.

Records that include Giovanna (Jennie) Mingolello(499) and/or Leonardo Anthony Altieri(499a):
- Bridgeport, CT Births June 1918 #380
- Bridgeport, CT, Births August 1919 #321
- "United States, Census, 1920", , FamilySearch (https://www.familysearch.org/ark:/61903/1:1:MCFW-53P : Fri Mar 08 23:09:26 UTC 2024), Entry for Anthony Altieri and Elsie Altieri, 1920.
- "United States, Census, 1930", , FamilySearch (https://www.familysearch.org/ark:/61903/1:1:XMP8-M1P : Wed Mar 06 09:36:34 UTC 2024), Entry for Joe Mingolello and Francis Mingolello, 1930.
- "United States, Census, 1930", , FamilySearch (https://www.familysearch.org/ark:/61903/1:1:XMG1-ZWL : Fri Mar 08 04:17:46 UTC 2024), Entry for Antonio Altieri and Elsie Altieri, 1930.
- "United States, Census, 1940", , FamilySearch (https://www.familysearch.org/ark:/61903/1:1:K71S-M9L : Fri Mar 08 16:03:19 UTC 2024), Entry for Joseph Mingolello and Jennie Mingolello, 1940.
- "United States, Census, 1940", , FamilySearch (https://www.familysearch.org/ark:/61903/1:1:KWMN-BSZ : Sun Mar 10 21:50:31 UTC 2024), Entry for Antonico Altieri and Elsie Altieri, 1940.

- "Connecticut, World War II Draft Registration Cards, 1940-1945", , FamilySearch (https://www.familysearch.org/ark:/61903/1:1:Q2CP-829M : Mon Jul 22 13:21:12 UTC 2024), Entry for Leonard Anthony Altieri and Antonio Altieri, 16 Oct 1940.
- "United States, World War II Army Enlistment Records, 1938-1946," database, FamilySearch (https://familysearch.org/ark:/61903/1:1:K8R3-JDX : 5 December 2014), Leonard A Altieri, enlisted 11 Apr 1944, Ft Devens, Massachusetts, United States; citing "Electronic Army Serial Number Merged File, ca. 1938-1946," database, The National Archives: Access to Archival Databases (AAD) (http://aad.archives.gov : National Archives and Records Administration, 2002); NARA NAID 1263923, National Archives at College Park, Maryland.
- "United States, Census, 1950", , FamilySearch (https://www.familysearch.org/ark:/61903/1:1:6FM6-4X8N : Wed Oct 04 15:40:02 UTC 2023), Entry for Leonard Altieri and Jennie Altieri, 25 April 1950.
- "Connecticut, Death Index, 1949-2001," , FamilySearch (https://familysearch.org/ark:/61903/1:1:VZPD-1VH : 9 December 2014), Jennie M Altieri, 07 Aug 1988; from "Connecticut Death Index, 1949-2001," database, Ancestry (http://www.ancestry.com : 2003); citing Bridgeport, Fairfield, Connecticut, Connecticut Department of Health, Hartfort.
- "United States, Social Security Death Index," database, FamilySearch (https://familysearch.org/ark:/61903/1:1:VMJ8-K3R : 7 January 2021), Jennie M Altieri, 07 Aug 1988; citing U.S. Social Security Administration, Death Master File, database (Alexandria, Virginia: National Technical Information Service, ongoing).
- "Find a Grave Index," database, FamilySearch (https://www.familysearch.org/ark:/61903/1:1:QL75-GP9Y : 13 June 2023), Jennie Altieri, ; Burial, Stratford, Fairfield, Connecticut, United States of America, Saint Michael's Cemetery; citing record ID 176842715, Find a Grave, http://www.findagrave.com.
- "Find a Grave Index," database, FamilySearch (https://www.familysearch.org/ark:/61903/1:1:QL75-GPSW : 13 June 2023), Leonard Altieri, ; Burial, Stratford, Fairfield, Connecticut, United States of America, Saint Michael's Cemetery; citing record ID 176842716, Find a Grave, http://www.findagrave.com.

500) Carmina Rinaldi

Carmina Rinaldi(500) was born in 1920, in Brazil, to Antonio DeDonato(303) and Maria Rinaldi(303a).

NOTE: I have a memo of finding a Brazilian baptism record from May 1920 that I have not been able to locate again.

501) Lucien Angelo Zarlenga [Staff Sergeant]

Lucien Angelo Zarlenga(501) was born on 25 July 1920 in St. Louis, MO, to Domenick Zarlenga(259a) and Clementina Anastasio(259). Lucien Angelo Zarlenga(501) enlisted in Co F 138th Infantry Missouri National Guard on 12 August 1937(listing 1919 as year of birth). On 12 August 1940 Lucien Angelo Zarlenga(501) enlisted as a corporal in Co F 138th Infantry Missouri National Guard. Lucien Angelo Zarlenga(501) died 18 November 1944 in battle near Raon l'Etape, France. Lucien Angelo Zarlenga(501) is buried at Epinal France. Lucien Angelo Zarlenga(501) was posthumously awarded the Purple Heart and Silver Star.

The President of the United States of America, authorized by Act of Congress July 9, 1918, takes Pride in presenting the Silver Star (Posthumously) to Staff Sergeant Lucian A. Zarlenga, United States Army, for conspicuous gallantry and intrepidity in action against the enemy while serving with Company A, 399th Infantry Regiment, 100th Infantry Division, in action at Baccarat, France, during World War II. Staff Sergeant Zarlenga's gallant actions and selfless devotion to duty, without regard for his own safety, were in keeping with the highest traditions of military service and reflect great credit upon himself, his unit, and the United States Army.
General Orders: Headquarters, 100th Infantry Division,

General Orders No. 34 (1944)
Action Date: World War II
Service: Army
Rank: Staff Sergeant
Company: Company A
Regiment: 399th Infantry Regiment
Division: 100th Infantry Division

He was killed in six days of bitter fighting in blinding rain and bitter cold when the 100th Division entered the line for the first time in the Vosges Mountains. Attacking SW out of the town of Baccarat their objective was to break the German entrenched positions along 1,200 to 1,500 foot high ridges covered with dense forest. By 18 Nov 44 they had outflanked the town of Raon l'Etape and broke the German winter lines in this sector which was intended by the Germans to hold out until April of 1945.

Records that include Lucien Angelo Zarlenga(501):
- "United States Census, 1930", , FamilySearch (https://www.familysearch.org/ark:/61903/1:1:XHJY-84K : Fri Mar 08 10:09:13 UTC 2024), Entry for Dominick Zarlingo and Clementine Zarlingo, 1930.
- "United States Census, 1940", , FamilySearch (https://www.familysearch.org/ark:/61903/1:1:K7HD-RP5 : Fri Mar 08 18:54:50 UTC 2024), Entry for Dominic Zarlenga and Clementine Zarlenga, 1940.
- "United States World War II Army Enlistment Records, 1938-1946," , FamilySearch (https://familysearch.org/ark:/61903/1:1:K8G5-94T : 5 December 2014), Lucian A Zarlenga, enlisted 23 Dec 1940, St Louis, Missouri, United States; citing "Electronic Army Serial Number Merged File, ca. 1938-1946," database, The National Archives: Access to Archival Databases (AAD) (http://aad.archives.gov : National Archives and Records Administration, 2002); NARA NAID 1263923, National Archives at College Park, Maryland.
- "Missouri, Pre-WWII Adjutant General Enlistment Contracts, 1900-1941", , FamilySearch (https://www.familysearch.org/ark:/61903/1:1:6CBL-3DGY : Sat Mar 09 08:46:39 UTC 2024), Entry for Lucian Angelo Zarlenga and Dominic Zarlenga, 12 Aug 1940.
- "Missouri, Pre-WWII Adjutant General Enlistment Contracts, 1900-1941," , FamilySearch (https://www.familysearch.org/ark:/61903/1:1:ZVB6-YP2M : 7 March 2022), Lucian A Zarlenga, ; citing Military Service, Missouri, United States, Missouri State Archives, Jefferson City; FHL microfilm .
- "Missouri, Pre-WWII Adjutant General Enlistment Contracts, 1900-1941", , FamilySearch (https://www.familysearch.org/ark:/61903/1:1:6CB2-NCK6 : Fri Mar 08 20:42:53 UTC 2024), Entry for Lucian A Zarlenga, 12 August 1937.
- "Missouri, Pre-WWII Adjutant General Enlistment Contracts, 1900-1941," , FamilySearch (https://www.familysearch.org/ark:/61903/1:1:ZVB6-YPT2 : 7 March 2022), Lucian Angelo Zarlenga, 12 Aug 1940; citing Military Service, Wahkon, Mille Lacs, Minnesota, United States, Missouri State Archives, Jefferson City; FHL microfilm .
- https://www.newspapers.com/article/st-louis-post-dispatch-lucian-a-zarleng/22658930/
- https://www.abmc.gov/decedent-search/zarlenga%3Dlucian
- "Find a Grave Index," database, FamilySearch (https://www.familysearch.org/ark:/61903/1:1:QVKR-GRTV : 13 June 2023), Lucian A Zarlenga, ; Burial, Epinal, Departement des Vosges, Lorraine, France, Epinal American Cemetery and Memorial; citing record ID 56376514, Find a Grave, http://www.findagrave.com.
- "Find a Grave Index," database, FamilySearch (https://www.familysearch.org/ark:/61903/1:1:4K4C-DN3Z : 5 August 2020), Lucian A Zarlenga, ; Burial, Saint Louis, St. Louis City, Missouri, United States of America, Calvary Cemetery and Mausoleum; citing record ID 202254168, Find a Grave, http://www.findagrave.com.

502) Josephine Giorgione/George

Josephine Giorgione/George(502) was born on 1 May 1920, in Middletown, NY, to Giuseppe Giorgione/George(263) and Margherita Adele Maria Marasco(263a). Josephine Giorgione/George(502) died 4 December 2019 in Rochester, NY.

Josephine Giorgione/George(502) married Alex Morganti(502a) around 1944.

Alex Morganti(502a) was born on 15 February 1922, in New York, to Anthony Morganti(502aF) and Felicia Ruccitti(502aM). Alex Morganti(502a) died on 9 August 2013 in Rochester, NY.

Josephine Giorgione/George(502) and Alex Morganti(502a) had child(ren).

Records that include Josephine Giorgione/George(502) and/or Alex Morganti(502a):

- "New York, Birth Indexes outside of New York City, 1881-1942", , FamilySearch (https://www.familysearch.org/ark:/61903/1:1:6XBF-LP1Y : Sat Mar 09 09:41:28 UTC 2024), Entry for Josephine I George, 1 May 1920.
- "United States Census, 1930", , FamilySearch (https://www.familysearch.org/ark:/61903/1:1:X78Q-X6G : Mon Mar 11 01:24:33 UTC 2024), Entry for Felice Morganti and Josephine Morganti, 1930.
- "United States Census, 1940", , FamilySearch (https://www.familysearch.org/ark:/61903/1:1:KQY5-9LC : Sat Mar 09 22:50:37 UTC 2024), Entry for Joseph George and Margret George, 1940.
- "United States Census, 1940", , FamilySearch (https://www.familysearch.org/ark:/61903/1:1:KQ58-598 : Sat Mar 09 14:49:35 UTC 2024), Entry for Felica Morganti and Joan Morganti, 1940.
- "United States Census, 1950", , FamilySearch (https://www.familysearch.org/ark:/61903/1:1:6XTY-M8YG : Thu Oct 05 23:34:30 UTC 2023), Entry for Joseph George and Margaret George, 13 April 1950.
- "United States Social Security Death Index," database, FamilySearch (https://familysearch.org/ark:/61903/1:1:K14R-GYS : 12 January 2021), Alex Morganti, 09 Aug 2013; citing U.S. Social Security Administration, Death Master File, database (Alexandria, Virginia: National Technical Information Service, ongoing).

503) Angelo James DeMeo JR

Angelo James DeMeo JR(503) was born on 1 June 1920, in Niskayuna, NY, to Angelo DeMeo(202a) and Maria Perrina(202). Angelo James DeMeo JR(503) died March 1969 in Schenectady, NY.

Angelo James DeMeo JR(503) married Carmela(503a).

Carmela(503a) was born in 1927. Carmela(503a) died in 2015.

Angelo James DeMeo JR(503) and Carmela(503a) had child(ren).

Records that include Angelo James DeMeo JR(503) and/or Carmela(503a):

- "New York, Birth Indexes outside of New York City, 1881-1942", , FamilySearch (https://www.familysearch.org/ark:/61903/1:1:6XBN-82V1 : Sat Mar 09 19:04:31 UTC 2024), Entry for Angelo V Demeo, 1 Jun 1920.
- "United States Census, 1930", , FamilySearch (https://www.familysearch.org/ark:/61903/1:1:X4TT-YB5 : Mon Mar 11 01:35:37 UTC 2024), Entry for Angelo De Meo and Mary De Meo, 1930.
- "New York, New York City, World War II Draft Registration Cards, 1940-1947", , FamilySearch (https://www.familysearch.org/ark:/61903/1:1:WW2N-2XN2 : Sat Mar 09 10:35:05 UTC 2024), Entry for Angelo James De Meo and Brinberg Body Builders, 01 Jul 1941.
- "United States 1950 Census", , FamilySearch (https://www.familysearch.org/ark:/61903/1:1:6XRQ-TK3W : Tue Mar 19 20:26:02 UTC 2024), Entry for Angelo De Meo, 10 April 1950.

- "United States Social Security Death Index," database, FamilySearch (https://familysearch.org/ark:/61903/1:1:JBR7-WTR : 7 January 2021), Angelo Demeo, Mar 1969; citing U.S. Social Security Administration, Death Master File, database (Alexandria, Virginia: National Technical Information Service, ongoing).
- "Find a Grave Index," database, FamilySearch (https://www.familysearch.org/ark:/61903/1:1:QGKM-H9NK : 7 August 2020), Carmela J. De Meo, ; Burial, Flushing, Queens, New York, United States of America, Mount Saint Mary Cemetery; citing record ID 184165572, Find a Grave, http://www.findagrave.com.
- "Find a Grave Index," database, FamilySearch (https://www.familysearch.org/ark:/61903/1:1:Q2SS-CVYM : 7 August 2020), Angelo J. De Meo, ; Burial, Flushing, Queens, New York, United States of America, Mount Saint Mary Cemetery; citing record ID 154135871, Find a Grave, http://www.findagrave.com.

504) Clara Evelyn Anastasio

Clara Evelyn Anastasio(504) was born on 9 August 1920, in Racine, WI, to Francesco (Frank) Paul Anastasio(166) and Hilda (Gilda) Marcotti(166a). Clara Evelyn Anastasio(504) died on 2 December 2009 in Racine, WI.

Clara Evelyn Anastasio(504) married Harlow Ferdinand Zebell(504a) on 17 March 1951 in Racine, WI.

Harlow Ferdinand Zebell(504a) was born on 23 February 1918, in Fort Atkinson, WI, to Edward Zebell(504aF) and Mary Traichel(504aM). Harlow Ferdinand Zebell(504a) died on 13 November 2003 in Mount Pleasant, WI.

Clara Evelyn Anastasio(504) and Harlow Ferdinand Zebell(504a) had child(ren).

Records that include Clara Evelyn Anastasio(504) and/or Harlow Ferdinand Zebell(504a):
- "United States Census, 1920", , FamilySearch (https://www.familysearch.org/ark:/61903/1:1:MFL9-YD1 : Fri Mar 08 16:21:58 UTC 2024), Entry for Edward C Gebelt and Mary J Gebert, 1920.
- "United States Census, 1930", , FamilySearch (https://www.familysearch.org/ark:/61903/1:1:X9SV-8LG : Sat Mar 09 06:47:12 UTC 2024), Entry for Edward C Zebell and Mary J Zebell, 1930.
- "United States Census, 1930", , FamilySearch (https://www.familysearch.org/ark:/61903/1:1:X9SJ-2LK : Sat Mar 09 02:41:12 UTC 2024), Entry for Frank Anastasio and Hilda Anastasio, 1930.
- "United States Census, 1940", , FamilySearch (https://www.familysearch.org/ark:/61903/1:1:K7J6-HTQ : Sat Mar 09 04:26:52 UTC 2024), Entry for Frank P Anastascio and Jilda Anastascio, 1940.
- "United States World War II Army Enlistment Records, 1938-1946," database, FamilySearch (https://familysearch.org/ark:/61903/1:1:K8Y2-ZCL : 5 December 2014), Harlow F Zebell, enlisted 20 Feb 1942, Ft Sheridan, Illinois, United States; citing "Electronic Army Serial Number Merged File, ca. 1938-1946," database, The National Archives: Access to Archival Databases (AAD) (http://aad.archives.gov : National Archives and Records Administration, 2002); NARA NAID 1263923, National Archives at College Park, Maryland.
- "United States 1950 Census", , FamilySearch (https://www.familysearch.org/ark:/61903/1:1:6FMB-ZH8X : Tue Oct 03 08:34:28 UTC 2023), Entry for Frank P Anastasio and Jilda Anastasio, April 3, 1950.
- "United States 1950 Census", , FamilySearch (https://www.familysearch.org/ark:/61903/1:1:6FMB-HWQ3 : Tue Oct 03 08:34:29 UTC 2023), Entry for Edward Zebell and Mary Zebell, April 3, 1950.
- https://journaltimes.newspapers.com/article/the-journal-times-obituary-for-frank-p/83018176/

- "United States Social Security Death Index," database, FamilySearch (https://familysearch.org/ark:/61903/1:1:J5GG-Z62 : 12 January 2021), Clara E Zebell, 02 Dec 2009; citing U.S. Social Security Administration, Death Master File, database (Alexandria, Virginia: National Technical Information Service, ongoing).
- "United States Social Security Death Index," database, FamilySearch (https://familysearch.org/ark:/61903/1:1:V37B-ZMF : 9 January 2021), Harlow F Zebell, 13 Nov 2003; citing U.S. Social Security Administration, Death Master File, database (Alexandria, Virginia: National Technical Information Service, ongoing).
- "United States, Social Security Numerical Identification Files (NUMIDENT), 1936-2007", database, FamilySearch (https://www.familysearch.org/ark:/61903/1:1:6KQ2-NWD3 : 10 February 2023), Harlow Ferdinand Zebell, .
- "Find a Grave Index," database, FamilySearch (https://www.familysearch.org/ark:/61903/1:1:6ZWQ-VWFK : 8 March 2021), Harlow F Zebell, ; Burial, Mount Pleasant, Racine, Wisconsin, United States of America, West Lawn Memorial Park; citing record ID 223106981, Find a Grave, http://www.findagrave.com.
- "Find a Grave Index," database, FamilySearch (https://www.familysearch.org/ark:/61903/1:1:QVKR-QMSP : 7 March 2024), Clara E. Anastasio Zebell, ; Burial, Mount Pleasant, Racine, Wisconsin, United States of America, West Lawn Memorial Park; citing record ID 45179537, Find a Grave, http://www.findagrave.com.

505) Eleanor Margaret Perrino

Eleanor Margaret Perrino(505) born on 21 January 1920, in Schenectady, NY, to Vittorio Perrino(187) and Carmela Ricci(187a). Eleanor Margaret Perrino(505) died 8 February 2006 in Schenectady, NY. Eleanor Margaret Perrino(505) was a restaurant owner and a government employee.

Eleanor Margaret Perrino(505) married Vincent Thomas (Jimmy) Angerami(505a) on 29 Jun 1947 in Schenectady, NY.

Vincent Thomas (Jimmy) Angerami(505a) was born on 1 October 1916, in Chicago, IL, to Rocco Angerami(505aF) and Mary Angela Christian(505aM). Vincent Thomas (Jimmy) Angerami(505a) died 13 September 2005 in Schenectady, NY. Vincent Thomas (Jimmy) Angerami(505a) was a Roller Derby Referee, Restaurant owner, and Government Employee.

Eleanor Margaret Perrino(505) and Vincent Thomas (Jimmy) Angerami(505a) had child(ren).

Records that include Eleanor Margaret Perrino(505) and/or Vincent Thomas (Jimmy) Angerami(505a):

- "New York, Birth Indexes outside of New York City, 1881-1942", , FamilySearch (https://www.familysearch.org/ark:/61903/1:1:6F9R-XGLG : Fri Mar 08 01:00:21 UTC 2024), Entry for Eleanor M Perrino, 25 Jan 1920.
- "St. Anthony, Schenectady, New York, Baptism (Sep 1912 - May 2007)", 2 Volumes American-Canadian Genealogical Society, Manchester, NH, page 693
- "United States Census, 1920", , FamilySearch (https://www.familysearch.org/ark:/61903/1:1:MJSN-S2M : Sun Mar 10 07:53:31 UTC 2024), Entry for Rocco Angerami and Mary Angerami, 1920.
- "United States Census, 1930", , FamilySearch (https://www.familysearch.org/ark:/61903/1:1:X4T1-VDJ : Mon Jul 08 19:59:28 UTC 2024), Entry for Victor C Perrino and Carrie Perrino, 1930.
- "United States Census, 1930", , FamilySearch (https://www.familysearch.org/ark:/61903/1:1:X4TY-2TB : Fri Mar 08 21:08:19 UTC 2024), Entry for Rocco Angerami and Mary Angerami, 1930.
- "United States Census, 1940", , FamilySearch (https://www.familysearch.org/ark:/61903/1:1:VYPF-7JJ : Thu Jul 11 13:40:31 UTC 2024), Entry for Vincent Angerami, 1940.

- "United States World War II Army Enlistment Records, 1938-1946,"
  database, FamilySearch
  (https://familysearch.org/ark:/61903/1:1:K8RW-4BJ : 5 December
  2014), Vincent T Angerami, enlisted 25 Apr 1941, Albany, New York,
  United States; citing "Electronic Army Serial Number Merged File,
  ca. 1938-1946," database, The National Archives: Access to Archival
  Databases (AAD) (http://aad.archives.gov : National Archives and
  Records Administration, 2002); NARA NAID 1263923, National Archives
  at College Park, Maryland.
- "United States Census, 1950", , FamilySearch
  (https://www.familysearch.org/ark:/61903/1:1:6XYM-F58N : Thu Oct 05
  05:13:14 UTC 2023), Entry for Vincent Angerami and Eleanor M
  Angerami, 4 April 1950.
- "United States, Social Security Numerical Identification Files
  (NUMIDENT), 1936-2007", database, FamilySearch
  (https://www.familysearch.org/ark:/61903/1:1:6K99-RNV1 : 10
  February 2023), Vincent Thomas Angerami, .
- "United States Social Security Death Index," database, FamilySearch
  (https://familysearch.org/ark:/61903/1:1:JTDB-4Z4 : 11 January
  2021), Vincent T Angerami, 13 Sep 2004; citing U.S. Social Security
  Administration, Death Master File, database (Alexandria, Virginia:
  National Technical Information Service, ongoing).
- "Find a Grave Index," database, FamilySearch
  (https://www.familysearch.org/ark:/61903/1:1:6LX4-HLX2 : 6 June
  2024), Jimmie, ; Burial, Colonie, Albany, New York, United States
  of America, Memory Gardens Cemetery and Memorial Park; citing
  record ID 256620544, Find a Grave, http://www.findagrave.com.
- "Find a Grave Index," database, FamilySearch
  (https://www.familysearch.org/ark:/61903/1:1:Q23B-CST2 : 6 June
  2024), Eleanor M. Perrino Angerami, ; Burial, Colonie, Albany, New
  York, United States of America, Memory Gardens Cemetery and
  Memorial Park; citing record ID 157987870, Find a Grave,
  http://www.findagrave.com.

506) Dorothy Lillian Perrino

Dorothy Lillian Perrino(506) born on 21 January 1920, in Schenectady, NY, to
Vittorio Perrino(187) and Carmela Ricci(187a). Dorothy Lillian Perrino(506)
died 25 January 1920 in Schenectady, NY.

Records that include Dorothy Lillian Perrino(506):
- "New York, Birth Indexes outside of New York City, 1881-1942", ,
  FamilySearch (https://www.familysearch.org/ark:/61903/1:1:6F9R-XGLL
  : Fri Mar 08 01:00:21 UTC 2024), Entry for Dorothy L Perrino, 21
  Jan 1920.
- "New York, State Death Index, 1880-1956", , FamilySearch
  (https://www.familysearch.org/ark:/61903/1:1:QPHW-SR32 : Sat Mar 09
  09:20:40 UTC 2024), Entry for Dorothy L Perrino, 25 Jan 1920.

507) Carmen Maria Lombardi

Carmen Maria Lombardi(507) was born on 13 September 1920, in Connecticut, to
Saverio Lombardi(261) and Giovanna Prezioso(261a).

Carmen Maria Lombardi(507) married George Francis Burgess(507a) on 10 July
1940 in Los Angeles, CA.

George Francis Burgess(507a) was born on 27 October 1920, in Albany, NY, to
Albert Burgess(507aF) and Sarah Jane McElroy(507aM). George Francis
Burgess(507a) died on 20 Dec 1989, in Los Angeles, CA.

Carmen Maria Lombardi(507) and George Francis Burgess(507a) had child(ren).

Records that include Carmen Maria Lombardi(507) and/or George Francis
Burgess(507a):
- "United States Census, 1930", , FamilySearch
  (https://www.familysearch.org/ark:/61903/1:1:XMPM-77Y : Fri Mar 08
  01:23:40 UTC 2024), Entry for James Lombardi and Carmello Lombardi,
  1930.

- "United States Census, 1940", , FamilySearch
  (https://www.familysearch.org/ark:/61903/1:1:K97H-NYF : Sat Mar 09
  03:29:53 UTC 2024), Entry for Sam Lombardis and Jennie Lombardis,
  1940.
- "California, World War II Draft Registration Cards, 1940-1945", ,
  FamilySearch (https://www.familysearch.org/ark:/61903/1:1:QGXB-57HL
  : Fri Mar 08 03:54:00 UTC 2024), Entry for George Francis Burgess
  and Sam Lombardi, 16 February 1942.
- "United States 1950 Census", , FamilySearch
  (https://www.familysearch.org/ark:/61903/1:1:6XG7-WDS9 : Thu Oct 05
  17:22:12 UTC 2023), Entry for George F Burgess and Carmine M
  Burgess, 10 April 1950.
- "United States, Social Security Numerical Identification Files
  (NUMIDENT), 1936-2007", database, FamilySearch
  (https://www.familysearch.org/ark:/61903/1:1:6K48-RC7H : 11
  February 2023), George Francis Burgess, .
- "California Death Index, 1940-1997," , FamilySearch
  (https://familysearch.org/ark:/61903/1:1:VPV4-CY3 : 26 November
  2014), George Francis Burgess, 20 Dec 1989; Department of Public
  Health Services, Sacramento.

508) Anthony (Tony) Mingolello

Anthony (Tony) Mingolello(508) was born 12 October 1920, in Bridgeport, CT, to
Joseph Mingolello(294a) and Francesca deDonato(294). Anthony (Tony)
Mingolello(508) served as a medic during WWII. Anthony (Tony) Mingolello(508)
died 13 January 2013 in Naples, FL.

Anthony (Tony) Mingolello(508) married Pauline Rose Patterson(508a).

Pauline Rose Patterson(508a) was born 11 September 1924, in Keene, NH, to
Anthony W. Patterson(508aF) and Exilda Adeline Gravel(508aM). Pauline Rose
Patterson(508a) died 19 August 2021, in Naples, FL.

Anthony (Tony) Mingolello(508) and Pauline Rose Patterson(508a) had
child(ren).

Records that include Anthony (Tony) Mingolello(508) and/or Pauline Rose
Patterson(508a):
- Bridgeport, CT, Births Oct 1920 #467
- "United States, Census, 1930", , FamilySearch
  (https://www.familysearch.org/ark:/61903/1:1:XMP8-M1P : Wed Mar 06
  09:36:34 UTC 2024), Entry for Joe Mingolello and Francis
  Mingolello, 1930.
- "United States, Census, 1930", , FamilySearch
  (https://www.familysearch.org/ark:/61903/1:1:X7NH-FC4 : Fri Mar 08
  22:19:06 UTC 2024), Entry for Anthony M Patterson and Elsie A
  Patterson, 1930.
- "United States, Census, 1940", , FamilySearch
  (https://www.familysearch.org/ark:/61903/1:1:VTMR-3XN : Sun Jul 14
  12:30:13 UTC 2024), Entry for Anthony W Patterson and Exilda A
  Patterson, 1940.
- "United States, Census, 1940", , FamilySearch
  (https://www.familysearch.org/ark:/61903/1:1:K71S-M9L : Fri Mar 08
  16:03:19 UTC 2024), Entry for Joseph Mingolello and Jennie
  Mingolello, 1940.
- "Connecticut, World War II Draft Registration Cards, 1940-1945", ,
  FamilySearch (https://www.familysearch.org/ark:/61903/1:1:Q2CR-2VX9
  : Wed Jul 17 14:03:11 UTC 2024), Entry for Columbus Anthony
  Mingolello and Joseph Mingolello, 16 Feb 1942.
- "United States, World War II Army Enlistment Records, 1938-1946," ,
  FamilySearch (https://familysearch.org/ark:/61903/1:1:K85R-BB5 : 5
  December 2014), Columbus A Mingolello, enlisted 01 Aug 1942,
  Hartford, Connecticut, United States; citing "Electronic Army
  Serial Number Merged File, ca. 1938-1946," database, The National
  Archives: Access to Archival Databases (AAD)
  (http://aad.archives.gov : National Archives and Records
  Administration, 2002); NARA NAID 1263923, National Archives at
  College Park, Maryland.

- "United States, Census, 1950", , FamilySearch
  (https://www.familysearch.org/ark:/61903/1:1:6FMF-NV69 : Tue Mar 19
  19:41:06 UTC 2024), Entry for Anthony Mingolello and Pauline
  Mingolello, 1950.
- "Find a Grave Index," database, FamilySearch
  (https://www.familysearch.org/ark:/61903/1:1:66MH-HSSW : 10
  September 2022), Pauline Rose Patterson Mingolello, ; Burial,
  Derby, New Haven, Connecticut, United States of America, Mount
  Saint Peter Cemetery; citing record ID 234208901, Find a Grave,
  http://www.findagrave.com.
- https://www.dignitymemorial.com/obituaries/monroe-ct/pauline-
  mingolello-10315090

509) Giuseppina Moschella

Giuseppina Moschella(509) was born about December 1920, in Ariano, Italy, to
Antonio Moschella(255a) and Mariangela Manganiello(255). Giuseppina
Moschella(509) died 28 July 1921 in Ariano, Italy.

Records that include Giuseppina Moschella(509):
- Ariano, Italy 1921 Death Act#200

510) Tommasina Pannese

Tommasina Pannese(510) was born on 23 January 1921, in Ariano, Italy, to
Angelo Pannese(213a) and Mariantonia Perrina(213).

Tommasina Pannese(510) married Giuseppe deLillo(510a) on 21 October 1937 in
Ariano, Italy.

Giuseppe deLillo(510a) was born on 19 March 1911, in Ariano, Italy, to
Pasquale deLillo(510aF) and Mariantonia Covotta(510aM).

Records that include Tommasina Pannese(510) and/or Giuseppe deLillo(510a):
- Ariano, Italy 1911 Birth Act #159
- Ariano, Italy 1921 Birth Act #61
- Ariano, Italy 1937 Marriage Act #P.IIA.160

511) Attilio Zecchino

Attilio Zecchino(511) was born on 10 January 1921, in Ariano, Italy, to
Giovanni Zecchino(291a) and Angela Miressi(291). Attilio Zecchino(511) died 13
January 1921 in Ariano, Italy.

Records that include Attilio Zecchino(511):
- Ariano, Italy 1921 Birth Act #35
- Ariano, Italy 1921 Death Act #17

512) Alfred Lorenzo Giorgione/George AKA Alfredo Lawrence Goodman

Alfred Lorenzo Giorgione/George(512) was born on 18 July 1921, in Middletown,
New York, to Giuseppe Giorgione/George(263) and Margherita Adele Maria
Marasco(263a). Alfred Lorenzo Giorgione/George(512) died on 11 August 1997 in
Lee, FL. Alfred Lorenzo Giorgione/George(512) also used the name Alfreddo
Lawrence Goodman.

Records that include Alfred Lorenzo Giorgione/George(512):
- "New York, Birth Indexes outside of New York City, 1881-1942", ,
  FamilySearch (https://www.familysearch.org/ark:/61903/1:1:6FB8-7ZV6
  : Fri Mar 08 06:52:15 UTC 2024), Entry for Alfreddo L Giorgone, 18
  Jul 1921.
- "United States Census, 1940", , FamilySearch
  (https://www.familysearch.org/ark:/61903/1:1:KQY5-9LC : Sat Mar 09
  22:50:37 UTC 2024), Entry for Joseph George and Margret George,
  1940.

- "United States World War II Army Enlistment Records, 1938-1946,"
  database, FamilySearch
  (https://familysearch.org/ark:/61903/1:1:KMXZ-B3Q : 5 December
  2014), Alfred L George, enlisted 09 Oct 1942, Rochester, New York,
  United States; citing "Electronic Army Serial Number Merged File,
  ca. 1938-1946," database, The National Archives: Access to Archival
  Databases (AAD) (http://aad.archives.gov : National Archives and
  Records Administration, 2002); NARA NAID 1263923, National Archives
  at College Park, Maryland.
- "United States Social Security Death Index," database, FamilySearch
  (https://familysearch.org/ark:/61903/1:1:VMVT-6PF : 7 January
  2021), Alfredo L Goodman, 11 Aug 1997; citing U.S. Social Security
  Administration, Death Master File, database (Alexandria, Virginia:
  National Technical Information Service, ongoing).
- "United States, Social Security Numerical Identification Files
  (NUMIDENT), 1936-2007", database, FamilySearch
  (https://www.familysearch.org/ark:/61903/1:1:6KMB-VGGV : 10
  February 2023), Joseph George in entry for Alfred Lorenzo George, .

513) Annette M. Stilo

Annette M. Stilo(513) was born on 4 October 1921, in Waterbury, CT, to Cosimo
Stilo(308a) and Helen Elvera Anastasio(308). Annette M. Stilo(513) died on 10
October 2002 in Plainfield, IN.

Annette M. Stilo(513) married William F Snyder(513a).

William F Snyder, LT. COL. USAF(513a) was born on 23 March 1921, in Racine,
WI, to William Oscar Snyder(513aF) and Anna Madera(513aM). William F
Snyder(513a) died on 29 May 2006, in Indianapolis, IN. William F Snyder(513a)
was buried in Maple Hill Mausoleum, Plainfield, IN. William F Snyder(513a) was
a Retired LT. Colonel in the United States Air Force.

Annette M. Stilo(513) and William F Snyder(513a) had child(ren).

Records that include Annette M. Stilo(513) and/or William F Snyder(513a):
- "United States Census, 1930", , FamilySearch
  (https://www.familysearch.org/ark:/61903/1:1:X7SP-TPK : Sun Mar 10
  23:23:02 UTC 2024), Entry for Causamo Stilo and Elvera Stilo, 1930.
- "United States Census, 1930", , FamilySearch
  (https://www.familysearch.org/ark:/61903/1:1:X9SJ-NY1 : Sat Mar 09
  21:20:43 UTC 2024), Entry for William O Snyder and Anna Snyder,
  1930.
- "United States Census, 1940", , FamilySearch
  (https://www.familysearch.org/ark:/61903/1:1:K7JD-8RF : Sun Mar 10
  04:22:47 UTC 2024), Entry for William O Synder and Anna Synder,
  1940.
- "United States Census, 1940", , FamilySearch
  (https://www.familysearch.org/ark:/61903/1:1:K7J8-X7Y : Sat Mar 09
  13:14:36 UTC 2024), Entry for Cosimo Stilo and Helen E Stilo, 1940.
- "United States, Social Security Numerical Identification Files
  (NUMIDENT), 1936-2007", database, FamilySearch
  (https://www.familysearch.org/ark:/61903/1:1:6KQF-GHM5 : 10
  February 2023), Annette Marie Stilo, .
- "United States, Social Security Numerical Identification Files
  (NUMIDENT), 1936-2007", database, FamilySearch
  (https://www.familysearch.org/ark:/61903/1:1:6KQK-19K8 : 10
  February 2023), William Francis Snyder, .
- "United States Social Security Death Index," database, FamilySearch
  (https://familysearch.org/ark:/61903/1:1:V3TD-RTB : 11 January
  2021), William F Snyder, 29 May 2006; citing U.S. Social Security
  Administration, Death Master File, database (Alexandria, Virginia:
  National Technical Information Service, ongoing).
- "Find a Grave Index," database, FamilySearch
  (https://www.familysearch.org/ark:/61903/1:1:QVLH-9JSY : 16
  December 2021), William F Snyder, ; Burial, Plainfield, Hendricks,
  Indiana, United States of America, Maple Hill Cemetery; citing
  record ID 89683914, Find a Grave, http://www.findagrave.com.

- "Find a Grave Index," database, FamilySearch
  (https://www.familysearch.org/ark:/61903/1:1:QVLH-9J91 : 1 April
  2023), Annette M Stilo Snyder, ; Burial, Plainfield, Hendricks,
  Indiana, United States of America, Maple Hill Cemetery; citing
  record ID 89683908, Find a Grave, http://www.findagrave.com.

514) Mary Jenuvieve Perrino

Mary Jenuvieve Perrino(514) was born on 29 May 1921 in Concord, NH, to
Liberatore Perrina(200) and Carmella Gammaroto(200a). Mary Jenuvieve
Perrino(514) died on 22 May 2002 in Concord, NH. Mary Jenuvieve Perrino(514)
was a concert pianist and piano teacher.

Mary Jenuvieve Perrino(514) married John Joseph Byrne(514a).

John Joseph Byrne(514a) was born about 1915 in Massachusetts.
NOTE: The information for John Joseph Byrne(514a) is from an undocumented
source and may not be correct.

Mary Jenuvieve Perrino(514) and John Joseph Byrne(514a) had child(ren).

Records that include Mary Jenuvieve Perrino(514) and/or John Joseph
Byrne(514a):
- "United States Census, 1930", , FamilySearch
  (https://www.familysearch.org/ark:/61903/1:1:X7NK-BXM : Sat Mar 09
  13:58:16 UTC 2024), Entry for Liberatone Perrino and Carmirella
  Perrino, 1930.
- "United States Census, 1940", , FamilySearch
  (https://www.familysearch.org/ark:/61903/1:1:VT94-72P : Sat Mar 09
  20:05:01 UTC 2024), Entry for Liberstore Perrins and Carmella
  Perrins, 1940.
- "United States 1950 Census", , FamilySearch
  (https://www.familysearch.org/ark:/61903/1:1:6F3Z-STDD : Wed Oct 04
  07:37:56 UTC 2023), Entry for Mary Perrino, 10 April 1950.
- "United States, Social Security Numerical Identification Files
  (NUMIDENT), 1936-2007", database, FamilySearch
  (https://www.familysearch.org/ark:/61903/1:1:6KM3-S7G1 : 10
  February 2023), Mary Perrino, .
- "Find a Grave Index," database, FamilySearch
  (https://www.familysearch.org/ark:/61903/1:1:731C-L7W2 : 8 November
  2023), Mary Perrino Byrne, ; Burial, Concord, Merrimack, New
  Hampshire, United States of America, Calvary Cemetery; citing
  record ID 194288057, Find a Grave, http://www.findagrave.com.

515) Eleanor Marie Tiso

Eleanor Marie Tiso(515) was born on 30 April 1921, in Newark, NJ, to Oto
(Ottone) Tiso(169) Mary Senese(169a). Eleanor Marie Tiso(515) died on 30 March
2004 in New Jersey.

Eleanor Marie Tiso(515) married Luis J. Rusca(515a).

Luis J. Rusca(515a) was born on 11 October 1916 to Frank Rusca(515aF) and
Pia(515aM). Luis J. Rusca(515a) died 3 April 1985 in Nutley, NJ.

Eleanor Marie Tiso(515) and Luis J. Rusca(515a) had child(ren).

Records that include Eleanor Marie Tiso(515) and/or Luis J. Rusca(515a):
- "New Jersey, Reclaim the Records, Geographic Birth Index, 1901-
  1929", , FamilySearch
  (https://www.familysearch.org/ark:/61903/1:1:6NMQ-DDCW : Sun Mar 10
  12:31:44 UTC 2024), Entry for Elonor M. O. Tiso, 30 Apr 1921.
- "United States Census, 1930", , FamilySearch
  (https://www.familysearch.org/ark:/61903/1:1:X4D5-94D : Sun Mar 10
  02:12:08 UTC 2024), Entry for Frank Roscoe and Piai Roscoe, 1930.
- "United States Census, 1930", , FamilySearch
  (https://www.familysearch.org/ark:/61903/1:1:X4DG-XPV : Fri Mar 08
  18:34:06 UTC 2024), Entry for Ottone Liso and Mary H Liso, 1930.

- "United States Census, 1940", , FamilySearch
  (https://www.familysearch.org/ark:/61903/1:1:K4BX-LGY : Sun Mar 10
  17:21:28 UTC 2024), Entry for William Sidoli and Mary Sidoli, 1940.
- "United States Census, 1940", , FamilySearch
  (https://www.familysearch.org/ark:/61903/1:1:K4BF-LBN : Sat Mar 09
  21:19:59 UTC 2024), Entry for Frank Rusca and Pia Rusca, 1940.
- "United States World War II Army Enlistment Records, 1938-1946,"
  database, FamilySearch
  (https://familysearch.org/ark:/61903/1:1:KMJQ-M3M : 5 December
  2014), Louis J Rusca, enlisted 13 Mar 1942, Ft Dix, New Jersey,
  United States; citing "Electronic Army Serial Number Merged File,
  ca. 1938-1946," database, The National Archives: Access to Archival
  Databases (AAD) (http://aad.archives.gov : National Archives and
  Records Administration, 2002); NARA NAID 1263923, National Archives
  at College Park, Maryland.
- "United States 1950 Census", , FamilySearch
  (https://www.familysearch.org/ark:/61903/1:1:6F9B-46PW : Wed Mar 20
  18:52:17 UTC 2024), Entry for Louis J Rusca and Eleanore M Rusca, 7
  April 1950.
- "United States, Social Security Numerical Identification Files
  (NUMIDENT), 1936-2007", database, FamilySearch
  (https://www.familysearch.org/ark:/61903/1:1:6K9Z-TQ1K : 10
  February 2023), Eleanor Marie Tiso, .
- "United States Social Security Death Index," database, FamilySearch
  (https://familysearch.org/ark:/61903/1:1:JBTF-BZD : 8 January
  2021), Louis Rusca, Apr 1985; citing U.S. Social Security
  Administration, Death Master File, database (Alexandria, Virginia:
  National Technical Information Service, ongoing).
- "United States Social Security Death Index," database, FamilySearch
  (https://familysearch.org/ark:/61903/1:1:VM3T-92Z : 11 January
  2021), Eleanor M Rusca, 30 Mar 2004; citing U.S. Social Security
  Administration, Death Master File, database (Alexandria, Virginia:
  National Technical Information Service, ongoing).
- "Find a Grave Index," database, FamilySearch
  (https://www.familysearch.org/ark:/61903/1:1:QVLZ-3KDH : 14 April
  2023), Eleanor Rusca, ; Burial, Bloomfield, Essex, New Jersey,
  United States of America, Glendale Cemetery; citing record ID
  90585429, Find a Grave, http://www.findagrave.com.
- "Find a Grave Index," database, FamilySearch
  (https://www.familysearch.org/ark:/61903/1:1:QVLZ-3KNP : 14 April
  2023), Louis J Rusca, ; Burial, Bloomfield, Essex, New Jersey,
  United States of America, Glendale Cemetery; citing record ID
  90585430, Find a Grave, http://www.findagrave.com.

516) Raymond Coari Lombardi

Raymond Coari Lombardi(516) was born on 26 September 1921, in Norwalk, CT, to
Feliciano (Phillip White) Lombardi(236) and Sylvia Noris Coari(236b).

Records that include Raymond Coari Lombardi(516):
- "United States Census, 1940", , FamilySearch
  (https://www.familysearch.org/ark:/61903/1:1:K7BP-XTQ : Sat Mar 09
  04:56:17 UTC 2024), Entry for Adolph Coari and Julia Connelly,
  1940.
- "United States World War II Army Enlistment Records, 1938-1946," ,
  FamilySearch (https://familysearch.org/ark:/61903/1:1:K8LF-XZ7 : 5
  December 2014), Raymond C Lombardi, enlisted 25 Mar 1943, Ft
  Devens, Massachusetts, United States; citing "Electronic Army
  Serial Number Merged File, ca. 1938-1946," database, The National
  Archives: Access to Archival Databases (AAD)
  (http://aad.archives.gov : National Archives and Records
  Administration, 2002); NARA NAID 1263923, National Archives at
  College Park, Maryland.
- "Connecticut, World War II Draft Registration Cards, 1940-1945", ,
  FamilySearch (https://www.familysearch.org/ark:/61903/1:1:Q2CR-JGGJ
  : Sat Mar 09 17:03:36 UTC 2024), Entry for Raymond Coari Lombardi
  and Julia Connelly, 16 Feb 1942.

- "United States 1950 Census", , FamilySearch
  (https://www.familysearch.org/ark:/61903/1:1:6XG2-FCGK : Thu Oct 05
  15:36:46 UTC 2023), Entry for Philip W Lombardi and Sylvia C
  Lombardi, 11 April 1950.
- https://www.lombardihouse.com/history/

517) Phillip Adam Lombardi

Phillip Adam Lombardi(517) was born on 14 November 1921, in Bridgeport, CT, to
Saverio Lombardi(261) and Giovanna Prezioso(261a). Phillip Adam Lombardi(517)
died on 4 January 2003 in Torrance, CA.

Phillip Adam Lombardi(517) married Louise Frances Saulsberry(517a), Lavone
Faye Ulhorn(517b), and Blanche E. Thompson(517c).

Phillip Adam Lombardi(517) married Louise Frances Saulsberry(517a) on 9
December 1945 in Orange, CA.

Louise Frances Saulsberry(517a) was born on 27 January 1922, in Payson, OK, to
Marion F. Saulsberry(517aF) and Minnie E. Gentry(517aM). Louise Frances
Saulsberry(517a) died August 1989 in Oklahoma. Louise Frances Saulsberry(517a)
also married William Thompson Gowing(517ab).

Phillip Adam Lombardi(517) married Lavone Faye Ulhorn(517b) on 31 August 1953
in Los Angeles, CA.

Lavone Faye Ulhorn(517b) was born about 1932 in North Dakota to Victor
Ulhorn(517bF) and Clara Martha Krause(517bM).

Phillip Adam Lombardi(517) married Blanche E. Thompson(517c) in 1962 in Los
Angeles, CA.

Blanche E. Thompson(517c) was born 30 March 1935, in Los Angeles, CA, to
Lowell Thompson(517cF) and Blanche Haugner(517cM). Blanche E. Thompson(517c)
died on 2 May 2009 in Whatcom, WA.

Phillip Adam Lombardi(517) and Blanche E. Thompson(517c) divorced in June 1967
in Los Angeles, CA.

Blanche E. Thompson(517c) was previously married to Erling Rossland(517cX).

Records that include Phillip Adam Lombardi(517), Louise Frances
Saulsberry(517a), Lavone Faye Ulhorn(517b), and/or Blanche E. Thompson(517c):
- "United States Census, 1930", , FamilySearch
  (https://www.familysearch.org/ark:/61903/1:1:XMPM-77Y : Fri Mar 08
  01:23:40 UTC 2024), Entry for James Lombardi and Carmello Lombardi,
  1930.
- "United States Census, 1930", , FamilySearch
  (https://www.familysearch.org/ark:/61903/1:1:XCW3-TNF : Mon Mar 11
  01:01:41 UTC 2024), Entry for Manuel Saulsberry and Minnie
  Saulsberry, 1930.
- "United States Census, 1940", , FamilySearch
  (https://www.familysearch.org/ark:/61903/1:1:K97H-NYF : Sat Mar 09
  03:29:53 UTC 2024), Entry for Sam Lombardis and Jennie Lombardis,
  1940.
- "United States Census, 1940", , FamilySearch
  (https://www.familysearch.org/ark:/61903/1:1:VBVJ-66S : Sat Mar 09
  22:59:06 UTC 2024), Entry for Marion ?ulsberry and Minnie ?
  ulsberry, 1940.
- "United States Census, 1940", , FamilySearch
  (https://www.familysearch.org/ark:/61903/1:1:K9Z8-NMS : Sat Mar 09
  13:08:21 UTC 2024), Entry for Lowell E Thompson and Blanche N
  Thompson, 1940.
- "California, World War II Draft Registration Cards, 1940-1945", ,
  FamilySearch (https://www.familysearch.org/ark:/61903/1:1:QGXY-LD9Q
  : Sat Mar 09 20:17:53 UTC 2024), Entry for Philip A Lombardi and
  Jennie Lombardi, 27 July 1945.

- "United States World War II Army Enlistment Records, 1938-1946," , FamilySearch (https://familysearch.org/ark:/61903/1:1:KMX1-5RH : 5 December 2014), Philip A Lombardi, enlisted 08 Jan 1942, Los Angeles, California, United States; citing "Electronic Army Serial Number Merged File, ca. 1938-1946," database, The National Archives: Access to Archival Databases (AAD) (http://aad.archives.gov : National Archives and Records Administration, 2002); NARA NAID 1263923, National Archives at College Park, Maryland.

- "California, County Marriages, 1850-1953", , FamilySearch (https://www.familysearch.org/ark:/61903/1:1:K8FP-W3J : Fri Mar 08 20:15:16 UTC 2024), Entry for Philip Adam Lombardi and Louise Frances Saulsberry, 9 December 1945.

- "United States 1950 Census", , FamilySearch (https://www.familysearch.org/ark:/61903/1:1:6XGS-KY77 : Tue Oct 03 01:04:12 UTC 2023), Entry for Louise F Lombardi, 3 April 1950.

- "United States 1950 Census", , FamilySearch (https://www.familysearch.org/ark:/61903/1:1:6XGZ-D71M : Wed Mar 20 23:24:02 UTC 2024), Entry for Philip A Lombardi, 1 May 1950.

- "United States Census, 1950", , FamilySearch (https://www.familysearch.org/ark:/61903/1:1:6XGN-ZHPC : Thu Oct 05 17:50:35 UTC 2023), Entry for Lowell E Thompson and Blanche N Thompson, April 12, 1950.

- "California Marriage Index, 1960-1985", , FamilySearch (https://www.familysearch.org/ark:/61903/1:1:V6FM-S3L : 26 January 2024), Philip A Lombardi, 1962.

- "California, County Marriages, 1850-1953", , FamilySearch (https://www.familysearch.org/ark:/61903/1:1:K86H-9PK : Sun Mar 10 11:35:48 UTC 2024), Entry for Philip Adam Lombardi and Lavone Faye Uhlhorn, 31 August 1953.

- "California Marriage Index, 1960-1985", database, FamilySearch (https://www.familysearch.org/ark:/61903/1:1:V6FM-S3L : 26 January 2024), Philip A Lombardi, 1962.

- "California Divorce Index, 1966-1984," , FamilySearch (https://familysearch.org/ark:/61903/1:1:VPBP-Y2V : 15 May 2014), Blanche E Rossland and Philip A Lombardi, Jul 1967; from "California Divorce Index, 1966-1984," database and images, Ancestry (http://www.ancestry.com : 2007); citing Los Angeles City, California, Health Statistics, California Department of Health Services, Sacramento.

- "United States, Social Security Numerical Identification Files (NUMIDENT), 1936-2007", database, FamilySearch (https://www.familysearch.org/ark:/61903/1:1:6K47-N8MX : 11 February 2023), Phillip Adam Lombardi, .

- "United States, Social Security Numerical Identification Files (NUMIDENT), 1936-2007", database, FamilySearch (https://www.familysearch.org/ark:/61903/1:1:6K49-8BGW : 10 February 2023), Louise Frances Saulsberry, .

- "United States Social Security Death Index," database, FamilySearch (https://familysearch.org/ark:/61903/1:1:JG79-HMP : 11 January 2021), Louise F Gowing, Aug 1989; citing U.S. Social Security Administration, Death Master File, database (Alexandria, Virginia: National Technical Information Service, ongoing).

- "United States Social Security Death Index," , FamilySearch (https://familysearch.org/ark:/61903/1:1:VMCV-44M : 12 January 2021), Blanche E Lombardi, 02 May 2009; citing U.S. Social Security Administration, Death Master File, database (Alexandria, Virginia: National Technical Information Service, ongoing).

- "Washington Death Index, 1965-2014," , FamilySearch (https://familysearch.org/ark:/61903/1:1:QLW9-PGP1 : 13 July 2017), Blanche E Lombardi, 02 May 2009, Whatcom, Washington, United States; from the Department of Health, Death Index, 1907-1960; 1965-2014, Washington State Archives, Digital Archives (https://www.digitalarchives.wa.gov/Collections/TitleInfo/472 : n.d.); Citing Washington State Department of Health.

- "Find a Grave Index," database, FamilySearch
  (https://www.familysearch.org/ark:/61903/1:1:QV2R-VCCD : 9
  September 2022), Louise Gowing, ; Burial, Lawton, Comanche,
  Oklahoma, United States of America, Sunset Memorial Gardens; citing
  record ID 76836096, Find a Grave, http://www.findagrave.com.

518) Angelo H Riccio

Angelo H Riccio(518) was born on 23 August 1920, in Schenectady, NY, to
Raffaele Riccio(221a) and Giovanna (Jenny) Ciasullo(221). Angelo H Riccio(518)
died 22 March 2013 in Camp Hill, PA.

Angelo H Riccio(518) married Mary Gerardi(518a).

Mary Gerardi(518a) was born on 20 February 1923, in Isnello, Italy, to
Giuseppe Gerardi(518aF) and Caterine Mazzella(518aF). Mary Gerardi(518a) died
24 September 1988 in Harrisburg, PA.

Angelo H Riccio(518) and Mary Gerardi(518a) had child(ren).

Records that include Angelo H Riccio(518) and/or Mary Gerardi(518a):
- "New York, Birth Indexes outside of New York City, 1881-1942", ,
  FamilySearch (https://www.familysearch.org/ark:/61903/1:1:6X1B-N3F1
  : Fri Mar 08 08:58:04 UTC 2024), Entry for Angelo Ricci, 23 Aug
  1920.
- "United States Census, 1930", , FamilySearch
  (https://www.familysearch.org/ark:/61903/1:1:X4TB-187 : Fri Mar 08
  12:10:26 UTC 2024), Entry for Ralph Riccio and Jennie Riccio, 1930.
- "United States Census, 1930", , FamilySearch
  (https://www.familysearch.org/ark:/61903/1:1:X4TB-1D5 : Sun Jul 14
  20:22:55 UTC 2024), Entry for Joseph Gerardi and Cathrine Gerardi,
  1930.
- "United States Census, 1940", , FamilySearch
  (https://www.familysearch.org/ark:/61903/1:1:K79V-TYQ : Sat Mar 09
  17:46:14 UTC 2024), Entry for Ralph Riccio and Jennie Riccio, 1940.
- "United States Census, 1940", , FamilySearch
  (https://www.familysearch.org/ark:/61903/1:1:K79V-TTR : Fri Mar 08
  22:52:54 UTC 2024), Entry for Joseph Gerardi and Catherine Gerardi,
  1940.
- "United States Census, 1950", , FamilySearch
  (https://www.familysearch.org/ark:/61903/1:1:6XRQ-YMHJ : Fri Oct 06
  09:40:25 UTC 2023), Entry for Angelo Riccio and Mary Riccio, 26
  April 1950.
- "United States, GenealogyBank Obituaries, Births, and Marriages
  1980-2014", , FamilySearch
  (https://www.familysearch.org/ark:/61903/1:1:QV54-TMPY : Fri Mar 08
  01:14:07 UTC 2024), Entry for Mary F Riccio and Angelo H Riccio, 24
  Sep 1988.
- "United States, GenealogyBank Obituaries, Births, and Marriages
  1980-2014", , FamilySearch
  (https://www.familysearch.org/ark:/61903/1:1:QKKT-CR6D : Mon Jun 03
  21:12:41 UTC 2024), Entry for Angelo H Riccio and John Alifano, 25
  Mar 2013.
- https://obits.pennlive.com/us/obituaries/pennlive/name/angelo-
  riccio-obituary?id=14403989

519) Josephine Bonelli

Josephine Bonelli(519) was born on 13 January 1922, in Detroit, MI, to Joseph
Bonelli(271a) and Concetta Anastasio(271). Josephine Bonelli(519) died 14 July
2002, in Michigan.

Josephine Bonelli(519) married Jerry Austin Jorgensen(519a), Lehr(519b), and
Robert Anthony Thomas(519c).

Josephine Bonelli(519) married Jerry Austin Jorgensen(519a) on 9 September
1939 in River Rouge, MI.

Jerry Austin Jorgensen(519a) was born 14 October 1919, in Detroit, MI, to
Jerry Peter Jorgensen(519aF) and Elmira Austin(519aM). Jerry Austin
Jorgensen(519a) died on 8 July 1955 in Michigan.

Josephine Bonelli(519) married Lehr(519b).

Lehr(519b) Only last name is known.

Josephine Bonelli(519) married Robert Anthony Thomas(519c).

Robert Anthony Thomas(519c) was born on 23 April 1931, in Detroit, MI, to Anthony R. Thomas(519cF) and Helen M. Key(519cM).

Josephine Bonelli(519) and Robert Anthony Thomas(519c) had child(ren).

Records that include Josephine Bonelli(519), Jerry Austin Jorgensen(519a), Lehr(519b), and/or Robert Anthony Thomas(519c).

- "United States Census, 1920", , FamilySearch (https://www.familysearch.org/ark:/61903/1:1:MZW1-1DX : Sat Mar 09 09:10:17 UTC 2024), Entry for Jerry P Jorgenson and Elmira Jorgenson, 1920.
- "United States Census, 1930", , FamilySearch (https://www.familysearch.org/ark:/61903/1:1:X7SD-KBS : Sun Mar 10 18:50:02 UTC 2024), Entry for Jerry Gorgensen and Elmira Gorgensen, 1930.
- "United States Census, 1930", , FamilySearch (https://www.familysearch.org/ark:/61903/1:1:X7SP-TPK : Sun Mar 10 23:23:02 UTC 2024), Entry for Causamo Stilo and Elvera Stilo, 1930.
- "United States Census, 1940", , FamilySearch (https://www.familysearch.org/ark:/61903/1:1:KM9W-K89 : Fri Mar 08 18:04:55 UTC 2024), Entry for Jerry Jorgenson and Josephene Jorgenson, 1940.
- "United States Census, 1940", , FamilySearch (https://www.familysearch.org/ark:/61903/1:1:KH95-G2T : Sat Mar 09 23:31:31 UTC 2024), Entry for Anthony Thomas and Helen Thomas, 1940.
- "North Dakota, World War II Draft Registration Cards, 1940-1947", , FamilySearch (https://www.familysearch.org/ark:/61903/1:1:W3R4-WC6Z : Sun Mar 10 13:11:54 UTC 2024), Entry for Jerry Austin Jorgensen and Harkins-Meyer, 16 Oct 1940.
- "North Dakota, World War II Draft Registration Cards, 1940-1947", , FamilySearch (https://www.familysearch.org/ark:/61903/1:1:W3P2-D13Z : Sat Mar 09 09:51:41 UTC 2024), Entry for Jerry Augtin Jorgensen and Hoskins-Meyer, 16 Oct 1940.
- "United States, Social Security Numerical Identification Files (NUMIDENT), 1936-2007", database, FamilySearch (https://www.familysearch.org/ark:/61903/1:1:6KQN-FGZL : 10 February 2023), Josephine Bonelli Jorgensen, .
- "United States Social Security Death Index," database, FamilySearch (https://familysearch.org/ark:/61903/1:1:V9Z3-QZD : 9 January 2021), Jerry Jorgensen, Jul 1955; citing U.S. Social Security Administration, Death Master File, database (Alexandria, Virginia: National Technical Information Service, ongoing).
- "United States Social Security Death Index," database, FamilySearch (https://familysearch.org/ark:/61903/1:1:J1X2-W4F : 9 January 2021), Josephine B Thomas, 14 Jul 2002; citing U.S. Social Security Administration, Death Master File, database (Alexandria, Virginia: National Technical Information Service, ongoing).
- "United States, Social Security Numerical Identification Files (NUMIDENT), 1936-2007", database, FamilySearch (https://www.familysearch.org/ark:/61903/1:1:6KQN-FGZL : 10 February 2023), Josephine Bonelli Jorgensen, .
- "United States, Social Security Numerical Identification Files (NUMIDENT), 1936-2007", database, FamilySearch (https://www.familysearch.org/ark:/61903/1:1:6KQJ-9HPN : 10 February 2023), Robert Anthony Thomas, .
- "United States Social Security Death Index," database, FamilySearch (https://familysearch.org/ark:/61903/1:1:JTDT-D2D : 11 January 2021), Robert A Thomas, 17 Nov 2005; citing U.S. Social Security Administration, Death Master File, database (Alexandria, Virginia: National Technical Information Service, ongoing).

- "United States, GenealogyBank Obituaries, Births, and Marriages 1980-2014," database with images, FamilySearch (https://familysearch.org/ark:/61903/1:1:QKL3-FZCF : accessed 28 April 2024), Robert Anthony Thomas, Florida, United States, 01 Dec 2005; from "Recent Newspaper Obituaries (1977 - Today)," database, GenealogyBank.com (http://www.genealogybank.com : 2014); citing Palm Beach Post, The, born-digital text.
- "United States, Social Security Numerical Identification Files (NUMIDENT), 1936-2007", database, FamilySearch (https://www.familysearch.org/ark:/61903/1:1:6KQJ-9HPN : 10 February 2023), Robert Anthony Thomas, .
- "Find a Grave Index," database, FamilySearch (https://www.familysearch.org/ark:/61903/1:1:6PXX-JBCZ : 5 October 2023), Josephine Beatrice Bonelli Thomas, ; Burial, Kalkaska, Kalkaska, Michigan, United States of America, Evergreen Cemetery; citing record ID 260202283, Find a Grave, http://www.findagrave.com.
- "Find a Grave Index," database, FamilySearch (https://www.familysearch.org/ark:/61903/1:1:6PXX-JBHL : 5 October 2023), Robert Anthony Thomas, ; Burial, Kalkaska, Kalkaska, Michigan, United States of America, Evergreen Cemetery; citing record ID 260202277, Find a Grave, http://www.findagrave.com.

520) Anthony Salvatore Scanzillo

Anthony Scanzillo(520) was born on 11 April 1922, in Bronx, NY, to Gaetano Scauzillo(164) and Giovanna Grasso(196). Anthony Scanzillo(520) died on 21 May 2007, in Trumbull, CT. Anthony Scanzillo(520) was a mail carrier.

Anthony Scanzillo(520) married Jane Pavia(520a).

Jane Pavia(520a) was born on 8 July 1921, in Bridgeport, CT, to Leonard Pavia(520aF) and Florence(520aM). Jane Pavia(520a) died on 19 April 1995 in Branford, CT.

Records that include Anthony Scanzillo(520) married Jane Pavia(520a):
- "United States Census, 1930", , FamilySearch (https://www.familysearch.org/ark:/61903/1:1:X7D4-SB4 : Sun Mar 10 21:34:02 UTC 2024), Entry for Gaetano Scanzillo and Guanina Scanzillo, 1930.
- "United States Census, 1940", , FamilySearch (https://www.familysearch.org/ark:/61903/1:1:KQBN-826 : Sat Mar 09 01:41:31 UTC 2024), Entry for Gaetano Scanzillo and Jennie Scanzillo, 1940.
- "United States Census, 1940", , FamilySearch (https://www.familysearch.org/ark:/61903/1:1:KWMJ-214 : Fri Mar 08 04:42:23 UTC 2024), Entry for Leonard Pavia and Florence Pavia, 1940.
- "New York, New York City, World War II Draft Registration Cards, 1940-1947", , FamilySearch (https://www.familysearch.org/ark:/61903/1:1:WQYH-HVMM : Sun Mar 10 10:38:46 UTC 2024), Entry for Anthony Salvatore Scanzillo and Montgomery Ward, 30 Jun 1942.
- "United States 1950 Census", , FamilySearch (https://www.familysearch.org/ark:/61903/1:1:6XYM-LFBY : Tue Oct 03 11:09:53 UTC 2023), Entry for Anthony Scanzillo and Jane Scanzello, 10 April 1950.
- "United States, Social Security Numerical Identification Files (NUMIDENT), 1936-2007", database, FamilySearch (https://www.familysearch.org/ark:/61903/1:1:6K9W-4986 : 10 February 2023), Anthony Scanzillo, .
- "Connecticut Death Index, 1949-2001," , FamilySearch (https://familysearch.org/ark:/61903/1:1:VZPZ-4D8 : 9 December 2014), Jane J Scanzillo, 19 Apr 1995; from "Connecticut Death Index, 1949-2001," database, Ancestry (http://www.ancestry.com : 2003); citing Branford, New Haven, Connecticut, Connecticut Department of Health, Hartfort.

- "United States Social Security Death Index," database, FamilySearch (https://familysearch.org/ark:/61903/1:1:JKJK-6T1 : 7 January 2021), Jane Scanzillo, 19 Apr 1995; citing U.S. Social Security Administration, Death Master File, database (Alexandria, Virginia: National Technical Information Service, ongoing).
- "United States, Social Security Numerical Identification Files (NUMIDENT), 1936-2007", database, FamilySearch (https://www.familysearch.org/ark:/61903/1:1:6KMV-DPV6 : 10 February 2023), Jane Jeanette Pavia, .
- "Find a Grave Index," database, FamilySearch (https://www.familysearch.org/ark:/61903/1:1:6K3W-1QYX : 13 June 2023), Jane Scanzillo, ; Burial, Stratford, Fairfield, Connecticut, United States of America, Saint Michael's Cemetery; citing record ID 185951736, Find a Grave, http://www.findagrave.com.
- "Find a Grave Index," database, FamilySearch (https://www.familysearch.org/ark:/61903/1:1:6K3W-1QYF : 13 June 2023), Anthony Scanzillo, ; Burial, Stratford, Fairfield, Connecticut, United States of America, Saint Michael's Cemetery; citing record ID 185951746, Find a Grave, http://www.findagrave.com.

521) Gaetano Zecchino

Gaetano Zecchino(521) was born in 1922, in Ariano, Italy, to Angela Miressi(291) and Giovanni Zecchino(291a). Gaetano Zecchino(521) died 6 August 1926 in Ariano, Italy.

Records that include Gaetano Zecchino(521):
- Ariano, Italy 1926 Death Act #293

522) Philomena [Filomena] B Riccio

Philomena (Filomena) B Riccio(522) was born on 21 Apr 1922, in Schenectady, NY, to Raffaele Riccio(221a) and Giovanna (Jenny) Ciasullo(221). Philomena (Filomena) B Riccio(522) died 8 January 2021 in Schenectady, NY. Philomena (Filomena) B Riccio(522) was buried at St's Cyril & Method Cemetery in Rotterdam, NY.

Philomena (Filomena) B Riccio(522) married Carmen Frisone(522a) about 1948.

Carmen Frisone(522a) was born on 28 November 1923, in Schenectady, NY, to Pasquale Frizone(522aF) and Jennie Pantalone(522aM). Carmen Frisone(522a) died 6 February 1995 in Schenectady, NY.

Philomena[Filomena] B Riccio and Carmen Frisone(522a) had child(ren).

Records that include Philomena (Filomena) B Riccio(522) and/or Carmen Frisone(522a):
- "United States Census, 1930", , FamilySearch (https://www.familysearch.org/ark:/61903/1:1:X4TB-187 : Fri Mar 08 12:10:26 UTC 2024), Entry for Ralph Riccio and Jennie Riccio, 1930.
- "United States Census, 1940", , FamilySearch (https://www.familysearch.org/ark:/61903/1:1:K79V-TYQ : Sat Mar 09 17:46:14 UTC 2024), Entry for Ralph Riccio and Jennie Riccio, 1940.
- "United States World War II Army Enlistment Records, 1938-1946," , FamilySearch (https://familysearch.org/ark:/61903/1:1:K8R2-FBD : 5 December 2014), Carmen Frisone, enlisted 13 Jan 1943, Albany, New York, United States; citing "Electronic Army Serial Number Merged File, ca. 1938-1946," database, The National Archives: Access to Archival Databases (AAD) (http://aad.archives.gov : National Archives and Records Administration, 2002); NARA NAID 1263923, National Archives at College Park, Maryland.
- "United States Census, 1950", , FamilySearch (https://www.familysearch.org/ark:/61903/1:1:6XYQ-DCGK : Tue Mar 19 10:45:05 UTC 2024), Entry for Carmen Frizone and Philomina Frizone, 11 April 1950.

- "United States Social Security Death Index," database, FamilySearch (https://familysearch.org/ark:/61903/1:1:JYMQ-HMX : 7 January 2021), Carmen Frisone, 06 Feb 1995; citing U.S. Social Security Administration, Death Master File, database (Alexandria, Virginia: National Technical Information Service, ongoing).
- "United States, Social Security Numerical Identification Files (NUMIDENT), 1936-2007", database, FamilySearch (https://www.familysearch.org/ark:/61903/1:1:6K9W-364H : 10 February 2023), Carmen Frizone, .
- "Find a Grave Index," database, FamilySearch (https://www.familysearch.org/ark:/61903/1:1:QVKW-CB85 : 6 March 2021), Carmen Frisone, ; Burial, Rotterdam, Schenectady, New York, United States of America, Saints Cyril and Method Cemetery; citing record ID 34496003, Find a Grave, http://www.findagrave.com.
- "Find a Grave Index," database, FamilySearch (https://www.familysearch.org/ark:/61903/1:1:6ZWM-F5VL : 8 March 2021), Filomena B. Riccio Frisone, ; Burial, Rotterdam, Schenectady, New York, United States of America, Saints Cyril and Method Cemetery; citing record ID 220875241, Find a Grave, http://www.findagrave.com.

523) Marcello Roque

Marcello Roque(523) was born on 19 August 1922, in Ribeirão Pires, São Paulo, Brasil, to Antonio DeDonato(303) and Maria Rinaldi(303a).

Records that include Marcello Roque(523):
- "Brasil, São Paulo, Registro Civil, 1925-2023", FamilySearch (https://www.familysearch.org/ark:/61903/1:1:6VWW-KZQ2 : Sat Aug 23 11:09:51 UTC 2025), Entry for Marcello Roque and Miguel Rinaldo, 19 de agosto de 1922.

524) Grace Delores Lombardi

Grace Delores Lombardi(524) was born on 30 October 1922, in Bridgeport, CT, to Saverio Lombardi(261) and Giovanna Prezioso(261a). Grace Delores Lombardi(524) died 21 December 1990 in Ventura, CA.

Grace Delores Lombardi(524) married Jack D. Duryea(524a) and Vincent Mike Pezzuto(524b).

Grace Delores Lombardi(524) married Jack D. Duryea(524a).

Jack D. Duryea(524a) AKA Jack Domenstein was born on 3 June 1920, in San Francisco, CA, to Robert Domenstein(524aF) and Gildie Duryea(524aM). Jack D. Duryea(524a) died 15 September 1998 in Los Angeles, CA.

Jack D. Duryea(524a) and Grace Delores Lombardi(524) divorced

Grace Delores Lombardi(524) married Vincent Mike Pezzuto(524b) on 11 September 1949 in Los Angeles, California.

Vincent Mike Pezzuto(524b) was born 11 February 1928, in Ontario, CA, to Antonio Pezzuto(524bF) and Vera Paz Mandella(524bM).

Grace Delores Lombardi(524) and Vincent Mike Pezzuto(524b) had child(ren).

Records that include Grace Delores Lombardi(524), Jack D. Duryea(524a), and/or Vincent Mike Pezzuto(524b):
- "California Birth Index, 1905-1995," , FamilySearch (https://familysearch.org/ark:/61903/1:1:VLBP-FPB : 27 November 2014), Jack Damenstein, 03 Jun 1920; citing San Francisco, California, United States, Department of Health Services, Vital Statistics Department, Sacramento.
- "United States Census, 1930", , FamilySearch (https://www.familysearch.org/ark:/61903/1:1:XMPM-77Y : Fri Mar 08 01:23:40 UTC 2024), Entry for James Lombardi and Carmello Lombardi, 1930.
- "United States Census, 1930", , FamilySearch (https://www.familysearch.org/ark:/61903/1:1:XC6W-JFT : Sun Mar 10 02:48:17 UTC 2024), Entry for Tony Pizzuta and Victoria Pizzuta, 1930.

- "United States Census, 1940", , FamilySearch
  (https://www.familysearch.org/ark:/61903/1:1:K97H-NYF : Sat Mar 09
  03:29:53 UTC 2024), Entry for Sam Lombardis and Jennie Lombardis,
  1940.
- "United States Census, 1940", , FamilySearch
  (https://www.familysearch.org/ark:/61903/1:1:K941-M3N : Sat Mar 09
  20:02:40 UTC 2024), Entry for Tony Pizzuto and Victoria Pizzuto,
  1940.
- "California, World War II Draft Registration Cards, 1940-1945", ,
  FamilySearch (https://www.familysearch.org/ark:/61903/1:1:QGF3-3DY6
  : Fri Mar 08 22:31:57 UTC 2024), Entry for Jack Damenstein and
  Harold Damenstein, 1 July 1941.
- "California, County Marriages, 1850-1953", , FamilySearch
  (https://www.familysearch.org/ark:/61903/1:1:K823-W2K : Fri Mar 08
  19:43:41 UTC 2024), Entry for Vincent Mike Pezzuto and Gloria
  Dalores Lombardi, 11 September 1949.
- "United States 1950 Census", , FamilySearch
  (https://www.familysearch.org/ark:/61903/1:1:6XGJ-LL7Z : Wed Oct 04
  02:47:40 UTC 2023), Entry for Vincent M Pizzuto and Dolores G
  Pizzuto, 10 April 1950.
- "California Death Index, 1940-1997," database, FamilySearch
  (https://familysearch.org/ark:/61903/1:1:VP96-DNF : 26 November
  2014), Gloria Dolores Pizzuto, 21 Dec 1990; Department of Public
  Health Services, Sacramento.
- "United States Social Security Death Index," database, FamilySearch
  (https://familysearch.org/ark:/61903/1:1:JG74-ZM3 : 11 January
  2021), Jack Duryea, 15 Sep 1998; citing U.S. Social Security
  Administration, Death Master File, database (Alexandria, Virginia:
  National Technical Information Service, ongoing).
- "United States, Social Security Numerical Identification Files
  (NUMIDENT), 1936-2007", database, FamilySearch
  (https://www.familysearch.org/ark:/61903/1:1:6K4Z-2MFW : 11
  February 2023), Jack Damenstein, .

525) Antonietta Moschella

Antonietta Moschella(525) was born about 1923, in Ariano, Italy, to Antonio
Moschella(255a) and Mariangela Manganiello(255). Antonietta Moschella(525)
died 14 July 1928 in Ariano, Italy.

Records that include Antonietta Moschella(525):
- Ariano, Italy 1928 Death Act #137

526) Concetta Mary Vernacchio

Concetta Mary Vernacchio(526) was born on 22 January 1923, in Ariano, Italy,
to Antonio Vernacchia(293a) and Assunta Ciasullo(293). On 29 October 1932
Concetta Mary Vernacchio(526) boarded the ship SS Conte Grande, in Naples,
Italy. Concetta Mary Vernacchio(526) arrived in New York, NY on 7 November
1932. Concetta Mary Vernacchio(526) died July 1980 in Schenectady, NY.

Concetta Mary Vernacchio(526) married Angelo A. Saccocio(526a).

Angelo A. Saccocio(526a) was born on 4 February 1921, in Schenectady, NY, to
Fred Saccocio(526aF) and Carmella Simone(526aM). Angelo A. Saccocio(526a) died
October 1986 in Schenectady, NY.

Concetta Mary Vernacchio(526) and Angelo A. Saccocio(526a) had child(ren).

Records that include Concetta Mary Vernacchio(526) and/or Angelo A.
Saccocio(526a):
- "New York, Birth Indexes outside of New York City, 1881-1942", ,
  FamilySearch (https://www.familysearch.org/ark:/61903/1:1:6FBD-45N9
  : Sat Mar 09 21:47:24 UTC 2024), Entry for Angelo Saccoish, 4 Feb
  1921.
- "New York, New York Passenger and Crew Lists, 1909, 1925-1957", ,
  FamilySearch (https://www.familysearch.org/ark:/61903/1:1:24JT-
  VFK : Sat Mar 09 03:39:25 UTC 2024), Entry for Concetta Vernacchio,
  1932.

- "United States Census, 1940", , FamilySearch
  (https://www.familysearch.org/ark:/61903/1:1:K79V-279 : Fri Mar 08
  09:15:07 UTC 2024), Entry for Tony Vernacchio and Assunda
  Vernacchio, 1940.
- "United States World War II Army Enlistment Records, 1938-1946," ,
  FamilySearch (https://familysearch.org/ark:/61903/1:1:K8RJ-5HX : 5
  December 2014), Angelo A Saccocio, enlisted 07 Oct 1942, Albany,
  New York, United States; citing "Electronic Army Serial Number
  Merged File, ca. 1938-1946," database, The National Archives:
  Access to Archival Databases (AAD) (http://aad.archives.gov :
  National Archives and Records Administration, 2002); NARA NAID
  1263923, National Archives at College Park, Maryland.
- "United States Census, 1950", , FamilySearch
  (https://www.familysearch.org/ark:/61903/1:1:6XP4-7JLP : Tue Oct 03
  16:28:17 UTC 2023), Entry for Angelo Saccocio and Concetta
  Saccocio, 19 April 1950.
- "United States, Social Security Numerical Identification Files
  (NUMIDENT), 1936-2007", database, FamilySearch
  (https://www.familysearch.org/ark:/61903/1:1:6KMY-CBF8 : 10
  February 2023), Concetta Mary Vernacchio, .
- "United States Social Security Death Index," database, FamilySearch
  (https://familysearch.org/ark:/61903/1:1:JTBP-6YX : 7 January
  2021), Concetta Saccocio, Jul 1980; citing U.S. Social Security
  Administration, Death Master File, database (Alexandria, Virginia:
  National Technical Information Service, ongoing).
- "Find a Grave Index," database, FamilySearch
  (https://www.familysearch.org/ark:/61903/1:1:6PX6-X6YD : 8 March
  2024), Concetta Mary Vernacchio Saccocio, ; Burial, Schenectady,
  Schenectady, New York, United States of America, Saint Joseph's
  Cemetery; citing record ID 259369980, Find a Grave,
  http://www.findagrave.com.
- "United States Social Security Death Index," database, FamilySearch
  (https://familysearch.org/ark:/61903/1:1:JKGS-J6G : 7 January
  2021), Angelo Saccocio, Oct 1986; citing U.S. Social Security
  Administration, Death Master File, database (Alexandria, Virginia:
  National Technical Information Service, ongoing).
- "Find a Grave Index," database, FamilySearch
  (https://www.familysearch.org/ark:/61903/1:1:6PX6-X6YV : 5 October
  2023), Angelo A. Saccocio, ; Burial, Schenectady, Schenectady, New
  York, United States of America, Saint Joseph's Cemetery; citing
  record ID 259369983, Find a Grave, http://www.findagrave.com.

527) Victoria Tiso

Victoria Tiso(527) was born on 13 July 1923 in Newark, NJ, to Oto (Ottone)
Tiso(169) and Mary Senese(169a). Victoria Tiso(527) died 9 October 2012 in
Bloomfield, NJ.

Victoria Tiso(527) married Jules B. Maioran(527a).

Jules B. Maioran(527a) was born on 10 July 1920 in Newark, NJ, to Benny
Maioran(527aF) and Mary Zarra(527aM). Jules B. Maioran(527a) died 12 April
1990 in Bloomfield, NJ.

Victoria Tiso(527) and Jules B. Maioran(527a) had child(ren).

Records that include Victoria Tiso(527) and/or Jules B. Maioran(527a):
- "New Jersey, Reclaim the Records, Geographic Birth Index, 1901-
  1929", , FamilySearch
  (https://www.familysearch.org/ark:/61903/1:1:6NS8-NK52 : Sun Mar 10
  05:03:10 UTC 2024), Entry for Julio B Maioran, 10 Jul 1920.
- "New Jersey, Reclaim the Records, Geographic Birth Index, 1901-
  1929", , FamilySearch
  (https://www.familysearch.org/ark:/61903/1:1:6NMB-9RN3 : Sat Mar 09
  04:29:05 UTC 2024), Entry for Victoria Tiso, 13 Jul 1923.
- "United States Census, 1930", , FamilySearch
  (https://www.familysearch.org/ark:/61903/1:1:X4DG-XPV : Fri Mar 08
  18:34:06 UTC 2024), Entry for Ottone Liso and Mary H Liso, 1930.

- "United States Census, 1940", , FamilySearch
  (https://www.familysearch.org/ark:/61903/1:1:K45L-1VZ : Fri Mar 08
  19:03:18 UTC 2024), Entry for Benjamin Maioran and Mary Maioran,
  1940.
- "United States Social Security Death Index," database, FamilySearch
  (https://familysearch.org/ark:/61903/1:1:JKTP-74Z : 8 January
  2021), Jules B Maioran, 12 Apr 1990; citing U.S. Social Security
  Administration, Death Master File, database (Alexandria, Virginia:
  National Technical Information Service, ongoing).
- "United States, Social Security Numerical Identification Files
  (NUMIDENT), 1936-2007", database, FamilySearch
  (https://www.familysearch.org/ark:/61903/1:1:6K96-N9WG : 10
  February 2023), Julius Maioran, .
- "Find a Grave Index," database, FamilySearch
  (https://www.familysearch.org/ark:/61903/1:1:DM47-XF6Z : 14 April
  2023), Jules B. Maioran, ; Burial, Upper Montclair, Essex, New
  Jersey, United States of America, Immaculate Conception Cemetery;
  citing record ID 181901443, Find a Grave,
  http://www.findagrave.com.
- "Find a Grave Index," database, FamilySearch
  (https://www.familysearch.org/ark:/61903/1:1:68N1-3FXP : 14 April
  2023), Victoria Tiso Maioran, ; Burial, Upper Montclair, Essex, New
  Jersey, United States of America, Immaculate Conception Cemetery;
  citing record ID 181901518, Find a Grave,
  http://www.findagrave.com.

528) Raimondo Manganiello

Raimondo Manganiello(528) was born about September 1923, in Ariano, Italy, to
Michele Manganiello(138) and Pasqualina Miniscalco(138a). Raimondo Manganiello
died 12 December 1924.

Records that include Raimondo Manganiello(528):
- Ariano, Italy 1924 Death Act #280

529) Rosa De Donato

Rosa De Donato(529) was born on 18 September 1923, in Ribeirão Pires, São
Paulo, Brasil, to Antonio DeDonato(303) and Maria Rinaldi(303a). Rosa De
Donato(529) died 6 October 1991 in Santo André, São Paulo, Brazil.

Rosa De Donato(529) married Pocetta(529a).

Pocetta(529a) only last name known - died before Rosa De Donato(529).

Records that include Rosa De Donato(529) and/or Pocetta(529a):
- "Brasil, São Paulo, Registro Civil, 1925-2023", FamilySearch
  (https://www.familysearch.org/ark:/61903/1:1:6VW7-R7DK : Sat Aug 23
  11:09:59 UTC 2025), Entry for Maria Olinaldi and Carmel- A Rinaldi,
  1923.
- "Brasil, São Paulo, Registro Civil, 1925-2023", FamilySearch
  (https://www.familysearch.org/ark:/61903/1:1:68JB-Q2NC : Wed Sep 03
  16:54:30 UTC 2025), Entry for and , 6 October 1991.

530) Ida Loretta Mingolello

Ida Loretta Mingolello(530) was born on 16 November 1923 in Queens, NY, to
Joseph Mingolello(294a) and Francesca deDonato(294). Ida Loretta
Mingolello(530) died on 9 July 2010 in Harlingen, TX.

Ida Loretta Mingolello(530) married Pasquale Francesco (Patsy F.)
Paradiso(530a) on 14 November 1942 in Stratford, CT.

Pasquale Francesco (Patsy F.) Paradiso(530a) was born on 18 November 1918, in
Bridgeport, CT, to Donato Paradiso(530aF) and Ann Vollotti(530aM). Pasquale
Francesco (Patsy F.) Paradiso(530a) served as an MP in the Unites States Army
during WWII. Pasquale Francesco (Patsy F.) Paradiso(530a) died 10 July 2010,
in Harlingen, TX.

Ida Loretta Mingolello(530) and Pasquale Francesco (Patsy F.) Paradiso(530a)
had child(ren).

Records that include Ida Loretta Mingolello(530) and/or Pasquale Francesco (Patsy F.) Paradiso(530a):

- City of Bridgeport, Births, November 1918 #214
- "United States, Census, 1930", , FamilySearch (https://www.familysearch.org/ark:/61903/1:1:XMP8-M1P : Wed Mar 06 09:36:34 UTC 2024), Entry for Joe Mingolello and Francis Mingolello, 1930.
- "United States, Census, 1930", , FamilySearch (https://www.familysearch.org/ark:/61903/1:1:XMGY-TTG : Sat Jul 06 14:21:03 UTC 2024), Entry for Daniel Paradiso and Anna Paradiso, 1930.
- "United States, Census, 1940", , FamilySearch (https://www.familysearch.org/ark:/61903/1:1:K71S-M9L : Fri Mar 08 16:03:19 UTC 2024), Entry for Joseph Mingolello and Jennie Mingolello, 1940.
- "Connecticut, World War II Draft Registration Cards, 1940-1945", , FamilySearch (https://www.familysearch.org/ark:/61903/1:1:Q2CR-PMKM : Mon Jul 22 16:21:10 UTC 2024), Entry for Patsy Francis Paradiso and Anna Paradiso, 16 Oct 1940.
- "Connecticut, World War II Draft Registration Cards, 1940-1945", , FamilySearch (https://www.familysearch.org/ark:/61903/1:1:Q2CR-2KCD : Sat Mar 09 10:41:48 UTC 2024), Entry for Ralph George Mingolello and Ida Paradiso, 17 Dec 1945.
- "United States, World War II Army Enlistment Records, 1938-1946," database, FamilySearch (https://familysearch.org/ark:/61903/1:1:K8R3-ZKF : 5 December 2014), Patsy F Paradiso, enlisted 02 Mar 1944, Ft Devens, Massachusetts, United States; citing "Electronic Army Serial Number Merged File, ca. 1938-1946," database, The National Archives: Access to Archival Databases (AAD) (http://aad.archives.gov : National Archives and Records Administration, 2002); NARA NAID 1263923, National Archives at College Park, Maryland.
- "United States, Social Security Death Index," , FamilySearch (https://familysearch.org/ark:/61903/1:1:VM8J-K61 : 12 January 2021), Ida Loretta Paradiso, 09 Jul 2010; citing U.S. Social Security Administration, Death Master File, database (Alexandria, Virginia: National Technical Information Service, ongoing).
- "Find a Grave Index," database, FamilySearch (https://www.familysearch.org/ark:/61903/1:1:QVKY-Q4D6 : 13 June 2023), Ida Loretta Mingolello Paradiso, ; Burial, Stratford, Fairfield, Connecticut, United States of America, Saint Michael's Cemetery; citing record ID 54986111, Find a Grave, http://www.findagrave.com.
- "United States, Social Security Death Index," database, FamilySearch (https://familysearch.org/ark:/61903/1:1:VQ3C-34M : 12 January 2021), Patsy F Paradiso, 10 Jul 2010; citing U.S. Social Security Administration, Death Master File, database (Alexandria, Virginia: National Technical Information Service, ongoing).
- "Find a Grave Index," database, FamilySearch (https://www.familysearch.org/ark:/61903/1:1:QVKY-Q4DX : 13 June 2023), Patsy F. Paradiso, ; Burial, Stratford, Fairfield, Connecticut, United States of America, Saint Michael's Cemetery; citing record ID 54986236, Find a Grave, http://www.findagrave.com.

531) Ralph Carmen Perrine

Ralph Carmen Perrine(531) was born on 1 December 1923 in Buffalo, NY, to Carmine Perrina(247) and Colomba di Pasquale(247a). Ralph Carmen Perrine(531) served as a Private First Class, 24th Cavalry Reconnaissance Squadron, U. S. Army during World War II. Ralph Carmen Perrine(531) died 21 December 1944(Killed in Action), near Bogheim, Germany. Ralph Carmen Perrine(531) was awarded the Purple Heart with 1 Oak Leaf Cluster.

Records that include Ralph Carmen Perrine(531):

- "United States Census, 1930", , FamilySearch (https://www.familysearch.org/ark:/61903/1:1:X7CK-1B8 : Fri Jul 05 22:27:03 UTC 2024), Entry for Carmino Perrine and Columbia Perrine, 1930.

- "United States Census, 1940", , FamilySearch
  (https://www.familysearch.org/ark:/61903/1:1:KQ53-VDG : Tue Jul 23
  10:44:20 UTC 2024), Entry for Carmen Perrone and Columba Perrone,
  1940.
- https://fieldsofhonor-database.com/index.php/en/american-war-
  cemetery-margraten-p/64649-perrine-ralph-c
- "Find a Grave Index," database, FamilySearch
  (https://www.familysearch.org/ark:/61903/1:1:QVKT-ZSW6 : 13 June
  2023), Ralph C Perrine, ; Burial, Margraten, Eijsden-Margraten
  Municipality, Limburg, Netherlands, Netherlands American Cemetery
  and Memorial; citing record ID 56302654, Find a Grave,
  http://www.findagrave.com.
- "Find a Grave Index," database, FamilySearch
  (https://www.familysearch.org/ark:/61903/1:1:QV2T-8J5D : 10 June
  2020), Ralph C Perrine, 1944; Burial, , ; citing record ID , Find a
  Grave, http://www.findagrave.com.
- https://www.newspapers.com/article/the-buffalo-news-perrine-
  colomba-nee-d/148955383/

532) Maria Costa

Maria Costa(532) was born on 20 September 1924, in Ribeirao, Brazil, to
Camillo Costa(333a) and Conceição DeDonato(333).

Records that include Maria Costa(532):
- "Brasil, São Paulo, Registro Civil, 1925-2023", FamilySearch
  (https://www.familysearch.org/ark:/61903/1:1:6VW4-MYVD : Sat Aug 23
  11:10:16 UTC 2025), Entry for Antenor Ferreira de Morais and Ca
  Millo Costa, 20 de setembro de 1924.

533) Angelo Perrina

Angelo Perrina(533) was born about 1924, in Ariano, Italy, to Salvatore
Perrina(302) and Carmela de Lillo(260). Angelo Perrina(533) died 5 January,
1932 in Ariano, Italy.

Records that include Angelo Perrina(533):
- Ariano, Italy 1932 Death Act #13

534) Antonio Zecchino

Antonio Zecchino(534) was born 19 January 1924, in Ariano, Italy, to Angela
Miressi(291) and Giovanni Zecchino(291a). Antonio Zecchino(534) died 30
September 1926 in Ariano, Italy.

Records that include Antonio Zecchino(534):
- Ariano, Italy 1926 Death Act #351

535) Anna M Dragoni

Anna M. Dragoni(535) was born on 7 March 1924, in Boston, MA, to Nicola
Giuseppe Amato Dragoni(324a) and Angela Maria D'Ausilio(324). Anna M.
Dragoni(535) died on 18 May 2011, in Beverly, MA.

Anna M. Dragoni(535) married Lawrence Otis Adams(535a).

Lawrence Otis Adams(535a) was born on 25 May 1923 in Ipswich, MA, to Lawrence
Otis Adams(535aF) and Madelene F. Holland(535aM). Lawrence Otis Adams(535a)
died 25 October 2009 in Ipswich, MA.

Anna M. Dragoni(327) and Lawrence Otis Adams(327a) had Child(ren).

Records that include Anna M. Dragoni(327) and/or Lawrence Otis Adams(327a):
- "Massachusetts State Vital Records, 1841-1925", database with
  images, FamilySearch
  (https://www.familysearch.org/ark:/61903/1:1:6ZSF-PC4H : 12 April
  2023), Lawrence Otis Adams, 1923.

- "United States Census, 1930", , FamilySearch
  (https://www.familysearch.org/ark:/61903/1:1:XQ5G-9DC : Thu Mar 07
  16:52:47 UTC 2024), Entry for Nicholas Dragoni and Angelina
  Dragoni, 1930.
- "United States Census, 1930", , FamilySearch
  (https://www.familysearch.org/ark:/61903/1:1:XQLX-2PP : Tue Oct 03
  20:00:41 UTC 2023), Entry for Laurence O Adams and Madaline F
  Adams, 1930.
- "United States Social Security Death Index," , FamilySearch
  (https://familysearch.org/ark:/61903/1:1:VQ3B-P3P : 12 January
  2021), Anna M Adams, 18 May 2011; citing U.S. Social Security
  Administration, Death Master File, database (Alexandria, Virginia:
  National Technical Information Service, ongoing).
- "United States Social Security Death Index," database, FamilySearch
  (https://familysearch.org/ark:/61903/1:1:JBFJ-X6N : 12 January
  2021), Lawrence O Adams, 25 Oct 2009; citing U.S. Social Security
  Administration, Death Master File, database (Alexandria, Virginia:
  National Technical Information Service, ongoing).
- "Find A Grave Index," database, FamilySearch
  (https://www.familysearch.org/ark:/61903/1:1:QV28-D9XV : 24 May
  2022), Anna M. Dragoni Adams, ; Burial, , ; citing record ID
  70290329, Find a Grave, http://www.findagrave.com.
- "Find A Grave Index," database, FamilySearch
  (https://www.familysearch.org/ark:/61903/1:1:QVKD-JLT5 : 13
  September 2020), Lawrence O. Adams, ; Burial, Ipswich, Essex,
  Massachusetts, United States of America, Highland Cemetery; citing
  record ID 43643534, Find a Grave, http://www.findagrave.com.

536) Phillip Vernacchio

Phillip Vernacchio(536) was born born on 2 April 1924, in Ariano, Italy, to
Antonio Vernacchia(293a) and Assunta Ciasullo(293). On 29 October 1932 Phillip
Vernacchio(536) boarded the ship SS Conte Grande, in Naples, Italy. Phillip
Vernacchio(536) arrived in New York, NY on 7 November 1932. Phillip
Vernacchio(536) died on 14 November 1959 in Schenectady, NY.

Records that include Phillip Vernacchio(536):
- "New York, New York Passenger and Crew Lists, 1909, 1925-1957", ,
  FamilySearch (https://www.familysearch.org/ark:/61903/1:1:24JT-
  VF2 : Sat Mar 09 03:39:25 UTC 2024), Entry for Filippo Vernacchio,
  1932.
- "United States Census, 1940", , FamilySearch
  (https://www.familysearch.org/ark:/61903/1:1:K79V-279 : Fri Mar 08
  09:15:07 UTC 2024), Entry for Tony Vernacchio and Assunda
  Vernacchio, 1940.
- "United States Census, 1950", , FamilySearch
  (https://www.familysearch.org/ark:/61903/1:1:6XP7-5F4V : Tue Oct 03
  16:28:17 UTC 2023), Entry for Anthony Vernacchio and Susan
  Vernacchio, 19 April 1950.
- "New York State Health Department, Genealogical Research Death
  Index, 1957-1963," , FamilySearch
  (https://familysearch.org/ark:/61903/1:1:2CHV-9V8 : 11 February
  2018), Philip Vernacchio, 14 Nov 1959; citing Death, Schenectady,
  Schenectady, New York, file #81042, New York State Department of
  Health—Vital Records Section, Albany.
- "Find a Grave Index," database, FamilySearch
  (https://www.familysearch.org/ark:/61903/1:1:QK1X-T6BR : 12 March
  2024), Philip Vernacchio, ; Burial, Schenectady, Schenectady, New
  York, United States of America, Saint Joseph's Cemetery; citing
  record ID 141889792, Find a Grave, http://www.findagrave.com.

537) Ralph M. Perrino

Ralph M. Perrino(537) was born on 25 June 1924, in Schenectady, NY, to
Michelangelo Perrina(275) and Rose Damiano(275a). Ralph M. Perrino(537) served
in the United States Army Air Corps from 1942 to 1946. Ralph M. Perrino(537)
died 10 June 2015 in Niskayuna, NY. Ralph M. Perrino(537) was a store and
restaurant owner.

Ralph M. Perrino(537) married Gilda E. Esposito(537a) on 24 August 1947 in Schenectady, NY.

Gilda E. Esposito(537a) was born on 4 December 1924, in Schenectady, NY, to Fiore Esposito(537aF) and Adreana Caiazzo(537aM). Gilda E. Esposito(537a) died on 18 October 2008 in Schenectady, NY.

Ralph M. Perrino(537) and Gilda E. Esposito(537a) had child(ren).

Records that include Ralph M. Perrino(537) and/or Gilda E. Esposito(537a):

- "United States Census, 1930", , FamilySearch (https://www.familysearch.org/ark:/61903/1:1:X4TT-MWS : Mon Jul 22 22:05:18 UTC 2024), Entry for Michael Purino and Rose Purino, 1930.
- "United States Census, 1930", , FamilySearch (https://www.familysearch.org/ark:/61903/1:1:X4TY-H1R : Sat Mar 09 08:45:34 UTC 2024), Entry for Fiore Epostio and Anna Epostio, 1930.
- "United States Census, 1940", , FamilySearch (https://www.familysearch.org/ark:/61903/1:1:KQ3C-F5Z : Sun Jul 14 04:45:47 UTC 2024), Entry for Michael Perrino and Rose Perrino, 1940.
- "United States Census, 1940", , FamilySearch (https://www.familysearch.org/ark:/61903/1:1:KQ3C-VQ3 : Sun Mar 10 19:02:23 UTC 2024), Entry for Fiore Esposito and Anna Esposito, 1940.
- "United States World War II Army Enlistment Records, 1938-1946," , FamilySearch (https://familysearch.org/ark:/61903/1:1:K8R2-XV3 : 5 December 2014), Ralph M Perrino, enlisted 06 Jan 1943, Albany, New York, United States; citing "Electronic Army Serial Number Merged File, ca. 1938-1946," database, The National Archives: Access to Archival Databases (AAD) (http://aad.archives.gov : National Archives and Records Administration, 2002); NARA NAID 1263923, National Archives at College Park, Maryland.
- "New York Records of the State National Guard, 1906-1954", , FamilySearch (https://www.familysearch.org/ark:/61903/1:1:QVJY-5B7S : Sun Mar 10 11:42:25 UTC 2024), Entry for Ralph M Perrino, 20 Jan 1949.
- "United States Census, 1950", , FamilySearch (https://www.familysearch.org/ark:/61903/1:1:6XT1-78XJ : Tue Mar 19 20:23:20 UTC 2024), Entry for Ralph M Perrino and Gilda E Perrino, 4 May 1950.
- "United States Social Security Death Index," database, FamilySearch (https://familysearch.org/ark:/61903/1:1:VMC9-JTL : 12 January 2021), Gilda Perrino, 18 Oct 2008; citing U.S. Social Security Administration, Death Master File, database (Alexandria, Virginia: National Technical Information Service, ongoing).
- "Find a Grave Index," database, FamilySearch (https://www.familysearch.org/ark:/61903/1:1:QK1G-JC84 : 16 December 2020), Gilda E. Esposito Perrino, ; Burial, Niskayuna, Schenectady, New York, United States of America, Most Holy Redeemer Cemetery; citing record ID 149228783, Find a Grave, http://www.findagrave.com.
- "Find a Grave Index," database, FamilySearch (https://www.familysearch.org/ark:/61903/1:1:QK1G-JCJC : 6 March 2021), Ralph M. Perrino, ; Burial, Niskayuna, Schenectady, New York, United States of America, Most Holy Redeemer Cemetery; citing record ID 147786597, Find a Grave, http://www.findagrave.com.
- "St. Anthony, Schenectady, New York, Marriages (Oct 1916 -Jul 2006)", 2 Volumes, American-Canadian Genealogical Society, Manchester, NH, page 589

538) Michael deDonato

Michael deDonato(538) was born on 29 July 1924, in Bridgeport, CT, to Domenico deDonato(319) and Anna Minotti(319a). Michael deDonato(538) died 13 March 2020 in Bridgeport, CT.

Michael deDonato(538) married Mary J. Zawacki(538a) around 1950.

Mary J. Zawacki(538a) was born on 19 June 1929 in Germantown, NY, to Ignacy Zawacki(538aF) and Helen Czujak(538aM). Mary J. Zawacki(538a) died on 23 November 2013 in Manhattan, NY.

Michael deDonato(538) and Mary J. Zawacki(538a) had child(ren):

Records that include Michael deDonato(538) and/or Mary J. Zawacki(538a):
- "United States Census, 1940", , FamilySearch
  (https://www.familysearch.org/ark:/61903/1:1:KWMV-T5X : Fri Mar 08
  07:43:14 UTC 2024), Entry for Domenick Dedonato and Anna Dedonato,
  1940.
- "Connecticut, World War II Draft Registration Cards, 1940-1945", ,
  FamilySearch (https://www.familysearch.org/ark:/61903/1:1:Q2CR-WFYM
  : Sat Feb 10 04:35:14 UTC 2024), Entry for Michael De Donato and
  Domenick De Donato, 12 Dec 1942.
- "Find A Grave Index," database, FamilySearch
  (https://www.familysearch.org/ark:/61903/1:1:Z5RH-J1MM : 13
  December 2022), Michael A. DeDonato, ; Burial, Trumbull, Fairfield,
  Connecticut, United States of America, Nichols Farm Burial Ground;
  citing record ID 208331147, Find a Grave,
  http://www.findagrave.com.
- "Find A Grave Index," database, FamilySearch
  (https://www.familysearch.org/ark:/61903/1:1:QL7T-7S2M : 16
  December 2021), Mary J. Zawacki DeDonato, ; Burial, Trumbull,
  Fairfield, Connecticut, United States of America, Nichols Farm
  Burial Ground; citing record ID 177740421, Find a Grave,
  http://www.findagrave.com.

539) Luiz de Donato

Luiz de Donato(539) was born on 11 October 1924, in Ribeirão Pires, São
Paulo, Brasil, to Antonio DeDonato(303) and Maria Rinaldi(303a). Luiz de
Donato(539) died around March 1925 in Ribeirão Pires, São Paulo, Brasil.

Records that include Luiz de Donato(539):
- "Brasil, São Paulo, Registro Civil, 1925-2023", FamilySearch
  (https://www.familysearch.org/ark:/61903/1:1:6VW4-2MFT : Sat Aug 23
  11:10:08 UTC 2025), Entry for Rosa de Donato and Antonio de Donato,
  11 de outubro de 1924.
- "Brasil, São Paulo, Registro Civil, 1925-2023", FamilySearch
  (https://www.familysearch.org/ark:/61903/1:1:65PV-BNRY : Sat Aug 23
  12:18:24 UTC 2025), Entry for Luiz de Donato and Antonio de Donato,
  1925.

540) John William Miressi

John William Miressi(540) was born on 24 December 1924, in Middletown NY, to
Giovanni Miressi(226) and Florence Emily Wilson(226a). John William
Miressi(540) died 17 December 1995 in Middletown, NY.

John William Miressi(540) married Ruth Ellner Barker(540a).

Ruth Ellner Barker(540a) was born on 13 June 1922, in Hamburg, NJ, to Arthur
Barker(540aF) and Ida Moore(540aM). Ruth Ellner Barker(540a) died 11 April
2012, in Middletown, NY.

John William Miressi(540) and Ruth Ellner Barker(540a) had child(ren).

Records that include John William Miressi(540) and/or Ruth Ellner
Barker(540a):
- "United States Census, 1930", , FamilySearch
  (https://www.familysearch.org/ark:/61903/1:1:X4R1-4DK : Wed Oct 04
  22:50:59 UTC 2023), Entry for Florence Miressi and Frances E Miressi,
  1930.
- "United States Census, 1930", , FamilySearch
  (https://www.familysearch.org/ark:/61903/1:1:X4R1-9FL : Sun Mar 10
  13:51:14 UTC 2024), Entry for Arthur S Barker and Ida P Barker, 1930.
- "United States Census, 1940", , FamilySearch
  (https://www.familysearch.org/ark:/61903/1:1:KQGP-K5S : Tue Nov 28
  08:13:17 UTC 2023), Entry for John Miressi and Florence Miressi, 1940.
- "United States Census, 1940", , FamilySearch
  (https://www.familysearch.org/ark:/61903/1:1:KQYZ-PZS : Sat Mar 09
  20:00:19 UTC 2024), Entry for Arthur Barker and Florence Barker, 1940.

- "United States Census, 1950", , FamilySearch (https://www.familysearch.org/ark:/61903/1:1:6XY3-XC5K : Wed Mar 20 03:16:35 UTC 2024), Entry for Kathleen Miressi and John Miressi, 11 April 1950.
- "United States, Social Security Numerical Identification Files (NUMIDENT), 1936-2007", database, FamilySearch (https://www.familysearch.org/ark:/61903/1:1:6KMR-JXNQ : 10 February 2023), John William Miressi, .
- "United States Social Security Death Index," database, FamilySearch (https://familysearch.org/ark:/61903/1:1:VSF2-DJ7 : 7 January 2021), John W Miressi, 17 Dec 1995; citing U.S. Social Security Administration, Death Master File, database (Alexandria, Virginia: National Technical Information Service, ongoing).
- "United States Social Security Death Index," database, FamilySearch (https://familysearch.org/ark:/61903/1:1:KMD4-X5P : 12 January 2021), Ruth Miressi, 11 Apr 2012; citing U.S. Social Security Administration, Death Master File, database (Alexandria, Virginia: National Technical Information Service, ongoing).
- "Find A Grave Index," database, FamilySearch (https://www.familysearch.org/ark:/61903/1:1:QVLZ-LQ8C : 1 April 2023), John W Miressi, ; Burial, Phillipsburg, Orange, New York, United States of America, Wallkill Cemetery; citing record ID 92908588, Find a Grave, http://www.findagrave.com.
- "Find a Grave Index," database, FamilySearch (https://www.familysearch.org/ark:/61903/1:1:QVLZ-LQ8Z : 1 April 2023), Ruth E Barker Miressi, ; Burial, Phillipsburg, Orange, New York, United States of America, Wallkill Cemetery; citing record ID 92908575, Find a Grave, http://www.findagrave.com.

541) Daniel Paul Stilo

Daniel Paul Stilo(541) was born 24 January 1925, in Racine, WI, to Cosimo Stilo(308a) and Helen Elvera Anastasio(308). Daniel Paul Stilo(541) served in the United States Navy during WWII. Daniel Paul Stilo(541) died 22 December 2012 in Easley, SC. Daniel Paul Stilo(541) was buried at Hillcrest Memorial Park and Gardens, Veteran's Garden.

Daniel Paul Stilo(541) married Rose Marie Scheuerman(541a) about 1951.

Rose Marie Scheuerman(541a) was born on 15 July 1930 , in Racine, WI, to John Scheuerman(541aF) and Mabel(541aM). Rose Marie Scheuerman(541a) died on 13 July 2023 in Easley, SC.

Daniel Paul Stilo(541) and Rose Marie Scheuerman(541a) had child(ren).

Records that include Daniel Paul Stilo(541) and/or Rose Marie Scheuerman(541a):

- "United States, Census, 1930", FamilySearch (https://www.familysearch.org/ark:/61903/1:1:X7SP-TPK : Sun Jan 19 00:36:31 UTC 2025), Entry for Causamo Stilo and Elvera Stilo, 1930.
- "United States, Census, 1940", FamilySearch (https://www.familysearch.org/ark:/61903/1:1:K7J8-X7Y : Wed Jan 22 06:44:17 UTC 2025), Entry for Cosimo Stilo and Helen E Stilo, 1940.
- "United States, Census, 1940", FamilySearch (https://www.familysearch.org/ark:/61903/1:1:K7J8-DLZ : Wed Jan 22 16:03:54 UTC 2025), Entry for John Schuerman and Mable Schuerman, 1940.
- "United States, Census, 1950", FamilySearch (https://www.familysearch.org/ark:/61903/1:1:6F9M-Q6TL : Wed Mar 20 07:07:01 UTC 2024), Entry for Cosimo Stilo and Helen E Stilo, April 1, 1950.
- "United States, Census, 1950", FamilySearch (https://www.familysearch.org/ark:/61903/1:1:6FMB-J5GV : Mon Mar 17 15:06:20 UTC 2025), Entry for Rose M Scheuermann and Caroline Scheuermann, 3 April 1950.
- https://www.dignitymemorial.com/en-ca/obituaries/pickens-sc/rose-stilo-11369935
- "Find a Grave Index", FamilySearch (https://www.familysearch.org/ark:/61903/1:1:QVLB-KJTL : Thu Aug 28 03:22:45 UTC 2025), Entry for Daniel Paul Stilo.

- "Find a Grave Index", FamilySearch
  (https://www.familysearch.org/ark:/61903/1:1:6LX4-XKPF : Wed Jun 18
  07:00:25 UTC 2025), Entry for Rose Marie Scheuerman Stilo.

542) Theresa Bonelli

Theresa Bonelli(542) was born on 13 March 1925, in Detroit, MI, to Joseph
Bonelli(271a) and Concetta Anastasio(271). Theresa Bonelli(542) died 11
October 2019 in Louisville, MS.

Theresa Bonelli(542) married Bernard Webster Fulton(542a) on 19 September 1942
in Hazel Park, MI.

Bernard Webster Fulton(542a) was born on 7 February 1923 in Louisville, MS, to
Daniel Webster Fulton(542aF) and Nina Alice Hatcher(542aM). Bernard Webster
Fulton(542a) died on 8 December 2020.

Theresa Bonelli(329) and Bernard Webster Fulton(329a) had child(ren).

Records that include Theresa Bonelli(542) and/or Bernard Webster Fulton(542a):
- "Mississippi Enumeration of Educable Children, 1850-1892; 1908-
  1957", , FamilySearch
  (https://www.familysearch.org/ark:/61903/1:1:QK6V-7MNS : Sat Dec 16
  00:30:58 UTC 2023), Entry for Benard Fulton and Webster Fulton,
  1929.
- "United States Census, 1930", , FamilySearch
  (https://www.familysearch.org/ark:/61903/1:1:X7SP-TPK : Fri Oct 06
  12:13:03 UTC 2023), Entry for Causamo Stilo and Elvera Stilo, 1930.
- "United States Census, 1930", , FamilySearch
  (https://www.familysearch.org/ark:/61903/1:1:X9MR-GKH : Tue Oct 03
  20:37:13 UTC 2023), Entry for D W Fulton and Nina A Fulton, 1930.
- "United States Census, 1940", , FamilySearch
  (https://www.familysearch.org/ark:/61903/1:1:KH9W-QLW : Tue Nov 28
  10:25:29 UTC 2023), Entry for Concetta H Athanas and Mary A
  Bonelli, 1940.
- "United States Census, 1940", , FamilySearch
  (https://www.familysearch.org/ark:/61903/1:1:VB3L-WP5 : Tue Nov 28
  18:18:41 UTC 2023), Entry for Daniel W Fulton and Nina A Fulton,
  1940.
- "United States 1950 Census", , FamilySearch
  (https://www.familysearch.org/ark:/61903/1:1:6FM4-HM11 : Wed Oct 04
  23:46:52 UTC 2023), Entry for Bernard W Fulton and Theresa B
  Fulton, April 12, 1950.
- "Find A Grave Index," database, FamilySearch
  (https://www.familysearch.org/ark:/61903/1:1:6Z7R-L2T5 : 14
  September 2023), Bernard Webster Fulton, ; Burial, Louisville,
  Winston, Mississippi, United States of America, Memorial Park;
  citing record ID 219549470, Find a Grave,
  http://www.findagrave.com.
- "Find A Grave Index," database, FamilySearch
  (https://www.familysearch.org/ark:/61903/1:1:4K82-VK6Z : 17
  December 2020), Theresa Bonelli Fulton, ; Burial, Louisville,
  Winston, Mississippi, United States of America, Memorial Park;
  citing record ID 203750556, Find a Grave,
  http://www.findagrave.com.

543) John Dragoni

John Dragoni(543) was born on 9 May 1925, in Boston, MA, to Nicola Giuseppe
Amato Dragoni(324a) and Angela Maria D'Ausilio(324). John Dragoni(543)
enlisted in the Army Air Corps, on 28 July 1943. John Dragoni(543) was a radar
navigator on B29s. John Dragoni(543) received two Air Medals, the China Medal
from the country of China and from the United States, five Battle Stars and
other medals. John Dragoni(543) died 13 December 2023 in Cape Girardeau. MO.

John Dragoni(543) married Ruth Erline Mackenzie(543a) in 1947.

Ruth Erline Mackenzie(543a) was born on 13 June 1926, in Ipswich, MA, to Alan
James Mackenzie(543aF) and Edna Mabel Alexander(543aM). Ruth Erline
Mackenzie(543a) died 28 May 2005 in Cape Girardeau, MO. Ruth Erline
Mackenzie(543a) was interred at Cape Girardeau Memorial Park Cemetery, Cape
Girardeau, MO.

John Dragoni(543) and Ruth Erline Mackenzie(543a) had child(ren).

Records that include John Dragoni(543) and/or Ruth Erline Mackenzie(543a):

- "Massachusetts State Vital Records, 1841-1925", , FamilySearch (https://www.familysearch.org/ark:/61903/1:1:6PND-NJKK : Thu May 23 03:52:51 UTC 2024), Entry for John Dragoni and Nicola, 9 May 1925.
- "United States Census, 1930", , FamilySearch (https://www.familysearch.org/ark:/61903/1:1:XQ5G-9DC : Tue Jul 23 16:54:53 UTC 2024), Entry for Nicholas Dragoni and Angelina Dragoni, 1930.
- "United States Census, 1930", , FamilySearch (https://www.familysearch.org/ark:/61903/1:1:XQLX-QHT : Sat Mar 09 16:53:03 UTC 2024), Entry for Allen I Mc Kenzie and Edna M Mc Kenzie, 1930.
- "United States Census, 1940", , FamilySearch (https://www.familysearch.org/ark:/61903/1:1:K4XD-RRZ : Sun Mar 10 03:15:01 UTC 2024), Entry for Allen J Mackenzie and Edna M Mackenzie, 1940.
- "United States World War II Army Enlistment Records, 1938-1946," , FamilySearch (https://familysearch.org/ark:/61903/1:1:K8R9-JX6 : 5 December 2014), John R Dragoni, enlisted 28 Jul 1943, Boston, Massachusetts, United States; citing "Electronic Army Serial Number Merged File, ca. 1938-1946," database, The National Archives: Access to Archival Databases (AAD) (http://aad.archives.gov : National Archives and Records Administration, 2002); NARA NAID 1263923, National Archives at College Park, Maryland.
- https://familysearch.org/ark:/61903/3:1:3Q9M-CSMV-FWGM-9?cat=1257420&i=844
- "United States Census, 1950", , FamilySearch (https://www.familysearch.org/ark:/61903/1:1:6F3Q-Z5FM : Fri Oct 06 09:19:08 UTC 2023), Entry for Ruth Dragoni and John Dragoni, Jr, April 13, 1950.
- "United States Social Security Death Index," database, FamilySearch (https://familysearch.org/ark:/61903/1:1:JTXM-D6F : 11 January 2021), Ruth Dragoni, 28 May 2005; citing U.S. Social Security Administration, Death Master File, database (Alexandria, Virginia: National Technical Information Service, ongoing).
- "United States, Social Security Numerical Identification Files (NUMIDENT), 1936-2007", database, FamilySearch (https://www.familysearch.org/ark:/61903/1:1:6KMS-H8XF : 10 February 2023), Ruth Erline Mackenzie, .
- "Find a Grave Index," database, FamilySearch (https://www.familysearch.org/ark:/61903/1:1:QVVD-BHFM : 16 July 2020), Ruth E Mackenzie Dragoni, 2005; Burial, , ; citing record ID , Find a Grave, http://www.findagrave.com.
- https://www.fordandsonsfuneralhome.com/obituaries/John-Dragoni/#!/Obituary
- Jolley, Laura R, et al. John R. Dragoni, Sr. Collection. 1943. Personal Narrative. Retrieved from the Library of Congress, <www.loc.gov/item/afc2001001.105183/>.
- "Find a Grave Index," database, FamilySearch (https://www.familysearch.org/ark:/61903/1:1:6RJ7-GSW2 : 29 January 2024), John R Dragoni, ; Burial, Cape Girardeau, Cape Girardeau, Missouri, United States of America, Cape County Memorial Park Cemetery; citing record ID 262248627, Find a Grave, http://www.findagrave.com.

544) Living person and/or spouse

545) Living person and/or spouse

546) Frances Roselyn George

Frances Roselyn George(546) was born on 20 April 1925, in Middletown, NY, to Carmine (Carmen Louis) Giorgione/George(290) and Bertha Michalowski(290a). Frances Roselyn George(546) died on 16 June 1991 in Chesapeake, VA.

Frances Roselyn George(546) married Charles Lewis Ludwig(546a).

Charles Lewis Ludwig(546a) was born on 16 March 1920, in Dennison, OH, to William A Ludwig(546aF) and Eula N Miller(546aM). Charles Lewis Ludwig(546a) died on 19 December 1988 in Chesapeake, VA.

Charles Lewis Ludwig(546a) previously married & divorced Natalie Marie Galluzzi(546aX).

Frances Roselyn George(546) and Charles Lewis Ludwig(546a) had child(ren).

Records that include Frances Roselyn George(546) and/or Charles Lewis Ludwig(546a):

- "United States Census, 1930", , FamilySearch (https://www.familysearch.org/ark:/61903/1:1:X4R1-RJV : Fri Sep 20 03:41:55 UTC 2024), Entry for Carmin L George and Bertha C George, 1930.
- "United States Census, 1930", , FamilySearch (https://www.familysearch.org/ark:/61903/1:1:X4ZV-CGP : Tue Jul 16 09:55:22 UTC 2024), Entry for William A Ludwig and Eulah N Ludwig, 1930.
- "United States Census, 1940", , FamilySearch (https://www.familysearch.org/ark:/61903/1:1:KQG5-SHX : Tue Jul 16 21:20:46 UTC 2024), Entry for Carmen George and Bertha M George, 1940.
- "United States Census, 1940", , FamilySearch (https://www.familysearch.org/ark:/61903/1:1:KWG6-9VS : Fri Mar 08 18:08:45 UTC 2024), Entry for William A Ludwig and Eulah Ludwig, 1940.
- "United States World War II Army Enlistment Records, 1938-1946," , FamilySearch (https://familysearch.org/ark:/61903/1:1:KMKS-GXH : 5 December 2014), Charles L Ludwig, enlisted 19 Jun 1946, Cleveland, Ohio, United States; citing "Electronic Army Serial Number Merged File, ca. 1938-1946," database, The National Archives: Access to Archival Databases (AAD) (http://aad.archives.gov : National Archives and Records Administration, 2002); NARA NAID 1263923, National Archives at College Park, Maryland.
- "United States Census, 1950", , FamilySearch (https://www.familysearch.org/ark:/61903/1:1:6XT1-73Y1 : Thu Oct 05 00:02:26 UTC 2023), Entry for Charles Ludwig and Natalie Ludwig, 4 April 1950.
- "Virginia, Marriage Certificates, 1936-1988", , FamilySearch (https://www.familysearch.org/ark:/61903/1:1:QK98-Y4BV : Fri Mar 08 04:10:36 UTC 2024), Entry for Charles Lewis Ludwig and Charles Lewis Ludwig, 04 Dec 1976.
- "United States Social Security Death Index," , FamilySearch (https://familysearch.org/ark:/61903/1:1:VSBL-3TY : 9 January 2021), Charles L Ludwig, 19 Dec 1988; citing U.S. Social Security Administration, Death Master File, database (Alexandria, Virginia: National Technical Information Service, ongoing).
- "United States, Social Security Numerical Identification Files (NUMIDENT), 1936-2007", database, FamilySearch (https://www.familysearch.org/ark:/61903/1:1:6K37-CKWX : 10 February 2023), Charles Lewis Ludwig, .
- "Find a Grave Index," database, FamilySearch (https://www.familysearch.org/ark:/61903/1:1:QVVH-GSJQ : 13 June 2023), Charles Lewis Ludwig, ; Burial, Hampton, Hampton City, Virginia, United States of America, Hampton National Cemetery; citing record ID 3087518, Find a Grave, http://www.findagrave.com.
- "United States Social Security Death Index," database, FamilySearch (https://familysearch.org/ark:/61903/1:1:JT1L-ZT5 : 7 January 2021), Frances G Ludwig, 16 Jul 1991; citing U.S. Social Security Administration, Death Master File, database (Alexandria, Virginia: National Technical Information Service, ongoing).
- "United States, Social Security Numerical Identification Files (NUMIDENT), 1936-2007", database, FamilySearch (https://www.familysearch.org/ark:/61903/1:1:6K9Q-14SQ : 10 February 2023), Frances Roselyn George, .

547) Living person and/or spouse

548) <u>Pedro Miguel de Donato</u>

Pedro Miguel de Donato(548) was born about 1926, in Brazil, to Antonio DeDonato(303) and Maria Rinaldi(303a). Pedro Miguel de Donato(548) died on 18 Jun 1976 in Santo André, São Paulo, Brasil.

Records that include Pedro Miguel de Donato(548):
- "Brazil, Cemetery Records, 1799-2024", FamilySearch (https://www.familysearch.org/ark:/61903/1:1:X3NY-KLF5 : Tue Jun 10 22:44:27 UTC 2025), Entry for Pedro Miguel de Donato and Antonio de Donato, 18 Jun 1976.

549) <u>Angelina Antoinette Amodio</u>

Angelina Antoinette Amodio(549) was born on 13 June 1926, in Middletown, NY, to Anthony Amodio(311a) and Maria Silveria Francesca (Frances) Giorgione/George(311). Angelina Antoinette Amodio(549) died 4 May 2001 in Goshen, NY.

Records that include Angelina Antoinette Amodio(549):
- "United States Census, 1930", , FamilySearch (https://www.familysearch.org/ark:/61903/1:1:X4R1-NC2 : Sun Jul 14 09:29:21 UTC 2024), Entry for Anthony Amodio and Frances Amodio, 1930.
- "United States Census, 1940", , FamilySearch (https://www.familysearch.org/ark:/61903/1:1:KQGP-8TT : Sat Mar 09 04:22:19 UTC 2024), Entry for Anthony Amodio and Frances Amodio, 1940.
- "United States Census, 1950", , FamilySearch (https://www.familysearch.org/ark:/61903/1:1:6XY7-1SV2 : Thu Oct 05 08:22:58 UTC 2023), Entry for Theodore T Garber and Rose L Garber, 5 April 1950.
- "United States Social Security Death Index," , FamilySearch (https://familysearch.org/ark:/61903/1:1:JT1K-KJW : 7 January 2021), Angelina A Amodio, 04 May 2001; citing U.S. Social Security Administration, Death Master File, database (Alexandria, Virginia: National Technical Information Service, ongoing).
- "Find a Grave Index," database, FamilySearch (https://www.familysearch.org/ark:/61903/1:1:QVVW-4JY7 : 1 April 2023), Angelina A. Amodio, ; Burial, Phillipsburg, Orange, New York, United States of America, Wallkill Cemetery; citing record ID 8871856, Find a Grave, http://www.findagrave.com.

550) Living person and/or spouse

551) <u>Theresa Ann Perrine</u>

Theresa Ann Perrine(551) was born on 15 July 1926, in Buffalo, NY, to Carmine Perrina(247) and Colomba di Pasquale(247a). Theresa Ann Perrine(551) died 14 September 1987.

Theresa Ann Perrine(551) married Joseph Grande(551a).

<u>Joseph Grande</u>(551a) was born on 17 September 1936. Joseph Grande(551a) died 27 September 2018 in New York.

Theresa Ann Perrine(551) and Joseph Grande(551a) had child(ren).

Records that include Theresa Ann Perrine(551) and/or Joseph Grande(551a):
- "United States Census, 1930", , FamilySearch (https://www.familysearch.org/ark:/61903/1:1:X7CK-1B8 : Fri Jul 05 22:27:03 UTC 2024), Entry for Carmino Perrine and Columbia Perrine, 1930.
- "United States Census, 1940", , FamilySearch (https://www.familysearch.org/ark:/61903/1:1:KQ53-VDG : Tue Jul 23 10:44:20 UTC 2024), Entry for Carmen Perrone and Columba Perrone, 1940.

- "United States Census, 1950", , FamilySearch
  (https://www.familysearch.org/ark:/61903/1:1:6XTT-79WW : Thu Mar 21
  00:15:09 UTC 2024), Entry for Carmine Perrino and Colombe Perrino,
  10 April 1950.
- https://www.newspapers.com/article/the-buffalo-news-perrine-colomba-nee-d/148955383/
- "United States, Social Security Numerical Identification Files
  (NUMIDENT), 1936-2007", , FamilySearch
  (https://www.familysearch.org/ark:/61903/1:1:6K99-DD6W : 10
  February 2023), Theresa Ann Perrine, .
- "Find a Grave Index," database, FamilySearch
  (https://www.familysearch.org/ark:/61903/1:1:4K6X-L1MM : 5 August
  2020), Theresa Grande, ; Burial, Cheektowaga, Erie, New York,
  United States of America, Holy Sepulchre Cemetery; citing record ID
  204212316, Find a Grave, http://www.findagrave.com.
- https://www.amigone.com/obituaries/Joseph-Grande?obId=12439655

552) Jennie Veronica Ciasullo

Jennie Veronica Ciasullo(552) was born in July of 1926, in Schenectady, NY, to
Giuseppe Ciasullo(262) and Grace Castaldi(262a). Jennie Veronica Ciasullo(552)
died 10 July 1958 in Schenectady, NY.

Jennie Veronica Ciasullo(552) married Edwin J. Zelazny(552a) in Schenectady,
NY.

Edwin J. Zelazny(552a) was born in 1926. Edwin J. Zelazny(552a) died 2
December 1964 in Schenectady, NY.

Edwin J. Zelazny(552a) also married Ethel Canders(552ab).

Records that include Jennie Veronica Ciasullo(552) and/or Edwin J.
Zelazny(552a):
- "United States Census, 1930", , FamilySearch
  (https://www.familysearch.org/ark:/61903/1:1:X4TY-PGH : Sat Mar 09
  21:13:12 UTC 2024), Entry for Joseph Ciasullo and Grace Ciasullo,
  1930.
- "United States Census, 1940", , FamilySearch
  (https://www.familysearch.org/ark:/61903/1:1:KQY5-9BR : Fri Mar 08
  20:57:12 UTC 2024), Entry for Joseph Ciasullo and Grace Ciasullo,
  1940.
- "New York State Health Department, Genealogical Research Death
  Index, 1957-1963," , FamilySearch
  (https://familysearch.org/ark:/61903/1:1:2CHK-95T : 11 February
  2018), Jennie Zelazny, 10 Jul 1958; citing Death, Schenectady,
  Schenectady, New York, file #50389, New York State Department of
  Health—Vital Records Section, Albany.
- "Find a Grave Index," database, FamilySearch
  (https://www.familysearch.org/ark:/61903/1:1:6PY3-M3PN : 8 March
  2024), Jennie V. Ciasullo Zelazny, ; Burial, Schenectady,
  Schenectady, New York, United States of America, Saint Joseph's
  Cemetery; citing record ID 260353442, Find a Grave,
  http://www.findagrave.com.
- "Find a Grave Index," database, FamilySearch
  (https://www.familysearch.org/ark:/61903/1:1:6PY3-M3PN : 8 March
  2024), Jennie V. Ciasullo Zelazny, ; Burial, Schenectady,
  Schenectady, New York, United States of America, Saint Joseph's
  Cemetery; citing record ID 260353442, Find a Grave,
  http://www.findagrave.com.
- https://www.findagrave.com/memorial/166334528/edwin_j_zelazny

553) Living person and/or spouse

554) Robert Otto Tiso

Robert Otto Tiso(554) was born on 9 October 1926, in Newark, NJ, to Oto
(Ottone) Tiso(169) and Mary Senese(169a). Robert Otto Tiso(554) died 5
December 2003 in Orange, FL.

Robert Otto Tiso(554) married Gudrun Ingrid Leikert(554a).

<u>Gudrun Ingrid Leikert</u>(554a) was born on 14 July 1929 in Germany. Gudrun Ingrid Leikert(554a) boarded the ship USS General Henry Tylor, as a "War Bride", on 22 June 1948, in Bremerhaven, Germany, arriving in New York City, on 22 June 1948. Gudrun Ingrid Leikert(554a) died on 8 August 1987, in Orlando, FL.

Robert Otto Tiso(554) and Gudrun Ingrid Leikert(554a) had child(ren).

Records that include Robert Otto Tiso(554) and/or Gudrun Ingrid Leikert(554a):
- "United States Census, 1930", , FamilySearch (https://www.familysearch.org/ark:/61903/1:1:X4DG-XPV : Fri Mar 08 18:34:06 UTC 2024), Entry for Ottone Liso and Mary H Liso, 1930.
- "United States Census, 1940", , FamilySearch (https://www.familysearch.org/ark:/61903/1:1:K4BX-LGY : Sun Mar 10 17:21:28 UTC 2024), Entry for William Sidoli and Mary Sidoli, 1940.
- "New York, New York Passenger and Crew Lists, 1909, 1925-1957", , FamilySearch (https://www.familysearch.org/ark:/61903/1:1:24PY-4X8 : Fri Jan 19 22:09:42 UTC 2024), Entry for Gudrun Tiso, 1948.
- "United States 1950 Census", , FamilySearch (https://www.familysearch.org/ark:/61903/1:1:6F9R-SGF9 : Sat Oct 07 00:34:28 UTC 2023), Entry for Robert O Tiso and Guerun Tiso, 13 April 1950.
- "United States, Social Security Numerical Identification Files (NUMIDENT), 1936-2007", database, FamilySearch (https://www.familysearch.org/ark:/61903/1:1:6K9V-68JL : 10 February 2023), Robert Tiso, .
- "United States Social Security Death Index," database, FamilySearch (https://familysearch.org/ark:/61903/1:1:VMPS-2ZN : 8 January 2021), Robert O Tiso, 05 Dec 2003; citing U.S. Social Security Administration, Death Master File, database (Alexandria, Virginia: National Technical Information Service, ongoing).
- "United States, GenealogyBank Obituaries, Births, and Marriages 1980-2014", , FamilySearch (https://www.familysearch.org/ark:/61903/1:1:QV53-THNW : Wed Oct 18 10:56:32 UTC 2023), Entry for Gudrun Ingrid Tiso and Robert, 09 Aug 1987.
- "United States Social Security Death Index," database, FamilySearch (https://familysearch.org/ark:/61903/1:1:J2M9-3JW : 8 January 2021), Gudrun Tiso, Aug 1987; citing U.S. Social Security Administration, Death Master File, database (Alexandria, Virginia: National Technical Information Service, ongoing).
- "Florida Death Index, 1877-1998," , FamilySearch (https://familysearch.org/ark:/61903/1:1:VV6H-9VB : 25 December 2014), Gudrun Ingrid Tiso, 08 Aug 1987; from "Florida Death Index, 1877-1998," index, Ancestry (www.ancestry.com : 2004); citing vol. , certificate number 82723, Florida Department of Health, Office of Vital Records, Jacksonville.

555) Living person and/or spouse

556) <u>Angelo Joseph Perrino</u>

Angelo Joseph Perrino(556) was born on 24 July 1927, in Brooklyn, NY, to Pasquale (Patsy) Perrino(287) and Fioritta (Fanny) Masucci(287a). Angelo Joseph Perrino(556) died 20 November 2001 in Fort Lauderdale, FL.

Angelo Joseph Perrino(556) married Margaret Mary McEntee(556a).

<u>Margaret Mary McEntee</u>(556a) was born on 27 May 1927, in Brooklyn, NY, to Francis H McEntee(556aF) and Frances H Mahoney(556aM). Margaret Mary McEntee(556a) died 1 July 2001 in Fort Lauderdale, FL.

Angelo Joseph Perrino(556) and Margaret Mary McEntee(556a) had child(ren).

Records that include Angelo Joseph Perrino(556) and/or Margaret Mary McEntee(556a):
- "United States Census, 1930", , FamilySearch (https://www.familysearch.org/ark:/61903/1:1:X4LJ-KDX : Fri Mar 08 21:55:42 UTC 2024), Entry for Patsy Perrino and Fannie Perrino, 1930.

- "United States Census, 1930", , FamilySearch (https://www.familysearch.org/ark:/61903/1:1:X4VN-NZK : Fri Mar 08 10:24:09 UTC 2024), Entry for Frank McEntee and Francis McEntee, 1930.
- "United States Census, 1940", , FamilySearch (https://www.familysearch.org/ark:/61903/1:1:KQLK-6DN : Sat Mar 09 18:14:25 UTC 2024), Entry for Pasquale Perrino and Fanny Perrino, 1940.
- "United States Census, 1940", , FamilySearch (https://www.familysearch.org/ark:/61903/1:1:K3TG-QXT : Sun Mar 10 06:42:02 UTC 2024), Entry for Frank McEntee and Frances McEntee, 1940.
- "New York, New York City, World War II Draft Registration Cards, 1940-1947", , FamilySearch (https://www.familysearch.org/ark:/61903/1:1:WZ9F-99W2 : Sat Mar 09 18:03:52 UTC 2024), Entry for Angelo Perrino and War Shipping Administration, 15 Nov 1945.
- "United States Census, 1950", , FamilySearch (https://www.familysearch.org/ark:/61903/1:1:6XRQ-T2GV : Wed Mar 20 21:41:17 UTC 2024), Entry for Patrick Perrino and Fannie Perrino, 8 April 1950.
- "New York Records of the State National Guard, 1906-1954", , FamilySearch (https://www.familysearch.org/ark:/61903/1:1:QVJY-5BQ1 : Fri Mar 08 13:39:46 UTC 2024), Entry for Angelo Joseph Perrino, 02 Nov 1950.
- "United States, Social Security Numerical Identification Files (NUMIDENT), 1936-2007", database, FamilySearch (https://www.familysearch.org/ark:/61903/1:1:6K97-JC4S : 10 February 2023), Margaret Mary McEntee, .
- "United States Social Security Death Index," database, FamilySearch (https://familysearch.org/ark:/61903/1:1:JT1C-6YZ : 7 January 2021), Margaret M Perrino, 01 Jul 2001; citing U.S. Social Security Administration, Death Master File, database (Alexandria, Virginia: National Technical Information Service, ongoing).
- "Find a Grave Index," database, FamilySearch (https://www.familysearch.org/ark:/61903/1:1:6K1Y-1TW9 : 10 May 2023), Margie, ; Burial, North Lauderdale, Broward, Florida, United States of America, Our Lady Queen of Heaven Cemetery; citing record ID 252056564, Find a Grave, http://www.findagrave.com.
- "Find a Grave Index," database, FamilySearch (https://www.familysearch.org/ark:/61903/1:1:6K1Y-1TQP : 10 May 2023), Sonny, ; Burial, North Lauderdale, Broward, Florida, United States of America, Our Lady Queen of Heaven Cemetery; citing record ID 252056551, Find a Grave, http://www.findagrave.com.
- "United States Social Security Death Index," database, FamilySearch (https://familysearch.org/ark:/61903/1:1:JBYQ-1TY : 7 January 2021), Angelo J Perrino, 20 Nov 2001; citing U.S. Social Security Administration, Death Master File, database (Alexandria, Virginia: National Technical Information Service, ongoing).
- https://www.legacy.com/us/obituaries/sunsentinel/name/angelo-perrino-obituary?id=28350379

557) Michael deDonato

Michael deDonato(557) was born on 21 October 1927, in Bridgeport, CT, to Filippo deDonato(327) and Florence Cerino(327a). Michael deDonato(557) died on February 1983 in Fairfield, CT. Michael deDonato(557) was buried in the Gate of Heaven Cemetery, Trumbull, CT.

Michael deDonato(557) married Raffaela Maria Delpercio(557a).

Raffaela Maria Delpercio(557a) was born on 15 December 1928, in Bridgeport, CT, to Matteo Delpercio(557aF) and Filomena Masucci(557aM). Raffaela Maria Delpercio(557a) died 15 November 2000 in Bridgeport, CT. Raffaela Maria Delpercio(557a) was buried in Gate of Heaven Cemetery, Trumbull, CT.

Michael deDonato(557) and Raffaela Maria Delpercio(557a) had child(ren).

Records that include Michael deDonato(557) and/or Raffaela Maria Delpercio(557a):

- "United States, Census, 1930", FamilySearch (https://www.familysearch.org/ark:/61903/1:1:XMPM-C9Q : Sun Jan 19 09:01:07 UTC 2025), Entry for Phillip Dedonato and Florence Dedonato, 1930.
- "United States, Census, 1940", FamilySearch (https://www.familysearch.org/ark:/61903/1:1:KWMK-MGQ : Wed Jan 22 10:36:11 UTC 2025), Entry for Philip Dedonato and Florence Dedonato, 1940.
- "Connecticut, World War II Draft Registration Cards, 1940-1945", FamilySearch (https://www.familysearch.org/ark:/61903/1:1:Q2CR-WN3X : Fri Apr 04 14:32:01 UTC 2025), Entry for Michael Joseph De Donato and Philip De Donato, 21 Aug 1945.
- "United States, Census, 1950", FamilySearch (https://www.familysearch.org/ark:/61903/1:1:6FMX-1KMM : Mon Mar 17 16:31:08 UTC 2025), Entry for Phillip De Donato and Florence De Donato, 10 April 1950.
- "United States, Social Security Death Index," , FamilySearch (https://familysearch.org/ark:/61903/1:1:JPQ2-X4F : 7 January 2021), Michael Dedonato, Feb 1983; citing U.S. Social Security Administration, Death Master File, database (Alexandria, Virginia: National Technical Information Service, ongoing).
- "Connecticut, Death Index, 1949-2001," , FamilySearch (https://familysearch.org/ark:/61903/1:1:VZPX-Q4J : 9 December 2014), Michael J Dedonato, 28 Feb 1983; from "Connecticut Death Index, 1949-2001," database, Ancestry (http://www.ancestry.com : 2003); citing Bridgeport, , Connecticut, Connecticut Department of Health, Hartfort.
- "Find a Grave Index", FamilySearch (https://www.familysearch.org/ark:/61903/1:1:6ZR9-7WTF : Tue Apr 01 13:14:30 UTC 2025), Entry for Michael J. Dedonato.
- "Connecticut, Death Index, 1949-2001," , FamilySearch (https://familysearch.org/ark:/61903/1:1:VZP8-H4Y : 9 December 2014), Raffaela Dedonato, 15 Nov 2000; from "Connecticut Death Index, 1949-2001," database, Ancestry (http://www.ancestry.com : 2003); citing Bridgeport, Fairfield, Connecticut, Connecticut Department of Health, Hartfort.
- "United States, Social Security Numerical Identification Files (NUMIDENT), 1936-2007", FamilySearch (https://www.familysearch.org/ark:/61903/1:1:6KMV-JWLK : Sat Apr 26 11:51:19 UTC 2025), Entry for Raffaela Maria Dedonato and Matteo Delpercio.
- "United States, Social Security Death Index," database, FamilySearch (https://familysearch.org/ark:/61903/1:1:JP3V-R6T : 7 January 2021), Raffaela Dedonato, 15 Nov 2000; citing U.S. Social Security Administration, Death Master File, database (Alexandria, Virginia: National Technical Information Service, ongoing).
- "Find a Grave Index", FamilySearch (https://www.familysearch.org/ark:/61903/1:1:6ZR9-7JLY : Tue Apr 01 18:11:25 UTC 2025), Entry for Raffaela M. Dedonato.

558) Ralph George Mingolello

Ralph George Mingolello(558) born on 16 December 1927, in Bridgeport, CT, to Joseph Mingolello(294a) and Francesca deDonato(294). Ralph George Mingolello(558) died before 2010.
NOTE: Name on Birth Certificate = Ralph Joseph Mingolelli.

Records that include Ralph George Mingolello(558):
Bridgeport, CT, Births Dec 1927 #406
- "United States, Census, 1930", , FamilySearch (https://www.familysearch.org/ark:/61903/1:1:XMP8-M1P : Wed Mar 06 09:36:34 UTC 2024), Entry for Joe Mingolello and Francis Mingolello, 1930.

- "United States, Census, 1940", , FamilySearch
  (https://www.familysearch.org/ark:/61903/1:1:K71S-M9L : Fri Mar 08
  16:03:19 UTC 2024), Entry for Joseph Mingolello and Jennie
  Mingolello, 1940.
- "Connecticut, World War II Draft Registration Cards, 1940-1945", ,
  FamilySearch (https://www.familysearch.org/ark:/61903/1:1:Q2CR-2KCD
  : Sat Mar 09 10:41:48 UTC 2024), Entry for Ralph George Mingolello
  and Ida Paradiso, 17 Dec 1945.
- "United States, Census, 1950", , FamilySearch
  (https://www.familysearch.org/ark:/61903/1:1:6FM6-4X8J : Wed Mar 20
  10:08:03 UTC 2024), Entry for Ralph Mingolello, 25 April 1950.

559) Jean Louine Garber

Jean Louise Garber(559) was born on 17 February 1928, in Middletown, NY, to
Theodore Taft Garber(339a) and Rose Louise Giorgione(339). Jean Louise
Garber(559) died 22 March 1989 in New York.

Jean Louise Garber(559) married Filoteo (Philip) John DelPizzo(559a) on 18
January 1953 in Middletown, NY.

Filoteo (Philip) John DelPizzo(559a) was born on 19 January 1927 in Nyack, NY,
to Domenick DelPizzo(559aF) and Josephine Caminti(559aM) Filoteo (Philip) John
DelPizzo(559a) died on September 1985 in New York.

Records that include Jean Louise Garber(559) and/or Filoteo (Philip) John
DelPizzo(559a):

- "United States Census, 1930", , FamilySearch
  (https://www.familysearch.org/ark:/61903/1:1:X4R1-NC5 : Mon Mar 11
  01:37:59 UTC 2024), Entry for Theodore Garber and Rose Garber,
  1930.
- "United States Census, 1930", , FamilySearch
  (https://www.familysearch.org/ark:/61903/1:1:X4TN-K3F : Thu Jul 18
  04:54:17 UTC 2024), Entry for Dominick Del Cuzzo and Josephine Del
  Cuzzo, 1930.
- "United States Census, 1940", , FamilySearch
  (https://www.familysearch.org/ark:/61903/1:1:KQGP-XN8 : Sun Mar 10
  21:26:22 UTC 2024), Entry for Anthony George and Joseph George,
  1940.
- "United States Census, 1950", , FamilySearch
  (https://www.familysearch.org/ark:/61903/1:1:6X54-7NYF : Tue Oct 03
  22:58:10 UTC 2023), Entry for Ruth Darlington and Connie McCarthy,
  3 April 1950.
- "United States Census, 1950", , FamilySearch
  (https://www.familysearch.org/ark:/61903/1:1:6X5W-TDH3 : Fri Oct 06
  20:01:39 UTC 2023), Entry for Micaela H Welch and Aeschleman Welch,
  3 April 1950.
- https://www.ancestry.com/discoveryui-content/view/1566370:61048
- "United States, Social Security Numerical Identification Files
  (NUMIDENT), 1936-2007", database, FamilySearch
  (https://www.familysearch.org/ark:/61903/1:1:6KMT-XB7M : 10
  February 2023), Jean Garber, .
- "United States Social Security Death Index," database, FamilySearch
  (https://familysearch.org/ark:/61903/1:1:VSX1-TZ4 : 7 January
  2021), Jean Delpizzo, 22 Mar 1989; citing U.S. Social Security
  Administration, Death Master File, database (Alexandria, Virginia:
  National Technical Information Service, ongoing).
- "Find a Grave Index," database, FamilySearch
  (https://www.familysearch.org/ark:/61903/1:1:QVVW-4V88 : 1 April
  2023), Jean L. Garber Del Pizzo, ; Burial, Phillipsburg, Orange,
  New York, United States of America, Wallkill Cemetery; citing
  record ID 9118331, Find a Grave, http://www.findagrave.com.
- "United States Social Security Death Index," database, FamilySearch
  (https://familysearch.org/ark:/61903/1:1:JRMZ-QZ3 : 7 January
  2021), Philip Delpizzo, Sep 1985; citing U.S. Social Security
  Administration, Death Master File, database (Alexandria, Virginia:
  National Technical Information Service, ongoing).

560) Living person and/or spouse

561) Marianna Riccio

Marianna Riccio(561) was born about 20 June 1928, in Ariano, Italy, to Angelo Maria Riccio(183a) and Raimonda Ciasullo(183). Marianna Riccio(561) died 22 August 1928 in Ariano, Italy.

Records that include Marianna Riccio(561):
- Ariano, Italy 1928 Death Act #172

562) Living person and/or spouse

563) Loretta DeDonato

Loretta DeDonato(563) was born on 12 June 1928, in Bridgeport, CT, to Domenico deDonato(319) and Anna Minotti(319a). Loretta DeDonato(563) died 31 July 2014 in Bridgeport, CT.

Loretta DeDonato(563) married Peter Victor Feola(563a).

Peter Victor Feola(563a) was born on 20 January 1925, in Stratford, CT, to Benjamin Feola(563aF) and Margherita DeCesare(563aM). Peter Victor Feola(563a) died 29 Jun 2006 in Trumbull, CT.

Records that include Loretta DeDonato(563) and/or Peter Victor Feola(563a):
- "United States Census, 1940", , FamilySearch (https://www.familysearch.org/ark:/61903/1:1:KWMV-T5X : Fri Mar 08 07:43:14 UTC 2024), Entry for Domenick Dedonato and Anna Dedonato, 1940.
- "United States Census, 1940", , FamilySearch (https://www.familysearch.org/ark:/61903/1:1:K719-P4R : Sun Mar 10 05:50:01 UTC 2024), Entry for Benny Peola and Margeriete Peola, 1940.
- "United States Census, 1950", , FamilySearch (https://www.familysearch.org/ark:/61903/1:1:6FMF-6VDT : Wed Mar 20 05:29:30 UTC 2024), Entry for Benjamin Feola and Margaret Feola, 12 April 1950.
- "Connecticut, World War II Draft Registration Cards, 1940-1945", , FamilySearch (https://www.familysearch.org/ark:/61903/1:1:Q2CR-C3G7 : Mon Mar 11 00:15:24 UTC 2024), Entry for Peter Vincent Feola and Benjamin Feola, 29 Jan 1943.
- "United States World War II Army Enlistment Records, 1938-1946," database, FamilySearch (https://familysearch.org/ark:/61903/1:1:K8RQ-YVN : 5 December 2014), Peter V Feola, enlisted 03 Apr 1946, New Haven, Connecticut, United States; citing "Electronic Army Serial Number Merged File, ca. 1938-1946," database, The National Archives: Access to Archival Databases (AAD) (http://aad.archives.gov : National Archives and Records Administration, 2002); NARA NAID 1263923, National Archives at College Park, Maryland.
- "United States Social Security Death Index," , FamilySearch (https://familysearch.org/ark:/61903/1:1:VS9M-SZ2 : 12 January 2021), Peter V Feola, 29 Jun 2006; citing U.S. Social Security Administration, Death Master File, database (Alexandria, Virginia: National Technical Information Service, ongoing).
- "United States, Social Security Numerical Identification Files (NUMIDENT), 1936-2007", database, FamilySearch (https://www.familysearch.org/ark:/61903/1:1:6KML-SPXT : 10 February 2023), Peter Vincent Feola, .
- "Find a Grave Index," database, FamilySearch (https://www.familysearch.org/ark:/61903/1:1:QPSH-DHDP : 13 June 2023), Loretta R DeDonato Feola, ; Burial, Stratford, Fairfield, Connecticut, United States of America, Saint Michael's Cemetery; citing record ID 186943194, Find a Grave, http://www.findagrave.com.
- "Find a Grave Index," database, FamilySearch (https://www.familysearch.org/ark:/61903/1:1:QVKZ-VR2H : 13 June 2023), Peter Vincent Feola, ; Burial, Stratford, Fairfield, Connecticut, United States of America, Saint Michael's Cemetery; citing record ID 39087925, Find a Grave, http://www.findagrave.com.

564) Anthony Joseph Stella

Anthony Joseph Stella(564) was born on 19 June 1928, in Bronx, NY, to Oto (Otino) Stella(289) and Maria Giovanna (Jennie) Merola(289a). Anthony Joseph Stella(564) died 9 October 1978. Anthony Joseph Stella(564) was a politician (New York State Assembly).

Records that include Anthony Joseph Stella(564):
- "United States Census, 1940", , FamilySearch (https://www.familysearch.org/ark:/61903/1:1:KQL9-GV9 : Sun Jul 14 11:25:30 UTC 2024), Entry for Otino Stella and Jennie Stella, 1940.
- "New York, New York City, World War II Draft Registration Cards, 1940-1947", , FamilySearch (https://www.familysearch.org/ark:/61903/1:1:WWBL-G5N2 : Fri Mar 08 23:28:02 UTC 2024), Entry for Anthony Stella and Cc Ny, 20 Jun 1946.
- "United States Census, 1950", , FamilySearch (https://www.familysearch.org/ark:/61903/1:1:6X5Z-K51C : Mon Mar 18 23:44:09 UTC 2024), Entry for Otino Stella and Jennie Stella, 18 April 1950.
- https://www.nytimes.com/1968/12/31/archives/stella-certified-as-election-winner.html
- "United States, Social Security Numerical Identification Files (NUMIDENT), 1936-2007", database, FamilySearch (https://www.familysearch.org/ark:/61903/1:1:6KMY-SK2V : 10 February 2023), Otino Stella in entry for Anthony Joseph Stella, .
- "United States Social Security Death Index," database, FamilySearch (https://familysearch.org/ark:/61903/1:1:JKLS-2MV : 7 January 2021), Anthony Stella, Oct 1978; citing U.S. Social Security Administration, Death Master File, database (Alexandria, Virginia: National Technical Information Service, ongoing).
- "Find a Grave Index," database, FamilySearch (https://www.familysearch.org/ark:/61903/1:1:6FNK-D4DY : 6 June 2024), Anthony J. Stella, ; Burial, Hartsdale, Westchester, New York, United States of America, Ferncliff Cemetery and Mausoleum; citing record ID 237232602, Find a Grave, http://www.findagrave.com.

565) Frances Michele Perrino

Frances Michele Perrino(565) was born on 20 July 1928 in Schenectady, NY, to Michelangelo Perrina(275) and Rose Damiano(275a). Frances Michele Perrino(565) died before 2004.

Frances Michele Perrino(565) married Elvera Civitello(565a) on 20 August 1950 in Schenectady, NY. Frances Michele Perrino(565) and Elvera Civitello(565a) divorced in 1972.

Elvera Civitello(565a) was born on 4 March 1927, in Schenectady, NY, to Ralph Civitello(565aF) and Rose Mastrianni(565aM). Elvera Civitello(565a) died 10 January 2011, in Schenectady, NY.

Frances Michele Perrino(565) and Elvera Civitello(565a) had child(ren).

Records that include Frances Michele Perrino(565) and/or Elvera Civitello(565a):
- "St. Anthony, Schenectady, New York, Baptism (Sep 1912 – May 2007)", 2 Volumes American-Canadian Genealogical Society, Manchester, NH, page 693
- "United States Census, 1930", , FamilySearch (https://www.familysearch.org/ark:/61903/1:1:X4TT-MWS : Mon Jul 22 22:05:18 UTC 2024), Entry for Michael Purino and Rose Purino, 1930.
- "United States Census, 1940", , FamilySearch (https://www.familysearch.org/ark:/61903/1:1:KQ3C-F5Z : Sun Jul 14 04:45:47 UTC 2024), Entry for Michael Perrino and Rose Perrino, 1940.
- "United States Census, 1940", , FamilySearch (https://www.familysearch.org/ark:/61903/1:1:KQS4-7NL : Sat Jul 20 23:23:48 UTC 2024), Entry for Erman Civitella and Anna Civitella, 1940.

- "United States Census, 1950", , FamilySearch
  (https://www.familysearch.org/ark:/61903/1:1:6XTY-YZ9F : Tue Mar 19
  20:23:20 UTC 2024), Entry for Francis M Perrino and Rose C Salerno,
  4 May 1950.
- "California Divorce Index, 1966-1984," , FamilySearch
  (https://familysearch.org/ark:/61903/1:1:VPBQ-8XS : 15 May 2014),
  Elvera T Civitello and Francis M Perrino, Feb 1972; from
  "California Divorce Index, 1966-1984," database and images,
  Ancestry (http://www.ancestry.com : 2007); citing Orange,
  California, Health Statistics, California Department of Health
  Services, Sacramento.
- "United States Social Security Death Index," database, FamilySearch
  (https://familysearch.org/ark:/61903/1:1:VMDQ-QJQ : 12 January
  2021), Elvera C Perrino, 10 Jan 2011; citing U.S. Social Security
  Administration, Death Master File, database (Alexandria, Virginia:
  National Technical Information Service, ongoing).
- "Find a Grave Index," database, FamilySearch
  (https://www.familysearch.org/ark:/61903/1:1:QK1G-JCZL : 6 March
  2021), Elvera Civitello Perrino, ; Burial, Niskayuna, Schenectady,
  New York, United States of America, Most Holy Redeemer Cemetery;
  citing record ID 147786756, Find a Grave,
  http://www.findagrave.com.
- "St. Anthony, Schenectady, New York, Marriages (Oct 1916 -Jul
  2006)", 2 Volumes, American-Canadian Genealogical Society,
  Manchester, NH, page 589

566) Armand O. Tiso

Armand O. Tiso(566) was born on 6 January 1929, in Newark, NJ, to Oto (Ottone)
Tiso(169) and Mary Senese(169a). Armand O. Tiso(566) died 2 January 2005 in
New Jersey.

Armand O. Tiso(566) married Elvira B. Cirminiello(566a) about 1944 in New
Jersey.

Elvira B. Cirminiello(566a) was born on 27 July 1932, in Newark, NJ, to
William Cirminiello(566aF) and Elvira D'Amato(566aM). Elvira B.
Cirminiello(566a) died 4 February 2021 in Jackson Township, NJ.

Armand O. Tiso(566) and Elvira B. Cirminiello(566a) had child(ren).

Records that include Armand O. Tiso(566) and/or Elvira B. Cirminiello(566a):
- "New Jersey, Reclaim the Records, Geographic Birth Index, 1901-
  1929", , FamilySearch
  (https://www.familysearch.org/ark:/61903/1:1:6N9T-6T3S : Wed Nov 15
  06:06:40 UTC 2023), Entry for Armando Tiso, 6 Jan 1929.
- "United States Census, 1930", , FamilySearch
  (https://www.familysearch.org/ark:/61903/1:1:X4DG-XPV : Fri Mar 08
  18:34:06 UTC 2024), Entry for Ottone Liso and Mary H Liso, 1930.
- "United States Census, 1940", , FamilySearch
  (https://www.familysearch.org/ark:/61903/1:1:K4BX-LGY : Sun Mar 10
  17:21:28 UTC 2024), Entry for William Sidoli and Mary Sidoli, 1940.
- "United States Census, 1950", , FamilySearch
  (https://www.familysearch.org/ark:/61903/1:1:6F9G-ZCCY : Tue Mar 19
  16:04:46 UTC 2024), Entry for William Cirminiello and Elvira
  Cirminiello, 5 April 1950.
- "United States Social Security Death Index," database, FamilySearch
  (https://familysearch.org/ark:/61903/1:1:JPMP-MYC : 11 January
  2021), Armand Tiso, 02 Jan 2005; citing U.S. Social Security
  Administration, Death Master File, database (Alexandria, Virginia:
  National Technical Information Service, ongoing).
- "United States, Social Security Numerical Identification Files
  (NUMIDENT), 1936-2007", database, FamilySearch
  (https://www.familysearch.org/ark:/61903/1:1:6K96-C5GF : 10
  February 2023), Armand Tiso, .

- "Find A Grave Index," database, FamilySearch (https://www.familysearch.org/ark:/61903/1:1:QVLS-QQ5B : 10 August 2022), Armand O. Tiso, ; Burial, Holmdel, Monmouth, New Jersey, United States of America, Holmdel Cemetery and Mausoleum; citing record ID 80323479, Find a Grave, http://www.findagrave.com.
- https://obits.nj.com/us/obituaries/starledger/name/armand-tiso-obituary?id=14878781
- https://www.tributearchive.com/obituaries/19892131/Elvira-B-Tiso

567) Felice Louis Amodio

Felice Louis Amodio(567) was born on 30 May 1929, in Middletown, NY, to Anthony Amodio(311a) and Maria Silveria Francesca (Frances) Giorgione/George(311). Felice Louis Amodio(567) died 5 July 1996 in Middletown, NY.

Felice Louis Amodio(567) married Kathleen Keyser(567a).

Kathleen Keyser(567a) was born on 15 August 1925, in Grafton, WV, to Gordon R. Keyser(567aF) and Susie M. Nestor(567aM). Kathleen Keyser(567a) died 15 May 2002 in Middletown, NY.

Felice Louis Amodio(567) and Kathleen Keyser(567a) had child(ren).

Records that include Felice Louis Amodio(567) and/or Kathleen Keyser(567a):
- "United States Census, 1930", , FamilySearch (https://www.familysearch.org/ark:/61903/1:1:X4R1-NC2 : Sun Jul 14 09:29:21 UTC 2024), Entry for Anthony Amodio and Frances Amodio, 1930.
- "United States Census, 1930", , FamilySearch (https://www.familysearch.org/ark:/61903/1:1:XMC4-QBL : Sun Mar 10 07:10:11 UTC 2024), Entry for Roscoe Keyser and Susie Keyser, 1930.
- "United States Census, 1940", , FamilySearch (https://www.familysearch.org/ark:/61903/1:1:KQGP-8TT : Sat Mar 09 04:22:19 UTC 2024), Entry for Anthony Amodio and Frances Amodio, 1940.
- "United States Census, 1940", , FamilySearch (https://www.familysearch.org/ark:/61903/1:1:K7Z1-B6M : Thu Mar 07 22:23:22 UTC 2024), Entry for Gordon Keyser and Susie Keyser, 1940.
- "United States Census, 1950", , FamilySearch (https://www.familysearch.org/ark:/61903/1:1:6XTR-V5QQ : Fri Oct 06 21:44:06 UTC 2023), Entry for Felice L Amodto and Kathleen Amodro, 5 April 1950.
- "Virginia, Marriage Certificates, 1936-1988", , FamilySearch (https://www.familysearch.org/ark:/61903/1:1:QK9D-5LYV : Sat Mar 09 15:02:05 UTC 2024), Entry for Warren Russell Lokey and Clarence Russell Lokey, 11 Dec 1972.
- "United States Social Security Death Index," database, FamilySearch (https://familysearch.org/ark:/61903/1:1:JYMW-L31 : 7 January 2021), Felice L Amodio, 05 Jul 1996; citing U.S. Social Security Administration, Death Master File, database (Alexandria, Virginia: National Technical Information Service, ongoing).
- "United States, Social Security Numerical Identification Files (NUMIDENT), 1936-2007", database, FamilySearch (https://www.familysearch.org/ark:/61903/1:1:6K9W-WF3D : 10 February 2023), Felice Louis Amodio, .
- https://www.recordonline.com/story/news/2002/05/21/may-21-2002/51175334007/
- "United States Social Security Death Index," , FamilySearch (https://familysearch.org/ark:/61903/1:1:JYWR-Z2H : 8 January 2021), Kathleen Amodio, 16 May 2002; citing U.S. Social Security Administration, Death Master File, database (Alexandria, Virginia: National Technical Information Service, ongoing).
- "United States, Social Security Numerical Identification Files (NUMIDENT), 1936-2007", database, FamilySearch (https://www.familysearch.org/ark:/61903/1:1:6KSZ-X9LC : 10 February 2023), Katie Kathleen Keyser, .

- "United States, Social Security Numerical Identification Files (NUMIDENT), 1936-2007", , FamilySearch (https://www.familysearch.org/ark:/61903/1:1:6K9W-WF3D : 10 February 2023), Felice Louis Amodio, .
- "United States, Social Security Numerical Identification Files (NUMIDENT), 1936-2007", database, FamilySearch (https://www.familysearch.org/ark:/61903/1:1:6KMR-X19B : 10 February 2023), Kathleen Keyser in entry for Anthony David Amodio, .

568) Joseph DeDonato Sr.

Joseph DeDonato Sr.(568) was born on 20 June 1929, in Bridgeport, CT, to Filippo deDonato(327) and Florence Cerino(327a). Joseph DeDonato Sr.(568) died on 23 August 2017, in Trumbull, CT.

Joseph DeDonato Sr.(568) married Elaine Mezick(568a).

Elaine Mezick(568a) was born on 17 May 1930, in Olyphant, PA, to John Mezick(568aF) and Elizabeth Anton(568aM). Elaine Mezick(568a) died on 8 July 2016 in Trumbull, CT.

Joseph DeDonato Sr.(568) and Elaine Mezick(568a) had child(ren).

Records that include Joseph DeDonato Sr.(568) and/or Elaine Mezick(568a):
- "United States Census, 1930", , FamilySearch (https://www.familysearch.org/ark:/61903/1:1:XMPM-C9Q : Tue Oct 03 10:11:57 UTC 2023), Entry for Phillip Dedonato and Florence Dedonato, 1930.
- "United States Census, 1940", , FamilySearch (https://www.familysearch.org/ark:/61903/1:1:KWMK-MGQ : Tue Nov 28 14:32:59 UTC 2023), Entry for Philip Dedonato and Florence Dedonato, 1940.
- "United States Census, 1940", , FamilySearch (https://www.familysearch.org/ark:/61903/1:1:KQDH-3C5 : Tue Nov 28 15:25:02 UTC 2023), Entry for John Mezick and Mary Mezick, 1940.
- "United States 1950 Census", , FamilySearch (https://www.familysearch.org/ark:/61903/1:1:6FMX-1KMM : Fri Oct 06 06:38:41 UTC 2023), Entry for Phillip De Donato and Florence De Donato, 1950.
- "United States 1950 Census", , FamilySearch (https://www.familysearch.org/ark:/61903/1:1:6FMD-Q6N5 : Tue Oct 03 19:41:02 UTC 2023), Entry for Peter Mezick and John Mezick, April 12, 1950.
- "Find A Grave Index," database, FamilySearch (https://www.familysearch.org/ark:/61903/1:1:Q2BB-WVGW : 13 June 2023), Elaine M. Mezick DeDonato, ; Burial, Trumbull, Fairfield, Connecticut, United States of America, Gate of Heaven Cemetery; citing record ID 175818665, Find a Grave, http://www.findagrave.com.
- "Find A Grave Index," database, FamilySearch (https://www.familysearch.org/ark:/61903/1:1:6ZRQ-HFM5 : 14 June 2023), Joseph A. DeDonato, ; Burial, Trumbull, Fairfield, Connecticut, United States of America, Gate of Heaven Cemetery; citing record ID 226941871, Find a Grave, http://www.findagrave.com.

569) Rena Perrine

Rena Perrine(569) was born 6 August 1929, in Buffalo, NY, to Carmine Perrina(247) and Colomba di Pasquale(247a). Rena Perrine(569) died 20 December 2011 in Buffalo, NY.

Rena Perrine(569) married Frank Martin Cino(569a).

Frank Martin Cino(569a) was born on 12 November 1927, in Buffalo, NY, to Charles Chino(569aF) and Jennie Failla(569aM). Frank Martin Cino(569a) died on December 12, 2005 in Buffalo, NY.

Rena Perrine(569) and Frank Martin Cino(569a) had child(ren).

Records that include Rena Perrine(569) and/or Frank Martin Cino(569a):
- "United States Census, 1930", , FamilySearch (https://www.familysearch.org/ark:/61903/1:1:X7CK-1B8 : Fri Jul 05 22:27:03 UTC 2024), Entry for Carmino Perrine and Columbia Perrine, 1930.
- "United States Census, 1930", , FamilySearch (https://www.familysearch.org/ark:/61903/1:1:X7ZS-RP3 : Sat Mar 09 09:40:12 UTC 2024), Entry for Charles Cino and Jennie Cino, 1930.
- "United States Census, 1940", , FamilySearch (https://www.familysearch.org/ark:/61903/1:1:KQ53-VDG : Tue Jul 23 10:44:20 UTC 2024), Entry for Carmen Perrone and Columba Perrone, 1940.
- "United States Census, 1940", , FamilySearch (https://www.familysearch.org/ark:/61903/1:1:KQBH-RXN : Sun Jul 07 06:16:07 UTC 2024), Entry for Charles Cino and Jennie Cino, 1940.
- "United States Census, 1950", , FamilySearch (https://www.familysearch.org/ark:/61903/1:1:6XTT-79WW : Thu Mar 21 00:15:09 UTC 2024), Entry for Carmine Perrino and Colombe Perrino, 10 April 1950.
- "United States Census, 1950", , FamilySearch (https://www.familysearch.org/ark:/61903/1:1:6XTG-VB84 : Sat Oct 07 01:05:16 UTC 2023), Entry for Charles Cino and Jenne Cino, 10 April 1950.
- https://www.newspapers.com/article/the-buffalo-news-perrine-colomba-nee-d/148955383/
- "United States, Social Security Numerical Identification Files (NUMIDENT), 1936-2007", database, FamilySearch (https://www.familysearch.org/ark:/61903/1:1:6KMY-VBDR : 10 February 2023), Frank Martin Cino, .
- "United States Social Security Death Index," database, FamilySearch (https://familysearch.org/ark:/61903/1:1:JBHB-TW5 : 11 January 2021), Frank M Cino, 12 Dec 2005; citing U.S. Social Security Administration, Death Master File, database (Alexandria, Virginia: National Technical Information Service, ongoing).
- https://www.legacy.com/us/obituaries/buffalonews/name/frank-cino-obituary?id=4672279
- "United States Social Security Death Index," database, FamilySearch (https://familysearch.org/ark:/61903/1:1:JBHB-TW5 : 11 January 2021), Frank M Cino, 12 Dec 2005; citing U.S. Social Security Administration, Death Master File, database (Alexandria, Virginia: National Technical Information Service, ongoing).
- https://www.legacy.com/us/obituaries/buffalonews/name/rena-cino-obituary?id=4767288

570) Louise George

Louise George(570) was born on 13 August 1929, in Middletown, NY, to Carmine (Carmen Louis) Giorgione/George(290) and Bertha Michalowski(290a). Louise George(570) died 23 June 2009 in Las Vegas, NV.

Louise George(570) married Edward Zaetz(570a).

Edward Zaetz(570a) was born on 30 May 1923, in Hampstead, NY, to Ignatz Zaetz(570aF) and Rozalia Kuszyk(570aM). Edward Zaetz(570a) died 30 December 1987 in Las Vegas, NV.

Louise George(570) and Edward Zaetz(570a) had child(ren).

Records that include Louise George(570) and/or Edward Zaetz(570a):
- "United States Census, 1930", , FamilySearch (https://www.familysearch.org/ark:/61903/1:1:X4R1-RJV : Fri Sep 20 03:41:55 UTC 2024), Entry for Carmin L George and Bertha C George, 1930.
- "United States Census, 1940", , FamilySearch (https://www.familysearch.org/ark:/61903/1:1:KQG5-SHX : Tue Jul 16 21:20:46 UTC 2024), Entry for Carmen George and Bertha M George, 1940.

- "United States Census, 1940", , FamilySearch
  (https://www.familysearch.org/ark:/61903/1:1:KQ3N-LYK : Fri Mar 08
  22:19:59 UTC 2024), Entry for Ignatz Zaetz and Rosa Zaetz, 1940.
- "United States Census, 1950", , FamilySearch
  (https://www.familysearch.org/ark:/61903/1:1:6XT5-S3N8 : Tue Mar 19
  04:47:32 UTC 2024), Entry for Carman L George and Bertha George, 5
  April 1950.
- "United States Census, 1950", , FamilySearch
  (https://www.familysearch.org/ark:/61903/1:1:6XY4-PPCJ : Tue Mar 19
  13:01:36 UTC 2024), Entry for Jennie Norwick and Peter Norwick, 10
  April 1950.
- "United States, Social Security Numerical Identification Files
  (NUMIDENT), 1936-2007", database, FamilySearch
  (https://www.familysearch.org/ark:/61903/1:1:6KMG-RXJ7 : 10
  February 2023), Edward Zaetz, .
- "United States, Social Security Numerical Identification Files
  (NUMIDENT), 1936-2007", database, FamilySearch
  (https://www.familysearch.org/ark:/61903/1:1:6KMG-RXJ7 : 10
  February 2023), Edward Zaetz, .
- "BillionGraves Index," , FamilySearch
  (https://familysearch.org/ark:/61903/1:1:QV3M-R49Z : 27 June 2019),
  Edward Zaetz, died 1987; citing BillionGraves
  (http://www.billiongraves.com : 2012), Burial at Palm Eastern
  Cemetery, Las Vegas, Clark, Nevada, United States.
- "Find a Grave Index," database, FamilySearch
  (https://www.familysearch.org/ark:/61903/1:1:QVV2-JNLD : 3 January
  2024), Edward Zaetz, ; Burial, Las Vegas, Clark, Nevada, United
  States of America, Palm Memorial Park; citing record ID 17201555,
  Find a Grave, http://www.findagrave.com.
- "United States, Social Security Numerical Identification Files
  (NUMIDENT), 1936-2007", , FamilySearch
  (https://www.familysearch.org/ark:/61903/1:1:6K9M-3W8M : 10
  February 2023), Edward Zaetz in entry for Michael Kevin Zaetz, .
- https://www.legacy.com/us/obituaries/lvrj/name/louise-zaetz-
  obituary?id=25923681
- "Find a Grave Index," database, FamilySearch
  (https://www.familysearch.org/ark:/61903/1:1:6NN6-9HC6 : 24 August
  2022), Louise Diana George Zaetz, ; Burial, Las Vegas, Clark,
  Nevada, United States of America, Palm Memorial Park; citing record
  ID 241910265, Find a Grave, http://www.findagrave.com.

571) Domenic Paul Zarlenga

Domenic Paul Zarlenga(571) was born on 28 September 1929 to Domenick
Zarlenga(259a) and Clementina Anastasio(259).

Domenic Paul Zarlenga(571) married Cathy Elizabeth Ferrario(571a) on 19
November 1955 in St. Louis, MO.

Cathy Elizabeth Ferrario(571a) was born on 6 Nov 1933, in St. Louis City, MO,
to Ambrogio Ferrario(571aF) and Giuseppina M. Venegoni(571aM). Cathy Elizabeth
Ferrario(571a) died on 17 Mar 2008 in St. Louis, MO.

Domenic Paul Zarlenga(571) and Cathy Elizabeth Ferrario(571a) had child(ren).

Records that include Domenic Paul Zarlenga(571) and/or Cathy Elizabeth
Ferrario(571a):
- "United States Census, 1930", , FamilySearch
  (https://www.familysearch.org/ark:/61903/1:1:XHJY-84K : Fri Mar 08
  10:09:13 UTC 2024), Entry for Dominick Zarlingo and Clementine
  Zarlingo, 1930.
- "United States Census, 1930", , FamilySearch
  (https://www.familysearch.org/ark:/61903/1:1:XHJY-84K : Fri Oct 06
  16:57:18 UTC 2023), Entry for Dominick Zarlingo and Clementine
  Zarlingo, 1930.
- "United States Census, 1940", , FamilySearch
  (https://www.familysearch.org/ark:/61903/1:1:K7HD-RP5 : Fri Mar 08
  18:54:50 UTC 2024), Entry for Dominic Zarlenga and Clementine Zarlenga,
  1940.

- "United States Census, 1940", , FamilySearch
  (https://www.familysearch.org/ark:/61903/1:1:K7HD-RP5 : Tue Nov 28
  07:59:30 UTC 2023), Entry for Dominic Zarlenga and Clementine Zarlenga,
  1940.
- "United States 1950 Census", , FamilySearch
  (https://www.familysearch.org/ark:/61903/1:1:6FM2-4LJD : Tue Oct 03
  08:02:25 UTC 2023), Entry for Dominick Zarlenga and Clementine
  Zarlenga, April 15, 1950.
- "Missouri, County Marriage, Naturalization, and Court Records, 1800-
  1991", , FamilySearch
  (https://www.familysearch.org/ark:/61903/1:1:66HX-G69H : Thu Mar 07
  20:48:15 UTC 2024), Entry for Dominic Paul Zarlenga and Catherine
  Elizabeth Ferrario, 19 Nov 1955.
- "Missouri, County Marriage, Naturalization, and Court Records, 1800-
  1991", , FamilySearch
  (https://www.familysearch.org/ark:/61903/1:1:66HX-G69H : Thu Mar 07
  20:48:15 UTC 2024), Entry for Dominic Paul Zarlenga and Catherine
  Elizabeth Ferrario, 19 Nov 1955.
- "Missouri, County Marriage, Naturalization, and Court Records, 1800-
  1991", , FamilySearch
  (https://www.familysearch.org/ark:/61903/1:1:669M-591T : Wed Oct 18
  13:05:38 UTC 2023), Entry for Dominic Paul Zarlenga and Catherine
  Elizabeth Ferrario, 19 Nov 1955.
- "United States, Social Security Numerical Identification Files
  (NUMIDENT), 1936-2007", database, FamilySearch
  (https://www.familysearch.org/ark:/61903/1:1:6KW7-LXLQ : 10 February
  2023), Dominic Paul Zarlenga, .
- "United States Social Security Death Index," database, FamilySearch
  (https://familysearch.org/ark:/61903/1:1:J52B-32R : 12 January 2021),
  Catherine E Zarlenga, 17 Mar 2008; citing U.S. Social Security
  Administration, Death Master File, database (Alexandria, Virginia:
  National Technical Information Service, ongoing).
- "United States Social Security Death Index," database, FamilySearch
  (https://familysearch.org/ark:/61903/1:1:V3F1-YNB : 10 January 2021),
  Dominic P Zarlenga, 23 Aug 2000; citing U.S. Social Security
  Administration, Death Master File, database (Alexandria, Virginia:
  National Technical Information Service, ongoing).
- "Find A Grave Index," database, FamilySearch
  (https://www.familysearch.org/ark:/61903/1:1:QVL9-V31S : 17 August
  2023), Dom, ; Burial, Lemay, St. Louis, Missouri, United States of
  America, Jefferson Barracks National Cemetery; citing record ID
  81109401, Find a Grave, http://www.findagrave.com.
- "Find a Grave Index," database, FamilySearch
  (https://www.familysearch.org/ark:/61903/1:1:QVGQ-NC8S : 2 August
  2020), Catherine E Ferrario Zarlenga, ; Burial, Lemay, St. Louis,
  Missouri, United States of America, Jefferson Barracks National
  Cemetery; citing record ID 109563749, Find a Grave,
  http://www.findagrave.com.

572) Eugenia Stella

Eugenia Stella(572) was born on 11 November 1929, in Bronx, NY, to Oto (Otino)
Stella(289) and Maria Giovanna (Jennie) Merola(289a). Eugenia Stella(572) died
20 September 2024, Scarsdale, NY.

Eugenia Stella(572) married Nicholas F. Lombardi(572a) in 1955 in Bronx, NY.

Nicholas F. Lombardi(572a) was born on 13 August 1924, in New York, NY, to
Frances Lombardo(572aF) and Fannie (572aM). Nicholas F. Lombardi(572a) died 5
January 1984 in Nassau, NY.

Eugenia Stella(572) and Nicholas F. Lombardi(572a) had child(ren).

Records that include Eugenia Stella(572) and/or Nicholas F. Lombardi(572a):
- "United States Census, 1930", , FamilySearch
  (https://www.familysearch.org/ark:/61903/1:1:X4PT-F3V : Sun Mar 10
  19:39:10 UTC 2024), Entry for Frank Lombardo and Annie Lombardo,
  1930.

- "United States Census, 1940", , FamilySearch
  (https://www.familysearch.org/ark:/61903/1:1:KQL9-GV9 : Sun Jul 14
  11:25:30 UTC 2024), Entry for Otino Stella and Jennie Stella, 1940.
- "United States Census, 1940", , FamilySearch
  (https://www.familysearch.org/ark:/61903/1:1:K79S-RMN : Sun Mar 10
  22:38:41 UTC 2024), Entry for Frank Lombardo and Fannie Lombardo,
  1940.
- "New York, New York City, World War II Draft Registration Cards,
  1940-1947", , FamilySearch
  (https://www.familysearch.org/ark:/61903/1:1:WWTC-XWT2 : Sun Mar 10
  07:59:53 UTC 2024), Entry for Nicholas Frank Lombardo and D
  Ginsberg and Sons, 11 Dec 1942.
- "United States World War II Army Enlistment Records, 1938-1946,"
  database, FamilySearch
  (https://familysearch.org/ark:/61903/1:1:K8RP-Q5T : 5 December
  2014), Nicholas F Lombardo, enlisted 17 Apr 1943, New York City,
  New York, United States; citing "Electronic Army Serial Number
  Merged File, ca. 1938-1946," database, The National Archives:
  Access to Archival Databases (AAD) (http://aad.archives.gov :
  National Archives and Records Administration, 2002); NARA NAID
  1263923, National Archives at College Park, Maryland.
- "United States Census, 1950", , FamilySearch
  (https://www.familysearch.org/ark:/61903/1:1:6X5Z-K51C : Mon Mar 18
  23:44:09 UTC 2024), Entry for Otino Stella and Jennie Stella, 18
  April 1950.
- "United States Census, 1950", , FamilySearch
  (https://www.familysearch.org/ark:/61903/1:1:6XRW-NBV1 : Wed Oct 04
  06:44:48 UTC 2023), Entry for Frank Lombardo and Fannie Lombardo,
  10 April 1950.
- "New York, New York City Marriage Licenses Index, 1950-1995," ,
  FamilySearch (https://www.familysearch.org/ark:/61903/1:1:QLS2-LP52
  : 16 February 2024), Eugenia Stella in entry for Nicholas Lombardi,
  1955, Bronx, New York City, New York, United States;Marriage,
  Bronx, New York City, New York, United States, from Reclaim the
  Records, The NYC Marriage Index (http://www.nycmarriageindex.com :
  2016); citing New York City Clerk's Office.
- "United States Social Security Death Index," database, FamilySearch
  (https://familysearch.org/ark:/61903/1:1:VMVY-S3F : 7 January
  2021), Nicholas Lombardo, Jan 1984; citing U.S. Social Security
  Administration, Death Master File, database (Alexandria, Virginia:
  National Technical Information Service, ongoing).
- "Find a Grave Index," database, FamilySearch
  (https://www.familysearch.org/ark:/61903/1:1:QVV7-RNBC : 13 June
  2023), Nicholas F. Lombardo, ; Burial, Calverton, Suffolk, New
  York, United States of America, Calverton National Cemetery; citing
  record ID 4052472, Find a Grave, http://www.findagrave.com.
- https://www.legacy.com/us/obituaries/name/eugenia-lombardi-
  obituary?id=56359477

573) John Louis D'Ausilio

John Louis D'Ausilio(573) was born on 2 December 1929, in Bridgeport, CT, to
Liberatore (Leon) D'Ausilio(335) and Helen Eleanor LaLuna(335a). John Louis
D'Ausilio(573) died June 25, 2023 in Stratford, CT. John Louis D'Ausilio(573)
served in the US Navy. John Louis D'Ausilio(573) was a fireman, liquor store
owner, travel agency owner, among other professions.

John Louis D'Ausilio(573) married to Nancy Rice(573a) and Cesira Elvina Rose
Scinto(573b).

John Louis D'Ausilio(573) married Nancy Rice(573a) on 4 April 1953 in San
Diego, California. They divorced.

Nancy Rice(573a) was born about 1933.

John Louis D'Ausilio(573) married Cesira Elvina Rose Scinto(573b) on 9 March
1956 in New Haven, CT.

Cesira Elvina Rose Scinto(573b) was born on 6 February 1930, in Bridgeport,
CT, to Peter Scinto(573bF) and Mamie Scarduzio(573bM). Cesira Elvina Rose
Scinto(573b) died on 18 September 2006, in Stratford, CT.

Cesira Elvina Rose Scinto(573b) was previously married to Charles Paul Kalakay(573bX) and had a child.

John Louis D'Ausilio(573) and Cesira Elvina Rose Scinto(573b) had child(ren).

Records containing information about John Louis D'Ausilio(573), Nancy Rice(573a),and/or Cesira Elvina Rose Scinto(573b):
- City of Bridgeport, Births December 1929 #12
- City of Bridgeport, Births February 1930 #35
- "United States Census, 1930", , FamilySearch (https://www.familysearch.org/ark:/61903/1:1:XMGY-ZDN : Wed Oct 04 19:20:17 UTC 2023), Entry for Libero Pavsilio and Helen Dansilio, 1930.
- "United States Census, 1930", , FamilySearch (https://www.familysearch.org/ark:/61903/1:1:XMGB-87G : Wed Oct 04 21:18:47 UTC 2023), Entry for Peter Scinto and Mamie Scinto, 1930.
- "United States Census, 1940", , FamilySearch (https://www.familysearch.org/ark:/61903/1:1:KWMF-GZ6 : Tue Nov 28 13:48:01 UTC 2023), Entry for Libero D Ansilio and Helen D Ansilio, 1940.
- "United States Census, 1940", , FamilySearch (https://www.familysearch.org/ark:/61903/1:1:KWMV-X8G : Tue Nov 28 08:11:24 UTC 2023), Entry for Peter Scinto and Mamie Scinto, 1940.
- "United States 1950 Census", , FamilySearch (https://www.familysearch.org/ark:/61903/1:1:6FM8-9K1V : Fri Oct 06 03:02:30 UTC 2023), Entry for Leon Dausilio and Rose Dausilio, 3 April 1950.
- "United States, Social Security Numerical Identification Files (NUMIDENT), 1936-2007", database, FamilySearch (https://www.familysearch.org/ark:/61903/1:1:6KMV-P2WP : 10 February 2023), Cesira Elvina Scinto, .
- "United States Social Security Death Index," , FamilySearch (https://familysearch.org/ark:/61903/1:1:JGNL-RJW : 12 January 2021), Elvina Dausilio, 18 Sep 2006; citing U.S. Social Security Administration, Death Master File, database (Alexandria, Virginia: National Technical Information Service, ongoing).
- "Find A Grave Index," database, FamilySearch (https://www.familysearch.org/ark:/61903/1:1:QVVZ-553N : 5 March 2021), Cesira Elvina Scinto D'Ausilio, ; Burial, Shelton, Fairfield, Connecticut, United States of America, Riverside Cemetery; citing record ID 15825783, Find a Grave, http://www.findagrave.com.
- https://www.legacy.com/us/obituaries/legacyremembers/john-d-ausilio-obituary?id=52447034
- Recollections of his Godson.

574) Giovanni Miressi

Giovanni Miressi(574) was born about March 1930, in Ariano, Italy, to Biagio Miressi(172) and Lucia Grasso(172a). Giovanni Miressi(574) died on 7 May 1931 in Ariano, Italy.

Records that include Giovanni Miressi(574):
- Ariano, Italy 1931 Death Act #102

575) Edigio Baviello

Edigio Baviello(575) was born about March 1930, in Ariano, Italy, to Angelo Maria Baviello(225a) and Maria Antonia di Lillo(225). Edigio Baviello(575) died on 11 May 1931 in Ariano, Italy.

Records that include Edigio Baviello(575):
- Ariano, Italy 1931 Death Act #104

576) Rita Dragoni

Rita Dragoni(576) was born on 22 April 1930, in East Boston, MA, to Nicola Giuseppe Amato Dragoni(324a) and Angela Maria D'Ausilio(324). Rita Dragoni(576) died 15 June 1997 in Amesbury, MA.

Rita Dragoni(576) may have married someone named Avelis, however, I have not
been able to locate any information about a marriage or spouse.

Records that include Rita Dragoni(576):
- "United States Census, 1950", , FamilySearch
  (https://www.familysearch.org/ark:/61903/1:1:6F38-C2LK : Fri Oct 06
  17:29:06 UTC 2023), Entry for Nick M Dragoni and Angela M Dragoni,
  10 April 1950.
- "United States Social Security Death Index," database, FamilySearch
  (https://familysearch.org/ark:/61903/1:1:JKXG-3MH : 7 January
  2021), Rita L Dragoni, 15 Jun 1997; citing U.S. Social Security
  Administration, Death Master File, database (Alexandria, Virginia:
  National Technical Information Service, ongoing).
- "United States, Social Security Numerical Identification Files
  (NUMIDENT), 1936-2007", database, FamilySearch
  (https://www.familysearch.org/ark:/61903/1:1:6KM3-RG5P : 10
  February 2023), Nicholas Dragoni in entry for Rita Dragoni, .
- "Massachusetts Death Index, 1970-2003", , FamilySearch
  (https://familysearch.org/ark:/61903/1:1:VZTN-Y93 : 13 June 2019),
  Rita L Dragoni, 1997.

577) Giovanni (John) Stella

Giovanni (John) Stella(577) was born on 11 January 1931, in Bronx, NY, to Oto
(Otino) Stella(289) and Maria Giovanna (Jennie) Merola(289a). Giovanni (John)
Stella(577) died 4 November 2021.

Giovanni (John) Stella(577) married Elaine Forte(577a) in 1960 in Bronx, NY.

Elaine Forte(577a) - no information at this time

Giovanni (John) Stella(577) and Elaine Forte(577a) had child(ren).

Records that include Giovanni (John) Stella(577) and/or Elaine Forte(577a):
- "United States Census, 1940", , FamilySearch
  (https://www.familysearch.org/ark:/61903/1:1:KQL9-GV9 : Sun Jul 14
  11:25:30 UTC 2024), Entry for Otino Stella and Jennie Stella, 1940.
- "United States Census, 1950", , FamilySearch
  (https://www.familysearch.org/ark:/61903/1:1:6X5Z-K51C : Mon Mar 18
  23:44:09 UTC 2024), Entry for Otino Stella and Jennie Stella, 18
  April 1950.
- "New York Records of the State National Guard, 1906-1954", ,
  FamilySearch (https://www.familysearch.org/ark:/61903/1:1:QVJY-QP65
  : Sat Mar 09 01:58:24 UTC 2024), Entry for John P Stella, 23 Feb
  1951.
- "New York Records of the State National Guard, 1906-1954", ,
  FamilySearch (https://www.familysearch.org/ark:/61903/1:1:QVJY-R4DP
  : Tue Jul 09 14:03:27 UTC 2024), Entry for John P Stella, 23 Feb
  1951.
- "New York, New York City Marriage Licenses Index, 1950-1995,"
  database, FamilySearch
  (https://www.familysearch.org/ark:/61903/1:1:QLST-R8RV : 16
  February 2024), John Stella and Elaine Forte, 1960, The Bronx, New
  York City, New York, United States;Marriage, The Bronx, New York
  City, New York, United States, from Reclaim the Records, The NYC
  Marriage Index (http://www.nycmarriageindex.com : 2016); citing New
  York City Clerk's Office.
- https://obits.nj.com/us/obituaries/starledger/name/gloria-liguori-
  obituary?id=31184874

578) Salvatore Bellofatto

Salvatore Bellofatto(578) was born on 7 February 1931, in Boston, MA, to Rocco
Louis Bellofatto(298a) and Concetta D'Ausilio(298). Salvatore Bellofatto(578)
died on 11 November 2000, in Massachusetts. Salvatore Bellofatto(578) was a
Linotype operator in 1950.

Salvatore Bellofatto(578) married Florence Melchiondo/Marchino(578a)in Boston,
MA in 1954.

Florence Melchiondo/Marchino(578a)[last name unsure] was born on 3 August 1934 in Massachusetts to (father's name unknown) and Mary C Anzalone(578aM). Florence Melchiondo/Marchino(578a) died on 21 December 2007 in Massachusetts.

Records that include Salvatore Bellofatto(578) and/or Florence Melchiondo/Marchino(578a):
- "United States Census, 1940", , FamilySearch (https://www.familysearch.org/ark:/61903/1:1:K4J6-N24 : Tue Nov 28 18:49:56 UTC 2023), Entry for Louis Bellorfatti and Concetta Bellorfatti, 1940.
- "United States Census, 1940", , FamilySearch (https://www.familysearch.org/ark:/61903/1:1:K4FD-58B : Tue Nov 28 18:42:23 UTC 2023), Entry for Victor Santelli and Mary Santelli, 1940.
- "United States 1950 Census", , FamilySearch (https://www.familysearch.org/ark:/61903/1:1:6F3N-BJZN : Fri Oct 06 09:08:13 UTC 2023), Entry for Louis Bellofatto and Concetta Billofette, April 13, 1950.
- "United States 1950 Census", , FamilySearch (https://www.familysearch.org/ark:/61903/1:1:6F3Q-71SP : Fri Oct 06 00:22:19 UTC 2023), Entry for Victor Santilli and Mary Santilli, 1 April 1950.
- https://www.newspapers.com/newspage/441088241/
- "Massachusetts Death Index, 1970-2003", , FamilySearch (https://familysearch.org/ark:/61903/1:1:VZR6-RQN : 13 June 2019), Salvator E E Bellofatto in entry for Florence Melchiondo, .
- "United States, Social Security Numerical Identification Files (NUMIDENT), 1936-2007", database, FamilySearch (https://www.familysearch.org/ark:/61903/1:1:6KM3-WRR6 : 10 February 2023), Salvatore P Bellofatto, .
- "United States Social Security Death Index," database, FamilySearch (https://familysearch.org/ark:/61903/1:1:JKJR-T2F : 7 January 2021), Salvatore P Bellofatto, 11 Nov 2000; citing U.S. Social Security Administration, Death Master File, database (Alexandria, Virginia: National Technical Information Service, ongoing).
- "United States Social Security Death Index," database, FamilySearch (https://familysearch.org/ark:/61903/1:1:JGV8-Z31 : 12 January 2021), Florence A Bellofatto, 21 Dec 2007; citing U.S. Social Security Administration, Death Master File, database (Alexandria, Virginia: National Technical Information Service, ongoing).
- https://www.legacy.com/us/obituaries/bostonglobe/name/florence-bellofatto-obituary?id=25214842
- "Find A Grave Index," database, FamilySearch (https://www.familysearch.org/ark:/61903/1:1:QVG2-4XC8 : 10 September 2021), Salvatore P Bellofatto, ; Burial, Bourne, Barnstable, Massachusetts, United States of America, Massachusetts National Cemetery; citing record ID 128986962, Find a Grave, http://www.findagrave.com.

579) Gloria Grasso

Gloria Grasso(579) was born on 21 February 1931, in New York, NY, to Antonio Grasso(276) and Mary Lombardi(276a). Gloria Grasso(579) died on 1 February 2017 in Allendale, NJ.

Gloria Grasso(579) married Albert LaBollita(579a).

Albert LaBollita(579a) was born on 29 June 1924, in New York, NY, to Joseph LaBollita(579aF) and Angelina Sardonia(579aM). Albert LaBollita(579a) died 9 February 2009 in Dumont, NJ.

Gloria Grasso(579) and Albert LaBollita(579a) had child(ren).

Records that include Gloria Grasso(579) and/or Albert LaBollita(579a):
- "New York, State Census, 1925", FamilySearch (https://www.familysearch.org/ark:/61903/1:1:KS79-HDC : Fri Jul 18 09:33:59 UTC 2025), Entry for Albert Labolleta, 1925.

- "United States, Census, 1930", FamilySearch
  (https://www.familysearch.org/ark:/61903/1:1:X4LS-B1J : Wed Jan 15
  12:53:37 UTC 2025), Entry for Joseph Labollita and Lena Labollita,
  1930.
- "United States, Census, 1940", FamilySearch
  (https://www.familysearch.org/ark:/61903/1:1:KQMD-V2P : Fri Jul 19
  06:08:08 UTC 2024), Entry for Anthony Grasso and Mary Grasso, 1940.
- "United States, Census, 1940", FamilySearch
  (https://www.familysearch.org/ark:/61903/1:1:KQS5-XSM : Thu Jan 16
  20:34:03 UTC 2025), Entry for Joseph Labollita and Angelina
  Labollita, 1940.
- "New York, New York City, World War II Draft Registration Cards,
  1940-1947", FamilySearch
  (https://www.familysearch.org/ark:/61903/1:1:WZHY-WWPZ : Sat Apr 12
  19:50:10 UTC 2025), Entry for Albert la Bollita and Landrau
  Chesterfield Hotel, 30 Jun 1942.
- "United States, Census, 1950", FamilySearch
  (https://www.familysearch.org/ark:/61903/1:1:6XT2-4X6Q : Tue Oct 03
  16:45:26 UTC 2023), Entry for Fred Grasso and Anthony Grasso, 10
  April 1950.
- "United States, Social Security Death Index," database,
  FamilySearch (https://familysearch.org/ark:/61903/1:1:J5GH-ZTT : 12
  January 2021), Albert La Bollita, 09 Feb 2009; citing U.S. Social
  Security Administration, Death Master File, database (Alexandria,
  Virginia: National Technical Information Service, ongoing).
- https://dailyvoice.com/new-
  jersey/northernhighlands/obituaries/gloria-labollita-85-allendale-
  resident/698458/

580) Anthony E. Dragoni

Anthony E. Dragoni(580) was born on 10 June 1931, in East Boston, MA, to
Nicola Giuseppe Amato Dragoni(324a) and Angela Maria D'Ausilio(324). On 21
February 1952 Anthony E. Dragoni(580) joined the United States Air Force. On
20 February 1960 Anthony E. Dragoni(580) was discharged from the United States
Air Force. Anthony E. Dragoni(580) died 11 August 2006 in Scarborough, ME.

Anthony E. Dragoni(580) married Ann K. Rawson(580a) on 29 October 1952.

Ann K. Rawson(580a) was born on 15 March 1933, in Salem MA, to John
Rawson(580aF) and Rose Nadeau(580aM). Ann K. Rawson(580a) died on 22 November
2016 in Scarborough, ME.

Anthony E. Dragoni(580) and Ann K. Rawson(580a) had child(ren).

Records that include Anthony E. Dragoni(580) and/or Ann K. Rawson(580a):
- "United States Census, 1940", , FamilySearch
  (https://www.familysearch.org/ark:/61903/1:1:K4X2-P8D : Sat Mar 09
  17:53:13 UTC 2024), Entry for John Rawson and Rose Rawson, 1940.
- "United States Census, 1950", , FamilySearch
  (https://www.familysearch.org/ark:/61903/1:1:6F38-C2LK : Fri Oct 06
  17:29:06 UTC 2023), Entry for Nick M Dragoni and Angela M Dragoni, 10
  April 1950.
- "United States Census, 1950", , FamilySearch
  (https://www.familysearch.org/ark:/61903/1:1:6F3Q-Z5YH : Wed Oct 04
  18:39:56 UTC 2023), Entry for John J Rawson and Rose Pawson, 10 April
  1950.
- "United States, Social Security Numerical Identification Files
  (NUMIDENT), 1936-2007", database, FamilySearch
  (https://www.familysearch.org/ark:/61903/1:1:6KMH-TXDL : 10 February
  2023), Anthony Edward Dragoni, .
- "United States, GenealogyBank Obituaries, Births, and Marriages 1980-
  2014", , FamilySearch
  (https://www.familysearch.org/ark:/61903/1:1:QKPC-4ZF5 : Mon Jun 03
  21:30:28 UTC 2024), Entry for Mr Anthony E Dragoni and Nicholas
  Dragoni, 17 Aug 2006.
- "United States, GenealogyBank Obituaries, Births, and Marriages 1980-
  2014", , FamilySearch
  (https://www.familysearch.org/ark:/61903/1:1:QKRR-DNMY : Mon Jun 03
  18:55:45 UTC 2024), Entry for Mr Anthony E Dragoni and Nicholas
  Dragoni, 17 Aug 2006.
- https://www.hobbsfuneralhome.com/obituary/5423510

581) Living person and/or spouse

582) Lillian Joyce D'Ausilio

Lillian Joyce D'Ausilio(582) was born on 17 August 1931, in Bridgeport, CT, to Liberatore (Leon) D'Ausilio(335) and Helen Eleanor LaLuna(335a). Lillian Joyce D'Ausilio(582) died on 18 January 1996, in Shelton, CT.

Lillian Joyce D'Ausilio(582) married Richard Irving Landau(582a) on 5 September 1949 in Bridgeport, Connecticut.

Richard Irving Landau(582a) was born on 3 April 1927, in Bridgeport, CT, to Maurice Landau(582aF) and Diana Brand(582aM). Richard Irving Landau(582a) died on 24 May 2009, in Shelton, CT.
NOTE: First name originally on Birth Certificate, 1930, & 1940 censuses is listed as Irving, birth certificate has note to indicate correction of middle name of Richard as first name.

Lillian Joyce D'Ausilio(582) and Richard Irving Landau(582a) had child(ren).

Records that include Lillian Joyce D'Ausilio(582) and/or Richard Irving Landau(582a):
- Bridgeport, CT April 1927 Births #310
- Bridgeport, CT August 1931 Births #142
- "United States Census, 1930", , FamilySearch (https://www.familysearch.org/ark:/61903/1:1:XMGB-5TB : Wed Oct 04 23:03:31 UTC 2023), Entry for Diana Landan and Seymour Landan, 1930.
- "United States Census, 1940", , FamilySearch (https://www.familysearch.org/ark:/61903/1:1:KWMX-TTY : Tue Nov 28 19:02:56 UTC 2023), Entry for Maurice Landau and Seymour Landau, 1940.
- "United States Census, 1940", , FamilySearch (https://www.familysearch.org/ark:/61903/1:1:KWMF-GZ6 : Tue Nov 28 13:48:01 UTC 2023), Entry for Libero D Ansilio and Helen D Ansilio, 1940.
- "Connecticut, World War II Draft Registration Cards, 1940-1945", , FamilySearch (https://www.familysearch.org/ark:/61903/1:1:Q2CR-N5BS : Sat Feb 10 05:24:04 UTC 2024), Entry for Richard Irving Landau and Beatrice Mirman, 19 Jul 1946.
- Bridgeport, CT, September 1949 Marriages #58
- "United States 1950 Census", , FamilySearch (https://www.familysearch.org/ark:/61903/1:1:6FMF-CB7K : Thu Oct 05 02:36:15 UTC 2023), Entry for Richard J Landaw and Lillian J Landaw, 6 April 1950.
- "United States 1950 Census", , FamilySearch (https://www.familysearch.org/ark:/61903/1:1:6FM8-9K1V : Fri Oct 06 03:02:30 UTC 2023), Entry for Leon Dausilio and Rose Dausilio, 3 April 1950.
- "Connecticut Death Index, 1949-2001," database, FamilySearch (https://familysearch.org/ark:/61903/1:1:VZPJ-NRL : 9 December 2014), Lillian D Landau, 21 Jan 1996; from "Connecticut Death Index, 1949-2001," database, Ancestry (http://www.ancestry.com : 2003); citing Shelton, Fairfield, Connecticut, Connecticut Department of Health, Hartfort.
- "United States Social Security Death Index," database, FamilySearch (https://familysearch.org/ark:/61903/1:1:VMN2-YM7 : 7 January 2021), Lillian J Landau, Jan 1996; citing U.S. Social Security Administration, Death Master File, database (Alexandria, Virginia: National Technical Information Service, ongoing).
- "United States Social Security Death Index," database, FamilySearch (https://familysearch.org/ark:/61903/1:1:JBX9-PPB : 12 January 2021), Richard Landau, 24 May 2009; citing U.S. Social Security Administration, Death Master File, database (Alexandria, Virginia: National Technical Information Service, ongoing).
- "United States, Social Security Numerical Identification Files (NUMIDENT), 1936-2007", database, FamilySearch (https://www.familysearch.org/ark:/61903/1:1:6KMF-JZ7N : 10 February 2023), Lillian Joyce Dausilio, .

- "Find A Grave Index," database, FamilySearch
  (https://www.familysearch.org/ark:/61903/1:1:6NND-M1NG : 24 August
  2022), Lillian D'Ausilio Landau, ; Burial, Middletown, Middlesex,
  Connecticut, United States of America, Connecticut State Veterans
  Cemetery; citing record ID 241235655, Find a Grave,
  http://www.findagrave.com.

583) Phyllis Marie DeDonato

Phyllis Marie DeDonato(583) was born on 17 September 1931, in Bridgeport, CT,
to Angelo deDonato(355) and Mary Cirella(355a). Phyllis Marie DeDonato(583)
died 6 September 2021 in Bridgeport, CT.

Phyllis Marie DeDonato(583) married Isadore (I) Anthony Mase(583a) around
1950.

Isadore (I) Anthony Mase(583a) was born on 10 March 1928, in Bridgeport, CT,
to Giovanni (John) Mase(583aF) and Mary DiBenedetto(583aM). Isadore (I)
Anthony Mase(583a) died on 5 October 1999 in Bridgeport, CT.

Phyllis Marie DeDonato(583) and Isadore (I) Anthony Mase(583a) had child(ren).

Records that include Phyllis Marie DeDonato(583) and/or Isadore (I) Anthony
Mase(583a):

- Bridgeport, CT, Births, March 1928 #88
- Bridgeport, CT, Births, September 1931 #146
- "United States Census, 1940", , FamilySearch
  (https://www.familysearch.org/ark:/61903/1:1:KWMJ-K2F : Sun Mar 10
  18:49:40 UTC 2024), Entry for Angelo Dedonato and Mary Dedonato,
  1940.
- "United States Census, 1940", , FamilySearch
  (https://www.familysearch.org/ark:/61903/1:1:KWMF-TX1 : Sat Mar 09
  04:34:58 UTC 2024), Entry for John Masi and Mary Masi, 1940.
- "Connecticut, World War II Draft Registration Cards, 1940-1945", ,
  FamilySearch (https://www.familysearch.org/ark:/61903/1:1:Q2CR-KZ2M
  : Sat Mar 09 20:17:35 UTC 2024), Entry for Isadore Anthony Mase and
  John Mase, 06 Sep 1946.
- Bridgeport, CT, deaths October 1999 #26
- "Connecticut Death Index, 1949-2001," , FamilySearch
  (https://familysearch.org/ark:/61903/1:1:VZP9-M61 : 9 December
  2014), I A Mase, 05 Oct 1999; from "Connecticut Death Index, 1949-
  2001," database, Ancestry (http://www.ancestry.com : 2003); citing
  Bridgeport, Fairfield, Connecticut, Connecticut Department of
  Health, Hartford.
- "United States Social Security Death Index," database, FamilySearch
  (https://familysearch.org/ark:/61903/1:1:JT5P-X5S : 7 January
  2021), I Anthony Mase, 05 Oct 1999; citing U.S. Social Security
  Administration, Death Master File, database (Alexandria, Virginia:
  National Technical Information Service, ongoing).
- "Find a Grave Index," database, FamilySearch
  (https://www.familysearch.org/ark:/61903/1:1:QV22-JLM5 : 9
  September 2022), I Anthony Mase, ; Burial, Trumbull, Fairfield,
  Connecticut, United States of America, Nichols Farm Burial Ground;
  citing record ID 77284588, Find a Grave, http://www.findagrave.com.
- Bridgeport, CT Deaths September 2021
- https://www.legacy.com/us/obituaries/ctpost/name/phyllis-mase-
  obituary?id=17732515

584) Joseph Domenic Bellofatto

Joseph Domenic Bellofatto(584) was born on 5 July 1932, to Rocco Louis
Bellofatto(298a) and Concetta D'Ausilio(298), in Chelsea, MA. Joseph Domenic
Bellofatto(584) died 25 June 2021 in Farmville, VA.

Joseph Domenic Bellofatto(584) married Anmarie Polleck(584a) and Doris
Cox(584b).

Anmarie Polleck(584a) was born on 31 May 1933, in Chelsea, MA, to Alphonse A.
Polleck(584aF) and Lillian M. Foley(584aM). Anmarie Polleck(584a) died 04 Jun
2015 in Tewksbury, MA. Anmarie Polleck(584a) was a Licensed Practical Nurse.
Anmarie Polleck(584a) and Joseph Domenic Bellofatto(584) divorced.

Joseph Domenic Bellofatto(584) and Anmarie Polleck(584a) had child(ren).

Joseph Domenic Bellofatto(584) married Doris Cox(584b) about 1981.

<u>Doris Cox</u>(584b) was born on 7 January 1938, in Catawba, NC, to Charles A. Cox(584bF) and Maggie Lawrence(584bM). Doris Cox(584b) died on September 4, 2019 in Farmville, VA. Doris Cox(584b) was a nurse.

Records that include Joseph Domenic Bellofatto(584), Anmarie Polleck(584a) and/or Doris Cox(584b):

- "North Carolina, Birth Index, 1800-2000", FamilySearch (https://www.familysearch.org/ark:/61903/1:1:VHYH-TZB : Tue Feb 25 08:37:23 UTC 2025), Entry for Doris Marie Cox and Charles Cox, 07 Jan 1938.
- "United States, Census, 1940", FamilySearch (https://www.familysearch.org/ark:/61903/1:1:K4J6-N24 : Wed Jan 22 14:29:04 UTC 2025), Entry for Louis Bellorfatti and Concetta Bellorfatti, 1940.
- "United States, Census, 1950", FamilySearch (https://www.familysearch.org/ark:/61903/1:1:6F3N-BJZN : Tue Mar 18 04:51:05 UTC 2025), Entry for Louis Bellofatto and Concetta Billofette, April 13, 1950.
- "Virginia, Marriage Certificates, 1936-1989", FamilySearch (https://www.familysearch.org/ark:/61903/1:1:QV1Q-5KPM : Wed Jan 15 13:04:57 UTC 2025), Entry for Dean Clinton Barnard and Dean Clinton Barnard, 26 Sep 1981.
- "Virginia, Marriage Certificates, 1936-1989", FamilySearch (https://www.familysearch.org/ark:/61903/1:1:QV13-7L8V : Tue Jan 21 12:51:51 UTC 2025), Entry for Robert Orvis Bradley and Robert Dewell Bradley, 10 Oct 1981.
- "Virginia, Marriage Certificates, 1936-1989", FamilySearch (https://www.familysearch.org/ark:/61903/1:1:QV19-YXLH : Sun Jan 19 18:07:10 UTC 2025), Entry for Carl William Gustafson and John Conrad Gustafson, 20 Mar 1982.
- "Virginia, Marriage Certificates, 1936-1989", FamilySearch (https://www.familysearch.org/ark:/61903/1:1:QV1S-H56S : Wed Jul 17 00:20:06 UTC 2024), Entry for Gary William Martin and William George Martin, 25 Feb 1984.
- "Virginia, Marriage Certificates, 1936-1989", FamilySearch (https://www.familysearch.org/ark:/61903/1:1:QV13-PV1X : Mon Jul 08 08:41:23 UTC 2024), Entry for Jeff Lynn Jones and Thomas Jefferson Jones, 20 Sep 1985.
- "Find a Grave Index", FamilySearch (https://www.familysearch.org/ark:/61903/1:1:QK1L-W8XZ : Tue Apr 01 11:30:56 UTC 2025), Entry for AnMarie Polleck Bellofatto.
- "United States, Obituary Records, 2014-2023", FamilySearch (https://www.familysearch.org/ark:/61903/1:1:61KQ-JYQZ : Fri Nov 08 04:11:39 UTC 2024), Entry for Doris Cox Bellofatto and Joseph Bellofatto, 25 October 2019.
- "United States, GenealogyBank Obituaries, Births, and Marriages, 1980-2015", FamilySearch (https://www.familysearch.org/ark:/61903/1:1:QKGK-KBR5 : Sat Jul 06 13:50:51 UTC 2024), Entry for Louis J Bellofatto and Maria, 01 May 2014.
- "Find a Grave Index", FamilySearch (https://www.familysearch.org/ark:/61903/1:1:68J9-LDQM : Thu Apr 03 03:31:40 UTC 2025), Entry for Joseph Domenic Bellofatto.
- "United States, Obituary Records, 2014-2023", , FamilySearch (https://www.familysearch.org/ark:/61903/1:1:XM41-V1J3 : Wed Nov 20 04:01:56 UTC 2024), Entry for Joseph Domenic Bellofatto and Rocco Luigi Bellofatto, 30 June 2021.

585) Living person and/or spouse

586) <u>Domenico Zarrillo</u>

Domenico Zarrillo(586) was born about December 1932 in Ariano, Italy to Antonio Zarrillo(223a) and Carmela Grasso(223). Domenico Zarrillo(586) died on 25 February 1933, in Ariano, Italy.

Records that include Domenico Zarrillo(586):
* Ariano, Italy 1933 Death Act #60

587) Living person and/or spouse

588) Rosa Zecchino

Rosa Zecchino(588) was born 22 April 1933, in Ariano, Italy, to Angela Miressi(291) and Giovanni Zecchino(291a). Rosa Zecchino(588) died 14 May 1933 in Ariano, Italy.

Records that include Rosa Zecchino(588):
* Ariano, Italy 1933 Death Act #138

589) Michael DeDonato

Michael DeDonato(589) was born 13 May 1933, in Bridgeport, CT to Anthony DeDonato(338) and Mary Cretella(338a). Michael DeDonato(589) died on 29 April 2013 in Bridgeport, CT. Michael DeDonato(589) was buried in St. Michael Cemetery, Stratford, CT.

Michael DeDonato(589) married Dorothy A. Holden(589a) about 1959.

Dorothy A. Holden(589a) was born 5 September 1935, in Bridgeport, CT, to Frederick Holden(589aF) and Mildred Squires(589aM). Dorothy A. Holden(589a) died 19 September 2015 in Stratford, CT. Dorothy A. Holden(589a) was buried in St. Michael Cemetery, Stratford, CT.

Michael DeDonato(589) and Dorothy Holden(589a) had child(ren).

Records that include Michael DeDonato(589) married Dorothy Holden(589a):
* Bridgeport, CT Births May 1933 #105
* Bridgeport, CT Deaths April 2013 #35
* "United States Census, 1940", , FamilySearch (https://www.familysearch.org/ark:/61903/1:1:K71S-C8W : Tue Nov 28 10:42:26 UTC 2023), Entry for Mary Dedonato and Micheal Dedonato, 1940.
* "United States, Census, 1940", FamilySearch (https://www.familysearch.org/ark:/61903/1:1:K719-KTY : Thu Jul 18 12:09:44 UTC 2024), Entry for Fredrick Holden and Mildred Holden, 1940.
* "United States 1950 Census", , FamilySearch (https://www.familysearch.org/ark:/61903/1:1:6FMX-JJ72 : Tue Oct 03 18:17:24 UTC 2023), Entry for Anthony Dedonato and Mary Dedonato, 22 April 1950.
* "United States, Census, 1950", FamilySearch (https://www.familysearch.org/ark:/61903/1:1:6FMD-MGJ8 : Fri Oct 06 05:00:10 UTC 2023), Entry for Mildred Holden and Janet C Holden, 25 April 1950.
* https://www.pisteyfuneralhome.com/obituaries/Michael-J-DeDonato?obId=577238
* "Find a Grave Index", FamilySearch (https://www.familysearch.org/ark:/61903/1:1:6ZRQ-88FR : Tue Apr 01 18:15:24 UTC 2025), Entry for Michael J. DeDonato.
* "United States, Obituary Records, 2014-2023", FamilySearch (https://www.familysearch.org/ark:/61903/1:1:61V5-3YQH : Thu Nov 07 16:16:18 UTC 2024), Entry for Dorothy A Dedonato, 18 September 2019.
* https://www.pisteyfuneralhome.com/obituaries/Dorothy-A-DeDonato?obId=623183

590) Living person and/or spouse

591) Living person and/or spouse

592) Deloris Ciasullo

Deloris Ciasullo(592) born on 9 August 1933, in Schenectady, NY, to Giuseppe Ciasullo(262) and Grace Castaldi(262a). Deloris Ciasullo(592) died 6 May 2013.

Deloris Ciasullo(592) married Lawrence R. Perkins(592a).

Lawrence R. Perkins(592a) was born on 18 March 1930, in Albany, NY, to John Perkins(592aF) and Margaret Howe(592aM). Lawrence R. Perkins(592a) died on 08 Apr 2014 in Schenectady, NY.

Records that include Deloris Ciasullo(592) and/or Lawrence R. Perkins(592a):
- "United States Census, 1930", , FamilySearch (https://www.familysearch.org/ark:/61903/1:1:X74B-T55 : Thu Jul 11 01:40:20 UTC 2024), Entry for John J Perkins and Margaret E Perkins, 1930.
- "United States Census, 1940", , FamilySearch (https://www.familysearch.org/ark:/61903/1:1:KQY5-9BR : Fri Mar 08 20:57:12 UTC 2024), Entry for Joseph Ciasullo and Grace Ciasullo, 1940.
- "United States Census, 1940", , FamilySearch (https://www.familysearch.org/ark:/61903/1:1:KQBD-2N3 : Sat Jul 13 11:08:01 UTC 2024), Entry for John Perkins and Margaret Perkins, 1940.
- "United States Census, 1950", , FamilySearch (https://www.familysearch.org/ark:/61903/1:1:6XT1-KBSD : Tue Mar 19 15:06:03 UTC 2024), Entry for Connie M Cisaullo and Joseph Ciasullo, 10 April 1950.
- "United States Social Security Death Index," database, FamilySearch (https://familysearch.org/ark:/61903/1:1:KNWH-8F5 : 12 January 2021), Dolores N Perkins, 06 May 2013; citing U.S. Social Security Administration, Death Master File, database (Alexandria, Virginia: National Technical Information Service, ongoing).
- https://www.findagrave.com/memorial/184462297/dolores_n_perkins
- https://www.demarcostonefuneralhome.com/obituary/Dolores-Perkins
- "Find a Grave Index," database, FamilySearch (https://www.familysearch.org/ark:/61903/1:1:QGV1-6MGL : 16 December 2020), Skip, ; Burial, Niskayuna, Schenectady, New York, United States of America, Most Holy Redeemer Cemetery; citing record ID 184461739, Find a Grave, http://www.findagrave.com.

593) Living person and/or spouse

594) Ferdinand (Fred Louis) Grasso

Ferdinand (Fred Louis) Grasso(594) was born on 7 January 1934, in Bronx, NY, to Antonio Grasso(276) and Mary Lombardi(276a). Ferdinand (Fred Louis) Grasso(594) served in the United States Military from 20 March 1952 to 1 June 1954. Ferdinand (Fred Louis) Grasso(594) died 25 February 2003 in Garden City, NY.

Records that include Ferdinand (Fred Louis) Grasso(594):
- "United States, Census, 1940", FamilySearch (https://www.familysearch.org/ark:/61903/1:1:KQMD-V2P : Fri Jul 19 06:08:08 UTC 2024), Entry for Anthony Grasso and Mary Grasso, 1940.
- "United States, Census, 1950", FamilySearch (https://www.familysearch.org/ark:/61903/1:1:6XT2-4X6Q : Tue Oct 03 16:45:26 UTC 2023), Entry for Fred Grasso and Anthony Grasso, 10 April 1950.
- "New York, Records of the State National Guard, 1906-1954", FamilySearch (https://www.familysearch.org/ark:/61903/1:1:QVJY-5C3Y : Sat Jan 18 17:29:39 UTC 2025), Entry for Fred Lewis Grasso, 20 Mar 1952.
- "United States, Social Security Death Index," , FamilySearch (https://familysearch.org/ark:/61903/1:1:JPH3-F3D : 7 January 2021), Fred L Grasso, 25 Feb 2003; citing U.S. Social Security Administration, Death Master File, database (Alexandria, Virginia: National Technical Information Service, ongoing).
- "United States, Social Security Numerical Identification Files (NUMIDENT), 1936-2007", FamilySearch (https://www.familysearch.org/ark:/61903/1:1:6K93-MKGZ : Fri Apr 25 19:28:26 UTC 2025), Entry for Fred L Grasso and Anthony Grasso.

595) Living person and/or spouse

596) Living person and/or spouse

597) <u>Eleanor Jane D'Ausilio</u>

Eleanor Jane D'ausilio(597) was born on 27 February 1935, in Bridgeport, CT, to Liberatore (Leon) D'Ausilio(335) and Helen Eleanor LaLuna(335a). Eleanor Jane D'ausilio(597) died on 18 March 2002, in Bridgeport, CT. Eleanor Jane D'ausilio(597) was buried on 21 March 2002 in Gate of Heaven Cemetery, Trumbull, CT.

Eleanor Jane D'ausilio(597) married James Frank DellaRocco(597a) and Joseph John Paris(597b).

Eleanor Jane D'ausilio(597) married James Frank DellaRocco(597a) on 20 November 1954 in Bridgeport, CT. They divorced.

<u>James Frank DellaRocco</u>(597a) was born on 7 April 1935, in Bridgeport, CT, to Frank DellaRocco(597aF) and Guiseppina Bellizzi(597aM). James Frank DellaRocco(597a) died on 3 August 2002, in Barefoot Bay, FL.

Eleanor Jane D'ausilio(597) and James Frank DellaRocco(597a) had child(ren).

Eleanor Jane D'ausilio(597) married Joseph John Paris(597b) on 7 March 1969 in Bridgeport, CT.

<u>Joseph John Paris</u>(597b) was born on 14 November 1931, in Bridgeport, Connecticut, to John Antonio Paris(597bF) and Mary Rizzo(597bM). Joseph John Paris(597b) died on 1 January 2013, in Bridgeport, CT. Joseph John Paris(597b) was buried in Gate of Heaven Cemetery, Trumbull, CT.

Eleanor Jane D'ausilio(597) and Joseph John Paris(597b) had child(ren).

Records that include Eleanor Jane D'ausilio(597), James Frank DellaRocco(597a), and/or Joseph John Paris(597b):
- City Of Bridgeport, Connecticut, Births November 1931 #101
- City Of Bridgeport, Connecticut, Births February 1935 #179
- City Of Bridgeport, Connecticut, Births April 1935 #50
- "United States Census, 1940", , FamilySearch (https://www.familysearch.org/ark:/61903/1:1:KWMF-GZ6 : Tue Nov 28 13:48:01 UTC 2023), Entry for Libero D Ansilio and Helen D Ansilio, 1940.
- "United States 1950 Census", , FamilySearch (https://www.familysearch.org/ark:/61903/1:1:6FM8-9K1V : Fri Oct 06 03:02:30 UTC 2023), Entry for Leon Dausilio and Rose Dausilio, 3 April 1950.
- "United States 1950 Census", , FamilySearch (https://www.familysearch.org/ark:/61903/1:1:6FM6-974V : Wed Oct 04 09:44:06 UTC 2023), Entry for Joseph I Monteiro and Mary R Monteiro, 5 April 1950.
- City of Bridgeport, CT, Marriages, November 1954
- City of Bridgeport, CT, Marriages, March 1969 #28
- City Of Bridgeport, Connecticut, Deaths March 2002 #108
- "United States, GenealogyBank Obituaries, Births, and Marriages 1980-2014", , FamilySearch (https://www.familysearch.org/ark:/61903/1:1:QK2J-ZLLC : Wed Oct 18 15:51:19 UTC 2023), Entry for Mr James Frank Dellarocco and Irma, 09 Aug 2002.
- "United States, Social Security Numerical Identification Files (NUMIDENT), 1936-2007", database, FamilySearch (https://www.familysearch.org/ark:/61903/1:1:6KML-M1F9 : 10 February 2023), James Frank Dellarocco, .
- "United States, Social Security Numerical Identification Files (NUMIDENT), 1936-2007", database, FamilySearch (https://www.familysearch.org/ark:/61903/1:1:6KMV-ZK31 : 10 February 2023), Eleanor Jane Dausilio, .

- "United States Social Security Death Index," database, FamilySearch (https://familysearch.org/ark:/61903/1:1:JKJR-XYH : 7 January 2021), James F Dellarocco, 04 Aug 2002; citing U.S. Social Security Administration, Death Master File, database (Alexandria, Virginia: National Technical Information Service, ongoing).
- "United States Social Security Death Index," database, FamilySearch (https://familysearch.org/ark:/61903/1:1:VMJR-QQ9 : 7 January 2021), Eleanor J Paris, 01 Mar 2002; citing U.S. Social Security Administration, Death Master File, database (Alexandria, Virginia: National Technical Information Service, ongoing).
- "Find A Grave Index," database, FamilySearch (https://www.familysearch.org/ark:/61903/1:1:68JQ-W3LR : 14 June 2023), Joseph John Paris, ; Burial, Trumbull, Fairfield, Connecticut, United States of America, Gate of Heaven Cemetery; citing record ID 229721579, Find a Grave, http://www.findagrave.com.
- "Find A Grave Index," database, FamilySearch (https://www.familysearch.org/ark:/61903/1:1:68JQ-W3LN : 14 June 2023), Eleanor J D'Ausillo Paris, ; Burial, Trumbull, Fairfield, Connecticut, United States of America, Gate of Heaven Cemetery; citing record ID 229721570, Find a Grave, http://www.findagrave.com.
- "Find A Grave Index," database, FamilySearch (https://www.familysearch.org/ark:/61903/1:1:66M9-9XX7 : 14 June 2023), James Frank Dellarocco, ; Burial, Bridgeport, Fairfield, Connecticut, United States of America, Lakeview Cemetery; citing record ID 231627864, Find a Grave, http://www.findagrave.com.

598) Living person and/or spouse

599) Antoinette DeDonato

Antoinette DeDonato(599) was born 29 December 1935 to Antonio deDonato(337) and Mary Rosaria Cretella(337a). Antoinette DeDonato(599) died in 1995, in Branford, CT.

Antoinette DeDonato(599) married Franc Dominick Federici(599a).

Franc Dominick Federici(599a) was born 1 March 1929 to Frank Federici(599aF) and Mary Matucgras(599aM). Franc Dominick Federici(599a) died March 1982

Records that include Antoinette DeDonato(599) and/or Franc Dominick Federici(599a):
- "United States Census, 1930", , FamilySearch (https://www.familysearch.org/ark:/61903/1:1:XMR3-MMB : Fri Oct 06 01:12:02 UTC 2023), Entry for Frank Federici and Albert Federici, 1930.
- "United States Census, 1940", , FamilySearch (https://www.familysearch.org/ark:/61903/1:1:K71S-C8W : Tue Nov 28 10:42:26 UTC 2023), Entry for Mary Dedonato and Micheal Dedonato, 1940.
- "United States 1950 Census", , FamilySearch (https://www.familysearch.org/ark:/61903/1:1:6FM8-9MSP : Fri Oct 06 21:42:55 UTC 2023), Entry for Frank Federici and Tericeo Federici, 4 April 1950.
- "United States 1950 Census", , FamilySearch (https://www.familysearch.org/ark:/61903/1:1:6FMX-JJ72 : Tue Oct 03 18:17:24 UTC 2023), Entry for Anthony Dedonato and Mary Dedonato, 22 April 1950.
- "United States, Social Security Numerical Identification Files (NUMIDENT), 1936-2007", database, FamilySearch (https://www.familysearch.org/ark:/61903/1:1:6KMF-2ZCH : 10 February 2023), Frank Federici, .
- "United States Social Security Death Index," database, FamilySearch (https://familysearch.org/ark:/61903/1:1:VMJF-C23 : 7 January 2021), Frank Federici, Mar 1982; citing U.S. Social Security Administration, Death Master File, database (Alexandria, Virginia: National Technical Information Service, ongoing).

- "Connecticut Death Index, 1949-2001," database, FamilySearch (https://familysearch.org/ark:/61903/1:1:VZGR-4B8 : 9 December 2014), Antoinette Federici, 1995; from "Connecticut Death Index, 1949-2001," database, Ancestry (http://www.ancestry.com : 2003); citing Branford, New Haven, Connecticut, Connecticut Department of Health, Hartfort.
- "Find A Grave Index," , FamilySearch (https://www.familysearch.org/ark:/61903/1:1:QK1K-KX58 : 13 June 2023), Antoinette Federici, ; Burial, Stratford, Fairfield, Connecticut, United States of America, Saint Michael's Cemetery; citing record ID 143668355, Find a Grave, http://www.findagrave.com.
- "Find A Grave Index," database, FamilySearch (https://www.familysearch.org/ark:/61903/1:1:QK1K-KF94 : 13 June 2023), Francis D. Federici, ; Burial, Stratford, Fairfield, Connecticut, United States of America, Saint Michael's Cemetery; citing record ID 143668321, Find a Grave, http://www.findagrave.com.

600) Living person and/or spouse

601) Living person and/or spouse

602) Gloria Stella

Gloria Stella(602) was born on 30 May 1939, in Bronx, NY, to Oto (Otino) Stella(289) and Maria Giovanna (Jennie) Merola(289a). Gloria Stella(602) died 28 October 2021 in Manalapan, FL.

Gloria Stella(602) married Gennaro Liguori(602a) about 1961.

Gennaro Liguori(602a) was born on 7 September 1938, in New York, NY, to Ciro Liguori(602aF) and Anna Migliucci(602aM). Gennaro Liguori(602a) died on 11 November 2014 in Manalapan, FL.

Gloria Stella(602) and Gennaro Liguori(602a) had child(ren).

Records that include Gloria Stella(602) and/or Gennaro Liguori(602a):
- "United States Census, 1940", , FamilySearch (https://www.familysearch.org/ark:/61903/1:1:KQL9-GV9 : Sun Jul 14 11:25:30 UTC 2024), Entry for Otino Stella and Jennie Stella, 1940.
- "United States Census, 1940", , FamilySearch (https://www.familysearch.org/ark:/61903/1:1:KQMK-DM9 : Tue Jul 09 01:47:07 UTC 2024), Entry for Ciro Ligouri and Anna Ligouri, 1940.
- "United States Census, 1950", , FamilySearch (https://www.familysearch.org/ark:/61903/1:1:6X5Z-K51C : Mon Mar 18 23:44:09 UTC 2024), Entry for Otino Stella and Jennie Stella, 18 April 1950.
- https://www.legacy.com/us/obituaries/app/name/gennaro-liguori-obituary?id=18651564
- "Find a Grave Index," database, FamilySearch (https://www.familysearch.org/ark:/61903/1:1:QK1D-2BTW : 10 August 2022), Gennaro Liguori, ; Burial, Lake Worth, Palm Beach, Florida, United States of America, South Florida National Cemetery; citing record ID 139845438, Find a Grave, http://www.findagrave.com.
- https://obits.nj.com/us/obituaries/starledger/name/gloria-liguori-obituary?id=31184874
- "Find a Grave Index," database, FamilySearch (https://www.familysearch.org/ark:/61903/1:1:668P-5VHF : 11 August 2022), Gloria C. Liguori, ; Burial, Lake Worth, Palm Beach, Florida, United States of America, South Florida National Cemetery; citing record ID 234803231, Find a Grave, http://www.findagrave.com.

603) Liberato Covotta

Liberato Covotta(603) was born on 30 August 1940, in Ariano, Italy, to Giuseppe Ciriaco Michele Covotta(342a) and Maria Libera deDonato(342). Liberato Covotta(603) died on 2 September 1940 in Ariano, Italy.

Records that include Liberato Covotta(603):
- Ariano, Italy 1940 Death Act #214

604) Living person and/or spouse

605) Living person and/or spouse

606) <u>Theodore Anthony Garber</u>

Theodore Anthony Garber(606) was born on 30 December 1941, in Middletown, NY, to Theodore Taft Garber(339a) and Rose Louise Giorgione(339). Theodore Anthony Garber(606) died on 23 November 2023 in Garland, TX. Theodore Anthony Garber(606) worked in Law Enforcement.

Theodore Anthony Garber(606) married Myra Ann Buford(606a).

<u>Myra Ann Buford</u>(606a) was born on 28 January 1938, in Sherman, TX, to Thomas C. Buford(606aF) and Idella Armstrong(606aM). Myra Ann Buford(606a) died 12 December 2013 in Garland, TX.

Theodore Anthony Garber(606) and Myra Ann Buford(606a) had child(ren).

Records that include Theodore Anthony Garber(606) and/or Myra Ann Buford(606a):
- "Texas Birth Index, 1903-1997," database, FamilySearch (https://familysearch.org/ark:/61903/1:1:V871-161 : 1 January 2015), Myra Ann Buford, 28 Jan 1938; from "Texas Birth Index, 1903-1997," database and images, Ancestry (http://www.ancestry.com : 2005); citing Texas Department of State Health Services.
- "United States Census, 1940", , FamilySearch (https://www.familysearch.org/ark:/61903/1:1:K4SY-KYQ : Sat Mar 09 23:31:09 UTC 2024), Entry for Tom Buford and Idella Buford, 1940.
- "United States Census, 1950", , FamilySearch (https://www.familysearch.org/ark:/61903/1:1:6XY7-1SV2 : Thu Oct 05 08:22:58 UTC 2023), Entry for Theodore T Garber and Rose L Garber, 5 April 1950.
- "United States Census, 1950", , FamilySearch (https://www.familysearch.org/ark:/61903/1:1:6XGB-C31S : Tue Mar 19 20:30:51 UTC 2024), Entry for Lom Buford and Idella Buford, 27 April 1950.
- "Find a Grave Index," database, FamilySearch (https://www.familysearch.org/ark:/61903/1:1:6RQ5-K8FG : 4 January 2024), Myra Ann Buford Garber, ; Burial, Dallas, Dallas, Texas, United States of America, Restland Memorial Park; citing record ID 261819355, Find a Grave, http://www.findagrave.com.
- "Find a Grave Index," database, FamilySearch (https://www.familysearch.org/ark:/61903/1:1:6RQ5-RDWC : 29 January 2024), Ted, ; Burial, Dallas, Dallas, Texas, United States of America, Restland Memorial Park; citing record ID 261828594, Find a Grave, http://www.findagrave.com.

607) Living person and/or spouse

608) Living person and/or spouse

609) Living person and/or spouse

610) Living person and/or spouse

611) Living person and/or spouse

612) Living person and/or spouse

613) Living person and/or spouse

614) Living person and/or spouse

615) Living person and/or spouse

616) Living person and/or spouse

Pasquale Bellofatto(298aF)
Rocco Louis Bellofatto(298a)
Salvatore Bellofatto(578)
Benedetto,
Antoinette Benedetto(335dM)
Benneditti,
Burisida Benneditti(341aM)
Bernardo,
Caterina Bernardo(55bM)
Bianchi,
Francesco Vincenzo Liberato
Bianchi(379)
Gerardino Bianchi(133a)
Liberato Amendeo Anselmo
Bianchi(406)
Oto Maria Carmelo (Otto M.)
Bianchi(422)
Oto Maria Carmine Bianchi(388)
Bilancione,
Rosa Bilancione(128a)
Bilotta,
Antonetta Bilotta(122a)
Serafino Bilotta(122aF)
Blaze,
Frank Blaze(344aF)
Laura Blaze(344a)
Bonelli,
Angelina Bonelli(468)
Angelo Bonelli(271aF)
Angelo Bonelli(496)
Joseph Bonelli(271a)
Josephine Bonelli(519)
Mary Ann Bonelli(484)
Theresa Bonelli(542)
Bongo,
Giuseppa Bongo(445aM)
Maria Giuseppa Bongo(410aM)
Bonusiewicz,
Joanne Catherine
Bonusiewicz(473a)
Stanley Bonusiewicz(473aF)
Borelli,
Michele Borelli(248a)
Borganali,
Agnese Borganali(19bcM)
Borgo,
Nicoletta Borgo(435b)
Borriello,
Luigi Borriello(398aF)
Michele Borriello(398a)
Brand,
Diana Brand(582aM)
Brotherson,
Agnita Brotherson(493aM)
Bruno,
Anna Maria Bruno(7aM)
Brzezinska,
Mary M Brzezinska(428aM)
Buci,
Avelina Buci(437aM)

Buford,
Myra Ann Buford(606a)
Thomas C. Buford(606aF)
Burgess,
Albert Burgess(507aF)
George Francis Burgess(507a)
Byrne,
John Joseph Byrne(514a)
Cacciatore,
Alfonsa Cacciatore(479bM)
Cacetare,
Luiz Cacetare(281a)
Caiazzo,
Adreana Caiazzo(537aM)
Calabrese,
Bennedetto Calabrese(408aF)
Joseph Calabrese(408a)
Caminti,
Josephine Caminti(559aM)
Campagnola,
Anna Maria Campagnola(159aM)
Capenone,
Federico Capenone(330a)
Capillo,
Mary Capillo(436aM)
Capozzi,
Maria Rosa Capozzi(165aM)
Cappabianca,
Antoinette (Alice)
Cappabianca(416a)
Frank Cappabianca(416aF)
Cappelluzzo,
Carmine Cappelluzzo(272a)
Vito Cappelluzzo(272aF)
Caputo,
Raimonda Caputo(48aM)
Caraglia,
Maria Grazia Caraglia(88a)
Michele Caraglia(88aF)
Carbone,
Antonio Carbone(418aF)
Raffaele (Ralph) Carbone(418a)
Cardinale,
Antonio Cardinale(9ab)
Domenico Cardinale(334aF)
Raffaele Cardinale(334a)
Cargano,
Antonetta Cargano(337aM)
Carmello,
Carmelia Carmello(402aM)
Carmosino,
Bridgida Carmosino(103a)
Casiodoro,
Domenico Luigi Casiodoro(382a)
Giovanni Casiodoro(382aF)
Caso,
Lorenzo Caso(132bF)
Maria Grazia Caso(305aM)
Maria Rosa Caso(132b)

Casozzo,
    Raffaela Casozzo(187aM)
Castaldi,
    Carmine Castaldi(262aF)
    Grace Castaldi(262a)
Castellano,
    Carmelo Castellano(479aF)
    Francesco (Frank) Charles
    Castellano(479a)
Castrogiovanni,
    Francesco Castrogiovanni(436aF)
    Giuseppe Castrogiovanni(436a)
Cerino,
    Florence Cerino(327a)
    Giuseppe Cerino(327aF)
Ceruolo,
    Maria Luigia Ceruolo(291aM)
Cesarini,
    Giovanni Cesarini(296a)
Cetrone,
    Maria Concetta Cetrone(293aM)
Chino,
    Charles Chino(569aF)
Christian,
    Mary Angela Christian(505aM)
Ciano,
    Eleonora Ciano(21aM)
    Generoso Ciano(212aF)
    Marianna Ciano(212a)
    Raffaella Ciano(45aM)
Ciasullo,
    Anna Ciasullo(280)
    Antonia Ciasullo(231)
    Assunta Ciasullo(293)
    Caterina Ciasullo(261aM)
    Deloris Ciasullo(592)
    Fedele Ciasullo(105aF)
    Fedele Ciasullo(254)
    Fedele Ciasullo(82aF)
    Filippo Ciasullo(105a)
    Filippo Ciasullo(204)
    Giovanna(Jenny) Ciasullo(221)
    Giuseppe Ciasullo(262)
    Jennie Veronica Ciasullo(552)
    Maria Archina Ciasullo(357)
    Mariangela Ciasullo(232)
    Mariangela Ciasullo(325)
    Michele Ciasullo(245)
    Michele Ciasullo(310)
    Michele Ciasullo(320)
    Michele Ciasullo(82a)
    Pasquale Ciasullo(306)
    Pasqualina Ciasullo(340)
    Pasqualina Ciasullo(346)
    Raimonda Ciasullo(183)
    Raimonda Ciasullo(332)
Ciccarelli,
    Antonietta Ciccarelli(442)
    Carmine Ciccarelli(309)
    Domenica Ciccarelli(461)

    Domenico Ciccarelli(69a)
    Giuseppantonio Ciccarelli(132dF)
    Mariantonia Ciccarelli(132d)
    Nicola Ciccarelli(241)
    Raffaele Ciccarelli(69aF)
    Vincenzo Ciccarelli(288)
    Brigida Ciccorelli(254aM)
Cino,
    Frank Martin Cino(569a)
Cirella,
    Andrew Cirella(355aF)
    Mary Cirella(355a)
Cirillo,
    Maria Luigia Cirillo(69aX)
Cirminiello,
    Elvira B. Cirminiello(566a)
    William Cirminiello(566aF)
Civitello,
    Elvera Civitello(565a)
    Ralph Civitello(565aF)
Clericuzio,
    Adelina Clericuzio(108)
    Angelo Antonio Clericuzio(30)
    Anna Maria Clericuzio(272aM)
    Colomba Clericuzio(11)
    Ferdinando Clericuzio(3b)
    Francesco Clericuzio(3bF)
    Francesco Saverio Clericuzio(10)
    Giuseppe Clericuzio(373aF)
    Giuseppe Vittorio Emmaneule
    Clericuzio(98)
    Maria Amalia Clericuzio(40)
    Maria Carmina Clericuzio(35)
    Maria Clericuzio(47aM)
    Maria Consiglia Clericuzio(38)
    Marietta Clericuzio(373a)
    Metilda Francesca Clericuzio(109)
    Nicolantonio Clericuzio(9)
    Nicoletta Clericuzio(33)
    Raffaele Clericuzio(12)
Coari,
    Luigi Noris Coari(236bF)
    Sylvia Noris Coari(236b)
Colacicco,
    Terese Colacicco(487aM)
Colangelo,
    Felico Colangelo(397a)
    Michele Colangelo(397aF)
Colucci,
    Giovanna Colucci(124a)
    Romualdo Colucci(124aF)
Comanzo,
    Maria Michele Comanzo(427a)
    Pietro Comanzo(427aF)
    Rosa Comanzo(393aM)
Comunale,
    Mary Antoinette Comunale(*483aM)
Condello,
    Domenick Condello(486a)
    Joseph Condello(486aF)

Constantino,
>   George Constantino(446a)
>   Orazio Constantino(446aF)

Contivire,
>   Carmella Contivire(303aM)

Coppola,
>   Anna Maria Coppola(61a)
>   Leonardo Coppola(61aF)

Corsano,
>   Lucrezia Corsano(427aM)

Costa,
>   Camillo Costa(333a)
>   Jose Luiz Costa(333aF)
>   Maria Costa(532)

Costanzo,
>   Antonia Costanzo(165a)
>   Crescenzo Costanzo(165aF)
>   Rosaria Costanzo(426aM)

Covotta,
>   Anna Maria Covotta(34)
>   Antonio Covotta(119)
>   Antonio Covotta(11a)
>   Filippo Covotta(342aF)
>   Gaetano Covotta(37)
>   Gaetano Covotta(39)
>   Gaetano Giuseppe Luciano
>   Covotta(358)
>   Giovannina Covotta(330)
>   Giuseppe Ciriaco Michele
>   Covotta(342a)
>   Giuseppe Covotta(11aF)
>   Leonardo Covotta(15bF)
>   Liberato Covotta(603)
>   Liberatore Covotta(15b)
>   Maria Covotta(129)
>   Mariantonia Covotta(510aM)
>   Michele Covotta(122)
>   Raffaele Covotta(125)
>   Raffaele Covotta(31)

Cox,
>   Charles A. Cox(584bF)
>   Doris Cox(584b)

Coyne,
>   Joseph Coyne(493aF)
>   Josephine L. Coyne(493a)

Cretella,
>   Antonio Cretella(337aF)
>   Mary Rosaria Cretella(337a)

Cuoco,
>   Gaetano Cuoco(478aF)
>   Giovanni Cuoco(478a)

Cusano,
>   Maria Liberia Cusano
>   Maria Michele Cusano(88aM)
>   Nicola Cusano(297aF)
>   Pasquale Cusano(297a)

Czujak,
>   Helen Czujak(538aM)

d'Agostino,
>   Andrew James D'Agostino(*483aF)

Aurelina D'Agostino(6a)
Evelyn D'Agostino(*483a)
Marianna d'Agostino(406aM)
Michele D'Agostino(6aF)

d'Alessandro,
>   Maria Giuseppa
>   d'Alessandro(351aM)

D'Amato,
>   Elvira D'Amato(566aM)

d'Amico,
>   Concordia d'Amico(212aM)

d'Anastasio,
>   Francesco Paulo d'Anastasio(72aF)

D'Angelo,
>   Josephine D'Angelo(479aM)

d'Antuono,
>   Angiolina d'Antuono(397)
>   Elena D'Antuono(384)
>   Gabriele d'Antuono(135aF)
>   Gabriele D'Antuono(372)
>   Gabriele D'Antuono(375)
>   Maria Archina D'Antuono(426)
>   Nicola Maria d'Antuono(135a)

D'Auria,
>   Carmela D'Auria(394aM)

D'Ausilio,
>   Alfredo D'Ausilio(295)
>   Alfredo D'Ausilio(307)
>   Angela Maria D'Ausilio(276)
>   Angela Maria D'Ausilio(324)
>   Angelo Maria D'Ausilio(24)
>   Anna Maria D'Ausilio(72)
>   Anna Saveria D'Ausilio(112)
>   Anna Saveria D'ausilio(92)
>   Carminantonio D'ausilio(127)
>   Concetta D'Ausilio(207)
>   Concetta D'Ausilio(298)
>   Concetta D'Ausilio(329)
>   Eleanor Jane D'ausilio(597)
>   Felice (Felix) D'Ausilio(344)
>   Francesco d'Ausilio(1)
>   Francesco Saverio d'Ausilio(5)
>   Gabriele D'ausilio(107)
>   Gabriele D'ausilio(56)
>   Gennaro d'Ausilio(2)
>   Gennaro D'Ausilio(26)
>   Giovanni Battista (John B.)
>   D'ausilio(120)
>   Giulio D'Ausilio(341)
>   John Louis D'Ausilio(573)
>   Leopoldo D'ausilio(190)
>   Leopoldo D'Ausilio(242)
>   Letizia (Leatrice) D'ausilio(351)
>   Liberatore (Leon) D'Ausilio(335)
>   Lillian Joyce D'Ausilio(582)
>   Maria Concetta D'Ausilio(220)
>   Maria Filomina D'Ausilio(21)
>   Maria Francesca D'Ausilio(117)
>   Maria Guiseppa D'ausilio(19)
>   Maria Silveria D'Ausilio(113)

Mariangela d'Ausilio(15)
Mario Carmelo (Carmine) D'ausilio(100)
Nicola Maria d'Ausilio(7)
Nicola Maria D'Ausilio(83)
Nicoletta d'Ausilio(3)
Oto Maria D'ausilio(99)
Pasquale D'Ausilio(315)
Pasquale D'ausilio(63)
Raimonda d'Ausilio(16)
Raimonda D'Ausilio(272)
Salvatore Antonio D'ausilio(124)
Vincenza d'Ausilio(4)

D'Onofrio,
Maria Giovanna D'Onofrio(119a)

Damiano,
Rose Damiano(275a)

Davis,
Dorothy Dale Davis(433a)
Henry Pierce Davis(433aF)

Dawson,
James R. Dawson(481aX)

de Donato,
Luiz de Donato(539)
Pedro Miguel de Donato(548)
Rosa De Donato(529)
Vincenza de Donato(144aM)

De Lillo,
Angela De Lillo(401)
Carmina de Lillo(297aM)
Elena De Lillo(498a)
Gabriele de Lillo(279a)
Michele de Lillo(279aF)
Tommaso De Lillo

de Marco,
Maria Giuseppa de Marco(19bX)

De Polo,
Antonieta De Polo(317aM)
Josefina Emma Fasanelli De Polo(317a)

de Stefano,
Rosaria de Stefano(138aM)

DeCesare,
Margherita DeCesare(563aM)

deDonato,
Agata deDonato(75)
Aldo deDonato(363)
Angela deDonato(114)
Angela deDonato(130)
Angela deDonato(194)
Angelina DeDonato(270)
Angelo deDonato(355)
Antoinette DeDonato(599)
Antonetta DeDonato(466)
Antonio DeDonato(303)
Antonio deDonato(337)
Carmella deDonato(281)
Clementina DeDonato(266)
Conceição DeDonato(333)
Concetta DeDonato(292)

Concetta deDonato(66)
Domenico deDonato(103)
Domenico deDonato(274)
Domenico deDonato(319)
Domenico deDonato(61)
Domenico deDonato(8a)
Domenico deDonato(94)
Elena deDonato(354)
Eustachio deDonato(121)
Filippo deDonato(327)
Filippo deDonato(8aF)
Francesca deDonato(294)
Francesco deDonato(362)
Francesco Saverio deDonato(36)
Generoso deDonato(197)
Generoso deDonato(210)
Giuseppe deDonato(234)
Giuseppe deDonato(364)
Guido Michele deDonato(361)
Joseph DeDonato Sr.(568)
Lorenza Concetta deDonato(360)
Loretta DeDonato(563)
Luigi Anselmo deDonato(175)
Luigi deDonato(126)
Luigi deDonato(201)
Luigi deDonato(219)
Luigi deDonato(27)
Marcello deDonato(78)
Marcello Francesco Saviero deDonato(32)
Maria Carmela deDonato(85)
Maria Libera deDonato(342)
Maria Luigia deDonato(253)
Maria Nicoletta deDonato(18)
Maria Raimonda deDonato(14)
Michael deDonato(538)
Michael deDonato(557)
Michael DeDonato(589)
Michele deDonato(106)
Michele deDonato(23)
Michele deDonato(343)
Pasquale deDonato(352)
Pasquale Leonardo Pietro deDonato(222)
Phyllis Marie DeDonato(583)
Pietro deDonato(128)
Raimonda deDonato(104)
Raimonda deDonato(96)
Rosaria deDonato(123)
Teresa Concetta deDonato(348)

DeFelice,
Albert DeFelice(437a)
Alexander DeFelice(437aF)

Del Grappo,
Mary Del Grappo(405aM)

Del Sardo,
Bernice Rosaria Del Sardo(458aM)
Francesco Antonio Del Sardo(304aF)
Guiseppe Del Sardo(304a)

del Vecchio,
    Camina del Vecchio(135aM)
deLillo,
    Giuseppe deLillo(510a)
    Pasquale deLillo(510aF)
DellaRocco,
    Frank DellaRocco(597aF)
    James Frank DellaRocco(597a)
Delorenzo,
    Carmella Delorenzo(471aM)
Delpercio,
    Matteo Delpercio(557aF)
    Raffaela Maria Delpercio(557a)
DelPizzo,
    Domenick DelPizzo(559aF)
    Filoteo (Philip) John
    DelPizzo(559a)
DeMeo,
    Angelo DeMeo(202a)
    Angelo James DeMeo JR(503)
    Concetta DeMeo(408aM)
    Giovanni Raffaele (John)
    DeMeo(438)
    Lucy DeMeo(386)
    Michael Angelo DeMeo(475)
    Ralph Pasquale DeMeo(456)
    Rosina (Rose) DeMeo(408)
    Teresina (Teresa) DeMeo(392)
DeMicco,
    Josephine (Julia) DeMicco(434a)
    Louis DeMicco(434aF)
DeRinaldi,
    Giuseppa DeRinaldi(263aM)
DeVito,
    Francesca DeVito(328a)
    Pasquale DeVito(328aF)
Di Franza,
    Giovanna Di Franza(39a)
    Michele di Franza(39aF)
di Iesu,
    Maria Teresa di Iesu(160aM)
di Liberto,
    Lucia di Liberto(112aM)
Di Lillo,
    Angelo Maria Di Lillo(170)
    Angelo Maria di Lillo(322)
    Angelo Michele Di Lillo(217)
    Carmela di Lillo(302a)
    Francesco Di Lillo(302aF)
    Francesco di Lillo(52aF)
    Francesco di Lillo(95aF)
    Giovanna Di Lillo(250)
    Maria Antonia di Lillo(225)
    Maria Carmela di Lillo(251)
    Maria Giuseppa Di Lillo(147)
    Mariantonia Di Lillo(155)
    Nicola Maria Di Lillo(52a)
    Pasquale Di Lillo(215)
    Pasquale Di Lillo(249)
    Raffaele Di Lillo(95a)

    Rosa di Lillo(279)
di Maina,
    Maddalena di Maina(184aM)
di Palma,
    Giuseppa di Palma(15bM)
di Paolo,
    Colomba di Paolo(35aM)
di Pasquale,
    Colomba di Pasquale(247a)
    Giovanni di Pasquale(247aF)
di Pippo,
    Maria Luisa di Pippo(300aM)
Di Stefano,
    Orsola Di Stefano(9aM)
Di Stephano,
    Antonia Maria Di Stephano(335aM)
Di Vitto,
    Antonio Di Vitto(84)
    Loreta di Vitto(106a)
    Pietro Paolo Di Vitto(93)
    Tobia di Vitto(106aF)
DiBenedetto,
    Mary DiBenedetto(583aM)
diDonato,
    Anna Maria diDonato(11aM)
    Maria Concordia diDonato(29)
diFuria,
    Mariantonia diFuria(63aM)
DiGrottola,
    Mariantonia DiGrottola(150aM)
    Anna diGruttola(14aM)
    Anna diGruttola(18aM)
DiLillo,
    Angelo Michele DiLillo(268)
    Francesco diLillo(184)
    Nicola diLillo(318)
diMaina,
    Ciriaco diMaina(460aF)
    Oto Maria diMaina(460a)
Dioguardi,
    Luigi Dioguardi(179aF)
    Maria Carmela Dioguardi(179a)
diPaola,
    Raffaele diPaola(184ab)
Dipasquale,
    Anthony Dipasquale(438aF)
    Lucy Mary Dipasquale(438a)
diStefano,
    Angela Maria diStefano(1a)
diTorio,
    Giuseppe (Joseph) diTorio(491aF)
    Marie diTorio(491a)
diVitto,
    Gennaro diVitto(50)
    Maria Rosa diVitto(59)
    Michele diVitto(16aF)
    Michele diVitto(54)
    Raimondo diVitto(16a)
    Saveria diVitto(460aM)

Domenstein,
        Jack Domenstein(524a)
        Robert Domenstein(524aF)
Domiano,
        Francesco Domiano(275aF)
Donisi,
        Eugenia Donisi(101a)
        Giuseppe Donisi(101aF)
Dos Santos,
        Luis Dos Santos(194a)
Dotolo,
        Giuseppe Dotolo(48aF)
        Maria Fransesca Paola
        Dotolo(48a)
Dragoni,
        Anna M. Dragoni(535)
        Anthony E. Dragoni(580)
        John Dragoni(543)
        Nicola Giuseppe Amato
        Dragoni(324a)
        Raffaele Dragoni(324aF)
        Rita Dragoni(576)
Duryea,
        Gildie Duryea(524aM)
        Jack D. Duryea(524a)
Errico,
        Marianna Errico(324aM)
Esposito,
        Fiore Esposito(537aF)
        Gilda E. Esposito(537a)
Evenson,
        Einer Evenson(477aF)
        June Elisabeth Evenson(477a)
Failla,
        Jennie Failla(569aM)
        Margaret Falvino(443aM)
Faratro,
        Rocco Faratro(419a)
Faretra,
        Carmina Faretra(225aM)
Farisco,
        Rosaria Farisco(352aM)
Federici,
        Franc Dominick Federici(599a)
        Frank Federici(599aF)
Feola,
        Benjamin Feola(563aF)
        Maria Constadina Feola(90bM)
        Peter Victor Feola(563a)
Feriero,
        Giovanni Feriero(265a)
        Giuseppe Feriero(265aF)
Ferrante,
        Concetta Ferrante(405a)
        Pasquale Ferrante(405aF)
Ferrara,
        Joseph Ferrara(450aF)
        Lucia Ferrara(348aM).
        Rose Ferrara(450a)

Ferrario,
        Ambrogio Ferrario(571aF)
        Cathy Elizabeth Ferrario(571a)
Ferraro,
        Carmela Ferraro(18ab)
        Filomena Ferraro(106aM)
Ferriero,
        Carmine Ferriero(415aF)
        Paolo Ferriero(415a)
Fiorenza,
        Antonio Fiorenza(111)
        Aurelia Fiorenza(55)
        Gaetano Fiorenza(13a)
        Giovanni Fiorenza(81)
        Maria Rosa Fiorenza(43)
        Maria Rosa Fiorenza(65)
        Mariantonia Fiorenza(91)
        Nicola Fiorenza(13aF)
        Nicola Fiorenza(47)
        Rosa Fiorenza(69)
Fodarella,
        Anna Maria Fodarella(57)
        Antonio Maria Fodarella(89)
        Carmela Fodarella(244)
        Domenico Fodarella(141)
        Domenico Fodarella(15a)
        Domenico Fodarella(174)
        Francesca Paula Fodarella(459)
        Giuseppantonio Fodarella(161)
        Giuseppe Fodarella(15aF)
        Giuseppe Fodarella(73)
        Lorenzo Fodarella(421)
        Lorenzo Fodarella(48)
        Luigi Fodarella(188)
        Maria Concordia Fodarella(42)
        Maria Francesca Fodarella(64)
        Maria Raimonda Fodarella(203)
        Mariangela Fodarella(146)
        Mariangela Fodarella(229)
        Mariantonia Fodarella(152)
        Mariantonia Fodarella(79)
        Nicola Fodarella(278aX)
        Oto Maria Fodarella(102)
        Raffaele Fodarella(41)
        Raffaele Fodarella(441)
Fodrella,
        Otomaria Fodrella(214)
Foley,
        Lillian M. Foley(584aM)
Ford,
        Bela L. Ford(451aM)
Forte,
        Elaine Forte(577a)
Fortunato,
        Antonietta Fortunato(376a)
        Vincenzo Fortunato(376aF)
Frisone,
        Carmen Frisone(522a)
        Pasquale Frizone(522aF)

Fulton,
        Bernard Webster Fulton(542a)
        Daniel Webster Fulton(542aF)
Gagliardo,
        Maria Assunta Gagliardo(459aM)
Gaina,
        Matthew Simon Gaina(271b)
Galdi,
        Anna Galdi(488aM)
Galluzzi,
        Natalie Marie Galluzzi(546aX)
Gammaroto,
        Carmenella Gammaroto(200a)
        Domenico A Gammaroto(200aF)
Garafano,
        Joseph T. Garafano(425aF)
        Louise Teresa Garafano(425a)
Garber,
        Jean Louise Garber(559)
        Theodore Anthony Garber(606)
        Theodore Taft Garber(339a)
        William Garber(339aF)
Gattis,
        (unknown) Gattis(433ac)
Gelormini,
        Maria Roseria Gelormini(322aM)
Gelormino,
        Carmina Gelormino(66aM)
        Luigi Gelormino(362aF)
        Saveria Gelormino(362a)
Genita,
        Antonia Genita(74aM)
Gentile,
        Angela Gentile(418)
        Maria Virginia Gentile(404)
        Pasquale Gentile(192a)
        Rosina Gentile(387)
Gentry,
        Minnie E. Gentry(517aM)
George,
        Frances Roselyn George(546)
        Louis William George(494)
        Louise George(570)
Gerardi,
        Giuseppe Gerardi(518aF)
        Mary Gerardi(518a)
Gerino,
        Giuseppe Gerino(328aF)
Gesa,
        Carmine Gesa(58aF)
        Maria Lucia Gesa(58a)
Giacabbe,
        Angela Felicia Giacabbe(304aM)
Giannario,
        Antonio Giannario(99aF)
        Maria Gabriella Giannario(99a)
        Isabella Gianpaolo(19aM)
Giardino,
        Francesco Paolo Giardino(132aF)
        Giovanna Giardino(132a)

        Vincenzo Giardino(296aSF)
Gibson,
        Charlie Thomas Gibson(484aF)
        Thomas Elmo Gibson(484a)
Gignac,
        Eugene J. Gignac(454aF)
        Mary A. Gignac(454a)
Giorgione/George,
        Alfred Lorenzo
        Giorgione/George(512)
        Antonio (Anthony)
        Giorgione/George(206)
        Carmine (Carmen Louis)
        Giorgione/George(290)
        Giuseppe (Joseph)
        Giorgione/George(263)
        Josephine Giorgione/George(502)
        Luigi (Louis)
        Giorgione/George(86)
        Maria Silveria Francesca
        (Frances) Giorgione/George(311)
        Raffaele (Ralph) Giorgione/
        George(490)
Giorgione,
        Antonia Giorgione(191)
        Antonio Giorgione(21a)
        Antonio Giorgione(278)
        Filomena Giorgione(216)
        Filomena Giorgione(248)
        Francesco Paolo Giorgione(328)
        Francesco Paulo Giorgione(97)
        Giuseppe Giorgione(228)
        Luigi Giorgione(71)
        Maria Giuseppa Giorgione(241aM)
        Maria Liberia Giorgione(60)
        Maria Luigia Giorgione(316)
        Michele Giorgione(264)
        Nicola Giorgione(356)
        Oto Giorgione(21aF)
        Raffaele Giorgione(233)
        Raffaele Giorgione(80)
        Rosa Giorgione(300)
        Rosa Giorgione(51)
        Rose Louise Giorgione(339)
Glovicko,
        Helen Marie Glovicko(476a)
        Steve Glovicko(476aF)
Gointa,
        Tomasina Gointa(355aM)
Goodman,
        Alfredo Lawrence Goodman(512)
Gowing,
        William Thompson Gowing(517ab)
Grande,
        Joseph Grande(551a)
Grass,
        Juliana Grass(477aM)
Grassie,
        Mabel Grassie(236a)

Grasso,
	Angelo Grasso(35aF)
	Anna Maria Grasso(132cM)
	Antonio Grasso(140)
	Antonio Grasso(276)
	Antonio Grasso(35a)
	Carmela Grasso(223)
	Carosino Grasso(39aM)
	Caterina Grasso(132dM)
	Caterina Grasso(382aM)
	Clorinda Grasso(131aM)
	Crescenzo Grasso(76a)
	Domenico Grasso(151a)
	Ferdinand (Fred Louis)
	Grasso(594)
	Floriano Grasso(258)
	Floriano Grasso(76aF)
	Gabriele Grasso(24aF)
	Giovanbattista Grasso(240)
	Giovanbattista Grasso(45aF)
	Giovanna Grasso(196)
	Giovanna Grasso(294aM)
	Giovanni Battista Grasso(162)
	Gloria Grasso(579)
	Lorenzo Grasso(45a)
	Lucia Grasso(149)
	Lucia Grasso(172a)
	Maria Concetta Grasso(24a)
	Maria Giovanna Grasso(99aM)
	Maria Giuseppa Grasso(167)
	Maria Grasso(296)
	Maria Grasso(8aM)
	Maria Raffaella Grasso(185)
	Maria Vincenza Grasso(293aX)
	Michele Grasso(151aF)
	Michele Grasso(211)
	Raffaella Grasso(173)
	Raimonda Grasso(158)
	Raimonda Grasso(177)
	Rosa Grasso(144)
	Rosa Grasso(403)
	Savino Grasso(172aF)
Gravel,
	Exilda Adeline Gravel(508aM)
Graziano,
	Loreta Graziano(42aM)
	Luigi Graziano(316a)
	Maria Michele Graziano(36aM)
	Michele Graziano(316aF)
Grillo,
	Maria Libera Grillo(124aM)
Guardabascio,
	Filomena Guardabascio(406a)
	Francesco Paolo
	Guardabascio(406aF)
	Raffaela Guardabascio(182aM)
	Raffaella Guardabascio(378aM)
Guarendi,
	Angelantonio (Angelo)
	Guarente/Guarendi(403a)

Guarente,
	Nicola Guarente(403aF)
Guarraci,
	Jennie Guarraci(379a)
Guerra,
	Elise Guerra(499aM)
	Julia Guerra(416aM)
Guide,
	Mary N. Guide(438aM)
Harlan,
	Felix Harlan(451ab)
Hatcher,
	Nina Alice Hatcher(542aM)
Haugner,
	Blanche Haugner(517cM)
Heater,
	Edith Heater(494aM)
Holden,
	Dorothy A. Holden(589a)
	Frederick Holden(589aF)
Holland,
	Madelene F. Holland(535aM)
Howe,
	Margaret Howe(592aM)
Iacoviello,
	Camilla Iacoviello(90aM)
Iannarona,
	Filomena Iannarona(87aM)
Iannarone,
	Angelo Iannarone(353a)
	Concetta Iannarone(69aM)
	Giocchino Iannarone(160aF)
	Maria Luigia Iannarone(160a)
	Maria Rosaria Iannarone(373aM)
	Raffaella Iannarone(251aM)
	Rosaria Iannarone(132aM)
	Sabato Iannarone(353aF)
Ianniciello,
	Alfonso Ianniciello(458a)
	Bartolomes Ianniciello(458aF)
Iannone,
	Giuseppe Iannone(47bF)
	Maria Carmela Iannone(47b)
Ienge,
	Carmina Ienge(2aM)
Impara,
	Carminella Impara(478aM)
Incerto,
	Gelsomina (Josephine)
	Incerto(434aM)
Inglese,
	Maria Inglese(360aM)
Iodice,
	Giustiniana Iodice(151aM)
Ionno,
	Lorenzo Ionno(47bX)
Janokowicz,
	Egnitz Janokowicz(409aF)
	Helen Janokowicz(409a)

Johnston,
        Virginia Mae Johnston(433aM)
Jorgensen,
        Jerry Austin Jorgensen(519a)
        Jerry Peter Jorgensen(519aF)
Jumper,
        Lillian Agnes Jumper(490aM)
Kalakay,
        Charles Paul Kalakay(573bX)
Kanetzke,
        Henry Kanetzke(414a)
        Julius Kanetzke(414aF)
Key,
        Helen M. Key(519cM)
Keyser,
        Gordon R. Keyser(567aF)
        Kathleen Keyser(567a)
Kiebel,
        Hulda Kiebel(414aM)
Knopa,
        Catherine Knopa(344aM)
Krause,
        Clara Martha Krause(517bM)
Kurtzenacker,
        John Terris Kurtzenacker
        III(335ab)
Kuszyk,
        Rozalia Kuszyk(570aM)
LaBollita,
        Albert LaBollita(579a)
        Joseph LaBollita(579aF)
Laluna,
        Francesco Laluna(335aF)
        Helen Eleanor LaLuna(335a)
        Maria Michele LaLuna(86aM)
Landau,
        Maurice Landau(582aF)
        Richard Irving Landau(582a)
Lanzi,
        Augusto Lanzi(341aF)
        Raffella Lanzi(341a)
Leggiadro,
        Giovannina (Jennie)
        Leggiadro(395)
        Luigi Leggiadro(167a)
Lehr,
        (unknown) Lehr(519b)
Leikert,
        Gudrun Ingrid Leikert(554a)
Leone,
        Giovanni Leone(90aF)
        Maria Cristina Sofia Leone(90a)
Liguori,
        Ciro Liguori(602aF)
        Gennaro Liguori(602a)
Lo Calzo,
        Pasquale Lo Calzo(305aF)
lo Conte,
        Antonia lo Conte(322a)
        Antonio Lo Conte(205aF)

Francesco Paolo Lo Conte(205a)
        Lucrezia Lo Conte(376aM)
        Rosaria Lo Conte(55aM)
        Serafina Lo Conte(51aM)
Lo Surdo,
        Vincenza Lo Surdo(213aM)
LoCalzo,
        Agata Maria LoCalzo(5aM)
        Agostino LoCalzo(305a)
LoConte,
        Angiolina LoConte(492)
        Antonetta LoConte(410a)
        Antonio LoConte(455)
        Eugenia LoConte(110a)
        Generoso LoConte(410aF)
        Generoso loConte(445aF)
        Giuseppe LoConte(435)
        Maria Liberata LoConte(415aM)
        Maria LoConte(398)
        Michele LoConte(110aF)
        Michele LoConte(322aF)
        Rosa loConte(223aM)
        Vincenza loConte(445a)
Loder,
        Clara Loder(417aM)
LoFrese,
        Joseph LoFrese(487aF)
        Robert Eustacchio LoFrese(487a)
Lombardi,
        Adamo Lombardi(282)
        Adamo (Adam Carl) Lombardi(312)
        Carmen Maria Lombardi(507)
        Eleanor Lombardi(436)
        Feliciano Lombardi(198)
        Feliciano Lombardi(218)
        Feliciano (Phillip White)
        Lombardi(236)
        Feliciano Lombardi(85aF)
        Ferdinand Lombardi(276aF)
        George Vincent Lombardi(473)
        Grace Delores Lombardi(524)
        Mariantonia Lombardi(16aM)
        Mary Lombardi(276a)
        Nicholas F. Lombardi(572a)
        Phillip Adam Lombardi(517)
        Raymond Coari Lombardi(516)
        Saverio Lombardi(252)
        Saverio Lombardi(261)
        Vincenzo (James) Lombardi(85a)
Lombardo,
        Frances Lombardo(572aF)
Ludwig,
        Charles Lewis Ludwig(546a)
        William A Ludwig(546aF)
Luongo,
        Cresenzo Luongo(291bF)
        Nicola Luongo(291b)
Macchiaverna,
        Giovanni Macchiaverna(39bF)
        Raffaela Macchiaverna(39b)

Mackenzie,
    Alan James Mackenzie(543aF)
    Ruth Erline Mackenzie(543a)
Madera,
    Anna Madera(513aM)
Maggese,
    Carmina Maggese(3bM)
Mainiero,
    Maria Rosa Mainiero(27aM)
    Mariah Leonarda Mainiero(420aM)
Maioran,
    Benny Maioran(527aF)
    Jules B. Maioran(527a)
Maioribus,
    Lucia Rachele Maioribus(319aM)
Maletesta,
    Catarina Maletesta(403aM)
Malinari,
    José Fasanelli Malinari(317aF)
Mancino,
    Agostino Mancino(150a)
    Amelia Mancino(420)
    Antonio Mancino(393)
    Luigi Mancino(150aF)
    Luigi Mancino(381)
Mancuso,
    Joseph Mancuso(403b)
Mandella,
    Vera Paz Mandella(524bM)
Manganiello,
    Carmela Manganiello(205)
    Ciriaco Manganiello(159)
    Ciriaco (Jerry) Manganiello(180)
    Ciriaco Manganiello(57aF)
    Ciriaco Manganiello(64aF)
    Concetta Manganiello(135)
    Concordia Manganiello(267)
    Genoveffa Carmna Maria
    Manganiello(419)
    Giuseppe Manganiello(64a)
    Ida Manganiello(467)
    Maria Annuziata Manganiello(148)
    Maria Carmela Manganiello(168)
    Maria Manganiello(378)
    Maria Michele Manganiello(137)
    Mariangela Manganiello(151)
    Mariangela Manganiello(255)
    Mariannina Manganiello(305)
    Mariantonia Manganiello(163)
    Mariantonia Manganiello(171)
    Michele Manganiello(138)
    Oto Manganiello(286)
    Raimondo Carmine
    Manganiello(427)
    Raimondo Manganiello(182)
    Raimondo Manganiello(79a)
    Raimondo Manganiello(528)
    Vincenzo Manganiello(193)
    Vincenzo Manganiello(57a)
    Vincenzo Manganiello(79aF)

    Virginia Manganiello(413)
Manna,
    Luigi Manna(352aF)
    Rosina Manna(352a)
Maraio,
    Carmina Maraio(168aM)
Marasciulo,
    Angelina Marasciulo(311aM)
Marasco,
    Margherita Adele Maria
    Marasco(263a)
    Orzono Marasco(263aF)
Marcotti,
    Hilda (Gilda) Marcotti(166a)

Mariano,
    Gabriele Mariano(83aF)
    Giustina Mariano(83a)
Marraffino,
    Antonio Marraffino(28)
    Francesco Saverio Marraffino(17)
    Francesco Saviero Marraffino(3a)
    Maria Angela Marraffino(8)
    Maria Michele Marraffino(25)
    Maria Rosaria Marraffino(20)
    Maria Rosaria Marraffino(22)
    Maria Vincenza Marraffino(13)
    Nicola Angelo Marraffino(6)
Marrone,
    Giuditta Marrone(188a)
Marseglia,
    Francesco Paolo Marseglia(351aF)
    Luigi Marseglia(351a)
Martin,
    Agnes M. Martin(454aM)
Martorana,
    Antonino Martorana(479bF)
    August Francis Martorana(479b)
Mase,
    Giovanni (John) Mase(583aF)
    Isadore (I) Anthony Mase(583a)
Massimiano,
    Carmina Massimiano(78aM)
Mastantuono,
    Marianna Mastantuono(179aM)
Mastrangelo,
    Angela Mastrangelo(298aM)
Masucci,
    Carmine Masucci(287aF)
    Filomena Masucci(557aM)
    Fioritta (Fanny)
        Masucci(287a)
Matucgras,
    Mary Matucgras(599aM)
Mature,
    Angelina Mature(472aM)
Mauro,
    Francesco Mauro(159aF)
    Maria Concetta Mauro(159a)

Mazzella,
    Caterine Mazzella(518aF)
McElroy,
    Sarah Jane McElroy(507aM)
McEntee,
    Francis H McEntee(556aF)
    Margaret Mary McEntee(556a)
Melchiondo/Marchino,
    Florence
    Melchiondo/Marchino(578a)
Mele,
    Josephine Mele(276aM)
Melito,
    Concetta Melito(36a)
    Joseph Melito(395aF)
    Maria Gabriella Melito(397aM)
    Maria Giovanna Melito(255aM)
    Maria Melito(463aM)
    Nicolantonio Melito(36aF)
    Otantonio (Anthony) Melito(395a)
Meninno,
    Francesca Meninno(200aM)
    Rosina Meninno(366aM)
Merlucci,
    Nicolina Merlucci(90b)
    Pasquale Merlucci(90bF)
Merola,
    Giovanni Merola(289aF)
    Maria Giovanna (Jennie)
        Merola(289a)
Messelotta,
    Fanny Messelotta(432aM)
Messina,
    Frank Messina(432a)
    Mariano Messina(432aF)
Mezick,
    Elaine Mezick(568a)
    John Mezick(568aF)
Michalowski,
    Bertha Michalowski(290a)
Miedico,
    Angela Maria Miedico(27a)
    Anna Maria Miedico(205aM)
    Filomena Miedico(435a)
    Giuseppe Miedico(27aF)
Migliucci,
    Anna Migliucci(602aM)
Miller,
    Eula N Miller(546aM)
Mincieli,
    Teresa Mincieli(407aM)
Mincolelli / Mingolello,
    Generoso (Joseph)
    Mincolelli/Mingolello(294a)
    Angela Maria Mincolelli(172aM)
    Antonio Mincolelli(241aF)
    Leonardantonio Mincolelli(294aF)
    Leonardo Antonio
    Mincolelli(254aF)
    Lucia Mincolelli(241a)

Rosaria Mincolelli(254a)
Concetta Mingolelli(214aM)
Mingolello,
    Anthony (Tony) Mingolello(508)
    Giovanna (Jennie)
    Mingolello(499)
    Ida Loretta Mingolello(530)
    Joseph Mingolello(294a)
    Ralph George Mingolello(558)
Miniscalco,
    Giuseppe Miniscalco(138aF)
    Pasqualina Miniscalco(138a)
Minotti,
    Anna Minotti(319a)
    Domenicantonio Minotti(319aF)
Miressi,
    Agata Miressi(142)
    Angela Miressi(291)
    Angelina Miressi(486)
    Angelo Maria Miressi(370)
    Biagio Miressi(172)
    Carmela Miressi (464)
    Ciriaco Miressi(273)
    Filomena Miressi(134)
    Frances Eva Miressi(487)
    Francesco Paolo Miressi(367)
    Generoso Miressi(145)
    Generoso Miressi(160)
    Giovanni Miressi(226)
    Giovanni Miressi(574)
    Giovannina Miressi(374)
    Giuseppe Miressi(368)
    Giuseppe Miressi(369)
    Giuseppe Miressi(383)
    Giuseppe Miressi(51a)
    John (Jack) Miressi(450)
    John William Miressi(540)
    Joseph Miressi(434)
    Maria Miressi(192)
    Maria Rosa Maria Domenica Maria
    Libera Miressi(390)
    Nicolangelo Miressi(51aF)
    Nicolantonio Miressi(132)
    Rosalind Miressi(497)
    Teresa Miressi(412)
    Virgilia Miressi(399)
Miseno,
    Bruno Miseno(472)
    Francesco Miseno(457)
    Lorenzo Miseno(238aF)
    Luciano Miseno(428)
    Ugo Miseno(238a)
    Ugo Ralph Miseno(485)
Miszkowski,
    Mary Miszkowski(409aM)
Monaco,
    Maria Michele Monaco(132c)
    Oto Maria Monaco(132cF)
    Raffaela Monaco(132bM)

Mondo,
      Rocco Mondo(407aF)
      Vito Rocco Mondo(407a)
Montecalvo,
      Caterina Montecalvo(126a)
Monteleone,
      Emilie Monteleone(472a)
      William Monteleone(472aF)
Moore,
      Ida Moore(540aM)
Morante,
      Elena Morante(193a)
Morganti,
      Alex Morganti(502a)
      Anthony Morganti(502aF)
Mortka,
      Stanley Mortka(392a)
Moscaritolo,
      Rosario Moscaritolo(353aM)
Moschella,
      Antonietta Moschella(525)
      Antonio Moschella(255a)
      Giovanna Moschella(452)
      Giuseppina Moschella(509)
      Michele Moschella(255aF)
      Michele Moschella(462)
Mosher,
      John Mosher(497a)
      John Mosher(497aF)
Muto,
      Elizabetta Muto(291bM)
Nadeau,
      Rose Nadeau(580aM)
Neri,
      Rosa Neri(236bM)
Nestor,
      Susie M. Nestor(567aM)
Ninfadoro,
      Anna Maria Ninfadoro(143)
      Anthony Ninfadoro(411)
      Antonio Ninfadoro(179)
      Concetta Ninfadoro(209)
      Edward Ninfadoro(471)
      Eleonora Ninfadoro(439)
      Enrico Ninfadoro(489)
      Gabriel Ninfadoro(402)
      Gabriele Giovanni Ninfadoro(474)
      Gabriele Ninfadoro(67a)
      Giovanni Ninfadoro(243)
      Maria Ninfadoro(156)
      Oto Ninfadoro(165)
Nuno,
      Frances Rico Nuno(312a)
      Guillermo Nuno(312aF)
Occhiuto,
      Louis Vincent Occhiuto(475aF)
      Marie Helen Occhiuto(475a)
Orlando,
      Antonio Orlando(19aF)
      Giuseppe Orlando(44)

      Pasquale Orlando(19a)
      Rosa Orlando(6aM)
Orton,
      Mary Ann Orton(226aM)
Paduano,
      Giuseppe Paduano(74aF)
      Tommasina Paduano(74a)
Pagano,
      Maria Liberia Pagano(110aM)
Palladino,
      Emma Palladino(474a)
      Nicola Palladino(474aF)
Pallini,
      Sabina Pallini(475aM)
Pallitto,
      Anthony Pallitto(482aF)
      Vincent James Pallitto(482a)
Pannese,
      Angelo Pannese(213a)
      Antonio Pannese(420a)
      Ciriaco Pannese(213aF)
      Giovanni Pannese(420aF)
      Maria Vincenza Pannese(448)
      Tommasina Pannese(510)
Pantalone,
      Jennie Pantalone(522aM)
Panza,
      Ciriaco Panza(152a)
      Francesco Panza(152aF)
      Francesco Panza(244aF)
      Giuseppe Panza(445)
      Lorenzo Panza(410)
      Maria Rosa Panza(382)
      Pasquale Panza(244a)
      Raffaele Panza(376)
Panzetta,
      Rosa Panzetta(13aM)
Paone,
      Giuseppe Paone(378a)
      Giuseppe Paone(378aF)
      Maria Giovanna Paone(182a)
      Pasquale Paone(467aF)
      Raffaele Paone(182aF)
      Vincenzo Paone(467a
Paracchia,
      Grazia Paracchia(412aM)
Paradiso,
      Donato Paradiso(530aF)
      Patsy F. Paradiso(530a)
Parcaro,
      Gerard (Jerry) P. Parcaro(443a)
      Ralph Parcaro(443aF)
Paris,
      John Antonio Paris(597bF)
      Joseph John Paris(597b)
Pastore,
      Nicoletta Pastore(396aM)
      Raffaele Pastore(396a)
Patterson,
      Anthony W. Patterson(508aF)

Pauline Rose Patterson(508a)

Pavia,
 Jane Pavia(520a)
 Leonard Pavia(520aF)

Peabody,
 Catherine Peabody(481aM)

Peluso,
 Angela Maria Peluso(2a)
 Nicola Peluso(2aF)

Pennacchio,
 Giovanni Antonio
 Pennacchio(285aF)
 Maria Saveria Pennacchio(58aM)
 Michele Pennacchio(285a)

Pepe,
 Loreta Pepe(346aM)

Perillo,
 Filomena (Fannie) Perillo(463a)
 Giuseppe Perillo(463aF)
 Giuseppe Perillo(86aF)
 Maria Giovanna Perillo(86a)

Perine,
 Violet Perine(485a)

Perini,
 Settemia Perini(358a)

Perkins,
 John Perkins(592aF)
 Lawrence R. Perkins(592a)

Perrina,
 Angela Perrina(52)
 Angelo Maria Perrina(74)
 Angelo Michele Perrina(444)
 Angelo Perrina(326)
 Angelo Perrina(533)
 Anna Maria Perrina(45)
 Anna Perrina(76)
 Antonio Perrina(139)
 Antonio Perrina(224)
 Antonio Perrina(260)
 Arminio Perrina(345)
 Arminio Perrina(359)
 Armino Perrina(366)
 Bennedetto Perrina(239a)
 Carmine Perrina(247)
 Ciriaco Perrina(62)
 Concetta Felicia Perrina(238)
 Concetta Perrina(157)
 Concetta Perrina(184a)
 Elisabetta Giovanna Perrina(301)
 Elisabetta Perrina(256)
 Emmiddio Giovanni Perrina(269)
 Filomena Perrina(53)
 Filomena Perrina(82)
 Francesco Paolo Perrina(68)
 Francesco Paolo Perrina(90)
 Giovanna Perrina(366aF)
 Giovannina Perrina(285)
 Giuseppa Perrina(297)
 Leonardantonio Perrina(14aF)
 Leonardantonio Perrina(18aF)

Leonardo Perrina(184aF)
Liberatore Perrina(18a)
Liberatore Perrina(200)
Lucia Perrina(52aM)
Lucia Perrina(95aM)
Luigi Ermino Perrina(314)
Luigi Perrina(277)
Maria Amalia Perrina(336)
Maria Amalia Perrina(353)
Maria Carssina Perrina(347)
Maria Felicita Perrina(239)
Maria Giovanna Perrina(105)
Maria Luigia Perrina(366a)
Maria Maddalena Perrina(458)
Maria Perrina(154)
Maria Perrina(202)
Maria Raimonda Perrina(304)
Maria Rosaria Perrina(334)
Mariangela Perrina(46)
Mariangela Perrina(49)
Mariangela Perrina(67)
Mariangela Perrina(77)
Mariantonia Perrina(213)
Michelangelo Perrina(176)
Michelangelo Perrina(275)
Michele Perrina(239aF)
Michele Perrina(88)
Oto Maria Perrina(14a)
Oto Maria Perrina(186)
Pasquale Perrina(246)
Pasqualina Perrina(265)
Raffaele Perrina(58)
Raffaele Perrine(480)
Raimonda Perrina(95)
Rosaria Perrina(227)
Salvatore Perrina(302)

Perrine,
 Anthony Carmen Perrine(488)
 Elena (Helen) Perrine(465)
 John Perrine(417)
 Paul (Frank) Perrine(433)
 Ralph Carmen Perrine(531)
 Rena Perrine(569)
 Sofia (Susie) Perrine(446)
 Theresa Ann Perrine(551)

Perrino,
 Angelo Joseph Perrino(556)
 Angelo Mario Perrino(481)
 Dorothy Lillian Perrino(506)
 Edward Laurie Perrino(454)
 Eleanor Margaret Perrino(505)
 Frances Michele Perrino(565)
 Mary Jenuvieve Perrino(514)
 Pasquale (Patsy) Perrino(287)
 Ralph M. Perrino(537)
 Teresa Alba Perrino(437)
 Victor Vincent Perrino(425)
 Vittorio Perrino(187)

Perrotta,
 Antonio Perrotta(12aF)

Pescatore,
  Concetta Pescatore(51aX)
Petrosino,
  Fillipo Petrosino(7aF)
  Saveria Maria Petrosino(7a)
Petruccelli,
  Aurelio Fedele Petruccelli(360a)
  Raffaele Petruccelli(360aF)
Pettinato,
  Gesuela Pettinato(298aX)
Pezzuto,
  Antonio Pezzuto(524bF)
  Vincent Mike Pezzuto(524b)
Pierro,
  Giuseppe Pierro(459a)
  Raffaele Pierro(459aF)
Pietracola,
  Antonio Pietracola(212)
  Maria Carmelo Pietracola(237)
  Mariangela Pietracola(189)
  Pasqualantonio Pietracola(55b)
  Pasquale Pietracola(453)
  Raffaele Pietracola(55bF)
Pocetta,
  Pocetta(529a)
Politano,
  Giuseppe Politano(78aF)
  Maria Rosa Politano(78a)
Polleck,
  Alphonse A. Polleck(584aF)
  Anmarie Polleck(584a)
Popolo,
  Angelina Popolo(395aM)
Portogallo,
  Bonaventura Portogallo(131aF)
  Giovanna Portogallo(131a)
Pratola,
  Rosa Pratola(152aM)
  Rosa Pratola(244aM)
Prezioso,
  Francesco Paolo Prezioso(261aF)
  Giovanna Prezioso(261a)
Prudente,
  Maria Teresa Prudente(247aM)
Puorro,
  Filippo Puorro(12aX)
  Giuseppe Puorro(426aF)
  Michele Puorro(426a)
Puzo,
  Maria Saveria Puzo(393a)
  Michele Puzo(393aF)
  Carmela Raso(403bX)
Rawson,
  Ann K. Rawson(580a)
  John Rawson(580aF)
Rendesi,
  Maria Clemenzia Rendesi(24aM)
Reynolds,
  Bryan W. Reynolds(451aF)

  Katherine Patricia
  Reynolds(451a)
Ricci,
  Carmela Ricci(187a)
  Vincenzo Ricci(187aF)
Riccio,
  Angela Maria Riccio(214a)
  Angelo H Riccio(518)
  Angelo Maria Riccio(183a)
  Anna Riccio(424)
  Anthony Riccio(483)
  Antonio Riccio(132dX)
  Concetta Riccio(381aM)
  Filomena Riccio(316aM)
  Filomena Riccio(447)
  Giovanni Riccio(214aF)
  Giovanni Riccio(251a)
  Maria Michela Riccio(460)
  Marianna Riccio(400)
  Marianna Riccio(561)
  Michael Sam Riccio(463)
  Michele Riccio(251aF)
  Peter Attilio Riccio(491)
  Philomena (Filomena) B
  Riccio(522)
  Pietro Riccio(183aF)(221aF)
  Pietro Riccio(440)
  Pietro Riccio(W183aF)(W221aF)
  Raffaele Riccio(221a)
Rice,
  Nancy Rice(573a)
Rico,
  Ester Rico(312aM)
Rinaldi,
  Carmina Rinaldi(500)
  Maria Rinaldi(303a)
  Miguel Rinaldi(303aF)
Rizzo,
  Mary Rizzo(597bM)
Rogazzo,
  Luigia Rogazzo(79aM)
  Vincenza Rogazzo(57ab)
Romagna,
  Concordia Romagna(418aM).
Romanella,
  Carmella Romanella(402a)
  Vincent Romanella(402aF)
Romanelli,
  Roslina Romanelli(471a)
  Vincenzo (James)
  Romanelli(471aF)
Romano,
  Generoso Romano(87aF)
  Margarita Galgothia Alfonsina
  Romano(87a)
Roque,
  Marcello Roque(523)
Rossland,
  Erling Rossland(517cX)

Roviello,
        Maria Teresa Roviello(265aM)
Rowley,
        Frances (Margaret) Rowley(494a)
        Frank Blaine Rowley(494aF)
Ruccitti,
        Felicia Ruccitti(502aM)
Ruffino,
        Jennie Ruffino(446aM)
Ruggerio,
        Gabriele Ruggerio(168aF)
        Concetta Ruggiero(47a)
        Domenico Ruggiero(47aF)
        Giovanni Ruggiero(168a)
Rundquist,
        Ramona Violet Josephine
        Rundquist(493b)
        Walter Rundquist(493bF)
Rusca,
        Frank Rusca(515aF)
        Luis J. Rusca(515a)
Rydoon,
        Hulda Josephena Sophina
        Rydoon(493bM)
Sabini,
        Elisa Sabini(474aM)
Saccocio,
        Angelo A. Saccocio(526a)
        Fred Saccocio(526aF)
Salvioli,
        Carmina Salvioli(80a)
Salza,
        Giuseppe Salza(5aF)
        Maria Rosa Salza(5a)
Sandridge,
        Carrie Sandridge(339aM)
Santolino,
        Maria Addolorata
        Santolino(279aM)
Sanzio,
        Giuseppe Sanzio(346aF)
        Vincenzo Sanzio(346a)
Sardella,
        Theresa Sardella(491aM)
Sardonia,
        Angelina Sardonia(579aM)
Saulsberry,
        Louise Frances Saulsberry(517a)
        Marion F. Saulsberry(517aF)
Savariello,
        Ludovico Savariello(300aF)
        Pietro Savariello(300a)
Savino,
        Adelina Savino(362aM)
        Giovanni Savino(286ab)
        Raimonda Savino(83aM)
Scafuri,
        Carolina Scafuri(289aM)
Scaglione,
        Filippo Scaglione(66aF)

Giuseppe Scaglione(66a)
        Luigi Scaglione(181)
        Tommaso Scaglione(199)
Scanzillo,
        Anthony Scanzillo(520)
        Aurelia Scanzillo(407)
        Carmela Scanzillo(394)
        Lorenzo Scanzillo(476)
        Virginia Scanzillo(431)
Scaperotta/Perotta,
        Maria Teresa
        Scaperotta/Perotta(12a)
Scaperrotta,
        Angela Scaperrotta(302aM)
Scarduzio,
        Mamie Scarduzio(573bM)
Scarpellino,
        Agata Scarpellino(8ab)
        Maddalena Scarpellino(239aM)
        Maria Raffaella
        Scarpellino(21ab)
Scauzillo,
        Gaetano Scauzillo(164)
        Lorenzo Scauzillo(389)
        Lorenzo Scauzillo(55a)
        Maria Loretta Scauzillo(63a)
        Maria Rosaria Scauzillo(150)
        Michele Scauzillo(63aF)
        Otantonio Scauzillo(55aF)
        Saveria Scauzillo(12aM)
Schaffer,
        Frank Schaffer(429aX)
Schettini,
        Mary S. Schettini(425aM)
Scheuerman,
        John Scheuerman(541aF)
        Rose Marie Scheuerman(541a)
Schiavo,
        Maria Clementina Schiavo(72aM)
Schiavonne,
        Raffaella Schiavonne(398aM)
Scinto,
        Cesira Elvina Rose Scinto(573b)
        Peter Scinto(573bF)
Scrima,
        Assunta Scrima(286a)
        Maria Michele Scrima(57aM)
        Maria Michele Scrima(64aM)
        Pasquale Scrima(286aF)
Sefcik,
        Mary Sefcik(476aM)
Senese,
        Mary Senese(169a)
Serluca,
        Maria Serluca(278aM)
Serpillo,
        Donato Serpillo(412aF)
        Vincenzo Serpillo(412a)
Shealy,
        Lillian Evetta Shealy(490a)

Pierce Rufus Shealy(490aF),
Sicuranza,
Concetta Angiolina
Sicuranza(430)
Francesco Sicuranza(203aF)
Francesco Sicuranza(449)
Maria Saveria Sicuranza(244aX)
Nicola Sicuranza(203a)
Sidoli,
Willam Sidoli(169ab)
Simone,
Carmella Simone(526aM)
Sisbarra,
Concetta Sisbarra(203aM)
Smith,
Alfred Smith(417aF)
June Smith(417a)
Snyder,
William F Snyder(513a)
William Oscar Snyder(513aF)
Solimene,
Frank Solimene(385a)
Joseph Solimene(385aF)
Soloman,
Osie Soloman(484aM)
Spagnoletto,
Maria Giuseppa
Spagnoletto(342aM)
Spagnuolo,
Faustina Spagnuolo(34aM)
Speranzo,
Emilio Speranzo(394aF)
Natalio Speranzo(394a)
Spinelli,
Anna Spinelli(488a)
Joseph Spinelli(488aF)
Squires,
Mildred Squires(589aM)
St Amand,
John H St Amand(481aF)
Lurline St Amand(481a)
Stark,
Carmela Stark(151ab)
Steinman,
Helen Steinman(429a)
Stella,
Agostino Stella(101)
Anthony Joseph Stella(564)
Antonio Stella(110)
Eugenia Stella(572)
Eugenio Stella(317)
Giovanni (John) Stella(577)
Gloria Stella(602)
Maria Stella(321)
Marianna Stella(116)
Marianna Stella(118)
Michele Stella(299)
Oto Emilio Stella(284)
Oto (Otino) Stella(289)
Oto Stella(34a)

Pellagrino Stella(34aF)
Vincenza Stella(313)
Stilo,
Annette M. Stilo(513)
Cosimo Stilo(308a)
Daniel Paul Stilo(541)
Victor Pasqual Stilo(493)
Vito Stilo(308aF)
Stiscia,
Maria Antonia Stiscia(47bM)
Summa,
Maria Summa(334aM)
Susia,
Francesca Susia(238aM)
Sweetman,
Margaret Sweetman(414aX)
Taselseth,
Angela Taselseth(271aM)
Tedeschi,
Geraldine L. Tedeschi(w479bX)
Terwilliger,
Alma Sharp Terwilliger(264a)
John Terwilliger(264aF)
Thomas,
Anthony R. Thomas(519cF)
Robert Anthony Thomas(519c)
Thompson,
Blanche E. Thompson(517c)
Lowell Thompson(517cF)
Tirano,
Anna Maria Tirano(57ac)
Tiso,
Alberto Tiso(495)
Angelina M. Tiso(482)
Anna M. Tiso(443)
Armand O. Tiso(566)
Carmela Tiso(415)
Clorinda Mariantonia Tiso(380)
Concordia Tiso(478)
Dora Tiso(423)
Eleanor Marie Tiso(515)
Filomena Tiso(136)
Gabriella Tiso(396)
Josephine Tiso(470)
Liberato Tiso(373)
Liberatore Tiso(42a)
Mariangela Tiso(133)
Mariangela Tiso(153)
Oto (Ottone) Tiso(169)
Robert Otto Tiso(554)
Victoria Tiso(527)
Vincenzo Tiso(131)
Vincenzo Tiso(42aF)
Traichel,
Mary Traichel(504aM)
Tropeano,
Angelina Tropeano(486aM)
Ulhorn,
Lavone Faye Ulhorn(517b)
Victor Ulhorn(517bF)

(unknown),
- Carmela (503a)
- Eugenia (456)
- Fannie (572aM)
- Florence (520aM)
- Mabel (541aM)
- Pia (515aM)

Uva,
- Dora Uva (450aM)

Valanta,
- Angelina Marie Valanta (120aM)

Vallillo,
- John Vallillo (335bF)
- Rose Vallillo (335b)

Van Dohlen,
- Katherine Van Dohlen (497aM)

Varasetta,
- Maria Varasetta (275aM)

Venegoni,
- Giuseppina M. Venegoni (571aM)

Verderamm,
- Lucy Verderamm (327aM)

Vernacchia,
- Angelo (Charles) Vernacchia (405)
- Angelo Vernacchia (144aF)
- Angelo Vernacchia (371)
- Anna Maria Vernacchia (328aM)
- Antonio Vernacchia (293a)
- Aurora (Mary) Vernacchia (432)
- Clementina Vernacchia (61aM)
- Francesco Paolo Vernacchia (144a)
- Francesco Paolo Vernacchia (278aF)
- Francesco Vernacchia (293aF)
- Giovanni (John) Vernacchia (416)
- Immacolota (Concetta) Vernacchia (391)
- John Vernacchia (377)
- Maria Liberata Vernacchia (278a)
- Rosa Vernacchia (76aM)
- Vincenza Vernacchia (385)

Vernacchio,
- Concetta Mary Vernacchio (526)
- Phillip Vernacchio (536)

Viola,
- Catherina Viola (120a)
- Nunzio Viola (120aF)

Viscio,
- Anna Maria Viscio (15aM)

Vitillo,
- Ciriaco Vitillo (381aF)
- Rosaria Vitillo (381a)

Vollotti,
- Ann Vollotti (530aM)

Walachowski,
- Laura Walachowski (473aM)

Wilson,
- Florence Emily Wilson (226a)
- William Henry Wilson (226aF)

Woznick,
- Paul J. Woznick (344ab)

Yacullo,
- Elizabeth Yacullo (482aM)

Yeredella,
- Florence Yeredella (385aM)

Zaetz,
- Edward Zaetz (570a)
- Ignatz Zaetz (570aF)

Zaklukiewicz / Zack,
- Clara C. [Zaklukiewicz] Zack (428a)

Zaklukiewicz,
- James Zaklukiewicz (428aF)

Zarlenga,
- Angela Zarlenga (259aM)
- Dan A Zarlenga (469)
- Domenic Paul Zarlenga (571)
- Domenick Zarlenga (259a)
- Donatangelo Zarlenga (259aF)
- Lucien Angelo Zarlenga (501)
- Mary Angela Ann Zarlenga (479)

Zarra,
- Mary Zarra (527aM)

Zarrillo,
- Antonio Zarrillo (223a)
- Domenico Zarrillo (586)
- Michelangelo Zarrillo (223aF)

Zawacki,
- Ignacy Zawacki (538aF)
- Mary J. Zawacki (538a)

Zebell,
- Edward Zebell (504aF)
- Harlow Ferdinand Zebell (504a)

Zecchino,
- Antonio Zecchino (534)
- Attilio Zecchino (511)
- Gaetano Zecchino (521)
- Giovanni Zecchino (291a)
- Michele Zecchino (291aF)
- Raimonda Zecchino (105aM)
- Raimonda Zecchino (82aM)
- Rosa Zecchino (588)

Zelazny,
- Edwin J. Zelazny (552a)

Zerella,
- Mariangela Zerella (39bM)

Zizzo,
- Mariantonia Zizzo (285aM)

Zullo,
- Filomena Zullo (85aM)

Zunino,
- Giovanni Battista Zunino (442a)
- Giovanni Battista Zunino (442aF)
- Luigia Zunino (442aM)

www.ingramcontent.com/pod-product-compliance
Lightning Source LLC
Chambersburg PA
CBHW080402270326
41927CB00015B/3316